Contents

How to Use the Guide

1 LOCATION

Place names are listed alphabetically within each county.

2 MAP REFERENCE

Each site is given a map reference for use in conjunction with the atlas section at the back of the guide. The map reference comprises the guide map page number, the National Grid location square and a two-figure map location reference.

For example: **Map 15 SJ52.**

15 refers to the page number of the map section at the back of the guide.

SJ is the National Grid lettered square (representing 100,000sq metres) in which the location will be found.

5 is the figure reading across the top or bottom of the map page.

2 is the figure reading down each side of the map page.

3 PLACES TO VISIT

Suggestions of nearby places to visit for adults and children.

4 AA CAMPING CARD SCHEME

See explanation on page 7.

5 RATING & SITE NAME

Campsites are listed in descending order of their Pennant Quality rating (see pages 10 & 11). Sites are rated from one to five pennants and are also awarded a score ranging from 50%-100% according to how they compare with other parks within the same pennant rating. Some sites are given a Holiday Centre grading. For a fuller explanation see page 10. A category for parks catering only for recreational vehicles (**RV**) has been created, (no toilet facilities are provided at these sites).

NEW indicates that the site is new in the guide this year. Where the name appears in *italic* type the information that follows has not been confirmed by the campsite for 2011.

6 6-FIGURE MAP REFERENCE

Each entry also includes a 6-figure National Grid reference as many sites are in remote locations. To help you find the precise location of a site the 6-figure map reference, based on the National Grid, can be used with the relevant Ordnance Survey maps in conjunction with the atlas at the back of the guide.

7 CONTACT DETAILS

---

1 WEM   **2** Map 15 SJ52

3 **Places to visit**

Hawkstone Historic Park and Follies, Weston-Under-Redcastle, 01948 841700, www.principal-hayley.co.uk

Great for kids: Shrewsbury Castle and Shropshire Regimental Museum, Shrewsbury, 01743 358516, www.shrewsburymuseums.com

4 **AA CAMPING CARD SITE**

5 ►►► 78% Lower Lacon Caravan Park

6 (SJ534304)   **18**   **17**

7 SY4 5RP
☎ 01939 232376   ▤ 01939 233606   **16**
e-mail: info@llcp.co.uk
web: www.llcp.co.uk
dir: *Take A49 to B5065. Site 3m on right*   **8**

9 * ⬛ £18-£28 ⬛ £18-£28 ▲ £18-£28

15

10 Open Apr-Oct (rs Nov-Mar club wknds only, toilets closed if frost) Last arrival 20.00hrs Last departure 16.00hrs

11 A large, spacious park with lively club facilities and an entertainments barn, set safely away from the main road. The park is particularly suited to families, with an outdoor swimming pool and farm animals. A 52 acre site with 270 touring pitches, 30 hardstandings and 50 statics.

12 **AA Pubs & Restaurants nearby:** Burlton Inn, Burlton 01939 270284

13
Leisure: ⬛ ⛰ ✎ ▢
Facilities: ⬛ ⬛ ⬛ ⬛ ✽ ⬛ ⬛ ⬛ ⬛
Services: ⬛ ⬛ ⬛ ⬛ ⬛ ⬛ ⬛ ⬛ ⬛ ⬛
Within 3 miles: ⬛ ⬛ ⬛ ⬛ ⬛

14 **Notes:** No skateboards, no commercial vehicles Crazy golf

---

8 DIRECTIONS

Brief directions from a recognisable point, such as a main road, are included in each entry. Please contact the individual site for more detailed directions or try the online AA Route Planner, **theAA.com**, and enter the postcode.

9 CHARGES

Rates are given after each appropriate symbol (⚏ Caravan, ⚏ Campervan, ▲ Tent) and are the overnight cost for one caravan or tent, one car and two adults, or one motorhome and two adults. The prices vary according to the number of people in the party, but some parks have a fixed fee per pitch regardless of the number of people. Please note that some sites charge separately for certain facilities, including showers; and some sites charge a different rate for pitches with or without electricity. Prices are supplied to us in good faith by the site operators and are as accurate as possible. They are, however, only a guide and are subject to change during the currency of this publication. * If this symbol appears before the prices, it indicates that the site has not advised us of the prices for 2011; they relate to 2010.

10 OPENING, ARRIVAL & DEPARTURE TIMES

Parks are not necessarily open all year and while most sites permit arrivals at any time, checking beforehand is advised (see page 12).

11 DESCRIPTION

These are based on information supplied by the AA inspector at the time of the last visit. The brief description of the site includes the number of touring pitches and hardstandings. We include the number of static caravan pitches in order to give an indication of the nature and size of the site.
Please note: The AA pennant classification is based on the touring pitches and the facilities only. AA inspectors do not visit or report on statics or chalets for hire under the AA Caravan & Camping quality standards scheme. The AA takes no responsibility for the condition of rented accommodation and can take no action in the event of complaints relating to these.

12 AA PUBS & RESTAURANTS

An entry may include suggestions for nearby pubs and/or restaurants recognised by the AA. Some of these establishments will have been awarded Rosettes for food excellence.

13 SYMBOLS & ABBREVIATIONS

These are divided into Leisure, Facilities, Services and Within 3 miles sections. Explanations can be found on page 9 and at the bottom of the pages throughout the guide.

14 NOTES

This includes information about any restrictions the site would like their visitors to be aware of and any additional facilities. As most sites now accept credit and debit cards, we have only indicated those that don't accept cards.

15 PHOTOGRAPH

Optional photograph supplied by the campsite.

16 COUNTRYSIDE DISCOVERY

 A group of over 30 family-run parks with fewer than 150 pitches, each sharing a common theme of tranquillity. **www.countryside-discovery.co.uk**

17 BEST OF BRITISH

Best of British A group of over 40 parks, both large and small, which focus on high quality facilities and amenities. **www.bob.org.uk**

18 DAVID BELLAMY AWARDS

 Many AA recognised sites are also recipients of a David Bellamy Award for Conservation. The awards are graded Gold, Silver and Bronze. The symbols we show indicate the 2009/10 winners as this was the most up-to-date information at the time of going to press. For the 2010/11 winners please contact:
British Holiday & Homes Parks Association Tel: 01452 526911

ROGER ALMOND AWARD   see page 21

The Most Improved Campsite of the Year award is a fitting tribute to Roger Almond who sadly passed away in 2009 following a battle with cancer.
Roger was the AA's Senior Campsite Inspector, with over 20 years of service, during which time he helped and encouraged many campsites to develop and improve their sites. He was well respected by everyone for his knowledge and guidance and is much missed.

Facilities for disabled visitors

The final stage (Part III) of the Disability Discrimination Act came into force in 2004. This means that service providers may be required to make permanent physical adjustments and adaptations to their premises; for example, the installation of ramps, hand rails and toilet and shower facilities suitable for use by visitors with restricted mobility.
& If a site has told us that they provide facilities for disabled visitors their entry in the guide will include this symbol. The sites in this guide should be aware of their responsibilities under the Act. However, we recommend that you always telephone in advance to ensure the site you have chosen has facilities to suit your needs. For further information see the government website **www.disability.gov.uk**

AA Camping Card Scheme

The New AA Camping Card

In this edition of the AA Caravan & Camping Guide Britain & Ireland you will find some sites highlighted with the **AA CAMPING CARD SITE** banner. This indicates that the site has signed up to our brand new Camping Card Scheme, and means they have agreed to offer reduced rates to campers who book in advance, citing the AA Camping Card, and show the card on arrival at the site. The offers are provided by and are available entirely at the discretion of participating campsites. Offers may include, for example, reduced pitch prices at certain times of the week or year. These discounts will only be available to those booking in advance, stating at the time of booking that an AA Camping Card is being used, and showing the card on arrival. Scheme terms and campsite terms of booking will apply.

You'll need to contact the site to find out what they are offering. We hope this will encourage you to visit sites and explore parts of the country you may not have considered before.

Terms and conditions

This card may be used at any campsite specified as accepting the AA Camping Card within the AA Caravan & Camping Guide Britain & Ireland 2011 and is valid for and may be applied to stays that expire before 31.1.2012.

To make use of the benefits of the AA Camping Card Scheme you must notify any participating campsite that you are a cardholder at your time of advance booking and provide details. Scheme Cards are issued and enclosed with your copy of AA Caravan & Camping Guide Britain & Ireland 2011 at the point of initial purchase.

The card entitles the bearer to any discount or other benefits being offered by the campsite under the scheme at the time of making an advance booking. Participating campsites may formulate, provide, vary or withdraw offers at their discretion. Offers may vary from campsite to campsite. Acceptance by you of any offer made by a campsite is an agreement between you and the campsite. Offers are subject to availability at time of booking and presentation of the booker person's AA Camping Card on arrival. Photocopies will not be accepted. Campsite terms and conditions will apply.

Only one card per person or party accepted. No change given. This card is valid during the period(s) specified by the campsites concerned, and will not be valid after 31 Jan 2012. This card cannot be used in conjunction with any other discount voucher or special offer. No cash alternative available.

This scheme will be governed by English law.

AA Camping Card

You can use this money-saving card when booking at sites that are marked as an **AA Camping Card Site** in the AA Caravan & Camping Guide Britain & Ireland 2011.

Terms and conditions apply.

For a list of sites that accept this card please see page 487

Symbols & Abbreviations

Facilities

- Bath
- Shower
- Electric Shaver
- Hairdryer
- Ice Pack Facility
- Disabled Facilities
- Public Telephone
- Shop on Site or within 200yds
- Mobile Shop (calling at least 5 days per week)
- BBQ Area
- Picnic Area
- Dog Exercise Area

Leisure

- Indoor Swimming Pool
- Outdoor Swimming Pool
- Tennis Court
- Games Room
- Children's Playground

- Stables & Horse Riding
- 9/18 hole Golf Course
- Boats for Hire
- Cinema
- Fishing
- Mini Golf
- Watersports
- Separate TV room

Services

- Toilet Fluid
- Café or Restaurant
- Fast Food/Takeaway
- Baby Care
- Electric Hook Up
- Motorvan Service Point
- Launderette
- Licensed Bar
- Calor Gas
- Camping Gaz
- Battery Charging

Abbreviations

BH	bank holiday/s
Etr	Easter
Whit	Whitsun
dep	departure
fr	from
hrs	hours
m	mile
mdnt	midnight
rdbt	roundabout
rs	restricted service
RV	Recreational Vehicles
U	rating not confirmed
wk	week
wknd	weekend

- no dogs
- no credit or debit cards

AA Pennant Classification

AA Pennant Rating and Holiday Centres

AA parks are classified on a 5-point scale according to their style and the range of facilities they offer. As the number of pennants increases, so the quality and variety of facilities is generally greater. There is also a separate category for Holiday Centres which provide full day and night holiday entertainment as well as offering complete touring facilities for campers and for caravanners.

What can you expect at an AA-rated park?

All AA parks must meet a minimum standard: they should be clean, well maintained and welcoming. In addition they must have a local authority site licence (unless specially exempted), and satisfy local authority fire regulations.

The AA inspection

Each campsite that applies for AA recognition receives an unannounced visit each year by one of the AA's highly qualified team of inspectors. They make a thorough check of the site's touring pitches, facilities and hospitality. The sites pay an annual fee for the inspection, the recognition and rating, and receive a text entry in the AA Caravan & Camping Guide Britain & Ireland. AA inspectors pay when they stay overnight on a site. The criteria used by the inspectors in awarding the AA Pennant rating is shown on the opposite page. **Please note:** the AA does not, under the AA Caravan and Camping quality standards scheme, inspect any statics or chalets that are for hire. The AA takes no responsibility for the condition of rented accommodation and can take no action in the event of complaints relating to these.

AA Quality % Score

AA Rated Campsites, Caravan Parks and Holiday Centres are awarded a percentage score alongside their pennant rating or holiday centre status. This is a qualitative assessment of various factors including customer care and hospitality, toilet facilities and park landscaping. The % score runs from 50% to 100% and indicates the relative quality of parks with the same number of pennants. For example, one 3-pennant park may score 60%, while another 3-pennant park may achieve 70%. Holiday Centres also receive a % score between 50% and 100% to differentiate between quality levels within this grading. Like the pennant rating, the percentage is reassessed annually.

Holiday Centres

In this category we distinguish parks which cater for all holiday needs including cooked meals and entertainment.

They provide:
- A wide range of on-site sports, leisure and recreational facilities
- Supervision and security at a very high level
- A choice of eating outlets
- Facilities for touring caravans that equal those available to rented holiday acommodation
- A maximum density of 25 pitches per acre
- Clubhouse with entertainment provided
- Laundry with automatic washing machines

AA Pennant Rating Guidelines

 ## One Pennant Parks

These parks offer a fairly simple standard of facilities including:

- No more than 30 pitches per acre
- At least 5% of the total pitches allocated to touring caravans
- An adequate drinking water supply and reasonable drainage
- Washroom with flush toilets and toilet paper provided, unless no sanitary facilities are provided in which case this should be clearly stated
- Chemical disposal arrangements, ideally with running water, unless tents only
- Adequate refuse disposal arrangements that are clearly signed
- Well-drained ground, and some level pitches
- Entrance and access roads of adequate width and surface
- Location of emergency telephone clearly signed
- Emergency telephone numbers fully displayed

Two Pennant Parks

Parks in this category should meet all of the above requirements, but offer an increased level of facilities, services, customer care, security and ground maintenance. They should include the following:

- Separate washrooms, including at least 2 male and 2 female WCs and washbasins per 30 pitches
- Hot and cold water direct to each basin
- Externally-lit toilet blocks
- Warden available during day, times to be indicated
- Whereabouts of shop/chemist clearly signed
- Dish-washing facilities, covered and lit
- Reception area

Three Pennant Parks

Many parks come within this rating and the range of facilities is wide. All parks will be of a very good standard and will meet the following minimum criteria:

- Facilities, services and park grounds are clean and well maintained, with buildings in good repair and attention paid to customer care and park security
- Evenly-surfaced roads and paths
- Clean modern toilet blocks with all-night lighting and containing toilet seats in good condition, soap and hand dryers or paper towels, mirrors, shelves and hooks, shaver & hairdryer points, and lidded waste bins in female toilets
- Modern shower cubicles with sufficient hot water and attached, private changing space
- Electric hook-ups
- Some hardstanding/wheel runs/firm, level ground
- Laundry with automatic washing and drying facilities, separate from toilets

- Children's playground with safe equipment
- 24 hours public telephone on site or nearby where mobile reception is poor
- Warden availability and 24-hour contact number clearly signed

Four Pennant Parks

These parks have achieved an excellent standard in all areas, including landscaping of grounds, natural screening and attractive park buildings, and customer care and park security.

Toilets are smart, modern and immaculately maintained, and generally offer the following facilities:

- Spacious vanitory-style washbasins, at least 2 male and 2 female per 25 pitches
- Fully-tiled shower cubicles with doors, dry areas, shelves and hooks, at least 1 male and 1 female per 30 pitches
- Availability of washbasins in lockable cubicles, or combined toilet/washing cubicles, or a private/family room with shower/toilet/washbasin

Other requirements are:

- Baby changing facilities
- A shop on site, or within reasonable distance
- Warden available 24 hours
- Reception area open during the day, with tourist information available
- Internal roads, paths and toilet blocks lit at night
- Maximum 25 pitches per campable acre
- Toilet blocks heated October to Easter
- Minimum 50% electric hook-ups
- Minimum 10% hardstandings where necessary
- Late arrivals enclosure

 ## Five Pennant Premier Parks

Premier parks are of an extremely high standard, set in attractive surroundings with superb mature landscaping. Facilities, security and customer care are of an exceptional quality. As well as the above they will also offer:

- First-class toilet facilities including several designated self-contained cubicles, ideally with WC, washbasin and shower.
- Electricity to most pitches
- Minimum 20% hardstandings (where necessary)
- Some fully-serviced 'super' pitches: of larger size and with water and electricity supplies connected
- A motorhome service point

Many Premier Parks will also provide:

- Heated swimming pool
- Well-equipped shop
- Café or restaurant and bar
- A designated walking area for dogs (if accepted)

Useful Information

Booking Information

It is advisable to book in advance during peak holiday seasons and in school or public holidays. It is also wise to check whether or not a reservation entitles you to a particular pitch. It does not necessarily follow that an early booking will secure the best pitch; you may simply have the choice of what is available at the time you check in.

Some parks may require a deposit on booking which may be non-returnable if you have to cancel your holiday. If you do have to cancel, notify the proprietor at once because you may be held legally responsible for partial or full payment unless the pitch can be re-let. Consider taking out insurance such as AA Travel Insurance, tel: 0800 085 7240 or visit the AA website: **theAA.com** for details to cover a lost deposit or compensation. Some parks will not accept overnight bookings unless payment for the full minimum period (e.g. two or three days) is made.

Last Arrival – Unless otherwise stated, parks will usually accept arrivals at any time of the day or night, but some have a special 'late arrivals' enclosure where you have to make temporary camp to avoid disturbing other people on the park. Please note that on some parks access to the toilet block is by key or pass card only, so if you know you will be late, do check what arrangements can be made.

Last Departure – Most parks will specify their overnight period – e.g. noon to noon. If you overstay the departure time you can be charged for an extra day.

Chemical Closet Disposal Point (cdp)

You will usually find one on every park, except those catering only for tents. It must be a specially constructed unit, or a WC permanently set aside for the purpose of chemical disposal and with adjacent rinsing and soak-away facilities. However, some local authorities are concerned about the effect of chemicals on bacteria in cesspools etc, and may prohibit or restrict provision of CDPs in their areas.

Complaints

Speak to the park proprietor or supervisor immediately if you have any complaints, so that the matter can be sorted out on the spot. If this personal approach fails, you may decide, if the matter is serious, to approach the local authority or tourist board. AA guide users may also write to:
The Co-ordinator, AA Caravan & Camping Scheme,
AA Lifestyle Guides, 13th floor, Fanum House, Basingstoke,
RG21 4EA

The AA may at its sole discretion investigate any complaints received from guide users for the purpose of making any necessary amendments to the guide. The AA will not in any circumstances act as representative or negotiator or undertake to obtain compensation or enter into further correspondence or deal with the matter in any other way whatsoever. The AA will not guarantee to take any specific action.

Dogs

Dogs may or may not be accepted at parks, and this is entirely at the owner's or warden's discretion (assistance dogs should be accepted). Even when the park states that they accept dogs, it is still discretionary, and certain breeds may not be considered as suitable, so we strongly advise that you check when you book.*
Dogs should always be kept on a lead and under control, and letting them sleep in cars is not encouraged.

*Some sites have told us they do not accept dangerous breeds.

The following breeds are covered under the Dangerous Dogs Act 1991 –
Pit Bull Terrier, Japanese Tosa, Dogo Argentino and Fila Brazilerio.

Electric Hook-Up

This is becoming more generally available at parks with three or more pennants, but if it is important to you, you should check before booking. The voltage is generally 240v AC, 50 cycles, although variations between 200v and 250v may still be found. All parks in the AA scheme which provide electric hook-ups do so in accordance with International Electrotechnical Commission regulations. Outlets are coloured blue and take the form of a lidded plug with recessed contacts, making it impossible to touch a live point by accident. They are also waterproof. A similar plug, but with protruding contacts which hook into the recessed plug, is on the end of the cable which connects the caravan to the source of supply, and is dead. This equipment can usually be hired on site, or a plug connector supplied to fit your own cable. You should ask for the male plug; the female plug is the one already fixed to the power supply. This supply is rated for either 5, 10 or 16 amps and this is usually displayed on a triangular yellow plate attached to source of supply. If it is not, be sure to check at the site reception. This is important because if you overload the circuit, the trip switch will operate to cut off the power supply. The trip switch can only be reset by a park official, who will first have to go round all the hook-ups on park to find the cause of the trip. This can take a long time and will make the culprit distinctly unpopular with all the other caravanners deprived of power, to say nothing of the park official. Tents and trailer tents are recommended to have a Residual Circuit Device (RCD) for safety reasons and to avoid overloading the circuit.

It is a relatively simple matter to calculate whether your appliances will overload the circuit. The amperage used by an appliance depends on its wattage and the total amperage used is the total of all the appliances in use at any one time. If you are not sure whether your camping or caravanning equipment can be used at a park, check beforehand.

Average amperage

Portable black & white TV 50 watts approx.	0.2 amp
Small colour TV 90 watts approx.	0.4 amp
Small fan heater 1000 watts (1kW) approx.	4.2 amp
One-bar electric fire NB each extra bar rates	
1000 watts (1kW)	4.2 amp
60 watt table lamp approx.	0.25 amp
100 watt light bulb approx.	0.4 amp
Battery charger 100 watts approx.	0.4 amp
Small fridge 125 watts approx.	0.4 amp
Domestic microwave 600 watts approx.	2.5 amp

Motor Caravans

At some parks motor caravans are only accepted if they remain static throughout the stay. Also check that there are suitable level pitches at the parks where you plan to stay.

Overflow Pitches

Campsites are legally entitled to use an overflow field which is not a normal part of their camping area for up to 28 days in any one year as an emergency method of coping with additional numbers at busy periods. When this 28 day rule is being invoked site owners should increase the numbers of sanitary facilities accordingly. In these circumstances the extra facilities are sometimes no more than temporary portacabins.

Parking

Some park operators insist that cars be put in a parking area separate from the pitches; others will not allow more than one car for each caravan or tent.

Park Restrictions

Many parks in our guide are selective about the categories of people they will accept on their parks. In the caravan and camping world there are many restrictions and some categories of visitor are banned altogether. Where a park has told us of a restriction/s this is included in notes in their entry.

On many parks in this guide, unaccompanied young people, single-sex groups, single adults, and motorcycle groups will not be accepted. The AA takes no stance in this matter, basing its pennant classification on facilities, quality and maintenance. On the other hand, some parks cater well for teenagers and offer magnificent sporting and leisure facilities as well as discos; others have only very simple amenities. A small number of parks in our guide exclude all children in order to create an environment aiming at holiday makers in search of total peace and quiet. (See p.45)

Pets Travel Scheme

The importation of animals into the UK is subject to strict controls. Penalties for trying to avoid these controls are severe. However, the Pet Travel Scheme (PETS) allows cats, dogs, ferrets and certain other pets coming from the EU and certain other countries to enter the UK without quarantine provided the appropriate conditions are met. For details:
www.defra.gov.uk/wildlife-pets/pets/travel/pets/index.htm
PETS HELPLINE on 0870 241 1710
E-mail: quarantine@animalhealth.gsi.gov.uk
Pets resident in the British Isles (UK, Republic of Ireland, Isle of Man and Channel Islands) are not subject to any quarantine or PETS rules when travelling within the British Isles.

Seasonal Touring Pitches

Some park operators allocate a number of their hardstanding pitches for long-term seasonal caravans. These pitches can be reserved for the whole period the campsite is open, generally between Easter and September, and a fixed fee is charged for keeping the caravan on the park for the season. These pitches are in great demand, especially in popular tourist areas, so enquire well in advance if you wish to book one.

Shops

The range of food and equipment in shops is usually in proportion to the size of the park. As far as our pennant requirements are concerned, a mobile shop calling several times a week, or a general store within easy walking distance of the park is acceptable.

Unisex Toilet Facilities

An ever-increasing number of parks now offer unisex toilet facilities instead of (or sometimes as well as) separate units for men and women. If the type of toilet facility is important to you, please check what the park has to offer at the time of booking.

Island Camping

Channel Islands

Tight controls are operated because of the narrow width of the mainly rural roads. On all of the islands tents can be hired on recognised campsites.

Alderney

Neither caravans nor motor caravans are allowed, and campers must have a confirmed booking on the one official camp site before they arrive.

Guernsey

Only islanders may own and use towed caravans, though motor caravans are allowed under strict conditions. A permit must be sought and received in advance, the vehicle must not be used for sleeping, and when not in use for transport the van must be left under cover at a camping park with prior permission. Tents and trailer tents are allowed provided you stay on official campsites; booking is strongly recommended during July and August.

Herm and Sark

These two small islands are traffic free. Herm has a small campsite for tents, and these can also be hired. Sark has three campsites. New arrivals are met off the boat by a tractor which carries people and luggage up the steep hill from the harbour. All travel is by foot, on bicycle, or by horse and cart.

Jersey

Visiting caravans are now allowed into Jersey, provided they are to be used as holiday accommodation only. Caravans will require a permit for travelling to and from the port and campsite on their arrival and departure days only. Motorvans may travel around the island on a daily basis, but must return to the campsite each night. Bookings should be made through the chosen campsite, who will also arrange for a permit. Early booking is strongly recommended during July and August.

Isle of Man

Motor caravans may enter with prior permission. Trailer caravans are generally only allowed in connection with trade shows and exhibitions, or for demonstration purposes, not for living accommodation. Written application for permission should be made to the Secretary, Planning Committee, Isle of Man Local Government Board, Murray House, Mount Havelock, Douglas. The shipping line cannot accept caravans without this written permission.

Isles of Scilly

Caravans and motor caravans are not allowed, and campers must stay at official sites. Booking is advisable on all sites, especially during school holidays.

Scottish Islands

Inner Isles (including Inner Hebrides)

Skye is accessible to caravans and motor caravans, and has official camping sites, but its sister isles of Rhum and Eigg have no car ferries, and take only backpackers. Official camping only is allowed at Rothsay on the Isle of Bute. The islands of Mull, Islay, Coll and Arran have official campsites, and welcome caravans, motor caravans and tenters. Offsite camping is also allowed with the usual permission. Iona is car free, and a backpacker's paradise, while Tiree does not accept caravans or motor caravans, and has no official sites. Colonsay and Cumbrae allow no caravanning or camping, although organized groups such as the Guides or Scouts may stay with official permission. Jura and Gigha allow neither camping nor caravanning, and Lismore bans caravans but permits camping, although there are no official sites and few suitable places.

Orkney

There are no camping and caravanning restrictions, and plenty of beauty spots in which to pitch camp.

Shetland

There are four official campsites on the Shetlands, but visitors can camp anywhere with prior permission. Caravans and motor caravans must stick to the main roads. Camping 'böds' offer budget accommodation in unisex dormitories for campers with their own bed rolls and sleeping bags. There is no camping or caravanning on Noss and Fair Isle, and the Tresta Links in Fetlar.

Western Isles (Outer Hebrides)

There are official campsites on these islands, but 'wild' camping is allowed within reason, and with the landowner's prior permission.

AA Campsites of the Year

ENGLAND & OVERALL WINNER OF THE AA BEST CAMPSITE OF THE YEAR

▶▶▶▶▶ **95%** SILVERDALE CARAVAN PARK

SILVERDALE, LANCASHIRE Page 221

The flagship park of the Holgate group, Silverdale is a superb holiday park situated on a rocky outcrop overlooking Morecambe Bay, yet within easy reach of the Lake District. There really is something for everyone on this well-managed park, from the first-class sporting and leisure facilities, which include a most attractive swimming pool, a sauna, and a fitness room, to the excellent facilities for children, which include a soft-play area, an adventure playground, and spacious, well tended grassy areas and extensive wooded areas in which to play in. The tasteful and spotless family restaurant and bar provide quality meals and, for those who wish to do their own cooking, there is an excellent on-site mini-market. Toilet facilities are top-notch – always spotlessly clean and well maintained. This is a top-class park, in an excellent location, where you will be well cared for by a most attentive and friendly team, who ensure the park always looks its best.

SCOTLAND

►►►►► 85% LINNHE LOCHSIDE HOLIDAYS
CORPACH, HIGHLAND Page 353

Just five miles from Fort William in the heart of the West Highlands, Linnhe Lochside Holidays offers quality touring facilities in a glorious setting on the shores of Loch Eil, with the wild and dramatic scenery of Ben Nevis to the east and the mountains of Sunart to the west. The owners have worked in harmony with nature to produce an idyllic environment, where they offer the highest standards of design and maintenance. Touring pitches, including 25 fully serviced pitches and some stunning loch-side tent pitches, enjoy equal status to statics in terms of prime location and taking in the wonderful views, and the maturity of the park, with its trees, mature shrubs, flowers and colourful combinations is quite breathtaking. Add immaculate maintenance across the park, a diligent approach to cleanliness, especially in the top quality toilet blocks, which offer a wealth of privacy cubicles, excellent play areas for both older and younger children, and the recent investment to create a loch-side beach and you have the perfect Highland hideaway.

WALES

►►►►► 91% THE PLASSEY LEISURE PARK
EYTON, WREXHAM Page 404

Fifty years ago the Brookshaw family started developing their farmland and buildings, set in 247 acres of park and woodland in the beautiful Dee Valley, into a Leisure Park. Today, the complex is thriving and features, among other activities, a craft and retail centre, golf course, garden centre, sauna, Tree Tops bar and restaurant and, at its heart, a superb touring park that offers quality facilities for both families and adults. Your can expect high standards of customer care and top-notch amenities, from luxury toilet blocks with individual cubicles for privacy and security, and 30 fully serviced 'super' pitches with hardstandings and TV connections, to excellent facilities for children, including a games room, a first-class outdoor adventure play area, and a farmland nature trail. There is plenty here to entertain the whole family, from scenic walks and swimming pool to free fishing, and use of the 9-hole golf course.

AA Campsites of the Year – Regional Award Winners

SOUTH WEST ENGLAND

▶▶▶▶▶ 83% OAKDOWN HOLIDAY PARK

SIDMOUTH, DEVON Page 167

A quality, friendly, well-maintained park set in a beautiful part of Devon, with superb landscaping and plenty of maturing trees that ensure it is well screened from the A3502. Pitches are grouped in paddocks surrounded by shrubs, with a stunning new 50-pitch development replete with an upmarket toilet block. The park's conservation areas, with their natural flora and fauna, offer attractive walks, and there is a hide by the Victorian reed bed for bird watchers. Additional features that make this park stand out are the good 9-hole golf course, the lovely café and the interesting field trail that leads to the nearby Donkey Sanctuary. A delightful park in every respect.

SOUTH EAST ENGLAND

91% SANDY BALLS HOLIDAY CENTRE

FORDINGBRIDGE, HAMPSHIRE Page 208

This superb holiday centre, set in the New Forest National Park, is the perfect getaway for families, couples and friends. The touring section of the park is excellent in its own right, with its spacious, fully serviced hardstanding pitches, which offer excellent privacy, the attractive summer camping fields, and the top quality toilet and shower facilities. Sandy Balls has something for everyone and the facilities and activities available are superb and include an indoor pool plus gym and fitness centre, a modern Italian pizza restaurant, a traditional pub, and a cycle centre for bike hire. It is certainly one of the best holiday centres in Britain, noted for its exceptional levels of customer care and its high standard and choice of leisure facilities.

HEART OF ENGLAND

▶▶▶▶▶ 86% TOWNSEND TOURING PARK

PEMBRIDGE, HEREFORDSHIRE Page 212

Opened in 2002 and now an outstanding, fully matured park, Townsend Touring Park stands in a beautiful location on the edge of one of Herefordshire's most beautiful 'Black and White' villages and makes an excellent base from which to explore the scenic village trail, Ludlow Castle and Ironbridge. The spacious, well-landscaped 12-acre park offers excellent facilities, including a fresh, clean and well-maintained toilet block, with quality showers and family rooms, as well as fully serviced hardstanding pitches, and a fishing lake. Popular with campers and locals is the award-winning, on-site farm shop and butchery, which sells traceable, locally-reared meats. Recent additions to this impressively run and well maintained park include three wooden camping pods.

AA Campsites of the Year – Regional Award Winners *continued*

NORTH WEST ENGLAND

▶▶▶▶ **88%** SKELWITH FOLD CARAVAN PARK

AMBLESIDE, CUMBRIA Page 120

Skelwith Fold is a top-notch family park set within secluded woodland in a beautiful Lakeland setting close to Lake Windermere and miles of stunning fell walks. Owner Henry Wild is driven by the desire to do things to the highest standard and this ethos pervades all aspects of the park, with ongoing renewal and upgrading of facilities, from landscaping the attractive pitches in peaceful glades and addition of 15 superb premium pitches, to internally refitting the toilet/amenity blocks, and creating two 'offices' with computers for visitors to keep tabs on their business interests. To complete the impressive picture, there is a 5-acre family recreation area that enjoys spectacular views of Loughrigg Fell. A class act in the Cumbrian fells.

NORTH EAST ENGLAND

▶▶▶▶▶ **80%** ORD HOUSE COUNTRY PARK

BERWICK-UPON-TWEED, NORTHUMBERLAND Page 241

Ord House Country Park is a high quality destination close to the glorious Northumberland coastline. Set in the grounds of an 18th-century country house, the beautifully landscaped touring park is well managed and this shows in all aspects of the park, from the time and effort taken to create the tasteful floral displays to the spotlessly clean and well maintained amenity blocks, which contain family bath and shower suites and first-class disabled rooms. All in all, the attention to detail in the presentation of this park is very impressive as is the ongoing investment to maintain quality in all areas, notably the excellent new children's play area installed by the reception building. A worthy winner.

ROGER ALMOND AWARD - MOST IMPROVED CAMPSITE*

▶▶▶▶ **84%** CHURCH FARM CARAVAN & CAMPING PARK

SIXPENNY HANDLEY, DORSET Page 192

This small, family run park, set in the beautiful Cranborne Chase, has seen major changes which have significantly improved the quality and feel of this popular site. The hands-on owners have invested in a new facility block, which includes good showers, toilets and family rooms, and an area that can be used as a café or function room, which leads out onto a patio area for alfresco eating. There is a variety of caravan or camping areas, which are well screened and offer good facilities for families as well as adults only. Roger Almond was instrumental is advising the owners about these improvements, so it is fitting that Church Farm is the first recipient of this AA award.

* See page 5

cool CORNISH

Following on from his 'Glamping' feature in the AA 2010 Caravan & Camping Guide, David Hancock ventures west to experience 'yurting' on one of Cornwall's 'coolest' campsites, set on an organic farm on Bodmin Moor.

For many, the thought of camping still conjures up vivid images of muddy fields, soggy tents, wet clothes, and the car crammed to the roof with sleeping bags, crockery and the leaky family tent, with, perhaps, just enough room for the kitchen sink and the kids. Today, however, if you crave your home comforts, even a little luxury, suffering in pursuit of a relaxing camping holiday can be avoided.

Outdoor living has never been more fun (and comfortable) since camping turned cool and glamorous with the arrival of a new genre of stylish alternative campsites, following the popularity of the luxury tents, carpeted cabins and customised double-decker buses that accommodate celebrities and the well-heeled festival-goer on Britain's flourishing festival circuit. 'Glamping', or posh camping, continues apace and savvy campers are seeking out these coolest of campsites, often on secluded farms deep in rolling countryside, where the nightmares of broken poles, missing pegs and soggy sleeping bags are a thing of the past.

Left: South Penquite Farm, Blisland, Cornwall ▷

CAMPING

> *…you stay in simple wooden camping pods or ready-erected Mongolian yurts, luxury bell tents, or Native American-style tipis…*

Above: Wooden wigwams at Woodclose Caravan Park, Kirkby Lonsdale, Cumbria

or you can choose to sleep in a converted shepherd's hut or a rustic stone barn. If sleeping under canvas is really not your thing, why not push the boat out and stay in a shiny American Airstream trailer, an upmarket timber lodge with private outdoor hot-tub, plus sauna and jacuzzi bath, or you can hire a re-conditioned VW campervan kitted out with Cath Kidston fabrics.

The ethos behind it all is that just because you're sleeping in a tent or trailer you don't have to abandon your senses of style and comfort, and you can still look good while experiencing the great outdoors and getting back to nature.

From a tap and loo, and Cornwall's best view…

Escaping the hustle and bustle of modern life and getting back to nature is difficult to achieve on this crowded island. However, at South Penquite Farm, a 200-acre working organic hill farm set amid the rugged pastures that fringe the wild and dramatic landscapes of Bodmin Moor, you can truly get away from it all and savour a unique Cornish camping experience. Although only short drive from the A30 (travelling west take the first right sign for St Breward), the farm can be found isolated down a rough stony track off a narrow moorland lane.

Having farmed the land since 1977, and achieving organic status in 2001, Dominic and Kathy Fairman diversified into camping in 1999, opening up a field with basic facilities for campers heading to Cornwall to witness the

A tent? They're so last year…..

'Boutique' campsites have made canvas chic and 'glamping' more accessible, and offer the ultimate eco-friendly and sustainable holiday experience. Here you stay in simple wooden camping pods or ready-erected Mongolian yurts, luxury bell tents, or Native American-style tipis, which are often heated by solar power. Some are filled with antiques, while others have private bedrooms and en suite toilets and showers, to avoid that midnight trudge across wet fields to the toilets. The latest in 'cool' is a palatial safari tent, replete with double beds, private compost loos and fireplace, and a luxury farm tent with its own field hot-tub,

eclipse. It obviously proved both successful and enjoyable, for the Fairmans have continued to develop the campsite over the past decade, adding toilets and showers, yet keeping it small, friendly and very much in tune with the local environment and their organic farming ethos. They co-exist in harmony and, in addition to keeping the camping traditional, the farm now has an educational centre for groups and schools to learn about farming on Bodmin Moor, a fascinating farm trail, where children will meet the Cheviot ewes and Galloway cattle reared on the farm, and the Fairmans also run family Bushcraft Courses during the summer.

To cool, eco-friendly family camping...

Swing left through the farm gate into the four lush grassy acres that are set aside for camping, push open the car door, breathe in the pure Bodmin air, savour the peace and quiet, marvel at the moorland views, and let the stress of the long drive ebb away. With the kids letting off pent-up steam in the recreation field, book in at the farmhouse and check out the facilities.

Unless you have booked one of the four Mongolian yurts, camping is a simple, no frills affair, so don't expect electric hook ups, landscaped and numbered pitches, or low level lighting. What you will get (if you book early) is a generous slice of one of the camping fields as, commendably, the Fairmans keep to a maximum of 120 campers, and super chic and very green toilet/shower facilities, which make the morning trudge (remember your wellies) to the farmyard toilets truly pleasurable. The kids won't mind waiting for you to finish your shower as they will

be entertained by the host of ducks, chickens, geese, pea-hens and turkeys that patrol the area.

The verandah-fronted shower block delivers solar-heated rainwater into family-sized cubicles lined with recycled plastic bottles and yoghurt pots, and you have use of phosphorate-free shower gel. Across the (often muddy) yard, which is lined with extensive recycling bins, the smart, pine-clad toilet block sports more compressed plastic bottles (beats tiling) and trendy round sinks that generally grace boutique hotel bathrooms. The

Above: Interior of a yurt at South Penquite Farm, Blisland, Cornwall

▷

Left: Interior of a yurt at
South Penquite Farm,
Blisland, Cornwall
Above: Washing facilities at
South Penquite Farm

laundry room next door has a fridge, freezer (for ice packs) and secure lockers with plugs for hairdryers and recharging your mobile phone. Naturally, the electricity is supplied courtesy of the local wind farm at Delabole.

Glamp it up in a Yurt

For that 'back to nature' experience on the farm, with all the home comforts you need and oodles of space to relax in, you can book one of the four yurts (Goldilocks and Daddy Bear, Mummy Bear, Baby Bear – for cosy couples) that stand tucked away in a peaceful meadow away from the campsite. A Mongolian-style yurt is the ultimate eco-tent for the 'cool' camper, a wood-lattice structure covered in canvas (traditionally thick felt in Mongolia), with a domed roof and a raised, wooden floor. Unsurprisingly, the yurts at South Penquite were made two

miles away by Yurtworks in St Breward (www.yurtworks.co.uk).

In keeping with the wild and unspoilt moorland setting of South Penquite, the yurts are simple and cosy, yet a stylish step up from sleeping in a pop-up dome or the family frame tent in the adjacent field, but don't expect en suite flush toilets and electricity. Like the other campers you too have the long walk to the eco-loos. However, you can expect a lesson in Bohemian chic as all the yurts are kitted out with futon-style beds, colourful, hand-made woollen rugs, throws and cushions, Moroccan lanterns, painted and tiled tables, a central wood-burning stove, and a fully-equipped campers' kitchen – think, gas cooker, enamel plates, bowls and mugs, and the luxury of a cool box. Added touches include candelabra and a wind-up radio and torch, the latter being essential for

that late-night trek to the farmyard. All you need to bring are your sleeping bags or some linen and duvets.

Daddy Bear, one of the two larger yurts, sleeps up to six close friends or family. There's plenty of space in which to relax during the day but come the night, when the three futon beds are laid out, it's certainly very cosy, especially if you have stoked up the wood-burning stove and the logs are glowing and crackling. Fine summer evenings should be spent eating alfresco, gathered round your own blazing fire pit, cooking and tucking into the delicious farm produced lamb and mint burgers and sausages. It's a great way to end a perfect day.

If the kids are content with meeting the menagerie of ducks and chickens that roam the campsite, or making good use of the swings and playing field, stressed out parents and couples looking for a

" ...or continue west to visit the impressive biomes at the Eden Project near St Austell. "

relaxing on-site experience can arrange for a deep tissue massage in the privacy of your tent or yurt. Now, how cool is that…?

Exploring Bodmin Moor

With the wild expanse of Bodmin Moor on your doorstep, you don't have to go far to get a real flavour of the area. Leave the car at the campsite, pick up the informative leaflet from the farmhouse and explore the fascinating farm trail, a 2.5 mile (4km) stroll across South Penquite's farmland, then along the banks of the De Lank River to disused quarries, before passing a standing stone and Bronze Age hut circle. And, if that's not enough, the views are stunning.

For a full day's walk head off into the heart of the moor and tackle Bodmin Moor's famous peaks, Brown Willy (Cornwall's highest point at 1,378ft) and Rough Tor, or follow paths from South Penquite to the Cheesewring, an amazing collection of weird granite slabs perched on a windswept hilltop.

Horse-lovers of all ages and abilities can enjoy a one or two hour trek or a half-day pub ride across the moors from Hallagenna Stables (www.hallagenna. co.uk), which is just a couple of miles from South Penquite Farm.

When it rains…

South Penquite's proximity to the A30 allows for an easy get-away when the mist and driving rain descend on Bodmin Moor, which it often does even in summer. On these inclement days head for Lanhydrock, a National Trust-owned Victorian mansion on a huge estate south of Bodmin, or continue west to visit the impressive biomes at the Eden Project near St Austell. Both Cornish coasts are within easy reach, with Port Isaac and Padstow, the latter famed for its restaurants, a short drive north, but best accessed via Bodmin and Wadebridge, unless you wish to negotiate tortuously narrow lanes through steep valleys. The charming fishing village of Fowey, with its upmarket shops and riverside cafés and restaurants, is worth the journey to the south coast.

THE ESSENTIALS

South Penquite Farm, Blisland, Bodmin, Cornwall PL30 4LH
01208 850491
Yurts: £290 to £360 for a week; 3 night weekend stays half price
No dogs allowed on the site but Penquite Petcare boarding kennels and cattery is next door.
AA-listed pubs nearby:
Blisland Inn, Blisland (1.5 miles)
01208 850739
The Old Inn, St Breward (2.5 miles)
01208 850711

Below: Rough Tor, Bodmin Moor

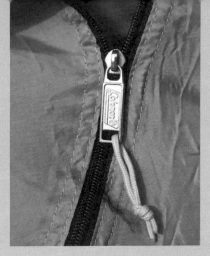

Camping for *all*

Time to escape the daily grind and enjoy the adventure of life under canvas, says Clive Garrett, Editor of Camping, the magazine for the UK tenting community. And here is his quick guide and top tips to get you started.

For many, camping offers a cost effective way to take a holiday. And a camping package promises to open the door on a myriad of adventures without too much impact on an already stressed wallet.

However, camping is more than this. Experienced campers find it offers the opportunity to spend quality time with family and friends, to explore new areas lacking more formal accommodation, expand experiences and create happy memories, and join a friendly network of fellow enthusiasts that is not defined by race, religion, politics or social standing.

And parents will find that their children will thrive in this community; making new friends, expending energy in play and enjoying a fun-filled day removed from the all consuming attraction of computers and the like. In fact, camping builds the many social skills needed to successfully see them through life.

But, let's dispel a myth. Camping these days is not cheap. However, the outlay required to purchase the quality gear required for years of top holidays does prove cost effective.

For instance, a four-berth tent costing £99 may need replacing after one season, whereas a quality tent costing £500 could last ten years. If the average family takes a two week camping holiday plus four weekends away per year then that means your £99 has provided you with 17 night's accommodation. That's £5.82 per night for a family of four.

However, if your up-market tent provides the same family accommodation but over ten years then each night will cost only £2.94 per night. How's that for long-term value!

There is nothing wrong with purchasing that cheap tent as long as you realise that it has limitations. It is a virtual certainty that, as you talk with fellow campers and take in a few specialist camping retailers, you'll soon want to upgrade to something with a little more room, comfort and stability. Yes, stability - you will eventually experience bad weather and while the rain falls and wind whistles around the ▷

> *Many of the modern tunnel and dome designs find their origin in lightweight tents favoured by backpackers.*

However, tents made out of cotton and polycotton, are making a comeback as campers realise that such tents last longer and provide condensation free accommodation that is cool in summer and warm in winter. It is hard to beat that emotive smell of cotton on a summer's day – pure camping heaven.

Pre angled pole joints are often the norm and these maintain height right up to the walls of the tent, creating far more useable space than earlier units. Although possibly not as stable as domes, tunnels are easier to pitch in windy conditions. This is because you insert and tension the poles at ground level and peg out some of the outer before raising the tent to the wind, whereas when you place a dome's poles under tension it is immediately raised into the wind and can take on the qualities of a hang glider. On a calm day, even a big tunnel can be pitched by a single fit camper – an important consideration if your partner is looking after children.

When searching for a tent do not be fooled by a manufacturer's claim as to how many it will sleep. A four-berth may sleep four but there will seldom be space for personal belongings or room in the living area for more than a table and chairs. Unless a backpacker, where weight and pack size are the priorities, an experienced camper will often go up a size or two in order to benefit from the increased in headroom and space.

Yet do not be tempted to buy the biggest tent possible. The increased weight of the fabric will need beefier poles, often steel. This makes the tent heavier still, bulkier to transport and a lot harder to pitch, dry, maintain and store – the latter three will be a concern if you live in a small house with little garden.

guy lines you'll be sitting snug in your tent thankful you paid out for a quality haven from the storm.

Choosing your tent

Tents come in many guises but designs are limited to just a few core styles. Many of the modern tunnel and dome designs find their origin in lightweight tents favoured by backpackers. And, while the ridge, frame and bell tents of old are enjoying a revival, such tunnels and domes make up the majority of tents that you will find on the market today.

Arguably, the market has been shaped by the use of synthetic fabrics in lightweight tents. Fibreglass poles can be placed under tension to provide the shape needed to create dome and tunnels. And, compared with traditional canvas, tents made out of lighter synthetic fabrics are easier to maintain, pitch and transport.

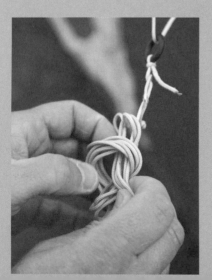

You might even have to consider towing a camping trailer to cart around all that extra camping gear. And some campsites may even charge you for two pitches...

It is far better to seek out a mid-size tent and purchase an optional awning to increase living space during longer camps. You will also find such a tent easier to pitch and maintain. Such versatility and features will encourage you to take more short term camping breaks and weekends away.

When buying a tent try to visit a specialist retailer during quiet times. They can then give you their full attention. Try to see your tent pitched and go over it with a fine-toothcomb, looking for faults and damage. Become familiar with your new purchase by pitching it a few times at home before you go camping. It could save you a lot of embarrassment...

Time with a retailer will allow you to check out if your tent has features like an electric cable port if you intend to use an electric hook-up. Vents are important to keep down condensation. You'll want good windows to keep the interior light and airy. A mesh backing to doors and windows will allow them to be opened for fresh air while keeping out bugs. A lot of tents now feature a fully sewn-in groundsheet which proves to be superb if you want a draught and creepy-crawly free tent.

Bedroom secrets

More important is having enough living space and that the bedroom suits your needs. A single bedroom split into two by a hanging curtain provides parental access to little kids while a vis-à-vis style arrangement, where the bedrooms are separated by the living area, or one where the bedrooms are divided by a gap (often a wardrobe) provides privacy.

Whatever you go for consider size. Is there room for an appropriately sized sleeping mat or air bed while providing enough space for personal belongings? Is there enough headroom and space to dress in the inner?

Most hardships met when camping can be overcome with a good night's sleep. A good bed can be made from a double airbed with sheet, pillows and duvet taken from home. There are plenty of good sleeping bags on the market, and ▷

a mummy-style bag that tapers towards the feet can provide a snug bed in colder conditions by limiting the amount of trapped air that the body has to heat.

However, most campers prefer oblong shaped bags that provide room to move. Most mummy and oblong bags can be zipped to another to create a double bag although you can buy double bags if you want to cuddle your partner. Whatever style chosen consider using an inner bag that can be removed for washing and that adds a little more insulation to your sleeping bag.

With night comes the need for a lantern that casts light over a wide area and is normally powered by electric or gas. A torch is useful for intimate work like cooking, washing-up or reading. Head torches are preferred as these leave hands free while lighting the work

area. LEDs have replaced bulbs - they are almost indestructible and require little battery power. Some lanterns and lights even incorporate solar panels and dynamos for recharging batteries, but while worthy often prove a bane when the light goes during some vital task like cooking – or making that late night trip to the toilet block.

Cooking on gas

Unless you are going to eat out you will need to take a cooker and the associated paraphernalia that makes up a campsite kitchen. This may be a simple meths stove to rustle up a quick brew, or a sophisticated two-ring gas stove with grill. Gas is the chosen fuel for many experienced campers. Not only is it clean and easy to use, but replacement canisters and cylinders are readily

available and can be found stocked on many larger campsites.

Gas purchased in a cylinder is cheaper than canisters but choose your supplier carefully. The two main suppliers, Campingaz and Calor, use different regulators. Although the cheaper option, Calor cannot be obtained abroad if you decide on a spot of continental camping.

While not an essential, a camp kitchen unit is handy. For a start its height makes cooking more comfortable and there is normally storage space underneath for food and pots. For safety, you can also make its vicinity a no go zone for kids. The general advice is that you do not cook inside a tent where there is a risk from fire and carbon monoxide poisoning. Experienced campers will use an awning or tarp/windbreak combination to create a kitchen out of doors – and this is especially useful if you decide to cook by barbecue.

Many cooking accessories, like pans and eating irons, can be raided from the kitchen cupboard at home. Only things like water containers may have to be purchased especially for camping. And if you do have to make a special purchase try to buy gear that can also be used at home – you want maximum return from your investment.

For instance, a table and chairs will improve the camping experience. They give a focal point for family meals, chats and games. And to sit back on a comfy lounger certainly beats lying on the ground. They can also be used with the barbecue for home entertainment. And you can use the cool box at home for the barbecue's beers as well as keeping food fresh when you defrost the fridge.

A choice of accessories is very personal – mine generally include a book, DAB

radio and multitool. But remember, every item you take has to be packed into your backpack or car. Always ask yourself: "Do I really need this item or is it a luxury that I can do without?"

Four things I would say are essential are a fire bucket, fire extinguisher, fire blanket and First Aid kit – along with the knowledge on how to use them. Fire is a camper's worse nightmare and this is why many campsites operate a 20ft rule between units as a fire break.

Perfect pitch

You've got your gear; now where are you going to go? From small simple sites in a pub beer garden to holiday parks with swimming pool, to all-singing, all-dancing resorts, there is something out there for you. And with literally thousands to choose from you should always find a pitch – if you are willing to try somewhere new rather than hit a holiday hotspot. Just thumb through a book like this AA guide and you will see what I mean. Keep an open mind and you'll find exploring our rich and diverse countryside provides rewards out of all expectations.

Finally, you arrive at your campsite, pitch the tent and break out your camping kit. But before you kick back with your well earned tipple of choice consider the site rules and etiquette. There should be a list of dos' and don'ts at the site's reception and the owners or managers should have pointed out those salient to the site's ethos. However, most are normally down to common sense and respect for fellow campers. For instance, we've already discussed the 20ft rule for safety, but a no noise policy between certain times ensures a good night's sleep. Keeping dogs under control and ensuring children do not play

From small simple sites in a pub beer garden to holiday parks with swimming pool, to all-singing, all-dancing resorts, there is something out there for you.

around other units are also respectful. And arrival/departure times are normally there for a good reason – whether to allow for cleaning or to ensure good access of small country roads.

At the end of the day, camping is all about adventure. It is an enjoyable learning curve that soothes our stressful lives. And one to be lived to the full. Don't brood over gear or worry about standards and rules.

Just get out there and go for it. You won't be disappointed.

CLIVE'S TOP TIP

Make a packing list and use it before and after your holiday to ensure everything goes into the car and that you do not forget vital kit like tent pegs and poles!

NEW TO CARAVAN

NING

With many years of camping experience, Colin Church, AA Camping Inspector, gives an outline of how to get started

Whether you have just bought a caravan or are still thinking about taking the plunge, the first thing to say is that you are about to embark on a wonderful, life-changing experience limited only by your imagination.

Britain has a huge diversity of campsites, ranging from the largest holiday complex - with everything from swimming pools and tennis courts to bars and entertainment - to the smaller and more humble basic site. Sites are often set in stunning locations, and you can pitch up on smart hardstandings with electricity and often waste water drains and TV as well, or just a simple grass pitch in an open field. The choice is yours. Many people taking up caravanning have come from a tenting background and see the caravan as a way of extending their travelling season and providing all the creature comforts of home, including heating, showers, fridges and cookers. There's nothing better than waking up on a bright winter's morning to find a layer of snow on the ground while you are snug in your warm caravan!　　　　　　　　　▷

...the key to good caravanning is to be prepared, work through a checklist before setting out and follow a good routine.

For anyone new to caravanning, or contemplating buying a caravan, there are often concerns about actually dragging that white box around behind your car. How difficult is it to tow, and is it safe - you hear so many horror stories about caravans turning over - and what do you need to take with you? How hard is it to get the caravan onto the pitch? The list of worries goes on.

All caravan owners have been through this stage, and, like anything else in life, after a while towing a caravan becomes second nature. However, the key to good caravanning is to be prepared, work through a checklist before setting out and follow a good routine. Taking note of a few basic rules and spending time getting things right from the start, will go a long way towards making caravanning a safe and enjoyable experience.

Towing safety - matching your car to your caravan

As a newcomer it is advisable to keep to the generally recommended guideline of towing a laden caravan weighing no more than 85% of the car's kerbweight. These weights can be found in the car and caravan handbooks. As you become more experienced, you can tow at a higher percentage, but the golden rule

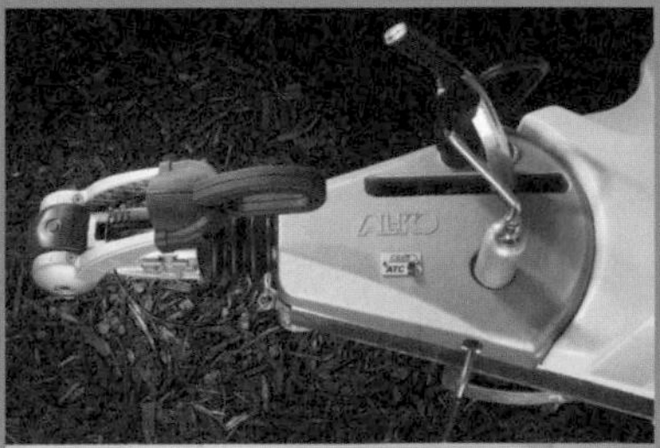

is NEVER go above 100%. You need to be aware of the car manufacturer's maximum towing limit. Sometimes this can be lower than the 85% guideline, if so you must take the lower figure.

What your car can tow is dependent on several things, namely the power of the engine and its torque (pulling power), whether is has automatic or manual gearbox, and whether it is a saloon, estate or 4x4. Diesel engines are favoured by many caravanners, as they tend to produce a lot of torque at low revs, which is just what you need to pull a caravan with ease. The majority of caravan dealers can run a suitability check of your car and/or caravan to check if it's a good match. This service can also be found on the internet.

Nose weight

Both the car and tow bracket manufacturer will give a nose weight limit, which is typically 75kg for a medium car to over 100kg for a 4x4. The nose weight limit is the maximum weight that the caravan should exert on the tow bar. It can be measured by a proprietary gauge or the careful use of bathroom scales and a wooden support. For good towing stability it is advised to be near this maximum but never above it. Too light a nose weight can cause instability, so keep to the advised maximum.

The stabiliser

The majority of modern caravans come with a fitted stabiliser (if not, you can get one fitted). The principle is that the stabiliser damps out lateral and vertical movement, aiding the outfit's stability. It is advisable to have one fitted - but it will not compensate for a badly loaded caravan.

Caravan loading

The loading of the caravan is very important in achieving a good stable outfit. The general rule is to load the heavy items low down and near to the caravan's axle. Normally the gas bottles in the front locker tend to make the caravan very nose heavy and you should not counter this by putting items at the very back of the caravan. You should make adjustments with the heavy items near the caravan axle. The aim is to achieve the recommended nose weight.

Tyre pressures, mirrors and accessories

It is very important to check the tyre pressures on both the caravan and car to ensure they are as recommended in the handbooks. Purchase a set of extension wing mirrors, which are fairly inexpensive, so that you can see along each side of the caravan, and it is a good idea to have some levelling blocks, which are used to level the caravan laterally if the pitch is not quite level.

Your caravan

Make sure you read the handbook and become familiar with the various controls, switches and functions of the caravan. My tip would be to make a simple list summarising the key items such as how to switch on the electric supply, how to turn on the gas supply, and how to switch on the fridge, space heater and water heater. Before you set out, make sure you are familiar with how to change a gas bottle, as they always seem to run out of gas whilst you're in the middle of cooking a meal, and it's probably raining and you have mislaid the torch!

What to take

The common mistake we all make when going away is that we take far too much. Just run through what you are likely to be doing and question the following - what clothes do you require; do you need to take food for the whole time you are away - it's best to take enough for one or two days and then buy when you get there; do you need cutlery and plates for six people when there are only two of you? Remember to plan ahead and travel as light as possible. As you gain experience you will quickly know what to take and what to leave behind. Don't forget the more you carry the higher the laden weight of the caravan will be and the more fuel your car will consume lugging all the kit around.

Your first trip

It is a good idea to plan your first trip close to home rather than give yourself a long and maybe tiring journey. Plan a short stay of a few days and you will pleasantly surprised how much confidence and knowledge you will gain. Connecting the caravan to the car is fairly straight forward; just back the car up until the tow bar is below the tow hitch of the caravan and, to make it easier, get someone to hold their arm vertically above the tow hitch to help you judge the distance more easily. Once in position just lower the caravan until it connects - most modern couplings have an indicator to ensure proper connection. Connect up the electric cable, then attach the breakaway cable to the car, and finally get someone to check the brake, indicator and side lights and you are ready for the off. Just make sure in your excitement to get going you have not forgotten your partner or the dog!

Towing guidelines

When turning corners don't forget you have a long caravan behind you so turn a bit later than normal to prevent cutting the corner. Brake a bit earlier to allow for the extra weight and try to drive as smoothly as possible; anticipating what is going on ahead. Mastering the art of towing a caravan will make you a much more aware and better driver. Before you set off make sure you have a clear understanding of the route to the campsite, especially the roads approaching the actual site, which can be tucked down narrow country lanes. Many campsites give instructions for how to get there, and it is a good idea to follow these rather than the Sat Nav directions (which can put a severe strain on your

relationship!). Remember the legal speed limits when towing – 50mph normal roads and 60mph on dual carriageways or motorways.

Arrival at the site

When you arrive at the campsite the owners or wardens are generally very helpful, especially to first timers. Once booked in, you are normally advised what pitch to go to and many wardens will actually see you to the pitch and help with reversing onto it. If you have any problems on site during your stay they will offer help and advice and even your neighbours will readily assist you if you ask them.

Setting up

Once onto the pitch the next stage is to get the caravan level. You may need to use a levelling block to get the lateral level right. Place the block in front of the wheel (which needs to be raised) and then ease the car and caravan forward up the block, until level. Then pull on the caravan brake and chock the wheels before uncoupling the car. Now a check with a simple spirit level on a flat surface in the caravan is all that's needed; the longitudinal levelling is easily obtained by adjusting the nose wheel until level. Then it's down with the corner steadies/jacks and you are ready to connect up the services.

Connect your electric cable to the caravan first and then to the electric hook-up on the site. This is far safer than connecting to the hook-up and walking around with a live cable on what might be wet grass! You can then switch on the supply in the caravan. Connect up your waste water container to the caravan and fill up your water container (Aquaroll or

similar) and connect it to the caravan's water pump. You can then prepare the cassette toilet by adding the chemicals and filling the water tank.

Now comes the good bit, take a seat and reward yourself with a nice cup of tea or maybe something stronger, especially if things have not gone to plan! If you have made some mistakes don't worry - it's all part of the learning curve.

Leaving the site

Make sure all the items are packed away securely and close all roof lights. Then it's just the reverse procedure of when you pitched up - disconnect electric, empty the water and waste water containers, and tackle the task of emptying the cassette toilet in the Chemical Disposal Point. Wind the corner steadies/jacks up and connect up the caravan to car, just as when you set off from home, check the lights and adjust mirrors and off you go, making sure that you have not left any rubbish on the pitch. Take it steady on the journey home and start planning your next trip!

These are just a few guidelines for the newcomer, but you can find a wealth of information on the internet, including some very useful downloads such as checklists and advice on towing, plus much more. A good way of fast tracking your knowledge and experience is to go on a caravan course which covers towing and manoeuvring. These are run by both The Caravan Club and The Camping & Caravanning Club and they are really worthwhile. It is also advisable to take out breakdown cover which includes the caravan just in case*.

Best for...

The AA thinks these are the best sites for...

...waterside pitches

ENGLAND

PENTEWAN SANDS HOLIDAY PARK, Pentewan, Cornwall
SOUTH END CARAVAN PARK, Barrow-in-Furness, Cumbria
SLENINGFORD WATERMILL CC PARK, North Stainley, North Yorkshire
SWALE VIEW CARAVAN PARK, Richmond, North Yorkshire

SCOTLAND

INVER MILL FARM CARAVAN PARK, Dunkeld, Perth & Kinross
SKYE C&C CLUB SITE, Edinbane, Isle of Skye

WALES

RIVERSIDE CAMPING, Caernarvon, Gwynedd

NORTHERN IRELAND

DRUMAHEGLIS MARINA & CARAVAN PARK, Ballymoney, Co Antrim

...stunning views

ENGLAND

TRISTRAM C&C PARK, Polzeath, Cornwall
TROUTBECK C&C CLUB SITE, Troutbeck, Cumbria
WOLDS WAY CARAVAN PARK, West Knapton, North Yorkshire

CHANNEL ISLANDS

SEAGULL CAMPSITE, Herm

SCOTLAND

OBAN C&C PARK, Oban, Argyll & Bute
LINNHE LOCHSIDE HOLIDAYS, Corpach, Highland
INVERCOE C&C PARK, Glencoe, Highland
JOHN O'GROATS CARAVAN SITE, John O'Groats, Highland

WALES

BRON-Y-WENDON CARAVAN PARK, Llanddulas, Conwy
BEACH VIEW CARAVAN PARK, Abersoch, Gwynedd
TRAWSDIR TOURING C&C PARK, Barmouth, Gwynedd
EISTEDDFA, Criccieth, Gwynedd
BARCDY TOURING C&C PARK, Talsarnau, Gwynedd
CARREGLWYD C&C PARK, Port Einon, Swansea

...good on-site restaurants

ENGLAND

STROUD HILL PARK, St Ives, Cambridgeshire
TRISTRAM C&C PARK, Polzeath, Cornwall
BAY VIEW HOLIDAY PARK, Bolton-Le-Sands, Lancashire
THE OLD BRICK KILNS, Barney, Norfolk
BEACONSFIELD FARM CARAVAN PARK, Shrewsbury, Shropshire

SCOTLAND

GLEN NEVIS C&C PARK, Fort William, Highland

...top toilets

ENGLAND

CARNON DOWNS C&C PARK, Truro, Cornwall
RIVERSIDE C&C PARK, South Molton, Devon
SHAMBA HOLIDAYS, St Leonards, Dorset
MOON & SIXPENCE, Woodbridge, Suffolk
RIVERSIDE CARAVAN PARK, High Bentham, North Yorkshire
WAYSIDE HOLIDAY PARK, Pickering, North Yorkshire
MOOR LODGE PARK, Bardsey, West Yorkshire

SCOTLAND

SKYE C&C CLUB SITE, Edinbane, Isle of Skye
BEECRAIGS C&C SITE, Linlithgow, West Lothian

...on-site fishing

ENGLAND

HEREFORD C&C CLUB SITE, Little Tarrington, Herefordshire
WOODLAND WATERS, Ancaster, Lincolnshire
SALTFLEETBY FISHERIES, Saltfleetby by Peter, Lincolnshire
LAKESIDE CARAVAN PARK & FISHERIES, Downham Market, Norfolk
MARSH FARM CARAVAN SITE, Saxmundham, Suffolk
SUMNERS PONDS FISHERY & CAMPSITE, Barns Green, West Sussex

SCOTLAND

HODDOM CASTLE CARAVAN PARK, Ecclefechan, Dumfries & Galloway
MILTON OF FONAB CARAVAN SITE, Pitlochry, Perth & Kinross
GART CARAVAN PARK, Callander, Stirling

WALES

AFON TEIFI C&C PARK, Newcastle Emlyn, Carmarthenshire
YNYSYMAENGWYN CARAVAN PARK, Tywyn, Gwynedd

...the kids

ENGLAND

TREVORNICK HOLIDAY PARK, Holywell Bay, Cornwall
EDEN VALLEY HOLIDAY PARK, Lostwithiel, Cornwall
GOLDEN VALLEY C&C PARK, Ripley, Derbyshire
FRESHWATER BEACH HOLIDAY PARK, Bridport, Dorset
SANDY BALLS HOLIDAY CENTRE, Fordingbridge, Hampshire
HEATHLAND BEACH CARAVAN PARK, Kessingland, Suffolk
GOLDEN SQUARE TOURING PARK, Helmsley, North Yorkshire
RIVERSIDE CARAVAN PARK, High Bentham, North Yorkshire
GOOSEWOOD CARAVAN PARK, Sutton-on-the-Forest, North Yorkshire

SCOTLAND

BLAIR CASTLE CARAVAN PARK, Blair Atholl, Perth & Kinross

WALES

HOME FARM CARAVAN PARK, Marian-Glas, Isle of Anglesey
HENDRE MYNACH TOURING C&C PARK, Barmouth, Gwynedd
TRAWSDIR TOURING C&C PARK, Barmouth, Gwynedd

...being eco-friendly

ENGLAND

SOUTH PENQUITE FARM, Blisland, Cornwall
RIVER DART COUNTRY PARK, Ashburton, Devon
BROOK LODGE FARM C&C PARK, Cowslip Green, Somerset

SCOTLAND

SHIELING HOLIDAYS, Craignure, Isle of Mull

WALES

CAERFAI BAY CARAVAN & TENT PARK, St David's, Pembrokeshire

...glamping it up

and staying in a pod or wigwam

ENGLAND

TREGOAD PARK, Looe, Cornwall
RUTHERN VALLEY HOLIDAYS, Ruthernbridge, Cornwall
LOW WRAY NATIONAL TRUST CAMPSITE, Ambleside Cumbria
WILD ROSE PARK, Appleby-in-Westmorland, Cumbria (wigwams)
ESKDALE C&C CLUB SITE, Boot, Cumbria
GREAT LANGDALE NATIONAL TRUST CAMPSITE, Great Langdale, Cumbria
WOODCLOSE CARAVAN PARK, Kirkby Lonsdale, Cumbria (wigwams)
WASDALE HEAD NATIONAL TRUST CAMPSITE, Wasdale Head, Cumbria
THE QUIET SITE, Watermillock, Cumbria
BELLINGHAM C&C CLUB SITE, Bellingham, Northumberland

COTSWOLD VIEW TOURING PARK, Charlbury, Oxfordshire

SCOTLAND

BARNSOUL FARM, Shawhead, Dumfries & Galloway
LINWATER CARAVAN PARK, East Calder, West Lothian

...or staying in a yurt

ENGLAND

SOUTH PENQUITE FARM, Blisland, Cornwall
GREAT LANGDALE NATIONAL TRUST CAMPSITE, Great Langdale, Cumbria
ACTON FIELD CAMPING SITE, Swanage, Dorset
HERSTON C&C PARK, Swanage, Dorset

...or staying in a tipi

ENGLAND

LOW WRAY NATIONAL TRUST CAMPSITE, Ambleside, Cumbria
SYKESIDE CAMPING PARK, Patterdale, Cumbria
SANDY BALLS HOLIDAY CENTRE, Fordingbridge, Hampshire
ROEBECK CAMPING & CARAVAN PARK, Ryde, Isle of Wight

WALES

EISTEDDFA, Criccieth, Gwynedd

Premier Parks ▶▶▶▶▶

ENGLAND

BERKSHIRE
HURLEY
Hurley Riverside Park

CAMBRIDGESHIRE
ST IVES
Stroud Hill Park

CHESHIRE
CODDINGTON
Manor Wood Country Caravan Park
WHITEGATE
Lamb Cottage Caravan Park

CORNWALL
BUDE
Wooda Farm Holiday Park
CARLYON BAY
Carlyon Bay Caravan & Camping Park
CRANTOCK
Trevella Tourist Park
GOONHAVERN
Silverbow Park
MEVAGISSEY
Seaview International Holiday Park
ST AUSTELL
River Valley Holiday Park
ST IVES
Polmanter Tourist Park
TRURO
Carnon Downs Caravan & Camping Park
Truro Caravan and Camping Park

CUMBRIA
APPLEBY-IN-WESTMORLAND
Wild Rose Park
BOOT
Eskdale Camping & Caravanning Club Site
KIRKBY LONSDALE
Woodclose Caravan Park
TROUTBECK [NEAR KESWICK]
Troutbeck Camping and Caravanning Club Site

DEVON
NEWTON ABBOT
Dornafield
Ross Park
SIDMOUTH
Oakdown Holiday Park

DORSET
BRIDPORT
Bingham Grange Touring & Camping Park
Highlands End Holiday Park
CHARMOUTH
Wood Farm Caravan & Camping Park
LYTCHETT MINSTER
South Lytchett Manor Caravan & Camping Park
ST LEONARDS
Shamba Holidays
WAREHAM
Wareham Forest Tourist Park
WEYMOUTH
East Fleet Farm Touring Park
WIMBORNE MINSTER
Merley Court
Wilksworth Farm Caravan Park

HAMPSHIRE
ROMSEY
Hill Farm Caravan Park

HEREFORDSHIRE
PEMBRIDGE
Townsend Touring Park

KENT
ASHFORD
Broadhembury Caravan & Camping Park
MARDEN
Tanner Farm Touring Caravan & Camping Park

LANCASHIRE
SILVERDALE
Silverdale Caravan Park

NORFOLK
CLIPPESBY
Clippesby Hall

NORTHUMBERLAND
BERWICK-UPON-TWEED
Ord House Country Park

NOTTINGHAMSHIRE
TEVERSAL
Teversal Camping & Caravanning Club Site

OXFORDSHIRE
HENLEY-ON-THAMES
Swiss Farm Touring & Camping
STANDLAKE
Lincoln Farm Park Oxfordshire

SHROPSHIRE
BRIDGNORTH
Stanmore Hall Touring Park
SHREWSBURY
Beaconsfield Farm Caravan Park
Oxon Hall Touring Park
TELFORD
Severn Gorge Park

SOMERSET
GLASTONBURY
The Old Oaks Touring Park
PORLOCK
Porlock Caravan Park
WIVELISCOMBE
Waterrow Touring Park

SUFFOLK
WOODBRIDGE
Moon & Sixpence

SUSSEX, EAST
BEXHILL
Kloofs Caravan Park

WIGHT, ISLE OF
NEWBRIDGE
Orchards Holiday Caravan Park
RYDE
Whitefield Forest Touring Park

YORKSHIRE, NORTH
ALLERSTON
Vale of Pickering Caravan Park
HARROGATE
Ripley Caravan Park
Rudding Holiday Park
HELMSLEY
Golden Square Touring Caravan Park
HIGH BENTHAM
Riverside Caravan Park
OSMOTHERLEY
Cote Ghyll Caravan & Camping Park
SCARBOROUGH
Jacobs Mount Caravan Park
SUTTON-ON-THE-FOREST
Goosewood Caravan Park
WYKEHAM
St Helens Caravan Park

CHANNEL ISLANDS

JERSEY
ST MARTIN,
Beuvelande Camp Site

SCOTLAND

ABERDEENSHIRE
HUNTLY
Huntly Castle Caravan Park

DUMFRIES & GALLOWAY
BRIGHOUSE BAY
Brighouse Bay Holiday Park
CREETOWN
Castle Cary Holiday Park
ECCLEFECHAN
Hoddom Castle Caravan Park

EAST LOTHIAN
DUNBAR
Thurston Manor Holiday Home Park

FIFE
ST ANDREWS
Craigtoun Meadows Holiday Park

HIGHLAND
CORPACH
Linnhe Lochside Holidays

PERTH & KINROSS
BLAIR ATHOLL
Blair Castle Caravan Park
River Tilt Caravan Park

WALES

ANGLESEY, ISLE OF
DULAS
Tyddyn Isaf Caravan Park
MARIAN-GLAS
Home Farm Caravan Park

CARMARTHENSHIRE
NEWCASTLE EMLYN
Cenarth Falls Holiday Park

CONWY
LLANDDULAS
Bron-Y-Wendon Caravan Park
LLANRWST
Bron Derw Touring Caravan Park

GWYNEDD
BARMOUTH
Hendre Mynach Touring Caravan &
Camping Park
Trawsdir Touring Caravans &
Camping Park
TAL-Y-BONT
Islawrffordd Caravan Park

MONMOUTHSHIRE
USK
Pont Kemys Caravan &
Camping Park

POWYS
BRECON
Pencelli Castle Caravan & Camping Park

WREXHAM
EYTON
The Plassey Leisure Park

NORTHERN IRELAND

CO ANTRIM
BUSHMILLS
Ballyness Caravan Park

CO FERMANAGH
BELCOO
Rushin House Caravan Park

Adults – No Children Parks

Over 40 of the parks in the AA pennant rating scheme have opted to provide facilities for adults only, and do not accept children. The minimum age for individual parks may be 18, or 21, while one or two pitch the limit even higher. For more information please contact the individual parks.

ENGLAND

CAMBRIDGESHIRE
Stanford Park, Burwell
Fields End Water CP, Doddington,
Stroud Hill Park, St Ives

CHESHIRE
Lamb Cottage Caravan Park, Whitegate

CORNWALL
St Day Holiday Park, St Day
Wayfarers C&C Park, St Hilary

CUMBRIA
Green Acres Caravan Park, Carlisle
Larches Caravan Park, Mealsgate

DERBYSHIRE
Clover Fields Touring CP, Buxton
Thornheyes Farm Campsite, Buxton

DEVON
Zeacombe House CP, East Anstey
Widdicombe Farm Touring Park, Torquay

DORSET
Bingham Grange T&CP, Bridport
Back of Beyond TP, St Leonards

GREATER MANCHESTER
Arrow Bank HP, Eardisland
Gelderwood Country Park, Rochdale

HEREFORDSHIRE
Cuckoo's Corner Campsite,
Moreton on Lugg

LINCOLNSHIRE
Long Acre CP, Boston
Orchard Park, Boston
Saltfleetby Fisheries, Saltfleetby St Peter

NORFOLK
Two Mills Touring Park, North Walsham
The Rickels C&C Park, Stanhoe
Breckland Meadows TP, Swaffham

NOTTINGHAMSHIRE
New Hall Farm Touring Park, Southwell

SHROPSHIRE
Beaconsfield Farm CP, Shrewsbury
Severn Gorge Park, Telford

SOMERSET
Exe Valley Caravan Site, Bridgetown
Cheddar Bridge Touring Park, Cheddar
The Old Oaks Touring Park, Glastonbury
Long Hazel Park, Sparkford
Greenacres Touring Park, Wellington
Homestead Park, Wells
Waterrow Touring Park, Wiveliscombe

SUFFOLK
Moat Barn Touring CP, Woodbridge

WEST MIDLANDS
Somers Wood Caravan Park, Meriden
WIGHT, ISLE OF
Riverside Paddock Camp Site, Newport

YORKSHIRE, NORTH
Shaws Trailer Park, Harrogate
Foxholme C&C Park, Helmsley
Maustin CP, Netherby

YORKSHIRE, WEST
Moor Lodge Park, Bardsey
St Helena's Caravan Park, Horsforth

SCOTLAND

FIFE
Woodland Gardens C&C Site,
Lundin Links

WALES

PEMBROKESHIRE
Rosebush Caravan Park, Rosebush

POWYS
Riverside C&C Park, Crickhowell
Dalmore C&C Park, Llandrindod Wells

AA Holiday Centres

ENGLAND

CORNWALL
HAYLE
St Ives Bay Holiday Park
HOLWELL BAY
Holywell Bay Holiday Park
Trevornick Holiday Park
LOOE
Tencreek Holiday Park
MULLION
Mullion Holiday Park
NEWQUAY
Hendra Holiday Park
Newquay Holiday Park
PENTEWAN
Pentewan Sands Holiday Park
PERRANPORTH
Perran Sands Holiday Park
REJERRAH
Monkey Tree Holiday Park
ST MERRYN
Harlyn Sands Holiday Park
WIDEMOUTH BAY
Widemouth Bay Caravan Park

CUMBRIA
FLOOKBURGH
Lakeland Leisure Park
POOLEY BRIDGE
Park Foot Caravan & Camping Park
SILLOTH
Stanwix Park Holiday Centre

DEVON
CROYDE BAY
Ruda Holiday Park
DAWLISH
Golden Sands Holiday Park
Lady's Mile Holiday Park
Peppermint Park
EXMOUTH
Devon Cliffs Holiday Park
MORTEHOE
Twitchen House Holiday Parc
PAIGNTON
Beverley Parks C&C Park
SHALDON
Coast View Holiday Park
WOOLACOMBE
Golden Coast Holiday Park
Woolacombe Bay Holiday Village
Woolacombe Sands Holiday Park

DORSET
BRIDPORT
Freshwater Beach Holiday Park
West Bay Holiday Park
HOLTON HEATH
Sandford Holiday Park
POOLE
Rockley Park
WEYMOUTH
Littlesea Holiday Park
Seaview Holiday Park

CO DURHAM
BLACKHALL COLLIERY
Crimdon Dene

ESSEX
CLACTON-ON-SEA
Martello Beach Holiday Park
Highfield Grange
MERSEA ISLAND
Waldegraves Holiday Park
ST LAWRENCE
Waterside St Lawrence Bay
ST OSYTH
Orchards Holiday Park
WALTON ON THE NAZE
Naze Marine

HAMPSHIRE
FORDINGBRIDGE
Sandy Balls Holiday Centre

KENT
EASTCHURCH
Warden Springs Caravan Park

LANCASHIRE
BLACKPOOL
Marton Mere Holiday Village

LINCOLNSHIRE
CLEETHORPES
Thorpe Park Holiday Centre ▷

AA Holiday Centres *continued*

LINCOLNSHIRE continued
MABLETHORPE
Golden Sands Holiday Park
SALTFLEET
Sunnydale

MERSEYSIDE
SOUTHPORT
Riverside Holiday Park

NORFOLK
BELTON
Wild Duck Holiday Park
BURGH CASTLE
Breydon Water
CAISTER-ON-SEA
Caister Holiday Park
GREAT YARMOUTH
Vauxhall Holiday Park
HUNSTANTON
Searles Leisure Resort

NORTHUMBERLAND
BERWICK-UPON-TWEED
Haggerston Castle
NORTH SEATON
Sandy Bay

SOMERSET
BREAN
Warren Farm Holiday Centre
BRIDGWATER
Mill Farm C&C Park
BURNHAM-ON-SEA
Burnham-on-Sea Holiday Village
CHEDDAR
Broadway House Holiday Park

SUFFOLK
KESSINGLAND
Kessingland Beach Holiday Park

SUSSEX, EAST
CAMBER
Camber Sands

SUSSEX, WEST
SELSEY
Warner Farm Touring Park

WIGHT, ISLE OF
COWES
Thorness Bay Holiday Park
ST HELENS
Nodes Point Holiday Park
SHANKLIN
Lower Hyde Holiday Park
WHITECLIFF BAY
Whitecliff Bay Holiday Park

YORKSHIRE, EAST RIDING OF
SKIPSEA
Low Skirlington Leisure Park
WITHERNSEA
Withernsea Sands

YORKSHIRE, NORTH
FILEY
Blue Dolphin Holiday Park
Flower of May Holiday Park
Primrose Valley Holiday Park
Reighton Sands Holiday Park

SCOTLAND

DUMFRIES & GALLOWAY
GATEHOUSE-OF-FLEET
Auchenlarie Holiday Park
SOUTHERNESS
Southerness Holiday Village

EAST LOTHIAN
LONGNIDDRY
Seton Sands Holiday Village

HIGHLAND
DORNOCH
Grannie's Heilan Hame HP
NAIRN
Nairn Lochroy Holiday Park

NORTH AYRSHIRE
SALTCOATS
Sandylands

PERTH & KINROSS
TUMMEL BRIDGE
Tummel Valley Holiday Park

SCOTTISH BORDERS
EYEMOUTH
Eyemouth

SOUTH AYRSHIRE
AYR
Craig Tara Holiday Park
COLYTON
Sundrum Castle Holiday Park

WALES

CEREDIGION
BORTH
Brynowen Holiday Park

CONWY
TOWYN
Ty Mawr Holiday Park

DENBIGHSHIRE
PRESTATYN
Presthaven Sands

GWYNEDD
PORTHMADOG
Greenacres
PWLLHELI
Hafan Y Mor Holiday Park

PEMBROKESHIRE
TENBY
Kiln Park Holiday Centre

SWANSEA
SWANSEA
Riverside Caravan Park

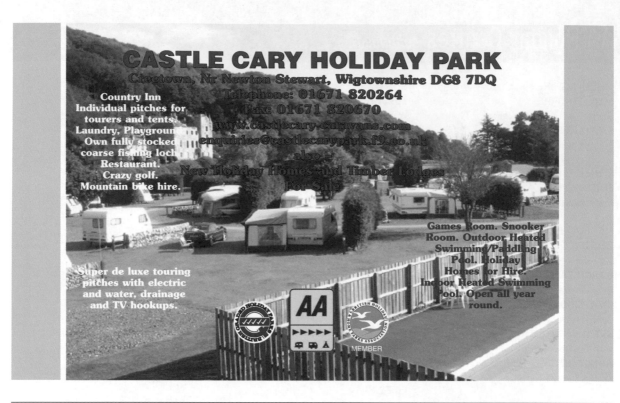

CASTLE CARY HOLIDAY PARK

Creetown, Nr Newton Stewart, Wigtownshire DG8 7DQ
Telephone: 01671 820264
Fax: 01671 820670
www.castlecary-caravans.com
enquiries@castlecarypark.f9.co.uk
also -
New Holiday Homes and Timber Lodges
For Sale

Country Inn
Individual pitches for
tourers and tents.
Laundry, Playground.
Own fully stocked
coarse fishing loch.
Restaurant.
Crazy golf.
Mountain bike hire.

Super de luxe touring
pitches with electric
and water, drainage
and TV hookups.

Games Room. Snooker
Room. Outdoor Heated
Swimming/Paddling
Pool. Holiday
Homes for Hire.
Indoor Heated Swimming
Pool. Open all year
round.

AA
▶▶▶▶▶

MEMBER

Quality-assured
accommodation at over
6,000 establishments
throughout the UK & Ireland

- Quality-assured accommodation
- Secure online booking process
- Extensive range and choice of accommodation
- Detailed, authoritative descriptions
- Exclusive discounts for AA Members

England

Cornham Brake, Exmoor National Park

ISLE OF - Places incorporating the words 'Isle of' of 'Isle' will be found under the actual name, eg Isle of Wight is listed under Wight, Isle of. Channel Islands and Isle of Man, however, are between England and Scotland, and there is also a section in the guide for Scottish Islands.

BERKSHIRE

FINCHAMPSTEAD — Map 5 SU76

Places to visit

West Green House Gardens, Hartley Wintney 01252 844611 www.westgreenhouse.co.uk

Museum of English Rural Life, Reading 0118 378 8660 www.merl.org.uk

Great for kids: The Look Out Discovery Centre, Bracknell 01344 354400 www.bracknell-forest.gov.uk/be

AA CAMPING CARD SITE

►►► 73% California Chalet & Touring Park *(SU788651)*

Nine Mile Ride RG40 4HU
☎ 0118 973 3928 0118 932 8720
e-mail: enquiries@californiapark.co.uk
dir: *From A321 (S of Wokingham), right onto B3016 to Finchampstead. Follow Country Park signs on Nine Mile Ride to site*

Open all year Last arrival 21.00hrs Last departure noon

A simple, peaceful woodland site with secluded pitches among the trees, adjacent to the country park. Several pitches have a prime position beside the lake with their own fishing area. Plans for the future include better hardstanding pitches, refurbished toilets and more lodges. A 5.5 acre site with 30 touring pitches, 30 hardstandings.

California Chalet & Touring Park

AA Pubs & Restaurants nearby: The Broad Street Tavern, Wokingham 0118 9773706

L'ortolan, Shinfield 0118 988 8500

Facilities: **Services:**

Within 3 miles:

Notes: No ground fires, no ball games, no washing of caravans

HURLEY

Places to visit

Cliveden (NT), Cliveden, 01628 605069 www.nationaltrust.org.uk

The Hell-Fire Caves, West Wycombe 01494 524411 (office) www.hellfirecaves.co.uk

Great for kids: Bekonscot Model Village & Railway, Beaconsfield 01494 672919 www.bekonscot.co.uk

HURLEY — Map 5 SU88

PREMIER PARK

►►►►► 81% Hurley Riverside Park *(SU826839)*

GOLD

Park Office SL6 5NE
☎ 01628 824493 & 823501 01628 825533
e-mail: info@hurleyriversidepark.co.uk
dir: *Signed off A4130 (Henley to Maidenhead road), just W of Hurley*

* £13-£21 £13-£21 £11-£21

Open Mar-Oct Last arrival 20.00hrs Last departure noon

A large Thames-side site with a good touring area close to river. Now a quality park following major investment, there are three beautifully refurbished toilet blocks, one of which houses quality, fully-serviced unisex facilities. Level grassy pitches are sited in small, sectioned areas, and this is a generally peaceful setting. There are furnished tents for hire. A 15 acre site with 200 touring pitches, 12 hardstandings and 290 statics.

AA Pubs & Restaurants nearby: Black Boys Inn, Hurley 01628 824212

Hotel du Vin, Henley-on-Thames 01491 848400

Facilities:

Services:

Within 3 miles:

Notes: No unsupervised children, dogs must be kept on leads, quiet park policy, fishing in season, slipway, gas sales, riverside picnic grounds, nature trail. Wi-fi

see advert below

NEWBURY Map 5 SU46

Places to visit

Highclere Castle & Gardens, Highclere 01635 253210 www.highclerecastle.co.uk

West Berkshire Museum, Newbury 01635 519231 westberkshiremuseum.org.uk

Great for kids: The Living Rainforest, Hampstead Norreys 01635 202444 www.livingrainforest.org

►►► 78% Bishops Green Farm Camp Site *(SU502630)*

Bishops Green RG20 4JP
☎ 01635 268365
dir: *Exit A339 (opp New Greenham Park) towards Bishops Green & Ecchinswell. Site on left, approx 0.5m by barn*

Open Apr-Oct Last arrival 21.30hrs

A sheltered and secluded meadowland park close to the Hampshire/Berkshire border, offering very clean and well-maintained facilities, including a new toilet block with a disabled/family room. There are woodland and riverside walks to be enjoyed around the farm, and coarse fishing is also available. A 1.5 acre site with 30 touring pitches.

AA Pubs & Restaurants nearby: Marco Pierre White's Yew Tree Inn, near Highclere 01635 253360

Facilities:
Services:
Within 3 miles:
Notes:

RISELEY

Places to visit

Basildon Park (NT), Lower Basildon 0118 984 3040 www.nationaltrust.org.uk/basildonpark

Mapledurham House 0118 972 3350 www.mapledurham.co.uk

Great for kids: Beale Park, Lower Basildon 0870 777 7160 www.bealepark.co.uk

RISELEY Map 5 SU76

►►► 84% Wellington Country Park

(SU728628)

Odiham Rd RG7 1SP
☎ 0118 932 6444 🖹 0118 932 6445
e-mail: info@wellington-country-park.co.uk
web: www.wellington-country-park.co.uk
dir: *M4 junct 11, A33 south towards Basingstoke. M3 junct 5, B3349 north towards Reading*

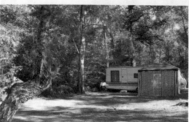

Open Mar-Nov Last arrival 17.30hrs Last departure 13.00hrs

A peaceful woodland site set within an extensive country park, which comes complete with lakes and nature trails, and these are accessible to campers after the country park closes. Toilet facilities were refurbished and modernised in 2010 and extra facilities, including family rooms and privacy cubicles are due to added for the 2011 season. There's also a herd of Red and Fallow deer that roam the meadow area. This site is ideal for those travelling on the M4. An 80 acre site with 72 touring pitches, 10 hardstandings.

AA Pubs & Restaurants nearby: The George & Dragon, Swallowfield 0118 988 4432

The Wellington Arms, Stratfield Turgis 01256 882214

Leisure: **Facilities:**
Services:
Within 3 miles:
Notes: No open fires, pets must be kept on leads. Miniature railway, crazy golf, maze, animal corner

BRISTOL

See Cowslip Green, Somerset

CAMBRIDGESHIRE

BURWELL Map 12 TL56

Places to visit

Anglesey Abbey, Gardens & Lode Mill (NT), Lode 01223 810080 www.nationaltrust.org.uk/angleseyabbey

National Horseracing Museum and Tours, Newmarket 01638 667333 www.nhrm.co.uk

►►► 69% *Stanford Park* *(TL578675)*

Weirs Drove CB25 0BP
☎ 01638 741547 & 07802 439997
e-mail: enquiries@stanfordcaravanpark.co.uk
dir: *Signed from B1102*

Open all year Last arrival 20.00hrs Last departure 11.00hrs

A secluded site on the outskirts of Burwell set in four large fields with several attractive trees. The amenities are modern and well kept, and there are eight hardstandings hedged with privet. A 20 acre site with 100 touring pitches, 20 hardstandings.

AA Pubs & Restaurants nearby: Dyke's End, Reach 01638 743816

Hole in the Wall, Little Wilbraham 01223 812282

Facilities:
Services:
Within 3 miles:
Notes: Adults only. No group bookings

COMBERTON Map 12 TL35

Places to visit

Imperial War Museum Duxford, Duxford 01223 835000 www.iwm.org.uk/duxford

Audley End House & Gardens, Audley End 01799 522842 www.english-heritage.org.uk

Great for kids: Linton Zoological Gardens, Linton 01223 891308 www.lintonzoo.co.uk

►►►► 91% *Highfield Farm Touring Park* *(TL389572)*

Best of British

Long Rd CB23 7DG
☎ 01223 262308 🖹 01223 262308
e-mail: enquiries@highfieldfarmtouringpark.co.uk
dir: *From M11 junct 12, take A603 (Sandy) for 0.5m, then right onto B1046 to Comberton*

LEISURE: Indoor swimming pool · Outdoor swimming pool · Children's playground · Tennis court · Games room · Separate TV room · 9/18 hole golf course · Boats for hire · Cinema · Fishing · Mini golf · Watersports · Stables **FACILITIES:** Bath · Shower · Electric shaver · Hairdryer · Ice Pack Facility · Disabled facilities · Public telephone · Shop on site or within 200yds · Mobile shop (calls at least 5 days a week) · BBQ area · Picnic area · Dog exercise area

Highfield Farm Touring Park

Open Apr-Oct Last arrival 22.00hrs Last departure 14.00hrs

Run by a very efficient and friendly family, the park is on a well-sheltered hilltop, with spacious pitches including a cosy backpackers/cyclists' area, and separate sections for couples and families. There is a one and a half mile marked walk around the family farm, with stunning views. An 8 acre site with 120 touring pitches, 52 hardstandings.

AA Pubs & Restaurants nearby: The Three Horseshoes, Madingley 01954 210221

Restaurant 22, Cambridge 01223 351880

Leisure: ⚑

Facilities: ⬛☉℘✳☾🛢🐾

Services: ⬛🅢🛒🚿🅣🍴⛽

Within 3 miles: ↧℘🛢🅢U

Notes: ⊛ Postbox. Wi-fi

DODDINGTON   Map 12 TL49

Places to visit

WWT Welney Wetland Centre, Welney 01353 860711 www.wwt.org.uk

Flag Fen Archaeology Park, Peterborough 01733 313414 www.flagfen.org

NEW ►►►► 85% Fields End Water Caravan Park & Fishery *(TL378908)*

Benwick Rd PE15 0TY
☎ **01354 740199**
e-mail: info@fieldsendfishing.co.uk
dir: *Exit A141, follow signs to Doddington. At clock tower in Doddington turn right into Benwick Rd. Site 1.5m on right after sharp bends*

* 🚐 £15-£16 🚏 £15-£16 ▲ £10-£12

Open all year Last arrival 20.30hrs Last departure noon

A new park developed to very high specifications. The 33 fully serviced pitches, all with very

generous hardstandings, are on elevated terraces with sweeping views of the surrounding Fenland countryside. The two toilet blocks contain several combined cubicle spaces and there are shady walks through mature deciduous woodland adjacent to two large and appealingly landscaped fishing lakes. A 20 acre site with 33 touring pitches, 10 hardstandings.

AA Pubs & Restaurants nearby: The Crown, Broughton 01487 824428

The Old Bridge Hotel, Huntingdon 01480 424300

Facilities: ⬛☉℘✳☾🛢🐾🪁

Services: ⬛🅢🅣🍴 **Within 3 miles:** ℘🛢🅢

Notes: Adults only. 2 fishing lakes. Wi-fi

HEMINGFORD ABBOTS   Map 12 TL27

►►► 77% Quiet Waters Caravan Park *(TL283712)*

PE28 9AJ
☎ **01480 463405**   ▤ **01480 463405**
e-mail: quietwaters.park@btopenworld.com
web: www.quietwaterscaravanpark.co.uk
dir: *Follow village signs off A14 junct 25, E of Huntingdon, site in village centre*

* 🚐 £14-£18 🚏 £14-£18 ▲ £14-£18

Open Apr-Oct Last arrival 20.00hrs Last dep noon

This attractive little riverside site is found in a most charming village just one mile from the A14, making an ideal centre to tour the Cambridgeshire area. There are nine holiday statics for hire. A 1 acre site with 20 touring pitches, 18 hardstandings and 40 statics.

AA Pubs & Restaurants nearby: The Cock Pub & Restaurant, Hemingford Grey 01480 463609

The Old Bridge Hotel, Huntingdon 01480 424300

Facilities: ⬛☉℘✳☾ **Services:** ⬛🅢🛒⌀
Within 3 miles: ↧🐾🍴℘🛢🅢U

Notes: Pets must be kept on leads. Fishing & boating. Wi-fi

HUNTINGDON   Map 12 TL27

Places to visit

Ramsey Abbey Gatehouse (NT), Ramsey 01480 301494 www.nationaltrust.org.uk

Fitzwilliam Museum, Cambridge 01223 332900 www.fitzmuseum.cam.ac.uk

Great for kids: The Raptor Foundation, Woodhurst 01487 741140 www.raptorfoundation.org.uk

►►► 79% Huntingdon Boathaven & Caravan Park *(TL249706)*

The Avenue, Godmanchester PE29 2AF
☎ **01480 411977**   ▤ **01480 411977**
e-mail: boathaven.hunts@virgin.net
dir: *S of town. Exit A14 at Godmanchester junct, through Godmanchester on B1043 to site (on left by River Ouse)*

* 🚐 £14-£17 🚏 £14-£17 ▲ £11-£18

Open all year (rs Open in winter when weather permits) Last arrival 21.00hrs

A small, well laid out site overlooking a boat marina and the River Ouse, set close to the A14 and within walking distance of Huntingdon town centre. The toilets are clean and well kept. A pretty area has been created for tents beside the marina, with wide views across the Ouse Valley. Weekend family activities are organised throughout the season. A 2 acre site with 24 touring pitches, 18 hardstandings.

AA Pubs & Restaurants nearby: The Old Bridge Hotel, Huntingdon 01480 424300

King William IV, Fenstanton 01480 462467

Facilities: ⬛☉℘✳☾🪑🪁

Services: ⬛🛢🅣🍴

Within 3 miles: ↧🐾🎯℘🛒🛢

Notes: ⊛ No cars by tents. Dogs on leads

An increasing number of parks do not accept children. For a full list of Adults-only parks see page 45

SERVICES: ⬛ Electric hook up   🅢 Launderette   🍸 Licensed bar   🛢 Calor Gas   ⌀ Camping Gaz   🅣 Toilet fluid   🍴 Café/Restaurant   🍟 Fast Food/Takeaway   🔋 Battery charging
🍼 Baby care   ⛽ Motorvan service point   **ABBREVIATIONS:** BH/bank hols-bank holidays   Etr-Easter   Whit-Whitsun   dep-departure   fr-from   hrs-hours   m-mile   mdnt-midnight
rdbt-roundabout   rs-restricted service   wk-week   wknd-weekend   ⊛ No credit cards   ⊗ no dogs   See page 7 for details of the AA Camping Card Scheme

HUNTINGDON continued

►►► 77% The Willows Caravan Park

(TL224708)

Bromholme Ln, Brampton PE28 4NE
☎ 01480 437566
e-mail: willows@willows33.freeserve.co.uk
dir: Exit A14/A1 signed Brampton, follow Huntingdon signs. Site on right close to Brampton Mill pub

⚐ £15-£16 ⛺ £15-£16 ▲ £14-£15

Open all year Last arrival 20.00hrs Last departure noon

A small, friendly site in a pleasant setting beside the River Ouse, on the Ouse Valley Walk. Bay areas have been provided for caravans and motorhomes, and planting for screening is gradually maturing. There are launching facilities and free river fishing. A 4 acre site with 50 touring pitches, 10 hardstandings.

AA Pubs & Restaurants nearby: The Old Bridge Hotel, Huntingdon 01480 424300

Leisure: ⚏

Facilities: ⚑☉✳♿

Services: ⚑◫🔒

Within 3 miles: ⚓⚒🎬✍🛒

Notes: ⊘ No cars by tents. Dogs must be on leads, ball games on field provided, no generators, no groundsheets, 5mph one-way system. Free book lending/exchange

ST IVES

Places to visit

The Farmland Museum and Denny Abbey, Waterbeach 01223 860988
www.dennyfarmlandmuseum.org.uk

Oliver Cromwell's House, Ely 01353 662062
www.visitely.org.uk

ST IVES   Map 12 TL37

PREMIER PARK

AA CAMPING CARD SITE

►►►►► 95% Stroud Hill Park

(TL335787)

Fen Rd PE28 3DE
☎ 01487 741333   📄 01487 741365
e-mail: stroudhillpark@btconnect.com
dir: Off B1040 in Pidley follow signs for Lakeside Lodge Complex, down Fen Rd. Site on right

⚐ £24-£26.50 ⛺ £24-£26.50 ▲ £16.50

Open all year Last arrival 20.00hrs Last dep noon

A superb adults-only caravan park designed to a very high specification in a secluded and sheltered spot not far from St Ives. A modern timber-framed barn houses the exceptional facilities. These include the beautifully tiled toilets with spacious cubicles, each containing a shower, washbasin and toilet. A bar and café, restaurant, small licensed shop, tennis court and course fishing are among the attractions. There are three pay-as-you-go golf courses plus ten-pin bowling nearby. A 6 acre site with 60 touring pitches, 44 hardstandings.

AA Pubs & Restaurants nearby: The Old Ferryboat Inn, Holywell 01480 463227

The Lazy Otter, Stretham 01353 649780

Leisure: ⚏   **Facilities:** ⚑☉☂✳♿⏰🖊🐴
Services: ⚑◫🍴🔒⚗Ⓣ🍽
Within 3 miles: ⚓🎬✍◎⚓🛒◫U
Notes: Adults only. No large motorhomes. Wi-fi

WISBECH   Map 12 TF40

Places to visit

Peckover House & Garden (NT), Wisbech 01945 583463
www.nationaltrust.org.uk/peckover

Sandringham House, Gardens & Museum, Sandringham 01533 612908
www.sandringham.co.uk

Great for kids: Butterfly & Wildlife Park, Spalding 01406 363833
www.butterflyandwildlifepark.co.uk

►►► 80% Little Ranch Leisure

(TF456062)

Begdale, Elm PE14 0AZ
☎ 01945 860066   📄 01945 860114
dir: From rdbt on A47 (SW of Wisbech) take Redmoor Lane to Begdale

⚐ £10-£15 ⛺ £10-£15 ▲ £10-£15

Open all year

A friendly family site set in an apple orchard, with 25 fully-serviced pitches and a beautifully designed, spacious toilet block. The site overlooks a large fishing lake, and the famous horticultural auctions at Wisbech are nearby. A 10 acre site with 25 touring pitches, 25 hardstandings.

AA Pubs & Restaurants nearby: The Moorings, Wisbech 01945 773391

The Hare Arms, Stow Bardolph 01366 382229

Facilities: ⚑☉☂✳♿🐴🐕
Services: ⚑◫⬇
Within 3 miles: ✍🛒
Notes: ⊘

CHESHIRE

CODDINGTON
Map 15 SJ45

Places to visit

Cholmondeley Castle Gardens, Cholmondeley
01829 720383 www.cholmondeleycastle.com

Hack Green Secret Nuclear Bunker, Nantwich
01270 629219 www.hackgreen.co.uk

Great for kids: Dewa Roman Experience,
Chester 01244 343407
www.dewaromanexperience.co.uk

PREMIER PARK

AA CAMPING CARD SITE

►►►►► 82% Manor Wood Country Caravan Park (SJ453553)

Manor Wood CH3 9EN
☎ 01829 782990 & 782442 📠 01829 782990
e-mail: info@manorwoodcaravans.co.uk
dir: From A534 at Barton, turn opposite Cock
O'Barton pub signed Coddington. Left in 100yds.
Site 0.5m on left

* 🚐 £12-£23 🚉 £12-£23 ⛺ £12-£23

Open all year (rs Oct-May swimming pool closed)
Last arrival 20.30hrs Last departure 11.00hrs

A secluded landscaped park in a tranquil country
setting with extensive views towards the Welsh
Hills across the Cheshire Plain. This park offers
fully serviced pitches, modern facilities, a heated
outdoor pool and tennis courts. Wildlife is
encouraged, and lake fishing with country walks
and pubs are added attractions. Generous pitch
density provides optimum privacy and the park is
immaculately maintained, with a diligent
approach to cleanliness throughout. Seasonal
touring pitches are available. An 8 acre site with
45 touring pitches, 38 hardstandings and 12
statics.

AA Pubs & Restaurants nearby: The Calveley
Arms, Handley 01829 770619

1851 Restaurant at Peckforton Castle, Peckforton
01829 260930

Leisure: 🏊 ⚲ ♨ ✎
Facilities: 🌣 ⊙ 🍴 ✳ ☕ ⛱
Services: 🔌 🔵 🅰 ⬇
Within 3 miles: ⚡ 🏌 🏬 🛒
Notes: No cars by caravans. Wi-fi

DELAMERE
Map 15 SJ56

Places to visit

Jodrell Bank Visitor Centre & Arboretum,
Jodrell Bank 01477 571339
www.manchester.ac.uk/jodrellbank

Little Moreton Hall (NT), Congleton
01260 272018 www.nationaltrust.org.uk

Great for kids: Chester Zoo, Chester
01244 380280 www.chesterzoo.org

AA CAMPING CARD SITE

►►► 87% Fishpool Farm Caravan Park (SJ567672)

Fishpool Rd CW8 2HP
☎ 01606 883970 & 07501 506583
📠 01606 301022
e-mail: enquiries@fishpoolfarmcaravanpark.co.uk
dir: From Tarporley take A49 towards Cuddington.
Left onto B5152. Continue on B5152 (now Fishpool
Rd). Site on right

* 🚐 fr £20 🚉 fr £20 ⛺ fr £15

Open 15 Feb-15 Jan Last arrival 19.00hrs Last
departure mdnt

Developed on a former hay field on the owner's
farm and opened in 2009, this excellent park has
a shop/reception, a superb purpose-built toilet
block with laundry facilities, a picnic area, and 50
spacious pitches, all with electric hook-up. Plans
for the future include a lakeside lodge, coarse
fishing and a nature walk. A 5.5 acre site with 50
touring pitches.

AA Pubs & Restaurants nearby: The Dysart Arms,
Bunbury 01829 260183

Alvanley Arms Inn, Tarporley 01829 760200

Leisure: ⚲
Facilities: 🌣 ⊙ 🍴 ✳ ☕ 🅰 ⛱
Services: 🔌 🔵 🅰 ⬇
Within 3 miles: ⚡ 🏌 ◎ ≋ 🏬 🛒 U
Notes: Dogs must be on leads. Dog walks
available

KNUTSFORD
Map 15 SJ77

►►► 75% Woodlands Park (SJ743710)

Wash Ln, Allostock WA16 9LG
☎ 01565 723429 & 01332 810818
dir: M6 junct 18 take A50 N to Holmes Chapel for
3m, turn into Wash Ln by Boundary Water Park.
Site 0.25m on left

* 🚐 fr £14 🚉 fr £14 ⛺ fr £12

Open Mar-6 Jan Last arrival 21.00hrs Last
departure 11.00hrs

A very tranquil and attractive park in the heart of
rural Cheshire, and set in 16 acres of mature
woodland. Tourers are located in three separate
wooded areas that teem with wildlife and you will
wake up to the sound of birdsong. This park is just
three miles from Jodrell Bank. A 16 acre site with
40 touring pitches and 140 statics.

AA Pubs & Restaurants nearby: The Dog Inn,
Knutsford 01625 861421

Facilities: 🌣 ⊙ ♿ **Services:** 🔌 🔵 🅰
Within 3 miles: ⚡ 🏌 🛒
Notes: 🐕 Pets must be on leads, no skateboards

WETTENHALL
Map 15 SJ66

AA CAMPING CARD SITE

NEW ►►► 82% New Farm Caravan Park (SJ613608)

Long Ln CW7 4DW
☎ 01270 528213 & 07970 221112
e-mail: info@newfarmcheshire.com
dir: A51 Alpraham near Tarpoley, signed

* 🚐 £16-£22 🚉 £16-£22

Open all year Last arrival 20.00hrs Last dep 14.00hrs

Diversification at New Farm has seen the
development of four fishing lakes, quality AA-listed
B&B accommodation in a newly converted milking
parlour, and the creation of a peaceful small touring
park. Only operational for a short period of time, the
proprietors are to be commended for their investment
to provide a very welcome touring destination within
this peaceful part of Cheshire. Expect good
landscaping, 17 generous hardstanding pitches, a
spotless new toilet block, and good attention to detail
throughout. Please note there is no laundry. A 40 acre
site with 24 touring pitches, 17 hardstandings.

AA Pubs & Restaurants nearby: The Nags Head,
Horton Moss 01829 260265

Facilities: 🌣 🍴 🅰 ⛱ **Services:** 🔌 🅰 ⊘ ⬆ ⬇
Within 3 miles: ⚡ ≋ 🏌 🛒 U
Notes: No cars by tents. Fishing

WHITEGATE
Map 15 SJ66

Places to visit

The Cheshire Military Museum,
Chester 01244 327617
www.chester.ac.uk/militarymuseum

Chester Cathedral, Chester 01244 324756
www.chestercathedral.com

PREMIER PARK

►►►►► 91% Lamb Cottage
Caravan Park (SJ613692)

GOLD

Dalefords Ln CW8 2BN
☎ 01606 882302 📠 01606 888491
e-mail: info@lambcottage.co.uk
dir: *From A556 turn at Sandiway lights into Dalefords Ln, signed Winsford. Site 1m on right*

🚐 🚑

Open Mar-Oct Last arrival 20.00hrs Last departure noon

A secluded and attractively landscaped adults-only park in a glorious location where the emphasis is on peace and relaxation. The serviced pitches are spacious with wide grass borders for sitting out and the high quality toilet block is spotlessly clean and immaculately maintained. A good central base for exploring this area, with access to nearby woodland walks and cycle trails. Seasonal touring pitches are available. A 6 acre site with 45 touring pitches, 28 hardstandings and 22 statics.

AA Pubs & Restaurants nearby: The Bear's Paw, Warmingham 01270 526317

Facilities: 🖙 ⊙ ℱ ᭺ ᳘ ㋛ 🐕

Services: 🚱 🖸 🛢

Within 3 miles: ᴫ 🏌 🛒 ∪

Notes: Adults only. No tents (except trailer tents), no commercial vehicles. Wi-fi

Cornwall

Known for its wild moorland landscapes, glorious river valleys, quaint towns and outstanding coastline, Cornwall is one of the country's most popular holiday destinations. Boasting the mildest and sunniest climate in the United Kingdom, as a result of its southerly latitude and the influence of the Gulf Stream, the county benefits from more than 1,500 hours of sunshine each year.

Bordered to the north and west by the Atlantic and to the south by the English Channel, the county boasts prehistoric sites, colourful mythology, a wealth of ancient traditions, a legacy of tin mining and impressive cultural diversity. Cornwall is acknowledged as one of the Celtic nations by many locals and use of the revived Cornish language has increased.

St Piran's flag is regarded by many as the national flag of Cornwall and an emblem of the Cornish people. It is said that St Piran, who is alleged to have discovered tin, adopted the flag's two colours – a white cross on a black background – after spotting the white tin amongst the black coals and ashes.

The coast

The Cornish coastline offers miles of breathtakingly beautiful scenery. The northern coast is open and exposed; the 735-ft High Cliff, between Boscastle

▶

St Ives

Rough Tor, Bodmin Moor

and St Gennys, represents the highest sheer drop cliff in the county. In contrast are long stretches of golden sandy beaches, including those at St Ives, and Newquay, now an internationally renowned surfing destination.

The Lizard, at Cornwall's most southerly point, is a geological masterpiece of towering cliffs, stacks and arches as is Land's End, on the county's south-west corner. The legendary 603-mile (970km) walk from this point to John O'Groats at the northern tip of Scotland creates a daunting challenge that numerous people, including sportsmen and TV personalities, have tackled with varying degrees of success over the years.

Truro is Cornwall's great cathedral city, with a wealth of Georgian buildings, quaint alleyways and historic streets adding to its charm. Compared to many cathedrals throughout the country, Truro's is relatively young; the foundation stones were laid in 1880 and the western towers were finally dedicated some thirty years later.

Inspirational Cornwall

Mysterious Bodmin Moor lies at the heart of Cornwall. In 1930 the writer Daphne du Maurier spent a night at Jamaica Inn in Bolventor, which inspired the famous novel of the same name; *Menabilly*, her home near Fowey, on Cornwall's south coast, was the inspiration for 'Manderley', the house in *Rebecca,* almost certainly her best-known and best-loved book. It is said that one day while out walking she spotted a flock of seagulls diving and wheeling above a newly ploughed field, which gave her the idea for the short story *The Birds,* which Alfred Hitchcock memorably turned into a horror film.

Walking and Cycling

Naturally, walking and cycling are very popular pursuits in Cornwall. The South West Coast Path offers many miles of rugged coastal grandeur and stunning views, while inland there is the chance to combine this most simple of outdoor pursuits with suitably green and environmentally friendly train travel. Tourist information centres provide leaflets showing a variety of linear or circular walks incorporating branch line stations; easy-to-follow maps are included. One popular route involves taking the train along the scenic Atlantic Coast line to Luxulyan, then cutting across country on foot for 2.5 miles (4km) to reach the Eden Project.

Festivals and Events

- The Newlyn Fish Festival takes place on August Bank Holiday Monday.
- Penzance hosts the Golowan Festival and Mazey Day for two weeks in mid-June.
- St Ives has its Feast Day in early February and the St Ives Festival of Music and the Arts for two weeks in early September.
- Victorian Day on Cotehele Quay near Calstock in mid-August is family fun and involves dressing up.
- Tamar Growers' Harvest at Cotehele Quay in mid-September. Here you will find local growers on the quay at an outdoor market.

CORNWALL & ISLES OF SCILLY

See Walk 1 & Cycle Ride 1 in the Walks & Cycle Ride section at the end of the guide.

ASHTON — Map 2 SW62

Places to visit

Godolphin House (NT),
Godolphin Cross 01736 763194
www.nationaltrust.org.uk/godolphin

Poldark Mine and Heritage Complex, Wendron
01326 573173 www.poldark-mine.com

Great for kids: The Flambards Experience,
Helston 01326 573404 www.flambards.co.uk

▶▶▶ 74% Boscrege Caravan & Camping Park (SW595305)

TR13 9TG
☎ 01736 762231   📠 01736 762152
e-mail: enquiries@caravanparkcornwall.com
dir: From Helston on A394 turn right in Ashton by Post Office into lane. Site in 1.5m, signed

🚐 🚗 Å

Open Mar-Nov Last arrival 22.00hrs Last departure 11.00hrs

A quiet and bright little touring park divided into small paddocks with hedges, and offering plenty of open spaces for children to play in. The family-owned park offers clean, well-painted and newly refurbished toilets facilities and neatly trimmed grass. In an Area of Outstanding Natural Beauty at the foot of Tregonning Hill. A 14 acre site with 50 touring pitches and 26 statics.

AA Pubs & Restaurants nearby: The Victoria Inn, Perranuthnoe 01736 710309

New Yard Restaurant, Helston 01326 221595

Leisure: 🅰 🔍 ▭
Facilities: 🅁 ⊙ ℘ ✳ ⓒ 🖉 ♨ 🄰 🐕 🕆
Services: 🄴 🄶 🄰 🄰 🅃 🄰
Within 3 miles: ↓ ↨ ℘ ◎ ⇘ 🄰 🄶 ↻
Notes: Recreation fields, microwave, nature trail. Wi-fi

see advert below

BLACKWATER

Places to visit

Royal Cornwall Museum, Truro 01872 272205
www.royalcornwallmuseum.org.uk

East Pool Mine (NT), Pool 01209 315027
www.nationaltrust.org.uk

Great for kids: National Maritime Museum Cornwall, Falmouth 01326 313388
www.nmmc.co.uk

BLACKWATER — Map 2 SW74

▶▶▶▶ 83% Chiverton Park

(SW743468)
East Hill TR4 8HS
☎ 01872 560667   📠 01872 560667
e-mail: chivertonpark@btopenworld.com
dir: Exit A30 at Chiverton rdbt (Starbucks) onto unclass road signed Blackwater (3rd exit). 1st right, site 300mtrs on right

* 🚐 £15-£20 🚗 £15-£22 Å £8-£20

Open 3 Mar-3 Nov (rs Mar-May & mid Sep-Nov limited stock kept in shop) Last arrival 21.00hrs Last departure noon

A small, well-maintained site with some mature hedges dividing pitches, sited midway between Truro and St Agnes. Facilities include a good toilet block and a steam room, sauna and gym. A games room with pool table, and children's outside play equipment prove popular with families. A 4 acre site with 12 touring pitches, 10 hardstandings and 50 statics.

AA Pubs & Restaurants nearby: Driftwood Spars, St Agnes 01872 552428

Leisure: 🅰 🔍 **Facilities:** 🅁 ⊙ ℘ ✳ ♿ ⓒ 🄰 ♨ 🄰
Services: 🄴 🄶 ♨ **Within 3 miles:** ↓ 🄷 ℘ ⇘ 🄰 🄶 ↻
Notes: No ball games. Drying lines. Wi-fi

LEISURE: 🏊 Indoor swimming pool 🏊 Outdoor swimming pool 🅰 Children's playground 🎾 Tennis court 🔍 Games room ▭ Separate TV room ⛳ 9/18 hole golf course 🚣 Boats for hire 🎬 Cinema 🎣 Fishing ◎ Mini golf 🏄 Watersports ↻ Stables **FACILITIES:** 🛁 Bath 🚿 Shower ⊙ Electric shaver ℘ Hairdryer ✳ Ice Pack Facility ♿ Disabled facilities ☎ Public telephone 🄰 Shop on site or within 200yds 🄰 Mobile shop (calls at least 5 days a week) ♨ BBQ area 🄰 Picnic area 🕆 Dog exercise area

▶▶▶▶ 80% Trevarth Holiday Park

(SW744468)

TR4 8HR
☎ 01872 560266   ▤ 01872 560379
e-mail: trevarth@btconnect.com
web: www.trevarth.co.uk
dir: *Exit A30 at Chiverton rdbt onto B3277 signed St Agnes. At next rdbt take road signed Blackwater. Site on right in 200mtrs*

* ⌂ £11-£17.50 ⌂ £11-£17.50 ▲ £11-£17.50

Open Apr-Oct Last arrival 22.00hrs Last departure 11.30hrs

A neat and compact park with touring pitches laid out on attractive, well-screened high ground adjacent to A30/A39 junction. This pleasant little park is centrally located for touring, and is maintained to a very good standard. Two seasonal touring pitches are available. A 4 acre site with 30 touring pitches, 10 hardstandings and 20 statics.

AA Pubs & Restaurants nearby: Driftwood Spars, St Agnes 01872 552428

Leisure: ⚔ 🔍   **Facilities:** ⋔ ⊙ ⌇ ✳ ☺ ▤
Services: ⌂ ▤ 🛢 ⌀ ⛽ 🍴
Within 3 miles: ⌇ ⛴ 🏦 ↻
Notes: Recycling facilities. Wi-fi

▶▶▶ 81% South Penquite Farm

(SX108751)

South Penquite PL30 4LH
☎ 01208 850491   ▤ 0870 1367926
e-mail: thefarm@bodminmoor.co.uk
dir: *From Exeter on A30 exit at 1st sign to St Breward on right, (from Bodmin 2nd sign on left). Follow narrow road across Bodmin Moor. Ignore left & right turns until South Penquite Farm Lane on right in 2m*

▲

Open May-Oct Last departure 14.00hrs

This 'cool camping' site is situated high on Bodmin Moor and on a farm committed to organic farming. As well as camping there are facilities to learn about conservation, organic farming and the local environment, including a fascinating and informative farm trail (pick up a leaflet). Toilet facilities have been considerably enhanced by the construction of an additional timber building with quality showers and a good disabled facility. There are home grown organic lamb burgers and sausages for sale and one field contains four Mongolian yurts, available for holiday lets. A 4 acre site with 40 touring pitches.

AA Pubs & Restaurants nearby: The Blisland Inn, Blisland 01208 850739

The Old Inn & Restaurant, St Breward 01208 850711

Leisure: ⚔
Facilities: ⋔ ⊙ ⌇ ✳ ☺ 🔫
Services: ▤
Within 3 miles: ⌇ ⛴ 🏦 ▤ ↻
Notes: ⊛ ⊗ No caravans. Organic produce available

▶▶▶ 74% Colliford Tavern Campsite

(SX171740)

Colliford Lake, St Neot PL14 6PZ
☎ 01208 821335   ▤ 01208 821661
e-mail: info@colliford.com
web: www.colliford.com
dir: *Exit A30 1.25m W of Bolventor onto unclass road signed Colliford Lake. Site 0.25m on left*

* ⌂ £14 ⌂ £14 ▲ £14

Open all year Last arrival 22.00hrs Last departure 11.00hrs

An oasis on Bodmin Moor, a small site with spacious grassy pitches, and the advantage of a comfortable lounge bar and restaurant in the tavern. Attractions for children are greatly enhanced by the merger of the site with the neighbouring children's play park. A 3.5 acre site with 40 touring pitches, 8 hardstandings.

AA Pubs & Restaurants nearby: Jamaica Inn, Bolventor 01566 86250

Leisure: ⚔
Facilities: ⋔ ⊙ ⌇ ✳ ☺ ☺ 🔫
Services: ⌂ ▤ 🍴 ⚒
Within 3 miles: ⌇
Notes: Dogs must be kept on leads, dog walking area

▶▶ 80% Lower Pennycrocker Farm

(SX125927)

PL35 0BY
☎ 01840 250257   ▤ 01840 250613
e-mail: karynheard@btinternet.com
dir: *Exit A39 at Marshgate onto B3263 towards Boscastle, site signed in 2m*

⌂ £10 ⌂ £10 ▲ £10

Open Etr-Oct Last arrival anytime Last departure anytime

Mature Cornish hedges provide shelter for this small, family-run site on a dairy farm. Spectacular scenery and the nearby coastal footpath are among the many attractions, along with fresh eggs, milk and home-made clotted cream for sale. The excellent, newly upgraded toilets and showers enhance this site's facilities, and there are plans for further modernisation. Two traditional Cornish cottages are available to let. A 6 acre site with 40 touring pitches.

AA Pubs & Restaurants nearby: The Port William, Tintagel 01840 770230

The Wellington Hotel, Boscastle 01840 250202

Facilities: ⋔ ⊙ ⌇ ✳ ☺ 🔫 🔫
Services: ⌂ ⚒ ⚑
Within 3 miles: ⛴ ⌇ ▤ ↻
Notes: ⊛

BRYHER (ISLES OF SCILLY)   Map 2 SV81

AA CAMPING CARD SITE

►►► 77% Bryher Camp Site
(SV880155)

TR23 0PR
☎ 01720 422559   📠 01720 423092
e-mail: relax@bryhercampsite.co.uk
web: www.bryhercampsite.co.uk
dir: *Accessed by boat from main island of St Marys*

⚊

Open Apr-Oct

Set on the smallest inhabited Scilly Isle with spectacular scenery and white beaches, this tent-only site is in a sheltered valley surrounded by hedges. Pitches are located in paddocks at the northern end of the island, and easily reached from the quay. There is a good modern toilet block, and plenty of peace and quiet. No pets allowed. A 2.25 acre site with 38 touring pitches.

AA Pubs & Restaurants nearby: Hell Bay Hotel, Bryher 01720 422947

Facilities: ⚙☉🍴⚹🖻 **Services:** 🛢🛒📶🍴
Within 3 miles: ⌂⚞🎣◎♨🍴🛒🅾↺

BUDE   Map 2 SS20

See also Kilkhampton & Bridgerule (Devon)

AA CAMPING CARD SITE

PREMIER PARK

►►►►► 90% Wooda Farm Holiday Park
(SS229080)

Best of British GOLD

Poughill EX23 9HJ
☎ 01288 352069   📠 01288 355258
e-mail: enquiries@wooda.co.uk
web: www.wooda.co.uk
dir: *2m E. From A39 at outskirts of Stratton follow unclassified road signed Poughill*

* 🚐 £14-£29 �"£12-£29 ⚊ £12-£24

Open Apr-Oct (rs Apr-May & mid Sep-Oct shop hours limited, bar & takeaway) Last arrival 20.00hrs Last departure noon

An attractive park set on raised ground overlooking Bude Bay, with lovely sea views. The park is divided into paddocks by hedges and mature trees, and offers high quality facilities in extensive colourful gardens. A variety of activities are provided by the large sports hall and hard tennis court, and there's a super children's playground. There are holiday static caravans for hire. A 50 acre site with 200 touring pitches, 80 hardstandings and 55 statics.

AA Pubs & Restaurants nearby: The Bush Inn, Morwenstow 01288 331242

The Castle Restaurant, Bude 01288 350543

Wooda Farm Holiday Park

Leisure: 🅰🏊🎱🖵
Facilities: ⬅⚙☉🍴⚹⚙🕐🖻🎋🐕
Services: 🛢🛒📶🚿🍴📶🍴🛒🐕
Within 3 miles: ⌂⚞🎣◎♨🍴🛒🅾↺

Notes: Restrictions on certain dog breeds, skateboards, rollerblades & scooters. Coarse fishing, clay pigeon shooting, pets corner, woodland walks. Wi-fi

AA CAMPING CARD SITE

►►►► 84% Widemouth Fields Caravan & Camping Park *(SS215010)*

Park Farm, Poundstock EX23 0NA
☎ 01288 361351   📠 01288 361115
e-mail: enquiries@widemouthbaytouring.co.uk
dir: *M5 junct 27 (signed Barnstaple). A361 to rdbt before Barnstaple. Take A39 signed Bideford & Bude. (NB do not exit A39 at Stratton). S for 3m, follow sign just past x-rds to Widemouth Bay. Into lay-by, entrance on left*

🚐 🚛 ⚊

Open Apr-end Oct Last arrival dusk Last dep noon

A new development set in a quiet location with far reaching views over the rolling countryside. It is only one mile from the golden beach at Widemouth Bay, and just three miles from the resort of Bude.

The park has a shop and small café/takeaway, and offers many hardstanding pitches. The toilets are of outstanding quality with a wealth of combined fully-serviced cubicles. The owner, having acquired Widemouth Bay Holiday Village, runs courtesy shuttle buses into Bude and to the Holiday Village, where the facilities can be used by the touring campers. Seasonal touring pitches are available. A 15 acre site with 156 touring pitches, 156 hardstandings.

Widemouth Fields Caravan & Camping Park

AA Pubs & Restaurants nearby: Bay View Inn, Widemouth Bay 01288 361273

Leisure: 🅰🖵
Facilities: ⬅⚙☉🍴⚹⚙🕐🖻🐕
Services: 🛢🛒📶🚿🍴📶🍴🛒🐕⚙
Within 3 miles: ⌂⚞🎣◎♨🍴🛒🅾↺

Notes: Entry to site by swipecard only, deposit taken when booking in. Wi-fi

►►►► 82% Budemeadows Touring Park *(SS215012)*

Widemouth Bay EX23 0NA
☎ 01288 361646   📠 0870 7064825
e-mail: holiday@budemeadows.com
dir: *3m S of Bude on A39. Follow signs after turn to Widemouth Bay. Site accessed via layby*

* 🚐 £10-£25 🚛 £10-£25 ⚊ £10-£25

Open all year (rs mid Sep-late May shop, bar & pool closed) Last arrival 21.00hrs Last departure 11.00hrs

A very well kept site of distinction, with good quality facilities, 30 hardstandings, eight new fully-serviced pitches and four seasonal touring pitches. Budemeadows is set on a gentle sheltered slope in nine acres of naturally landscaped parkland, surrounded by mature hedges. Just one mile from Widemouth Bay, and three miles from the unspoilt resort of Bude. A 9 acre site with 145 touring pitches, 24 hardstandings.

AA Pubs & Restaurants nearby: Bay View Inn, Widemouth Bay 01288 361273

The Castle Restaurant, Bude 01288 350543

Budemeadows Touring Park

Leisure: ⚓ 🏛 🎯 ▢

Facilities: 🚽 🐾 ⊙ 🅿 ✳ ⚄ 🕒 🛒 🍴 🪑

Services: 🔌 🗑 🍺 🔥 🚿 ⛽ 🔋 👶 ⚙

Within 3 miles: 🚣 🎣 🏇 🎿 ◎ ⛳ 🎯 🎳 ⟳

Notes: Table tennis, giant chess, baby changing facility. Wi-fi

---

▶▶▶▶ **76% Willow Valley Holiday Park** *(SS236078)*

Bush EX23 9LB
☎ **01288 353104**
e-mail: willowvalley@talk21.com
dir: *On A39, 0.5m N of junct with A3072 at Stratton*

🚐 £9-£16 🚌 ⚊

Open Mar-end Oct Last arrival 21.00hrs Last departure 11.00hrs

A small sheltered park in the Strat Valley with level grassy pitches and a stream running through it. The friendly family owners have improved all

areas of this attractive park, including a smart toilet block and a new reception/shop. The park has direct access off the A39, and is only two miles from the sandy beaches at Bude. There are four pine lodges for holiday hire. A 4 acre site with 41 touring pitches and 4 statics.

AA Pubs & Restaurants nearby: The Bickford Arms, Holsworthy 01409 221318

The Castle Restaurant, Bude 01288 350543

Leisure: 🏛

Facilities: 🐾 ⊙ 🅿 ✳ ⚄ 🕒 🛒 🍴 🪑

Services: 🔌 🗑 🔥 ⛽ 🚿

Within 3 miles: 🚣 🎣 🏇 🎿 ◎ ⛳ 🎯 🎳 ⟳

Notes: 🚭

▶▶▶ **79% Upper Lynstone Caravan Park** *(SS205053)*

Lynstone EX23 0LP
☎ 01288 352017   📄 01288 359034
e-mail: reception@upperlynstone.co.uk
dir: *0.75m S of Bude on coastal road to Widemouth Bay*

✳ 🚐 £12.50-£20 🚌 £12.50-£20 ⚊ £12.50-£20

Open Apr-Oct Last arrival 22.00hrs Last departure 10.00hrs

There are extensive views over Bude to be enjoyed from this quiet family-run park set on sheltered ground. There is a new reception/shop selling basic food supplies and camping spares, a children's playground, and static caravans for holiday hire. A path leads directly to the coastal footpath with its stunning sea views, and the old Bude Canal is a stroll away. A 6 acre site with 65 touring pitches and 41 statics.

AA Pubs & Restaurants nearby: The Castle Restaurant, Bude 01288 350543

Leisure: 🏛

Facilities: 🐾 ⊙ 🅿 ✳ ⚄ 🛒 🪑

Services: 🔌 🗑 🔥 ⛽ 🚿

Within 3 miles: 🚣 🎣 🏇 🎿 ◎ ⛳ 🎯 🎳 ⟳

Notes: No groups. Baby changing room

▶▶▶▶ **85% Juliot's Well Holiday Park** *(SX095829)*

PL32 9RF
☎ **01840 213302**   📄 **01840 212700**
e-mail: juliotswell@breaksincornwall.com
web: www.juliotswell.com
dir: *Through Camelford, A39 at Valley Truckle turn right onto B3266, then 1st left signed Lanteglos, site 300yds on right*

🚐 🚌 ⚊

Open all year Last arrival 20.00hrs Last departure 11.00hrs

Set in the wooded grounds of an old manor house, this quiet site enjoys lovely and extensive views across the countryside. A rustic inn on site offers occasional entertainment, and there is plenty to do, both on the park and in the vicinity. The superb, fully-serviced toilet facilities are very impressive. There are also self-catering pine lodges, static caravans and five cottages. A 33 acre site with 39 touring pitches and 82 statics.

AA Pubs & Restaurants nearby: The Mill House Inn, Trebarwith 01840 770200

Leisure: ⚓ 🏛 🎯

Facilities: 🚽 🐾 🅿 ⚄ 🕒 🛒 🪑

Services: 🔌 🗑 🍺 🍽 👶

Within 3 miles: 🚣 🏇 🎯 🎳 ⟳

Notes: Free cots/high chairs available. Wi-fi

The quality percentage score for all parks ranges from 50%-100%

CAMELFORD *continued*

►►► 74% Lakefield Caravan Park

(SX095853)

Lower Pendavey Farm PL32 9TX
☎ 01840 213279
e-mail: lakefieldcaravanpark@btconnect.com
dir: *From A39 in Camelford turn right onto B3266, then right at T-junct, site 1.5m on left*

🚐 🚙 Å

Open Etr or Apr-Sep Last arrival 22.00hrs Last departure 11.00hrs

Set in a rural location, this friendly park is part of a specialist equestrian centre, and offers good quality services. Riding lessons and hacks always available, with a BHS qualified instructor. A 5 acre site with 40 touring pitches.

AA Pubs & Restaurants nearby: The Old House Inn & Restaurant, St Breward 01208 850711

Facilities: 🖳 ⊙ 🃏 ✳ 🃟 🖈
Services: 🖭 🖨 💧 T 🍴 🖳
Within 3 miles: 🌡 🖉 🛥 ♻ ∪

Notes: Dogs must be kept on leads. On-site lake

CARLYON BAY   Map 2 SX05

Places to visit

Charlestown Shipwreck & Heritage Centre, St Austell 01726 69897 www.shipwreckcharlestown.com

Eden Project, St Austell 01726 811911 www.edenproject.com

Great for kids: The China Clay Country Park, St Austell 01726 850362 www.wheal-martyn.com

PREMIER PARK

►►►►► 87% *Carlyon Bay Caravan & Camping Park* (SX052526)

Bethesda, Cypress Av PL25 3RE
☎ 01726 812735 📠 01726 815496
e-mail: holidays@carlyonbay.net
dir: *Off A390 W of St Blazey, left onto A3092 for Par, right in 0.5m. On private road to Carlyon Bay*

🚐 🚙 Å

Open Etr-3 Oct (rs Etr-mid May & mid Sep-3 Oct swimming pool, takeaway & shop closed) Last arrival 21.00hrs Last departure 11.00hrs

An attractive, secluded site set amongst a belt of trees with background woodland. The spacious grassy park is beautifully landscaped and offers quality toilet and shower facilities and plenty of on-site attractions, including a well-equipped games room, TV room, café, an inviting swimming pool, and occasional family entertainment. It is less than half a mile from a sandy beach and the Eden Project is only two miles away. A 35 acre site with 180 touring pitches, 6 hardstandings.

AA Pubs & Restaurants nearby: The Royal Inn, Tywardreath 01726 815601

Austell's, St Austell 01726 813888

Leisure: 🛥 🎠 🎱 🎯 ⌷
Facilities: 🖳 ⊙ 🃏 ✳ 🕘 🖨 🖩 🖈
Services: 🖭 🖨 💧 🕯 T 🖳 🖳
Within 3 miles: 🌡 🕈 🖽 🖉 ◎ 🛥 ♻ 🖽 ∪

Notes: Crazy golf, children's entertainment in Jul & Aug

►►► 80% East Crinnis Camping & Caravan Park *(SX062528)*

Lantyan, East Crinnis PL24 2SQ
☎ 01726 813023 & 07950 614780
📠 01726 813023
e-mail: eastcrinnis@btconnect.com
dir: *From A390 (Lostwithiel to St Austell) take A3082 signed Fowey at rdbt by Britannia Inn, site on left*

* 🚐 £10-£18 🚙 £10-£18 Å £10-£18

Open Etr-Oct Last arrival 21.00hrs Last departure 11.00hrs

A small rural park with spacious pitches set in individual bays about one mile from the beaches at Carlyon Bay, and just two miles from the Eden Project. The friendly owners keep the site very clean and well maintained and also offer three self-catering holiday lodges. A 2 acre site with 25 touring pitches, 6 hardstandings.

AA Pubs & Restaurants nearby: The Rashleigh Inn, Polkerris 01726 813991

Austell's, St Austell 01726 813888

Leisure: 🎠
Facilities: 🖳 ⊙ ✳ 🕘 🖨 🖩 🖽 🖈
Services: 🖭 🖨
Within 3 miles: 🌡 🕈 🖽 🖉 ◎ 🛥 ♻ 🖽 ∪

Notes: Dogs must be kept on leads at all times. Coarse fishing, wildlife & pond area with dog walk. Wi-fi

COVERACK   Map 2 SW71

Places to visit

Trevarno Estate Garden & Museum of Gardening, Helston 01326 574274 www.trevarno.co.uk

Goonhilly Satellite Earth Station Experience, Helston 0800 679593 www.goonhilly.bt.com

Great for kids: National Seal Sanctuary, Gweek 0871 423 2110 www.sealsanctuary.co.uk

►►► 79% Little Trevothan Caravan & Camping Park *(SW772179)*

Trevothan TR12 6SD
☎ 01326 280260
e-mail: sales@littletrevothan.co.uk
web: www.littletrevothan.co.uk
dir: *A3083 onto B3293 signed Coverack, approx 2m after Goonhilly ESS, right at Zoar Garage onto unclass road. Approx 1m, 3rd left. Site 0.5m on left*

* 🚐 £10-£13 🚙 £10-£13 Å £10-£13

Open Mar-Oct Last arrival 21.00hrs Last dep noon

A secluded site near the unspoilt fishing village of Coverack, with a large recreation area. The nearby sandy beach has lots of rock pools for children to play in, and the many walks both from the park and the village offer stunning scenery. A 10.5 acre site with 70 touring pitches, 10 hardstandings and 40 statics.

AA Pubs & Restaurants nearby: The New Inn, Manaccan 01326 231323

Leisure: 🎠 🎯 ⌷ **Facilities:** 🖳 ⊙ 🃏 ✳ 🕘 🖨 🖈
Services: 🖭 🖨 💧 T 🖳
Within 3 miles: 🖉 🛥 🖨 🖩

Notes: 🐾 Dogs must be kept on leads

CRACKINGTON HAVEN   Map 2 SX19

►►► 75% *Hentervene Holiday Park*

(SX155944)

EX23 0LF
☎ 01840 230365
e-mail: contact@hentervene.co.uk
dir: *Exit A39 approx 10m SW of Bude (1.5m beyond Wainhouse Corner) onto B3263 signed Boscastle & Crackington Haven. 0.75m to Tresparret Posts junct, right signed Hentervene. Site 0.75m on right*

🚐 🚙

Open Mar-Oct Last arrival 21.00hrs Last dep 11.00hrs

LEISURE: 🏊 Indoor swimming pool 🏊 Outdoor swimming pool 🎠 Children's playground 🎾 Tennis court 🎱 Games room ⌷ Separate TV room ⛳ 9/18 hole golf course
⛵ Boats for hire 🎬 Cinema 🎣 Fishing ◎ Mini golf 🏄 Watersports ∪ Stables **FACILITIES:** 🛁 Bath 🚿 Shower 🔌 Electric shaver 💈 Hairdryer ✳ Ice Pack Facility
♿ Disabled facilities 📞 Public telephone 🛒 Shop on site or within 200yds 🚚 Mobile shop (calls at least 5 days a week) 🍴 BBQ area 🌲 Picnic area 🐕 Dog exercise area

This much improved park is set in a rural location a short drive from a golden sandy beach. It is in an Area of Outstanding Natural Beauty, and pitches are in paddocks which are bordered by mature hedges, with a small stream running past. Some pitches are on level terraces, and there are also hardstandings. Static caravans and three pine lodges for self-catering holiday hire. An 11 acre site with 8 touring pitches, 8 hardstandings and 24 statics.

Leisure: ⚙ 🎣 🎱 ▯

Facilities: ⌐ ⊙ ⌇ ✳ ⊙ 🐾

Services: ⚡ 🗑 🛢 🧺 🛅

Within 3 miles: 🖉 ⛵ 🏠 🎣 ↻

Notes: Baby bathroom. Microwave & freezer for campers. Wi-fi

CRANTOCK (NEAR NEWQUAY)   Map 2 SW76

PREMIER PARK

►►►►► 85% *Trevella Tourist Park* (SW801599)

GOLD

TR8 5EW

☎ 01637 830308   📄 01637 830155
e-mail: holidays@trevella.co.uk
dir: *Between Crantock & A3075*

🚐 🚏 Å

Open Etr-Oct

A well established and very well run family site, with outstanding floral displays. Set in a rural area close to Newquay, this attractive park boasts three teeming fishing lakes for the experienced and novice angler, and a superb outdoor swimming pool and paddling area. Toilet facilities have now been refurbished and include excellent en suite wet rooms. All areas are neat and clean and the whole park looked stunning at our last inspection. A 15 acre site with 313 touring pitches, 53 hardstandings.

AA Pubs & Restaurants nearby: The Smugglers' Den Inn, Cubert 01637 830209

The Lewinnick Lodge Bar & Restaurant, Newquay 01637 878117

Sand Brasserie, Headland Hotel, Newquay 01637 872211

Leisure: 🌊 ⚙ 🎣 ▯

Facilities: ⌐ ⊙ ⌇ ✳ ᰵ ⊙ 🖥 🛅 🐾

Services: ⚡ 🗑 🛢 🧺 🛢 🧴 T ▯○▯ 🍔 🚚 ↯

Within 3 miles: 🚴 ⛵ 🖉 ◎ 🎣 🏠 ↻

Notes: Crazy golf, badminton

see advert on page 87

►►► 83% *Treago Farm Caravan Site*

(SW782601)

TR8 5QS

☎ 01637 830277   📄 01637 830277
e-mail: treagofarm@aol.com
dir: *From A3075 (W of Newquay) turn right for Crantock. Site signed beyond village*

🚐 🚏 Å

Open mid May-mid Sep Last arrival 22.00hrs Last departure 18.00hrs

A grass site in open farmland in a south-facing sheltered valley. This friendly family park has direct access to Crantock and Polly Joke beaches, National Trust land and many natural beauty spots. A 5 acre site with 90 touring pitches and 10 statics.

AA Pubs & Restaurants nearby: The Smugglers' Den Inn, Cubert 01637 830209

The Lewinnick Lodge Bar & Restaurant, Newquay 01637 878117

Sand Brasserie, Headland Hotel, Newquay 01637 872211

Leisure: 🎣 ▯

Facilities: ⌐ ⊙ ⌇ ✳ ⊙ 🖥 🛅 🐾

Services: ⚡ 🗑 🛢 🛢 🧺 T 🛅

Within 3 miles: 🚴 ⛵ 🖉 ◎ 🎣 🏠 ↻

►►► 80% Crantock Plains Camping & Caravan Park (SW805589)

TR8 5PH

☎ 01637 830955   & 07967 956897
e-mail: matthew-milburn@btconnect.com
dir: *Exit Newquay on A3075, 2nd right signed to park & Crantock. Site on left in 0.75m on narrow road*

🚐 🚏 Å

Open Last arrival 22.00hrs Last departure noon

A small rural park with pitches on either side of a narrow lane, surrounded by mature trees for shelter. This spacious, family-run park has good modern toilet facilities and is ideal for campers who appreciate peace and quiet and is situated approximately 1.2 miles from pretty Crantock, and Newquay is within easy reach. A 6 acre site with 60 touring pitches.

AA Pubs & Restaurants nearby: The Smugglers' Den Inn, Cubert 01637 830209

The Lewinnick Lodge Bar & Restaurant, Newquay 01637 878117

Sand Brasserie, Headland Hotel, Newquay 01637 872211

Leisure: ⚙ 🎣

Facilities: ⌐ ⊙ ⌇ ✳ ᰵ ⊙ 🖥 🐾

Services: ⚡ 🗑 🧺 🛅

Within 3 miles: 🚴 ⛵ 🖉 🎣 🏠 ↻

Notes: No skateboards, dogs on leads at all times

►►► 80% Quarryfield Holiday Park

(SW793608)

TR8 5RJ

☎ 01637 872792   & 830338   📄 01637 872792
e-mail: quarryfield@crantockcaravans. orangehome.co.uk
dir: *From A3075 (Newquay-Redruth road) follow Crantock signs. Site signed*

* 🚐 £14-£20 🚏 £14-£20 Å £14-£20

Open Etr to end Oct (rs May/Sep pool closed) Last arrival 23.00hrs Last departure 10.00hrs

This park has a private path down to the dunes and golden sands of Crantock Beach, about ten minutes away, and it is within easy reach of all that Newquay has to offer, particularly for families. The park has new, very modern facilities, and provides plenty of amenities. A 10 acre site with 145 touring pitches and 43 statics.

AA Pubs & Restaurants nearby: The Smugglers' Den Inn, Cubert 01637 830209

The Lewinnick Lodge Bar & Restaurant, Newquay 01637 878117

Sand Brasserie, Headland Hotel, Newquay 01637 872211

Leisure: 🌊 ⚙ 🎣

Facilities: ⌐ ⊙ ⌇ ✳ ᰵ ⊙ 🖥 🛅 🐾

Services: ⚡ 🗑 🛢 🛢 🧺 ▯○▯ 🛅 🚚 ↯

Within 3 miles: 🚴 ⛵ 🖉 ◎ 🏠 ↻

Notes: No campfires, quiet after 22.30hrs

CUBERT · Map 2 SW75

Places to visit

Blue Reef Aquarium, Newquay 01637 878134
www.bluereefaquarium.co.uk

Trerice (NT), Trerice 01637 875404
www.nationaltrust.org.uk

Great for kids: Dairy Land Farm World,
Newquay 01872 510246
www.dairylandfarmworld.com

▶▶▶ 80% Cottage Farm Touring Park (SW786589)

Treworgans TR8 5HH
☎ 01637 831083
web: www.cottagefarmpark.co.uk
dir: From A392 towards Newquay, left onto A3075 towards Redruth. In 2m right signed Cubert, right again in 1.5m signed Crantock, left in 0.5m

* ⌂ £12-£16 ⌂ £12-£16 ▲ £12-£16

Open Apr-Oct Last arrival 22.30hrs Last departure noon

A small grassy touring park nestling in the tiny hamlet of Treworgans, in sheltered open countryside close to a lovely beach at Holywell Bay. This quiet family-run park boasts very good quality facilities. A 2 acre site with 45 touring pitches, 2 hardstandings and 1 static.

AA Pubs & Restaurants nearby: The Smugglers' Den Inn, Cubert 01637 830209

The Plume of Feathers, Mitchell 01872 510387

Facilities: ↖ ⊙ ⌐ ✳ 🛁

Services: 🖭 🗑 🚽 🚿

Within 3 miles: ⌂ ⌂ 🎣 🎣 ◎ ⌂ 🛒 🗄 🗄 ∪

EDGCUMBE

Places to visit

Poldark Mine and Heritage Complex, Wendron 01326 573173 www.poldark-mine.com

Trevarno Estate Garden & Museum of Gardening, Helston 01326 574274
www.trevarno.co.uk

Great for kids: National Seal Sanctuary, Gweek 0871 423 2110 www.sealsanctuary.co.uk

EDGCUMBE · Map 2 SW73

▶▶▶ 78% Retanna Holiday Park (SW711327)

TR13 0EJ
☎ 01326 340643 📠 01326 340643
e-mail: retannaholpark@btconnect.com
web: www.retanna.co.uk
dir: On A394 towards Helston, site signed on right. Site in 100mtrs

* ⌂ £16-£22 ▲ £16-£22

Open Apr-Oct Last arrival 21.00hrs Last departure noon

A small family-owned and run park in a rural location midway between Falmouth and Helston. Its well-sheltered grassy pitches make this an ideal location for visiting the lovely beaches and towns nearby. An 8 acre site with 24 touring pitches and 23 statics.

AA Pubs & Restaurants nearby: Trengilly Wartha Inn, Constantine 01326 340332

The Gweek Inn, Gweek 01326 221502

Leisure: ⌂ ⌐ ⌐

Facilities: ↖ ⊙ ✳ ⌐ ⌐ 🛁 ⌐

Services: 🖭 🗑 🚽 ⊤ 🛒 🚿 🚿

Within 3 miles: ⌂ 🎣 ◎ ⌂ 🗄 🗄

Notes: No pets, no disposable BBQs, no open fires. Free use of fridge/freezer in laundry room

FALMOUTH · Map 2 SW83

Places to visit

Pendennis Castle, Falmouth 01326 316594
www.english-heritage.org.uk

Trebah Garden, Mawnan Smith 01326 252200
www.trebah-garden.co.uk

Great for kids: National Maritime Museum Cornwall, Falmouth 01326 313388
www.nmmc.co.uk

▶▶▶ 78% Pennance Mill Farm Touring Park (SW792307)

Maenporth TR11 5HJ
☎ 01326 317431 📠 01326 317431
dir: From A39 (Truro to Falmouth road) follow brown camping signs towards Maenporth Beach. At Hill Head rdbt take 2nd exit for Maenporth Beach

⌂ ⌂ ▲

Open Etr-Xmas Last arrival 22.00hrs Last departure 10.00hrs

Set approximately half a mile from the safe, sandy bay at Maenporth, accessed by a private woodland walk direct from the park, this is a mainly level, grassy park in a rural location sheltered by mature trees and shrubs and divided into three meadows. It has a modern toilet block. A 6 acre site with 75 touring pitches, 8 hardstandings and 4 statics.

AA Pubs & Restaurants nearby: Trengilly Wartha Inn, Constantine 01326 340332

Budock Vean - Hotel on the River, Mawnan Smith 01326 252100

Leisure: ⌂ 🎾 🎱

Facilities: ↖ ⊙ ✳ 🕐 🛁 ⌐

Services: 🖭 🗑 🚽 🗑 🛒 🗄 🚿 🚿

Within 3 miles: ⌂ 🎣 ⌂ 🎣 ◎ ⌂ 🛒 🗄 🗄 ∪

Notes: ⌂ 0.5m private path to walk or cycle to beach

▶▶ 78% Tregedna Farm Touring Caravan & Tent Park (SW785305)

Maenporth TR11 5HL
☎ 01326 250529
e-mail: enquiries@tregednafarmholidays.co.uk
dir: Take A39 from Truro to Falmouth. Turn right at Hill Head rdbt. Site 2.5m on right

⌂ ⌂ ▲

Open Apr-Sep Last arrival 22.00hrs Last departure 13.00hrs

Set in the picturesque Maen Valley, this gently-sloping, south-facing park is part of a 100-acre farm. It is surrounded by beautiful wooded countryside just minutes from the beach, with spacious pitches and well-kept facilities. A 12 acre site with 40 touring pitches.

AA Pubs & Restaurants nearby: Trengilly Wartha Inn, Constantine 01326 340332

Budock Vean - Hotel on the River, Mawnan Smith 01326 252100

Leisure: ⌂

Facilities: ↖ ⊙ ✳ 🕐 🛁 ⌐

Services: 🖭 🗑 🚿 🗑

Within 3 miles: ⌂ 🎣 🎣 ◎ ⌂ 🗄 🗄

Notes: ⌂ One dog only per pitch

LEISURE: 🏊 Indoor swimming pool 🏊 Outdoor swimming pool ⌂ Children's playground 🎾 Tennis court 🎱 Games room 📺 Separate TV room ⛳ 9/18 hole golf course
🚣 Boats for hire 🎦 Cinema 🎣 Fishing ⌾ Mini golf 🏄 Watersports ∪ Stables **FACILITIES:** 🛁 Bath ↖ Shower ⊙ Electric shaver ⌐ Hairdryer ✳ Ice Pack Facility
♿ Disabled facilities 🕐 Public telephone 🛒 Shop on site or within 200yds 🚐 Mobile shop (calls at least 5 days a week) 🍖 BBQ area 🪑 Picnic area 🐕 Dog exercise area

FOWEY — Map 2 SX15

Places to visit

St Catherine's Castle, Fowey
www.english-heritage.org.uk

Restormel Castle, Restormel 01208 872687
www.english-heritage.org.uk

Great for kids: The China Clay Country Park,
St Austell 01726 850362
www.wheal-martyn.com

►►► 80% Penmarlam Caravan & Camping Park (SX134526)

Bodinnick PL23 1LZ
☎ 01726 870088 📠 01726 870082
e-mail: info@penmarlampark.co.uk
dir: *From A390 at East Taphouse take B3359 signed Looe & Polperro. Follow signs for Bodinnick & Fowey, via ferry. Site on right at entrance to Bodinnick*

Open Apr-Oct Last departure noon

This tranquil park set above the Fowey Estuary in an Area of Outstanding Natural Beauty, with access to the water, continues to improve with the addition of six more fully-serviced pitches. Pitches are level, and sheltered by trees and bushes in two paddocks, while the toilets are spotlessly clean and well maintained. A 4 acre site with 63 touring pitches and 1 static.

AA Pubs & Restaurants nearby: Old Ferry Inn, Bodinnick 01726 870237

The Ship Inn, Fowey 01726 832230

Facilities: ♣ ⊙ ⌾ ✳ ᕀ 🖻 🎪 🐕

Services: ⊞ 🖻 🛢 🖉 T 🎫

Within 3 miles: ↨ ✝ ⛳ ℐ 🚴 ⛴ 🛒 U

Notes: Private slipway, small boat storage, internet access. Wi-fi

GOONHAVERN

See also Rejerrah

Places to visit

Trerice (NT), Trerice 01637 875404
www.nationaltrust.org.uk

Blue Reef Aquarium, Newquay 01637 878134
www.bluereefaquarium.co.uk

Great for kids: Dairy Land Farm World, Newquay 01872 510246
www.dairylandfarmworld.com

GOONHAVERN — Map 2 SW75

►►►►► 82% Silverbow Park (SW782531)

GOLD

Perranwell TR4 9NX
☎ 01872 572347
dir: *Adjacent to A3075, 0.5m S of village*

🚐 🚙 Å

Open May-end Sep Last arrival 22.00hrs Last departure 10.30hrs

This park has a quiet garden atmosphere, and appeals to families with young children. The superb landscaped grounds and good quality toilet facilities, housed in an attractive chalet-style building, including four family rooms, are maintained to a very high standard with attention paid to detail. Leisure facilities include two inviting swimming pools (outdoor and indoor), a bowling green and a nature reserve. A 14 acre site with 100 touring pitches, 2 hardstandings and 15 statics.

AA Pubs & Restaurants nearby: The Smugglers' Den Inn, Cubert 01637 830209

The Plume of Feathers, Mitchell 01872 510387

Leisure: 🏊 🎱 🔍

Facilities: 🛏 ♣ ⊙ ⌾ ✳ ᕀ 🖻 🎪 🎪 🐕

Services: ⊞ 🖻 🛢 🖉 T 🚿

Within 3 miles: ↨ ✝ ⛳ ◎ 🚴 🛒 U

Notes: No cycling, no skateboards. Short mat bowls rink, conservation/information area, indoor/outdoor table tennis

see advert below

GOONHAVERN *continued*

AA CAMPING CARD SITE

►►►► 82% Penrose Holiday Park

(SW795534)

TR4 9QF
☎ 01872 573185　📄 01872 571972
e-mail: info@penroseholidaypark.com
web: www.penroseholidaypark.com
dir: *From Exeter take A30, past Bodmin & Indian Queens. Just after Wind Farm take B3285 towards Perranporth, site on left on entering Goonhavern*

🚐🚌⛺

Open Etr or Apr-Oct Last arrival 21.30hrs

A quiet sheltered park set in five paddocks divided by hedges and shrubs, only a short walk from the village. Lovely floral displays enhance the park's appearance, and the grass and hedges are neatly trimmed. Four cubicled family rooms are very popular, and there is a good laundry, and a smart new reception building. Seasonal touring pitches are available. A 9 acre site with 110 touring pitches, 48 hardstandings and 24 statics.

AA Pubs & Restaurants nearby: The Smugglers' Den Inn, Cubert 01637 830209

The Plume of Feathers, Mitchell 01872 510387

Leisure: 🅰

Facilities: 🅵☉🅿✳🅱🕒🅱🚿🍴🚻

Services: 🚫🔋🛢🖉🅃🍴🎪🛒♿

Within 3 miles: ↓🎣⛴🏇🎯U

Notes: Families & couples only. Disabled wet room, family bathrooms. Wi-fi

see advert below

►►► 77% Sunny Meadows Tourist Park *(SW782542)*

Rosehill TR4 9JT
☎ 01872 571333　📄 01872 571491
dir: *From A30 onto B3285 signed Perranporth. At Goonhavern turn left at T-junct, then right at rdbt to Perranporth. Site on left*

🚐🚌⛺

Open Etr-Oct

A gently-sloping park in a peaceful, rural location, with mostly level pitches set into three small hedge-lined paddocks. Run by a friendly family, the park is just two miles from the long sandy beach at Perranporth. A 14.5 acre site with 100 touring pitches, 1 hardstanding.

AA Pubs & Restaurants nearby: The Smugglers' Den Inn, Cubert 01637 830209

The Plume of Feathers, Mitchell 01872 510387

Leisure: 🅰

Facilities: 🅵☉✳🅱🐾🚿

Services: 🚫🔋🖉🅃🎪

Within 3 miles: ↓🎣⛴🎯U

Notes: ⊗ Dogs must be kept on leads. Pool table & family TV room, washing machine & tumble dryer

see advert on opposite page

AA CAMPING CARD SITE

►►► 75% Roseville Holiday Park

(SW787540)

TR4 9LA
☎ 01872 572448　📄 01872 572448
dir: *From mini-rdbt in Goonhavern follow B3285 towards Perranporth, site 0.5m on right*

🚐🚌⛺

Open Whit-Oct (rs Apr-Jul, Sep-Oct shop closed)
Last arrival 21.30hrs Last departure 11.00hrs

A family park set in a rural location with sheltered grassy pitches, some gently sloping. The toilet facilities are modern, and there is an attractive outdoor swimming pool complex. This park is approximately two miles from the long sandy beach at Perranporth. An 8 acre site with 95 touring pitches and 5 statics.

AA Pubs & Restaurants nearby: The Smugglers' Den Inn, Cubert 01637 830209

The Plume of Feathers, Mitchell 01872 510387

Leisure: 🏊🅰🔍　**Facilities:** 🅵☉🅿✳🅱🐾

Services: 🚫🔋🛢🖉🅃🎪

Within 3 miles: ↓🎣☉🏇🎯U

Notes: ⊗ Families only. Off-licence in shop

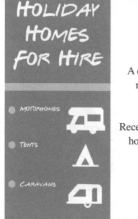

LEISURE: 🅰 Indoor swimming pool　🏊 Outdoor swimming pool　🅰 Children's playground　🎾 Tennis court　🎱 Games room　📺 Separate TV room　⛳ 9/18 hole golf course　⛴ Boats for hire　🎬 Cinema　🎣 Fishing　⛳ Mini golf　🏄 Watersports　U Stables　**FACILITIES:** 🛁 Bath　🚿 Shower　☉ Electric shaver　🅿 Hairdryer　✳ Ice Pack Facility　🅱 Disabled facilities　🕒 Public telephone　🛒 Shop on site or within 200yds　🚐 Mobile shop (calls at least 5 days a week)　🍴 BBQ area　🍴 Picnic area　🐾 Dog exercise area

►► 79% Little Treamble Farm Touring Park (SW785560)

Rose TR4 9PR
☎ 01872 573823 & 07971 070760
e-mail: info@treamble.co.uk
dir: A30 onto B3285 signed Perranporth. Approx 0.5m right into Scotland Rd signed Newquay. Approx 2m to T-junct, right onto A3075 signed Newquay. 0.25m left at Rejerrah sign. Site signed 0.75m on right

🚐 fr £13 🚐 fr £13 ▲ fr £13

Open all year Last departure noon

This site is set in a quiet rural location with extensive countryside views across an undulating valley. There is a small toilet block and a well-stocked shop. This working farm is next to a Caravan Club site. A 1.5 acre site with 20 touring pitches.

AA Pubs & Restaurants nearby: The Smugglers' Den Inn, Cubert 01637 830209

The Plume of Feathers, Mitchell 01872 510387

Facilities: 🌂 ✳ 🖳   Services: 🖳 🖹 🚐
Within 3 miles: 🎣 🐾 ◎ 🖳 ∪

GORRAN   Map 2 SW94

►►► 80% Treveague Farm Caravan & Camping Site (SX002410)

PL26 6NY
☎ 01726 842295 🖷 01726 842295
e-mail: treveague@btconnect.com
web: www.treveaguefarm.co.uk
dir: From St Austell take B3273 towards Mevagissey, past Pentewan at top of hill, turn right signed Gorran. Past Heligan Gardens towards Gorran Churchtown. Follow brown tourist signs from fork in road

* 🚐 £7.50-£18 🚐 £7.50-£18 ▲ £6-£15

Open Apr-Oct Last arrival 21.00hrs Last dep noon

Spectacular panoramic coastal views can be enjoyed from this rural park, which is set on an organic farm and well equipped with modern facilities. A stone-faced toilet block with a Cornish slate roof is an attractive and welcome feature, as is the new building that houses the smart reception, café and shop, which sells meat produced on the farm. A footpath leads to the fishing village of Gorran Haven in one direction, and the secluded sandy Vault Beach in the other. A 4 acre site with 40 touring pitches.

AA Pubs & Restaurants nearby: The Ship Inn, Mevagissey 01726 843324

The Crown Inn, St Ewe 01726 843322

Leisure: ⚠ Facilities: 🌂◎🖳✳🖳❀🖳🖳
Services: 🖳🖹🚐🖳🖳🖳🖳🖳🖳🖳
Within 3 miles: 🎣🐾🖳🖳
Notes: 🚭 Bird hide with observation cameras

►►► 77% Treveor Farm Caravan & Camping Site (SW988418)

PL26 6LW
☎ 01726 842387 🖷 01726 842387
e-mail: info@treveorfarm.co.uk
web: www.treveorfarm.co.uk
dir: From St Austell bypass left onto B3273 for Mevagissey. On hilltop before descent to village turn right on unclass road for Gorran. Right in 3.5m, site on right

* 🚐 £8.50-£16.50 🚐 £8.50-£16.50
▲ £5.50-£13.50

Open Apr-Oct Last arrival 20.00hrs Last dep 11.00hrs

A small family-run camping park set on a working farm, with grassy pitches backing onto mature hedging. This quiet site, with good facilities, is close to beaches and offers a large coarse fishing lake. A 4 acre site with 50 touring pitches.

AA Pubs & Restaurants nearby: The Ship Inn, Mevagissey 01726 843324

The Crown Inn, St Ewe 01726 843322

Leisure: ⚠ Facilities: 🌂◎🖳✳
Services: 🖳🖹🚐 Within 3 miles: 🎣🐾🖳🖳
Notes: 🚭 No hard ball, kites or frizbees

GORRAN HAVEN — Map 2 SX04

Places to visit

Caerhays Castle Gardens, Gorran
01872 501144 www.caerhays.co.uk

The Lost Gardens of Heligan, Pentewan
01726 845100 www.heligan.com

Great for kids: The China Clay Country Park,
St Austell 01726 850362
www.wheal-martyn.com

►► 74% Trelispen Caravan & Camping Park (SX008421)

PL26 6NT
☎ 01726 843501 📠 01726 843501
e-mail: trelispen@care4free.net
dir: B3273 from St Austell towards Mevagissey, on
hilltop at x-roads before descent into Mevagissey
turn right on unclass road to Gorran. Through
village, 2nd right towards Gorran Haven, site
signed on left in 250mtrs

* ⚏ £14-£18 ⛺ £14-£18 ▲ £14-£18

Open Etr & Apr-Oct Last arrival 22.00hrs Last
departure noon

A quiet rural site set in three paddocks, and
sheltered by mature trees and hedges. The simple
toilets have plenty of hot water, and there is a
small laundry. Sandy beaches, pubs and shops
are nearby, and Mevagissey is two miles away. A 2
acre site with 40 touring pitches.

AA Pubs & Restaurants nearby: The Ship Inn,
Mevagissey 01726 843324

The Crown Inn, St Ewe 01726 843322

Leisure: 🄰 **Facilities:** 🌣☉✳
Services: 🔌🔵 **Within 3 miles:** ⚓🎣🛒🅿
Notes: ☺ 30-acre nature reserve

GWITHIAN — Map 2 SW54

Places to visit

East Pool Mine (NT), Pool 01209 315027
www.nationaltrust.org.uk

►►►► 81% Gwithian Farm Campsite
(SW586412)

Gwithian Farm TR27 5BX
☎ 01736 753127
e-mail: camping@gwithianfarm.co.uk
dir: Exit A30 at Hayle rdbt, take 4th exit signed
Hayle, 100mtrs. At 1st mini-rdbt turn right
onto B3301 signed Portreath. Site 2m on left on
entering village

⚏ £15.50-£24 ⛺ £15.50-£24 ▲ £12-£20.50

Open 31 Mar-1 Oct Last arrival 22.00hrs Last
departure 17.00hrs

An unspoilt site located behind the sand dunes of
Gwithian's golden beach, which can be reached
directly by footpath from the site. The site boasts
stunning floral displays, a superb toilet block with
excellent facilities, including a bathroom and
baby-changing unit, and new first-class
hardstanding pitches. There is a good pub
opposite. A 7.5 acre site with 87 touring pitches,
12 hardstandings.

AA Pubs & Restaurants nearby: The Basset Arms,
Portreath 01209 842077

Porthminster Beach, St Ives 01736 795352

Facilities: 🌣☉✳🅿♿🅿🚿🚻🅿🐕
Services: 🔌🔵🅿✏🅃🔵⚱
Within 3 miles: ⚓🎣☉♨🛒🅿⛴
Notes: Surf board & wet suit hire, table tennis

HAYLE — Map 2 SW53

Places to visit

Tate St Ives, St Ives 01736 796226
www.tate.org.uk/stives

Barbara Hepworth Museum & Sculpture
Garden, St Ives 01736 796226
www.tate.org.uk/stives

80% St Ives Bay Holiday Park (SW577398)

73 Loggans Rd, Upton Towans TR27 5BH
☎ 01736 752274 📠 01736 754523
e-mail: stivesbay@btconnect.com
web: www.stivesbay.co.uk
dir: Exit A30 at Hayle then immediate right onto
B3301 at mini-rdbts. Site entrance 0.5m on left

* ⚏ £10-£32 ⛺ £10-£32 ▲ £10-£32

Open Etr-1 Oct Last arrival 21.00hrs Last
departure 09.00hrs

An extremely well maintained holiday park
with a relaxed atmosphere, built on sand
dunes adjacent to a three mile beach. The
touring section forms a number of separate
locations around this extensive park. The park
is specially geared for families and couples,
and as well as the large indoor swimming
pool there are two pubs with seasonal
entertainment. A 90 acre site with 240 touring
pitches and 250 statics.

AA Pubs & Restaurants nearby: White Hart,
Ludgvan 01736 740574

Porthminster Beach, St Ives 01736 795352

Leisure: 🏊🄰⚓♨🛒📺
Facilities: 🌣☉✳♿🅿🔵🚿
Services: 🔌🔵🅿🍺✏🅃🍽🅿⛴⚱
Within 3 miles: ⚓🎣🛒🔵🅿⛴
Notes: No pets. Crazy golf, video room. Wi-fi

AA CAMPING CARD SITE

►►► 83% Higher Trevaskis Caravan & Camping Park (SW611381)

Gwinear Rd, Connor Downs TR27 5JQ
☎ 01209 831736
dir: At Hayle rdbt on A30 take exit signed Connor
Downs, in 1m turn right signed Carnhell Green.
Site 0.75m just past level crossing

⚏ £10-£19 ⛺ £10-£19 ▲ £10-£19

Open mid Apr-Sep Last arrival 20.00hrs Last
departure 10.30hrs

An attractive paddocked park in a sheltered rural
position with views towards St Ives. This secluded
park is personally run by owners who keep it quiet
and welcoming. Three unisex showers are a great
hit with visitors. Fluent German is spoken. A 6.5
acre site with 82 touring pitches, 3 hardstandings.

AA Pubs & Restaurants nearby: White Hart,
Ludgvan 01736 740574

Porthminster Beach, St Ives 01736 795352

Leisure: 🄰
Facilities: 🌣☉✳♿🔵🅿
Services: 🔌🔵🅿✏🅃⛴
Within 3 miles: ⚓🎣☉♨🛒🅿
Notes: ☺ Max speed 5mph, max 2 dogs, no
dangerous dogs, balls on field only. Football/sport
field

LEISURE: 🏊 Indoor swimming pool ⚓ Outdoor swimming pool 🄰 Children's playground ♨ Tennis court ⚓ Games room 📺 Separate TV room ⚓ 9/18 hole golf course
⚓ Boats for hire 🎬 Cinema 🎣 Fishing ☉ Mini golf ⚓ Watersports ♨ Stables **FACILITIES:** 🚿 Bath 🌣 Shower ☉ Electric shaver 🅿 Hairdryer ✳ Ice Pack Facility
♿ Disabled facilities 🔵 Public telephone 🛒 Shop on site or within 200yds 🅿 Mobile shop (calls at least 5 days a week) 🅿 BBQ area 🅿 Picnic area 🐕 Dog exercise area

▶▶▶ 81% *Atlantic Coast Caravan Park* (NW580400)

53 Upton Towans, Gwithian TR27 5BL
☎ 01736 752071 ▤ 01736 758100
e-mail: enquiries@atlanticcoastpark.co.uk
dir: *From A30 into Hayle, turn right at double rdbt. Site 1.5m on left*

🚐 🚙 Å

Open Mar-early Jan Last arrival 20.00hrs Last departure 11.00hrs

Fringed by the sand-dunes of St Ives Bay and close to the golden sands of Gwithian Beach, the small, friendly touring area offers fully serviced pitches. There's freshly baked bread, a takeaway and a bar next door. This park is ideally situated for visitors to enjoy the natural coastal beauty and attractions of south-west Cornwall. Static caravans for holiday hire. A 4.5 acre site with 15 touring pitches and 50 statics.

AA Pubs & Restaurants nearby: White Hart, Ludgvan 01736 740574

Porthminster Beach, St Ives 01736 795352

Facilities: 🅿️ ⊙ 🄿 ✳ 🛆 🕒 🖻
Services: 🔌 🖥 🅃 🍴 🍔 🚼
Within 3 miles: ↨ 🎣 ◎ 🛥 🖻 🖥 ↻

Notes: No commercial vehicles, gazebos or day tents. Wi-fi

▶▶▶ 79% Parbola Holiday Park

(SW612366)

Wall, Gwinear TR27 5LE
☎ 01209 831503
e-mail: bookings@parbola.co.uk
dir: *At Hayle rdbt on A30 take Connor Downs exit. In 1m turn right signed Carnhell Green. In village right to Wall. Site in village on left*

* 🚐 £12-£22 🚙 £12-£22 Å £12-£22

Open all year (rs Etr-end of Jun & Sep shop closed, unheated pool) Last arrival 21.00hrs Last departure 10.00hrs

Pitches are provided in both woodland and open areas in this spacious park in Cornish downland. The park is centrally located for touring the seaside resorts and towns in the area, especially nearby Hayle with its three miles of golden sands. A 16.5 acre site with 110 touring pitches, 4 hardstandings and 28 statics.

AA Pubs & Restaurants nearby: White Hart, Ludgvan 01736 740574

Porthminster Beach, St Ives 01736 795352

Leisure: 🏊 ⚑ 🔍
Facilities: 🅿️ ⊙ 🄿 ✳ 🛆 🖻 🖥
Services: 🔌 🖥 🅗 🌱 🛒 🚼
Within 3 miles: ↨ 🎣 ◎ 🖻 🖥 ↻

Notes: Dogs not allowed Jul-Aug. Crazy golf & table tennis, giant chess & draughts, hairdressing, make-up room, herb garden

▶▶▶ 77% Treglisson Touring Park

(SW581367)

Wheal Alfred Rd TR27 5JT
☎ 01736 753141
e-mail: enquiries@treglisson.co.uk
dir: *4th exit off rdbt on A30 at Hayle. 100mtrs, left at 1st mini-rdbt. Approx 1.5m past golf course, site sign on left*

🚐 £9.50-£16.50 🚙 £9.50-£16.50
Å £9.50-£16.50

Open Etr-Sep Last arrival 20.00hrs Last departure 11.00hrs

A small secluded site in a peaceful wooded meadow, a former apple and pear orchard. This quiet rural site has level grass pitches and a well-planned modern toilet block, and is just two miles from the glorious beach at Hayle with its vast stretch of golden sand. A 3 acre site with 26 touring pitches, 3 hardstandings.

AA Pubs & Restaurants nearby: White Hart, Ludgvan 01736 740574

Porthminster Beach, St Ives 01736 795352

Leisure: 🏊 ⚑
Facilities: 🅿️ ⊙ 🄿 ✳ 🛆 🕒 🖻 🚼 🐾
Services: 🔌 🖥 🛒
Within 3 miles: ↨ 🎣 🛥 🖻 🖥

Notes: Max 6 people to one pitch, dogs must be on leads at all times. Tourist information, milk deliveries

NEW ▶▶▶ 71% Lavender Fields Touring Park (SW623377)

Penhale Rd, Carnhell Green TR14 0LU
☎ 01209 832188 & 07855 227773
e-mail: info@lavenderfieldstouring.co.uk
dir: *Exit A30 at Camborne W junct. At top of slip road left at rdbt, 2nd exit through Roseworthy, left after Roseworthy signed Carnhell Green, over level crossing to T-junct, turn left. Site 750yds on right*

🚐 🚙 Å

Open all year Last arrival 21.00hrs Last departure 10.00hrs

A family owned and run park in the heart of the Cornish countryside on the outskirts of the idyllic village of Carnhell Green, yet only a short car or bus ride to glorious golden beaches and towns. Developed on an old mine waste site, the park is maturing well and has some good hardstandings for larger units. Dogs are very welcome here. Five seasonal touring pitches are available. A 5 acre site with 45 touring pitches, 21 hardstandings.

Facilities: 🅿️ ⊙ ✳ 🛆 🖻 🐾
Services: 🔌 🖥 🅗 ↺
Within 3 miles: ↨ 🎋 🎣 ◎ 🖻 🖥 ↻

Notes: Dogs must be kept on leads

HELSTON

See also Ashton

Places to visit

Trevarno Estate Garden & Museum of Gardening, Helston 01326 574274
www.trevarno.co.uk

Goonhilly Satellite Earth Station Experience, Helston 0800 679593 www.goonhilly.bt.com

Great for kids: The Flambards Experience, Helston 01326 573404 www.flambards.co.uk

Not all campsites accept pets.
It is advisable to check at the time of booking

HELSTON — Map 2 SW62

►►► 80% Lower Polladras Touring Park (SW617308)

Carleen, Breage TR13 9NX
☎ 01736 762220 📠 01736 762220
e-mail: lowerpolladras@btinternet.com
web: www.lower-polladras.co.uk
dir: *From Helston take A394 then B3302 (Hayle road) at Ward Garage, 2nd left to Carleen, site 2m on right*

* 🚐 £10-£20 🚏 £10-£19 ▲ £10-£19

Open Apr-Jan Last arrival 22.00hrs Last departure noon

An attractive rural park with extensive views of surrounding fields, appealing to families who enjoy the countryside. The planted trees and shrubs are maturing, and help to divide the area into paddocks with spacious grassy pitches. Improvements include a new dishwashing area, a new games room, a dog and nature walk and also Wi-fi, with plans for campers' kitchen and two fully-serviced family rooms for 2011. A 4 acre site with 39 touring pitches, 23 hardstandings and 3 statics.

AA Pubs & Restaurants nearby: The Ship Inn, Porthleven 01326 564204

The Kota Restaurant with Rooms, Porthleven 01326 562407

The New Yard Restaurant, Helston 01326 221595

Leisure: 🅰 🎱
Facilities: 🌂⊙℔✳🚿🔥📷🍴🚻🐕
Services: 🔌🚐🛒🖊🅃🧺🛒♿
Within 3 miles: ↓⛳🕽ᐟ🎣◎🐎🛥🎣🐕♻
Notes: 🐾 Caravan storage area. Wi-fi

AA CAMPING CARD SITE

►►► 77% Poldown Caravan Park (SW629298)

Poldown, Carleen TR13 9NN
☎ 01326 574560
e-mail: stay@poldown.co.uk
dir: *From Helston follow Penzance signs for 1m, right onto B3302 to Hayle, 2nd left to Carleen, 0.5m to site*

* 🚐 £10-£15.50 🚏 £10-£15.50 ▲ £10-£15.50

Open Apr-Sep Last arrival 21.00hrs Last departure noon

A small, quiet site set in attractive countryside with bright toilet facilities. All of the level grass pitches have electricity. This sunny park is sheltered by mature trees and shrubs. A 2 acre site with 13 touring pitches, 2 hardstandings and 7 statics.

AA Pubs & Restaurants nearby: The Ship Inn, Porthleven 01326 564204

The Kota Restaurant with Rooms, Porthleven 01326 562407

The New Yard Restaurant, Helston 01326 221595

Leisure: 🅰
Facilities: 🌂⊙℔✳🚿🔥📷🍴🚻🐕
Services: 🔌🖊🧺
Within 3 miles: ↓⛳🕽ᐟ🎣🐎🛥🎣🐕♻
Notes: 🐾 Table tennis. Wi-fi

►►► 76% Skyburriowe Farm (SW698227)

Garras TR12 6LR
☎ 01326 221646
e-mail: bkbenney@hotmail.co.uk
web: www.skyburriowefarm.co.uk
dir: *From Helston A3083 to The Lizard. After Culdrose Naval Airbase continue straight at rdbt, in 1m left at Skyburriowe Ln sign. In 0.5m right at Skyburriowe B&B/Campsite sign. Pass bungalow to farmhouse. Site on left*

🚐 £12-£16 🚏 £12-£16 ▲ £10-£14

Open Apr-Oct Last arrival 22.00hrs Last departure 11.00hrs

A leafy no-through road leads to this picturesque farm park in a rural location on the Lizard Peninsula. A newly-built toilet block offers excellent quality facilities, and most pitches have electric hook-ups. There are some beautiful coves and beaches nearby. A 4 acre site with 30 touring pitches, 2 hardstandings.

Skyburriowe Farm

AA Pubs & Restaurants nearby: The Ship Inn, Porthleven 01326 564204

The Kota Restaurant with Rooms, Porthleven 01326 562407

The New Yard Restaurant, Helston 01326 221595

Skyburriowe Farm

Facilities: 🌂⊙✳🔥🐕
Services: 🔌🧺
Within 3 miles: ↓🕽ᐟ🎣🐎🛥🎣🐕♻
Notes: 🐾 Dogs must be kept on leads, quiet after 23.00hrs

HOLYWELL BAY

Places to visit

Trerice (NT), Trerice 01637 875404
www.nationaltrust.org.uk

Blue Reef Aquarium, Newquay 01637 878134
www.bluereefaquarium.co.uk

Great for kids: Newquay Zoo, Newquay
0844 474 2244 www.newquayzoo.org.uk

HOLYWELL BAY　　　　　　Map 2 SW75

94% *Trevornick Holiday Park*
(SW776586)

TR8 5PW
☎ 01637 830531　▤ 01637 831000
e-mail: info@trevornick.co.uk
web: www.trevornick.co.uk
dir: *3m from Newquay off A3075 towards Redruth. Follow Cubert & Holywell Bay signs*

🚐 🚗 🅰

Open Etr & mid May-mid Sep Last arrival 21.00hrs Last departure 10.00hrs

A large seaside holiday complex with excellent facilities and amenities. There is plenty of entertainment including a children's club and an evening cabaret, adding up to a full holiday experience for all the family. A sandy beach is just a 15-minute footpath walk away. The park has 68 ready-erected tents for hire. A 20 acre site with 593 touring pitches, 6 hardstandings.

AA Pubs & Restaurants nearby: The Smugglers' Den Inn, Cubert 01637 830209

Leisure: 🏊 ⚄ 🎣
Facilities: 🚿 🌂 ⊙ ℗ ✳ ⚄ 🚽 🍴 🎫 ⛱
Services: 🔌 🚻 🚮 🛢 ⊘ 🚾 🍴 🛒 🎁 🚿
Within 3 miles: 🚴 ⚡ 🏊 ◎ ⛴ 🎣 🎁 ∪

Notes: Families & couples only. Fishing, golf course, entertainment

see advert on page 87

77% Holywell Bay Holiday Park *(SW773582)*

TR8 5PR
☎ 0844 335 3756　▤ 01637 831166
e-mail: touringandcamping@parkdeanholidays.com
web: www.parkdeantouring.com
dir: *Exit A30 onto A392, take A3075 signed Redruth, right in 2m signed Holywell/Cubert. Through Cubert past Trevornick to site on left*

🚐 £14-£40　🚗 £14-£40　🅰 £11-£35

Open Mar-Oct (rs May-19 Sep pool open) Last arrival 21.00hrs Last departure 10.00hrs

Close to lovely beaches in a rural location, this level grassy park borders on National Trust land, and is only a short distance from the Cornish Coastal Path. The park provides a popular entertainment programme for the whole family (including evening entertainment), and there is an outdoor pool with a waterslide and children's clubs. Newquay is just a few miles away. A 40 acre site with 40 touring pitches and 162 statics.

AA Pubs & Restaurants nearby: The Smugglers' Den Inn, Cubert 01637 830209

Leisure: 🏊 ⚄ 🎣　**Facilities:** 🚿 ⊙ ⚄ 🚽 🍴 ⛱
Services: 🔌 🚻 🚮 🛢 🚾 🍴 🛒 🎁
Within 3 miles: 🚴 ⚡ ◎ ⛴ 🎣 🎁 ∪

Notes: No pets. Family entertainment, children's clubs, surf school & hire shop, adventure playground

see advert in preliminary section

INDIAN QUEENS　　　　　　Map 2 SW95

Places to visit

Lanhydrock (NT), Lanhydrock 01208 265950
www.nationaltrust.org.uk

Charlestown Shipwreck & Heritage Centre, St Austell 01726 69897
www.shipwreckcharlestown.com

Great for kids: Eden Project, St Austell 01726 811911 www.edenproject.com

▶▶▶ 74% Gnome World Caravan & Camping Site *(SW890599)*

Moorland Rd TR9 6HN
☎ 01726 860812　& 860101　▤ 01726 861749
e-mail: gnomesworld@btconnect.com
dir: *Signed from slip road at A30 & A39 rdbt in village of Indian Queens - site on old A30, now unclassified road*

* 🚐 £7-£9　🚗 £7-£9　🅰 £7-£9

Open Mar-Dec Last arrival 22.00hrs Last departure noon

continued

SERVICES: 🔌 Electric hook up　🚻 Launderette　🍸 Licensed bar　🛢 Calor Gas　⊘ Camping Gaz　🚾 Toilet fluid　🍴 Café/Restaurant　🍔 Fast Food/Takeaway　🔋 Battery charging
🍼 Baby care　⚡ Motorvan service point　**ABBREVIATIONS:** BH/bank hols-bank holidays　Etr-Easter　Whit-Whitsun　dep-departure　fr-from　hrs-hours　m-mile　mdnt-midnight
rdbt-roundabout　rs-restricted service　wk-week　wknd-weekend　⊗ No credit cards　⊗ no dogs　See page 7 for details of the AA Camping Card Scheme

INDIAN QUEENS *continued*

Set in open countryside, this spacious park is set on level grassy land only half a mile from the A30 (Cornwall's main arterial route) and in a central holiday location for touring the county. There are no narrow lanes to negotiate. Seasonal touring pitches are available. A 4.5 acre site with 50 touring pitches, 25 hardstandings and 60 statics.

Leisure: ⚑

Facilities: ⌂⊙✻⌂⌂⌂

Services: ⊡⊡⊟

Within 3 miles: ⌂⌂⊟∪

Notes: Dogs must be kept on leads. Nature trail

see advert on page 79

JACOBSTOW Map 2 SX19

Places to visit

Launceston Castle, Launceston 01566 772365 www.english-heritage.org.uk

Tamar Otter & Wildlife Centre, Launceston 01566 785646 www.tamarotters.co.uk

Great for kids: Launceston Steam Railway, Launceston 01566 775665 www.launcestonsr.co.uk

---

▶▶▶ 76% *Edmore Tourist Park*

(SX184955)

Edgar Rd, Wainhouse Corner EX23 0BJ
☎ 01840 230467 ▤ 01840 230467
e-mail: enquiries@cornwallvisited.co.uk
dir: *Exit A39 at Wainhouse Corner onto Edgar Rd, site signed on right in 200yds*

⊡⊡⚊

Open 1 wk before Etr-Oct Last arrival 21.00hrs Last departure noon

A quiet family-owned site in a rural location with extensive views, set close to the sandy surfing beaches of Bude, and the unspoilt sandy beach and rock pools at Crackington Haven. Friendly owners keep all facilities in a very good condition and recent improvements include new hardstanding pitches and new gravel access roads. A 3 acre site with 28 touring pitches.

AA Pubs & Restaurants nearby: Bay View Inn, Widemouth Bay 01288 361273

Leisure: ⚑ **Facilities:** ⌂⊙⌂✻⊙⊟

Services: ⊡⊟⚊

Within 3 miles: ⊟

Notes: ⊛

KENNACK SANDS Map 2 SW71

Places to visit

National Seal Sanctuary, Gweek 0871 423 2110 www.sealsanctuary.co.uk

Trevarno Estate Garden & Museum of Gardening, Helston 01326 574274 www.trevarno.co.uk

Great for kids: Goonhilly Satellite Earth Station Experience, Helston 0800 679593 www.goonhilly.bt.com

---

▶▶▶ 78% *Chy Carne Holiday Park*

(SW725164)

Kuggar, Ruan Minor TR12 7LX
☎ 01326 290200 & 291161
e-mail: enquiries@camping-cornwall.com
web: www.camping-cornwall.com
dir: *From A3083 turn left on B3293 after Culdrose Naval Air Station. At Goonhilly ESS right onto unclass road signed Kennack Sands. Left in 3m at junct*

⊡⊡⚊

Open Etr-Oct Last arrival dusk

A small but spacious park in a quiet, sheltered spot with extensive sea and coastal views from the grassy touring area. A village pub with restaurant is a short walk by footpath from the touring area, and a sandy beach is less than half a mile away. A 12 acre site with 30 touring pitches, 4 hardstandings and 18 statics.

AA Pubs & Restaurants nearby: Cadgwith Cove Inn, Cadgwith 01326 290513

Leisure: ⚑ ⚈

Facilities: ⌂⊙⌂✻⊙⊟⌂⌂⌂

Services: ⊡⊟⚊⊘⊤⊙⚊⚊

Within 3 miles: ⌂✦⌂⊚⊟⊟∪

Notes: Wi-fi

▶▶▶ 76% *Silver Sands Holiday Park* (SW727166)

Gwendreath TR12 7LZ
☎ 01326 290631 ▤ 01326 290434
e-mail: info@silversandsholidaypark.co.uk
dir: *From Helston follow signs to Future World Goonhilly. After 300yds turn right at x-roads signed Kennack Sands, 1m, left at Gwendreath sign, site 1m*

⊡⊡⚊

A small park in a remote location, with individually screened pitches providing sheltered suntraps. New owners are gradually upgrading the park, improving the landscaping, access roads, toilets and general detail around the park, notably the lovely floral displays that greet you on arrival. A footpath through the woods from the family-owned park leads to the beach and the local pub. A 9 acre site with 34 touring pitches.

AA Pubs & Restaurants nearby: Cadgwith Cove Inn, Cadgwith 01326 290513

▶▶▶ 72% Gwendreath Farm Holiday Park (SW738168)

TR12 7LZ
☎ 01326 290666
e-mail: tom.gibson@virgin.net
dir: *From A3083 turn left past Culdrose Naval Air Station onto B3293. Right past Goonhilly Earth Station signed Kennack Sands, left in 1m. At end of lane turn right over cattle grid. Right, through Seaview to 2nd reception*

⊡⚊

Open May-Sep Last arrival 21.00hrs Last departure 10.00hrs

A grassy park in an elevated position with extensive sea and coastal views, and the beach just a short walk through the woods. Campers can use the bar and takeaway at an adjoining site. It is advisable to telephone ahead and book before arrival. A 5 acre site with 10 touring pitches and 17 statics.

AA Pubs & Restaurants nearby: Cadgwith Cove Inn, Cadgwith 01326 290513

Leisure: ⚑

Facilities: ⌂⊙✻⊙⊟⌂

Services: ⊡⊟⚊⊘⚊

Within 3 miles: ⌂⌂⊟⊟∪

Notes: ⊛

KILKHAMPTON — Map 2 SS21

Places to visit

Dartington Crystal, Great Torrington 01805 626242 www.dartington.co.uk

RHS Garden Rosemoor, Great Torrington 01805 624067 www.rhs.org.uk/rosemoor

Great for kids: The Milky Way Adventure Park, Clovelly 01237 431255 www.themilkyway.co.uk

AA CAMPING CARD SITE

►► 72% Upper Tamar Lake *(SS288118)*

Upper Tamar Lake EX23 9SB
☎ **01288 321712**
e-mail: info@swlakestrust.org.uk
dir: *From A39 at Kilkhampton onto B3254, left in 0.5m onto unclass road, follow signs approx 4m to site*

Å

Open Apr-Oct

A well-trimmed, slightly sloping site overlooking the lake and surrounding countryside, with several signed walks. The site benefits from the excellent facilities provided for the watersports centre and coarse anglers, with a rescue launch on the lake when the flags are flying. A good family site, with Bude's beaches and surfing waves only eight miles away. A 2 acre site with 36 touring pitches.

AA Pubs & Restaurants nearby: The Bush Inn, Morwenstow 01288 331242

Leisure: 🅰

Facilities: 🌾🇵♿🅾️🚻🎠

Services: 🍽💧

Within 3 miles: 🚴🎣🅿⛴🎣🎯U

Notes: Dogs must be kept on leads. Watersports centre, canoeing, sailing, windsurfing

LANDRAKE — Map 3 SX36

Places to visit

Cotehele (NT), Calstock 01579 351346 www.nationaltrust.org.uk

Mount Edgcumbe House & Country Park, Torpoint 01752 822236 www.mountedgcumbe.gov.uk

Great for kids: The Monkey Sanctuary, Looe 01503 262532 www.monkeysanctuary.org

AA CAMPING CARD SITE

►►►► 82% Dolbeare Park Caravan and Camping *(SX363616)*

Best of British — SILVER

St Ive Rd PL12 5AF
☎ **01752 851332** 📠 **01752 547871**
e-mail: reception@dolbeare.co.uk
web: www.dolbeare.co.uk
dir: *A38 to Landrake, 4m W of Saltash. At footbridge over A38 turn right, follow signs to site (0.75m from A38)*

🚐 £14.50-£22.60 🚚 £14.50-£22.60
Å £11-£22.60

Open all year Last arrival 18.00hrs Last departure noon

A mainly level grass site with trees and bushes set in meadowland. The keen and friendly owners set high standards, and the park is always neat and clean. The refurbished toilet block with its new inviting interior and spacious family rooms is particularly impressive. A 9 acre site with 60 touring pitches, 54 hardstandings.

AA Pubs & Restaurants nearby: The Crooked Inn, Saltash 01752 848177

The Farmhouse, Saltash 01752 854664

Leisure: 🅰

Facilities: 🌾🅾️🇵♿🅾️🕐🚻🎠

Services: 🔌🅾️🛢🚿🅃🔋💧♻️

Within 3 miles: 🚴🎣🅿⛴🎯U

Notes: No cycling, no kite flying, dogs on leads. Info centre, off licence, free fridge & freezer. Wi-fi

see advert on page 86

LANIVET — Map 2 SX06

Places to visit

Restormel Castle, Restormel 01208 872687 www.english-heritage.org.uk

Eden Project, St Austell 01726 811911 www.edenproject.com

AA CAMPING CARD SITE

►►► 79% Mena Caravan & Camping Park *(SW041626)*

PL30 5HW
☎ **01208 831845** 📠 **01208 831845**
e-mail: mena@campsitesincornwall.co.uk
dir: *Exit A30 onto A389 N signed Lanivet & Wadebridge. In 0.5m 1st right & pass under A30. 1st left signed Lostwithiel & Fowey. In 0.25m right at top of hill. 0.5m then 1st right. Entrance 100yds on right*

🚐🚚Å

Open all year Last arrival 22.00hrs Last departure noon

Set in a secluded, elevated location with high hedges for shelter, and plenty of peace. This grassy site is about four miles from the Eden Project and midway between the north and south Cornish coasts. There is a small coarse fishing lake on site, additional new hardstanding pitches, and two static caravans for holiday hire. A 15 acre site with 25 touring pitches, 1 hardstanding and 2 statics.

AA Pubs & Restaurants nearby: The Borough Arms, Dunmere 01208 73118

Trehellas House Hotel & Restaurant, Bodmin 01208 72700

Leisure: 🅰🎣

Facilities: 🌾🅾️🇵♿🅾️🚻🎠

Services: 🔌🅾️🛢🚿🅃💧

Within 3 miles: 🚴🅿⛴🎣🎯U

LEEDSTOWN (NEAR HAYLE)   Map 2 SW63

Places to visit

East Pool Mine (NT), Pool 01209 315027
www.nationaltrust.org.uk

Godolphin House (NT), Godolphin Cross 01736
763194 www.nationaltrust.org.uk/godolphin

▶▶▶▶ **80%** *Calloose Caravan &*
Camping Park (SW597352)

TR27 5ET
☎ 01736 850431 & 0800 328 7589
📠 01736 850431
e-mail: calloose@hotmail.com
dir: *From Hayle take B3302 to Leedstown, turn left*
opposite village hall, before entering village. Site
0.5m on left at bottom of hill

🚐 🚙 ⛺

Open Mar-Nov, Xmas & New Year (rs Mar-mid May
& late Sep-Nov swimming pool closed) Last arrival
22.00hrs Last departure 11.00hrs

A comprehensively equipped leisure park in a
remote rural setting in a small river valley. This
very good park is busy and bustling, and offers
bright, clean and newly upgraded toilet facilities,
an excellent games room, an inviting pool, a good
children's play area, and log cabins and static
caravans for holiday hire. A 12.5 acre site with
109 touring pitches, 29 hardstandings and 25
statics.

AA Pubs & Restaurants nearby: Mount Haven
Hotel & Restaurant, Marazion 01736 710249

Leisure: 🏊 🎢 ⛳ 🎱 🖥
Facilities: 🚿 ⊙ ✂ ☀ ♿ 🕐 🏪 🍴 🐕
Services: 🔌 🗑 🚿 💧 🚰 T 🍴 🎫 🛒
Within 3 miles: 🎣 🏪 🛒
Notes: Crazy golf, skittle alley

LOOE

Places to visit

Antony House (NT), Torpoint 01752 812191
www.nationaltrust.org.uk/antony

Mount Edgcumbe House & Country Park,
Torpoint 01752 822236
www.mountedgcumbe.gov.uk

Great for kids: The Monkey Sanctuary, Looe
01503 262532 www.monkeysanctuary.org

LOOE   Map 2 SX25

AA CAMPING CARD SITE

68% Tencreek Holiday Park
(SX233525)

Polperro Rd PL13 2JR
☎ 01503 262447   📠 01503 262760
e-mail: reception@tencreek.co.uk
web: www.dolphinholidays.co.uk
dir: *Take A387 1.25m from Looe. Site on left*

* 🚐 £10.50-£19.50 🚙 £10.50-£19.50
⛺ £10.50-£19.50

Open all year Last arrival 23.00hrs Last
departure 10.00hrs

Occupying a lovely position with extensive
countryside and sea views, this holiday
centre is in a rural spot but close to Looe and
Polperro. There is a full family entertainment
programme, with indoor and outdoor swimming
pools, an adventure playground and an exciting
children's club. The two new toilet blocks on the
touring area are exceptional and include two
superb family/disabled cubicles. A 24 acre site
with 254 touring pitches and 101 statics.

AA Pubs & Restaurants nearby: Barclay House,
Looe 01503 262929

Trelaske Hotel & Restaurant, Looe
01503 262159

Leisure: 🏊 🏊 🎢 🎱
Facilities: 🚿 ⊙ ✂ ☀ ♿ 🕐 🏪 🐕
Services: 🔌 🗑 🚿 💧 🚰 T 🍴 🎫 🛒 🚮
Within 3 miles: 🎣 🚴 🎬 🎣 ◎ 🛥 🏪 🛒 ⛵
Notes: Families & couples only. Nightly
entertainment, 45-metre pool flume

▶▶▶▶ **78%** *Camping Caradon*
Touring Park (SX218539)

Trelawne PL13 2NA
☎ 01503 272388   📠 01503 272858
e-mail: enquiries@campingcaradon.co.uk
dir: *Site signed from B3359 near junct with A387,*
between Looe & Polperro

🚐 🚙 ⛺

Open all year (rs Nov-Mar by booking only) Last
arrival 22.00hrs Last departure noon

Set in a quiet rural location between the popular
coastal resorts of Looe and Polperro, this family-
run and developing eco-friendly park is just one

and half miles from the beach at Talland Bay. The
hands-on owners have upgraded the bar and
restaurant (food can also be delivered to your
pitch), and added two fully-serviced family/
disabled wet rooms. The toilet facilities will be
refurbished and upgraded for the 2011 season. A
3.5 acre site with 85 touring pitches, 23
hardstandings.

AA Pubs & Restaurants nearby: Old Mill House
Inn, Polperro 01503 272362

Barclay House, Looe 01503 262929

Leisure: 🎢 🎱 🖥
Facilities: 🚿 ⊙ ✂ ☀ ♿ 🏪 🐕
Services: 🔌 🗑 🚿 💧 🚰 T 🍴 🎫 🚮
Within 3 miles: 🎣 🚴 🛥 🏪 🛒
Notes: Wi-fi

▶▶▶▶ **77%** *Tregoad Park* (SX272560)

St Martin PL13 1PB
☎ 01503 262718   📠 01503 264777
e-mail: info@tregoadpark.co.uk
web: www.tregoadpark.co.uk
dir: *Signed with direct access from B3253, or from*
E on A387 follow B3253 for 1.75m towards Looe.
Site on left

🚐 🚙 ⛺

Open all year Last arrival 20.00hrs Last departure
11.00hrs

Investment continues at this smart, terraced park
with extensive sea and rural views, about a mile
and a half from Looe. All pitches are level. The
facilities are well maintained and spotlessly clean
(one toilet block has now been refurbished), and
there is a swimming pool with adjacent jacuzzi
and sun patio, and a licensed bar where bar
meals are served in the conservatory. American
trailers, static caravans, holiday cottages and two
camping pods for holiday hire, and there's an
excellent new camping barn that sleeps 30. A 55
acre site with 200 touring pitches, 60
hardstandings and 7 statics.

AA Pubs & Restaurants nearby: Barclay House,
Looe 01503 262929

Trelaske Hotel & Restaurant, Looe 01503 262159

Leisure: 🏊 🎢 🎱 🖥
Facilities: 🛁 🚿 ⊙ ✂ ☀ ♿ 🕐 🏪 🐕
Services: 🔌 🗑 🚿 💧 🚰 T 🍴 🎫 🚮 🚮 ⛽
Within 3 miles: 🎣 🚴 🎬 🎣 ◎ 🛥 🏪 🛒 ⛵
Notes: Pets on leads at all times. Fishing lake,
crazy golf, ball sports area. Wi-fi

▶▶▶ 80% Polborder House Caravan & Camping Park *(SX283557)*

Bucklawren Rd, St Martin PL13 1NZ
☎ 01503 240265
e-mail: reception@polborderhouse.co.uk
dir: *Approach Looe from E on A387, follow B3253 for 1m, left at Polborder & Monkey Sanctuary sign. Site 0.5m on right*

🚐 🚏 Å

Open all year Last arrival 22.00hrs Last departure 11.00hrs

A very neat and well-kept small grassy site on high ground above Looe in a peaceful rural setting. Friendly and enthusiastic owners continue to invest in the park, refurbishing the toilet facilities with upmarket fittings (note the infra-red operated taps and under floor heating) and adding new roadways. The whole park looked immaculate at our last inspection. A 3.3 acre site with 31 touring pitches, 19 hardstandings and 5 statics.

AA Pubs & Restaurants nearby: Barclay House, Looe 01503 262929

Trelaske Hotel & Restaurant, Looe 01503 262159

Leisure: 🏊
Facilities: 🌂⊙🄿✳🕭🕐🅰️🎿
Services: 🔌🅶🄰🖊🅃🎿🚼
Within 3 miles: 🏌🏇🎣🚴🎣🄰🅱️⟲
Notes: Dogs allowed but no exercise area. Washing/food prep sinks, information centre. Wi-fi

▶▶▶ 79% Trelay Farmpark *(SX210544)*

Pelynt PL13 2JX
☎ 01503 220900   📠 01503 220902
e-mail: stay@trelay.co.uk
dir: *From A390 at East Taphouse, take B3359 S towards Looe. After Pelynt, site 0.5m on left*

🚐 £7.50-£13.50   🚏 £7.50-£13.50
Å £7.50-£13.50

Open Dec-Oct Last arrival 21.00hrs Last departure 11.00hrs

A small site with a friendly atmosphere set in a pretty rural area with extensive views. The good-size grass pitches are on slightly-sloping ground, and the toilets are immaculately kept, with the addition of an excellent washing-up room in 2010. Looe and Polperro are just three miles away. A 4.5 acre site with 66 touring pitches and 45 statics.

AA Pubs & Restaurants nearby: Old Mill House Inn, Polperro 01503 272362

Barclay House, Looe 01503 262929

Leisure: 🏊
Facilities: 🌂⊙🄿✳🕭🕐🅰️🎿
Services: 🔌🅶🄰🖊🅃🎿🚼🅅
Within 3 miles: 🏇🎣🚴🄰🅱️⟲
Notes: No skateboards, ball games or kites. Fridge & freezer. Wi-fi

---

| LOSTWITHIEL | Map 2 SX15 |

Places to visit

Restormel Castle, Restormel 01208 872687
www.english-heritage.org.uk

Eden Project, St Austell 01726 811911
www.edenproject.com

▶▶▶▶ 80% Eden Valley Holiday Park *(SX083593)*

PL30 5BU
☎ 01208 872277   📠 01208 871236
e-mail: enquiries@edenvalleyholidaypark.co.uk
dir: *1.5m SW of Lostwithiel on A390 turn right at brown/white sign in 400mtrs*

🚐 £11-£15   🚏 £11-£15   Å £11-£15

Open Etr or Apr-Oct Last arrival 22.00hrs Last departure 11.30hrs

A grassy park set in attractive paddocks with mature trees. A gradual upgrading of facilities continues, and both buildings and grounds are carefully maintained and contain an impressive children's play area. Recent improvements include new cinder roadways and a large motorhome service point. This park is ideally located for visiting the Eden Project, the nearby golden beaches and sailing at Fowey. There are also two self-catering lodges and seasonal touring pitches. A 12 acre site with 56 touring pitches, 12 hardstandings and 38 statics.

AA Pubs & Restaurants nearby: The Royal Oak, Lostwithiel 01208 872552

The Crown Inn, Lanlivery 01208 872707

Leisure: 🏊🎣▭
Facilities: 🌂⊙🄿✳🕭🕐 🎿
Services: 🔌🅶🄰🖊🎿
Within 3 miles: 🏌🏇🎣◎🚴🄰🅱️⟲
Notes: Badminton, soft tennis, putting green

| LUXULYAN | Map 2 SX05 |

Places to visit

Restormel Castle, Restormel 01208 872687
www.english-heritage.org.uk

Eden Project, St Austell 01726 811911
www.edenproject.com

▶▶▶ 77% Croft Farm Holiday Park *(SX044568)*

PL30 5EQ
☎ 01726 850228   📠 01726 850498
e-mail: enquiries@croftfarm.co.uk
dir: *Exit A30 at Bodmin onto A391 towards St Austell. In 7m left at double rdbt onto unclass road towards Luxulyan/Eden Project, continue to rdbt at Eden, left signed Luxulyan. Site 1m on left. (NB Do not approach any other way as roads are very narrow)*

* 🚐 £11-£17   🚏 £11-£17   Å £11-£17

Open 21 Mar-21 Jan Last arrival 18.00hrs Last departure 11.00hrs

A peaceful, picturesque setting at the edge of a wooded valley, and only one mile from The Eden Project. Facilities include a well-maintained toilet block, a well-equipped dishwashing area, replete with freezer and microwave, and a newly revamped children's play area reached via an attractive woodland trail. A 10.5 acre site with 52 touring pitches, 42 hardstandings and 45 statics.

AA Pubs & Restaurants nearby: The Royal Oak, Lostwithiel 01208 872552

The Crown Inn, Lanlivery 01208 872707

Leisure: 🏊🎣
Facilities: 🚿🌂⊙🄿✳🕐🅰️🎿🎿
Services: 🔌🅶🄰🖊🅃🎿🅅
Within 3 miles: 🏌🏇🎣🍴🚴◎🄰🅱️
Notes: No skateboarding, ball games only in playing field, quiet between 23.00hrs-07.00hrs. Woodland walk, crazy golf, information room. Wi-fi

---

MARAZION Map 2 SW53

See also St Hilary & Praa Sands

Places to visit

St Michael's Mount, Marazion 01736 710507 www.stmichaelsmount.co.uk

Trengwainton Garden (NT), Penzance 01736 363148 www.nationaltrust.org.uk

AA CAMPING CARD SITE

►►► 76% Wheal Rodney Holiday Park *(SW525315)*

Gwallon Ln TR17 0HL
☎ 01736 710605
e-mail: reception@whealrodney.co.uk
dir: *Exit A30 at Crowlas, signed Rospeath. Site 1.5m on right. From Marazion centre turn opposite Fire Engine Inn, site 500mtrs on left*

🚃 £15-£21 🚐 £15-£21 ⛺ £12-£17

Open Etr-Oct Last arrival 20.00hrs Last dep 11.00hrs

Set in a quiet rural location surrounded by farmland, with level grass pitches and well-kept facilities. Within half a mile are the beach at Marazion and the causeway or ferry to St Michael's Mount. A cycle route is just 400 yards away. A 2.5 acre site with 30 touring pitches.

AA Pubs & Restaurants nearby: Godolphin Arms, Marazion 01736 710202

Mount Haven Hotel & Restaurant, Marazion 01736 710249

Leisure: 🏊 **Facilities:** 🚿🪒💨❄📞🏪

Services: 🔌🧼🍟🔋

Within 3 miles: ⛳🎣◎🏄🏪🧼🐴

Notes: Quiet after 22.00hrs. Wi-fi

MAWGAN PORTH Map 2 SW86

►►►► 77% Sun Haven Valley Holiday Park *(SW861669)*

TR8 4BQ
☎ 01637 860373 📠 01637 860373
e-mail: sunhaven@sunhavenvalley.com
dir: *Exit A30 at Highgate Hill junct for Newquay follow signs for airport. At T-junct turn right. At beach level in Mawgan Porth take only road inland, then 0.25m. Site 0.5m beyond S bend*

🚃 🚐 ⛺

Open Apr-Oct Last arrival 22.00hrs Last dep 10.30hrs

An attractive site with level pitches on the side of a river valley. The very high quality facilities include a TV lounge and a games room in a Swedish-style chalet, and a well-kept adventure playground. Trees and hedges fringe the park, and the ground is well drained. A 5 acre site with 109 touring pitches and 38 statics.

AA Pubs & Restaurants nearby: The Falcon Inn, St Mawgan 01637 860225

The Scarlet Hotel, Mawgan Porth 01637 861800

Leisure: 🛝🎱📺

Facilities: 🛁🚿🪒💨❄♿📞🏪🍖

Services: 🔌🧼⛽🔥[T]

Within 3 miles: ⛳🎣◎🏄🏪🧼🐴

Notes: Families and couples only. Wi-fi

►►► 79% Trevarrian Holiday Park *(SW853661)*

TR8 4AQ
☎ 01637 860381 & 0845 2255910
e-mail: holiday@trevarrian.co.uk
dir: *From A39 at St Columb rdbt turn right onto A3059 towards Newquay. Fork right in approx 2m for St Mawgan onto B3276. Turn right, site on left*

🚃 🚐 ⛺

Open all year Last arrival 22.00hrs Last dep 11.00hrs

A well-established and well-run holiday park overlooking Mawgan Porth beach. This park has a wide range of attractions including a free entertainment programme in peak season and a new 10-pin bowling alley with licensed bar. A 7 acre site with 185 touring pitches, 10 hardstandings.

AA Pubs & Restaurants nearby: The Falcon Inn, St Mawgan 01637 860225

Bedruthan Steps Hotel, Mawgan Porth 01637 860555

Leisure: 🏖🛝🎾🎱📺

Facilities: 🛁🚿🪒💨❄📞🏪🐕

Services: 🔌🧼🍺⛽🔥[T]🍴🍟👶🛠

Within 3 miles: ⛳⛵🎬🎣◎🏪🧼🐴

Notes: Sports field, pitch 'n' putt

MEVAGISSEY Map 2 SX04

See also Gorran & Pentewan

PREMIER PARK

AA CAMPING CARD SITE

►►►►► 91% Seaview International Holiday Park *(SW990412)*

Boswinger PL26 6LL
☎ 01726 843425 📠 01726 843358
e-mail: holidays@seaviewinternational.com
web: www.seaviewinternational.com
dir: *From St Austell take B3273 signed Mevagissey. Turn right before entering village. Follow brown tourist signs to site*

* 🚃 £6-£34 🚐 £6-£34 ⛺ £6-£30

Open Mar-Oct Last arrival 21.00hrs Last departure 10.00hrs

An attractive holiday park set in a beautiful environment overlooking Veryan Bay, with colourful landscaping, including attractive flowers and shrubs. It continues to offer an outstanding holiday experience, with its luxury family pitches, super toilet facilities, takeaway and shop, static caravans for holiday hire and ten seasonal touring pitches. The beach and sea are just half a mile away. A 28 acre site with 189 touring pitches, 18 hardstandings and 38 statics.

AA Pubs & Restaurants nearby: The Ship Inn, Mevagissey 01726 843324

Leisure: 🏖🛝🎾🎱

Facilities: 🛁🚿🪒❄♿🏪🍖🧺🐕

Services: 🔌🧼⛽🔥[T]🍴👶🛠

Within 3 miles: ⛵🎣◎🏄🏪🧼

Notes: Restrictions on certain dog breeds. Crazy golf, volleyball, badminton, tennis, scuba diving. Wi-fi

see advert in preliminary section

MULLION   Map 2 SW61

Places to visit

Trevarno Estate Garden & Museum of Gardening, Helston 01326 574274 www.trevarno.co.uk

Goonhilly Satellite Earth Station Experience, Helston 0800 679593 www.goonhilly.bt.com

Great for kids: National Seal Sanctuary, Gweek 0871 423 2110 www.sealsanctuary.co.uk

76% Mullion Holiday Park *(SW699182)*

Ruan Minor TR12 7LJ
☎ 0844 335 3756 📠 01326 241141
e-mail: touringandcamping@parkdeanholidays.com
web: www.parkdeantouring.com
dir: *A30 onto A39 through Truro towards Falmouth. A394 to Helston, A3083 for The Lizard. Site 7m on left*

🚐🚌🅰

Open Apr-Oct (rs 17 May-20 Sep outdoor pool open) Last arrival 22.00hrs Last dep 10.00hrs

A comprehensively-equipped leisure park geared mainly for self-catering holidays, and set close to the sandy beaches, coves and fishing villages on The Lizard peninsula. There is plenty of on-site entertainment for all ages, with indoor and outdoor swimming pools and a bar and grill. A 49 acre site with 69 touring pitches, 9 hardstandings and 305 statics.

AA Pubs & Restaurants nearby: The Halzephron Inn, Gunwalloe 01326 240406

Leisure: 🏊⛱🎬🎯🖥

Facilities: 🔦☉🥤✳🔥🛁🚻🖉

Services: 🔌🔲🔧💰🚿🍽🛒🐾

Within 3 miles: 🚴🅿◎🚏🛢🔴🎡🦽

Notes: Scuba diving, football pitch, surf & cycle hire, multi-sports court. Wi-fi

see advert in preliminary section

►►► 75% 'Franchis' Holiday Park
(SW698203)

Cury Cross Lanes TR12 7AZ
☎ 01326 240301
e-mail: enquiries@franchis.co.uk
web: www.franchis.co.uk
dir: *Off A3083 on left 0.5m past Wheel Inn PH, between Helston & The Lizard*

* 🚐 £12-£16 🚌 £12-£16 🅰 £10-£16

Open Apr-Oct Last arrival 20.00hrs Last departure 10.30hrs

A grassy site surrounded by hedges and coppices, and divided into two paddocks for tourers, in an ideal position for exploring the Lizard Peninsula. The pitches are a mixture of level and slightly sloping. A 16 acre site with 70 touring pitches and 12 statics.

AA Pubs & Restaurants nearby: The Halzephron Inn, Gunwalloe 01326 240406

Facilities: 🔦☉✳🛁🎣

Services: 🔌🔲💰🖉🛢🔧

Within 3 miles: 🚴🎣🅿🛢🔴🦽

Notes: Woodland walks. Wi-fi

NEWQUAY

See also Rejerrah

Places to visit

Blue Reef Aquarium, Newquay 01637 878134 www.bluereefaquarium.co.uk

Newquay Zoo, Newquay 0844 474 2244 www.newquayzoo.org.uk

Great for kids: Dairy Land Farm World, Newquay 01872 510246 www.dairylandfarmworld.com

---

NEWQUAY   Map 2 SW86

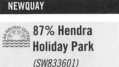

87% Hendra Holiday Park
(SW833601)

TR8 4NY
☎ 01637 875778 📠 01637 879017
e-mail: enquiries@hendra-holidays.com
dir: *A30 onto A392 signed Newquay. At Quintrell Downs over rdbt, signed Lane, site 0.5m on left*

* 🚐 £11.30-£19.90 🚌 £11.30-£19.90 🅰 £11.30-£19.90

Open Apr-Oct (rs Apr-Spring BH, Sep-Oct outdoor pool closed) Last arrival dusk Last departure 10.00hrs

A large complex with holiday statics and superb facilities including an indoor fun pool and an outdoor pool. There is a children's club for the over 6s, and evening entertainment during high season. The touring pitches are set amongst mature trees and shrubs, and some have fully-serviced facilities. All amenities are open to the public. An 80 acre site with 548 touring pitches, 28 hardstandings and 283 statics.

AA Pubs & Restaurants nearby: Lewinnick Lodge Bar & Restaurant, Pentire Headland, Newquay 01637 878117

Sand Brasserie, Headland Hotel, Newquay 01637 872211

Leisure: 🏊⛱🎬🎯🖥

Facilities: 🔦☉🥤✳🛁🎡🔥🛒🚻🖉🎣

Services: 🔌🔲🔧💰🖉🍽🛒🚿🛢🦽

Within 3 miles: 🚴🎣🎗🅿◎🚏🛢🔴🦽

Notes: Families and couples only. Solarium, fish bar, kids' club, train rides. Wi-fi

see advert on page 89

Campsites in popular areas get very crowded at busy times – it is advisable to book well in advance

---

NEWQUAY *continued*

78% Newquay Holiday Park *(SW853626)*

TR8 4HS
☎ 0844 335 3756 📠 01637 850818
e-mail:
touringandcamping@parkdeanholidays.com
web: www.parkdeantouring.com
dir: *From Bodmin on A30, under low bridge, right towards RAF St Mawgan. Take A3059 towards Newquay, site past Treloy Golf Club*

🚐 £11-£39 🚙 £11-£39 ⛺ £11-£39

Open Mar-Oct (rs May-19 Sep outdoor pool complex open) Last arrival 21.00hrs Last departure 10.00hrs

A well-maintained park with a wide range of indoor and outdoor activities. A children's playground and bar and grill enhance the facilities, and the club and bars offer quality entertainment. Three heated outdoor pools and a giant waterslide are very popular. A 60 acre site with 50 touring pitches, 10 hardstandings and 262 statics.

AA Pubs & Restaurants nearby: Lewinnick Lodge Bar & Restaurant, Pentire Headland, Newquay 01637 878117

Sand Brasserie, Headland Hotel, Newquay 01637 872211

Leisure: 🏊 🎢 🎱 📺
Facilities: 🚿⊙🅿✳⚫🕐🅱🍴🐾
Services: 🔌🍴🚰🔒🚿🚽🍴🛒🏪
Within 3 miles: 🎣🏇🅿◎🅱🛒U

Notes: Pool room, family entertainment, children's clubs. Wi-fi

see advert in preliminary section

►►►► 80% Trencreek Holiday Park *(SW828609)*

Hillcrest, Higher Trencreek TR8 4NS
☎ 01637 874210 📠 01637 879526
e-mail: trencreek@btconnect.com
dir: *A392 to Quintrell Downs, right towards Newquay, left at 2 mini-rdbts into Trevenson Rd to site*

* 🚐 £10.40-£16.80 🚙 £10.40-£16.80
⛺ £10.40-£16.80

Open Whit-mid Sep Last arrival 22.00hrs Last departure noon

An attractively landscaped park in the village of Trencreek, with modern toilet facilities of a very high standard. Two well-stocked fishing lakes, and evening entertainment in the licensed clubhouse, are extra draws. Located about two miles from Newquay with its beaches and surfing. A 10 acre site with 194 touring pitches, 8 hardstandings and 6 statics.

AA Pubs & Restaurants nearby: Lewinnick Lodge Bar & Restaurant, Pentire Headland, Newquay 01637 878117

Sand Brasserie, Headland Hotel, Newquay 01637 872211

Leisure: 🏊 🎢 🎱 📺
Facilities: 🚿⊙🅿✳⚫🕐🅱🍴🐾
Services: 🔌🍴🚰🔒🚿🚽🍴🛒🏪
Within 3 miles: 🎣🏇🅿◎🅱🛒U

Notes: 🚭🐕 Families and couples only. Free coarse fishing on site

---

►►►► 78% Porth Beach Tourist Park *(SW834629)*

Porth TR7 3NH
☎ 01637 876531 📠 01637 871227
e-mail: info@porthbeach.co.uk
dir: *1m NE off B3276 towards Padstow*

* 🚐 £14-£28 🚙 £14-£28 ⛺ £9-£37

Open Mar-Nov Last arrival 18.00hrs Last departure 10.00hrs

This attractive, popular park offers level, grassy pitches in neat and tidy surroundings. A well-run site set in meadowland and adjacent to sea and a fine sandy beach. A 6 acre site with 200 touring pitches, 19 hardstandings and 18 statics.

AA Pubs & Restaurants nearby: Lewinnick Lodge Bar & Restaurant, Pentire Headland, Newquay 01637 878117

Sand Brasserie, Headland Hotel, Newquay 01637 872211

Leisure: 🎢 **Facilities:** 🚿⊙⚫🕐🅱
Services: 🔌🍴🚰🚽🏪
Within 3 miles: 🎣🏇🅿◎🅱🛒U

Notes: Families and couples only

see advert on page 88

►►► 82% Treloy Touring Park *(SW858625)*

TR8 4JN
☎ 01637 872063 & 876279 📠 01637 872063
e-mail: treloy.tp@btconnect.com
web: www.treloy.co.uk
dir: *Off A3059 (St Columb Major-Newquay road)*

🚐 🚙 ⛺

Open May-15 Sep (rs Sep pool, takeaway, shop & bar) Last arrival 21.00hrs Last departure 10.00hrs

An attractive site with fine countryside views, that is within easy reach of resorts and beaches. The pitches are set in four paddocks with mainly level but some slightly sloping grassy areas. Maintenance and cleanliness are very high. An 18 acre site with 223 touring pitches, 24 hardstandings.

AA Pubs & Restaurants nearby: Lewinnick Lodge Bar & Restaurant, Pentire Headland, Newquay 01637 878117

Sand Brasserie, Headland Hotel, Newquay 01637 872211

Leisure: 🏊 🎢 🎱 📺 **Facilities:** 🚿⊙🅿✳⚫🕐🅱🐾
Services: 🔌🍴🚰🔒🚿🍴🛒🏪
Within 3 miles: 🎣🏇🅿🅱🛒U

Notes: Concessionary green fees for golf, entertainment. Wi-fi

see advert on page 88

►►► 80% Trebellan Park (SW790571)

Cubert TR8 5PY
☎ 01637 830522   📠 01637 830277
e-mail: enquiries@trebellan.co.uk
dir: *4m S of Newquay, turn W off A3075 at Cubert sign. Left in 0.75m onto unclass road*

* 🚐 £17-£24 🚙 £17-£24 ⛺ £13-£22

Open May-Oct Last arrival 21.00hrs Last departure 10.00hrs

A terraced grassy rural park within a picturesque valley with views of Cubert Common, and adjacent to the Smuggler's Den, a 16th-century thatched inn. This park has three well-stocked coarse fishing lakes on site. An 8 acre site with 150 touring pitches and 7 statics.

AA Pubs & Restaurants nearby: Lewinnick Lodge Bar & Restaurant, Pentire Headland, Newquay 01637 878117

Sand Brasserie, Headland Hotel, Newquay 01637 872211

Leisure: 🏊 🎣 🎱 🎮 **Facilities:** ↖ ⊙ 🍴 ✳ 🔥 🕐 🛢 🛗
Services: 🔌 🛗 🛒 **Within 3 miles:** ↓ 🌊 ✎ ◎ 🍴 🛖 🛢 🎣 ∪
Notes: Families and couples only

►►► 79% Trethiggey Touring Park (SW846596)

GOLD

Quintrell Downs TR8 4QR
☎ 01637 877672   📠 01637 879706
e-mail: enquiries@trethiggey.co.uk
dir: *A30 onto A392 signed Newquay at Quintrell Downs rdbt, left onto A3058, pass Newquay Pearl centre. Site 0.5m on left*

🚐 🚙 ⛺

Open Mar-Dec Last arrival 22.00hrs Last departure 10.30hrs

A family-owned park in a rural setting that is ideal for touring this part of Cornwall. It is pleasantly divided into paddocks with maturing trees and shrubs, and offering coarse fishing and tackle hire. A 15 acre site with 145 touring pitches, 35 hardstandings and 12 statics.

AA Pubs & Restaurants nearby: Lewinnick Lodge Bar & Restaurant, Pentire Headland, Newquay 01637 878117

Sand Brasserie, Headland Hotel, Newquay 01637 872211

Leisure: 🎱 🎣 🎮
Facilities: ↖ ↖ ⊙ 🍴 ✳ 🔥 🕐 🛢 🎣 🛗 🛒
Services: 🔌 🛗 🛒 🛢 🚿 ⌷ 🍴 🛗 🚼 ⛽
Within 3 miles: ↓ 🌊 ✎ ◎ 🍴 🛖 🛢 🎣 ∪
Notes: Off licence, recreation field, fishing. Wi-fi

see advert on page 86

►►► 77% Riverside Holiday Park (SW829592)

Gwills Ln TR8 4PE
☎ 01637 873617   📠 01637 877051
e-mail: info@riversideholidaypark.co.uk
web: www.riversideholidaypark.co.uk
dir: *A30 onto A392 signed Newquay. At Quintrell Downs cross rdbt signed Lane. 2nd left in 0.5m onto unclass road signed Gwills. Site in 400yds*

🚐 🚙 ⛺

Open Mar-Oct Last arrival 22.00hrs Last departure 10.00hrs

A sheltered valley beside a river in a quiet location is the idyllic setting for this lightly wooded park. The fairly simple facilities continue to be upgraded, and the park caters for families and couples only. The site is close to the wide variety of attractions offered by this major resort and the park has self-catering lodges, cabins and static vans for hire. An 11 acre site with 65 touring pitches and 65 statics.

AA Pubs & Restaurants nearby: Lewinnick Lodge Bar & Restaurant, Pentire Headland, Newquay 01637 878117

Sand Brasserie, Headland Hotel, Newquay 01637 872211

Leisure: 🏊 🎱 🎣 🎮 **Facilities:** ↖ ⊙ 🍴 ✳ 🔥 🕐 🛢
Services: 🔌 🛗 🛒 🛢 🚿 ⌷ ⌷ 🍴 🚼 ⛽
Within 3 miles: ↓ 🌊 ✎ ◎ 🍴 🛖 🛢 🎣 ∪
Notes: Families and couples only

►►► 76% Trenance Holiday Park (SW818612)

Edgcumbe Av TR7 2JY
☎ 01637 873447   📠 01637 852677
e-mail: enquiries@trenanceholidaypark.co.uk
dir: *Off A3075 near viaduct. Site by boating lake rdbt*

* 🚐 £15-£18 🚙 £15-£18 ⛺ £15-£18

Open 26 May-Oct Last arrival 22.00hrs Last departure 10.00hrs

A mainly static park popular with tenters, close to Newquay's vibrant nightlife, and serving excellent

breakfasts and takeaways. Set on high ground in an urban area of town, with cheerful owners and clean facilities. A 12 acre site with 50 touring pitches and 190 statics.

AA Pubs & Restaurants nearby: Lewinnick Lodge Bar & Restaurant, Pentire Headland, Newquay 01637 878117

Sand Brasserie, Headland Hotel, Newquay 01637 872211

Leisure: 🎣
Facilities: ↖ ⊙ 🍴 ✳ 🕐 🛢
Services: 🔌 🛗 🛒 🛢 🚿 ⌷ 🍴 🚼 ⛽
Within 3 miles: ↓ 🌊 ✎ ◎ 🍴 🛖 🛢 🎣 ∪
Notes: No pets

►►► 78% St Tinney Farm Holidays (SX169906)

GOLD

PL32 9TA
☎ 01840 261274
e-mail: info@st-tinney.co.uk
dir: *Signed 1m off A39 via unclass road signed Otterham*

🚐 🚙 ⛺

Open Etr-Oct Last arrival 21.00hrs Last departure 10.00hrs

A family-run farm site in a rural area with nature trails, lakes, valleys and offering complete seclusion. Visitors are free to walk around the farmland lakes and lose themselves in the countryside. A 34 acre site with 20 touring pitches and 15 statics.

AA Pubs & Restaurants nearby: The Wellington Hotel, Boscastle 01840 250202

Leisure: 🏊 🎱 🎣
Facilities: ↖ ⊙ 🍴 ✳ 🛢 🐾
Services: 🔌 🛗 🛒 🛢 🚿 ⌷ ⌷ 🍴 ⛽
Within 3 miles: ✎ 🛢
Notes: Coarse fishing. Wi-fi

PADSTOW
Map 2 SW97

See also Rumford

Places to visit

Prideaux Place, Padstow 01841 532411
www.prideauxplace.co.uk

▶▶▶▶ 85% Padstow Touring Park (SW913738)

SILVER

PL28 8LE
☎ 01841 532061
e-mail: mail@padstowtouringpark.co.uk
dir: *1m S of Padstow, on E side of A389 (Padstow to Wadebridge road)*

* ⛺ £10-£15.50 ⛺ £10-£15.50 ▲ £10-£15.50

Open all year Last arrival 21.00hrs Last departure 11.00hrs

Improvements continue apace at this popular park set in open countryside above the quaint fishing town of Padstow, which can be approached by footpath directly from the park. It is divided into paddocks by maturing bushes and hedges to create a peaceful and relaxing holiday atmosphere. Planned for 2011 are more hardstanding pitches, an improved entrance, refurbished toilets, better landscaping, and a new dishwashing area. A 13.5 acre site with 150 touring pitches, 27 hardstandings.

AA Pubs & Restaurants nearby: The Cornish Arms, St Merryn 01841 520288

Paul Ainsworth at No 6, Padstow 01841 532093
Rosel & Co, Padstow 01841 521289

Leisure: 🅰 **Facilities:** 🅁⊙🄵✳🄰🅾🄱🄰
Services: 🄰🄰🄱🄰🅃🄰🄰
Within 3 miles: 🄻✚🄷🄿⊚🄰🄰🄰🅄
Notes: No groups. Wi-fi

▶▶▶ 76% Dennis Cove Camping (SW919743)

Dennis Ln PL28 8DR
☎ 01841 532349
e-mail: denniscove@freeuk.com
dir: *Approach Padstow on A389, right at Tesco into Sarah's Ln, 2nd right to Dennis Ln, follow to site at end*

⛺ ⛺ ▲

Open Apr-end Sep Last arrival 21.00hrs Last departure 11.00hrs

Set in meadowland with mature trees, this site overlooks Padstow Bay, with access to the Camel Estuary and the nearby beach. The centre of town is just a 10-minute walk away, and bike hire is available on site, with the famous Camel Trail beginning right outside. A 3 acre site with 42 touring pitches.

AA Pubs & Restaurants nearby: Margot's, Padstow 01841 533441

The Seafood Restaurant, Padstow 01841 532700

Facilities: 🅁⊙🄵✳🄷 **Services:** 🄰🄰🄱🄰🄰
Within 3 miles: 🄻✚🄷🄿⊚🄰🄰🄰🅄
Notes: 🄰 Arrivals from 14.00hrs

▶▶▶ 74% Padstow Holiday Park (SW009073)

Cliffdowne PL28 8LB
☎ 01841 532289 📠 01841 532289
e-mail: mail@padstowholidaypark.co.uk
dir: *On B3274/A389 into Padstow. Signed 1.5m before Padstow*

* ⛺ £15.50 ⛺ £15.50 ▲ £15.50

Open Mar-Dec Last arrival 17.00hrs Last departure noon

A mainly static park with some touring pitches in a small paddock and others in an open field. This quiet holiday site is only a mile from Padstow and can be reached by a footpath. Three holiday letting caravans are available. A 5.5 acre site with 27 touring pitches and 74 statics.

AA Pubs & Restaurants nearby: The Cornish Arms, St Merryn 01841 520288

Custard, Padstow 01841 532565

Leisure: 🅰 **Facilities:** ⛭🅁⊙🄵✳⊙🄰
Services: 🄰🄰🄱🄰🅃
Within 3 miles: 🄻✚🄷🄿⊚🄰🄰🄰🅄
Notes: 🄰. Wi-fi

PENTEWAN

Places to visit

The Lost Gardens of Heligan, Pentewan 01726 845100 www.heligan.com

Charlestown Shipwreck & Heritage Centre, St Austell 01726 69897
www.shipwreckcharlestown.com

Great for kids: Eden Project, St Austell 01726 811911 www.edenproject.com

PENTEWAN
Map 2 SX04

90% Pentewan Sands Holiday Park (SX018468)

PL26 6BT
☎ 01726 843485 📠 01726 844142
e-mail: info@pentewan.co.uk
dir: *On B3273 4m S of St Austell*

⛺ ⛺ ▲

Open Apr-Oct Last arrival 22.00hrs Last departure 10.30hrs

A large holiday park with a wide range of amenities, set on grassy pitches beside a private beach where plenty of aquatic activities are available. A short stroll leads to the pretty village of Pentewan, and other attractions are a short drive away. The new and very impressive 'Seahorse Complex' comprises swimming pools, a well-stocked bar and restaurant, with a choice of dining options, a kids' zone, a fully-equipped gym, and outside terraces with stunning sea views. A 32 acre site with 500 touring pitches and 120 statics.

AA Pubs & Restaurants nearby: The Ship Inn, Mevagissey 01726 843324

Leisure: 🄰🄰🄰
Facilities: ⛭🅁⊙✳🄰🅾🄱🄰
Services: 🄰🄰🄱🄰🄰🅃🄾🄰🄰🄰
Within 3 miles: 🄻✚🄿🄰🄰🄰🅄
Notes: 🄰 No jet skis. Cycles, boat launch, water sports, caravan store. Wi-fi

▶▶▶▶ 81% Sun Valley Holiday Park (SX005486)

Best of British

GOLD

Pentewan Rd PL26 6DJ
☎ 01726 843266 & 844393 📠 01726 843266
e-mail: reception@sunvalley-holidays.co.uk
dir: *From St Austell take B3273 towards Mevagissey. Site 2m on right*

⛺ ⛺ ▲

Open all year (rs Winter pool, restaurant & touring field) Last arrival 22.00hrs Last dep 10.30hrs

In a picturesque valley amongst woodland, this neat park is kept to a high standard. The extensive amenities include tennis courts, indoor swimming pool, licensed clubhouse and restaurant. The sea is just a mile away, and can be accessed via a footpath and cycle path along the river bank. A 20 acre site with 29 touring pitches, 13 hardstandings and 75 statics.

AA Pubs & Restaurants nearby: The Crown Inn, St Ewe 01726 843322

Leisure: 🏊🎣🎿🎯

Facilities: 🚿⊙📶✖🔥🕐💲🎏🐾

Services: 🔌🧺🎪🛢🚿🍽💧🚮🚐♻

Within 3 miles: 🚶🎣🎯🎿📶⚓💲🛒🎣U

Notes: Certain pet restrictions apply, please contact the site for details. No motorised scooters, skateboards or bikes at night. Pets' corner, bike hire, outdoor & indoor play areas

---

►►► 82% Heligan Woods *(SW998470)*

PL26 6BT
☎ 01726 842714 & 844414   📠 01726 844142
e-mail: info@pentewan.co.uk
dir: *From A390 take B3273 for Mevagissey at x-roads signed 'No caravans beyond this point'. Right onto unclass road towards Gorran, site 0.75m on left*

🚐🚌⛺

Open 16 Jan-26 Nov Last arrival 22.30hrs Last departure 10.30hrs

A pleasant peaceful park adjacent to the Lost Gardens of Heligan, with views over St Austell Bay, and well-maintained facilities. Guests can also use the extensive amenities at the sister park, Pentewan Sands, and there's a footpath with direct access to Heligan Gardens. Three seasonal touring pitches are available. A 12 acre site with 89 touring pitches, 24 hardstandings and 17 statics.

AA Pubs & Restaurants nearby: Austell's, St Austell 01726 813888

Leisure: 🎿

Facilities: 🛁🚿⊙📶🕐💲🎏

Services: 🔌🧺🛢🚿🍽💧♻

Within 3 miles: 🚶🎣🎯📶⚓💲🛒🎣U

PENZANCE

See also Rosudgeon

Places to visit

Trengwainton Garden (NT), Penzance 01736 363148 www.nationaltrust.org.uk

St Michael's Mount, Marazion 01736 710507 www.stmichaelsmount.co.uk

---

PENZANCE Map 2 SW43

►►►► 77% Higher Chellew Holiday Park *(SW496353)*

Higher Trenowin, Nancledra TR20 8BD
☎ 01736 364532 & 07818 025884
e-mail: higherchellew@btinternet.com
web: www.higherchellewcamping.co.uk
dir: *From A30 turn towards St Ives, left at mini-rdbt towards Nancledra. Left at B3311 junct, through Nancledra. Site 0.5m on left*

* 🚐 £10-£16 🚌 £10-£16 ⛺ £10-£16

Open Fri before Etr-Oct Last departure 10.30hrs

A small rural park quietly located just four miles from the golden beaches at St Ives, and a similar distance from Penzance. This well sheltered park occupies an elevated location, and all pitches are level. A 1.25 acre site with 30 touring pitches.

AA Pubs & Restaurants nearby: Turk's Head Inn, Penzance 01736 363093

The Navy Inn, Penzance 01736 333232

Facilities: 🚿⊙📶✖🔥🕐💲

Services: 🔌🧺   **Within 3 miles:** 💲🛒U

Notes: ⊗ No pets. Microwave, freezer

►►► 76% Bone Valley Caravan & Camping Park *(SW472316)*

Heamoor TR20 8UJ
☎ 01736 360313   📠 01736 360313
e-mail: wardmandie@yahoo.co.uk
dir: *Exit A30 at Heamoor/Madron rdbt. 4th on right into Josephs Lane. 800yds left into Bone Valley. Entrance 200yds on left*

🚐🚌⛺

Open all year Last arrival 22.00hrs Last departure 10.00hrs

A compact grassy park on the outskirts of Penzance, with well maintained facilities. It is divided into paddocks by mature hedges, and a small stream runs alongside. A 1 acre site with 17 touring pitches, 6 hardstandings and 3 statics.

AA Pubs & Restaurants nearby: Dolphin Tavern, Penzance 01736 364106

Harris's Restaurant, Penzance 01736 364408

Leisure: 🎱

Facilities: 🛁🚿⊙📶✖🔥🕐💲🎏🐾

Services: 🔌🧺🛢🚿🎈

Within 3 miles: 🚶🎯📶💲🛒U

Notes: No cars by tents. Dogs must be kept on leads. Campers' lounge, kitchen & laundry room

---

PERRANPORTH Map 2 SW75

See also Rejerrah

Places to visit

Royal Cornwall Museum, Truro 01872 272205 www.royalcornwallmuseum.org.uk

Trerice (NT), Trerice 01637 875404 www.nationaltrust.org.uk

Great for kids: Blue Reef Aquarium, Newquay 01637 878134 www.bluereefaquarium.co.uk

---

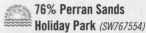 ### 76% Perran Sands Holiday Park *(SW767554)*

TR6 0AQ
☎ 01872 573511   📠 01872 571158
e-mail: nick.cooke@bourne-leisure.co.uk
dir: *A30 onto B3285 towards Perranporth. Site on right before descent on hill into Perranporth*

🚐🚌⛺

Open mid Mar-Oct (rs mid Mar-May & Sep-Oct some facilities may be reduced) Last arrival 22.00hrs Last departure 10.00hrs

Nestling amid 500 acres of protected dune grassland, and with a footpath through to the surf and three miles of golden sandy beach, this lively park is set in a large village-style complex. It offers a complete range of on-site facilities and entertainment for all the family, which makes it an extremely popular park. A 550 acre site with 360 touring pitches, 20 hardstandings and 600 statics.

AA Pubs & Restaurants nearby: Driftwood Spars, St Agnes 01872 552428

Leisure: 🏊🎿🎱

Facilities: 🛁🚿⊙📶✖🔥🕐💲

Services: 🔌🧺🎪🛢🚿🍽🚮♻

Within 3 miles: 🚶📶⚓💲🛒🎣U

Notes: Families & couples only, certain dog breeds banned. Wi-fi

see advert on page 94

LEISURE: ⌇ Indoor swimming pool ⌇ Outdoor swimming pool ⋀ Children's playground ⌇ Tennis court ⌇ Games room ⌇ Separate TV room ⌇ 9/18 hole golf course ⌇ Boats for hire ⌇ Cinema ⌇ Fishing ⌇ Mini golf ⌇ Watersports ⌇ Stables **FACILITIES:** ⌇ Bath ⌇ Shower ⌇ Electric shaver ⌇ Hairdryer ⌇ Ice Pack Facility ⌇ Disabled facilities ⌇ Public telephone ⌇ Shop on site or within 200yds ⌇ Mobile shop (calls at least 5 days a week) ⌇ BBQ area ⌇ Picnic area ⌇ Dog exercise area

PERRANPORTH *continued*

►►►► 80% Tollgate Farm Caravan & Camping Park *(SW768547)*

Budnick Hill TR6 0AD
☎ 01872 572130 & 0845 166 2126
e-mail: enquiries@tollgatefarm.co.uk
dir: *Off A30 onto B3285 to Perranporth. Site on right 1.5m after Goonhavern*

🚐 £16-£27 🚌 £16-£27 ⛺ £13-£27

Open Etr-Sep Last arrival 21.00hrs Last departure 11.00hrs

A quiet site in a rural location with spectacular coastal views. Pitches are divided into four paddocks sheltered and screened by mature hedges. Children will enjoy the play equipment and pets' corner. The three miles of sand at Perran Bay are just a walk away through the sand dunes, or by car it will be a three-quarter mile drive. A 10 acre site with 102 touring pitches, 10 hardstandings.

AA Pubs & Restaurants nearby: Driftwood Spars, St Agnes 01872 552428

Leisure: ⚏

Facilities: 🅿⊙🅿✳🕭🅾🆖🚿🛒🔥

Services: 🔌🅾🍴🖨🛢🚰

Within 3 miles: ⚡✈🅿◎🛍🎣🅾U

Notes: No large groups. Family shower rooms with baby changing facilities. Wi-fi

see advert on opposite page

►►► 78% Higher Golla Touring & Caravan Park *(SW756514)*

Penhallow TR4 9LZ
☎ 01872 573963 & 572116 📠 01872 572116
e-mail: cornish.hair@btconnect.com
web: www.highergollatouringpark.co.uk
dir: *A30 onto B3284 towards Perranporth. (Straight on at junct with A3075). Approx 2m. Site signed on right*

🚐 £12-£18 🚌 £12-£18 ⛺ £7-£12

Open Etr-mid Oct Last arrival 20.00hrs Last departure 10.30hrs

Extensive country views can be enjoyed from all pitches on this quietly located site, which now has new high quality and immaculate toilet facilities. Every pitch has electricity and a water tap and this peaceful park is just two miles from Perranporth and its stunning beach. A 1.5 acre site with 18 touring pitches and 2 statics.

Facilities: 🅿⊙🅿🔥🛒

Services: 🔌🅾🚰

Within 3 miles: ⚡🅿◎🛍🎣🅾U

Notes: No kite flying, quiet between 21.00hrs-08.00hrs, dogs must be kept on leads on the site

►►► 69% *Perranporth Camping & Touring Park (SW768542)*

Budnick Rd TR6 0DB
☎ 01872 572174 📠 01872 572174
dir: *0.5m E off B3285*

🚐 🚌 ⛺

Open Whit-Sep (rs Etr & end Sep shop & club facilities closed) Last arrival 23.00hrs Last departure noon

A mainly tenting site with few level pitches, located high above a fine sandy beach, which is much-frequented by surfers. The park is attractive to young people, and is set in a lively town on a spectacular part of the coast. 9 static caravans for holiday hire. A 6 acre site with 120 touring pitches, 4 hardstandings and 9 statics.

AA Pubs & Restaurants nearby: Driftwood Spars, St Agnes 01872 552428

Leisure: ⚏⚏🎱⌷

Facilities: 🛏🅿⊙🅿✳🕭🅾🆖🚿🔥

Services: 🔌🅾🍴🛢🚰🖨🚰⚡

Within 3 miles: ⚡✈🅿◎🛍🅾🅾U

Notes: Dogs must be kept on leads, no noise after 23.00hrs

see advert below

POLPERRO | Map 2 SX25

Places to visit

Restormel Castle, Restormel 01208 872687
www.english-heritage.org.uk

Great for kids: The Monkey Sanctuary, Looe
01503 262532 www.monkeysanctuary.org

▶▶ 77% Great Kellow Farm Caravan & Camping Site (SX201522)

Lansallos PL13 2QL
☎ 01503 272387 🖹 01503 272387
e-mail: kellow.farm@virgin.net
dir: From Looe to Pelynt. In Pelynt left at church follow Lansallos sign. Left at x-rds, 0.75m. At staggered x-rds left, follow site signs

* 🚐 £10-£12 🚙 £10-£12 ▲ £10-£12

Open Mar-3 Jan Last arrival 22.00hrs Last departure noon

Set on a high level grassy paddock with extensive views of Polperro Bay, this attractive site is on a working dairy and beef farm, and close to National Trust properties and gardens. It is situated in a very peaceful location close to the fishing village of Polperro. A 3 acre site with 30 touring pitches and 10 statics.

AA Pubs & Restaurants nearby: Old Mill House Inn, Polperro 01503 272362

Barclay House, Looe 01503 262929

Facilities: �☉✻🐾
Services: 🚐
Within 3 miles: ⭐🎣🏪
Notes: ⊗

POLRUAN

Places to visit

Restormel Castle, Restormel 01208 872687
www.english-heritage.org.uk

Great for kids: The Monkey Sanctuary, Looe
01503 262532 www.monkeysanctuary.org

POLRUAN | Map 2 SX15

AA CAMPING CARD SITE

▶▶▶ 81% Polruan Holidays-Camping & Caravanning (SX133509)

Polruan-by-Fowey PL23 1QH
☎ 01726 870263
e-mail: polholiday@aol.com
web: www.polruanholidays.co.uk
dir: A38 to Dobwalls, left onto A390 to East Taphouse. Left onto B3359. Right in 4.5m signed Polruan

🚐 🚙 ▲

Open Etr-Oct Last arrival 21.00hrs Last departure noon

A very rural and quiet site in a lovely elevated position above the village, with good views of the sea. The River Fowey passenger ferry is close by, and the site has a good shop, and barbecues to borrow. A 3 acre site with 47 touring pitches, 7 hardstandings and 10 statics.

AA Pubs & Restaurants nearby: Old Ferry Inn, Bodinnick 01726 870237

The Ship Inn, Fowey 01726 832230

Leisure: ⌂
Facilities: ⌂☉🅿✻☉🖥🍴🎪
Services: 🚐🖴🎂🧺🅃🎁🛒
Within 3 miles: 🎣🌊🏪🎯🎣🎳🎡🐎
Notes: No skateboards, rollerskates, bikes, water pistols or water bombs. Tourist information

POLZEATH | Map 2 SW97

▶▶▶ 82% South Winds Caravan & Camping Park (SW948790)

Polzeath Rd PL27 6QU
☎ 01208 863267 🖹 01208 862080
e-mail: info@southwindscamping.co.uk
web: www.polzeathcamping.co.uk
dir: Exit B3314 onto unclass road signed Polzeath, site on right just past turn to New Polzeath

* 🚐 £16-£40 🚙 £16-£40 ▲ £16-£40

Open Mar-Sep Last arrival 21.00hrs Last departure 10.30hrs

A peaceful site with beautiful sea and panoramic rural views, within walking distance of a golf complex, and just three quarters of a mile from

beach and village. New in 2010 - an impressive reception building, replete with tourist information, TV, settees and a range of camping spares. A 16 acre site with 100 touring pitches.

AA Pubs & Restaurants nearby: Restaurant Nathan Outlaw, Rock 01208 863394

Leisure: ⌂
Facilities: ⌂☉🅿✻🅆☉🖥🎪🎯🎳
Services: 🚐🖴🎂🖉🅃🛒🛠
Within 3 miles: 🎯⭐🎣🎣🎡🌊🏪🎳🎡🐎
Notes: No disposable BBQs, no noise 23.00hrs-07.00hrs, dogs on leads at all times, families & couples only. Wi-fi

see advert on opposite page

▶▶▶ 82% Tristram Caravan & Camping Park (SW936790)

PL27 6TP
☎ 01208 862215 🖹 01208 862080
e-mail: info@tristramcampsite.co.uk
web: www.polzeathcamping.co.uk
dir: From B3314 onto unclassified road signed Polzeath. Through village, up hill, site 2nd right

* 🚐 £30-£48 🚙 £30-£48 ▲ £15-£48

Open Mar-Nov Last arrival 21.00hrs Last departure 10.00hrs

An ideal family site, positioned on a gently sloping cliff with grassy pitches and glorious sea views, which are best enjoyed from the terraced premier pitches, or over lunch at the Salt Water Café adjacent to the reception/shop. There is direct, gated access to the beach, where surfing is very popular, and the park has a holiday bungalow for rent. The local amenities of the village are only a few hundred yards away. A 10 acre site with 100 touring pitches.

AA Pubs & Restaurants nearby: Restaurant Nathan Outlaw, Rock 01208 863394

Facilities: ⌂☉🅿✻🅆☉🖥🎪
Services: 🚐🖴🎂🖉🍴🛒
Within 3 miles: 🎯⭐🎣🎣🎡🌊🏪🎳🎡🐎
Notes: No ball games, no disposable BBQs, no noise between 23.00hrs-07.00hrs, dogs must be kept on leads at all times. Surf equipment hire. Wi-fi

see advert on opposite page

PORTHTOWAN Map 2 SW64

►►►► 83% Porthtowan Tourist Park *(SW693473)*

SILVER

Mile Hill TR4 8TY
☎ 01209 890256
e-mail: admin@porthtowantouristpark.co.uk
web: www.porthtowantouristpark.co.uk
dir: *Exit A30 at junct signed Redruth/Porthtowan. Take 3rd exit at rdbt. 2m, right at T-junct. Site on left at top of hill*

* £9-£16.50 £9-£16.50 £9-£16.50

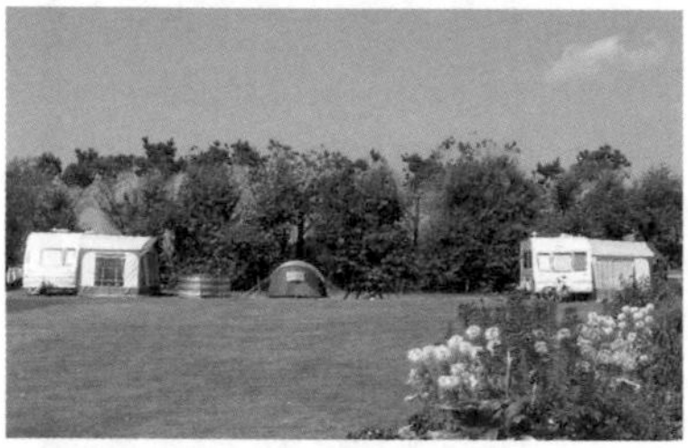

Open Apr-Sep Last arrival 21.30hrs Last departure 11.00hrs

A neat, level grassy site on high ground above Porthtowan, with plenty of shelter from mature trees and shrubs. The superb toilet facilities considerably enhance the appeal of this peaceful rural park, which is almost midway between the small seaside resorts of Portreath and Porthtowan, with their beaches and surfing. A 5 acre site with 80 touring pitches, 2 hardstandings.

AA Pubs & Restaurants nearby: Driftwood Spars, St Agnes 01872 552428

Leisure:

Facilities:

Services:

Within 3 miles:

Notes: No bikes/skateboards during Jul-Aug

AA CAMPING CARD SITE

►►► 81% Wheal Rose Caravan & Camping Park *(SW717449)*

Wheal Rose TR16 5DD
☎ 01209 891496
e-mail: whealrose@aol.com
dir: *Exit A30 at Scorrier sign, follow signs to Wheal Rose. Site 0.5m on left (Wheal Rose to Porthtowan road)*

* £10-£17 £10-£17 £10-£17

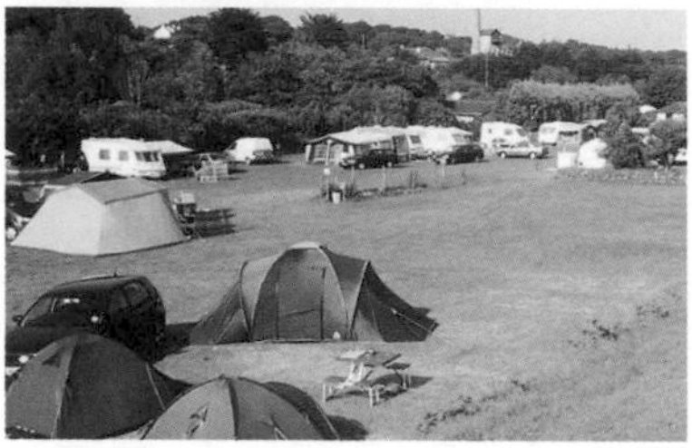

Open Mar-Dec Last arrival 21.00hrs Last departure 11.00hrs

A quiet, peaceful park in a secluded valley setting, central for beaches and countryside, and two miles from the surfing beaches of Porthtowan. The friendly owners work hard to keep this park immaculate, with a bright toilet block and well-trimmed pitches. A 6 acre site with 50 touring pitches, 6 hardstandings and 3 statics.

Leisure:

Facilities:

Services:

Within 3 miles:

Notes: 5mph speed limit, dogs must be kept on leads, minimum noise after 23.00hrs, gates locked 23.00hrs. Family bathroom

PORTREATH

Places to visit

East Pool Mine (NT), Pool 01209 315027 www.nationaltrust.org.uk

Remember that prices and opening times are liable to change within the currency of this guide. It is always best to phone in advance

PORTREATH Map 2 SW64

AA CAMPING CARD SITE

►►► 82% Tehidy Holiday Park *(SW682432)*

GOLD

Harris Mill, Illogan TR16 4JQ
☎ 01209 216489 📠 01209 216489
e-mail: holiday@tehidy.co.uk
web: www.tehidy.co.uk
dir: *Exit A30 at Redruth/Portreath junct onto A3047 to 1st rdbt. Left onto B3300. At junct straight over signed Tehidy Holiday Park. Past Cornish Arms pub, site 800yds at bottom of hill on left*

* £12-£18 £12-£18 £12-£18

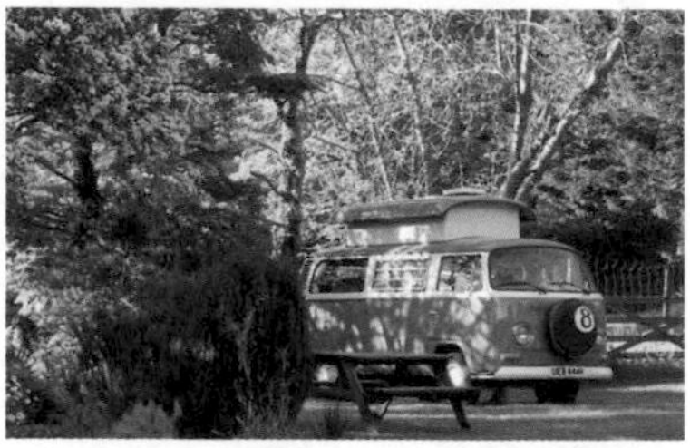

Open all year (rs Nov-Mar part of shower block & shop closed) Last arrival 20.00hrs Last departure 10.00hrs

An attractive wooded location in a quiet rural area only two and half miles from popular beaches. Mostly level pitches on tiered ground, and the toilet facilities are bright and modern. Holiday static caravans for hire. A 4.5 acre site with 18 touring pitches, 11 hardstandings and 32 statics.

AA Pubs & Restaurants nearby: The Basset Arms, Portreath 01209 842077

Leisure:

Facilities:

Services:

Within 3 miles:

Notes: No pets. Trampoline, off-licence. Wi-fi

see advert on page 86

PORTSCATHO

Places to visit

St Mawes Castle, St Mawes 01326 270526 www.english-heritage.org.uk

Trelissick Garden (NT), Trelissick Garden 01872 862090 www.nationaltrust.org.uk

PORTSCATHO — Map 2 SW83

▶▶▶ 78% Trewince Farm Touring Park (SW868339)

TR2 5ET
☎ 01872 580430 📠 01872 580430
e-mail: info@trewincefarm.co.uk
dir: From St Austell take A390 towards Truro. Left on B3287 to Tregony, following signs to St Mawes. At Trewithian, turn left to St Anthony. Site 0.75m past church

* 🚐 £11-£18 🚏 £11-£18 ▲ £11-£18

Open May-Sep Last arrival 23.00hrs Last departure 11.00hrs

A site on a working farm with spectacular sea views from its elevated position. There are many quiet golden sandy beaches close by, and boat launching facilities and mooring can be arranged at the nearby Percuil River Boatyard. The village of Portscatho with shops and pubs and attractive harbour is approximately one mile away. A 3 acre site with 25 touring pitches.

AA Pubs & Restaurants nearby: The New Inn, Veryan 01872 501362

The Quarterdeck at The Nare, Veryan 01872 501111

Facilities: 🐾⊙🅿☀🏠🎣📞
Services: 🔌🅾🔋
Within 3 miles: 🎣🚵🚴🏄⛵♨
Notes: 🐕

▶▶ 77% *Treloan Coastal Holidays* (SW876348)

Treloan Ln TR2 5EF
☎ 01872 580989
e-mail: info@treloancoastalholidays.co.uk
dir: From A3078 (Tregony to St Mawes road) take unclass road to Gerrans. Immediately after Gerrans church, road divides, take Treloan Lane by Royal Standard pub to site

🚐🚏▲

Open all year

This stunningly located, rather rustic coastal park, known as 'Arthurs Field', offers much improved toilet facilities (with the complete refurbishment of one block in 2010), a new fireside area for communal barbeques plus a very friendly welcome. There arc spectacular sea views and it is close to quiet sandy beaches with access to the Cornish Coastal Footpath. The villages of Gerrans

and Portscatho are a beautiful, short stroll away. A 7 acre site with 57 touring pitches.

AA Pubs & Restaurants nearby: The New Inn, Veryan 01872 501362

Driftwood, Porthscatho 01872 580644

PRAA SANDS — Map 2 SW52

Places to visit

Trevarno Estate Garden & Museum of Gardening, Helston 01326 574274 www.trevarno.co.uk

Goonhilly Satellite Earth Station Experience, Helston 0800 679593 www.goonhilly.bt.com

Great for kids: The Flambards Experience, Helston 01326 573404 www.flambards.co.uk

▶▶ 69% *Higher Pentreath Farm Campsite* (SW570280)

Higher Pentreath TR20 9TL
☎ 01736 763222
e-mail: d.spencer@btinternet.com
dir: Off A394 approx midway between Helston & Penzance, signed on unclass rd to Pentreath

🚐🚏▲

Set midway between Helston and Penzance, this simple campsite is set in two grassy paddocks, and enjoys extensive views over Praa Sands and its superb long sandy beach. The village also boasts a variety of cafés and gift shops, and a pub with adjoining restaurant. 90 touring pitches.

AA Pubs & Restaurants nearby: The Victoria Inn, Perranuthnoe 01736 710309

The Ship Inn, Porthleven 01326 564204

REDRUTH — Map 2 SW64

Places to visit

East Pool Mine (NT), Pool 01209 315027 www.nationaltrust.org.uk

Pendennis Castle, Falmouth Tel: 01326 316594 www.english-heritage.org.uk

Great for kids: National Maritime Museum Cornwall, Falmouth 01326 313388 www.nmmc.co.uk

▶▶▶▶ 81% Globe Vale Holiday Park (SW708447)

Radnor TR16 4BH
☎ 01209 891183 📠 01209 890590
e-mail: info@globevale.co.uk
dir: A30 take Redruth/Porthtowan exit then Portreath/North Country exit from rdbt, right at x-rds into Radnor Rd, left after 0.5m, site on left after 0.5m

🚐🚏▲

Open all year Last arrival 20.00hrs Last departure 10.00hrs

A family owned and run park set in a quiet rural location yet close to some stunning beaches and coastline. The park has a newly created touring area with a number of full facility hardstanding pitches, a new high quality toilet block, a comfortable lounge bar serving bar meals, and holiday static caravans. A 13 acre site with 77 touring pitches, 19 hardstandings and 7 statics.

AA Pubs & Restaurants nearby: The Basset Arms, Portreath 01209 842077

Leisure: 🎱🎣
Facilities: 🐾☀♿🎣
Services: 🔌🅾🍴🛢🚿🚰📞🍽️📮🛒⛽
Within 3 miles: 🎣🎯🏄🏠🎣
Notes: Pets must be kept on leads throughout the park

REDRUTH continued

►►► 80% *Lanyon Holiday Park*

(SW684387)

Loscombe Ln, Four Lanes TR16 6LP
☎ 01209 313474
e-mail: info@lanyonholidaypark.co.uk
web: www.lanyonholidaypark.co.uk
dir: *Signed 0.5m off B2397 on Helston side of Four Lanes village*

Open Mar-Oct Last arrival 21.00hrs Last dep noon
Small, friendly rural park in an elevated position with fine views to distant St Ives Bay. This family owned and run park continues to be upgraded in all areas, with newly refurbished toilet blocks and two holiday lodges, and is close to a cycling trail. Stithian's Reservoir for fishing, sailing and windsurfing is two miles away. A 14 acre site with 25 touring pitches and 49 statics.

AA Pubs & Restaurants nearby: The Basset Arms, Portreath 01209 842077

Leisure: 🏊 △ 🎱 ▢ **Facilities:** ⛭ 🔥 ☉ 🅿 ✳ 🛒 🐕
Services: 🔌 🔲 🛢 🍴 🍽 🖳 ⛲
Within 3 miles: ⬇ 🚤 🎣 🏌 ◎ 🏊 🏪 🐴 ⛵

Notes: Family park. Take-away service, all-day games room. Wi-fi

►►► 79% Cambrose Touring Park

(SW684453)

Portreath Rd TR16 4HT
☎ 01209 890747
e-mail: cambrosetouringpark@supanet.com
dir: *A30 onto B3300 towards Portreath. Approx 0.75m at 1st rdbt right onto B3300. Take unclass road on right signed Porthtowan. Site 200yds on left*

* 🚐 £9-£16 🚙 £9-£16 ▲ £9-£16

Open Apr-Oct Last arrival 22.00hrs Last departure 11.30hrs

Situated in a rural setting surrounded by trees and shrubs, this park is divided into grassy paddocks. It is situated about two miles from the harbour village of Portreath. A 6 acre site with 60 touring pitches.

AA Pubs & Restaurants nearby: The Basset Arms, Portreath 01209 842077

Leisure: 🏊 △ 🎱 **Facilities:** ⛭ 🔥 ☉ 🅿 ✳ 🛒 🐕
Services: 🔌 🔲 🛢 🍴 🖳 ⛲
Within 3 miles: ⬇ 🏌 🎣 ◎ 🏪 ⛵

Notes: Mini football pitch, family shower room

REJERRAH   Map 2 SW75

Places to visit
Trerice (NT), Trerice 01637 875404
www.nationaltrust.org.uk

Blue Reef Aquarium, Newquay 01637 878134
www.bluereefaquarium.co.uk

Great for kids: Newquay Zoo, Newquay
0844 474 2244 www.newquayzoo.org.uk

82% Monkey Tree Holiday Park *(SW803545)*

Scotland Rd TR8 5QR
☎ 01872 572032   📠 01872 573577
e-mail: enquiries@monkeytreeholidaypark.co.uk
web: www.monkeytreeholidaypark.co.uk
dir: *Exit A30 onto B3285 to Perranporth, 0.25m right into Scotland Rd, site on left in 1.5m*

Open all year Last arrival 22.00hrs Last departure 10.00hrs

A busy holiday park with plenty of activities and a jolly holiday atmosphere. Set close to lovely beaches between Newquay and Perranporth, it offers an outdoor swimming pool, children's playground, two bars with entertainment, and a good choice of eating outlets including a restaurant and a takeaway. A 56 acre site with 505 touring pitches, 17 hardstandings and 48 statics.

AA Pubs & Restaurants nearby: The Smugglers' Den Inn, Cubert 01637 830209

Leisure: 🏊 △ 🎱
Facilities: ⛭ 🔥 ☉ ✳ 🛒 🐕
Services: 🔌 🔲 🛢 🍴 🖳 ⛲
Within 3 miles: ⬇ 🎣 ◎ 🏪 ⛵

Notes: Family & couples park. Mini diggers, amusement arcade, aqua-blaster, remote control cars/boats, indoor soft play area

►►►► 87% Newperran Holiday Park

(SW801555)

TR8 5QJ
☎ 01872 572407   📠 01872 571254
e-mail: holidays@newperran.co.uk
dir: *4m SE of Newquay & 1m S of Rejerrah on A3075. Or A30 Redruth, exit B3275 Perranporth, at 1st T-junct right onto A3075 towards Newquay, site 300mtrs on left*

Open Etr-Oct Last arrival mdnt Last departure 10.00hrs

A family site in a lovely rural position near several beaches and bays. This airy park offers screening to some pitches, which are set in paddocks on level ground. High season entertainment is available in the park's country inn, and the café has an extensive menu. A 25 acre site with 357 touring pitches, 14 hardstandings and 6 statics.

AA Pubs & Restaurants nearby: The Smugglers' Den Inn, Cubert 01637 830209

Leisure: 🏊 △ 🎱
Facilities: 🔥 ☉ 🅿 ✳ 🛒 🐕
Services: 🔌 🔲 🛢 🍴 🖳 ⛲
Within 3 miles: ⬇ 🎣 🏌 ◎ 🏪 ⛵

Notes: Families & couples only. No skateboards. Dogs must be kept on leads. Adventure playground

see advert on page 89

ROSUDGEON

Places to visit
Trengwainton Garden (NT), Penzance
01736 363148 www.nationaltrust.org.uk

Goonhilly Satellite Earth Station Experience, Helston 0800 679593 www.goonhilly.bt.com

Great for kids: The Flambards Experience, Helston 01326 573404 www.flambards.co.uk

---

ROSUDGEON — Map 2 SW52

▶▶▶ 80% Kenneggy Cove Holiday Park (SW562287)

Higher Kenneggy TR20 9AU
☎ 01736 763453
e-mail: enquiries@kenneggycove.co.uk
web: www.kenneggycove.co.uk
dir: On A394 between Penzance & Helston, turn S into signed lane to site & Higher Kenneggy

⌂ ⛺ Å

Open 17 May-4 Oct Last arrival 21.00hrs Last departure 11.00hrs

Set in an Area of Outstanding Natural Beauty with spectacular sea views, this family-owned park is quiet and well kept, with a well-equipped children's play area, clean, well maintained toilets (due for refurbishment for 2011), and a new takeaway food facility offering home-cooked meals. A short walk along a country footpath leads to the Cornish Coastal Path, and on to the golden sandy beach at Kenneggy Cove. A 4 acre site with 50 touring pitches and 7 statics.

AA Pubs & Restaurants nearby: The Victoria Inn, Perranuthnoe 01736 710309

The Ship Inn, Porthleven 01326 564204

Leisure: ⚑
Facilities: ⛱ ⌂ ⊙ ⌱ ✳ ⊙ ⓢ ▤
Services: ⚡ ⓢ ⓐ ⌀ Ⓣ ▬ ⚙
Within 3 miles: ⌱ ⚡ ⌱ ⚓ ⓢ ⓢ ∪

Notes: No large groups. Fresh bakery items & homemade takeaway food

RUMFORD

Places to visit
Prideaux Place, Padstow 01841 532411
www.prideauxplace.co.uk

RUMFORD — Map 2 SW87

▶▶▶ 80% Music Water Touring Park (SW906685)

PL27 7SJ
☎ 01841 540257
dir: A39 at Winnards Perch rdbt onto B3274 signed Padstow. Left in 2m onto unclass road signed Rumford & St Eval. Site 500mtrs on right

* ⛺ £9-£16 ⛺ £9-£16 Å £9-£16

Open Apr-Oct Last arrival 23.00hrs Last dep 11.00hrs

Set in a peaceful location yet only a short drive to the pretty fishing town of Padstow, and many sandy beaches and coves. This family owned and run park has grassy paddocks, and there is a quiet lounge bar and a separate children's games room. An 8 acre site with 55 touring pitches, 2 hardstandings and 2 statics.

AA Pubs & Restaurants nearby: The Cornish Arms, St Merryn 01841 520288

Leisure: ⚓ ⚑ ⚒ Facilities: ⌂ ⊙ ⌱ ✳ ▤ ⛱
Services: ⚡ ⓢ ⓔ ⓐ ⌀ ▬
Within 3 miles: ⌸ ⚡ ⌱ ⓢ ⓢ ∪

Notes: ⊘ Maximum 2 dogs, one tent per pitch. Pets corner (donkeys)

RUTHERNBRIDGE — Map 2 SX06

Places to visit
Prideaux Place, Padstow 01841 532411
www.prideauxplace.co.uk

Cornwall's Regimental Museum, Bodmin 01208 72810

Great for kids: Pencarrow, Bodmin 01208 841369 www.pencarrow.co.uk

▶▶▶ 76% Ruthern Valley Holidays (SX014665)

PL30 5LU
☎ 01208 831395
e-mail: camping@ruthernvalley.com
web: www.ruthernvalley.com
dir: A389 through Bodmin, follow St Austell signs, then Lanivet signs. At top of hill turn right on unclass road signed Ruthernbridge. Follow signs

* ⛺ £15-£19 ⛺ £15-£19 Å £15-£19

Open all year Last arrival 20.30hrs Last dep noon

An attractive woodland site peacefully located in a small river valley west of Bodmin Moor. This away-from-it-all park is ideal for those wanting a quiet holiday, and the informal pitches are spread in

four natural areas, with plenty of sheltered space. There are also 12 lodges, two heated wooden wigwams, three camping pods, and static holiday vans for hire. A 7.5 acre site with 26 touring pitches, 2 hardstandings and 4 statics.

AA Pubs & Restaurants nearby: The Swan, Wadebridge 01208 812526

Trehellas House Hotel & Restaurant, Bodmin 01208 72700

Leisure: ⚑ Facilities: ⌂ ⊙ ✳ ⊙ ⓢ ▤ ⛱
Services: ⚡ ⓢ ⓔ ⌀ Ⓣ ▬ ⚙
Within 3 miles: ⌱ ⚡ ⓢ ⓢ ∪

Notes: No dogs in camping pods or wigwams or in Jul & Aug. Woodland area, children's play area. Wi-fi

ST AGNES — Map 2 SW75

Places to visit
Royal Cornwall Museum, Truro 01872 272205
www.royalcornwallmuseum.org.uk

Trerice (NT), Trerice 01637 875404
www.nationaltrust.org.uk

AA CAMPING CARD SITE

▶▶▶▶ 76% Beacon Cottage Farm Touring Park (SW705502)

Beacon Dr TR5 0NU
☎ 01872 552347 & 553381
e-mail: beaconcottagefarm@lineone.net
web: www.beaconcottagefarmholidays.co.uk
dir: From A30 at Threeburrows rdbt take B3277 to St Agnes, left into Goonvrea Rd, right into Beacon Drive, follow brown sign to site

* ⛺ £15-£21 ⛺ £15-£21 Å £15-£21

Open Apr-Oct (rs Etr-Whit shop closed) Last arrival 20.00hrs Last departure noon

A neat and compact site on a working farm, utilizing a cottage and outhouses, an old orchard and adjoining walled paddock. The unique location on a headland looking north-east along the coast comes with stunning views towards St Ives, and the keen friendly family owners keep all areas very well maintained. A 5 acre site with 70 touring pitches.

AA Pubs & Restaurants nearby: Driftwood Spars, St Agnes 01872 552428

Leisure: ⚑ Facilities: ⌂ ⊙ ⌱ ✳ ⓢ ⛱
Services: ⚡ ⓢ ⓔ ⌀ ▬ ⚙
Within 3 miles: ⌱ ⚡ ⌱ ⊙ ⓢ ⓢ ⓢ ∪

Notes: No large groups. Secure year-round caravan storage

ST AGNES *continued*

►►► 82% Presingoll Farm Caravan & Camping Park *(SW721494)*

TR5 0PB

☎ 01872 552333 📱 01872 552333

e-mail: pam@presingollfarm.co.uk

dir: *From A30 Chiverton rdbt take B3277 towards St Agnes. Site 3m on right*

* ⛺ fr £13 ⛟ fr £13 ▲ fr £13

Open Etr/Apr-Oct Last departure 10.00hrs

An attractive rural park adjoining farmland, with extensive views of the coast beyond. Family owned and run, with level grass pitches, and modernised toilet block in smart converted farm buildings. There is also a campers' room with microwave, freezer, kettle and free coffee and tea, and a newly equipped children's play area. A 5 acre site with 90 touring pitches, 6 hardstandings.

AA Pubs & Restaurants nearby: Driftwood Spars, St Agnes 01872 552428

Leisure: ⚄ **Facilities:** ⚗☉ℱ☀⚙◐🅱📷🎣🚻

Services: ⚡🅱🍴 **Within 3 miles:** ✎🅱↺

Notes: ⊛ No large groups. Microwave & freezer facility, tea & coffee

---

ST AUSTELL Map 2 SX05

See also Carlyon Bay

Places to visit

Charlestown Shipwreck & Heritage Centre, St Austell 01726 69897
www.shipwreckcharlestown.com

Eden Project, St Austell 01726 811911
www.edenproject.com

Great for kids: The China Clay Country Park, St Austell 01726 850362
www.wheal-martyn.com

PREMIER PARK

►►►►► 81% River Valley Holiday Park *(SX010503)*

London Apprentice PL26 7AP

☎ 01726 73533

e-mail: mail@cornwall-holidays.co.uk

web: www.rivervalleyholidaypark.co.uk

dir: *Direct access to site signed on B3273 from St Austell at London Apprentice*

⛺ £15-£27 ⛟ £15-£27 ▲ £15-£27

Open Apr-end of Sep Last arrival 21.00hrs Last departure 11.00hrs

A neat, well-maintained family-run park set in a pleasant river valley. The quality toilet block and attractively landscaped grounds make this a delightful base for a holiday. All pitches are hardstanding, mostly divided by low fencing and neatly trimmed hedges, and the park offers a good range of leisure facilities, including an inviting swimming pool, a games room, an internet room, and an excellent children's play area. There is direct access to river walks and the cycle trail to the beach at Pentewan. A 2 acre site with 45 touring pitches, 45 hardstandings and 40 statics.

AA Pubs & Restaurants nearby: The Royal Inn, Tywardreath 01726 815601

Austell's, St Austell 01726 813888

Leisure: ⚄⚄⚄🎱 **Facilities:** ⚗☉ℱ☀⚙◐🅱🎣

Services: ⚡🅱 **Within 3 miles:** ↕✦🅱✎⚞🅱🅱

Notes: Cycle trail to beach-off road. Wi-fi

see advert below

►►► 78% Court Farm Holidays *(SW953524)*

St Stephen PL26 7LE

☎ 01726 823684 📱 01726 823684

e-mail: truscott@ctfarm.freeserve.co.uk

dir: *From St Austell take A3058 towards Newquay. Through St Stephen (pass Peugeot garage). Right at St Stephen/Coombe Hay/Langreth/Industrial site sign. 400yds, site on right*

⛺ ⛟ ▲

Open Apr-Sep Last arrival by dark Last departure 11.00hrs

Set in a peaceful rural location, this large camping field offers plenty of space, and is handy for the Eden Project and the Lost Gardens of Heligan. Coarse fishing and star-gazing facilities at the Roseland Observatory are among the on-site attractions. A 4 acre site with 20 touring pitches, 5 hardstandings.

LEISURE: 🏊 Indoor swimming pool 🏊 Outdoor swimming pool ⚄ Children's playground ⚟ Tennis court 🎱 Games room ▭ Separate TV room ⛳ 9/18 hole golf course ⛵ Boats for hire ⊞ Cinema ℱ Fishing ⊕ Mini golf ⚄ Watersports ↺ Stables **FACILITIES:** ⚗ Bath ⚗ Shower ☉ Electric shaver ℱ Hairdryer ☀ Ice Pack Facility ⚙ Disabled facilities ◐ Public telephone 🅱 Shop on site or within 200yds 🚚 Mobile shop (calls at least 5 days a week) ▤ BBQ area 🅱 Picnic area 🎣 Dog exercise area

AA Pubs & Restaurants nearby: The Royal Inn, Tywardreath 01726 815601

Austell's, St Austell 01726 813888

Leisure: ⚙️ **Facilities:** 🌂⊙✳🎋🚶

Services: 🔌🚉 **Within 3 miles:** ⚓️🎡🏧🛒🎯U

Notes: No noisy behaviour after dark. Astronomy lectures, observatory, solar observatory. Wi-fi

---

►►► 76% *Meadow Lakes* (SW966485)

Hewas Water PL26 7JG
☎ 01726 882540 📠 01726 883254
dir: *from A390 4m SW of St Austell onto B3287. 1m, site on left*

🚐🚙⛺

Set in a quiet rural area, this park is divided into paddocks with mature hedges and trees, and with its own coarse fishing lake. This friendly, family park has new owners, who plan significant changes, including new roads, better landscaping and a new toilet block. There is a new reception area and the park offers organised activities for children indoors (a new, well-equipped games room) and out in the summer holidays, and at other times caters for adult breaks. There are animals in pens, which children can enter. Self-catering lodges, static caravans and nine bungalows are also found at this site. A 56 acre site with 108 touring pitches.

AA Pubs & Restaurants nearby: The Royal Inn, Tywardreath 01726 815601

Austell's, St Austell 01726 813888

►►► 82% Doubletrees Farm
(SX060540)

Luxulyan Rd PL24 2EH
☎ 01726 812266
e-mail: doubletrees@eids.co.uk
dir: *On A390 at Blazey Gate. Turn by Leek Seed Chapel, almost opposite BP filling station. After approx 300yds turn right by public bench into site*

🚐 fr £16 🚙 fr £16 ⛺ fr £15.50

Open all year Last arrival 22.30hrs Last departure 11.30hrs

A popular park with terraced pitches offering superb sea and coastal views. Close to beaches, and the nearest park to the Eden Project, it is very well maintained by friendly owners. A 1.57 acre site with 32 touring pitches, 6 hardstandings.

AA Pubs & Restaurants nearby: The Royal Inn, Tywardreath 01726 815601

Austell's, St Austell 01726 813888

Facilities: 🌂⊙✳♿🚻🎋🚶 **Services:** 🔌🛒🚉

Within 3 miles: ⚓️🎡◎🏧🛒U

Notes: ⊛

NEW ►►► 83% Treverven Touring Caravan & Camping Park (SW410237)

Treverven Farm TR19 6DL
☎ 01736 810200 & 810318 📠 01736 810200
e-mail: trevervenpark@btconnect.com
dir: *Exit A30 onto B3283 1.5m after St Buryan, left onto B3315. Site on right in 1m*

🚐🚙⛺

Open Etr-Oct Last departure noon

Situated in a quiet Area of Outstanding Natural Beauty, with panoramic sea and country views, this family-owned site is located off a traffic-free lane leading directly to the coastal path. The toilet facilities are very good, and Treverven is ideally placed for exploring west Cornwall. A 6 acre site with 115 touring pitches.

Leisure: ⚙️

Facilities: 🌂⊙🌭✳♿🕐🏧🎋🚶

Services: 🔌🛒🍴🚽🚉🛒⬇

Within 3 miles: 🎡🏧🚣🛒🎯

Notes: Toaster & kettle available. Wi-fi

►►► 79% *Southleigh Manor Naturist Park* (SW918623)

TR9 6HY
☎ 01637 880938 📠 01637 881108
e-mail: enquiries@southleigh-manor.com
dir: *Exit A30 at junct with A39 signed Wadebridge. At Highgate Hill rdbt take A39. At Halloon rdbt take A39. At Trekenning rdbt take 4th exit. Site 500mtrs on right*

🚐🚙⛺

Open Etr-Oct (rs Peak times shop open) Last arrival 20.00hrs Last departure 10.30hrs

A very well maintained, naturist park in the heart of the Cornish countryside, catering for families and couples only. Seclusion and security are very well planned, and the lovely gardens provide a calm setting. There are two lodges and static caravans for holiday hire. A 4 acre site with 50 touring pitches.

Leisure: 🏊 ⚙️ **Facilities:** 🌂⊙🌭✳🕐🏧🎋

Services: 🔌🛒🍴🔋🎿🚽🍴🚉

Within 3 miles: 🎡🏧🛒🎯U

Notes: ⊛ Sauna, spa bath, pool table, putting green

►►► 80% St Day Touring Park
(SW733422)

Church Hill TR16 5LE
☎ 01209 821086 & 07989 996175
e-mail: jo@stdaytouringpark.co.uk
dir: *From A30 at Scorrier onto B3298 towards Falmouth. Site signed on right in 2m*

🚐 £14 🚙 £14 ⛺ £8-£14

Open Etr & Apr-Oct Last departure noon

A very good touring area with modern toilet facilities. This rurally located park with keen friendly owners is situated in a quiet area between Falmouth and Newquay and within close walking distance of the attractive village of St Day. Nine seasonal touring pitches are available. A 4 acre site with 30 touring pitches, 9 hardstandings.

Facilities: 🌂⊙🌭✳♿🕐🏧 **Services:** 🔌🛒🚉

Within 3 miles: ⚓️🎡🏧◎🚣🛒🎯U

Notes: ⊛ Adults only. No ball games, dogs must be kept on leads. Wi-fi

ST GILES-ON-THE-HEATH

See Chapmans Well (Devon)

ST HILARY   Map 2 SW53

Places to visit

Godolphin House (NT),
Godolphin Cross 01736 763194
www.nationaltrust.org.uk/godolphin

▶▶▶▶ 81% Wayfarers Caravan & Camping Park *(SW558314)*

Relubbus Ln TR20 9EF
☎ 01736 763326
e-mail: elaine@wayfarerspark.co.uk
dir: *Exit A30 onto A394 towards Helston. Left at rdbt onto B3280 after 2m. Site 1.5m on left*

⊞ £15-£21 ⊞ £15-£21 ▲ £13-£18

Open May-Sep Last arrival 19.00hrs Last departure 11.00hrs

A quiet sheltered park in a peaceful rural setting within two and half miles of St Michael's Mount. It offers spacious, well-drained pitches and very well cared for facilities. A 4.8 acre site with 39 touring pitches, 25 hardstandings and 3 statics.

AA Pubs & Restaurants nearby: Trevelyan Arms, Goldsithney 01736 710453

Godolphin Arms, Marazion 01736 710202

Facilities: 🅿️⊙🅿️✳️👌🕒🅱️🍴🎋

Services: 🕒🅱️🛒🖨️🗑️

Within 3 miles: ↕️🚶🎣◎🚴🅱️🅱️♨️

Notes: ⓐ Adults only. No pets. Tourist information room

▶▶▶ 77% Trevair Touring Park

(SW548326)

South Treveneague TR20 9BY
☎ 01736 740647
e-mail: info@trevairtouringpark.co.uk
dir: *A30 onto A394 signed Helston. 2m to rdbt, left onto B3280. Through Goldsithney. Left at brown site sign. Through 20mph zone to site, 1m on right*

⊞ £10-£15 ⊞ £10-£15 ▲ £10-£15

Open Etr-Nov Last arrival 22.00hrs Last departure 11.00hrs

Set in a rural location adjacent to woodland, this park is level and secluded, with grassy pitches. Marazion's beaches and the famous St Michael's Mount are just three miles away. The friendly owners live at the farmhouse on the park. A 3.5 acre site with 40 touring pitches and 2 statics.

AA Pubs & Restaurants nearby: Trevelyan Arms, Goldsithney 01736 710453

Godolphin Arms, Marazion 01736 710202

Facilities: 🅿️⊙✳️🍴

Services: 🕒🅱️🛒🖨️

Within 3 miles: ↕️🎣🚴🅱️♨️

Notes: ⓐ

ST IVES   Map 2 SW54

Places to visit

Barbara Hepworth Museum & Sculpture Garden, St Ives 01736 796226
www.tate.org.uk/stives

Tate St Ives, St Ives 01736 796226
www.tate.org.uk/stives

PREMIER PARK

▶▶▶▶▶ 94% Polmanter Tourist Park *(SW510388)*

Best of British

Halsetown TR26 3LX
☎ 01736 795640
e-mail: reception@polmanter.com
dir: *Signed off B3311 at Halsetown*

⊞ ⊞ ▲

Open Whit-10 Sep (rs Whit shop, pool, bar & takeaway food closed) Last arrival 21.00hrs Last departure 10.00hrs

A well-developed touring park on high ground, Polmanter offers high quality in all areas, from the immaculate modern toilet blocks to the outdoor swimming pool and hard tennis courts. Pitches are individually marked and sited in meadows, and the park has been tastefully landscaped, which includes a new field with full-facility hardstanding pitches to accommodate larger caravans and motorhomes. The fishing port and beaches of St Ives are just a mile and a half away, and there is a bus service in high season. A 20 acre site with 270 touring pitches, 60 hardstandings.

AA Pubs & Restaurants nearby: The Tinners Arms, Zennor 01736 796927

The Gurnard's Head, Zennor 01736 796928

Leisure: 🏊🎠🎱🎯

Facilities: 🅿️⊙🅿️✳️👌🕒🅱️🐕

Services: 🕒🅱️🍴🛒🗑️🖨️🍽️🛒🐴🗑️

Within 3 miles: ↕️🚶🅱️🎣◎🚴🅱️🅱️♨️

Notes: No skateboards, roller blades or heelys. Putting, sports field, 7 family shower rooms. Wi-fi

▶▶▶▶ 90% *Ayr Holiday Park*

(SW509408)

TR26 1EJ
☎ 01736 795855   📠 01736 798797
e-mail: recept@ayrholidaypark.co.uk
dir: *From A30 follow St Ives 'large vehicles' route via B3311 through Halsetown onto B3306. Site signed towards St Ives town centre*

⊞ ⊞ ▲

Open all year Last arrival 22.00hrs Last departure 10.00hrs

A well-established park on a cliff side overlooking St Ives Bay, with a heated toilet block that makes winter holidaying more attractive. There are stunning views from most pitches, and the town centre, harbour and beach are only half a mile away, with direct access to the coastal footpath. A 4 acre site with 40 touring pitches, 20 hardstandings.

AA Pubs & Restaurants nearby: The Watermill, Hayle 01736 757912

Alba Restaurant, St Ives 01736 797222

Leisure: 🎠🎯

Facilities: 🛁🅿️⊙🅿️✳️👌🕒🅱️🅱️🍴🐕

Services: 🕒🅱️🛒🖨️🗑️🖨️🗑️

Within 3 miles: ↕️🚶🅱️🎣🚴🅱️🅱️♨️

Notes: Wi-fi

see advert on opposite page

▶▶▶▶ **86% Little Trevarrack Holiday Park** (SW525379)

Laity Ln, Carbis Bay TR26 3HW
☎ 01736 797580
e-mail: info@littletrevarrack.co.uk
dir: *A30 onto A3074 signed 'Carbis Bay & St Ives'. Left opposite turn to beach. 150yds, over x-rds, site 2nd on right*

* 🚐 £13.50-£29.25 🚐 £13.50-£29.25
🛖 £13.50-£29.25

Open Apr-Sep (rs Etr-Whit, mid-end Sep games room & pool closed) Last arrival 21.00hrs Last departure 10.00hrs

A pleasant grass park set in countryside but close to beaches and local amenities. Plenty of tree planting has resulted in more shelter and privacy in this landscaped park, and there are superb sea views. There are impressive floral displays, well maintained toilets, a good children's play area, and a spacious games field. A private bus service runs to St Ives in high season. A 20 acre site with 200 touring pitches.

AA Pubs & Restaurants nearby: The Watermill, Hayle 01736 757912

The Wave Restaurant, St Ives 01736 796661

Leisure: 🏊 🎱 🎣 **Facilities:** 🚿⊙🅿✳⚡🕐🐾
Services: 🔌🧺💰🚿🛢️🚽
Within 3 miles: ⛳🎣🐴🚵🎯🛒⛴️🏪🏬🎳⛵

Notes: No groups. Sports area, recycling, night warden. Wi-fi

▶▶▶▶ **78% Trevalgan Touring Park** (SW490402)

Trevalgan TR26 3BJ
☎ 01736 792048
e-mail: recept@trevalgantouringpark.co.uk
dir: *From A30 follow holiday route to St Ives. B3311 through Halsetown to B3306. Left towards Land's End. Site signed 0.5m on right*

🚐 🚐 🛖

Open Etr-Sep Last arrival 22.00hrs Last departure 10.00hrs

An open park next to a working farm in a rural area on the coastal road from St Ives to Zennor. The park is surrounded by mature hedges, but there are extensive views over the sea. There are very good toilet facilities including family rooms, and a large TV lounge and recreation room with drinks machine. A 4.9 acre site with 120 touring pitches.

AA Pubs & Restaurants nearby: The Tinners Arms, Zennor 01736 796927

The Gurnard's Head, Zennor 01736 796928

Leisure: 🎱 🎣 📺
Facilities: 🚿⊙🅿✳⚡🕐🏪🏬🎪
Services: 🔌🧺💰🚿🚽🍴🍔♨️⛽
Within 3 miles: ⛳🎣🐴🚵🎯🛒⛴️🏪🏬🎳⛵

Notes: Farm trail, crazy golf

All the campsites in this guide are inspected annually by a team of experienced inspectors

SERVICES: 🔌 Electric hook up 🧺 Launderette 🍷 Licensed bar 💰 Calor Gas 🚗 Camping Gaz 🚽 Toilet fluid 🍴 Café/Restaurant 🍔 Fast Food/Takeaway ♨️ Battery charging
🍼 Baby care ⛽ Motorvan service point ABBREVIATIONS: BH/bank hols-bank holidays Etr-Easter Whit-Whitsun dep-departure fr-from hrs-hours m-mile mdnt-midnight
rdbt-roundabout rs-restricted service wk-week wknd-weekend No credit cards no dogs See page 7 for details of the AA Camping Card Scheme

ST IVES continued

▶▶▶ 86% Penderleath Caravan & Camping Park (SW496375)

Towednack TR26 3AF
☎ 01736 798403
e-mail: holidays@penderleath.co.uk
dir: From A30 take A3074 towards St Ives. Left at 2nd mini-rdbt, approx 3m to T-junct. Left then immediately right. Next left

* 🚐 £13-£23 🚐 £13-£23 ▲ £13-£23

Open Etr-Oct Last arrival 21.30hrs Last departure 10.30hrs

Set in a rugged rural location, this tranquil park has extensive views towards St Ives Bay and the north coast. Facilities are all housed in modernised granite barns, and include spotless, upgraded toilets, including new fully-serviced shower rooms, and there's a quiet licensed bar with beer garden, breakfast room and bar meals. The owners are welcoming and helpful and have now opened a food takeaway facility. A 10 acre site with 75 touring pitches.

AA Pubs & Restaurants nearby: The Watermill, Hayle 01736 757912

Alba Restaurant, St Ives 01736 797222

Leisure: 🅰 🐟 **Facilities:** 🚻⊙🅿✳♿⏰🖳🎣🍽
Services: 🚐🖳🔧🔒🚿🚽🍴🍺🛒
Within 3 miles: ↓✚🅗🎣◎♨🛒🎣U

Notes: Dogs must be well behaved & kept on leads at all times. Bus to St Ives in high season

▶▶ 85% Balnoon Camping Site
(SW509382)

Halsetown TR26 3JA
☎ 01736 795431
e-mail: nat@balnoon.fsnet.co.uk
dir: From A30 take A3074, at 2nd mini-rdbt 1st left signed Tate/St Ives. In 3m right after Balnoon Inn

* 🚐 £10-£15 🚐 £10-£15 ▲ £10-£15
Open Etr-Oct Last arrival 20.00hrs Last dep 11.00hrs

Small, quiet and friendly, this sheltered site offers superb views of the adjacent rolling hills. The two paddocks are surrounded by mature hedges, and the toilet facilities are kept spotlessly clean. The beaches of Carbis Bay and St Ives are about two miles away. A 1 acre site with 23 touring pitches.

AA Pubs & Restaurants nearby: The Tinners Arms, Zennor 01736 796927

The Gurnard's Head, Zennor 01736 796928

Facilities: 🚻⊙🅿✳🖳
Services: 🚐🔒🚿🖳🛒
Within 3 miles: ↓✚🅗🎣◎🛒🎣U
Notes: 🐕

ST JUST (NEAR LAND'S END)   Map 2 SW33

Places to visit

Geevor Tin Mine, Pendeen 01736 788662 www.geevor.com

Carn Euny Ancient Village, Sancreed www.english-heritage.org.uk

▶▶▶ 80% Roselands Caravan and Camping Park (SW387305)

Dowran TR19 7RS
☎ 01736 788571
e-mail: info@roselands.co.uk
dir: From A30 Penzance bypass turn right for St Just on A3071. 5m, turn left at sign after tin mine chimney, follow signs to site

🚐🚐▲

Open all year Last arrival 21.00hrs Last departure 11.00hrs

A small, friendly park in a sheltered rural setting, an ideal location for a quiet family holiday. The owners continue to upgrade the park, and in addition to the attractive little bar there is an indoor games room, children's playground, and good toilet facilities. A 3 acre site with 15 touring pitches and 15 statics.

AA Pubs & Restaurants nearby: The Wellington, St Just 01736 787319

Harris's Restaurant, Penzance 01736 364408

The Navy Inn, Penzance 01736 333232

Leisure: 🅰 🐟 ⏹
Facilities: 🚻⊙🅿✳⏰🖳🎣
Services: 🚐🖳🔧🔒🚿🚽🖳🛒🚗
Within 3 miles: ↓🎣♨🛒🎣U
Notes: No cars by caravans. Wi-fi

▶▶▶ 78% Kelynack Caravan & Camping Park (SW374301)

Kelynack TR19 7RE
☎ 01736 787633   📠 01736 787633
e-mail: kelynackholidays@tiscali.co.uk
dir: 1m S of St Just, 5m N of Land's End on B3306

🚐🚐▲

Open Apr-Oct Last arrival 22.00hrs Last departure 10.00hrs

A small secluded park nestling alongside a stream in an unspoilt rural location. The level grass pitches are in two areas, and the park is close to many coves, beaches, and ancient villages. The camping barn has been converted into B&B accommodation. A 3 acre site with 20 touring pitches, 3 hardstandings and 13 statics.

AA Pubs & Restaurants nearby: The Wellington, St Just 01736 787319

Harris's Restaurant, Penzance 01736 364408

The Navy Inn, Penzance 01736 333232

Leisure: 🅰 🐟
Facilities: 🚻⊙🅿✳♿⏰🖳🎣
Services: 🚐🖳🔧🚿🖳🛒🚗🖳
Within 3 miles: ↓🎣♨🛒U
Notes: Dining & cooking shelter. Wi-fi

AA CAMPING CARD SITE

►►► 76% Trevaylor Caravan & Camping Park *(SW368222)*

Botallack TR19 7PU
☎ 01736 787016
e-mail: trevaylor@cornishcamping.co.uk
dir: *On B3306 (St Just-St Ives road), site on right 0.75m from St Just*

Open Fri before Etr-Oct Last departure 11.00hrs

A sheltered grassy site located off the beaten track in a peaceful location at the western tip of Cornwall. The dramatic coastline and the pretty villages nearby are truly unspoilt. Clean, well-maintained facilities and a good shop are offered along with a bar serving meals. A 6 acre site with 50 touring pitches and 5 statics.

AA Pubs & Restaurants nearby: The Wellington, St Just 01736 787319

Harris's Restaurant, Penzance 01736 364408

The Navy Inn, Penzance 01736 333232

Leisure: **Facilities:**
Services:
Within 3 miles: **Notes:** Wi-fi

AA CAMPING CARD SITE

►►► 75% Secret Garden Caravan & Camping Park *(SW370305)*

Bosavern House TR19 7RD
☎ 01736 788301
e-mail: mail@bosavern.com
web: www.secretbosavern.com
dir: *Exit A3071 near St Just onto B3306 Land's End road. Site 0.5m on left*

* £14 £14 £14

Open Mar-Oct Last arrival 22.00hrs Last dep noon

A neat little site in a walled garden behind a guest house, where visitors can enjoy breakfast and snacks in the bar in the evening. This site is in a fairly sheltered location with all grassy pitches. Please note that there is no children's playground. A 1.5 acre site with 12 touring pitches.

AA Pubs & Restaurants nearby: The Wellington, St Just 01736 787319

Harris's Restaurant, Penzance 01736 364408

The Navy Inn, Penzance 01736 333232

Leisure: **Facilities:**
Services:
Within 3 miles:
Notes: No pets. Wi-fi

ST JUST-IN-ROSELAND — Map 2 SW83

Places to visit

St Mawes Castle, St Mawes 01326 270526 www.english-heritage.org.uk

Trelissick Garden (NT), Feock 01872 862090 www.nationaltrust.org.uk

►►►► 89% Trethem Mill Touring Park *(SW860365)*

Best of British

TR2 5JF
☎ 01872 580504 📠 01872 580968
e-mail: reception@trethem.com
dir: *From Tregony on A3078 to St Mawes. 2m after Trewithian, follow signs to site*

* £16-£23 £16-£23 £16-£23

Open Apr-mid Oct Last arrival 20.00hrs Last departure 11.00hrs

A quality park in all areas, with upgraded amenities including a reception, shop, laundry, and disabled/family room. This carefully-tended and sheltered park is in a lovely rural setting, with spacious pitches separated by young trees and shrubs. The very keen family who own the site are continually looking for ways to enhance its facilities. An 11 acre site with 84 touring pitches, 50 hardstandings.

AA Pubs & Restaurants nearby: The Victory Inn, St Mawes 01326 270324

Hotel Tresanton, St Mawes 01326 270055

Driftwood, Porthscatho 01872 580644

Leisure:

Facilities:

Services:

Within 3 miles:

Notes: Information centre. Wi-fi

ST MARY'S (ISLES OF SCILLY) — Map 2 SV91

Places to visit

Isles of Scilly Museum, St Mary's 01720 422337 www.iosmuseum.org

►►► 79% Garrison Campsite *(SV897104)*

Tower Cottage, The Garrison TR21 0LS
☎ 01720 422670 📠 01720 422670
e-mail: tedmoulson@aol.com
dir: *10 mins' walk from quay to site*

* £14.50-£19.50

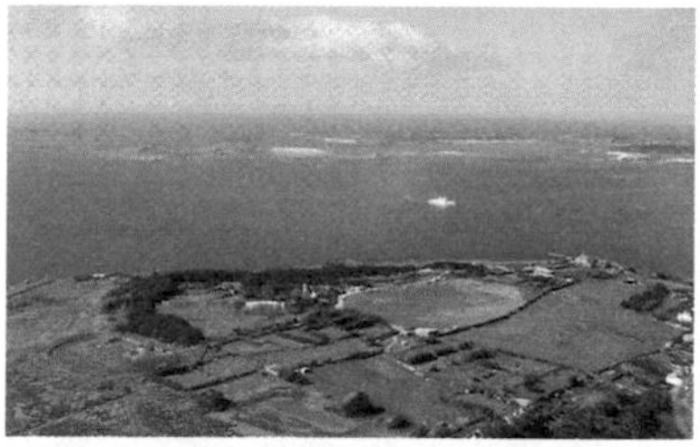

Open Etr-Oct Last arrival 20.00hrs Last departure 19.00hrs

Set on the top of an old fort with superb views, this park offers tent-only pitches in a choice of well-sheltered paddocks. There are modern toilet facilities (with powerful new showers), a superb children's play area, and a good shop at this attractive site, which is only ten minutes from the town, the quay and the nearest beaches. A 9.5 acre site with 120 touring pitches.

AA Pubs & Restaurants nearby: St Mary's Hall Hotel, St Mary's 01720 422316

Facilities:

Services:

Within 3 miles:

Notes: No cars on site, no pets, no open fires. Playground adjacent to site

78% Harlyn Sands Holiday Park (SW873752)

Lighthouse Rd, Trevose Head PL28 8SQ
☎ 01841 520720   📠 01841 521251
e-mail: enquiries@harlynsands.co.uk
web: www.harlynsands.co.uk
dir: *Exit B3276 in St Merryn centre onto unclassified road towards Harlyn Sands & Trevose Head. Follow brown site signs for approx 1m. (NB Do not turn right to Harlyn Sands)*

* 🚐 £8-£30 🚏 £8-£30 ▲ £8-£30

Open Etr-Nov Last arrival 22.00hrs Last departure 10.00hrs

A family park for 'bucket and spade' holidays, surrounded by seven bays each with its own sandy beach. On site entertainment for children and adults is extensive, and there is an indoor swimming pool complex, excellent restaurant and takeaway, and a quiet over-30s lounge bar. A 21 acre site with 160 touring pitches, 6 hardstandings and 350 statics.

AA Pubs & Restaurants nearby: The Cornish Arms, St Merryn 01841 520288

Leisure: 🏊 🅼 🎱
Facilities: 🖍 ⊙ 🅿 ✳ 🔥 🚿 🕗 🛍 🛒 🎋 🏕
Services: 🔌 🍴 🍺 🏧 🔥 🎽 🛒
Within 3 miles: ↧ 🎬 🎣 🛍 🐴 ⛵
Notes: Families only. Arcade, clubhouse, chip shop. Wi-fi

80% Carnevas Holiday Park & Farm Cottages (SW862728)

Carnevas Farm PL28 8PN
☎ 01841 520230 & 521209 📠 01841 520230
e-mail: carnevascampsite@aol.com
dir: *From St Merryn on B3276 towards Porthcothan Bay. Approx 2m turn right at site sign onto unclass road opposite Tredrea Inn. Site 0.25m on right*

* 🚐 £9.50-£16.50 🚏 £9.50-£16.50
▲ £9.50-£16.50

Open Apr-Oct (rs Apr-Whit & mid Sep-Oct shop, bar & restaurant closed)

A family-run park on a working farm, divided into four paddocks on slightly sloping grass. The toilets are central to all areas, and there is a small licensed bar serving bar meals. An 8 acre site with 195 touring pitches and 14 statics.

Carnevas Holiday Park & Farm Cottages

AA Pubs & Restaurants nearby: The Cornish Arms, St Merryn 01841 520288

Leisure: 🅼 🎱   **Facilities:** 🖍 ⊙ 🅿 ✳ 🔥 🚿 🕗 🛍
Services: 🔌 🍴 🍺 🏧 🔥 🛒 🎋 🏕
Within 3 miles: ↧ 🎣 🛍 🐴 ⛵
Notes: ⊗ No skateboards. 2 family bathrooms. Wi-fi

78% Atlantic Bays Holiday Park (SW890717)

St Merryn PL28 8PY
☎ 01841 520855   📠 01841 520419
e-mail: info@atlanticbaysholidaypark.com
dir: *Take B3274 towards Padstow, in 3m left onto unclassified road to St Merryn, follow brown signs to park*

* 🚐 £10-£32 🚏 £10-£32 ▲ £10-£32

Open Mar- 2 Jan Last arrival 19.00hrs Last departure 10.00hrs

Atlantic Bays has been completely re-developed and opened for the 2010 season, with a mix of hardstanding and grass pitches, a new high quality toilet/shower block and a comfortable bar/restaurant. The park is set in a rural area yet only two miles from the coast and beautiful sandy beaches, and within easy reach of the quaint fishing village of Padstow. A 27 acre site with 70 touring pitches, 50 hardstandings and 171 statics.

AA Pubs & Restaurants nearby: The Cornish Arms, St Merryn 01841 520288

Leisure: 🅼 🎱   **Facilities:** 🖍 ⊙ 🅿 ✳ 🔥 🛍 🎋
Services: 🔌 🍴 🍺 🛒 🎋
Within 3 miles: ↧ 🎣 🎣 🛍 ⊙ 🛍 🐴 ⛵
Notes: No pets. Wi-fi

78% Trevean Caravan & Camping Park (SW875724)

Trevean Ln PL28 8PR
☎ 01841 520772   📠 01841 520772
e-mail: trevean.info@virgin.net
dir: *From St Merryn take B3276 to Newquay for 1m. Turn left for Rumford. Site 0.25m on right*

* 🚐 £8-£12 🚏 £8-£12 ▲ £8-£12

Open Apr-Oct (rs Whit-Sep shop open) Last arrival 22.00hrs Last departure 11.00hrs

A small working farm site with level grassy pitches in open countryside. The toilet facilities are clean and well kept, and there is a laundry and good children's playground. A 1.5 acre site with 68 touring pitches and 3 statics.

AA Pubs & Restaurants nearby: The Cornish Arms, St Merryn 01841 520288

Leisure: 🅼   **Facilities:** 🖍 ⊙ 🅿 ✳ 🔥 🚿 🕗 🛍 🎋 🐕
Services: 🔌 🍴 🔥 🎋
Within 3 miles: ↧ 🎣 🎣 ⊙ 🛍 🐴 ⛵

80% Tregavone Touring Park (SW898732)

Tregavone Farm PL28 8JZ
☎ 01841 520148
e-mail: info@tregavone.co.uk
dir: *From A389 towards Padstow, right after Little Petherick. In 1m just beyond Padstow Holiday Park turn left into unclass road signed Tregavone. Site on left, approx 1m*

* 🚐 £9.50-£11.50 🚏 £9.50-£11.50 ▲ £9.50-£11.50

Open Mar-Oct

Situated on a working farm with unspoilt country views, this spacious grassy park, run by friendly family owners, makes an ideal base for exploring the north Cornish coast and the seven local golden beaches with surfing areas, or for enjoying quiet country walks from the park. A 3 acre site with 40 touring pitches.

AA Pubs & Restaurants nearby: The Cornish Arms, St Merryn 01841 520288

Facilities: 🖍 ⊙ ✳ 🐕   **Services:** 🔌 🍴 🎋
Within 3 miles: ↧ 🎣 🎬 🎣 ⊙ 🛍 🐴 ⛵
Notes: ⊗

LEISURE: 🏊 Indoor swimming pool 🏊 Outdoor swimming pool 🅼 Children's playground 🎾 Tennis court 🎱 Games room 📺 Separate TV room ⛳ 9/18 hole golf course
⛵ Boats for hire 🎬 Cinema 🎣 Fishing ⊙ Mini golf 🏄 Watersports 🐴 Stables **FACILITIES:** 🛁 Bath 🚿 Shower ⊙ Electric shaver 🅿 Hairdryer ✳ Ice Pack Facility
🔥 Disabled facilities 🕗 Public telephone 🛍 Shop on site or within 200yds 🚚 Mobile shop (calls at least 5 days a week) 🍴 BBQ area 🎋 Picnic area 🐕 Dog exercise area

ST MINVER
Map 2 SW97

►►►► 80% Gunvenna Caravan Park
(SW969782)

PL27 6QN
☎ **01208 862405** ▤ **01208 869107**
dir: *From A39 N of Wadebridge take B3314 (Port Isaac road), site 4m on right*

* ⛺ £14-£27 ⛺ £14-£27 ▲ £14-£27

Open Etr-Oct Last arrival 21.00hrs Last departure 11.00hrs

An attractive park with extensive rural views in a quiet country location, yet within three miles of Polzeath. This popular park is family owned and run, and provides good facilities in an ideal position for touring north Cornwall. The park has new hardstanding pitches, improved landscaping, and static caravans and a cottage for holiday hire. A 10 acre site with 75 touring pitches, 5 hardstandings and 44 statics.

AA Pubs & Restaurants nearby: The Swan, Wadebridge 01208 812526

Restaurant Nathan Outlaw, Rock 01208 863394

Leisure: ⌂ ⋀ ⚲
Facilities: ⛟ ⋔ ⊙ ☞ ⚡ ⚿ ⚀ ⛺ ⋔
Services: ⌸ ⌷ ⛽ ⊘ ⊤ ⌇ ⚲
Within 3 miles: ⚿ ⚄ ⚲ ⚄ ⚄ ⚄ ⚄
Notes: Dogs must be on leads at all times. Wi-fi

SENNEN
Map 2 SW32

Places to visit
Geevor Tin Mine, Pendeen 01736 788662
www.geevor.com

Carn Euny Ancient Village, Sancreed
www.english-heritage.org.uk

►►► 79% Trevedra Farm Caravan & Camping Site *(SW368276)*

TR19 7BE
☎ **01736 871818 & 871835**
e-mail: trevedra@btconnect.com
dir: *Take A30 towards Land's End. After junct with B3306 turn right into farm lane. NB Sat Nav directs past site entrance to next lane which is unsuitable for caravans*

⛺ ⛺ ▲

Open Etr or Apr-Oct Last arrival 19.00hrs Last departure 10.30hrs

A working farm with dramatic sea views over to the Scilly Isles, just a mile from Land's End. The popular campsite offers well appointed toilets, a well-stocked shop, and a cooked breakfast or evening meal from the food bar. There is direct access to the coastal footpath, and two beautiful beaches are a short walk away. An 8 acre site with 100 touring pitches.

AA Pubs & Restaurants nearby: The Old Success Inn, Sennan 01736 871232

Facilities: ⋔ ⊙ ☞ ⚡ ⚿ ⚀ ⚄
Services: ⌸ ⌷ ⛽ ⊘ ⊤ ⛴ ⛴ ⚲
Within 3 miles: ⚿ ⚲ ⚄ ⚄ ⚄
Notes: Dogs must be kept on a lead at all times, no open fires. Wi-fi

SUMMERCOURT
Map 2 SW85

Places to visit
Trerice (NT), Trerice 01637 875404
www.nationaltrust.org.uk

Blue Reef Aquarium, Newquay 01637 878134
www.bluereefaquarium.co.uk

Great for kids: Dairyland Farmworld, Newquay 01872 510246 www.dairylandfarmworld.com

AA CAMPING CARD SITE

RV ►►►► 95% Carvynick Country Club *(SW878564)*

TR8 5AF
☎ **01872 510716** ▤ **01872 510172**
e-mail: info@carvynick.co.uk
web: www.carvynick.co.uk
dir: *Off A3058*

⛺

Open all year (rs Jan-early Feb restricted leisure facilities)

Set within the gardens of an attractive country estate this spacious dedicated American RV Park (also home to the 'Itchy Feet' retail company) provides all full facility pitches on hardstandings. The extensive on-site amenities, shared by the high quality time share village, include an excellent restaurant with lounge bar, indoor leisure area with swimming pool, fitness suite and badminton court. 47 touring pitches.

AA Pubs & Restaurants nearby: The Plume of Feathers, Mitchell 01872 510387

Leisure: ⌂ ⋀ ⚲
Facilities: ⋔ ⊙ ☞
Services: ⌸ ⌷ ⛽ ⊤ ⊚ ⚲
Within 3 miles: ⚿ ⚄ ⚄
Notes: Dogs must be exercised off site

see advert on page 110

TINTAGEL   Map 2 SX08

See also Camelford

Places to visit

Tintagel Castle, Tintagel 01840 770328
www.english-heritage.org.uk

Tintagel Old Post Office (NT), Tintagel
01840 770024
www.nationaltrust.org.uk/
main/w-tintageloldpostoffice

Great for kids: Tamar Otter & Wildlife Centre, Launceston 01566 785646 www.tamarotters.co.uk

►►► 74% Headland Caravan & Camping Park (SX056887)

Atlantic Rd PL34 0DE
☎ 01840 770239   📱 01840 770925
e-mail: headland.caravan@talktalkbusiness.net
dir: From B3263 follow brown tourist signs through village to Headland

🚐 🚏 Å

Open Etr-Oct Last arrival 21.00hrs

A peaceful family-run site in the mystical village of Tintagel, close to the ruins of King Arthur's Castle.

There are two well terraced camping areas with sea and countryside views, immaculately clean and newly updated toilet facilities, and good, colourful planting across the park. The Cornish coastal path and the spectacular scenery are just two of the attractions here, and there are safe bathing beaches nearby. There are holiday statics for hire. A 5 acre site with 62 touring pitches and 28 statics.

Headland Caravan & Camping Park

AA Pubs & Restaurants nearby: The Port William, Tintagel 01840 770230

Leisure: � **Facilities:** 📶 ⊙ 🅿 ✳ 🕒 🖸 🚻
Services: 🔌 🖸 🛢 🖉 🚽 🖀 🖐
Within 3 miles: ⚡ 🖋 🚴 🖸 🖸 ∪
Notes: Dogs must be kept on short leads & exercised off site, quiet after 23.00hrs

TORPOINT   Map 3 SX45

Places to visit

Antony House, Torpoint 01752 812191
www.nationaltrust.org.uk/antony

Mount Edgcumbe House & Country Park, Torpoint 01752 822236
www.mountedgcumbe.gov.uk

Great for kids: The Monkey Sanctuary, Looe 01503 262532 www.monkeysanctuary.org

AA CAMPING CARD SITE

►►►► 78% Whitsand Bay Lodge & Touring Park (SX410515)

Millbrook PL10 1JZ
☎ 01752 822597   📱 01752 823444
e-mail: enquiries@whitsandbayholidays.co.uk
dir: From Torpoint take A374, turn left at Anthony onto B3247 for 1.25m to T-junct. Turn left, 0.25m then right onto Cliff Rd. Site 2m on left

* 🚐 £10-£30 🚏 £10-£30 Å £10-£23

Open all year (rs Sep-Mar opening hours shop/pool restricted) Last arrival 19.00hrs Last departure 10.00hrs

---

LEISURE: 🏊 Indoor swimming pool 🏊 Outdoor swimming pool 🎠 Children's playground 🎾 Tennis court 🎱 Games room 📺 Separate TV room ⛳ 9/18 hole golf course ⛵ Boats for hire 🎬 Cinema 🎣 Fishing ⛳ Mini golf 🏄 Watersports ∪ Stables   **FACILITIES:** 🛁 Bath 🚿 Shower ⊙ Electric shaver 🅿 Hairdryer ✳ Ice Pack Facility ♿ Disabled facilities ☎ Public telephone 🛒 Shop on site or within 200yds 🚚 Mobile shop (calls at least 5 days a week) 🍖 BBQ area 🪑 Picnic area 🐕 Dog exercise area

A very well equipped park with panoramic coastal, sea and countryside views from its terraced pitches. An ambitious programme of development has resulted in a very high quality park with upmarket toilet facilities and other amenities. A 27 acre site with 49 touring pitches, 30 hardstandings and 5 statics.

AA Pubs & Restaurants nearby: The Halfway House Inn, Kingsland 01752 822279

Leisure:

Facilities:

Services:

Within 3 miles:

Notes: Families & couples only. Sauna, gym, entertainment, putting, chapel, library. Wi-fi

TRURO — Map 2 SW84

See also Portscatho

Places to visit

Royal Cornwall Museum, Truro 01872 272205 www.royalcornwallmuseum.org.uk

Trewithen Gardens, Probus 01726 883647 www.trewithengardens.co.uk

Great for kids: Pencarrow, Bodmin 01208 841369 www.pencarrow.co.uk

PREMIER PARK

►►►►► 92% Carnon Downs Caravan & Camping Park *(SW805406)*

DAVID BELLAMY CONSERVATION AWARD GOLD

Carnon Downs TR3 6JJ
☎ 01872 862283 01872 870820
e-mail: info@carnon-downs-caravanpark.co.uk
dir: *Take A39 from Truro towards Falmouth. Site just off main Carnon Downs rdbt, on left*

* £18.50-£25.50 £18.50-£25.50 £18.50-£22.50

Open all year Last arrival 22.00hrs Last departure 11.00hrs

A beautifully upgraded, mature park set in meadowland and woodland close to the village amenities of Carnon Downs. The four toilet blocks provide exceptional facilities in bright modern surroundings. An extensive landscaping programme has been carried out to give more spacious pitch sizes, and there is an exciting children's playground with modern equipment, and a football pitch. A 33 acre site with 150 touring pitches, 80 hardstandings and 1 static.

AA Pubs & Restaurants nearby: The Pandora Inn, Mylor Bridge 01326 372678

Tabb's, Truro 01872 262110

Leisure:

Facilities:

Services:

Within 3 miles:

Notes: No children's bikes in Jul & Aug. Baby & child bathroom, 3 family bathrooms

PREMIER PARK

►►►►► 82% Truro Caravan and Camping Park *(SW772452)*

TR4 8QN
☎ 01872 560274 01872 561413
e-mail: info@trurocaravanandcampingpark.co.uk
dir: *Exit A390 at Threemilestone rdbt onto unclass road towards Chacewater. Site signed on right in 0.5m*

* £18.50-£25.50 £18.50-£25.50 £18.50-£25.50

Open all year Last arrival 19.00hrs Last departure 10.30hrs

An attractive south-facing and well laid out park with spacious pitches, including new hardstandings, and quality modern toilets that are kept spotlessly clean. It is situated on the edge of the city of Truro yet close to many beaches, with St Agnes being just ten minutes away by car. It is equidistant from both the rugged north coast and the calmer south coastal areas. There is a good bus service from the gate of the park to Truro. An 8.5 acre site with 51 touring pitches, 26 hardstandings and 49 statics.

AA Pubs & Restaurants nearby: The Wig & Pen Inn, Truro 01872 273028

Probus Lamplighter Restaurant, Probus 01726 882453

Facilities:

Services:

Within 3 miles:

Notes: Wi-fi

see advert on page 112

AA CAMPING CARD SITE

►►►► 81% Cosawes Park *(SW768376)*

Perranarworthal TR3 7QS
☎ 01872 863724 01872 870268
e-mail: info@cosawes.com
dir: *Exit A39 midway between Truro & Falmouth. Direct access at site sign after Perranarworthal*

* £14-£18 £16-£22 £12-£16

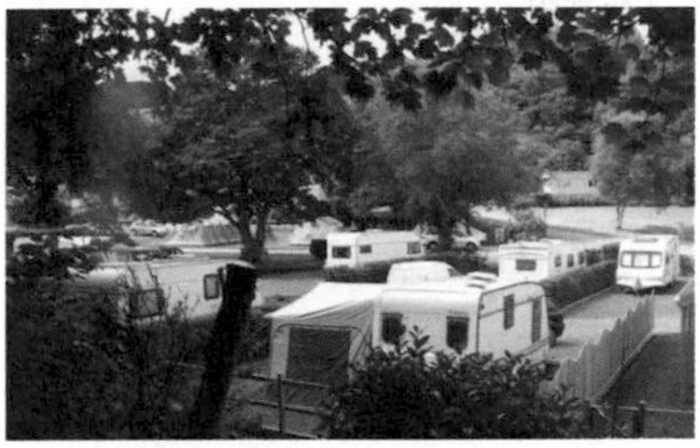

Open all year Last departure noon

A small touring park in a peaceful wooded valley, midway between Truro and Falmouth, with new toilet facilities that include two smart family rooms. Its stunning location is ideal for visiting the many nearby hamlets and villages close to the Carrick Roads, a stretch of tidal water, which is a centre for sailing and other boats. A 2 acre site with 40 touring pitches, 25 hardstandings.

AA Pubs & Restaurants nearby: The Pandora Inn, Mylor Bridge 01326 372678

Facilities:

Services:

Within 3 miles:

Notes: Dogs must be kept on leads at all times. Underfloor heating, vanity cubicles. Fish & chips every Thursday evening. Wi-fi

see advert on page 113

Truro Caravan & Camping Park

TRURO, Cornwall TR4 8QN

"Location!   Location!   Location!"

Tel: 01872 560274   Fax: 01872 561413

email: info@trurocaravanandcampingpark.co.uk

- Wide main road easy access to Park with Barrier access/exit
- Open throughout the year
- Secure, clean landscape surroundings with scenic views set within 8.5 acres
- Hard road surfaces with lighting leading to Pitches
- Large level Caravan, Motor home, RV and Camping Super pitches
- Modern Heated Ablution Blocks, Disabled facilities, Washing up area and Chemical Disposal points
- Information Room, Calor Gas, Wi-Fi access and a well equipped laundry
- Children's play area. Dog walk, Recycling Bins
- Motor Home and RV Service point "Sani-Station"
- Bus stop outside, Park & Ride within walking distance
- Beaches, Retail Park, Supermarket, Pubs, Cycle Trails, Walks, Fishing and Attractions nearby
- Caravan, Motor Home and RV Storage Facilities. Seasonal Pitches.

Located in the centre of Cornwall on the fringe of TRURO close to the City Centre

Directions: Take the A30 to the Chiverton Cross roundabout, turn on to the A390 towards Truro, continue to the roundabout and take the 3rd exit. Continue to the next roundabout and take the 2nd exit. Go past the Oak Tree Inn and the Retail Park (on your right). You will then arrive at the Truro Caravan & Camping Park exit and Entrance.

Book online at trurocaravanandcampingpark.co.uk or telephone 01872 560274

Caravan, Motor Home, RV and Camping Pitches from £15.00 per day depending on Season

TRURO *continued*

▶▶▶ 80% Summer Valley *(SW800479)*

Shortlanesend TR4 9DW
☎ 01872 277878
e-mail: res@summervalley.co.uk
dir: *3m NW off B3284*

🚐 £13-£16 🚏 £13-£16 ▲ £13-£16

Open Apr-Oct Last arrival 20.00hrs Last departure noon

A very attractive and secluded site in a rural setting midway between the A30 and the cathedral city of Truro. The keen owners maintain the facilities to a good standard. A 3 acre site with 60 touring pitches.

AA Pubs & Restaurants nearby: Old Ale House, Truro 01872 271122

Bustophers Bar Bistro, Truro 01872 279029

Leisure: 🅰
Facilities: 🄽⊙🄿✳🕘🄶🚿🐾
Services: 🄾🄶🄰🄰🄣🄴
Within 3 miles: 🚴🄷🄿◎🄶🄶🅄

Notes: Campers' lounge

WADEBRIDGE Map 2 SW97

Places to visit
Prideaux Place, Padstow 01841 532411 www.prideauxplace.co.uk

Cornwall's Regimental Museum, Bodmin 01208 72810

Great for kids: Pencarrow, Bodmin 01208 841369 www.pencarrow.co.uk

---

AA CAMPING CARD SITE

▶▶▶ 86% St Mabyn Holiday Park

(SX055733)

Longstone Rd, St Mabyn PL30 3BY
☎ 01208 841677 📠 01208 841514
e-mail: info@stmabyn.co.uk
web: www.stmabynholidaypark.co.uk
dir: *S of Camelford on A39, left after BP garage onto B3266 to Bodmin, 6m to Longstone, right at x-rds to St Mabyn, site approx 400mtrs on right*

* 🚐 £12-£24 🚏 £12-£24 ▲ £8-£16

Open 15 Mar-Oct (rs 15 Mar-Spring BH & mid Sep-Oct swimming pool may be closed) Last arrival 22.00hrs Last departure noon

A family run site ideally situated close to the picturesque market town of Wadebridge, and within easy reach of Bodmin. The park offers peace and tranquillity in a country setting and at the same time provides plenty of on-site activities including a swimming pool and children's play areas. Holiday chalets and fully-equipped holiday homes are available to rent, along with a choice of pitches. Seasonal touring pitches are available. A 12 acre site with 120 touring pitches, 49 hardstandings and 20 statics.

AA Pubs & Restaurants nearby: The Swan, Wadebridge 01208 812526

The Borough Arms, Dunmere 01208 73118

Leisure: 🏊🅰🎣🖵
Facilities: 🄽⊙🄿✳🕘🄶🚿🐾
Services: 🄾🄶🄰🄰🄣🐾
Within 3 miles: 🚴🄿🄶🄶🅄

Notes: Quiet from 23.00hrs-07.00hrs. Information book given on arrival. Small animal area with goats, ducks & chickens. Wi-fi

For full details of the pennant rating scheme see pages 10 & 11

SERVICES: 🔌 Electric hook up 🧺 Launderette 🍺 Licensed bar 🔥 Calor Gas ⛽ Camping Gaz 🚽 Toilet fluid 🍽 Café/Restaurant 🍟 Fast Food/Takeaway 🔋 Battery charging 🍼 Baby care ♿ Motorvan service point **ABBREVIATIONS:** BH/bank hols-bank holidays Etr-Easter Whit-Whitsun dep-departure fr-from hrs-hours m-mile mdnt-midnight rdbt-roundabout rs-restricted service wk-week wknd-weekend 🚫 No credit cards 🚫 no dogs See page 7 for details of the AA Camping Card Scheme

WADEBRIDGE *continued*

►►► 82% *The Laurels Holiday Park*
(SW957715)

Padstow Rd, Whitecross PL27 7JQ
☎ 01209 313474
e-mail: info@thelaurelsholidaypark.co.uk
web: www.thelaurelsholidaypark.co.uk
dir: *Off A389 (Padstow road) near junct with A39, W of Wadebridge*

Open Apr or Etr-Oct Last arrival 20.00hrs Last departure 11.00hrs

A very smart and well-equipped park with individual pitches screened by hedges and young shrubs. The enclosed dog walk is of great benefit to pet owners, and the Camel cycle trail and Padstow are not far away. A 2.2 acre site with 30 touring pitches, 2 hardstandings.

AA Pubs & Restaurants nearby: The Swan, Wadebridge 01208 812526

Leisure:

Facilities:

Services:

Within 3 miles:

Notes: No group bookings, family park, dogs must be kept on leads. Wet suit dunking bath & drying area

►►► 79% Little Bodieve Holiday Park (SW995734)

Bodieve Rd PL27 6EG
☎ 01208 812323
e-mail: info@littlebodieve.co.uk
dir: *From A39 rdbt on Wadebridge by-pass take B3314 signed Rock/Port Isaac, site 0.25m on right*

Open Apr-Oct (rs Early & late season pool, shop & clubhouse closed) Last arrival 21.00hrs Last departure 11.00hrs

Rurally located with pitches in three large grassy paddocks, this family park is close to the Camel Estuary. The licensed clubhouse provides bar meals, with an entertainment programme in high season, and there is a swimming pool with sun terrace plus a separate waterslide and splash pool, and 7 static holiday caravans. A 22 acre site with 195 touring pitches and 75 statics.

AA Pubs & Restaurants nearby: The Swan, Wadebridge 01208 812526

Leisure:

Facilities:

Services:

Within 3 miles:

Notes: Families & couples only. Crazy golf, water shute/splash pool, pets' corner

AA CAMPING CARD SITE

►►►► 83% Watergate Bay Touring Park (SW850653)

TR8 4AD
☎ 01637 860387   📠 0871 661 7549
e-mail: email@watergatebaytouringpark.co.uk
web: www.watergatebaytouringpark.co.uk
dir: *4m N of Newquay on B3276 (coast road)*

* 🚐 £11-£20 🚙 £11-£20 ▲ £11-£20

Open all year (rs Oct-Etr restricted bar, café, shop & pool) Last arrival 22.00hrs Last departure noon

A well-established park above Watergate Bay, where acres of golden sand, rock pools and surf are seen as a holidaymakers' paradise. The toilet facilities are appointed to a high standard, and there is a new well-stocked shop and café, an inviting swimming pool, and a wide range of activities including tennis courts and outdoor facilities for all ages, and a regular entertainment programme in the clubhouse. A 30 acre site with 171 touring pitches, 14 hardstandings and 2 statics.

AA Pubs & Restaurants nearby: Fifteen Cornwall, Watergate Bay 01637 861000

Leisure:

Facilities:

Services:

Within 3 miles:

Notes: Entertainment, free minibus to beach. Wi-fi

see advert below

WIDEMOUTH BAY — Map 2 SS20

71% Widemouth Bay Caravan Park (SS199008)

EX23 0DF
☎ 01271 866766 📄 01271 866791
e-mail: bookings@jfhols.co.uk
dir: *Take Widemouth Bay coastal road off A39, turn left. Site on left*

* 🚐 £11-£38 🚐 £11-£38 ⛺ £9-£26

Open Etr-Oct Last arrival dusk Last departure 10.00hrs

A partly sloping rural site set in countryside overlooking the sea and one of Cornwall's finest beaches. Nightly entertainment in high season with emphasis on children's and family club programmes. This park is located less than half a mile from the sandy beaches of Widemouth Bay. A 58 acre site with 220 touring pitches, 90 hardstandings and 200 statics.

AA Pubs & Restaurants nearby: The Bay View Inn, Widemouth Bay 01288 361273

Castle Restaurant, Bude 01288 350543

Leisure: 🐟 🎢 🎣
Facilities: 🏊 ⊙ 🅿 ✳ ⅄ 🔌 🖻 🪑 ⛽
Services: 🚐 🗑 🍴 🍽 🚿
Within 3 miles: ↨ 🚲 🎿 🎣 ⊚ 🚌 🖻 U

Notes: Crazy golf, entertainment, kids' club, play area. Wi-fi

---

AA CAMPING CARD SITE

►►► 74% Cornish Coasts Caravan & Camping Park (SS202981)

Middle Penlean, Poundstock, Bude EX23 0EE
☎ 01288 361380
e-mail: enquiries5@cornishcoasts.co.uk
dir: *5m S of Bude on A39, 0.5m S of Rebel Cinema on right*

* 🚐 £12-£15 🚐 £12-£15 ⛺ £7-£15

Open Apr-Oct Last arrival 22.00hrs Last departure 10.30hrs

New owners have taken over this quiet park, with lovely terraced pitches making the most of the stunning views over the countryside to the sea at Widemouth Bay. The reception is in a 13th-century cottage, and the park is well equipped and tidy, with the well maintained and quirky toilet facilities (note the mosaic vanity units) housed in a freshly painted older-style building. At the time of our last inspection the planned improvements for this small and friendly park sounded very positive. A 3.5 acre site with 46 touring pitches, 5 hardstandings and 4 statics.

AA Pubs & Restaurants nearby: The Bay View Inn, Widemouth Bay 01288 361273

Castle Restaurant, Bude 01288 350543

Leisure: 🎢
Facilities: 🏊 ⊙ 🅿 ✳ ⅄ 🖻 ⛽
Services: 🚐 🗑 🛢 🚿 🍴 🚌 🚙
Within 3 miles: 🎿 🎣 ⊚ 🚌 🖻 U

Notes: Quiet after 22.00hrs. Post office

►►► 74% Penhalt Farm Holiday Park (SS194003)

EX23 0DG
☎ 01288 361210 📄 01288 361210
e-mail: denandjennie@penhaltfarm.fsnet.co.uk
web: www.penhaltfarm.co.uk
dir: *From Bude take 2nd right to Widemouth Bay road off A39, left at end by Widemouth Manor signed Millook onto coastal road. Site 0.75m on left*

🚐 🚐 ⛺

Open Etr-Oct

Splendid views of the sea and coast can be enjoyed from all pitches on this sloping but partly level site, set in a lovely rural area on a working farm. About one mile away is one of Cornwall's finest beaches which prove popular with all the family as well as surfers. An 8 acre site with 100 touring pitches.

AA Pubs & Restaurants nearby: The Bay View Inn, Widemouth Bay 01288 361273

Castle Restaurant, Bude 01288 350543

Leisure: 🎢 🎣 **Facilities:** 🏊 ⊙ 🅿 ✳ ⅄ 🔌 🖻 ⛽
Services: 🚐 🗑 🛢 🚿 🚙
Within 3 miles: ↨ 🎿 🎣 🚌 🖻 U

Notes: Pool table, netball & football posts, air hockey & table tennis

● Derwent Water

Cumbria

Think of Cumbria and you immediately picture a rumpled landscape of magical lakes and mountains and high green fells. For sheer natural beauty and grandeur, the English Lake District is hard to beat, and despite traffic congestion and high visitor numbers, this enchanting corner of the country manages to retain its unique individuality and sense of otherness.

Even on a glorious summer's day, you can still escape the 'madding crowd' and discover Lakeland's true heart and face. It is a fascinating place, characterised by ever changing moods and a timeless air of mystery. By applying a little effort and leaving the tourist hotspots and the busy roads far behind, you can reach and appreciate the Lake District that inspired William Wordsworth, Samuel Taylor Coleridge, Arthur Ransome and Robert Southey.

Derwentwater – the 'Queen of the English Lakes' is one of the most popular lakes in the region and certainly the widest. Shelley described it as 'smooth and dark as a plain of polished jet.' Windermere, to

the south, is the largest lake and the town of the same name is a popular tourist base; this is one of the few places in the Lake District that has a railway. Away from the lakes and the various watersports are miles of country for the adventurous to explore. The towering summits of Helvellyn, Scafell, Scafell Pike and Great Gable are the highest peaks in England.

Along the eastern edge of the 866-square mile National Park and handy for the West Coast main line and the M6 are several well-known towns – Kendal and Penrith. To the north is the ancient and historic city of Carlisle; once a Roman camp – its wall still runs north of the city – it was captured during the Jacobean rising of 1745. The cathedral dates back to the early 12th century.

The southern half of Cumbria is often bypassed and overlooked in favour of the more obvious attractions of the Lake District. Visitors who do journey beyond the park boundaries are usually impressed and inspired in equal measure by its wealth of delights. The Lune Valley, for example, remains as lovely as it was when Turner came here to paint, and the 19th-century writer John Ruskin described the view from 'The Brow,' a walk running behind Kirkby Lonsdale's parish church, as 'one of the loveliest scenes in England.'

▶

● Wast Water

Walking and Cycling

Walkers are spoilt for choice in Cumbria and the Lake District. Numerous paths and trails crisscross this rugged mountain landscape. That is part of its appeal – the chance to get up close and personal with Mother Nature. For something even more ambitious and adventurous, there are several long-distance trails.

The 70-mile (112km) Cumbria Way follows the valley floors rather than the mountain summits, while the 190-mile (305km) Coast to Coast has just about every kind of landscape and terrain imaginable. The route, pioneered by the well-known walker and writer, Alfred Wainwright, cuts across the Lake District, the Yorkshire Dales and the North York Moors, spanning the width of England between St Bees on the Cumbrian west coast, and Robin Hood's Bay on the North Yorkshire and Cleveland Heritage Coast.

The region also offers a walk with a difference and one which brings a true sense of drama and adventure. At the extreme southern end of Cumbria, in the reassuring company of official guide Cedric Robinson, MBE, you can cross the treacherous, deceptively beautiful sands of Morecambe Bay on foot. The bay, which is Britain's largest continuous intertidal area, is renowned for its quick sand and shifting channels. Many lives have been lost here over the years but in Cedric's expert hands, it is safe to cross.

The region is also popular with cyclists with lots of cycle hire outlets and plenty of routes to choose from. The 12-mile Wast Water to Santon Bridge cycle route passes England's deepest lake and is reputed to offer the finest view of the Lake District. It's quite a tough challenge and not suitable for under-11s. There are also waymarked bike trails in Grizedale Forest and Whinlatter Forest.

Festivals and Events

Cumbria offers something in the region of 500 festivals and events throughout the year.
The choice includes:

- Ambleside Daffodil and Spring Flower Festival in late March.
- Ulverston Walking Festival at the end of March and beginning of April.
- Model Railway and Transport Exhibition at Barrow-in-Furness, also in April.
- In July there is the Coniston Water Festival, famous for its Duck Race at Church Bridge; the Carlisle Festival of Nations; the Carlisle Summer Classical Music Festival at the cathedral.
- In August there is the 'Made in Cumbria Food and Craft Fair'.
- The Westmorland County Show takes place at Crooklands, near Kendal, in early September while the Dickensian Festival is staged in Ulverston in late November.
- There are winter lighting events along Hadrian's Wall in November and December; and Christmas at the Castle at Muncaster Castle, Ravenglass.

CUMBRIA

See Walk 2 & Cycle Ride 2 in the Walks & Cycle Rides section at the end of the guide

AMBLESIDE — Map 18 NY30

Places to visit

The Armitt Collection, Ambleside
015394 31212 www.armitt.com

Beatrix Potter Gallery (NT), Hawkshead
015394 36269 www.nationaltrust.org.uk

Great for kids: Lakes Aquarium, Lakeside
015395 30153 www.lakesaquarium.co.uk

**Regional Winner –
AA North West of England
Campsite of the Year 2011**

▶▶▶▶ 88% *Skelwith Fold Caravan Park* (NY355029)

LA22 0HX
☎ 015394 32277 📠 015394 34344
e-mail: info@skelwith.com
dir: *From Ambleside on A593 towards Coniston, left at Clappersgate onto B5286 (Hawkshead road). Site 1m on right*

🚐 🚙

Open Mar-15 Nov Last arrival dusk Last departure noon

In the grounds of a former mansion, this park is in a beautiful setting close to Lake Windermere. Touring areas are dotted in paddocks around the extensively wooded grounds, and the all-weather pitches are set close to the many facility buildings. The premium pitches are quite superb. There is a five-acre family recreation area, which has spectacular views of Loughrigg Fell. A 130 acre site with 150 touring pitches, 150 hardstandings and 300 statics.

AA Pubs & Restaurants nearby: Wateredge Inn, Ambleside 015394 32332

Drunken Duck Inn, Ambleside 015394 36347

Leisure: 🅰 ⛱
Facilities: 🍴 ☉ ☂ ✳ ⚿ ⏰ 🛄 🔥 🎾 🐕
Services: 🔌 🛢 🛁 🚿 T 🚮 ♻
Within 3 miles: ⚓ 🎣 🎪 ⛳ ◎ 🚴 🛄 🛒 U
Notes: Family recreation area. Wi-fi

▶▶▶ 72% Low Wray National Trust Campsite (NY372013)

Low Wray LA22 0JA
☎ 015394 63862 📠 015394 32684
e-mail: campsite.bookings@nationaltrust.org.uk
dir: *3m SW of Ambleside on A593 to Clappersgate, then B5286. Approx 1m turn left at Wray sign. Site less than 1m on left*

* 🚐 £12.50-£26 ⛺ £12.50-£34.50

Open wk before Etr-Oct Last arrival 19.00hrs (21:00hrs on Fri) Last departure 11.00hrs

Picturesquely set on the wooded shores of Lake Windermere, this site is a favourite with tenters and watersports enthusiasts. The well-maintained facilities are housed in wooden cabins, and tents can be pitched in wooded glades with lake views or open grassland, here there are wooden camping pods, and a mini-reservation of tipis and solar-heated bell tents. Off-road biking, walks and pubs serving food are all nearby. A 10 acre site with 140 touring pitches.

AA Pubs & Restaurants nearby: Wateredge Inn, Ambleside 015394 32332

Drunken Duck Inn, Ambleside 015394 36347

Kings Arms, Hawkshead 015394 36372

Leisure: 🅰
Facilities: 🍴 ☉ ✳ ⚿ ⏰ 🛄
Services: ◎
Within 3 miles: ⚓ 🎣 🎪 ⛳ ◎ 🚴 🛄
Notes: No groups of more than 4 unless a family group with children. Launching for sailing craft

APPLEBY-IN-WESTMORLAND

Places to visit

Brougham Castle, Brougham 01768 862488
www.english-heritage.org.uk

Acorn Bank Garden and Watermill (NT), Temple Sowerby 017683 61893
www.nationaltrust.org.uk

Great for kids: Wetheriggs Animal Rescue & Conservation Centre, Penrith 01768 866657
www.wetheriggsanimalrescue.co.uk

APPLEBY-IN-WESTMORLAND — Map 18 NY62

PREMIER PARK

AA CAMPING CARD SITE

▶▶▶▶▶ 91% Wild Rose Park (NY698165)

Ormside CA16 6EJ
☎ 017683 51077 📠 017683 52551
e-mail: reception@wildrose.co.uk
web: www.wildrose.co.uk
dir: *Signed on unclass road to Great Ormside, off B6260*

* 🚐 £18-£32.50 🚙 £18-£32.50 ⛺ £18-£32.50

Open all year (rs Nov-Mar shop & pool closed, restaurant rs) Last arrival 22.00hrs Last departure noon

Situated in the Eden Valley, this large family-run park has been carefully landscaped and offers superb facilities maintained to an extremely high standard, including four wooden wigwams for hire. There are several individual pitches, and extensive views from most areas of the park. Traditional stone walls and the planting of lots of indigenous trees help it to blend into the environment, and wildlife is actively encouraged. An 85 acre site with 226 touring pitches, 140 hardstandings and 273 statics.

AA Pubs & Restaurants nearby: Royal Oak, Appleby-in-Westmorland 017683 51463

Tufton Arms Hotel, Appleby-in-Westmorland 017683 51593

Leisure: ⛱ 🅰 🎱 🖥
Facilities: 🍴 ☉ 🅿 ✳ ⚿ ⏰ 🛄 🐕
Services: 🔌 🛢 🛁 🚿 T 🍴 🚮 ♻ ⬇
Within 3 miles: 🎣 ⛳ ◎ 🛄 🛒
Notes: No unaccompanied teenagers, no group bookings, no dangerous dogs. Tourist information, pitch & putt

see advert on opposite page

AYSIDE

Places to visit

Hill Top (NT), Near Sawrey 015394 36269
www.nationaltrust.org.uk

Levens Hall, Levens 015395 60321
www.levenshall.co.uk

Great for kids: Lakes Aquarium, Lakeside
015395 30153 www.lakesaquarium.co.uk

LEISURE: 🏊 Indoor swimming pool 🏊 Outdoor swimming pool 🅰 Children's playground ⛱ Tennis court 🎱 Games room 🖥 Separate TV room ⛳ 9/18 hole golf course ⚓ Boats for hire 🎬 Cinema 🎣 Fishing ◎ Mini golf 🚴 Watersports U Stables **FACILITIES:** 🛁 Bath 🍴 Shower ☉ Electric shaver 🅿 Hairdryer ✳ Ice Pack Facility ⚿ Disabled facilities ⏰ Public telephone 🛄 Shop on site or within 200yds 🛒 Mobile shop (calls at least 5 days a week) 🔥 BBQ area 🌲 Picnic area 🐕 Dog exercise area

AYSIDE
Map 18 SD38

▶▶▶ 74% Oak Head Caravan Park
(SD389839)

LA11 6JA
☎ **015395 31475**
web: www.oakheadcaravanpark.co.uk
dir: *M6 junct 36, A590 towards Newby Bridge, 14m. From A590 bypass follow signs for Ayside*

⛺ 🚐 ⛺

Open Mar-Oct Last arrival 22.00hrs Last departure noon

A pleasant terraced site with two separate areas - grass for tents and all gravel pitches for caravans and motorhomes. The site is enclosed within mature woodland and surrounded by hills. This site is located in a less busy area but convenient for all the Lake District attractions. A 3 acre site with 60 touring pitches, 30 hardstandings and 71 statics.

AA Pubs & Restaurants nearby: White Hart Inn, Bouth 01229 861229
Rogan & Company Bar & Restaurant, Cartmel 015395 35917

Facilities: 🅿 ⊙ ⌾ ✳ ⚸ 🕒
Services: 🔌 🗄 🍴 🛢 ⌀ 🚿
Within 3 miles: ⚹ 🏌 ⛵ 🔥 ∪
Notes: ⊛ No open fires

BARROW-IN-FURNESS
Map 18 SD26

Places to visit

The Dock Museum, Barrow-in-Furness
01229 876400 www.dockmuseum.org.uk

Furness Abbey, Barrow-in-Furness
01229 823420 www.english-heritage.org.uk

Great for kids: South Lakes Wild Animal Park, Dalton-in-Furness 01229 466086
www.wildanimalpark.co.uk

▶▶▶ 82% South End Caravan Park
(SD208628)

Walney Island LA14 3YQ
☎ **01229 472823 & 471556** 📠 **01229 472822**
e-mail: enquiries@secp.co.uk
web: www.walneyislandcaravanpark.co.uk
dir: *M6 junct 36, A590 to Barrow, follow signs for Walney Island. Cross bridge, turn left. Site 6m south*

⛺ 🚐

Open Mar-Oct (rs Mar-Etr & Oct pool closed) Last arrival 22.00hrs Last departure noon

A friendly family-owned and run park next to the sea and close to a nature reserve, on the southern end of Walney Island. It offers an extensive range of quality amenities including an adult lounge, and high standards of cleanliness and maintenance. A 7 acre site with 50 touring pitches, 20 hardstandings and 250 statics.

South End Caravan Park

Leisure: 🏊 ⌂ ♨ 🎣 ▫
Facilities: 🅿 ⊙ ✳ ⚸ 🐕 🚼
Services: 🔌 🗄 🍴 🛢 ⌀ 🛒 🎡
Within 3 miles: ⚹ 🏌 🐟 🔥 ∪
Notes: Bowling green, snooker table

BASSENTHWAITE LAKE

See map for locations of sites in the vicinity

SERVICES: 🔌 Electric hook up 🗄 Launderette 🍴 Licensed bar 🛢 Calor Gas ⌀ Camping Gaz 🚽 Toilet fluid 🍴 Café/Restaurant 🍔 Fast Food/Takeaway 🔋 Battery charging 🚼 Baby care ⚡ Motorvan service point **ABBREVIATIONS:** BH/bank hols-bank holidays Etr-Easter Whit-Whitsun dep-departure fr-from hrs-hours m-mile mdnt-midnight rdbt-roundabout rs-restricted service wk-week wknd-weekend ⊛ No credit cards ⊗ no dogs See page 7 for details of the AA Camping Card Scheme

BOOT
Map 18 NY10

Places to visit
Steam Yacht Gondola (NT), Coniston 015394 41288 www.nationaltrust.org.uk/gondola

The Ruskin Museum, Coniston 015394 41164 www.ruskinmuseum.com

Great for kids: Ravenglass & Eskdale Railway, Ravenglass 01229 717171 www.ravenglass-railway.co.uk

PREMIER PARK

►►►►► 82% Eskdale Camping & Caravanning Club Site (NY178011)

CA19 1TH
☎ 019467 23253 & 0845 130 7633
dir: Exit A595 at Gosforth or Holmbrook to Eskdale Green & then to Boot. Site on left towards Hardknott Pass after railway

🚐 £7.50-£9 🚐 £7.50-£9 ▲ £7.50-£9

Open Mar-14 Jan Last arrival 20.00hrs Last departure noon

Stunningly located in Eskdale, a feeling of peace and tranquillity prevails at this top quality Club site, with the sounds of running water and birdsong the only welcome distractions. Although mainly geared to campers, the facilities here are very impressive, with a smart amenities block, equipped with efficient modern facilities including an excellent fully-serviced wet room-style family room with power shower, and the surroundings of mountains, mature trees and shrubs create a wonderful 'back to nature' feeling. There's a nest of camping pods under the trees, with gravel access paths and barbeques, and a new adults-only backpackers' area. Expect great attention to detail and a high level of customer care. The park is only a quarter of a mile from Boot station on the Ravenglass/Eskdale railway ('Ratty'). An 8 acre site with 80 touring pitches.

AA Pubs & Restaurants nearby: Boot Inn, Boot 019467 23224

Brook House Inn, Boot 019467 23288

Leisure: ⚊
Facilities: ⚏✳❤◔🖨
Services: ◐🗑🔒⌂🍴↯
Notes: Site gates closed 23.00hrs-07.00hrs. Wi-fi

BOWNESS-ON-WINDERMERE
Sites are listed under Windermere

CARLISLE
Map 18 NY35

Places to visit
Carlisle Castle, Carlisle 01228 591992 www.english-heritage.org.uk

Tullie House Museum & Art Gallery, Carlisle 01228 618718 www.tulliehouse.co.uk

Great for kids: Trotters World of Animals, Bassenthwaite 017687 76239 www.trottersworld.com

►►► 85% Dandy Dinmont Caravan & Camping Park (NY399620)

Blackford CA6 4EA
☎ 01228 674611 📄 01228 674611
e-mail: dandydinmont@btopenworld.com
dir: *M6 junct 44, A7 N. Site 1.5m on right, after Blackford sign*

🚐 fr £13 🚐 fr £13 ▲ £11-£12

Open Mar-Oct Last arrival 21.00hrs Last departure 14.00hrs

A sheltered, rural site, screened on two sides by hedgerows and only one mile from the M6 and Carlisle. The grass pitches are immaculately kept, and there are some larger hardstandings for motor homes. This park attracts mainly adults; please note that cycling and ball games are not allowed. A 4 acre site with 47 touring pitches, 14 hardstandings and 15 statics.

Facilities: ⚏✳❤🖨
Services: ◐🗑🔒
Within 3 miles: ↯🖉◎🏧🗑↺
Notes: Dogs must be kept on leads at all times & exercised off site. Children's activities are restricted. Covered dishwashing area

►►► 84% Green Acres Caravan Park (NY416614)

High Knells, Houghton CA6 4JW
☎ 01228 675418
e-mail: info@caravanpark-cumbria.com
dir: *Exit M6/A74(M) junct 44, A689 towards Brampton for 1m. Left at Scaleby sign. Site 1m on left*

* 🚐 £13-£14 🚐 £13-£14 ▲ £10-£13

Open Apr-Oct Last arrival 21.00hrs Last departure noon

A small touring park in rural surroundings close to the M6 with distant views of the fells. A convenient stopover, this pretty park is run by keen, friendly owners who maintain high standards throughout. Seasonal touring pitches are available. A 3 acre site with 30 touring pitches, 30 hardstandings.

Facilities: ⚏☺✳❤
Services: ◐🗑
Within 3 miles: ↯🗑
Notes: Adults only. Open field for games such as football & kite flying

CARTMEL
Map 18 SD37

Places to visit
Holker Hall & Gardens, Holker 015395 58328 www.holker.co.uk

Hill Top (NT), Near Sawrey 015394 36269 www.nationaltrust.org.uk

Great for kids: Lakes Aquarium, Lakeside 015395 30153 www.lakesaquarium.co.uk

►►► 75% Greaves Farm Caravan Park (SD391823)

Field Broughton LA11 6HU
☎ 015395 36329 & 36587
dir: *M6 junct 36 onto A590 signed Barrow. Approx 1m before Newby Bridge, turn left at x-roads signed Cartmel/Staveley. Site 2m on left just before church*

🚐 £16-£18 🚐 £16-£18 ▲ £14-£16

Open Mar-Oct Last arrival 21.00hrs Last departure noon

A small family-owned park close to a working farm in a peaceful rural area. Motorhomes are parked in a paddock, and there is a large field for tents and caravans. This simple park is carefully maintained, offers electric pitches (6amp), and there is always a sparkle to the toilet facilities. Static holiday caravans for hire. A 3 acre site with 12 touring pitches and 20 statics.

AA Pubs & Restaurants nearby: Cavendish Arms, Cartmel 015395 36240

Rogan & Company Bar & Restaurant, Cartmel 015395 35917

Facilities: ⚓☉👤✕⏰🚿 **Services:** 🔌🛁

Within 3 miles: 🎣✕🅿🏊🎣U

Notes: ⊗ Separate chalet for dishwashing. Small freezer & fridge available

---

CROOKLANDS   Map 18 SD58

Places to visit

Levens Hall, Levens 015395 60321
www.levenshall.co.uk

RSPB Leighton Moss Nature Reserve, Silverdale 01524 701601 www.rspb.org.uk

Great for kids: South Lakes Wild Animal Park, Dalton-in-Furness 01229 466086
www.wildanimalpark.co.uk

▶▶▶ 83% Waters Edge Caravan Park

(SD533838)

LA7 7NN
☎ 015395 67708
e-mail: dennis@watersedgecaravanpark.co.uk
dir: *M6 junct 36 take A65 towards Kirkby Lonsdale, at 2nd rdbt follow signs for Crooklands/ Endmoor. Site 1m on right at Crooklands garage, just beyond 40mph limit*

* 🚐 £14.80-£21.40 🚐 £14.80-£21.40 ▲ £11-£25

Open Mar-14 Nov (rs Low season bar not always open on week days) Last arrival 22.00hrs Last departure noon

A peaceful, well-run park close to the M6, pleasantly bordered by streams and woodland. A Lakeland-style building houses a shop and bar, and the attractive toilet block is clean and modern. This is ideal either as a stopover or for longer stays. A 3 acre site with 26 touring pitches, 18 hardstandings and 20 statics.

Leisure: ▪🖥 **Facilities:** ⚓☉👤✕♿🍴🛁🚻

Services: 🔌🛁🍴🛢⊘⊤

Within 3 miles: 🅿🎣U

Notes: Dogs must be kept on a lead at all times

CUMWHITTON

Places to visit

Nenthead Mines, Alston 01434 382294
www.npht.com/nentheadmines

Lanercost Priory, Brampton 01697 73030
www.english-heritage.org.uk

CUMWHITTON   Map 18 NY55

▶▶▶ 69% Cairndale Caravan Park

(NY518523)

CA8 9BZ
☎ 01768 896280
dir: *Exit A69 at Warwick Bridge on unclass road through Great Corby to Cumwhitton, left at village sign, site 1m*

🚐 £9-£10 🚐 £9-£10

Open Mar-Oct Last arrival 22.00hrs

Lovely grass site set in the tranquil Eden Valley with good views to distant hills. The all-weather touring pitches have electricity, and are located close to the immaculately maintained toilet facilities. Static holiday caravans for hire. A 2 acre site with 5 touring pitches, 5 hardstandings and 15 statics.

AA Pubs & Restaurants nearby: String of Horses Inn, Faugh 01228 670297

Facilities: ⚓☉✕ **Services:** 🔌🛁🛢

Within 3 miles: 🎣✕🅿🏊 **Notes:** ⊗

DALSTON   Map 18 NY35

Places to visit

Carlisle Cathedral, Carlisle 01228 535169
www.carlislecathedral.org.uk

The Guildhall Museum, Carlisle 01228 625400
www.tulliehouse.co.uk

Great for kids: Trotters World of Animals, Bassenthwaite 017687 76239
www.trotlersworld.com

▶▶▶ 77% Dalston Hall Holiday Park

(NY378519)

Dalston Hall CA5 7JX
☎ 01228 710165
e-mail: info@dalstonhoildaypark.com
dir: *M6 junct 42 signed for Dalston. 2.5m SW of Carlisle, just off B5299*

* 🚐 fr £15 🚐 fr £15 ▲ £5-£12

Open Mar-Jan Last arrival 22.00hrs Last departure noon

A neat, well-maintained site on level grass in the grounds of an estate located between Carlisle and Dalston. All facilities are to a good standard, and ongoing improvements include new hardstanding pitches and extra hook-ups. Amenities include a 9-hole golf course, a bar and clubhouse serving breakfast and bar meals, and salmon and trout fly

---

fishing. A 5 acre site with 70 touring pitches, 50 hardstandings and 32 statics.

AA Pubs & Restaurants nearby: Oddfellows Arms, Caldbeck 016974 /8227

Leisure: ⚑ **Facilities:** ⚓☉👤✕🛁🚻🚻

Services: 🔌🛁🍴🛢⊘⊤🍴🍴💧⚡

Within 3 miles: 🎣🗓🅿🛁🎣

Notes: No commercial vans, gates closed 22.00hrs-07.00hrs. Water hook point to every pitch. Wi-fi

---

FLOOKBURGH   Map 18 SD37

Places to visit

Holker Hall & Gardens, Holker 015395 58328
www.holker.co.uk

Hill Top (NT), Near Sawrey 015394 36269
www.nationaltrust.org.uk

Great for kids: Lakes Aquarium, Lakeside 015395 30153 www.lakesaquarium.co.uk

---

76% Lakeland Leisure Park *(SD372743)*

Moor Ln LA11 7LT
☎ 01539 558556 🖨 01539 558559
dir: *On B5277 through Grange-over-Sands to Flookburgh. Left at village square, site 1m*

🚐 🚐 ▲

Open mid Mar-Oct (rs Mar-May & Sep-Oct reduced activities, outdoor pool closed) Last arrival anytime Last departure 10.00hrs

A complete leisure park with full range of activities and entertainments, making this flat, grassy site ideal for families. The touring area, which has a newly upgraded toilet block, is quietly situated away from the main amenities, but the swimming pools, all-weather bowling green and evening entertainment are just a short stroll away. A 105 acre site with 190 touring pitches and 800 statics.

AA Pubs & Restaurants nearby: Cavendish Arms, Cartmel 015395 36240

Rogan & Company Bar & Restaurant, Cartmel 015395 35917

Leisure: 🏊🏊⚑🎱

Facilities: ⚓☉✕♿🍴🛁🚻

Services: 🔌🛁🍴🛢⊤🍴🍴💧⚡

Within 3 miles: 🎣🗓🅿🛁🎣🎣U

Notes: No cars by caravans or tents. Family park. Wi-fi   *see advert on page 124*

GRANGE-OVER-SANDS

See Cartmel

GREAT LANGDALE   Map 18 NY20

Places to visit

Dove Cottage and The Wordsworth Museum, Grasmere 015394 35544
www.wordsworth.org.uk

Honister Slate Mine, Borrowdale 01768 777230
www.honister.com

Great for kids: Cars of the Stars Motor Museum, Keswick 017687 73757
www.carsofthestars.com

▶▶▶ **76% Great Langdale National Trust Campsite** (NY286059)

LA22 9JU
☎ 015394 63862
e-mail: campsite.bookings@nationaltrust.org.uk
web: www.ntlakescampsites.org.uk
dir: *From Ambleside, A593 to Skelwith Bridge, right onto B5343, approx 5m to New Dungeon Ghyll Hotel. Site on left just before hotel*

* ⚌ £12.50-£16 ▲ £12.50-£25

Open all year Last departure 11.00hrs

Nestling in a green valley, sheltered by mature trees and surrounded by stunning fell views, this site is an ideal base for campers, climbers and fell walkers. The large grass tent area has some gravel parking for cars, and there is a separate area for groups, and one for families with a children's play area. Attractive wooden cabins

house the toilets, a shop, and drying rooms, and there are wooden camping pods and two yurts for hire. A 9 acre site with 220 touring pitches.

AA Pubs & Restaurants nearby: New Dungeon Ghyll Hotel, Great Langdale 015394 37213

Britannia Inn, Elterwater 015394 37210

Purdy's at Langdale Hotel & Country Club 015394 37302

Leisure: ⚑

Facilities: ⚑☉✳⚑⚑⚑⚑

Services: ⚑⚑⚑

Within 3 miles: ⚑⚑

Notes: No noise between 23.00hrs-07.00hrs, no groups of 4 or more unless a family with children

HOLMROOK

Places to visit

The Beacon, Whitehaven 01946 592302
www.thebeacon-whitehaven.co.uk

The Rum Story, Whitehaven 01946 592933
www.rumstory.co.uk

Great for kids: Ravenglass & Eskdale Railway, Ravenglass 01229 717171
www.ravenglass-railway.co.uk

HOLMROOK   Map 18 SD09

AA CAMPING CARD SITE

▶▶▶ **73% Seven Acres Caravan Park** (NY078014)

CA19 1YD
☎ 01946 822777   📠 01946 824442
e-mail: reception@seacote.com
dir: *Off A595 between Holmrook & Gosforth*

* ⚌ £18-£21 ⚌ £18-£21 ▲ £10-£15

Open Mar-15 Jan Last arrival 21.00hrs Last departure 10.30hrs

This sheltered park is close to the quiet West Cumbrian coastal villages and beaches, and handy for Eskdale and Wasdale. There is a good choice of pitches, some with hedged bays for privacy, and some with coastal views. The park has a heated toilet block, and a children's play area, and there is plenty to do and see in the area. A 7 acre site with 37 touring pitches, 20 hardstandings and 16 statics.

AA Pubs & Restaurants nearby: Bower House Inn, Eskdale Green 019467 23244

Cumbrian Lodge, Seascale 019467 27309

Facilities: ⚑⚑☉⚑✳⚑⚑

Services: ⚑⚑⚑

Within 3 miles: ⚑⚑☉⚑⚑

LEISURE: 🏊 Indoor swimming pool   🏊 Outdoor swimming pool   ⚑ Children's playground   🎾 Tennis court   ♣ Games room   📺 Separate TV room   ⛳ 9/18 hole golf course
⛵ Boats for hire   🎬 Cinema   🎣 Fishing   ⛳ Mini golf   🏄 Watersports   ♻ Stables   **FACILITIES:** 🛁 Bath   🚿 Shower   ☉ Electric shaver   ✂ Hairdryer   ✳ Ice Pack Facility
♿ Disabled facilities   ☎ Public telephone   🛒 Shop on site or within 200yds   🚐 Mobile shop (calls at least 5 days a week)   🍖 BBQ area   🌲 Picnic area   🐕 Dog exercise area

KESWICK

Map 18 NY22

Places to visit

Cumberland Pencil Museum, Keswick
017687 73626 www.pencilmuseum.co.uk

Keswick Museum & Art Gallery,
Keswick 017687 73263
www.allerdale.gov.uk/keswick-museum

Great for kids: Mirehouse, Keswick
017687 72287 www.mirehouse.com

►►►► 94% Castlerigg Hall Caravan & Camping Park

GOLD

(NY282227)

Castlerigg Hall CA12 4TE
☎ 017687 74499 📄 017687 74499
e-mail: info@castlerigg.co.uk
dir: 1.5m SE of Keswick on A591, turn right at sign. Site 200mtrs on right past Heights Hotel

🚐 £22-£25 🚚 £22-£25 ▲ £15.50-£19.50

Open mid Mar-7 Nov Last arrival 21.00hrs Last departure 11.30hrs

Spectacular views over Derwentwater to the mountains beyond are among the many attractions at this lovely Lakeland park. Old farm buildings have been tastefully converted into excellent toilets with private washing and family bathroom, reception and a well-equipped shop, and there is a kitchen/dining area for campers, and a restaurant/takeaway. There is a superb toilet block and wooden camping pods in the tent field, and a further ten all-weather pitches have been created. An 8 acre site with 48 touring pitches, 48 hardstandings and 30 statics.

AA Pubs & Restaurants nearby: Kings Head, Keswick 017687 72393

Leisure: 🞐 **Facilities:** 🛠🐾☉📎☀🚻🕐📷🐕

Services: 🔌🔥🛢🕥📻🎬🍽🔋🚮♿

Within 3 miles: ⚓🚴🎯🎣📎◎🐟🎣🎢↺

Notes: Dogs must be kept on leads & not left unattended. Campers' kitchen, sitting room. Wi-fi

►►►► 77% Gill Head Farm Caravan & Camping Park (NY380269)

Troutbeck CA11 0ST
☎ 017687 79652 📄 017687 79130
e-mail: enquiries@gillheadfarm.co.uk
web: www.gillheadfarm.co.uk
dir: M6 junct 40 take A66, then A5091 towards Troutbeck. Right after 100yds, then right again

🚐 🚚 ▲

Open Apr-Oct Last arrival 22.30hrs Last departure noon

A family-run park on a working hill farm with lovely fell views. It has level touring pitches, and a log cabin dining room that is popular with families. Tent pitches are gently sloping in a separate field with glorious views towards Keswick. B&B accommodation is available at the farmhouse. A 5.5 acre site with 42 touring pitches, 21 hardstandings and 17 statics.

AA Pubs & Restaurants nearby: The George, Keswick 017687 72076

Leisure: 🞐🞐

Facilities: 🛠☉📎☀🕐📷🚻🕐🐕

Services: 🔌🛢🔋📎

Within 3 miles: ⚓🚴📎🐟🎣↺

Notes: 🞐 No fires

►►► 82% Castlerigg Farm Camping & Caravan Site (NY283225)

Castlerigg Farm CA12 4TE
☎ 017687 72479
e-mail: info@castleriggfarm.com
dir: From Keswick on A591 towards Windermere, turn right at top of hill at camping sign. Farm 2nd site on left

▲

Open Mar-Nov (rs At quiet times café & shop restricted hours) Last arrival 21.30hrs Last departure 11.30hrs

Nestling at the foot of Walla Crag, this tranquil fell-side park enjoys lake views, and is popular with families and couples seeking a quiet base for fell walking. The modern facilities include a shop, laundry and spotless toilet facilities, and a café in a converted barn. Castlerigg Stone Circle and the attractions of Keswick are nearby. A 3 acre site with 48 touring pitches.

AA Pubs & Restaurants nearby: Horse & Farrier Inn, Keswick 017687 79688

The Swinside Inn, Keswick 017687 78253

Facilities: 🛠☉📎☀🕐📷🚻

Services: 🔌🛢🔋🎬

Within 3 miles: ⚓🚴🎯🎣📎◎🐟🎣🎢↺

Notes: No noise after 22.30hrs, no fires on the ground, dogs must be kept on leads. Cycle storage. Wi-fi

►►► 77% Burns Farm Caravan Park

(NY307244)

St Johns in the Vale CA12 4RR
☎ 017687 79225 & 79112
e-mail: linda@burns-farm.co.uk
dir: Exit A66 signed Castlerigg Stone Circle/Youth Centre/Burns Farm. Site on right in 0.5m

🚐 🚚 ▲

Open Mar-4 Nov Last departure noon

Lovely views of Blencathra and Skiddaw can be enjoyed from this secluded park, set on a working farm which extends a warm welcome to families. This is a good choice for exploring the beautiful and interesting countryside. Food can be found in the pub at Threlkeld. A 2.5 acre site with 32 touring pitches.

AA Pubs & Restaurants nearby: The Farmers, Keswick 01768 773442

Facilities: 🛠☉☀♿🕐🚻

Services: 🔌🛢🔋🎬

Within 3 miles: ⚓🚴🎯🎣📎◎🐟🎣🎢↺

Notes: 🞐 Wi-fi

KIRKBY LONSDALE

Places to visit

Sizergh Castle & Garden (NT), Sizergh
015395 60951 www.nationaltrust.org.uk

Kendal Museum, Kendal 01539 815597
www.kendalmuseum.org.uk

Great for kids: Dales Countryside Museum & National Park Centre, Hawes 01969 666210
www.yorkshiredales.org.uk

KIRKBY LONSDALE
Map 18 SD67

PREMIER PARK

▶▶▶▶▶ 80% Woodclose Caravan Park *(SD618786)*

GOLD

High Casterton LA6 2SE
☎ 01524 271597 📄 01524 272301
e-mail: info@woodclosepark.com
web: www.woodclosepark.com
dir: *On A65, 0.25m after Kirkby Lonsdale towards Skipton, on left*

Open Mar-Oct Last arrival 21.00hrs Last departure noon

A peaceful park with excellent toilet facilities set in idyllic countryside in the beautiful Lune Valley. Ideal for those seeking quiet relaxation, and for visiting the Lakes and Dales, with the riverside walks at Devil's Bridge, and historic Kirkby Lonsdale both an easy walk from the park. You can hire one of the three wigwam cabins and Freeview TV is available via a booster cable from reception. An increased number of fully-serviced all weather pitches are planned for 2011. A 9 acre site with 29 touring pitches, 8 hardstandings and 54 statics.

AA Pubs & Restaurants nearby: Sun Inn, Kirkby Lonsdale 015242 71965

The Whoop Hall, Kirkby Lonsdale 015242 71284

Pheasant Inn, Kirkby Lonsdale 01524 271230

Leisure: 🅰
Facilities: 🏕⊙🄿✳⚹🕙🚻🛒
Services: 🚽🔲🛢⌗
Within 3 miles: ↨🕹🖥🔟🅾

Notes: No arrivals before 13.00hrs. Cycle hire, internet access, wigwams & crock boxes for hire. Wi-fi

---

▶▶▶▶ 79% New House Caravan Park *(SD628774)*

LA6 2HR
☎ 015242 71590
e-mail: colinpreece9@aol.com
dir: *1m SE of Kirkby Lonsdale on A65, turn right into site entrance 300yds past Whoop Hall Inn*

✱ 🚐 £16 🚌 £16

Open Mar-Oct Last arrival 20.00hrs

A very pleasant base in which to relax or tour the surrounding area, developed around a former farm. The excellent toilet facilities are purpose built, and there are good roads and hardstandings, all in a lovely rural setting. A 3 acre site with 50 touring pitches, 50 hardstandings.

AA Pubs & Restaurants nearby: Sun Inn, Kirkby Lonsdale 015242 71965

The Whoop Hall, Kirkby Lonsdale 015242 71284

Pheasant Inn, Kirkby Lonsdale 01524 271230

Facilities: 🏕⊙🄿✳⚹🕙🚻
Services: 🚽🔲🛢⌗🔲🛒⛟
Within 3 miles: ↨🕹🖥🔟

Notes: ⊛ No cycling. Wi-fi

LONGTOWN
Map 21 NY36

Places to visit
Carlisle Castle, Carlisle 01228 591992 www.english-heritage.org.uk

Tullie House Museum & Art Gallery, Carlisle 01228 618718 www.tulliehouse.co.uk

---

▶▶ 75% Camelot Caravan Park *(NY391666)*

CA6 5SZ
☎ 01228 791248
dir: *M6 junct 44/A7, site 5m N & 1m S of Longtown*

🚐 🚌 🅰

Open Mar-Oct Last arrival 22.00hrs Last departure noon

A very pleasant level grassy site in a wooded setting near the M6, with direct access from the A7, and simple, clean toilet facilities. The park is an ideal stopover site. A 1.5 acre site with 20 touring pitches and 2 statics.

Facilities: 🏕⊙✳🚻 **Services:** 🚽🛢
Within 3 miles: 🕹🖥🔟🅾 **Notes:** ⊛

MEALSGATE
Map 18 NY24

Places to visit
Jennings Brewery Tour and Shop, Cockermouth 0845 129 7190 www.jenningsbrewery.co.uk

Wordsworth House, Cockermouth 01900 820882 www.wordsworthhouse.org.uk

---

▶▶▶▶ 78% Larches Caravan Park *(NY205415)*

CA7 1LQ
☎ 016973 71379 & 71803 📄 016973 71782
dir: *On A595 (Carlisle to Cockermouth road)*

✱ 🚐 £15.90-£18.90 🚌 £15.90-£18.90
🅰 £13-£18.90

Open Mar-Oct (rs Early & late season) Last arrival 21.30hrs Last departure noon

This over 18s-only park is set in wooded rural surroundings on the fringe of the Lake District National Park. Touring units are spread out over two sections. The friendly family-run park offers well cared for facilities, and a small indoor swimming pool. A 20 acre site with 73 touring pitches, 30 hardstandings.

AA Pubs & Restaurants nearby: Oddfellows Arms, Caldbeck 016974 78227

Leisure: 🏊
Facilities: 🏕⊙🄿✳⚹🕙🖥🚻
Services: 🚽🔲🛢⌗🔲🛒
Within 3 miles: ↨🕹🔟🅾

Notes: Adults only. ⊛

MILNTHORPE

Places to visit
Levens Hall, Levens 015395 60321 www.levenshall.co.uk

RSPB Leighton Moss Nature Reserve, Silverdale 01524 701601 www.rspb.org.uk

Great for kids: Lakes Aquarium, Lakeside 015395 30153 www.lakesaquarium.co.uk

---

MILNTHORPE — Map 18 SD48

▶▶▶ 75% Hall More Caravan Park (SD502771)

Hale LA7 7BP
☎ 01524 781453 📠 01524 782243
e-mail: enquiries@pureleisure-holidays.co.uk
dir: M6 junct 35 onto A6 towards Milnthorpe for 4m. Left at Lakeland Wildlife Oasis, follow brown signs

🚐 🚑 Å

Open Mar-Jan Last arrival 22.00hrs Last departure 10.00hrs

A pleasant meadowland site with hardstanding and grass pitches in two neat and tidy hedged areas, simple, well maintained toilet facilities, and seven wooden cabins for hire. It is close to a farm and stables offering pony trekking, and there is trout fishing nearby. A 4 acre site with 44 touring pitches, 7 hardstandings and 60 statics.

AA Pubs & Restaurants nearby: The Wheatsheaf, Beetham 015395 62123

Facilities: 🅁 ⊙ 🅟 ✳ ⊙ 🖤 📌
Services: 🔌 🖴 🍴 🔋 🖉 🔧
Within 3 miles: ⌦ 🖉 🖤 🖴 U

PATTERDALE — Map 18 NY31

AA CAMPING CARD SITE

▶▶▶ 78% Sykeside Camping Park

(NY403119)

Brotherswater CA11 0NZ
☎ 017684 82239 📠 017684 82239
e-mail: info@sykeside.co.uk
dir: Direct access off A592 (Windermere to Ullswater road) at foot of Kirkstone Pass

* 🚐 £20-£25.50 🚑 £20-£25.50 Å £13-£19.50

Open all year Last arrival 22.30hrs Last departure 14.00hrs

A camper's delight, this family-run park is sited at the foot of Kirkstone Pass, under the 2,000ft Hartsop Dodd in a spectacular area with breathtaking views. The park has mainly grass pitches with a few hardstandings, an area with tipis for hire, and for those campers without a tent there is bunkhouse accommodation. There's a small campers' kitchen and the bar serves breakfast and bar meals. There is abundant wildlife. A 5 acre site with 86 touring pitches, 5 hardstandings.

AA Pubs & Restaurants nearby: Inn on the Lake, Glenridding 017684 82444

The Brackenrigg, Watermillock 017684 86206

Leisure: 🅰
Facilities: 🅁 ⊙ 🅟 ✳ ⊙ 🖤 📌 🖤 📌
Services: 🔌 🖴 🍴 🔋 🖉 🔧 T 🍽 📷 🔩
Within 3 miles: ⌦ 🖉 🖴 🖤 🖴
Notes: Laundry & drying room

PENRITH — Map 18 NY53

Places to visit

Dalemain Mansion & Historic Gardens, Dalemain 017684 86450 www.dalemain.com

Shap Abbey, Shap www.english-heritage.org.uk

Great for kids: The Rheged Centre, Penrith 01768 868000 www.rheged.com

▶▶▶▶ 84% Lowther Holiday Park (NY527265)

Eamont Bridge CA10 2JB
☎ 01768 863631 📠 01768 868126
e-mail: sales@lowther-holidaypark.co.uk
dir: 3m S of Penrith on A6

* 🚐 £22.50-£26 🚑 £22.50-£26 Å £22.50-£26

Open mid Mar-mid Nov Last arrival 22.00hrs Last departure 22.00hrs

A secluded natural woodland site with lovely riverside walks and glorious countryside surroundings. The park is home to a rare colony of red squirrels, and trout fishing is available on the two-mile stretch of the River Lowther which runs through it. A 50 acre site with 180 touring pitches, 50 hardstandings and 403 statics.

AA Pubs & Restaurants nearby: Yanwath Gate Inn, Yanwath 01768 862386

Queen's Head Inn, Tirril 01768 863219

Martindale Restaurant, Penrith 01768 868111

Leisure: 🅰
Facilities: 🚿 🅁 ⊙ 🅟 ✳ ⊙ ⅚ 🖤 📌
Services: 🔌 🖴 🍴 🔋 🖉 T 🍽 📷 🔩 🔧
Within 3 miles: ⌦ 🅗 🖉 ⊙ 🖴 🖤 🖴 U
Notes: Families only, no cats, rollerblades, skateboards or commercial vehicles

see advert on page 128

AA CAMPING CARD SITE

▶▶▶▶ 80% Flusco Wood

(NY345529)

Flusco CA11 0JB
☎ 017684 80020 📠 017684 80794
e-mail: info@fluscowood.co.uk
dir: From Penrith to Keswick on A66 turn right signed Flusco. Approx 800mtrs, up short incline to right. Site on left

* 🚐 £17.50-£20.50 🚑 £17.50-£20.50

Open all year (rs Etr-Nov tourers & motorhomes) Last arrival 20.00hrs Last departure noon

Flusco Wood is set in mixed woodland with outstanding views towards Blencathra and the fells around Keswick. It combines two distinct areas, one of which has been designed specifically for touring caravans in neat glades with hardstandings, all within close proximity of the excellent log cabin-style toilet facilities. A 24 acre site with 53 touring pitches, 53 hardstandings.

AA Pubs & Restaurants nearby: Yanwath Gate Inn, Yanwath 01768 862386

Queen's Head Inn, Tirril 01768 863219

Martindale Restaurant, Penrith 01768 868111

Leisure: 🅰
Facilities: 🅁 ⊙ 🅟 ✳ ⅚ ⊙ 🖤 📌 🖤
Services: 🔌 🖴 🔋 T
Notes: Quiet site, not suitable for large groups

To find out more about the AA Camping Card and reduced camping fees see page 7

All the campsites in this guide are inspected annually by a team of experienced inspectors

LOWTHER
HOLIDAY PARK

Lowther Holiday Park Limited
Eamont Bridge, Penrith, Cumbria CA10 2JB

Set in 50 acres of woodland and parkland, this river fronted park abounds with wildlife and easy reach of charming Lakeland villages and five miles from the best lake of them all, Ullswater.

The park is a mix of caravan holiday homes and timber lodges that are all for private use and available for sale as per our sales list on the web site. The touring area is served by two toilet/shower blocks and is a mix of hard standing and grass, all with electric hook up.

There is a well stocked mini market for all your needs and the Squirrel Inn will satisfy your thirst and hunger.

www.lowther-holidaypark.co.uk
Email sales@lowther-holidaypark.co.uk
Phone 01768 863631

Holiday Homes and lodges for sale
E-mail alastair@lowther-holidaypark.co.uk

PENRUDDOCK — Map 18 NY42

►►► 78% Beckses Caravan Park

(NY419278)

CA11 0RX
☎ 01768 483224 📄 01768 483006
dir: *M6 junct 40 onto A66 towards Keswick. Approx 6m at caravan park sign turn right onto B5288. Site on right in 0.25m*

🚐🚗⛺

Open Etr-Oct Last arrival 20.00hrs Last departure 11.00hrs

A small, pleasant site on sloping ground with level pitches and views of distant fells, on the edge of the National Park. This sheltered park is in a good location for touring the North Lakes. A 4 acre site with 23 touring pitches and 18 statics.

AA Pubs & Restaurants nearby: Queen's Head, Troutbeck 015394 32174

Leisure: 🅰
Facilities: 🅁⊙🄿✳🕔🕳
Services: 🄴🅐🚿🅃🔋
Within 3 miles: 🄿∪

PENTON — Map 21 NY47

NEW ►►► 74% Twin Willows

(NY449771)

The Beeches CA6 5QD
☎ 01228 577313 & 07850 713958
e-mail: davidson_b@btconnect.com
dir: *M6 junct 44/A7 Longtown, right onto Netherby St, 6m to Bridge Inn pub. Right then 1st left, site 300yds on right*

🚐 £20-£25 🚗 £20-£25 ⛺ £15-£20

Open all year Last arrival 22.00hrs Last departure 10.00hrs

Twin Willows is a newly created, spacious park in a rural location on a ridge overlooking the Scottish border. All facilities, including all-weather pitches, are brand new and are of a high quality. The park is suited to those who enjoy being away-

from-it-all yet at the same time being able to explore the rich history of this part of the Borders. The attractive city of Carlisle is 20 miles from the park. Ten seasonal touring pitches are available. A 3 acre site with 10 touring pitches, 10 hardstandings.

Facilities: 🅁⊙🄿✳🕔🕳🅃🔋🚻
Services: 🄴🅐🚿🅃🔋
Within 3 miles: 🄿🅑∪ **Notes:** 🚫

POOLEY BRIDGE — Map 18 NY42

AA CAMPING CARD SITE

83% Park Foot Caravan & Camping Park *(NY469235)*

Howtown Rd CA10 2NA
☎ 017684 86309 📄 017684 86041
e-mail: holidays@parkfootullswater.co.uk
web: www.parkfootullswater.co.uk
dir: *M6 junct 40, A66 towards Keswick, then A592 to Ullswater. Turn left for Pooley Bridge, right at church, right at x-roads signed Howtown*

* 🚐 £20-£34 🚗 £20-£34 ⛺ £13-£30

Open Mar-Oct (rs Mar-Apr, mid Sep-Oct clubhouse open wknds only) Last arrival 22.00hrs Last departure noon

A lively park with good outdoor sports facilities, and boats can be launched directly onto Lake Ullswater. The attractive mainly tenting park has many mature trees and lovely views across the lake. The Country Club bar and restaurant provides good meals, as well as discos, live music and entertainment in a glorious location. There are lodges and static caravans for holiday hire. An 18 acre site with 323 touring pitches and 131 statics.

AA Pubs & Restaurants nearby:
The Brackenrigg, Watermillock 017684 86206

Leisure: 🅰🌊🎣🖥
Facilities: 🅁⊙🄿✳🕔🕳🄴🚻
Services: 🄴🅑🚿🅐🅃🔋🍽🔋🍔🔌
Within 3 miles: 🚣🄿🚴🄴🅑∪

Notes: Families & couples only. Boat launch, pony trekking, pool table, table tennis, bike hire. Wi-fi

►►► 80% Waterfoot Caravan Park *(NY462246)*

CA11 0JF
☎ 017684 86302 📄 017684 86728
e-mail: enquiries@waterfootpark.co.uk
web: www.waterfootpark.co.uk
dir: *M6 junct 40, A66 for 1m, then A592 for 4m, site on right before lake. (NB do not leave A592 until site entrance Sat Nav not compatible)*

🚐🚗

Open Mar-14 Nov Last arrival dusk Last departure noon

A quality touring park with neat, hardstanding pitches in a grassy glade within the wooded grounds of an elegant Georgian mansion. Toilets facilities are clean and well maintained, and the lounge bar with a separate family room enjoys lake views, and there is a path to Ullswater. Aira Force waterfall, Dalemain House and Gardens and Pooley Bridge are all close by. Please note that there is no access via Dacre. A 22 acre site with 34 touring pitches, 30 hardstandings and 146 statics.

AA Pubs & Restaurants nearby: The Brackenrigg, Watermillock 017684 86206

Leisure: 🅰🎣
Facilities: 🅁⊙🄿✳🕔🕳🄴🚻
Services: 🄴🅑🍽🅐🅃🔋🔌
Within 3 miles: 🚣🄿🚴🄴🅑∪

Notes: Families only, no tents, no large RVS

SANTON BRIDGE
Map 18 NY10

Places to visit

Brantwood, Coniston 015394 41396
www.brantwood.org.uk

▶▶▶ 75% The Old Post Office
Campsite *(NY110016)*

CA19 1UY
☎ 01946 726286 & 01785 822866
e-mail: enquiries@theoldpostofficecampsite.co.uk
dir: *A595 to Holmrook and Santon Bridge, 2.5m*

🚐 fr £20 🚚 fr £18 ▲ fr £16.50

Open Mar-15 Nov Last departure noon

A family-run campsite in a delightful riverside
setting next to an attractive stone bridge, with
very pretty pitches. The enthusiastic owner is
steadily upgrading the park and has now
upgraded the toilets. Permits for salmon, sea and
brown trout fishing are available, and there is an
adjacent pub serving excellent meals. A 2.2 acre
site with 40 touring pitches, 5 hardstandings.

AA Pubs & Restaurants nearby: Bower House Inn,
Eskdale Green 019467 23244

Wasdale Head Inn, Wasdale Head 019467 26229

Leisure: 🎠 **Facilities:** 🚿⊙☂✳🚻🏧🐕
Services: 🔌🛢🛒 **Within 3 miles:** 🎣🏧U
Notes: 🐾

SILLOTH
Map 18 NY15

90% Stanwix Park Holiday
Centre *(NY108527)*

Greenrow CA7 4HH
☎ 016973 32666 📠 016973 32555
e-mail: enquiries@stanwix.com
dir: *1m SW on B5300. From A596 (Wigton
bypass), follow signs to Silloth on B5302. In
Silloth follow signs to site, approx 1m on B5300*

* 🚐 £20.40-£25.70 🚚 £20.40-£25.70
▲ £20.40-£25.70

Open all year (rs Nov-Feb (ex New Year) no
entertainment/shop closed) Last arrival
21.00hrs Last departure 11.00hrs

A large well-run family park within easy
reach of the Lake District. Attractively laid
out, with lots of amenities to ensure a lively
holiday, including a 4-lane automatic, 10-pin
bowling alley. Excellent touring areas with
hardstandings, one in a peaceful glade well
away from the main leisure complex, and
there's a campers' kitchen and clean, well
maintained toilet facilities. A 4 acre site with
121 touring pitches, 100 hardstandings and
212 statics.

AA Pubs & Restaurants nearby: New Inn,
Blencogo 016973 61091

Leisure: 🏊🏄🎠🎾🕹🖥
Facilities: 🛁🚿⊙☂✳🚻🕐🏧
Services: 🔌🛢🍴🛢⌀🚻🍽🚮🚼⊔
Within 3 miles: ⚓🎣◎🏧🛢

Notes: Families only. Amusement arcade, gym,
ten pin bowling, kitchen

see advert below

LEISURE: 🖝 Indoor swimming pool 🖝 Outdoor swimming pool 🎠 Children's playground 🎾 Tennis court 🕹 Games room 🖥 Separate TV room ⚑ 9/18 hole golf course 🚣 Boats for hire 🎬 Cinema 🎣 Fishing ◎ Mini golf 🏄 Watersports ♘ Stables **FACILITIES:** 🛁 Bath 🚿 Shower ⊙ Electric shaver ☂ Hairdryer ✳ Ice Pack Facility 🖝 Disabled facilities 🕐 Public telephone 🏧 Shop on site or within 200yds 🚐 Mobile shop (calls at least 5 days a week) 🍽 BBQ area 🌲 Picnic area 🐕 Dog exercise area

►►►► 86% Hylton Caravan Park

(NY113533)

Eden St CA7 4AY
☎ 016973 31707 & 32666 📠 016973 32555
e-mail: enquiries@stanwix.com
dir: On entering Silloth on B5302 follow signs Hylton Caravan Park, approx 0.5m on left, (end of Eden St)

* ⚑ £18-£22.10 ⇔ £18-£22.10 ▲ £18-£22.10

Open Mar-15 Nov Last arrival 21.00hrs Last departure 11.00hrs

A smart, modern touring park with excellent toilet facilities including several bathrooms. This high quality park is a sister site to Stanwix Park, which is just a mile away and offers all the amenities of a holiday centre, which are available to Hylton tourers. An 18 acre site with 90 touring pitches and 213 statics.

AA Pubs & Restaurants nearby: New Inn, Blencogo 016973 61091

Leisure: ⚗

Facilities: ⊪ ⏃ ⊙ 🌂 ⅍ ⊛ 🚽

Services: ⚑ 🗑 🖴 🧴 ⏚

Within 3 miles: ↧ 🖉 ◎ 🖴🖽

Notes: Families only Use of facilities at Stanwix Park Holiday Centre

TEBAY　　　　　　　Map 18 NY60

►►► 75% Westmorland Caravan Park *(NY609060)*

Orton CA10 3SB
☎ 01539 711322 📠 015396 24944
e-mail: caravans@westmorland.com
web: www.westmorland.com/caravan
dir: Exit M6 at Westmorland Services, 1m from junct 38. Site accessed through service area from either N'bound or S'bound carriageways. Follow park signs

* ⚑ £17-£20 ⇔ £17-£20

Open Mar-Oct Last arrival anytime Last departure noon

An ideal stopover site adjacent to the Tebay service station on the M6, and handy for touring the Lake District. The park is screened by high grass banks, bushes and trees, and is within walking distance of an excellent farm shop and restaurant. A 4 acre site with 70 touring pitches, 70 hardstandings and 7 statics.

AA Pubs & Restaurants nearby: Fat Lamb Country Inn, Ravenstonedale 015396 23242
Black Swan, Ravenstonedale 015396 23204

Facilities: ⏃ ⊙ 🌂 ⚹ ⅍ ⊛ 🖴 🚽

Services: ⚑ 🗑 🍴 🍺 T ⅋ ⚙

Within 3 miles: 🖉 🖴🖽

TROUTBECK (NEAR KESWICK)　　Map 18 NY32

PREMIER PARK

►►►►► 80% Troutbeck Camping and Caravanning Club Site *(NY365271)*

Hutton Moor End CA11 0SX
☎ 017687 79149
dir: M6 junct 40, take A66 towards Keswick. After 9.5m take sharp left for Wallthwaite

* ⚑ £22.40-£29.20 ⇔ £22.40-£29.20
▲ £22.40-£29.20

Open 4 Mar-12 Nov Last arrival 20.00hrs Last departure noon

Beautifully situated between Penrith and Keswick, this quiet, well managed Lakeland park offers two immaculate touring areas, one a sheltered paddock for caravans and motorhomes, with serviced hardstanding pitches, and a newly developed and maturing lower field, which has spacious hardstanding pitches and a superb and very popular small tenting area that enjoys stunning and extensive views of the surrounding fells. The toilet block is appointed to a very high standard and includes two family cubicles, and the log cabin reception/shop stocks local and organic produce. The enthusiastic franchisees offer high levels of customer care and are constantly improving the park, which is well-placed for visited Keswick, Ullswater and the north lakes. A 4.5 acre site with 54 touring pitches, 36 hardstandings and 20 statics.

Leisure: ⚗

Facilities: ⏃ ⊙ 🌂 ⚹ ⅍ 🖴 🖽

Services: ⚑ 🗑 🍴 ⅋ T 🍺 ⚙

Within 3 miles: ↧ ∪

Notes: Site gates closed 23.00hrs-07.00hrs. Dog walk. Wi-fi

ULVERSTON　　　　　Map 18 SD27

Places to visit

The Dock Museum, Barrow-in-Furness
01229 876400 www.dockmuseum.org.uk

Furness Abbey, Barrow-in-Furness
01229 823420 www.english-heritage.org.uk

Great for kids: South Lakes Wild Animal Park, Dalton-in-Furness 01229 466086
www.wildanimalpark.co.uk

►►►► 85% Bardsea Leisure Park

(SD292765)

Priory Rd LA12 9QE
☎ 01229 584712 📠 01229 580413
e-mail: reception@bardsealeisure.co.uk
dir: Off A5087

* ⚑ £13-£31.50 ⇔ £13-£31.50

Open all year Last arrival 21.00hrs Last departure 18.00hrs

An attractively landscaped former quarry, making a quiet and very sheltered site. Many of the generously-sized pitches offer all-weather full facilities, and a luxury toilet block provides plenty of fully-serviced cubicles. Set on the southern edge of the town, it is convenient for both the coast and the Lake District. Please note that this site no longer accepts tents. A 5 acre site with 83 touring pitches, 83 hardstandings and 83 statics.

AA Pubs & Restaurants nearby: Farmers Arms, Ulverston 01229 584469

Leisure: ⚗ **Facilities:** ⏃ ⊙ 🌂 ⚹ ⅍ ⊛ 🖴 🖽

Services: ⚑ 🗑 🍴 ⅋ T 🍺 ⚙

Within 3 miles: ↧ 🅗 🖉 🖴🖽 ∪

WASDALE HEAD　　　　Map 18 NY10

►►► 76% Wasdale Head National Trust Campsite *(NY183076)*

CA20 1EX
☎ 015394 63862
e-mail: campsite.bookings@nationaltrust.org.uk
web: www.ntlakescampsites.org.uk
dir: From A595(N) left at Gosforth; from A595(S) right at Holmrook for Santon Bridge, follow signs to Wasdale Head

* ⇔ £12.50-£16 ▲ £12.50-£25

Open all year (rs Wknds Nov-Feb shop open) Last departure 11.00hrs

Set in a remote and beautiful spot at Wasdale Head, under the stunning Scafell peaks at the

continued

WASDALE HEAD ***continued***

head of the deepest lake in England. Clean, well-kept facilities are set centrally amongst open grass pitches and trees, where camping pods are also located. The renowned Wasdale Head Inn is close by. A 5 acre site with 120 touring pitches.

AA Pubs & Restaurants nearby: Wasdale Head Inn, Wasdale Head 019467 26229

Facilities: 🚿⊙💨❄✆🛒 **Services:** 🚰🫧🔥🍃

Notes: No groups of more than 4 unless a family with children. Small shop, washing machine & dryer 3

WATERMILLOCK — Map 18 NY42

►►►► 85% The Quiet Site

(NY431236)

GOLD

Ullswater CA11 0LS

☎ **07768 727016**

e-mail: info@thequietsite.co.uk

dir: *M6 junct 40, A592 towards Ullswater. Right at lake junct, then right at Brackenrigg Hotel. Site 1.5m on right*

* 🚐 £12-£30 🚌 £12-£30 ⛺ £12-£30

Open all year (rs Low season park open wknds only) Last arrival 22.00hrs Last departure noon

A well-maintained site in a lovely, peaceful location, with good terraced pitches offering great fells views, very good, newly refurbished toilet facilities including family bathrooms, and a charming 'olde-worlde' bar. There are wooden camping pods for hire, a newly-refurbished self-catering stone cottage and seasonal touring pitches. A 10 acre site with 100 touring pitches, 60 hardstandings and 23 statics.

AA Pubs & Restaurants nearby: The Brackenrigg, Watermillock 017684 86206

Leisure: 🛝🎱📺

Facilities: 🛁🚿⊙💨❄♿✆🛒🧺🐕

Services: 🚰🫧🍷🔥🍃[T]🍽🍴

Within 3 miles: ⛵🎣🏄🛒🫧🐎

Notes: Quiet from 22.00hrs onwards. Pets corner, pool/darts (for adults), caravan storage. Wi-fi

►►► 82% Ullswater Caravan, Camping & Marine Park *(NY438232)*

High Longthwaite CA11 0LR

☎ **017684 86666** 📠 **017684 86095**

e-mail: info@uccmp.co.uk

web: www.ullswatercaravanpark.co.uk

dir: *M6 junct 40 take A592, W for Ullswater for 5m. Right alongside Ullswater for 2m, then right at phone box. Site 0.5m on right*

🚐🚌⛺

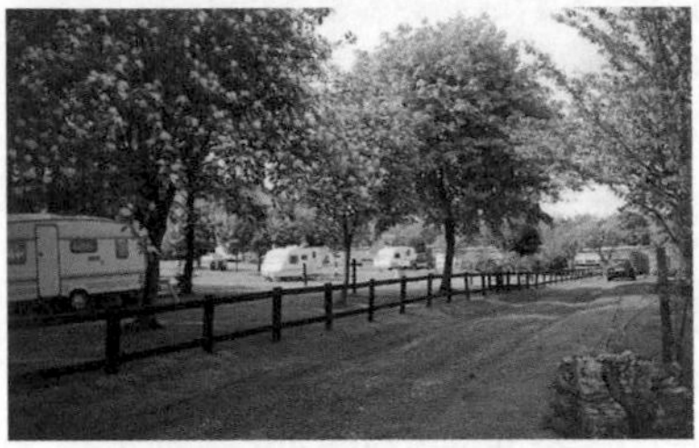

Open Mar-Nov (rs Low season bar open wknds only) Last arrival 21.00hrs Last departure noon

A pleasant rural site with its own nearby boat launching and marine storage facility, making it ideal for sailors. The family-owned and run park enjoys fell and lake views, and there is a bar, café and shop on site. Many of the pitches are fully serviced and there are two wooden cabins with barbecues. Please note that the Marine PArk is one mile from the camping area. A 12 acre site with 160 touring pitches, 58 hardstandings and 55 statics.

AA Pubs & Restaurants nearby: The Brackenrigg, Watermillock 017684 86206

Leisure: 🛝🎱📺 **Facilities:** 🚿⊙💨❄♿🛒🐕

Services: 🚰🫧🍷🔥🍃[T]🍽

Within 3 miles: ⛵🎣🏄🛒🐎

Notes: No open fires. Boat launching & moorings 1m. Wi-fi

AA CAMPING CARD SITE

►►► 79% Cove Caravan & Camping Park *(NY431236)*

Ullswater CA11 0LS

☎ **017684 86549** 📠 **017684 86549**

e-mail: info@cove-park.co.uk

dir: *M6 junct 40 take A592 for Ullswater. Right at lake junct, then right at Brackenrigg Hotel. Site 1.5m on left*

* 🚐 £18-£28 🚌 £18-£28 ⛺ £12-£25

Open Mar-Oct Last arrival 21.00hrs Last departure noon

A peaceful family site in an attractive and elevated position with extensive fell views and glimpses of Ullswater Lake. The ground is gently sloping grass, but there are also hardstandings for motorhomes and caravans, and simple toilet facilities are fresh, clean and well maintained by enthusiastic and welcoming wardens. A 3 acre site with 50 touring pitches, 17 hardstandings and 39 statics.

AA Pubs & Restaurants nearby: The Brackenrigg, Watermillock 017684 86206

Leisure: 🛝 **Facilities:** 🚿⊙💨❄♿🛒🧺🐕

Services: 🚰🫧🔥🍃

Within 3 miles: ⛵🎣🏄🛒🫧

Notes: 🚫 No open fires

see advert on oppposite page

WINDERMERE — Map 18 SD49

Places to visit

Holehird Gardens, Windermere 015394 46008 www.holehirdgardens.org.uk

Blackwell The Arts & Crafts House, Bowness-on-Windermere 015394 46139 www.blackwell.org.uk

Great for kids: Lake District Visitor Centre at Brockhole, Windermere 015394 46601 www.lake-district.gov.uk

►►►► 85% Fallbarrow Park

(SD401973)

GOLD

Rayrigg Rd LA23 3DL

☎ **015394 44422** 📠 **015394 88736**

e-mail: enquiries@southlakelandparks.co.uk

dir: *0.5m N of Windermere on A591. At mini-rdbt take road to Bowness Bay & the Lake. Site 1.3m on right*

🚐 £18.50-£30 🚌

Open Mar-mid Nov Last arrival 22.00hrs Last departure 10.00hrs

A park set in impressive surroundings just a few minutes' walk from Bowness on the shore of Lake Windermere. There is direct access to the lake through the park. The site has good, hedged, fully serviced pitches, quality toilet facilities, a deli and café serving meals using locally sourced produce, and 30 holiday hire statics. A 32 acre site with 38 touring pitches and 269 statics.

AA Pubs & Restaurants nearby: Eagle & Child Inn, Staveley 01539 821320

Jerichos at The Waverley, Windermere 015394 42522

LEISURE: 🏊 Indoor swimming pool 🌊 Outdoor swimming pool 🛝 Children's playground 🎾 Tennis court 🎱 Games room 📺 Separate TV room ⛳ 9/18 hole golf course ⛵ Boats for hire 🎬 Cinema 🎣 Fishing ◎ Mini golf 🏄 Watersports 🐎 Stables **FACILITIES:** 🛁 Bath 🚿 Shower ⊙ Electric shaver 💨 Hairdryer ❄ Ice Pack Facility ♿ Disabled facilities ✆ Public telephone 🛒 Shop on site or within 200yds 🚚 Mobile shop (calls at least 5 days a week) 🍖 BBQ area 🧺 Picnic area 🐕 Dog exercise area

Leisure: ⚕ ⚲ ▢

Facilities: ⌸ ⊙ ⌿ ✳ ◔ ⌂ ⋤

Services: ⊟ ▤ ⌸ ▮ ⌾ ◉ ⇩ ⇲

Within 3 miles: ⤙ ⤚ ⌘ ⌟ ⓞ ⤳ ⌂ ▣ ◑ ∪

Notes: ⊗ No tents, no cycling, no scooters. Boat launching. Wi-fi

---

►►►► 85% Park Cliffe Camping & Caravan Estate *(SD391912)*

Birks Rd, Tower Wood LA23 3PG
☎ 01539 531344   📠 01539 531971
e-mail: info@parkcliffe.co.uk
dir: M6 junct 36, A590. Right at Newby Bridge onto A592. 3.6m right into site. (NB due to difficult access from main road this is only advised direction for approaching site)

* 🚐 £24.50-£28 🚙 £24.50-£28 ▲ £19.50-£33

Open Mar-14 Nov (rs Wknds/school hols facilities open fully) Last arrival 22.00hrs Last departure noon

---

►►►► 78% Hill of Oaks & Blakeholme *(SD386899)*

LA12 8NR
☎ 015395 31578   📠 015395 30431
e-mail: enquiries@hillofoaks.co.uk
web: www.hillofoaks.co.uk
dir: M6 junct 36 onto A590 towards Barrow. At rdbt signed Bowness turn right onto A592. Site approx 3m on left

🚐 🚙

Open Mar-14 Nov Last departure noon

A lovely hillside park set in 25 secluded acres of fell land. The camping area is sloping and uneven in places, but well drained and sheltered

some pitches have spectacular views of Lake Windermere and the Langdales. The park is very well equipped for families, and there is an attractive bar lounge, and three static holiday caravans. A 25 acre site with 60 touring pitches, 60 hardstandings and 55 statics.

AA Pubs & Restaurants nearby: Eagle & Child Inn, Staveley 01539 821320

Jerichos at The Waverley, Windermere 015394 42522

Leisure: ⚕ ⚲

Facilities: ⇌ ⌸ ⊙ ⌿ ✳ ⓑ ◔ ⌂ ⋤ ⇥

Services: ⊟ ▤ ⌸ ▮ ⊘ ⌗ 🅃 ⌾ ◉ ⇩ ⇲

Within 3 miles: ⤙ ⤚ ⌘ ⌟ ⓞ ⤳ ⌂ ▣ ◑ ∪

Notes: No noise 22.30hrs-07.30hrs. Off-licence, playground. Wi-fi

---

A secluded, heavily wooded park on the shores of Lake Windermere. Pretty lakeside picnic areas, woodland walks and a play area make this a delightful park for families, with excellent serviced pitches, a licensed shop and a heated toilet block. Watersports include sailing and canoeing, with private jetties for boat launching. Combined toilet/wash-hand basin cubicles are planned for 2011. A 31 acre site with 43 touring pitches and 215 statics.

Hill of Oaks & Blakeholme

AA Pubs & Restaurants nearby: Eagle & Child Inn, Staveley 01539 821320

Jerichos at The Waverley, Windermere 015394 42522

Leisure: ⚕

Facilities: ⌸ ⊙ ⌿ ✳ ⓑ ◔ ⌂ ⋤ ⇥

Services: ⊟ ▤ ▮ 🅃 ⇲

Within 3 miles: ⤙ ⤚ ⌘ ⌟ ⓞ ⤳ ⌂ ▣ ◑ ∪

Derbyshire

Think of Derbyshire and you instantly think of the Peak District, the first of Britain's glorious and much-loved National Parks and still the most popular. This is where the rugged, sometimes inhospitable landscape of north England meets the gentler beauty of the Midland counties.

Within the National Park lies the upland country of the Dark Peak, shaped over the centuries by silt from the region's great rivers, and where gritstone outcrops act as monuments to the splendour and magic of geology. History was made in this corner of Derbyshire in 1932 when 500 ramblers spilled on to Kinder Scout to argue for the right of public access to the countryside.

Southern landscape

To the south is the White Peak, different in both character and appearance. This is a land of limestone, of deep wooded gorges, underground caves and high pastures crisscrossed by traditional drystone walls. There are dales, too – the most famous among them being Dovedale, the haunt of countless writers and artists over the years. Not surprisingly, Wordsworth and Tennyson sought inspiration here and much of it retains a rare, magical quality.

● Peak District, overlooking Kinder Reservoir

● Chatsworth House

Fine buildings

Look in and around the Peak District National Park and you'll find an impressive range of fine buildings. Calke Abbey (NT) is not an abbey at all but a magnificent baroque mansion dating back to the beginning of the 18th century.

World-famous Chatsworth, the palatial home of the Duke of Devonshire, is one of Derbyshire's most cherished visitor attractions. Work began on the original building in 1549 and the house has been substantially altered and enlarged over the years. The 1,000-acre park is the jewel in Chatsworth's crown; designed by 'Capability' Brown, it includes rare trees, a maze and the highest gravity-fed fountain in the world.

Towns and villages

As well as the county's palatial houses, there is an impressive array of quaint villages and historic towns. Chesterfield is known for the crooked spire of its church, while Buxton is acknowledged as one of the country's loveliest spa towns. Bakewell introduced the tradition of the Bakewell Pudding and the villagers of Tissington still maintain the old custom of well dressing on Ascension Day.

Walking and Cycling

Derbyshire is just the place for exhilarating walking where almost every person you pass is pleasant and friendly. The Peak District offers more demanding and adventurous routes, including the High Peak Trail, which runs from Hurdlow to Cromford, and the Monsal Trail, which extends from Haddon Park to Topley Pike. There is also the 26-mile (42km) Limestone Way from Matlock to Castleton and the 35-mile (56km) Gritstone Trail from Disley to Kidsgrove. Derbyshire's most famous walk is undoubtedly the Pennine Way, which starts at Edale in the Peak District and runs north for 251 miles (404km) to Kirk Yetholm in Scotland.

In common with other parts of the country, the Peak District includes a number of disused railway tracks that have been adapted to user-friendly cycle trails. Among many popular cycle trails are several family routes around Derwent reservoir, where 617 Squadron, 'The Dambusters', famously practised low-level flying during the Second World War.

Festivals and Events

Among many fixtures are the following:

- The Ashbourne Shrovetide Football on Shrove Tuesday and Ash Wednesday.
- The Bamford Sheep Dog Trials, the Chatsworth Horse Trials and the Castleton Garland Ceremony in May.
- In July there is the Bakewell Carnival, the Padley Pilgrimage and the Buxton Festival.
- September sees the Matlock Bath Illuminations and Firework Display and December the Castleton Christmas Lights and the Boxing Day Raft Race at Matlock Bath.

DERBYSHIRE

See Walk 3 & Cycle Ride 3 in the Walks & Cycle Rides Section at the end of the guide.

ASHBOURNE   Map 10 SK14

Places to visit

Kedleston Hall (NT), Kedleston Hall
01332 842191 www.nationaltrust.org.uk

Wirksworth Heritage Centre, Wirksworth
01629 825225 www.storyofwirksworth.co.uk

Great for kids: Crich Tramway Village, Crich
01773 854321 www.tramway.co.uk

►► 83% Carsington Fields Caravan Park (SK251493)

Millfields Ln, Nr Carsington Water DE6 3JS
☎ 01335 372872
dir: *From Belper towards Ashbourne on A517, turn right approx 0.25m past Hulland Ward into Dog Ln. 0.75m right at x-roads signed Carsington. Site on right approx 0.75m*

🚐🚌🏕

Open Etr-end Sep Last arrival 21.00hrs Last departure 18.00hrs

A very well presented and spacious park with a good toilet block, open views and a large fenced pond that attracts plenty of wildlife. The popular tourist attraction of Carsington Water is a short stroll away, with its variety of leisure facilities including fishing, sailing, windsurfing and children's play area. The park is also a good base for walkers. A 6 acre site with 10 touring pitches, 10 hardstandings.

AA Pubs & Restaurants nearby: Barley Mow Inn, Ashbourne 01335 370306

The Dining Room, Ashbourne 01335 300666

Facilities: 🏕⊙🔥🐎🕂

Services: 🚐

Within 3 miles: ⚓🎣🚣🖩🖩U

Notes: No large groups or group bookings. Wi-fi

BAKEWELL

Places to visit

Chatsworth, Nr Bakewell 01246 565300
www.chatsworth.org

Chesterfield Museum and Art Gallery, Chesterfield 01246 345727
www.visitchesterfield.info

BAKEWELL   Map 16 SK26

AA CAMPING CARD SITE

►►► 78% Greenhills Holiday Park (SK202693)

Crowhill Ln DE45 1PX
☎ 01629 813052 & 813467 📠 01629 815760
e-mail: info@greenhillsholidaypark.co.uk
web: www.greenhillsholidaypark.co.uk
dir: *1m NW of Bakewell on A6. Signed before Ashford-in-the-Water, 50yds along unclass road on right*

* 🚐 £30 🚌 £30 🏕 £30

Open Feb-Nov (rs Mar, Apr & Oct bar & shop closed) Last arrival 22.00hrs Last departure noon

A well-established park set in lovely countryside within the Peak District National Park. Many pitches enjoy uninterrupted views, and there is easy accessibility to all facilities. A clubhouse, shop and children's playground are popular features. An 8 acre site with 172 touring pitches, 30 hardstandings and 63 statics.

AA Pubs & Restaurants nearby: Bull's Head, Bakewell 01629 812931 Piedaniel's, Bakewell 01629 812687

Leisure: 🅰

Facilities: 🏕⊙🔥🐎🕂🔥🕐🖩🐎

Services: 🚐🖩🍴🛢🖊🖩🍽🚿

Within 3 miles: 🎣🖊🖩🖩U

Notes: Wi-fi

BUXTON   Map 16 SK07

Places to visit

Eyam Hall, Eyam 01433 631976
www.eyamhall.com

Poole's Cavern (Buxton Country Park), Buxton 01298 26978 www.poolescavern.co.uk

AA CAMPING CARD SITE

►►►► 83% Lime Tree Park (SK070725)

Dukes Dr SK17 9RP
☎ 01298 22988 📠 01298 22988
e-mail: info@limetreeparkbuxton.co.uk
dir: *1m S of Buxton, between A515 & A6*

* 🚐 £20-£23 🚌 £20 🏕 £10-£18

Open Mar-Oct Last arrival 21.00hrs Last departure noon

A most attractive and well-designed site, set on the side of a narrow valley in an elevated location, with separate, neatly landscaped areas for statics, tents, touring caravans and now motorhomes. There's good attention to detail throughout including the clean toilets with refurbished showers. Its backdrop of magnificent old railway viaduct and views over Buxton and the surrounding hills make this a sought-after destination. There are eight static caravans, a pine lodge and two apartments available for holiday lets. A 10.5 acre site with 106 touring pitches, 22 hardstandings and 43 statics.

AA Pubs & Restaurants nearby: Queen Anne Inn, Buxton 01298 871246

Leisure: 🅰🎱🖵

Facilities: 🏕⊙🔥🐎🕂🔥🕐🖩🐎

Services: 🚐🖩🛢🖊🖩🚿🚿

Within 3 miles: ⚓⊙🚣🖩🖩U

►►► 80% Clover Fields Touring Caravan Park (SK075704)

1 Heath View, Harpur Hill SK17 9PU
☎ 01298 78731
e-mail: cloverfields@tiscali.co.uk
dir: *A515, B5053, then immediately right. Site 0.5m on left*

🚐🚌🏕

Open all year Last departure 18.00hrs

A developing and spacious adults-only park with very good facilities, including an upmarket, timber chalet-style toilet block, just over a mile from the attractions of Buxton. All pitches are fully serviced including individual barbecues, and are set out on terraces, each with extensive views over the countryside. Swathes of natural meadow grasses and flowers cloak the terraces and surrounding fields. A 12 acre site with 25 touring pitches, 25 hardstandings.

AA Pubs & Restaurants nearby: Queen Anne Inn, Buxton 01298 871246

Facilities: 🏕⊙🔥🐎🕐🖩🐎🕂

Services: 🚐🖩🛢🖊🖩🚿

Within 3 miles: 🎣🖩🖩U

Notes: Adults only. No cars by tents. No commercial vehicles

AA CAMPING CARD SITE

►► 78% Beech Croft Farm (SK122720)

Beech Croft, Blackwell in the Peak SK17 9TQ
☎ 01298 85330
e-mail: mail@beechcroftfarm.net
dir: Off A6 midway between Buxton & Bakewell. Site signed

* ⚙ £14-£17 ⚙ £14-£17 ▲ £11-£13

Open mid Mar-Nov (rs Mar hook-up & water tap only, Elsan disposal) Last arrival 21.30hrs

A small terraced site in an attractive farm setting with lovely views. Hardstandings are provided for caravans, and there is a separate field for tents. An ideal site for those touring or walking in the Peak District. A 3 acre site with 30 touring pitches, 25 hardstandings.

AA Pubs & Restaurants nearby: Queen Anne Inn, Buxton 01298 871246

Facilities: ⚙⊙✷⚙

Services: ⚙⚙⚙⊤

Notes: Wi-fi

►► 71% Thornheyes Farm Campsite
(SK084761)

Thornheyes Farm, Longridge Ln, Peak Dale SK17 8AD
☎ 01298 26421
dir: 1.5m from Buxton on A6 turn E for Peak Dale. After 0.5m S at x-rds to site on right

* ⚙ fr £12 ⚙ fr £12 ▲ fr £12

Open Etr-Oct Last arrival 21.30hrs Last departure noon

A pleasant mainly-sloping farm site run by a friendly family team in the central Peak District. Toilet and other facilities are very simple but extremely clean. A 2 acre site with 10 touring pitches.

AA Pubs & Restaurants nearby: Queen Anne Inn, Buxton 01298 871246

Facilities: ⚙✷

Services: ⚙⚙⚙

Within 3 miles: ⚙⚙⚙⚙U

Notes: ⊘ Adults only. No ball games, dogs must be kept on leads at all times

---

►► 69% Coopers Camp & Caravan Park (SK121859)

Newfold Farm, Edale Village S33 7ZD
☎ 01433 670372
dir: From A6187 at Hope take minor road for 4m to Edale. Right onto unclassified road, site on left in 800yds opposite school

* ⚙ fr £11 ⚙ fr £11 ▲ fr £11

Open all year Last arrival 23.30hrs Last departure 15.00hrs

Rising grassland behind a working farm, divided by a wall into two fields, culminating in the 2,062ft Edale Moor. Facilities have been converted from original farm buildings, and include a café for backpackers, and a well-stocked shop. A 6 acre site with 135 touring pitches and 11 statics.

AA Pubs & Restaurants nearby: Cheshire Cheese Inn, Hope 01433 620381

Ye Olde Nag's Head, Castleton 01433 620248

The Peaks Inn, Castleton 01433 620247

Facilities: ⚙⊙⚙✷⊙⚙⚙

Services: ⚙⚙⚙⚙⚙

Within 3 miles: ⚙U

Notes: ⊘

►► 76% Pindale Farm Outdoor Centre (SK163825)

Pindale Rd S33 6RN
☎ 01433 620111   🖷 01433 620729
e-mail: pindalefarm@btconnect.com
dir: On A6187 in Hope, turn south between church & Woodrough pub. Centre 1m on left

* ▲ £10-£12

Open Mar-Oct

Set around a 13th-century farmhouse and a former lead mine pump house (now converted to a self-contained bunkhouse for up to 60 people), this simple, off-the-beaten track site is an ideal base for walking, climbing, caving and various outdoor pursuits. Around the farm are several deeply wooded closes available for tents, and old stone buildings that have been well converted to house modern toilet facilities. A 4 acre site with 60 touring pitches.

AA Pubs & Restaurants nearby: Cheshire Cheese Inn, Hope 01433 620381

Ye Olde Nag's Head, Castleton 01433 620248

The Peaks Inn, Castleton 01433 620247

Facilities: ⚙⊙✷

Services: ⚙⚙

Within 3 miles: ⚙U

Notes: ⊘ No anti-social behaviour, noise must be kept to minimum after 21.00hrs, no fires

---

MATLOCK
Map 16 SK35

▶▶▶▶ 80% Lickpenny Caravan Site
(SK339597)

Lickpenny Ln, Tansley DE4 5GF
☎ 01629 583040 📠 01629 583040
e-mail: lickpenny@btinternet.com
dir: *From Matlock take A615 towards Alfreton for 3m. Site signed to left, into Lickpenny Ln, right into site near end of road*

✱ ⬛ £15-£24 ⬛ £15-£24

Open all year Last arrival 20.00hrs Last departure noon

A picturesque site in the grounds of an old plant nursery with areas broken up and screened by a variety of shrubs, and spectacular views, which are best enjoyed from the upper terraced areas. Pitches, several fully serviced, are spacious, well screened and well marked, and facilities are to a very good standard. The bistro/coffee shop is popular with visitors. Seasonal touring pitches are available. A 16 acre site with 80 touring pitches, 80 hardstandings.

AA Pubs & Restaurants nearby: Red Lion, Matlock 01629 584888

Stones Restaurant, Matlock 01629 56061

Leisure: 🅰
Facilities: 🖮⊙℗⬛🕓⬛🚿🎿
Services: 🔌⬛🔒⬛🚽🖥⬛
Within 3 miles: ⬛🎣🖉⊚⬛⬛🎠
Notes: Child bath available

NEWHAVEN
Map 16 SK16

Places to visit
Middleton Top Engine House, Middleton 01629 823204
www.derbyshire.gov.uk/countryside

Peak District Mining Museum, Matlock Bath 01629 583834 www.peakmines.co.uk

▶▶▶ 77% Newhaven Caravan & Camping Park *(SK167602)*

SK17 0DT
☎ 01298 84300 📠 01332 726027
e-mail: newhavencaravanpark@btconnect.com
web: www.newhavencaravanpark.co.uk
dir: *Between Ashbourne & Buxton at A515 & A5012 junct*

✱ ⬛ £11.25-£16.50 ⬛ £11.25-£16.50
⬛ £11.25-£16.50

Open Mar-Oct Last arrival 21.00hrs

Pleasantly situated within the Peak District National Park, this park has mature trees screening the three touring areas. Very good toilet facilities, newly repainted and with updated showers, cater for touring vans and a large tent field, and there's a restaurant adjacent to the site. A 30 acre site with 125 touring pitches, 18 hardstandings and 73 statics.

AA Pubs & Restaurants nearby: Red Lion Inn, Birchover 01629 650363

Druid Inn, Birchover 01629 650302

Leisure: 🅰🎱
Facilities: 🖮⊙℗🎿🕓⬛🚿🎿🎿
Services: 🔌⬛🔒⬛🚽🖥⬛
Within 3 miles: 🎿🖉🎿⬛⬛🎠

RIPLEY
Map 16 SK35

Places to visit
Midland Railway Butterley, Ripley 01773 747674
www.midlandrailwaycentre.co.uk

Denby Pottery Visitor Centre, 01773 740799
www.denbyvisitorcentre.co.uk

▶▶▶▶ 77% Golden Valley Caravan & Camping Park

GOLD

(SK408513)

Coach Rd DE55 4ES
☎ 01773 513881 & 746786 📠 01773 746786
e-mail: enquiries@goldenvalleycaravanpark.co.uk
web: www.goldenvalleycaravanpark.co.uk
dir: *M1 junct 26, A610 to Codnor. Right at lights, then right onto Alfreton Rd. In 1m left onto Coach Rd, park on left. (NB it is advised that Sat Nav is ignored for last few miles & guide directions are followed)*

✱ ⬛ £20-£27 ⬛ £20-£25 ⬛ £15-£25

Open all year (rs Wknds only in low season bar/cafe open) Last arrival 21.00hrs Last departure noon

This superbly landscaped park is set within 30 acres of woodland in the Amber Valley. The fully-serviced pitches are set out in informal groups in clearings amongst the trees. The park has a cosy bar and bistro with outside patio, a fully stocked fishing lake, an innovative and well-equipped play area, an on-site jacuzzi and fully equipped fitness suite. There is also a wildlife pond and a nature trail. A 30 acre site with 45 touring pitches, 45 hardstandings and 1 static.

AA Pubs & Restaurants nearby: Moss Cottage Hotel, Ripley 01773 742555

Leisure: 🅰🎱⬛
Facilities: 🛁🖮⊙℗🎿🕓⬛🚿🎿🎿
Services: 🔌⬛🔒⬛🚽🖥🍴⬛⬛⬛
Within 3 miles: 🎿🎿🖉⬛⬛🎠

Notes: No open fires or disposable BBQs, no noise after 22.30hrs, no vehicles on grass. Gym, jacuzzi, zip slide, donkey rides, tractor train. Wi-fi

ROSLISTON
Map 10 SK21

Places to visit
Sudbury Hall and Museum of Childhood (NT), Sudbury 01283 585305
www.nationaltrust.org.uk

Ashby-de-la-Zouch Castle, Ashby-de-la-Zouch 01530 413343 www.english-heritage.org.uk

Great for kids: Conkers, Moira 01283 216633 www.visitconkers.com

▶▶ 83% Beehive Woodland Lakes
(SK249161)

DE12 8HZ
☎ 01283 763981 📠 01283 763981
e-mail: info@beehivefarm-woodlandlakes.co.uk
dir: *Turn S off A444 at Castle Gresley onto Mount Pleasant Rd, follow Rosliston signs for 3.5m through Linton to T-junct. Turn left signed Beehive Farms*

⬛ ⬛ ⬛

Open Mar-Nov Last arrival 20.00hrs Last departure 10.30hrs

A small, informal and rapidly developing caravan area secluded from an extensive woodland park in the heart of the National Forest National Park. Young children will enjoy the on-site animal farm and playground, whilst anglers will appreciate fishing the three lakes within the park, and bikes can be hired. The Honey Pot tearoom provides snacks and is open most days. A 2.5 acre site with 25 touring pitches, 12 hardstandings.

AA Pubs & Restaurants nearby: Horseshoe Inn, Tatenhill 01283 564913

Leisure:

Facilities:

Services:

Within 3 miles:

Notes: 3 coarse fishing lakes, takeaway food delivered to site

ROWSLEY — Map 16 SK26

Places to visit

Hardwick Hall (NT), Chesterfield 01246 850430 www.nationaltrust.org.uk/main/w-hardwickhall

Temple Mine, Matlock Bath 01629 583834 www.peakmines.co.uk

Great for kids: The Heights of Abraham Cable Cars, Caverns & Hilltop Park, Matlock Bath 01629 582365 www.heightsofabraham.com

►►► 73% Grouse & Claret *(SK258660)*

Station Rd DE4 2EB

01629 733233 01629 735194

e-mail: grouseandclaret.matlock@marstons.co.uk

dir: *M1 junct 29. Site on A6, 5m from Matlock & 3m from Bakewell*

Open all year Last arrival 20.00hrs Last departure noon

A well-designed, purpose-built park at the rear of an eating house on the A6 between Bakewell and Chatsworth, and adjacent to the New Peak Shopping Village. The park comprises a level grassy area running down to the river, and all pitches have hardstandings and electric hook-ups. A 2.5 acre site with 26 touring pitches, 26 hardstandings.

AA Pubs & Restaurants nearby: Grouse & Claret (on site)

Peacock at Rowsley 01629 733518

Leisure:

Facilities:

Services:

Within 3 miles:

Notes: No cars by tents. Dogs must be under strict control. Wi-fi

SHARDLOW — Map 11 SK43

Places to visit

Melbourne Hall & Gardens, Melbourne 01332 862502 www.melbournehall.com

The Silk Mill - Derby's Museum of Industry and History, Derby 01332 255308 www.derby.gov.uk/museums

►►► 69% Shardlow Marina Caravan Park *(SK444303)*

London Rd DE72 2GL

01332 792832 01332 792832

dir: *M1 junct 24a, take A50 Derby. Exit junct 1 at rdbt signed Shardlow. Site 1m on right*

* £12-£16 £12-£16 £12-£20

Open Mar-Jan (rs Office closed between 13.00-14.00hrs) Last arrival 17.00hrs Last departure noon

A large marina site with restaurant facilities, situated on the Trent/Merseyside Canal. Pitches are on grass surrounded by mature trees, and for the keen angler the site offers fishing within the marina. The attractive grass touring area overlooks the marina. Five seasonal touring pitches are available. A 25 acre site with 35 touring pitches, 10 hardstandings and 73 statics.

AA Pubs & Restaurants nearby: Old Crown Inn, Shardlow 01332 792392

Priest House on the River, Castle Donington 01332 810649

Facilities:

Services:

Within 3 miles:

Notes: Max 2 dogs per unit & max 1 child per unit

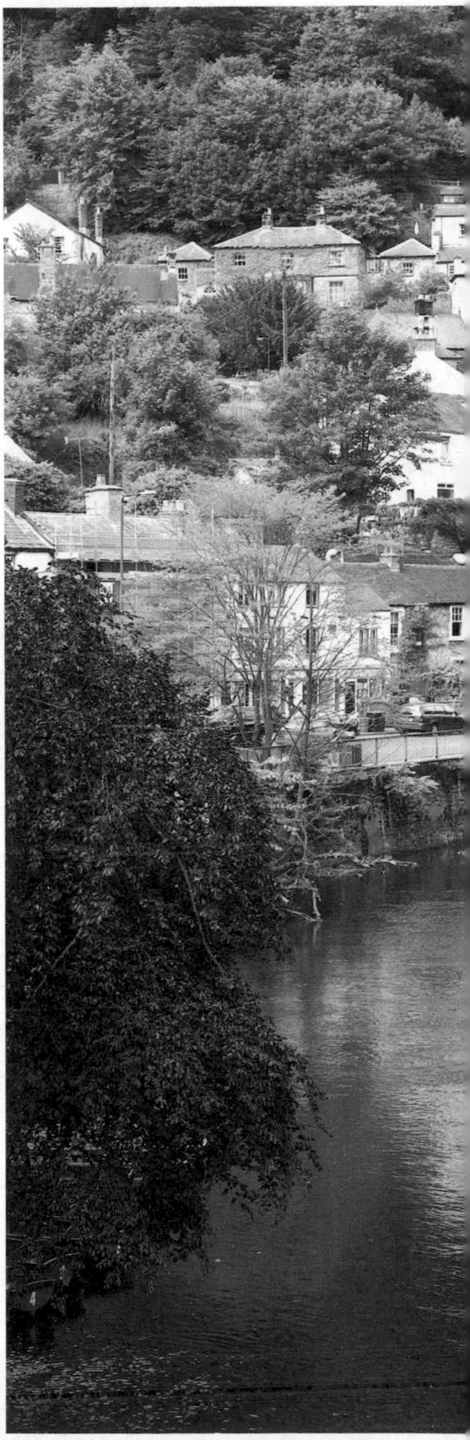

Kingsbridge estuary

Devon

With two magnificent coastlines, two historic cities and a world-famous national park, Devon sums up all that is best about the British landscape. For centuries it has been a fashionable and much-loved holiday destination – especially south Devon's glorious English Riviera.

The largest and most famous seaside resort on the southern coast is Torquay, created in the 19th century and still retaining a tangible air of Victorian charm mixed with a pleasing hint of the Mediterranean. Palm trees grace the bustling harbour where colourful yachts and cabin cruisers vie for space and the weather is pleasantly warm and sunny for long hours in the summer.

In and around Torquay

In recent years television and literature have helped to boost Torquay's holiday image. The hotel that was the inspiration for *Fawlty Towers*, starring the

Crockern Tor, near Two Bridges, Dartmoor

incomparable John Cleese, is located in the town, while Agatha Christie, the Queen of Crime, was born and raised in Torquay. A bust of her, unveiled in 1990 to mark the centenary of her birth, stands near the harbour and tourist information centre.

Greenway, Christie's splendid holiday home, now managed by the National Trust and open to the public, lies outside the town, overlooking a glorious sweep of the River Dart. By taking a nostalgic ride on the Paignton and Dartmouth Steam Railway you can wallow in the world of Poirot and Miss Marple, Christie's famous sleuths, passing close to the house and its glorious grounds.

Dartmoor

One of Agatha Christie's favourite Devon landscapes was Dartmoor. The National Park which contains it covers 365 square miles and includes vast moorland stretches, isolated granite tors and two summits exceeding 2,000 feet. This bleak and brooding landscape is the largest tract of open wilderness left in southern England. More than 100 years ago Sir Arthur Conan Doyle gave Dartmoor something of a boost when he set his classic and most famous Sherlock Holmes' story, *The Hound of the Baskervilles*, in this romantic and adventurous area.

Wheal Betsy Tin Mine, Dartmoor

South Devon

Plymouth lies in Devon's south-west corner and is a fine city and naval port with a wide range of visitor attractions, including the Plymouth Mayflower, overlooking Sutton Harbour, an interactive exhibition explaining the city's history. There is particular emphasis on the Spanish Armada and the voyage of the Pilgrim Fathers to America. The ancient city of Exeter can also occupy many hours of sightseeing. As well as the famous cathedral with its Norman twin towers, there is the Guildhall, which includes a Mayor's Parlour with five original Tudor windows, and the Quay House Visitor Centre where the history of the city is illustrated.

Walking and Cycling

The beauty of Devon, of course, is also appreciated on foot. The Dart Valley Trail offers views of the river at its best, while at Dartmouth you can join the South West Coast Path, renowned for its stunning views and breezy cliff-top walking. The trail heads along the coast to South Hams, a rural farming district where gently rolling hills sweep down to the majestic coastline. One of the area's great landmarks is Salcombe, a bustling fishing port with a magnificent natural harbour.

Another popular trail is the 103-mile (164km) Two Moors Way which begins at Ivybridge and crosses Dartmoor before passing through the delightful hidden landscape of R.D.Blackmoor's classic novel *Lorna Doone* to reach Exmoor, which straddles the Devon/Somerset border. On reaching picturesque Lynton and Lynmouth you can link up with the South Coast Path again to explore north Devon's stunning coastline. Don't miss the Valley of Rocks, an extraordinary collection of peaks and outcrops which add a wonderful sense of drama to this stretch of coast.

There are various leaflets and booklets on cycling available from tourist information centres throughout the county. The Dartmoor Way is a great introduction to the National Park with a choice of off-road cycle routes; there is also a range of cycle trails in the Exmoor National Park.

Festivals and Events

- The Ashburton Carnival takes place at Ashburton in early July and there is a Winter Carnival in early November.
- Chagford has an Agricultural and Flower show in August.
- During July, Honiton hosts a Fair with the Hot Pennies ceremony; in August there is an Agricultural Show and in October a carnival.
- Ilfracombe is the setting for the North Devon Festival and there is evening entertainment on the seafront throughout the summer. July & August sees the local Sea Fishing Festival.
- Plymouth Navy Days takes place on the August Bank Holiday weekend.

DEVON

ASHBURTON
Map 3 SX77

Places to visit

Compton Castle (NT), Compton 01803 661906
www.nationaltrust.org.uk/devoncornwall

Tuckers Maltings, Newton Abbot 01626 334734
www.tuckersmaltings.com

Great for kids: Prickly Ball Farm and Hedgehog Hospital, Newton Abbot 01626 362319
www.pricklyballfarm.com

►►►► 82% Parkers Farm Holiday Park (SX779713)

Higher Mead Farm TQ13 7LJ
☎ 01364 654869 📄 01364 654004
e-mail: parkersfarm@btconnect.com
dir: From Exeter on A38, take 2nd left after Plymouth 26m sign, signed Woodland-Denbury. From Plymouth on A38 take A383 Newton Abbot exit, turn right across bridge, rejoin A38, then as above

* 🚐 £9-£24 � £9-£24 ▲ £9-£24

Open Etr-end Oct (rs Wknds only bar/restaurant open out of season) Last arrival 22.00hrs Last departure 10.00hrs

A well-developed site terraced into rising ground. Part of a working farm, this park offers beautifully maintained, good quality facilities. Large family rooms with two shower cubicles, a large sink and a toilet are especially appreciated by families with small children. There are regular farm walks when all the family can meet and feed the various animals. A 25 acre site with 100 touring pitches, 20 hardstandings and 18 statics.

AA Pubs & Restaurants nearby: Dartbridge Inn, Buckfastleigh 01364 642214

Agaric, Ashburton 01364 654478

Leisure: 🅰 🔍 ⯅
Facilities: 🔦 ⊙ ✳ ⅗ ⓒ 🖀 🖩 🎋 🐾
Services: 🔌 🖥 🍴 🖴 🖉 🖽 🍽 🛒 🖕 ⯆
Within 3 miles: 🖉 🖥 🖩
Notes: Large field for dog walking

AA CAMPING CARD SITE

►►►► 82% River Dart Country Park
(SX734700)

Holne Park TQ13 7NP
☎ 01364 652511 📄 01364 652020
e-mail: info@riverdart.co.uk
web: www.riverdart.co.uk
dir: M5 junct 31, A38 towards Plymouth. In Ashburton at Peartree junct follow brown site signs. Site 1m on left. (NB Peartree junct is 2nd exit at Ashburton - do not exit at Linhay junct as narrow roads are unsuitable for caravans)

* 🚐 £16-£26.50 🚐 £16-£26.50 ▲ £16-£26.50

Open Apr-Sep (rs Low season café bar restricted opening hours) Last arrival 21.00hrs Last departure 11.00hrs

Set in 90 acres of magnificent parkland that was once part of a Victorian estate, with many specimen and exotic trees, and in spring a blaze of colour from the many azaleas and rhododendrons. There are numerous outdoor activities for all ages including abseiling, caving and canoeing, plus high quality, well-maintained facilities. The open moorland of Dartmoor is only a few minutes away. A 90 acre site with 170 touring pitches, 23 hardstandings.

AA Pubs & Restaurants nearby: Dartbridge Inn, Buckfastleigh 01364 642214

Agaric, Ashburton 01364 654478

Leisure: 🖉 🅰 🎱 🔍
Facilities: 🔦 🔯 ⊙ 🖉 ✳ ⅗ ⓒ 🖀 🎋 🐾
Services: 🔌 🖥 🍴 🖴 🖉 🖽 🍽 🛒 🖕
Within 3 miles: 🖉 🖉 🖥 🖩 ⓤ
Notes: Dogs to be kept on leads. Adventure playground, climbing, canoeing. Wi-fi

---

AXMINSTER

Places to visit

Branscombe - The Old Bakery, Manor Mill and Forge (NT), Branscombe 01752 346585
www.nationaltrust.org.uk

Allhallows Museum, Honiton 01404 44966
www.honitonmuseum.co.uk

Great for kids: Pecorama Pleasure Gardens, Beer 01297 21542 www.peco-uk.com

---

AXMINSTER
Map 4 SY29

►►►► 82% Andrewshayes Caravan Park (ST248088)

Dalwood EX13 7DY
☎ 01404 831225 📄 01404 831893
e-mail: info@andrewshayes.co.uk
web: www.andrewshayes.co.uk
dir: On A35, 3m from Axminster. Turn N at Taunton Cross signed Stockland/Dalwood. Site 150mtrs on right

* 🚐 £12-£26 🚐 £12-£26 ▲ £12-£26

Open Mar-Nov (rs Sep-Nov shop, bar hours limited, pool closed Sep-mid May) Last arrival 22.00hrs Last departure 11.00hrs

An attractive family park within easy reach of Lyme Regis, Seaton, Branscombe and Sidmouth in an ideal touring location. This popular park offers modern toilet facilities, an outdoor swimming pool and a quiet, cosy bar with a widescreen TV. A 12 acre site with 150 touring pitches, 105 hardstandings and 80 statics.

AA Pubs & Restaurants nearby: Tuckers Arms, Dalwood 01404 881342

Leisure: 🖉 🅰 🔍 ⯅
Facilities: 🔯 ⊙ 🖉 ✳ ⅗ ⓒ 🖀 🐾
Services: 🔌 🖥 🍴 🖴 🖉 🛒 🖕
Within 3 miles: 🖉 🖥 🖩
Notes: Dogs must be kept on leads

AA CAMPING CARD SITE

►►► 81% Hawkchurch Country Park
(SY344985)

Hawkchurch EX13 5UL
☎ 01297 678402
e-mail: enquiries@hawkchurchpark.co.uk
dir: From Axminster towards Charmouth on A35 left onto B3165. Left onto Wareham Rd, site on left, follow signs. (NB the lanes near Hawkchurch are narrow)

🚐 🚐 ▲

Open 15 Feb-4 Jan Last arrival 18.00hrs Last departure 10.00hrs

This peaceful park is set in mature woodlands right on the Devon and Dorset border, with easy access to the Jurassic Coast Heritage Site, Lyme Regis, Charmouth and West Bay. The site has huge potential, with hardstandings plus tent and rally fields. A 12 acre site with 369 touring pitches, 225 hardstandings.

AA Pubs & Restaurants nearby: Bottle Inn, Marshwood 01297 678254

Leisure: 🅐 🔍

Facilities: 🅝 ☉ ℱ ✻ Ꮣ ☺ 🄶 🄰 🖈

Services: 🕀 🖥 🍽 🔋 🔌 T 🍽 🔌

Within 3 miles: 🎣 🎢 🏇 🚣 🏰 🛒 U

Notes: Wi-fi

BERRYNARBOR

Places to visit

Arlington Court (NT), Arlington 01271 850296
www.nationaltrust.org.uk/
main/w-arlingtoncourt

Exmoor Zoological Park, Blackmoor Gate
01598 763352 www.exmoorzoo.co.uk

Great for kids: Combe Martin Wildlife Park & Dinosaur Park, Combe Martin 01271 882486
www.dinosaur-park.com

BERRYNARBOR   Map 3 SS54

AA CAMPING CARD SITE

▶▶▶ **84% Mill Park** *(SS559471)*

Mill Ln EX34 9SH
☎ **01271 882647**
e-mail: millparkdevon@btconnect.com
dir: *M5 junct 27 onto A361 towards Barnstaple. Right onto A399 towards Combe Martin. At Sawmills Inn take turn opposite for Berrynarbor*

* 🚐 £13-£21 🚏 £13-£21 ⛺ £4.50-£18

Open Mar-30 Oct (High season on-site facilities open) Last arrival 22.00hrs Last departure 10.00hrs

This family owned and run park is set in an attractive wooded valley with a stream running into a lake where coarse fishing is available. There is a quiet bar/restaurant with a family room. The park is two miles from Combe Martin and Ilfracombe and just a stroll across the road from the small harbour at Watermouth. A 23 acre site with 178 touring pitches, 20 hardstandings and 1 static.

AA Pubs & Restaurants nearby: George & Dragon, Ilfracombe 01271 863851

The Quay, Ilfracombe 01271 868090

Leisure: 🅐 🔍

Facilities: 🅝 ☉ ℱ ✻ Ꮣ ☺ 🄶 🄰 🖈

Services: 🕀 🖥 🍽 🔋 🔌 T 🍽 🔌

Within 3 miles: 🎢 🏇 🏰 🛒 U

Notes: No large groups. Wi-fi

BICKINGTON (NEAR ASHBURTON)   Map 3 SX87

Places to visit

Bradley Manor (NT),
Newton Abbot 01803 843235
www.nationaltrust.org.uk/devoncornwall

Great for kids: Living Coasts, Torquay
01803 202470 www.livingcoasts.org.uk

▶▶▶▶ **80% Lemonford Caravan Park** *(SX793723)*

TQ12 6JR
☎ **01626 821242**
e-mail: info@lemonford.co.uk
web: www.lemonford.co.uk
dir: *From Exeter on A38 take A382, then 3rd exit at rdbt, follow Bickington signs*

* 🚐 £10-£18.50 🚏 £10-£18.50 ⛺ £10-£16.50

Open all year Last arrival 22.00hrs Last dep 11.00hrs

Small, secluded and well-maintained park with a good mixture of attractively laid out pitches. The friendly owners pay a great deal of attention to detail, and the toilets in particular are kept spotlessly clean. This good touring base is only one mile from Dartmoor and ten miles from the seaside at Torbay. A 7 acre site with 82 touring pitches, 55 hardstandings and 44 statics.

AA Pubs & Restaurants nearby: Wild Goose Inn, Combeinteignhead 01626 872241

Agaric, Ashburton 01364 654478

Leisure: 🅐 **Facilities:** 🛁 🅝 ☉ ℱ ✻ Ꮣ 🄶 🄰 🖈

Services: 🕀 🖥 🔋 🔌 T 🍽 🚼 ♿

Within 3 miles: 🎢 🏰 🛒 U

Notes: Clothes drying area

see advert below

SERVICES: 🕀 Electric hook up 🖥 Launderette 🍽 Licensed bar 🔋 Calor Gas ⌀ Camping Gaz T Toilet fluid 🍽 Café/Restaurant 🔌 Fast Food/Takeaway 🔋 Battery charging
🚼 Baby care ♿ Motorvan service point   **ABBREVIATIONS:** BH/bank hols-bank holidays Etr-Easter Whit-Whitsun dep-departure fr-from hrs-hours m-mile mdnt-midnight
rdbt-roundabout rs-restricted service wk-week wknd-weekend 🚫 No credit cards 🚫 no dogs See page 7 for details of the AA Camping Card Scheme

BICKINGTON (NEAR ASHBURTON) *continued*

►►► 74% The Dartmoor Halfway Inn Caravan Park *(SX801721)*

TQ12 6JW
☎ 01626 821270 📠 01626 821820
e-mail: info@dartmoor-halfway-inn.co.uk
dir: *Direct access from A383, 1m from A38 (Exeter-Plymouth road)*

🚐 🚙

Open all year Last arrival 23.00hrs Last departure 10.00hrs

A well-developed park tucked away on the edge of Dartmoor, beside the River Lemon and adjacent to the Halfway Inn. The neat and compact park has a small toilet block with immaculate facilities, and pitches separated by mature shrubs. An extensive menu at the inn offers reasonably-priced food all day and evening. A 2 acre site with 25 touring pitches, 25 hardstandings.

AA Pubs & Restaurants nearby: Wild Goose Inn, Combeinteignhead 01626 872241

Agaric, Ashburton 01364 654478

Leisure: ⚄ **Facilities:** 🎣⊙&🚿⊙🚻🐎
Services: 🚐🔌🍽🍴♨🛒
Within 3 miles: ↓🎿🌳🎣🛒🍺∪

►►►► 85% *Hidden Valley Park* *(SS499408)*

West Down EX34 8NU
☎ 01271 813837
dir: *Direct access off A361, 8m from Barnstaple & 2m from Mullacott Cross*

🚐 🚙 Å

A delightful, well-appointed family site set in a wooded valley, with superb facilities and a café. The park is set in a very rural, natural location not far from the beautiful coastline around Ilfracombe. A 25 acre site with 115 touring pitches.

AA Pubs & Restaurants nearby: The Williams Arms, Braunton 01271 812360

►►► 78% Lobb Fields Caravan & Camping Park *(SS475378)*

Saunton Rd EX33 1HG
☎ 01271 812090 📠 01271 812090
e-mail: info@lobbfields.com
dir: *At x-rds in Braunton take B3231 to Croyde. Site signed on right leaving Braunton*

* 🚐 £9-£27 🚙 £9-£27 Å £9-£27

Open Mar-Oct Last arrival 22.00hrs Last departure 10.30hrs

A bright, tree-lined park with the gently-sloping grass pitches divided into two open areas and a camping field in August. Braunton is an easy walk away, and the golden beaches of Saunton Sands and Croyde are within easy reach. A 14 acre site with 180 touring pitches, 6 hardstandings.

AA Pubs & Restaurants nearby: The Williams Arms, Braunton 01271 812360

Leisure: ⚄

Facilities: 🎣⊙🍴🚿&⊙🐎

Services: 🚐🔌♨🍴♨🛒

Within 3 miles: ↓🎣🌊🛒🍺∪

Notes: No under 18s unless accompanied by an adult. Baby changing facilities, surfing, boards & wet suits for hire, wet suit washing areas

---

►►► 75% Bridestowe Caravan Park *(SX519893)*

EX20 4ER
☎ 01837 861261
e-mail: ali.young53@btinternet.com
dir: *Exit A30 at A386/Sourton Cross junct, follow B3278 signed Bridestowe, turn left in 3m. In village centre, left down unclass road for 0.5m*

* 🚐 £12.50-£17.50 🚙 £12.50-£17.50 Å £9.50-£14.50

Open Mar-Dec Last arrival 22.30hrs Last departure noon

A small, well-established park in a rural setting close to Dartmoor National Park. This mainly static park has a small, peaceful touring space, and there are many activities to enjoy in the area including fishing and riding. Part of the National Cycle Route 27 - the Devon coast to coast - passes close to this park. A 1 acre site with 13 touring pitches, 3 hardstandings and 40 statics.

AA Pubs & Restaurants nearby: Highwayman Inn, Sourton 01837 861243

Lewtrenchard Manor, Lewdown 01566 783222

Leisure: ⚄🎣 **Facilities:** 🎣⊙❄🍴
Services: 🚐🛢🍴🚽📶
Within 3 miles: 🎣🛒∪
Notes: 🐕

►►► 82% *Hedleywood Caravan & Camping Park* *(SS262013)*

EX22 7ED
☎ 01288 381404 📠 01288 382011
e-mail: alan@hedleywood.co.uk
dir: *From B3254 take Widemouth road (unclass) at the Devon/Cornwall border*

🚐 🚙 Å

Open all year (Main hols bar/restaurant open) Last arrival anytime Last departure anytime

---

Set in a very rural location about four miles from Bude, this relaxed family-owned site has a peaceful, easy-going atmosphere. Pitches are in separate paddocks, some with extensive views, and this wooded park is quite sheltered in the lower areas. A 16.5 acre site with 120 touring pitches, 14 hardstandings and 16 statics.

AA Pubs & Restaurants nearby: The Bickford Arms, Holsworthy 01409 221318

Bay View Inn, Widemouth Bay 01288 361273

Leisure: ⚑ ⚄ ▭

Facilities: ⛄ ⊙ ⌿ ✳ ⛴ ⓒ 🖫 🎋 ⌷ 🐾

Services: ⚡ 🖥 ⛽ 🍴 ⌀ Ⓣ 🍽 ⌷ ⛟ ⚓

Within 3 miles: ⚹ 🏋 ⌿ 🖥 🖫 ↻

Notes: ⊛ Dog kennels, nature trail/dog walk. Wi-fi

►► 89% Highfield House Camping & Caravanning (SS279035)

Holsworthy EX22 7EE
☎ **01288 381480**
e-mail: nikki@highfieldholidays.freeserve.co.uk
dir: *Exit A3072 at Red Post x-rds onto B3254 towards Launceston. Direct access just over Devon border on right*

⛺ 🚐 Å

Open all year

Set in a quiet and peaceful rural location, this park has extensive views over the valley to the sea at Bude, five miles away. The friendly young owners, with small children of their own, offer a relaxing holiday for families, with the simple facilities carefully looked after. A 4 acre site with 20 touring pitches and 4 statics.

AA Pubs & Restaurants nearby: The Bickford Arms, Holsworthy 01409 221318

Bay View Inn, Widemouth Bay 01288 361273

Facilities: ⛄ ⊙ ✳ ⛴ 🎋 🐾

Services: ⚡ 🖥 **Within 3 miles:** ⚹ ⌿ ◎ ⛟ 🖫

Notes: ⊛

BRIXHAM Map 3 SX95

Places to visit

Greenway (NT), Churston Ferrers 01803 842382
www.nationaltrust.org.uk/devoncornwall

Great for kids: Paignton Zoo Environmental Park, Paignton 0844 474 2222
www.paigntonzoo.org.uk

►►► 78% Galmpton Touring Park (SX885558)

Greenway Rd TQ5 0EP
☎ **01803 842066**
e-mail: galmptontouringpark@hotmail.com
dir: *Signed from A3022 (Torbay to Brixham road) at Churston*

* ⛺ £14.70-£19.50 🚐 £14.70-£19.50
Å £14.70-£19.50

Open Etr-Sep Last arrival 21.00hrs Last departure 11.00hrs

An excellent location on high ground overlooking the River Dart, with outstanding views of the creek and anchorage. Pitches are set on level terraces, and facilities are bright and clean. A 10 acre site with 120 touring pitches, 15 hardstandings.

AA Pubs & Restaurants nearby: Ship Inn, Kingswear 01803 752348

Quayside Hotel, Brixham 01803 855751

Leisure: ⚑

Facilities: ⛄ ⊙ ⌿ ✳ ⛴ ⓒ 🖫 🐾

Services: ⚡ 🖥 ⛽ ⌀ Ⓣ

Within 3 miles: ⚹ 🏋 ⌷ ⌿ ◎ ⛟ 🖫 🖥

Notes: Families & couples only, no dogs during peak season. Bathroom for under 5s (charges apply)

BRIXTON Map 3 SX55

Places to visit

Saltram (NT), Plympton 01752 333500
www.nationaltrust.org.uk

Plymouth City Museum & Art Gallery, Plymouth 01752 304774 www.plymouthmuseum.gov.uk

►► 72% *Brixton Caravan & Camping Park* (SX550520)

Venn Farm PL8 2AX
☎ **01752 880378** 📠 **01752 880378**
e-mail: info@vennfarm.co.uk
dir: *In Plymouth exit A38 at Marsh Mills rdbt onto A379, signed Modbury & Kingsbridge. Approx 4m right at mini-rdbt in village centre, right into private road, site signed*

⛺ 🚐 Å

Open 15 Mar-14 Oct (rs May, Jul-Aug warden on site) Last arrival 23.00hrs Last departure noon

A small park adjacent to a farm in the village, in a quiet rural area. The park is divided into two paddocks, and is just 100 yards from the village services. A 2 acre site with 43 touring pitches.

AA Pubs & Restaurants nearby: Rose & Crown, Yealmpton 01752 880223

Facilities: ⌷ ⛄ ⊙ ✳ 🖫 🐾

Services: ⚡ 🍽 ⛟

Within 3 miles: ⚹ 🏋 ⌷ ⌿ 🖫 🖥 ↻

BROADWOODWIDGER

Places to visit

Museum of Dartmoor Life, Okehampton 01837 52295
www.museumofdartmoorlife.eclipse.co.uk

Finch Foundry (NT), Sticklepath 01837 840046
www.nationaltrust.org.uk

BROADWOODWIDGER — Map 3 SX48

AA CAMPING CARD SITE

▶▶▶ 75% Roadford Lake (SX421900)

Lower Goodacre PL16 0JL
☎ 01409 211507 ▤ 01566 778503
e-mail: info@swlaketrust.org.uk
dir: Exit A30 between Okehampton & Launceston at Roadford Lake signs, across dam wall, watersports centre 0.25m on right

⌂ Å

Open Apr-Oct

Located right at the edge of Devon's largest inland water, this popular rural park is well screened by mature trees and shrubs. It boasts an excellent watersports school (sailing, windsurfing, rowing and kayaking) with hire and day launch facilities, and is an ideal location for fly fishing for brown trout. A 1.5 acre site with 30 touring pitches, 4 hardstandings.

AA Pubs & Restaurants nearby: Arundell Arms, Lifton 01566 784666

Facilities: ⌂⊙℘✳⚁🚿🖻
Services: ⌂🍽
Within 3 miles: ⚞℘⚟
Notes: Dogs must be kept on leads

BUCKFASTLEIGH

Places to visit
Buckfast Abbey, Buckfastleigh 01364 645500
www.buckfast.org.uk

Great for kids: Buckfast Butterfly Farm & Dartmoor Otter Sanctuary, Buckfastleigh 01364 642916 www.ottersandbutterflies.co.uk

BUCKFASTLEIGH — Map 3 SX76

▶ 86% Churchill Farm Campsite (SX743664)

TQ11 0EZ
☎ 01364 642844 & 07964 730578
e-mail: apedrick@btinternet.com
dir: From A38 Dart Bridge exit for Buckfastleigh/Totnes towards Buckfast Abbey. Pass Abbey entrance, proceed up hill, then left at x-roads to site opposite Holy Trinity church

* ⌂ £11-£14 ⌂ £11-£14 Å £11-£14

Open Etr-Sep Last arrival 22.00hrs

A working family farm in a relaxed and peaceful setting, with keen, friendly owners. Set on the hills above Buckfast Abbey, this attractive park is maintained to a good standard. The spacious pitches in the neatly trimmed paddock enjoy extensive country views, and the clean, simple toilet facilities have modern showers. A 3 acre site with 25 touring pitches.

AA Pubs & Restaurants nearby: Dartbridge Inn, Buckfastleigh 01364 642214

Facilities: ⌂⊙✳⚁ Services: ⌂🖻
Within 3 miles: 🖻
Notes: ⊜ Dogs must be kept on leads (working farm), no ball games. Within a Site of Special Scientific Interest

▶ 84% Beara Farm Caravan & Camping Site (SX751645)

Colston Rd TQ11 0LW
☎ 01364 642234
dir: From Exeter take Buckfastleigh exit at Dart Bridge, follow South Devon Steam Railway/Butterfly Farm signs. In 200mtrs 1st left to Old Totnes Rd, 0.5m right at brick cottages signed Beara Farm

* ⌂ fr £10 ⌂ fr £10 Å fr £10

Open all year

A very good farm park with clean unisex facilities and very keen and friendly owners. A well-trimmed camping field offers peace and quiet. Close to the River Dart and the Dart Valley steam railway line, within easy reach of sea and moors. Please note that the approach to the site is narrow, with passing places, and care needs to be taken. A 3.63 acre site with 30 touring pitches, 1 hardstanding.

AA Pubs & Restaurants nearby: Dartbridge Inn, Buckfastleigh 01364 642214

Facilities: ⌂⊙✳🚿🐾 Services: 🖻
Within 3 miles: ℘🖻 Notes: ⊜

BUDLEIGH SALTERTON — Map 3 SY08

Places to visit
Otterton Mill, Otterton 01392 568521
www.ottertonmill.com

Great for kids: Bicton Park Botanical Gardens, Bicton 01395 568465
www.bictongardens.co.uk

▶▶ 81% Pooh Cottage Holiday Park (SY053831)

Bear Ln EX9 7AQ
☎ 01395 442354
e-mail: info@poohcottage.co.uk
web: www.poohcottage.co.uk
dir: M5 junct 30 onto A376 towards Exmouth. Left onto B3179 towards Woodbury & Budleigh Salterton. Left into Knowle on B3178. Through village, at brow of hill take sharp left into Bear Lane (very narrow). Site 200yds

⌂ ⌂ Å

Open Apr-Oct Last arrival 20.00hrs Last departure 11.00hrs

A rural park with widespread views of the sea and surrounding peaceful countryside. Expect a friendly welcome to this attractive site, with its lovely play area, and easy access to plenty of walks, as well as the Buzzard Cycle Way. An 8 acre site with 52 touring pitches, 5 hardstandings and 3 statics.

AA Pubs & Restaurants nearby: The Blue Ball, Sidford 01395 514062

Salty Monk, Sidford 01395 513174

Leisure: 🎠
Facilities: ⌂⊙✳⚁🚿🐾
Services: ⌂🖻
Within 3 miles: ⚞⚞🎡℘◎⚟🖻🖻∪
Notes: Cycle track, dog walk

CHAPMANS WELL — Map 3 SX39

Places to visit

Launceston Steam Railway, Launceston 01566 775665 www.launcestonsr.co.uk

Launceston Castle, Launceston 01566 772365 www.english-heritage.org.uk

Great for kids: Tamar Otter & Wildlife Centre, Launceston 01566 785646 www.tamarotters.co.uk

AA CAMPING CARD SITE

▶▶▶ 84% *Chapmanswell Caravan Park (SX354931)*

St Giles-on-the-Heath PL15 9SG
☎ 01409 211382 📠 01409 211154
e-mail: george@chapmanswellcaravanpark.co.uk
web: www.chapmanswellcaravanpark.co.uk
dir: *Take A338 from Launceston towards Holsworthy, 6m. Site on left at Chapmans Well*

🚐 🚏 ▲

Open all year

Set on the borders of Devon and Cornwall in peaceful countryside, this park is just waiting to be discovered. It enjoys extensive views towards Dartmoor from level pitches, and is within easy driving distance of Launceston (7 miles) and the golden beaches at Bude (14 miles). A 10 acre site with 50 touring pitches, 35 hardstandings and 50 statics.

AA Pubs & Restaurants nearby: The Bickford Arms, Holsworthy 01409 221318

Blagdon Manor, Ashwater 01409 211224

Leisure: 🅰
Facilities: ↖⊙✳🕭◐🖢
Services: 🚐🖳🎪🔥📷⊤🍴🍴⛟⛺
Within 3 miles: ↧🎣🥾♨🐴🖢◐U
Notes: Wi-fi

CHUDLEIGH

Places to visit

Canonteign Falls, Chudleigh 01647 252434 www.canonteignfalls.com

Exeter's Underground Passages, Exeter 01392 665887 www.exeter.gov.uk/passages

Great for kids: Prickly Ball Farm and Hedgehog Hospital, Newton Abbot 01626 362319 www.pricklyballfarm.com

CHUDLEIGH — Map 3 SX87

▶▶▶ 80% Holmans Wood Holiday Park *(SX881812)*

Harcombe Cross TQ13 0DZ
☎ 01626 853785 📠 01626 853792
e-mail: enquiries@holmanswood.co.uk
dir: *Follow M5 past Exeter onto A38 after racecourse at top of Haldon Hill. Left at BP petrol station signed Chudleigh, site entrance on left of slip road*

* 🚐 £17-£22 🚏 £17-£22 ▲ £12-£16

Open mid Mar-end Oct Last arrival 22.00hrs Last departure 11.00hrs

A delightful small park set back from the A38 in a secluded wooded area, handy for touring Dartmoor National Park, and the lanes and beaches of South Devon. The facilities are bright and clean, and the grounds are attractively landscaped. A 12 acre site with 73 touring pitches, 71 hardstandings and 34 statics.

AA Pubs & Restaurants nearby: The Cridford Inn, Trusham 01626 853694

Leisure: 🅰 **Facilities:** ↖⊙✳✳🕭◐🖢
Services: 🚐🖳🔥🔥 **Within 3 miles:** 🖢◐U
Notes: No pets. Information room

COMBE MARTIN — Map 3 SS54

See also Berrynarbor

Places to visit

Arlington Court (NT), Arlington 01271 850296 www.nationaltrust.org.uk/main/w-arlingtoncourt

Great for kids: Combe Martin Wildlife Park & Dinosaur Park, Combe Martin 01271 882486 www.dinosaur-park.com

▶▶▶▶ 88% Stowford Farm Meadows *(SS560427)*

Berry Down EX34 0PW
☎ 01271 882476 📠 01271 883053
e-mail: enquiries@stowford.co.uk
dir: *M5 junct 27 onto A361 to Barnstaple. Take A39 from town centre towards Lynton, in 1m turn left onto B3230. Right at garage at Lynton Cross onto A3123, site 1.5m on right*

* 🚐 £8.40-£22 🚏 £9.40-£23 ▲ £8.40-£28

Open all year (rs Winter pool & bars closed) Last arrival 20.00hrs Last departure 10.00hrs

Very gently sloping, grassy, sheltered and south-facing site approached down a wide, well-kept driveway. This large farm park is set in 500 acres, and offers many quality amenities, including a large swimming pool, horse riding and crazy golf. A 60-acre wooded nature trail is an added attraction, as is the mini zoo with its stock of friendly animals. A 100 acre site with 700 touring pitches, 115 hardstandings.

AA Pubs & Restaurants nearby: George & Dragon, Ilfracombe 01271 863851

Fox & Goose, Parracombe 01598 763239

The Quay, Ilfracombe 01271 868090

Leisure: 🏊🅰🎣
Facilities: ↖↖⊙🅿✳🕭◐🖢🚻
Services: 🚐🖳🎪🔥📷⊤🍴⛟⛟
Within 3 miles: ↧🎣◐🖢◐U
Notes: Caravan accessory shop/storage/workshop/sales. Wi-fi

see advert on page 152

AA CAMPING CARD SITE

▶▶▶▶ 77% Newberry Valley Park *(SS576473)*

Woodlands EX34 0AT
☎ 01271 882334
e-mail: relax@newberryvalleypark.co.uk
dir: *M5 junct 27, A361 to North Aller rdbt. Right onto A399, through Combe Martin to sea. Left into site*

🚐 £14-£38 🚏 £9-£38 ▲ £9-£38

Open Mar-Sep Last arrival 20.45hrs Last departure 10.00hrs

A family owned and run touring park on the edge of Combe Martin, with all its amenities just a five-minute walk away. The park is set in a wooded valley with its own coarse fishing lake. The safe beaches of Newberry and Combe Martin are reached by a short footpath opposite the park entrance, where the South West Coast Path is located. A 20 acre site with 120 touring pitches.

AA Pubs & Restaurants nearby: George & Dragon, Ilfracombe 01271 863851

Fox & Goose, Parracombe 01598 763239

The Quay, Ilfracombe 01271 868090

Leisure: 🅰
Facilities: ↖🅿✳🕭◐🖢🚻🍴🚻
Services: 🚐🖳⊤⛟ **Within 3 miles:** ↧♨🥾🖢
Notes: No camp fires. Wi-fi

CROYDE
Map 3 SS43

Places to visit

Marwood Hill Gardens, Barnstaple
01271 342528 www.marwoodhillgarden.co.uk

Great for kids: Watermouth Castle & Family Theme Park, Ilfracombe 01271 863879
www.watermouthcastle.com

►►► 79% Bay View Farm Caravan & Camping Park (SS443388)

EX33 1PN
☎ 01271 890501
dir: *M5 junct 27 onto A361, through Barnstaple to Braunton, turn left onto B3231. Site at entry to Croyde village*

Open Mar-Oct Last arrival 21.30hrs Last departure 11.00hrs

A very busy and popular park close to surfing beaches and rock pools, with a public footpath leading directly to the sea. Set in a stunning location with views out over the Atlantic to Lundy Island, it is just a short stroll from Croyde. Facilities are clean and well maintained, and there is a fish and chip shop on site. Please note that no dogs are allowed. A 10 acre site with 70 touring pitches, 38 hardstandings and 3 statics.

AA Pubs & Restaurants nearby: The Williams Arms, Braunton 01271 812360

George & Dragon, Ilfracombe 01271 863851

The Quay, Ilfracombe 01271 868090

Leisure: 🅰

Facilities: ↖⊙♥☀☕♨🔥

Services: ⊕🔲🔒🚿🚽🍽️🔋🚰

Within 3 miles: ⬇🎣🏌⊙🚴🍺🔥🏇U

Notes: ⊕⊗

CROYDE BAY
Map 3 SS43

84% Ruda Holiday Park (SS438397)
GOLD

EX33 1NY
☎ 0844 335 3756 ▤ 01271 890656
e-mail: touringandcamping@parkdeanholidays.com
web: www.parkdeantouring.com
dir: *M5 junct 27, A361 to Braunton. Left at main lights, follow Croyde signs*

🚐 £17.50-£45 🚙 £17.50-£45 ⛺ £14.50-£42

Open mid Mar-Oct Last arrival 21.00hrs Last departure 10.00hrs

A spacious, well-managed park with its own glorious award-winning sandy beach, a surfers' paradise. Set in well-landscaped grounds, and with a full leisure programme plus daytime and evening entertainment for all the family. Cascades tropical adventure pool and an entertainment lounge are very popular features. A 220 acre site with 306 touring pitches and 289 statics.

AA Pubs & Restaurants nearby: The Williams Arms, Braunton 01271 812360

George & Dragon, Ilfracombe 01271 863851

The Quay, Ilfracombe 01271 868090

Leisure: 🏊🅰🎿🎯🖥

Facilities: ↖↖⊙♥☀♨🔥🍴

Services: ⊕🔲🔦🔒🚿🍽️🔋🚰

Within 3 miles: 🎣🚴🔥U

Notes: No pets. Family entertainment, children's clubs, Coast Bar & Kitchen. Wi-fi

see advert in preliminary section

CULLOMPTON

See Kentisbeare

DARTMOUTH
Map 3 SX85

Places to visit

Dartmouth Castle, Dartmouth 01803 833588
www.english-heritage.org.uk

Coleton Fishacre House & Garden (NT), Kingswear 01803 752466
www.nationaltrust.org.uk

Great for kids: Woodlands Family Theme Park, Dartmouth 01803 712598
www.woodlandspark.com

AA CAMPING CARD SITE

►►►► 92% Woodlands Grove Caravan & Camping Park (SX813522)
Best of British

Blackawton TQ9 7DQ
☎ 01803 712598 ▤ 01803 712680
e-mail: holiday@woodlandsgrove.com
web: www.woodlands-caravanpark.com
dir: *4m from Dartmouth on A3122. From A38 take turn for Totnes & follow brown tourist signs*

* 🚐 £13.50-£21 🚙 £13.50-£21 ⛺ £13.50-£21

Open Etr-7 Nov Last departure 11.00hrs

A quality caravan or tent park with excellent facilities, spacious pitches and good attention to detail, all set in an extensive woodland environment with a terraced grass camping area. Free entry to the adjoining Woodlands Theme Park makes an excellent package holiday for families but also good for adults travelling without children seeking a low season break. Wi-fi is now available. A 16 acre site with 350 touring pitches, 50 hardstandings.

AA Pubs & Restaurants nearby: The Seahorse, Dartmouth 01803 835147

Jan and Freddies Brasserie, Dartmouth 01803 832491

Leisure: 🅰🎯🖥

Facilities: ↖↖⊙♥☀♨🔥🍴🏇

Services: ⊕🔲🔒🚿🚽🍽️🔋🚰

Within 3 miles: ⬇⊙🔥🔥

Notes: Falconry centre, woodland walk, free entry to theme park. Wi-fi

see advert on page 154

DARTMOUTH *continued*

►►►► 81% Little Cotton Caravan Park *(SX858508)*

Little Cotton TQ6 0LB
☎ 01803 832558 📠 01803 834887
e-mail: enquiries@littlecotton.co.uk
dir: *Exit A38 at Buckfastleigh, A384 to Totnes, A381 to Halwell, then A3122 Dartmouth Rd, site on right at entrance to town*

* 🚐 £14.75-£20 🚙 £14.75-£20 ▲ £14.75-£20

Open 15 Mar-Oct Last arrival 22.00hrs Last departure 11.00hrs

A very good grassy touring park set on high ground above Dartmouth, with quality facilities, and park-and-ride to the town from the gate. The toilet blocks are heated and superbly maintained. The friendly owners are happy to offer advice on touring in this pretty area. Excellent base for visiting Totnes, Slapton Sands, and Kingsbridge. A 7.5 acre site with 95 touring pitches, 42 hardstandings.

AA Pubs & Restaurants nearby: The Seahorse, Dartmouth 01803 835147

Jan and Freddies Brasserie, Dartmouth 01803 832491

Facilities: 🅿️ ⊙ 🄿 ✳ ⚡ ⚙ ☖ 🍴 🐾
Services: 🔌 🄶 🄰 🄰 🌀 🅃 ⚡
Within 3 miles: ⚓ 🎣 🅗 🅟 ⊚ ⚓ ☖ 🄶

DAWLISH Map 3 SX97

AA CAMPING CARD SITE

 ## 82% Lady's Mile Holiday Park *(SX968784)*

EX7 0LX
☎ 0845 026 7252 📠 01626 888689
e-mail: info@ladysmile.co.uk
dir: *1m N of Dawlish on A379*

🚐 🚙 ▲

Open 17 Mar-27 Oct Last arrival 20.00hrs Last departure 11.00hrs

A holiday site with a wide variety of touring pitches, including some new, fully serviced pitches. There are plenty of activities for everyone, including two swimming pools with waterslides, a large adventure playground, 9-hole golf course, and a bar with entertainment in high season all add to the enjoyment of a stay here. Facilities are kept very clean, and the surrounding beaches are easily accessed. Holiday homes are also available. A 16 acre site with 243 touring pitches, 30 hardstandings and 43 statics.

AA Pubs & Restaurants nearby: The Elizabethan Inn, Luton 01626 775425

Anchor Inn, Cockwood 01626 890203

Leisure: 🏊 🏊 ⚑ 🎣
Facilities: 🚿 🅿️ ⊙ ⚡ ☖ 🍴 🄷 🐾
Services: 🔌 🄶 🄴 🄰 🄰 🅃 🍴 🄰 🍴
Within 3 miles: ⚓ 🎣 🅗 🅟 ⊚ ⚓ ☖ 🄶 ⛳
Notes: Wi-fi *see advert on page 156*

78% Peppermint Park *(SX978788)*

Warren Rd EX7 0PQ
☎ 01626 863436 📠 01626 866482
e-mail: peppermint@parkholidaysuk.com
web: www.parkholidaysuk.com
dir: *From A379 at Dawlish follow signs for Dawlish Warren. Site 1m on left at bottom of hill*

* 🚐 £13-£28 🚙 £13-£28 ▲ £13-£22

Open Etr-end Oct Last arrival 18.00hrs Last departure 10.00hrs

Well managed, attractive park close to the coast, with excellent facilities including a club and bar, which are well away from pitches. Nestling close to sandy beaches, the park offers

individually marked pitches on level terraces in pleasant, sheltered grassland. The many amenities include a heated swimming pool and water chute, coarse fishing and a launderette. A 26 acre site with 180 touring pitches, 15 hardstandings and 82 statics.

AA Pubs & Restaurants nearby:
The Elizabethan Inn, Luton 01626 775425

Anchor Inn, Cockwood 01626 890203

Leisure: ⚑
Facilities: 🚿 ✳ ⚡ ☖ 🍴 🐾
Services: 🔌 🄶 🄰 🌀 🄰 🍴
Within 3 miles: ⚓ 🅟 ⊚ ⚓ ☖ 🄶
Notes: Families & couples only. Wi-fi

74% Golden Sands Holiday Park *(SX968784)*

Week Ln EX7 0LZ
☎ 01626 863099 📠 01626 867149
dir: *M5 junct 30 onto A379 signed Dawlish. After 6m pass small harbour at Cockwood, signed on left in 2m*

* 🚐 £13-£28 🚙 £13-£28 ▲ £13-£28

Open 21 Mar-Oct Last arrival noon Last departure 10.00hrs

A holiday centre for all the family, offering a wide range of entertainment. The small touring area is surrounded by mature trees and hedges in a pleasant area, and visitors enjoy free use of the licensed club, and heated swimming pools. Organised children's activities are a popular feature, and the facilities of neighbouring Peppermint Park are open to all visitors. A 12 acre site with 28 touring pitches.

AA Pubs & Restaurants nearby:
The Elizabethan Inn, Luton 01626 775425

Anchor Inn, Cockwood 01626 890203

Leisure: 🏊 🏊 ⚑ 🎣
Facilities: 🚿 ⊙ ✳ ⚡ ☖ 🍴 🄷 🐾
Services: 🔌 🄶 🄴 🍴 🄰 🍴 🄰 🍴
Within 3 miles: ⚓ 🅟 ⊚ ☖ 🄶 ⛳
Notes: Wi-fi

SERVICES: 🔌 Electric hook up 🄶 Launderette 🄴 Licensed bar 🄰 Calor Gas 🄰 Camping Gaz 🅃 Toilet fluid 🍴 Café/Restaurant 🍴 Fast Food/Takeaway 🄰 Battery charging
🍼 Baby care ⚡ Motorvan service point **ABBREVIATIONS:** BH/bank hols-bank holidays Etr-Easter Whit-Whitsun dep-departure fr-from hrs-hours m-mile mdnt-midnight
rdbt-roundabout rs-restricted service wk-week wknd-weekend ⊘ No credit cards ⊗ no dogs See page 7 for details of the AA Camping Card Scheme

DAWLISH *continued*

►►►► 82% Cofton Country Holidays *(SX967801)*

GOLD

Starcross EX6 8RP
☎ 01626 890111 & 0800 085 8649
📄 01626 890160
e-mail: info@coftonholidays.co.uk
dir: *On A379 (Exeter/Dawlish road) 3m from Dawlish*

* 🚐 £13-£33.50 🚏 £13-£33.50 ▲ £13-£27.50

Open all year (rs Spring BH-mid Sep pool open; Etr-end Oct bar & shop open) Last arrival 20.00hrs Last departure 11.00hrs

This park is set in a rural location surrounded by spacious open grassland, with plenty of well-kept flowerbeds throughout. Most pitches overlook either the swimming pool complex or the fishing lakes and woodlands. An on-site pub serves drinks, meals and snacks for all the family, and a mini-market caters for most shopping needs. Seasonal touring pitches are available. A 45 acre site with 450 touring pitches, 30 hardstandings and 76 statics.

AA Pubs & Restaurants nearby: The Elizabethan Inn, Luton 01626 775425

Anchor Inn, Cockwood 01626 890203

Leisure: 🏊 🎪 🔍
Facilities: 🚻 🎣 ☺ 🍴 ✳ 🅗 ⏰ 🅢 🎾 🎿
Services: 🔌 🅑 🍺 🛢 🚿 🔧 ⓣ 🍴 🔋 🛒 🚼
Within 3 miles: 🚶 🎿 🎣 ◎ 🅢 🅢
Notes: Coarse fishing, pub with family room, camping orchard, takeaway, games room. Wi-fi
see advert on opposite page

►►► 76% Leadstone Camping
(SX974782)

Warren Rd EX7 0NG
☎ 01626 864411 📄 01626 873833
e-mail: info@leadstonecamping.co.uk
web: www.leadstonecamping.co.uk
dir: *M5 junct 30, A379 to Dawlish. Before village turn left on brow of hill, signed Dawlish Warren. Site 0.5m on right*

* 🚐 £17-£21 🚏 £13-£17 ▲ £13-£17

Open 10 Jun-4 Sep Last arrival 22.00hrs Last departure noon

A traditional, mainly level grassy camping park approximately a half mile walk from sands and dunes at Dawlish Warren, an Area of Outstanding Natural Beauty. This mainly tented park has been run by the same friendly family for many years, and is an ideal base for touring south Devon. A regular bus service from outside the gate takes in a wide area. Wi-fi is now available. An 8 acre site with 137 touring pitches.

AA Pubs & Restaurants nearby: The Elizabethan Inn, Luton 01626 775425

Anchor Inn, Cockwood 01626 890203

Leisure: 🎪
Facilities: 🎣 ☺ 🍴 ✳ 🅢
Services: 🔌 🛢 🚿 🔧 🔋
Within 3 miles: 🎿 🎣 ◎ 🅢 🅢
Notes: No noise after 23.00hrs. Portable/disposable BBQs allowed. Wi-fi

Places to visit

Coleton Fishacre House & Garden (NT), Kingswear 01803 752466 www.nationaltrust.org.uk

Cookworthy Museum of Rural Life, 01548 853235 www.kingsbridgemuseum.net

Great for kids: Woodlands Family Theme Park, Dartmouth 01803 712598 www.woodlandspark.com

►►► 74% Mounts Farm Touring Park
(SX757488)

The Mounts TQ9 7QJ
☎ 01548 521591
e-mail: mounts.farm@lineone.net
web: www.mountsfarm.co.uk
dir: *A381 from Totnes towards Kingsbridge (NB ignore signs for East Allington). At 'Mounts', site 0.5m on left*

🚐 £10-£24 🚏 £10-£24 ▲ £10-£24

Open 15 Mar-Oct Last arrival anytime Last departure anytime

A neat grassy park divided into four paddocks by mature natural hedges. Three of the paddocks house the tourers and campers, and the fourth is the children's play area. The laundry and well-stocked little shop are in converted farm buildings. A 7 acre site with 50 touring pitches.

AA Pubs & Restaurants nearby: Fortescue Arms, East Allington 01548 521215

Tower Inn, Slapton 01548 580216

Leisure: 🎪
Facilities: 🎣 ☺ 🍴 ✳ 🅢
Services: 🔌 🛢 🍺 🔧 ⓣ 🔋
Within 3 miles: 🎿 🍴 🎣 🛒 🅢 🅢 ⛳
Notes: Provisions & camping accessories shop on site

EAST ANSTEY — Map 3 SS82

Places to visit

Quince Honey Farm, South Molton
01769 572401 www.quincehoney.com

Tiverton Museum of Mid Devon Life, Tiverton
01884 256295 www.tivertonmuseum.org.uk

AA CAMPING CARD SITE

▶▶▶▶ 86% Zeacombe House Caravan Park (SS860240)

Blackerton Cross EX16 9JU
☎ 01398 341279
e-mail: enquiries@zeacombeadultretreat.co.uk
dir: M5 junct 27, A361 signed Barnstaple, right at next rdbt onto A396 signed Dulverton & Minehead. In 5m at Exeter Inn left, 1.5m, at Black Cat junct left onto B3227 towards South Molton, site 7m on left

☞ £16-£20 ☞ £16-£20 ▲ £16-£20

Open 7 Mar-Oct Last arrival 21.00hrs Last departure noon

Set on the southern fringes of Exmoor National Park, this 'garden' park is nicely landscaped in a tranquil location, and enjoys panoramic views towards Exmoor. This adult-only park offers a choice of grass or hardstanding pitches, and a unique restaurant-style delivery service allows you to eat an evening meal in the comfort of your own unit. A 5 acre site with 50 touring pitches, 12 hardstandings.

AA Pubs & Restaurants nearby: London Inn, Molland 01769 550269

Facilities: 📶⊙℘✳♿🅱🐾
Services: 🔌🅱🛢⌷⌷🚮🚽
Within 3 miles: ⚡℘🚴🅱🛍♻
Notes: Adults only. Dogs must be kept on leads

An increasing number of parks do not accept children. For a full list of Adults-only parks see page 45

EAST WORLINGTON — Map 3 SS71

▶▶▶▶ 78% Yeatheridge Farm Caravan Park (SS768110)

EX17 4TN
☎ 01884 860330
e-mail: yeatheridge@talk21.com
dir: M5 junct 27, A361, at 1st rdbt at Tiverton take B3137 for 9m towards Witheridge. Fork left 1m past Nomansland onto B3042. Site on left in 3.5m. (NB Do not go to East Worlington)

* ☞ £8.75-£16.50 ☞ £8.75-£16.50
▲ £8.75-£16.50

Open Etr-Sep Last arrival 22.00hrs Last departure 10.00hrs

Gently sloping grass site with mature trees, set in meadowland in rural Devon. There are good views of distant Dartmoor, and the site is of great appeal to families with its farm animals, horse riding, and two indoor swimming pools, one with flume. There are many attractive villages in this area. A 9 acre site with 85 touring pitches and 12 statics.

Leisure: 🏊🅰🎱⌷
Facilities: 🚿📶⊙℘✳♿🅱🐾
Services: 🔌🅱🛢🛢⌷⌷🍽🚮🚽
Within 3 miles: ℘🅱🛍♻
Notes: Fishing, pool table, horse riding. Wi-fi

EXETER

See Kennford

EXMOUTH

See also Woodbury Salterton

Places to visit

A la Ronde (NT), Exmouth 01395 265514
www.nationaltrust.org.uk

Bicton Park Botanical Gardens, Bicton
01395 568465 www.bictongardens.co.uk

Great for kids: The World of Country Life, Exmouth 01395 274533
www.worldofcountrylife.co.uk

EXMOUTH — Map 3 SY08

90% Devon Cliffs Holiday Park (SY036807)

Sandy Bay EX8 5BT
☎ 01395 226226   📠 01395 226267
e-mail: bob.sleighton@bourne-leisure.co.uk
dir: M5 junct 30/A376 towards Exmouth, follow brown signs to Sandy Bay

☞ ☞ ▲

Open mid Mar-Oct (rs mid Mar-May & Sep-Oct some facilities may be reduced) Last arrival anytime Last departure 10.00hrs

A large and exciting holiday park on a hillside setting close to Exmouth, with spectacular views across Sandy Bay. The all-action park offers a superb entertainment programme for all ages throughout the day, with the very modern sports and leisure facilities available for everyone. An internet café is just one of the quality amenities, and though some visitors may enjoy relaxing and watching others play, the temptation to join in is overpowering. A 163 acre site with 193 touring pitches, 43 hardstandings and 1800 statics.

AA Pubs & Restaurants nearby: Globe Inn, Lympstone 01395 263166

Les Saveurs at The Seafood Restaurant, Exmouth 01395 269459

Leisure: 🏊🏊🅰
Facilities: 🚿📶⊙℘♿🅲🅱🐾🔦
Services: 🔌🅱🛢🛢🅰🍽🚮
Within 3 miles: ⚡🎬℘◎🚴🅱🛍♻
Notes: No cars by tents. Dogs must be on leads, certain dog breeds banned, tents only in Aug. Crazy golf. Wi-fi

▶▶ 80% Prattshayes Farm National Trust Campsite (SY030810)

Maer Ln EX8 5DB
☎ 01395 276626   📠 01395 276626
dir: A376 Exmouth, follow signs towards Sandy Bay. Right at narrow bridge by Clinton Arms pub, site 0.5m on right

* ☞ £8-£10 ☞ £8-£10 ▲ £8-£10

Open Apr-Oct Last arrival 21.00hrs Last departure 10.30hrs

Set in a quiet rural location, with grassy pitches surrounded by mature hedging. Converted farm buildings house the good toilet/shower facilities.

There is also a National Trust 'Base Camp' with dormitories, kitchen and wet rooms available for groups or families. Takeaway breakfasts are also available at certain times. An ideal spot for exploring the Jurassic Coast. 30 touring pitches.

AA Pubs & Restaurants nearby: Globe Inn, Lympstone 01395 263166

Les Saveurs at The Seafood Restaurant, Exmouth 01395 269459

Facilities: ♠⊙♂✕🕭🕓🖻🖩🎪 **Services:** ⊟

Within 3 miles: ⏸🕹目🖉◎🍴🛒🛍🖩U

Notes: ⊛ Dogs not to be exercised on site, no generators, no open fires or ground level BBQs

---

HOLSWORTHY   Map 3 SS30

Places to visit

Dartington Crystal, Great Torrington 01805 626242 www.dartington.co.uk

RHS Garden Rosemoor, Great Torrington 01805 624067 www.rhs.org.uk/rosemoor

Great for kids: The Milky Way Adventure Park, Clovelly 01237 431255 www.themilkyway.co.uk

---

AA CAMPING CARD SITE

▶▶▶ **77% Headon Farm Caravan Site** (SS367023)

Headon Farm, Hollacombe EX22 6NN
☎ 01409 254477   📄 0870 705 9052
e-mail: reader@headonfarm.co.uk
dir: Exit A388, 0.75m into Staddon Rd, 1m, right follow Ashwater sign. In 0.75m left follow Hollacombe sign. Site on left in 50yds

* ⊞ £13.50-£15.50 ⊞ £13.50-£15.50

Open all year Last arrival 19.00hrs Last dep noon

Set on a working farm in a quiet rural location. All pitches have extensive views of the Devon countryside, yet the park is only two and a half miles from the market town of Holsworthy, and within easy reach of roads to the coast and beaches of north Cornwall. A 2 acre site with 19 touring pitches, 5 hardstandings.

AA Pubs & Restaurants nearby: The Bickford Arms, Holsworthy 01409 221318

Leisure: ⚓ **Facilities:** ♠⊙✕🎪🐾

Services: ⊟🖩🛍🚿

Within 3 miles: ⏸🖉🛒🖩U

Notes: ⊛ Breathable groundsheets only, pets must be kept on leads on site. Secure caravan & motorhome storage. Wi-fi

---

AA CAMPING CARD SITE

▶▶ **75% Tamarstone Farm** (SS286056)

Bude Rd, Pancrasweek EX22 7JT
☎ 01288 381734
e-mail: camping@tamarstone.co.uk
dir: A30 to Launceston, then B3254 towards Bude, approx 14m. Right onto A3072 towards Holsworthy, approx 1.5m, site on left

⊞ £8-£10 ⊞ £8-£10 ▲ £8-£10

Open Etr-end Oct Last arrival 22.00hrs Last departure noon

Four acres of river-bordered meadow and woodland providing a wildlife haven for those who enjoy peace and seclusion. The wide, sandy beaches of Bude are just five miles away, and coarse fishing is provided free on site for visitors. A 1 acre site with 16 touring pitches and 1 static.

AA Pubs & Restaurants nearby: The Bickford Arms, Holsworthy 01409 221318

Leisure: 🎣

Facilities: ♠⊙✕🎪🐾

Services: ⊟

Within 3 miles: ⏸🖉🛍

Notes: ⊛ Dogs must be kept on leads at all times

▶ **75% Noteworthy Caravan and Campsite** (SS303052)

Noteworthy, Bude Rd EX22 7JB
☎ 01409 253731
e-mail: enquiries@noteworthy-devon.co.uk
dir: On A3072 between Holsworthy & Bude. 3m from Holsworthy on right

⊞ ⊞ ▲

Open all year

This campsite is owned by a friendly young couple with their own small children. There are good views from the quiet rural location, and simple toilet facilities. A 5 acre site with 5 touring pitches and 1 static.

AA Pubs & Restaurants nearby: The Bickford Arms, Holsworthy 01409 221318

Leisure: ⚓

Facilities: ♠⊙✕🕓🐾

Services: ⊟🚙

Within 3 miles: ⏸🖉🛒🖩U

Notes: ⊛ No open fires. Dog grooming

ILFRACOMBE   Map 3 SS54

See also Berrynarbor

Places to visit

Arlington Court (NT), Arlington 01271 850296 www.nationaltrust.org.uk/main/w-arlingtoncourt

Exmoor Zoological Park, Blackmoor Gate 01598 763352 www.exmoorzoo.co.uk

Great for kids: Watermouth Castle & Family Theme Park, Ilfracombe 01271 863879 www.watermouthcastle.com

---

AA CAMPING CARD SITE

▶▶▶▶ **82% Hele Valley Holiday Park** (SS533472)

Hele Bay EX34 9RD
☎ 01271 862460   📄 01271 867926
e-mail: holidays@helevalley.co.uk
dir: M5 junct 27 onto A361. Through Barnstaple & Braunton to Ilfracombe. Then A399 towards Combe Martin. Follow brown Hele Valley signs. 400mtrs sharp right, then to T-junct. Reception on left

⊞ £13-£33 ⊞ £13-£33 ▲ £13-£33

Open Etr-Oct Last arrival 18.00hrs Last departure 11.00hrs

A deceptively spacious park set in a picturesque valley with glorious tree-lined hilly views from most pitches. High quality toilet facilities are provided, and the park is close to a lovely beach, with the harbour and other attractions of Ilfracombe just a mile away. A 17 acre site with 50 touring pitches, 18 hardstandings and 80 statics.

AA Pubs & Restaurants nearby: George & Dragon, Ilfracombe 01271 863851

The Quay, Ilfracombe 01271 868090

Leisure: ⚓

Facilities: ♠⊙♂✕🕭🕓🖻🖩🎪🐾

Services: ⊟🖩🛍🖉🚿🚻🚮

Within 3 miles: ⏸🕹目🖉◎🍴🛒🖩U

Notes: Groups by arrangement only. Post collection, internet access, information service

---

KENNFORD   Map 3 SX98

Places to visit

St Nicholas Priory, Exeter 01392 665858
www.exeter.gov.uk/priory

Quay House Visitor Centre, Exeter
01392 271611 www.exeter.gov.uk/quayhous

Great for kids: Crealy Adventure Park, Clyst St
Mary 01395 233200 www.crealy.co.uk

▶▶▶▶ 78% Kennford International Caravan Park (SX912857)

EX6 7YN
☎ 01392 833046   🖷 01392 833046
e-mail: ian@kennfordinternational.com
web: www.kennfordinternational.co.uk
dir: At end of M5, take A38, site signed at
Kennford slip road

🚐 🚙 ⚕

Open all year (rs Winter arrival times change) Last
arrival 21.00hrs Last departure 11.00hrs

Screened from the A38 by trees and shrubs, this
park offers many pitches divided by hedging for
privacy. A high quality toilet block complements

the park's facilities. A good, centrally-located
base for touring the coast and countryside of
Devon, and Exeter is easily accessible via a nearby
bus stop. A 15 acre site with 96 touring pitches
and 53 statics.

AA Pubs & Restaurants nearby: Swans Nest,
Exminster 01392 832371

Leisure: 🄰 🔍 **Facilities:** 🛁 🌂 ⊙ ⚡ ⊙ 🖉 🖍
Services: 🕮 🖥 🍴 🍺 🖽 🚽 🛢 ↧
Within 3 miles: ↧ 🐟 🎌 🅿 🖥 🖥 ↺

KENTISBEARE   Map 3 ST00

Places to visit

Killerton House & Garden (NT) 01392 881345
www.nationaltrust.org.uk

Allhallows Museum, Honiton 01404 44966
www.honitonmuseum.co.uk

Great for kids: Diggerland, Cullompton
0871 227 7007 www.diggerland.com

AA CAMPING CARD SITE

▶▶▶▶ 77% Forest Glade Holiday Park (ST101073)

EX15 2DT
☎ 01404 841381   🖷 01404 841593
e-mail: enquiries@forest-glade.co.uk
dir: Tent traffic: from A373 signed at Keepers
Cottage Inn (2.5m E of M5 junct 28). Touring
caravans: via Honiton/Dunkeswell road: please
phone for access details

🚐 🚙 ⚕

Open mid Mar-end Oct (rs Low season limited
shop hours) Last arrival 21.00hrs Last departure
noon

A quiet, attractive park in a forest clearing with
well-kept gardens and beech hedge screening.
One of the main attractions is the immediate
proximity of the forest, which offers magnificent
hillside walks with surprising views over the
valleys. Please telephone for route details. A 15
acre site with 80 touring pitches, 40
hardstandings and 57 statics.

AA Pubs & Restaurants nearby: Five Bells Inn,
Clyst Hydon 01884 277288

Leisure: 🄰 🄰 🍃 🔍
Facilities: 🌂 ⊙ 🖉 ✳ ⚡ ⊙ 🖥 🖍 🖍
Services: 🕮 🖥 🖉 🖽 🚽 🛢 🚚 ↧
Within 3 miles: 🅿 🖥 🖥 ↺

Notes: Families and couples only. Adventure play
area, paddling/ball pools, wildlife information
room. Wi-fi

see advert below

LYNTON

See also Oare (Somerset)

Places to visit

Arlington Court (NT), Arlington 01271 850296
www.nationaltrust.org.uk/
main/w-arlingtoncourt

Great for kids: Exmoor Zoological Park,
Blackmoor Gate 01598 763352
www.exmoorzoo.co.uk

LYNTON
Map 3 SS74

AA CAMPING CARD SITE

►►►► 71% Channel View Caravan and Camping Park

(SS724482)

Manor Farm EX35 6LD
☎ 01598 753349 📠 01598 752777
e-mail: relax@channel-view.co.uk
web: www.channel-view.co.uk
dir: *A39 E for 0.5m on left past Barbrook*

* 🚐 £11-£19 🚐 £11-£19 ▲ £11-£19

Open 15 Mar-15 Nov Last arrival 22.00hrs Last departure noon

On the top of the cliffs overlooking the Bristol Channel, a well-maintained park on the edge of Exmoor, and close to both Lynton and Lynmouth. Pitches can be selected from a hidden hedged area, or with panoramic views over the coast. A 6 acre site with 76 touring pitches, 15 hardstandings and 31 statics.

AA Pubs & Restaurants nearby: Bridge Inn, Lynton 01598 753425

Beggars Roost, Barbrook 01598 752404

Leisure: 🅰

Facilities: 🖕🅵☺🅵✳🕹🅕🖥🎣🚻

Services: 🔌🅶🅰🖉🅃🍴🚮♨

Within 3 miles: 🕗🅿◎🛥🅰🅶🅄

Notes: Groups by prior arrangement only. Parent & baby room. Wi-fi

see advert below

►►► 76% Sunny Lyn Holiday Park

(SS719486)

Lynbridge EX35 6NS
☎ 01598 753384 📠 01598 753273
e-mail: info@caravandevon.co.uk
web: www.caravandevon.co.uk
dir: *M5 junct 27, A361 to South Molton. Right onto A399 to Blackmoor Gate, right onto A39, left onto B3234 towards Lynmouth. Site 1m on right*

* 🚐 £12.50-£15.50 🚐 £12.50-£15.50 ▲ £11.50-£12.50

Open Mar-Oct Last arrival 20.00hrs Last departure 11.00hrs

Set in a sheltered riverside location in a wooded combe within a mile of the sea, in Exmoor National Park. This family-run park offers good facilities including an excellent café. A 4.5 acre site with 9 touring pitches, 5 hardstandings and 7 statics.

AA Pubs & Restaurants nearby: Bridge Inn, Lynton 01598 753425

Beggars Roost, Barbrook 01598 752404

Facilities: 🅵☺🅵✳🅕🅕🖥🎣

Services: 🔌🅶🅰🖉🍴🚮🕭

Within 3 miles: ♨🕗🅿◎🅰🅶🅄

Notes: No cars by tents. No wood fires. Wi-fi

MODBURY
Map 3 SX65

Places to visit
Cookworthy Museum of Rural Life, Kingsbridge 01548 853235 www.kingsbridgemuseum.net

Great for kids: National Marine Aquarium, Plymouth 01752 600301 www.national-aquarium.co.uk

►►► 81% Pennymoor Camping & Caravan Park *(SX685516)*

PL21 0SB
☎ 01548 830542 & 830020 📠 01548 830542
e-mail: enquiries@pennymoor-camping.co.uk
dir: *Exit A38 at Wrangaton Cross. Left & straight over x-roads. Then 4m, pass petrol station & 2nd left. Site 1.5m on right*

* 🚐 £8-£15 🚐 £6-£12 ▲ £8-£15

Open 15 Mar-15 Nov (rs 15 Mar-mid May one toilet & shower block only open) Last arrival 20.00hrs Last departure 10.00hrs

A well-established rural park on part level, part gently sloping grass with good views over distant Dartmoor and the countryside in between. The park has been owned and run by the same family since 1935, and is very carefully tended, with a relaxing atmosphere. A 12.5 acre site with 119 touring pitches and 76 statics.

AA Pubs & Restaurants nearby: California Country Inn, Modbury 01548 821449

Rose & Crown, Yealmpton 01752 880223

Leisure: 🅰 **Facilities:** 🅵☺🅵✳🅕🅕🖥🎣

Services: 🔌🅶🅰🖉🅃🚮

Within 3 miles: 🅰🅶 **Notes:** ⊗ No skateboards

see advert on page 162

CHANNEL VIEW CARAVAN & CAMPING PARK

BARBROOK, LYNTON, NORTH DEVON EX35 6LD

Tel: (01598) 753349 Fax: (01598) 752777

www.channel-view.co.uk

Email: relax@channel-view.co.uk

A warm welcome awaits you at this quiet family run site, which is situated on the edge of Exmoor National Park, overlooking Lynton and Lynmouth and the Bristol Channel. With some of the most spectacular views in the area. First class camping and touring facilities. Electric hook-ups, fully serviced pitches, site shop, site café, public telephone, launderette. Dogs welcome. WiFi Available.

MORTEHOE
Map 3 SS44

See also Woolacombe

Places to visit

Marwood Hill Gardens, Barnstaple
01271 342528 www.marwoodhillgarden.co.uk

Great for kids: Watermouth Castle & Family
Theme Park, Ilfracombe 01271 863879
www.watermouthcastle.com

AA CAMPING CARD SITE

83% Twitchen House Holiday Park (SS465447)

Station Rd EX34 7ES
☎ 01271 870343   📠 01271 870089
e-mail: goodtimes@woolacombe.com
dir: From Mullacott Cross rdbt take B3343
(Woolacombe road) to Turnpike Cross junct.
Take right fork, site 1.5m on left

* 🚐 £15.75-£60 🚙 £15.75-£60 ▲ £10.50-£38

Open Mar-Oct (rs mid May & mid Sep outdoor
pool closed) Last arrival mdnt Last departure
10.00hrs

A very attractive park with good leisure
facilities. Visitors can use the amenities at all
three of Woolacombe Bay holiday parks, and a
bus service connects them all with the beach.
The touring area features pitches with either
sea views or a woodland countryside outlook.
A 45 acre site with 334 touring pitches, 110
hardstandings and 278 statics.

AA Pubs & Restaurants nearby: George &
Dragon, Ilfracombe 01271 863851

The Quay, Ilfracombe 01271 868090

Leisure: 🏊♨️⛱🎱▢

Facilities: ⚡☉℘✳♿🚻🚿🎠⌁

Services: 🚐🔌🍴🛢🖉Ⓣ🍽🛒👕♨

Within 3 miles: ⚓🎣☰℘◎🚴🏪🛒U

Notes: Table tennis, sauna, kids' clubs,
swimming & surfing lessons. Wi-fi

►►►► 82% Warcombe Farm Caravan & Camping Park (SS478445)

GOLD

Station Rd EX34 7EJ
☎ 01271 870690 & 07774 428770
📠 01271 871070
e-mail: info@warcombefarm.co.uk
web: www.warcombefarm.co.uk
dir: On B3343 towards Woolacombe turn right
towards Mortehoe. Site less than 2m on right

* 🚐 £14-£31 🚙 £14-£31 ▲ £12-£27.50

Open 15 Mar-Oct (rs Low season no takeaway
food) Last arrival 21.00hrs Last departure
11.00hrs

Extensive views over the Bristol Channel can be
enjoyed from the open areas of this attractive
park, while other pitches are sheltered in
paddocks with maturing trees. The superb sandy
beach with a Blue Flag award at Woolacombe Bay
is only a mile and a half away, and there is a
fishing lake with direct access from some pitches.

A 19 acre site with 250 touring pitches, 10
hardstandings.

AA Pubs & Restaurants nearby: George & Dragon,
Ilfracombe 01271 863851

The Quay, Ilfracombe 01271 868090

Leisure: ⛱

Facilities: ⚡☉℘✳♿🚻🚿🎠⌁

Services: 🚐🔌🛢🖉Ⓣ🍽🛒♨

Within 3 miles: ⚓☰℘◎🏪🛒U

Notes: No groups unless booked in advance.
Private fishing, internet access. Wi-fi

►►► 85% North Morte Farm Caravan & Camping Park (SS462455)

North Morte Rd EX34 7EG
☎ 01271 870381   📠 01271 870115
e-mail: info@northmortefarm.co.uk
dir: From B3343 into Mortehoe, right at post office.
Site 500yds on left

🚐 🚙 ▲

Open Apr-Oct Last arrival 22.30hrs Last departure
noon

LEISURE: 🏊 Indoor swimming pool ♨️ Outdoor swimming pool 🎠 Children's playground 🎾 Tennis court 🎱 Games room ▢ Separate TV room ⛳ 9/18 hole golf course ⛵ Boats for hire 🎬 Cinema 🎣 Fishing ◎ Mini golf 🏄 Watersports U Stables **FACILITIES:** 🛁 Bath 🚿 Shower ⊙ Electric shaver ℘ Hairdryer ✳ Ice Pack Facility ♿ Disabled facilities 🕐 Public telephone 🏪 Shop on site or within 200yds 🚐 Mobile shop (calls at least 5 days a week) 🍖 BBQ area 🎋 Picnic area 🐕 Dog exercise area

Set in spectacular coastal countryside close to National Trust land and 500 yards from Rockham Beach. This attractive park is very well run and maintained by friendly family owners, and the quaint village of Mortehoe with its cafés, shops and pubs, is just a five-minute walk away. A 22 acre site with 180 touring pitches, 18 hardstandings and 73 statics.

AA Pubs & Restaurants nearby: George & Dragon, Ilfracombe 01271 863851

The Quay, Ilfracombe 01271 868090

Leisure: ⚏

Facilities: ⚏⚏⚏⚏⚏⚏⚏⚏

Services: ⚏⚏⚏⚏⚏⚏⚏⚏

Within 3 miles: ⚏⚏⚏⚏⚏

Notes: No large groups, dogs must be kept on leads at all times. Wi-fi

AA CAMPING CARD SITE

►►► 78% Easewell Farm Holiday Park & Golf Club (SS465455)

EX34 7EH
☎ 01271 870343 📠 01271 870089
e-mail: goodtimes@woolacombe.com
dir: B3343 to Mortehoe. Turn right at fork, site 2m on right

* ⚏ £15-£55 ⚏ £15-£55 ⚏ £10-£36.60

Open Mar-Oct (rs Etr) Last arrival 22.00hrs Last departure 10.00hrs

A peaceful cliff-top park with full facility pitches for caravans and motorhomes, and superb views. The park offers a range of activities including indoor bowling and a 9-hole golf course, and all the facilities at the three other nearby holiday centres within this group are open to everyone. A 17 acre site with 302 touring pitches, 50 hardstandings and 1 static.

AA Pubs & Restaurants nearby: George & Dragon, Ilfracombe 01271 863851

The Quay, Ilfracombe 01271 868090

Leisure: ⚏⚏⚏⚏

Facilities: ⚏⚏⚏⚏⚏⚏⚏⚏⚏

Services: ⚏⚏⚏⚏⚏⚏⚏⚏⚏

Within 3 miles: ⚏⚏⚏⚏⚏⚏⚏⚏⚏

Notes: Indoor bowls, snooker. Wi-fi

NEWTON ABBOT
Map 3 SX87

See also Bickington

Places to visit

Tuckers Maltings, Newton Abbot 01626 334734 www.tuckersmaltings.com

Bradley Manor (NT), Newton Abbot 01803 843235 www.nationaltrust.org.uk/devoncornwall

Great for kids: Prickly Ball Farm and Hedgehog Hospital, Newton Abbot 01626 362319 www.pricklyballfarm.com

PREMIER PARK

AA CAMPING CARD SITE

►►►►► 96% Ross Park (SX845671)

Park Hill Farm, Ipplepen
TQ12 5TT
☎ 01803 812983 📠 01803 812983
e-mail: enquiries@rossparkcaravanpark.co.uk
web: www.rossparkcaravanpark.co.uk
dir: Off A381, 3m from Newton Abbot towards Totnes, signed opposite Texaco garage towards 'Woodland'

* ⚏ £13-£24.95 ⚏ £13-£24.95 ⚏ £12-£24.95

Open Mar-2 Jan (rs Nov-Jan & 1st 3 wks of Mar restaurant/bar closed (ex Xmas/New Year)) Last arrival 21.00hrs Last departure 10.00hrs

A top-class park in every way, with large secluded pitches, high quality toilet facilities and lovely floral displays throughout. The beautiful tropical conservatory also offers a breathtaking show of colour. This very rural park enjoys superb views of Dartmoor, and good quality meals to suit all tastes and pockets are served in the restaurant. A park that manages to get better each year. A 32 acre site with 110 touring pitches, 94 hardstandings.

AA Pubs & Restaurants nearby: Sampsons Farm & Restaurant, Newton Abbot 01626 354913

Union Inn, Denbury 01803 812595

Leisure: ⚏⚏⚏

Facilities: ⚏⚏⚏⚏⚏⚏⚏⚏⚏

Services: ⚏⚏⚏⚏⚏⚏⚏⚏⚏⚏

Within 3 miles: ⚏⚏⚏⚏⚏

Notes: Bikes, skateboards/scooters only allowed on leisure field. Snooker, table tennis, badminton, croquet. Wi-fi

PREMIER PARK

AA CAMPING CARD SITE

►►►►► 94%
Dornafield (SX838683)

Dornafield Farm, Two Mile Oak TQ12 6DD
☎ 01803 812732 📠 01803 812032
e-mail: enquiries@dornafield.com
web: www.dornafield.com
dir: Take A381 (Newton Abbot-Totnes) for 2m. At Two Mile Oak Inn turn right, then left at x-roads in 0.5m to site on right

* ⚏ £15-£29 ⚏ £15-£29 ⚏ £14-£25

Open 17 Mar-4 Jan Last arrival 22.00hrs Last departure 11.00hrs

An immaculately kept park in a tranquil wooded valley between Dartmoor and Torbay, offering either deluxe or fully-serviced pitches. A lovely 15th-century farmhouse sits at the entrance, and the park is divided into three separate areas, served by two superb, ultra-modern toilet blocks. The friendly family owners are always available. Well positioned for visiting nearby Totnes or the resorts of Torbay. A 30 acre site with 135 touring pitches, 119 hardstandings.

AA Pubs & Restaurants nearby: Sampsons Farm & Restaurant, Newton Abbot 01626 354913

Union Inn, Denbury 01803 812595

Leisure: ⚏⚏⚏

Facilities: ⚏⚏⚏⚏⚏⚏⚏⚏⚏

Services: ⚏⚏⚏⚏⚏⚏⚏⚏

Within 3 miles: ⚏⚏⚏⚏⚏

Notes: Caravan storage (all year). Wi-fi

NEWTON ABBOT *continued*

►►► 78% Twelve Oaks Farm Caravan Park *(SX852737)*

Teigngrace TQ12 6QT
☎ 01626 352769 01626 352769
e-mail: info@twelveoaksfarm.co.uk
dir: *A38 from Exeter left signed Teigngrace (only), 0.25m before Drumbridges rdbt. 1.5m, through village, site on left. From Plymouth pass Drumbridges rdbt, take slip road for Chudleigh Knighton. Right over bridge, rejoin A38 towards Plymouth. Left for Teigngrace (only), then as above*

* £8.50-£15 £8.50-£15 £8.50-£15

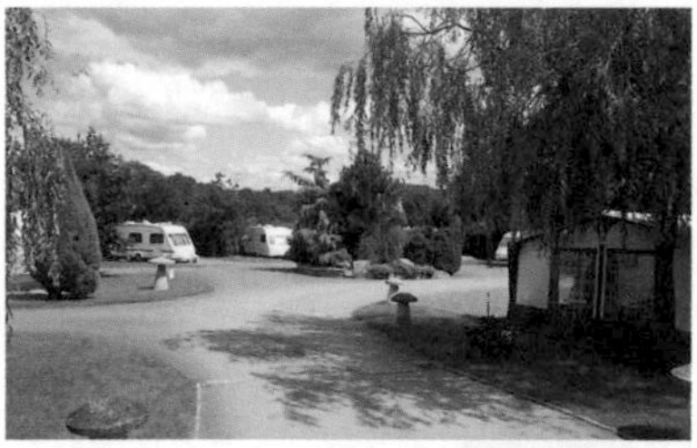

Open all year Last arrival 21.00hrs Last departure 11.00hrs

An attractive small park on a working farm close to Dartmoor National Park, and bordered by the River Teign. The tidy pitches are located amongst trees and shrubs, and the modern facilities are very well maintained. Children will enjoy all the farm animals, and nearby is the Templar Way walking route. A 2 acre site with 35 touring pitches, 17 hardstandings.

AA Pubs & Restaurants nearby: Sampsons Farm & Restaurant, Newton Abbot 01626 354913

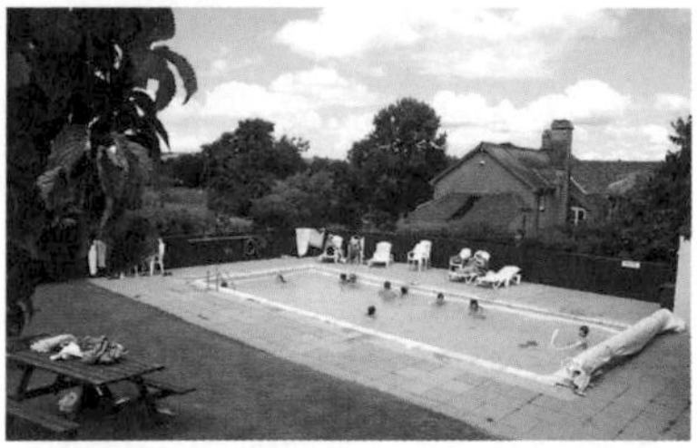

Leisure:
Facilities:
Services:
Within 3 miles:

PAIGNTON — Map 3 SX86

Places to visit

Dartmouth Steam Railway & River Boat Company, Paignton 01803 555872
www.dartmouthrailriver.co.uk

Kents Cavern, Torquay 01803 215136
www.kents-cavern.co.uk

Great for kids: Paignton Zoo Environmental Park, Paignton 0844 474 2222
www.paigntonzoo.org.uk

AA CAMPING CARD SITE

88% Beverley Parks Caravan & Camping Park *(SX886582)*

Best of British — GOLD

Goodrington Rd TQ4 7JE
☎ 01803 661979 01803 845427
e-mail: info@beverley-holidays.co.uk
dir: *On A380/A3022, 2m S of Paignton turn left into Goodrington Road. Beverley Park on right*

£15.50-£38.50 £15.50-£38.50
£13-£28.50

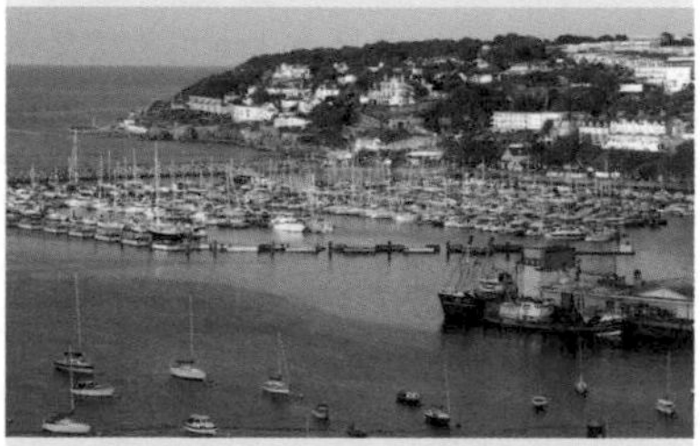

Open all year Last arrival 21.00hrs Last departure 10.00hrs

A high quality family-run park with extensive views of the bay and plenty of on-site amenities. The park boasts indoor and outdoor heated swimming pools, plus tasteful bars and restaurants. The toilet facilities are modern and very clean. The park complex is attractively laid out with the touring areas divided into nicely screened areas. Seasonal touring pitches are available. A 12 acre site with 172 touring pitches, 49 hardstandings.

AA Pubs & Restaurants nearby: Church House Inn, Marldon 01803 558279

Elephant Restaurant & Brasserie, Torquay 01803 200044

No 7 Fish Bistro, Torquay 01803 295055

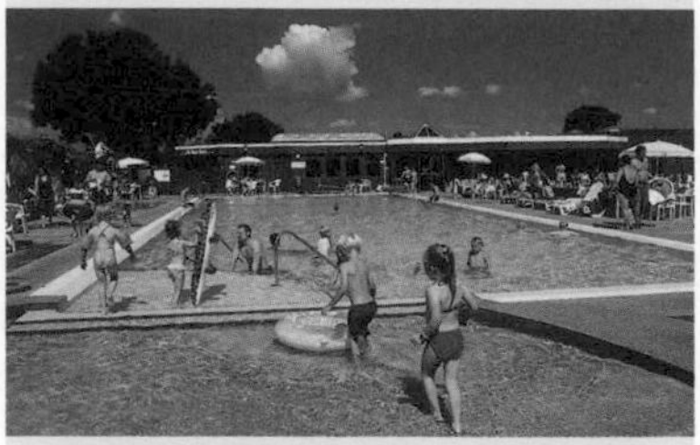

Beverley Parks Caravan & Camping Park

Leisure:
Facilities:
Services:
Within 3 miles:
Notes: No pets. Table tennis, pool, spa bath, sauna, crazy golf, gym, letter box trail. Wi-fi

►►►► 79% *Widend Touring* Park *(SX852619)*

GOLD

Berry Pomeroy Rd, Marldon TQ3 1RT
☎ 01803 550116 01803 550116
dir: *Signed from Torbay ring road*

Open Apr-end Sep (rs Apr-mid May & mid Sep swimming pool & club house closed) Last arrival 20.00hrs Last departure 10.00hrs

A terraced grass park divided into paddocks and screened on high ground overlooking Torbay with views of Dartmoor. This attractive park is well laid out, divided up by mature trees and bushes but with plenty of open grassy areas. Facilities are of a high standard and offer a heated outdoor swimming pool with sunbathing area, a small lounge bar and a well-stocked shop. A 22 acre site with 207 touring pitches, 6 hardstandings and 16 statics.

AA Pubs & Restaurants nearby: Church House Inn, Marldon 01803 558279

Elephant Restaurant & Brasserie, Torquay 01803 200044

No 7 Fish Bistro, Torquay 01803 295055

Leisure:
Facilities:
Services:
Within 3 miles:
Notes: No dogs mid Jul-Aug

AA CAMPING CARD SITE

►►► 84% Whitehill Country Park (SX857588)

GOLD

Stoke Rd TQ4 7PF
☎ 01803 782338 📄 01803 782722
e-mail: info@whitehill-park.co.uk
dir: A385 through Totnes towards Paignton. Turn right by Parkers Arms onto Stoke Rd towards Stoke Gabriel. Site on left after approx 1.5m

🚐 £15-£29 🚐 £15-£29 ▲ £13-£23.50

Open Etr-Sep Last arrival 21.00hrs Last departure 10.00hrs

A family-owned and run park set in rolling countryside, with many scenic beaches just a short drive away. This extensive country park covers 40 acres with woodland walks, and plenty of flora and fauna. It offers ideal facilities, including new luxury lodges, for an excellent holiday. A 40 acre site with 260 touring pitches and 60 statics.

AA Pubs & Restaurants nearby: Church House Inn, Marldon 01803 558279

Elephant Restaurant & Brasserie, Torquay 01803 200044

No 7 Fish Bistro, Torquay 01803 295055

Leisure: 🏖 ⚄ 🔍 🖵
Facilities: 🎣 ✳ ♿ 🕐 🚿 🛒
Services: 🔌 🗄 🚽 🛢 🕎 🍴 🚮 🚿
Within 3 miles: 🛴 🚴 🎯 🌊 🎣 🕎 🕒 ∪

Notes: Dogs allowed at certain times only (phone to check). Walking & cycling trails, letter box trail, craft room, table tennis. Wi-fi

►►► 79% Byslades International Touring & Camping Park (SX853603)

Totnes Rd TQ4 7PY
☎ 01803 666930 & 555072 📄 01803 555669
e-mail: info@byslades.co.uk
dir: On A385, halfway between Paignton & Totnes

✱ 🚐 £10-£18 🚐 £10-£18 ▲ £10-£18

Open Whit-Aug BH Last arrival 18.00hrs Last departure 10.00hrs

A well-kept terraced park, now owned by Haulfryn Leisure, in beautiful countryside, only two miles from Paignton. It offers a good mix of amenities, including the famous 17th-century Blagdon Inn at the adjoining holiday park home estate. There is access through this to a full bar, snacks and restaurant service. A 23 acre site with 190 touring pitches, 40 hardstandings.

AA Pubs & Restaurants nearby: Church House Inn, Marldon 01803 558279

Elephant Restaurant & Brasserie, Torquay 01803 200044

No 7 Fish Bistro, Torquay 01803 295055

Leisure: 🏖 ⚄ 🔍 🔍
Facilities: 🎣 🕐 ✳ ✳ ♿ 🕐 🚿 🛒
Services: 🔌 🗄 🚽 🛢 🕎 🍴 🚮 🚿
Within 3 miles: 🛴 🚴 🎯 🌊 🕎 🕒

Notes: No commercial vehicles. Crazy golf. Wi-fi

►►►► 80% Riverside Caravan Park (SX515575)

Leigham Manor Dr PL6 8LL
☎ 01752 344122 📄 01752 344122
e-mail: info@riversidecaravanpark.com
dir: A38 follow signs at Marsh Mills rdbt, take 3rd exit, then left. 400yds turn right (keep River Plym on right) to site

🚐 🚐 ▲

Open all year (rs Oct-Etr bar, restaurant, takeaway & pool closed) Last arrival 22.00hrs Last departure 10.00hrs

A well-groomed site on the outskirts of Plymouth on the banks of the River Plym, in a quiet location surrounded by woodland. The toilet facilities are to a very good standard, and include private cubicles. This park is an ideal stopover for the ferries to France and Spain, and makes an excellent base for touring Dartmoor and the coast. An 11 acre site with 259 touring pitches and 22 statics.

AA Pubs & Restaurants nearby: Fishermans Arms, Plymouth 01752 661457

Tanners, Plymouth 01752 252001

Artillery Tower Restaurant, Plymouth 01752 257610

Leisure: 🏖 ⚄ 🔍 🖵
Facilities: 🎣 🕐 ✳ ✳ ♿ 🕐 🚿 🛒
Services: 🔌 🗄 🚽 🛢 🕎 🅃 🍴 🚮 🚿
Within 3 miles: 🛴 🚴 🎯 🌊 🕎 🕒 ∪

PRINCETOWN   Map 3 SX57

►► 76% *The Plume of Feathers Inn*

(SX592734)

PL20 6QQ
☎ **01822 890240**
dir: *Site accessed directly from B3212 rdbt
(beside Plume of Feathers Inn) in centre of
Princetown*

⌸ Å

Open all year Last arrival 23.30hrs Last dep 11.00hrs

Set amidst the rugged beauty of Dartmoor not far
from the notorious prison, this campsite boasts
good toilet facilities and all the amenities of the
inn. The Plume of Feathers is Princetown's oldest
building, and serves all day food in an
atmospheric setting - try the 'camp and breakfast'
deal that's on offer. The campsite is mainly for
tents. A 3 acre site with 85 touring pitches.

Leisure: ⚁   **Facilities:** ⚄☀☺⚅⛲⚑⚏⚐
Services: ⚑⚏⚒
Within 3 miles: ⚄⚑⚏⚑⚒⚏⚐⚑
Notes: No caravans

SALCOMBE   Map 3 SX73

Places to visit
Overbeck's (NT), Salcombe 01548 842893
www.nationaltrust.org.uk
Cookworthy Museum of Rural Life, Kingsbridge
01548 853235 www.kingsbridgemuseum.net

►►► 79% Karrageen Caravan & Camping Park *(SX686395)*

Bolberry, Malborough TQ7 3EN
☎ **01548 561230**   🖷 **01548 560192**
e-mail: phil@karrageen.co.uk
dir: *At Malborough on A381, turn sharp right
through village, after 0.6m right again, after 0.9m
site on right*

* ⌸ £13-£22 ⌸ £13-£22 Å £12-£27

Open Etr-Sep Last arrival 21.00hrs Last dep 11.30hrs

A small friendly, family-run park with terraced
grass pitches giving extensive sea and country
views. There is a varied takeaway menu available
every evening, and a well-stocked shop. This park
is just one mile from the beach and pretty hamlet
of Hope Cove. A 7.5 acre site with 70 touring
pitches and 25 statics.

AA Pubs & Restaurants nearby: Victoria Inn,
Salcombe 01548 842604

Soar Mill Cove Hotel, Salcombe 01548 561566

Facilities: ⚄☺⚑☀⚅⚐⚅⚏⚒
Services: ⚑⚏⚐⚒⛲⚏⚒
Within 3 miles: ⚏⚑⚒⚐⚏
Notes: ⚏ Licensed shop, 2 play areas, family
shower room

►►► 78% Higher Rew Caravan & Camping Park *(SX714383)*

Higher Rew, Malborough TQ7 3BW
☎ **01548 842681**   🖷 **01548 843681**
e-mail: enquiries@higherrew.co.uk
dir: *A381 to Malborough. Right at Townsend Cross,
follow signs to Soar for 1m. Left at Rew Cross*

* ⌸ £12-£18 ⌸ £12-£18 Å £11-£16

Open Etr-Oct Last arrival 22.00hrs Last departure
noon

A long-established park in a remote location
within sight of the sea. The spacious, open touring
field has some tiered pitches in the sloping grass,
and there are lovely countryside or sea views from
every pitch. Friendly family owners are continually
improving the facilities. A 5 acre site with 85
touring pitches.

AA Pubs & Restaurants nearby: Victoria Inn,
Salcombe 01548 842604

Soar Mill Cove Hotel, Salcombe 01548 561566

Leisure: ⚄⚑   **Facilities:** ⚄☺⚑☀⚅⚐⚑
Services: ⚑⚏⚐⚒⛲⚏⚒
Within 3 miles: ⚏⚑⚒⚐⚏
Notes: ⚏ Play barn

►►► 74% Bolberry House Farm Caravan & Camping Park *(SX687395)*

Bolberry TQ7 3DY
☎ **01548 561251**
e-mail: enquiries@bolberryparks.co.uk
dir: *At Malborough on A381 turn right signed Hope
Cove/Bolberry. Take left fork after village signed
Soar/Bolberry. 0.6m right again. Site signed in
0.5m*

* ⌸ £12-£21 ⌸ £12-£21 Å £8-£21

Open Etr-Oct Last arrival 20.00hrs Last departure
11.30hrs

A very popular park in a peaceful setting on a
coastal farm with sea views, fine cliff walks and
nearby beaches. There's a discount in low season
for senior citizens. Customers are assured of a
warm welcome. A 6 acre site with 70 touring
pitches and 10 statics.

AA Pubs & Restaurants nearby: Victoria Inn,
Salcombe 01548 842604

Soar Mill Cove Hotel, Salcombe 01548 561566

Leisure: ⚑   **Facilities:** ⚄☺⚑☀⚅⚐⚑
Services: ⚑⚏⚒
Within 3 miles: ⚄⚏⚑⚒⚑⚐⚏⚑
Notes: ⚏

►► 69% Alston Camping and Caravan Site *(SX716406)*

Malborough, Kingsbridge TQ7 3BJ
☎ **01548 561260**   & **0780 803 0921**
e-mail: info@alstoncampsite.co.uk
dir: *1.5m W of town off A381 towards Malborough*

* ⌸ £11-£19 ⌸ £10-£19 Å £10-£19

Open 15 Mar-Oct

An established farm site in a rural location
adjacent to the Kingsbridge/Salcombe estuary.
The site is well sheltered and screened, and
approached down a long, well-surfaced narrow
farm lane with passing places. The toilet facilities
are basic. A 16 acre site with 90 touring pitches
and 58 statics.

AA Pubs & Restaurants nearby: Victoria Inn,
Salcombe 01548 842604

Soar Mill Cove Hotel, Salcombe 01548 561566

Leisure: ⚑   **Facilities:** ⚄☺⚑☀⚅⚐⚑⚏⚑
Services: ⚑⚏⚐⚒⛲⚏⚒
Within 3 miles: ⚄⚏⚑⚒⚑⚐⚏
Notes: ⚏

LEISURE: ⚁ Indoor swimming pool   ⚂ Outdoor swimming pool   ⚁ Children's playground   ⚃ Tennis court   ⚄ Games room   ⚅ Separate TV room   ⚆ 9/18 hole golf course
⚇ Boats for hire   ⚈ Cinema   ⚉ Fishing   ◎ Mini golf   ⚑ Watersports   U Stables   **FACILITIES:** ⚒ Bath   ⚄ Shower   ☺ Electric shaver   ⚐ Hairdryer   ☀ Ice Pack Facility
⚅ Disabled facilities   ⚅ Public telephone   ⚅ Shop on site or within 200yds   ⚏ Mobile shop (calls at least 5 days a week)   ⚑ BBQ area   ⚑ Picnic area   ⚑ Dog exercise area

SAMPFORD PEVERELL — Map 3 ST01

Places to visit

Tiverton Castle, Tiverton 01884 253200
www.tivertoncastle.com

Tiverton Museum of Mid Devon Life, Tiverton
01884 256295 www.tivertonmuseum.org.uk

Great for kids: Diggerland, Cullompton
0871 227 7007 www.diggerland.com

►►►► 87% Minnows Touring Park

(SS042148)

Holbrook Ln EX16 7EN
☎ 01884 821770 📠 01884 829199
dir: *M5 junct 27 take A361 signed Tiverton &
Barnstaple. In 600yds take 1st slip road, then
right over bridge, site ahead*

* 🚐 £12.70-£23.40 � £12.70-£23.40
🅰 £11.20-£14.20

Open 7 Mar-7 Nov Last arrival 20.00hrs Last
departure 11.30hrs

A small, well-sheltered park, peacefully located
amidst fields and mature trees. The toilet
facilities are of a high quality in keeping with the
rest of the park, and there is a good laundry. The
park has direct gated access to the canal
towpath. All pitches have hardstandings. A 5.5
acre site with 59 touring pitches, 59
hardstandings and 1 static.

Leisure: 🅰

Facilities: 🕭⊙🅿✳️❄️🕒⬛🎋

Services: 🔌🅱️🅐🅐🅣🔋⬇️

Within 3 miles: 🚴🏊‍♂️♨️⛴️💲

Notes: No cycling, no groundsheets on grass.
Tourist information centre

SHALDON

Places to visit

Bradley Manor (NT),
Newton Abbot 01803 843235
www.nationaltrust.org.uk/devoncornwall

'Bygones', Torquay 01803 326108
www.bygones.co.uk

Great for kids: Babbacombe Model Village,
Torquay 01803 315315
www.model-village.co.uk

SHALDON — Map 3 SX97

AA CAMPING CARD SITE

76% Coast View Holiday Park

(SX935716)

Torquay Rd TQ14 0BG
☎ 01626 872392 📠 01626 872719
e-mail: info@coastview.co.uk
dir: *M5 junct 31, A38 then A380 towards
Torquay. Then A381 towards Teignmouth. Right
in 4m at lights, over Shaldon Bridge. 0.75m, up
hill, site on right*

🚐�🅰

Open 15 Mar-1 Nov Last arrival 21.00hrs Last
departure 10.30hrs

This park has stunning sea views from its
spacious pitches. The family-run park has a full
entertainment programme every night for all
the family, plus outdoor and indoor activities
for children; this site will certainly appeal to
lively families. A 17 acre site with 110 touring
pitches, 6 hardstandings and 86 statics.

AA Pubs & Restaurants nearby: ODE, Shaldon
01626 873977

Leisure: 🏊‍♂️🅰🎣

Facilities: 🕭⊙🅿✳️❄️🕒⬛🎋🎋🐕

Services: 🔌🅱️🖥️🅐🅐🅣🍽️

Within 3 miles: 🚴🏊‍♂️♨️♨️🅿️◎⛴️💲🔵

Notes: Crazy golf, assault course, indoor soft
play areas. Wi-fi

SIDMOUTH

Places to visit

Branscombe - The Old Bakery, Manor Mill and
Forge (NT), Branscombe 01752 346585
www.nationaltrust.org.uk

Otterton Mill, Otterton 01392 568521
www.ottertonmill.com

Great for kids: Pecorama Pleasure Gardens,
Beer 01297 21542 www.peco-uk.com

SIDMOUTH — Map 3 SY18

**Regional Winner – AA South West of
England Campsite of the Year 2011**

PREMIER PARK

AA CAMPING CARD SITE

►►►►► 83% Oakdown Holiday Park

(SY167902)

Best of British

Gatedown Ln, Weston EX10 0PT
☎ 01297 680387 📠 01297 680541
e-mail: enquiries@oakdown.co.uk
web: www.oakdown.co.uk
dir: *Off A3052, 2.5m E of junct with A375*

* 🚐 £11.30-£27.50 � £11.30-£27.50
🅰 £11.30-£22

Open Apr-Oct Last arr 22.00hrs Last dep 10.30hrs

A quality, friendly, well-maintained park with
good landscaping and plenty of maturing
trees that makes it well screened from the
A3502. Pitches are grouped in paddocks
surrounded by shrubs, with a new 50-pitch
development replete with an upmarket toilet
block. The park's conservation areas, with
their natural flora and fauna, offer attractive
walks, and there is a hide by the Victorian
reed bed for both casual and dedicated bird
watchers. A delightful park in every respect. A
16 acre site with 150 touring pitches, 90
hardstandings and 62 statics.

AA Pubs & Restaurants nearby: The Blue
Ball, Sidford 01395 514062

The Salty Monk, Sidford 01395 513174

Dukes, Sidmouth 01395 513320

Leisure: 🅰🎣🛝

Facilities: ➡️🕭⊙🅿✳️❄️🕒⬛🐕

Services: 🔌🅱️🅐🅐🅣🍽️🔋⬇️

Within 3 miles: 🚴🏊‍♂️♨️♨️🅿️◎⛴️💲🔵🔵🔵

Notes: Dogs must be kept on leads, no bikes/
skateboards or kite flying. Use of microwave,
field trail to donkey sanctuary. Wi-fi

SERVICES: 🔌 Electric hook up 🅱️ Launderette 🍺 Licensed bar 🅐 Calor Gas ⛽ Camping Gaz 🅣 Toilet fluid 🍽️ Café/Restaurant 🍟 Fast Food/Takeaway 🔋 Battery charging
🍼 Baby care ⬇️ Motorvan service point **ABBREVIATIONS:** BH/bank hols-bank holidays Etr-Easter Whit-Whitsun dep-departure fr-from hrs-hours m-mile mdnt-midnight
rdbt-roundabout rs-restricted service wk-week wknd-weekend ⊛ No credit cards ⊗ no dogs See page 7 for details of the AA Camping Card Scheme

SIDMOUTH *continued*

►►► 83% Salcombe Regis Caravan & Camping Park *(SY153892)*

Salcombe Regis EX10 0JH
☎ **01395 514303** 📄 **01395 514314**
e-mail: contact@salcombe-regis.co.uk
web: www.salcombe-regis.co.uk
dir: *Off A3052 1m E of junct with A375. From opposite direction turn left past Donkey Sanctuary*

* 🚐 £11.50-£22 ⛺ £11.50-£22 ⛺ £11.50-£22

Open Etr-end Oct Last arrival 20.15hrs Last departure 10.30hrs

Set in quiet countryside with glorious views, this spacious park has well-maintained facilities, and a good mix of grass and hardstanding pitches. There is a self-catering holiday cottage and static caravans for hire. A footpath runs from the park to the coastal path and the beach. A 16 acre site with 100 touring pitches, 40 hardstandings and 10 statics.

AA Pubs & Restaurants nearby: The Blue Ball, Sidford 01395 514062

The Salty Monk, Sidford 01395 513174

Dukes, Sidmouth 01395 513320

Salcombe Regis Caravan & Camping Park

Leisure: 🅰
Facilities: 🚿 ⚡ ☺ 🅿 ✳ ⏰ 🛒 🎾 🐕
Services: 🚐 🔵 🛢 ⌀ 🅃 🚽 ⬇
Within 3 miles: ⚓ 🎣 🎬 🅿 ◎ ⚓ 🛒 🔵 ♻
Notes: Putting. Wi-fi

►►► 76% Kings Down Tail Caravan & Camping Park *(SY173907)*

Salcombe Regis EX10 0PD
☎ **01297 680313** 📄 **01297 680313**
e-mail: info@kingsdowntail.co.uk
dir: *Off A3052 3m E of junct with A375*

* 🚐 £16.50-£18.50 ⛺ £16.50-£18.50
⛺ £13.50-£15.50

Open 15 Mar-15 Nov Last arrival 22.00hrs Last departure noon

A well-kept site on level ground in a tree-sheltered spot on the side of the Sid Valley. This neat family-run park makes a good base for exploring the east Devon coast. A 5 acre site with 102 touring pitches, 61 hardstandings.

AA Pubs & Restaurants nearby: The Blue Ball, Sidford 01395 514062

The Salty Monk, Sidford 01395 513174

Dukes, Sidmouth 01395 513320

Leisure: 🅰 🎾 **Facilities:** ⚡ ☺ 🅿 ✳ ♿ 🛒 🐕
Services: 🚐 🔵 🛢 🅃 🛒
Within 3 miles: ⚓ 🎣 🎬 🅿 🔵 🔵 ♻

Notes: Dogs must be kep on leads at all times. Wet room for disabled or family use

see advert below

►►► 78% Bundu Camping & Caravan Park *(SX546916)*

EX20 4HT
☎ **01837 861611**
e-mail: frances@bundu.plus.com
dir: *W on A30, past Okehampton. Take A386 to Tavistock. Take 1st left & left again*

* 🚐 £12-£15 ⛺ £12-£15 ⛺ £8-£12

Open all year Last arrival 23.30hrs Last departure 14.00hrs

LEISURE: 🏊 Indoor swimming pool 🏊 Outdoor swimming pool 🅰 Children's playground 🎾 Tennis court 🎯 Games room 📺 Separate TV room ⛳ 9/18 hole golf course
⛵ Boats for hire 🎬 Cinema 🎣 Fishing ◎ Mini golf 🏄 Watersports ♻ Stables **FACILITIES:** 🛁 Bath 🚿 Shower ☺ Electric shaver 🅿 Hairdryer ✳ Ice Pack Facility
♿ Disabled facilities ☎ Public telephone 🛒 Shop on site or within 200yds 🚚 Mobile shop (calls at least 5 days a week) 🍖 BBQ area 🌲 Picnic area 🐕 Dog exercise area

Welcoming, friendly owners set the tone for this well-maintained site, ideally positioned on the border of the Dartmoor National Park. Along with fine views and level grassy pitches, the Granite Way cycle track from Lydford to Okehampton along the old railway line (part of the Devon Coast to Coast cycle trail) passes the edge of the park. A 4.5 acre site with 38 touring pitches, 11 hardstandings.

AA Pubs & Restaurants nearby: Highwayman Inn, Sourton 01837 861243

Facilities: ⋔ ☉ ⌗ ✻ ⛽ 🅑 🎣 ⌂

Services: 🔌 🅢 🅐 🥫 🅣 🔋

Within 3 miles: ⊟ 🅢 🅢 **Notes:** ⊛

SOUTH MOLTON   Map 3 SS72

Places to visit

Quince Honey Farm, South Molton 01769 572401 www.quincehoney.com

Great for kids: Exmoor Zoological Park, Blackmoor Gate 01598 763352 www.exmoorzoo.co.uk

---

AA CAMPING CARD SITE

►►►► 88% Riverside Caravan & Camping Park (SS723274)

Marsh Ln, North Molton Rd EX36 3HQ
☎ 01769 579269   📠 01769 574853
e-mail: relax@exmoorriverside.co.uk
web: www.exmoorriverside.co.uk
dir: M5 junct 27 onto A361 towards Barnstaple. Site signed 1m before South Molton on right

* 🚐 £15-£21 🚙 £15-£21 ▲ £10-£18

Open all year Last arrival 22.00hrs Last dep 11.00hrs

A newly developed family-run park, set alongside the River Mole, where supervised children can play, and fishing is available. This is an ideal base for exploring Exmoor, as well as north Devon's golden beaches. The site has an award for the excellence of the toilets. There are now tea rooms offering hot meals and takeaways. A 40 acre site with 42 touring pitches, 42 hardstandings.

AA Pubs & Restaurants nearby: The Rising Sun Inn, Umberleigh 01769 560447

Leisure: ⛰ **Facilities:** ⋔ ☉ ⌗ ✻ ⛽ 🅞 🅑 ⌂ 🎣
Services: 🔌 🅢 🅐 🥫 🅣 🔋 ⛽
Within 3 miles: ⊟ 🅟 🍴 🅢 🅢 ⛳

Notes: Pets must be on leads. Fishing. Storage available

STARCROSS

See Dawlish

STOKE GABRIEL   Map 3 SX85

Places to visit

Berry Pomeroy Castle, Totnes 01803 866618 www.english-heritage.org.uk

Totnes Museum, Totnes 01803 863821 www.devonmuseums.net/totnes

Great for kids: Paignton Zoo Environmental Park, Paignton 0844 474 2222 www.paigntonzoo.org.uk

►►► 84% Higher Well Farm Holiday Park (SX857577)

Waddeton Rd TQ9 6RN
☎ 01803 782289
e-mail: higherwell@talk21.com
dir: From Exeter A380 to Torbay, turn right onto A385 for Totnes, in 0.5m left for Stoke Gabriel, follow signs

🚐 £10.50-£17 🚙 £10.50-£17 ▲ £10.50-£17

Open 8 Apr-30 Oct Last arrival 22.00hrs Last departure 10.00hrs

Set on a quiet farm yet only four miles from Paignton, this rural holiday park is on the outskirts of the picturesque village of Stoke Gabriel. A toilet block, with some en suite facilities, is an excellent amenity, and tourers are housed in an open field with some very good views. A 10 acre site with 80 touring pitches, 3 hardstandings and 19 statics.

AA Pubs & Restaurants nearby: Durant Arms, Ashprington 01803 732240

Steam Packet Inn,Totnes 01803 863880

White Hart, Totnes 01803 847111

Facilities: ⋔ ☉ ⌗ ✻ ⛽ 🅞 🅑 🎣
Services: 🔌 🅢 🅐 🥫 🅣 🔋 ⛽
Within 3 miles: 🅟 🅢 🅢

Notes: No commercial vehicles

►►► 80% Broadleigh Farm Park (SX851587)

Coombe House Ln, Aish TQ9 6PU
☎ 01803 782422
e-mail: enquiries@broadleighfarm.co.uk
web: www.broadleighfarm.co.uk
dir: From Exeter on A38 then A380 towards Torbay. Right onto A385 for Totnes. In 0.5m right at Whitehill Country Park. Site approx 0.75m on left

* 🚐 £10.50-£19.50 🚙 £10.50-£19.50
▲ £10.50-£19.50

Open Mar-Oct Last arrival 21.00hrs Last departure 11.30hrs

Set in a very rural location on a working farm bordering Paignton and Stoke Gabriel. The large sloping field with a timber-clad toilet block in the centre is sheltered and peaceful, surrounded by rolling countryside but handy for the beaches. There is also an excellent rally field with good toilets and showers. A 7 acre site with 80 touring pitches.

AA Pubs & Restaurants nearby: Rumour, Totnes 01803 864682

Royal Seven Stars Hotel, Totnes 01803 862125

Facilities: ⋔ ☉ ⌗ ✻ ⛽ 🎣 **Services:** 🔌 🅢 🔋
Within 3 miles: 🅟 ⊟ 🅟 ◎ 🍴 🅢 🅢 **Notes:** ⊛

STOKENHAM   Map 3 SX84

Places to visit

Cookworthy Museum of Rural Life, Kingsbridge 01548 853235 www.kingsbridgemuseum.net

►►► 80% Old Cotmore Farm

(SX804417)

TQ7 2LR
☎ 01548 580240
e-mail: info@holiday-in-devon.com
dir: From Kingsbridge take A379 towards Dartmouth, through Frogmore & Chillington to mini rdbt at Stokenham. Right towards Beesands, site 1m on right

🚐 🚙 ▲

Open 15 Mar-Oct Last arrival 20.00hrs Last departure 11.00hrs

A small and peaceful, family run touring caravan and camp site well located in the South Hams region of Devon, close to Slapton and within easy reach of Salcombe and Dartmouth. Facilities are very clean and well maintained and there is a basic shop and small play area. Pebble and sandy beaches with cliff walks through woods and fields are within walking distance. Self-catering cottages are available. A 22 acre site with 30 touring pitches, 25 hardstandings.

AA Pubs & Restaurants nearby: Start Bay Inn, Torcross 01548 580553

The Cricket Inn, Beesands 01548 580215

Leisure: ⛰ 🎣 **Facilities:** ⋔ ✻ ⛽ 🅞 🅑 ⌂ 🎣
Services: 🔌 🅢 🅐 🥫 🔋 ⛽
Within 3 miles: 🍴 🅟 🍴 🅢 🅢
Notes: Wi-fi

TAVISTOCK — Map 3 SX47

Places to visit

Morwellham Quay, Morwellham 01822 832766
www.morwellham-quay.co.uk

Yelverton Paperweight Centre, Yelverton
01822 854250 www.paperweightcentre.co.uk

Great for kids: National Marine Aquarium,
Plymouth 01752 600301
www.national-aquarium.co.uk

►►►► 85% Woodovis Park

(SX431745)

Gulworthy PL19 8NY
☎ 01822 832968 📠 01822 832948
e-mail: info@woodovis.com
dir: *A390 from Tavistock signed Callington
& Gunnislake. At hill top right at rdbt signed
Lamerton & Chipshop. Site 1m on left*

* 🚐 £15-£30 🚌 £15-£30 ▲ £15-£30

Open 26 Mar-29 Oct Last arrival 20.00hrs Last
departure noon

A well-kept park in a remote woodland setting on
the edge of the Tamar Valley. This peacefully-
located park is set at the end of a private, half-
mile, tree-lined road, and has lots of on-site
facilities. The toilets are excellent, and there is an
indoor swimming pool, all in a friendly, purposeful
atmosphere. Four seasonal touring pitches are
available. A 14.5 acre site with 50 touring pitches,
20 hardstandings and 35 statics.

AA Pubs & Restaurants nearby: Dartmoor Inn,
Lydford 01822 820221

Royal Inn, Horsebridge 01822 870214

Leisure: 🏊♨️Ⓜ️🔍

Facilities: 🚿🚻⊙℘✳️🔥⚡🛎️🖶🚻

Services: 🔌🛢️🍳⌀🚽🛒🚮

Within 3 miles: 🎣℘◎🏄🛒🛍️♻️U

Notes: Dogs must be kept on leads. Mini golf,
jacuzzi, archery, water-walking, physiotherm
infra-red therapy cabin. Wi-fi

AA CAMPING CARD SITE

►►►► 79% Langstone Manor Camping & Caravan Park *(SX524738)*

Moortown PL19 9JZ
☎ 01822 613371 📠 01822 613371
e-mail: jane@langstone-manor.co.uk
web: www.langstone-manor.co.uk
dir: *Take B3357 from Tavistock to Princetown.
Approx 1.5m turn right at x-rds, follow signs. Over
bridge, cattle grid, up hill, left at sign, left again.
Follow lane to park*

🚐 £13.50-£17 🚌 £13.50-£17 ▲ £13.50-£17

Open 15 Mar-Oct (rs Wkdys in low season
restricted hours in bar & restaurant) Last arrival
22.00hrs Last departure 11.00hrs

A secluded site set in the well-maintained
grounds of a manor house in Dartmoor National
Park. Many attractive mature trees provide a
screen within the park, and there is a popular
lounge bar with an excellent menu of reasonably
priced evening meals. Plenty of activities and
places of interest can be found within the
surrounding moorland. A 6.5 acre site with 40
touring pitches, 10 hardstandings and 25 statics.

AA Pubs & Restaurants nearby: Dartmoor Inn,
Lydford 01822 820221

Royal Inn, Horsebridge 01822 870214

Leisure: Ⓜ️🔍

Facilities: 🚿⊙℘✳️⚡🔥🖶

Services: 🔌🛢️🍳⌀🚽🍽️🛒🚮

Within 3 miles: 🎣🏇℘◎🏄🛒🛍️♻️U

Notes: No skateboards, scooters, cycles, ball
games. Baguettes, croissants & pain au chocolate
available

AA CAMPING CARD SITE

►►► 82% Harford Bridge Holiday Park *(SX504767)*

Peter Tavy PL19 9LS
☎ 01822 810349 📠 01822 810028
e-mail: enquiry@harfordbridge.co.uk
web: www.harfordbridge.co.uk
dir: *2m N of Tavistock, off A386 Okehampton Rd,
take Peter Tavy turn, entrance 200yds on right*

* 🚐 fr £12.75 🚌 fr £12.75 ▲ fr £12.75

Open all year (rs Nov-Mar statics only & 5
hardstandings) Last arrival 21.00hrs Last
departure noon

This beautiful spacious park is set beside the
River Tavy in the Dartmoor National Park. Pitches
are located beside the river and around the
copses, and the park is very well equipped for the
holidaymaker. An adventure playground and
games room entertain children, and there is fly-
fishing and a free tennis court. A 16 acre site with
120 touring pitches, 5 hardstandings and 80
statics.

AA Pubs & Restaurants nearby: Dartmoor Inn,
Lydford 01822 820221

Royal Inn, Horsebridge 01822 870214

Leisure: Ⓜ️🎾🔍🖥️

Facilities: 🚿⊙℘✳️⚡🔥🖶🚻

Services: 🔌🛢️🍳⌀🚽🛒🚮

Within 3 miles: 🎣🏇℘🛒🛍️U

Notes: No large groups. Fly fishing. Wi-fi

TEDBURN ST MARY
Map 3 SX89

Places to visit
Finch Foundry (NT), Sticklepath 01837 840046 www.nationaltrust.org.uk

Castle Drogo (NT), Drewsteignton 01647 433306 www.nationaltrust.org.uk/main

Great for kids: Prickly Ball Farm and Hedgehog Hospital, Newton Abbot 01626 362319 www.pricklyballfarm.com

AA CAMPING CARD SITE

▶▶▶▶ 80% Springfield Holiday Park (SX788935)

EX6 6EW
☎ 01647 24242
e-mail: enquiries@springfieldholidaypark.co.uk
dir: M5 junct 31, A30 towards Okehampton, exit at junct, signed to Cheriton Bishop. Follow brown tourist signs to site. (For Sat Nav use postcode EX6 6JN)

🚐 £15-£20 🚏 £15-£25 ▲ £10-£15

Open 15 Mar-15 Nov Last arrival 22.00hrs Last departure noon

Set in a quiet rural location with countryside views, this park continues to be upgraded to a smart standard. It has the advantage of being located close to Dartmoor National Park, with village pubs and stores just two miles away. A 9 acre site with 48 touring pitches, 38 hardstandings and 49 statics.

AA Pubs & Restaurants nearby: Old Thatch Inn, Cheriton Bishop 01647 24204

Leisure: 🏊 🎢 🔍
Facilities: 🌲 ☺ ⚹ 🍴 🎏 🐕
Services: 🔌 🗑 🛢 🚿
Within 3 miles: ⚓ 🚴 🐢 🎣
Notes: Dogs must be kept on leads. Family shower rooms

TIVERTON

See East Worlington

TORQUAY
Map 3 SX96

See also Newton Abbot

Places to visit
Torre Abbey, Torquay 01803 293593 www.torre-abbey.org.uk

'Bygones', Torquay 01803 326108 www.bygones.co.uk

Great for kids: Living Coasts, Torquay 01803 202470 www.livingcoasts.org.uk

▶▶▶▶ 81% Widdicombe Farm Touring Park (SX876643)

Marldon TQ3 1ST
☎ 01803 558325 📠 01803 559526
e-mail: info@widdicombefarm.co.uk
dir: On A380, midway between Torquay & Paignton ring road

🚐 🚏 ▲

Open mid Mar-mid Oct Last arrival 20.00hrs Last departure 10.00hrs

A friendly family-run park on a working farm with good quality facilities and extensive views. The level pitches are terraced to take advantage of the views towards the coast and Dartmoor. This is the only touring park within Torquay, and is also handy for Paignton and Brixham. Wi-fi is now available and there's a new bus service from the park to the local shopping centre and Torquay's harbour. There is a well-stocked shop, a restaurant and a lounge bar. An 8 acre site with 180 touring pitches, 180 hardstandings and 3 statics.

AA Pubs & Restaurants nearby: Church House Inn, Marldon 01803 558279

Elephant Restaurant & Brasserie, Torquay 01803 200044

No 7 Fish Bistro, Torquay 01803 295055

Facilities: 🌲 ☺ 🍽 ⚹ 🚿 🍴 🎏 🐕
Services: 🔌 🗑 🍽 🛢 🚿 🔧 🍴 🚮 ⛽
Within 3 miles: ⚓ 🚴 🐢 🎣 ◎ 🏊 🎣
Notes: Adults only. Most dog breeds accepted. Dog exercise area, entertainment

WOODBURY SALTERTON
Map 3 SY08

Places to visit
The World of Country Life, Exmouth 01395 274533 www.worldofcountrylife.co.uk

A la Ronde (NT), Exmouth 01395 265514 www.nationaltrust.org.uk

Great for kids: Crealy Adventure Park, Clyst St Mary 01395 233200 www.crealy.co.uk

▶▶▶ 86% Browns Farm Caravan Park (SY016885)

Browns Farm EX5 1PS
☎ 01395 232895
dir: M5 junct 30, A3052 for 3.7m. Right at White Horse Inn follow sign to Woodbury, right at x-rds in village centre, site 1.25m on left

* 🚐 £10-£13 🚏 £10-£13 ▲ £10-£13

Open all year Last departure 11.00hrs

A small farm park adjoining a 14th-century thatched farmhouse, and located in a quiet village. Pitches back onto hedgerows, and friendly owners keep the excellent facilities very clean. The tourist information and games room, with table tennis, chess etc, is housed in a purpose-built building. The park is just a mile from the historic heathland of Woodbury Common with its superb views. A 2.5 acre site with 29 touring pitches, 24 hardstandings.

AA Pubs & Restaurants nearby: Golden Lion Inn, Tipton St John 01404 812881

Moore's Restaurant & Rooms, Newton Poppleford 01395 568100

Leisure: 🔍 🖵
Facilities: 🌲 ☺ 🍽 ⚹ 🚿 🕐
Services: 🔌 🗑 🛢 🚿 ⛽
Within 3 miles: ⚓ 🐢 🎣 ↻
Notes: ⊛ No ground sheets in awnings, no music. Hardstandings for winter period, caravan storage

WOOLACOMBE
Map 3 SS44

See also Mortehoe

Places to visit

Arlington Court (NT), Arlington 01271 850296
www.nationaltrust.org.uk/
main/w-arlingtoncourt

Great for kids: Watermouth Castle & Family
Theme Park, Ilfracombe 01271 863879
www.watermouthcastle.com

AA CAMPING CARD SITE

**80% Woolacombe Bay Holiday
Village** (SS465442)

Sandy Ln EX34 7AH
☎ 01271 870343 📠 01271 870089
e-mail: goodtimes@woolacombe.com
dir: From Mullacott Cross rdbt take B3343
(Woolacombe road) to Turnpike Cross junct.
Right towards Mortehoe, site approx 1m on left

* 🚐 🚗 ▲ £10.50-£38

Open Mar-Oct (rs Mar-mid May, mid Sep-Oct
no touring, camping only available) Last arrival
mdnt Last departure 10.00hrs

A well-developed touring section in a holiday
complex with a full entertainment and leisure
programme. This park offers excellent facilities
including a steam room and sauna. For a small
charge a bus takes holidaymakers to the other
Woolacombe Bay holiday centres where they can
take part in any of the activities offered, and
there is also a bus to the beach. An 8 acre site
with 180 touring pitches and 237 statics.

AA Pubs & Restaurants nearby: George &
Dragon, Ilfracombe 01271 863851

The Quay, Ilfracombe 01271 868090

The Williams Arms, Braunton 01271 812360

Leisure: 🏊🏊⛰🎱🔍📺

Facilities: 🎣☉👁✳🔥♿⏰🛒🚿🔫🚻

Services: 🔌🚽🍴🛢🧹🍽🍔🔋

Within 3 miles: 🚴⛳🎯🏇🚶◎🏄🐟🎣🎱⛵

Notes: Entertainment, kids' club, health suite,
surfing & swimming lessons

see advert on opposite page

WOOLACOMBE *continued*

AA CAMPING CARD SITE

78% Golden Coast Holiday Park *(SS482436)*

Station Rd EX34 7HW
☎ 01271 870343 📄 01271 870089
e-mail: goodtimes@woolacombe.com
dir: *From Mullacott Cross towards Woolacombe Bay, site 1.5m on left*

* 🚐 £15.75-£60 🚌 £15.75-£60 ⛺ £10.50-£38

Open Feb-Dec (rs mid Sep-May outdoor pools closed) Last arrival mdnt Last departure 10.00hrs

A holiday village offering excellent leisure facilities together with the amenities available at the other Woolacombe Bay holiday parks. There is a neat touring area with a unisex toilet block, maintained to a high standard. Bowling alleys, a number of bars and plenty of activities add to the holiday experience. A 10 acre site with 91 touring pitches, 53 hardstandings and 444 statics.

AA Pubs & Restaurants nearby: George & Dragon, Ilfracombe 01271 863851

The Quay, Ilfracombe 01271 868090

The Williams Arms, Braunton 01271 812360

Leisure: 🏊 🏊 🎢 🎱 🏌 📺
Facilities: 🚿 ⊙ 🅿 ✳ ⚕ 🕐 🛒 🍽 🎋
Services: 🚱 🔧 🍴 🛢 ⊘ 📞 🍽 🛒 🛆 ⚡ ⛽
Within 3 miles: ⚓ 🎿 🎪 🎣 ⊚ ⛵ 🛒 🎿 🎠 ⛲

Notes: No pets on touring pitches. Sauna, solarium, golf, fishing, snooker, cinema, kids' clubs, swimming & surfing lessons. Wi-fi

---

76% Woolacombe Sands Holiday Park *(SS471434)*

Beach Rd EX34 7AF
☎ 01271 870569 📄 01271 870606
e-mail: lifesabeach@woolacombe-sands.co.uk
dir: *M5 junct 27, A361 to Barnstaple. Follow Ilfracombe signs, until Mullacott Cross. Turn left onto B3343 to Woolacombe. Site on left*

🚐 £10-£30 🚌 £10-£30 ⛺ £10-£30

Open Apr-Oct Last arrival 22.00hrs Last departure 10.00hrs

Set in rolling countryside with grassy terraced pitches, most with spectacular views overlooking the sea at Woolacombe. The lovely Blue Flag beach can be accessed directly by footpath in 10-15 minutes, and there is a full entertainment programme for all the family in high season. A 20 acre site with 200 touring pitches, 50 hardstandings and 80 statics.

AA Pubs & Restaurants nearby: George & Dragon, Ilfracombe 01271 863851

The Quay, Ilfracombe 01271 868090

The Williams Arms, Braunton 01271 812360

Leisure: 🏊 🏊 🎢 🎱
Facilities: 🚿 ⊙ 🅿 ✳ ⚕ 🕐 🛒 🎋
Services: 🚱 🔧 🍴 🛢 ⊘ 📞 🍽 🛒 🛆 ⚡
Within 3 miles: ⚓ 🎣 ⊚ 🎿 🎠 🛒 ⛲

Notes: Kids' club, crazy golf. Wi-fi

see advert on page 173

▶▶▶ **77% *Europa Park*** *(SS475435)*

Beach Rd EX34 7AN
☎ 01271 871425 📄 01271 871425
e-mail: europaparkwoolacombe@yahoo.co.uk
dir: *M5 junct 27, A361 through Barnstaple to Mullacott Cross. Left onto B3343 signed Woolacombe. Site on right at Spa shop/garage*

🚐 🚌 ⛺

Open all year Last arrival 23.00hrs

A very lively family-run site handy for the beach at Woolacombe, and catering well for surfers but maybe not suitable for a quieter type of stay. Set in a stunning location high above the bay, it provides a wide range of accommodation including surf cabins, and generous touring pitches. Visitors can enjoy the indoor pool and sauna, games room, restaurant/café/bar and clubhouse. Please make sure the site is suitable for you before making your booking. A 16 acre site with 200 touring pitches, 20 hardstandings and 22 statics.

AA Pubs & Restaurants nearby: George & Dragon, Ilfracombe 01271 863851

The Quay, Ilfracombe 01271 868090

The Williams Arms, Braunton 01271 812360

Leisure: 🏊 🎢 🎱 📺
Facilities: 🚿 ⊙ ✳ 🕐 🛒 🎋
Services: 🚱 🔧 🍴 🛢 ⊘ 📞 🍽 🛒 ⛽
Within 3 miles: 🎣 ⊚ 🎿 🎠 🛒 ⛲

Notes: Beer deck, off licence, pub, big screen TV

SERVICES: ⚡ Electric hook up ▣ Launderette 🍸 Licensed bar 🔵 Calor Gas ⊘ Camping Gaz 🅃 Toilet fluid 🍴 Café/Restaurant 🍟 Fast Food/Takeaway 🔋 Battery charging
🍼 Baby care ↧ Motorvan service point **ABBREVIATIONS:** BH/bank hols-bank holidays Etr-Easter Whit-Whitsun dep-departure fr-from hrs-hours m-mile mdnt-midnight
rdbt-roundabout rs-restricted service wk-week wknd-weekend ⊛ No credit cards ⊗ no dogs See page 7 for details of the AA Camping Card Scheme

Dorset

Dorset means rugged varied coastline and high chalk downland, with more than a hint of Thomas Hardy, its most famous son. The coastal grandeur is breathtaking with two famous local landmarks, Lulworth Cove and Durdle Door, shaped and sculpted to perfection by the elements. Squeezed in among the cliffs and set amid some of Britain's most beautiful scenery is a chain of picturesque villages and occasionally seaside towns.

Most prominent among these seaside towns is Lyme Regis, with its sturdy breakwater, known as the Cobb, made famous by Jane Austen in *Persuasion*, and John Fowles in *The French Lieutenant's Woman*. It's the sort of place where Georgian houses and quaint cottages jostle with historic pubs and independently run shops. With its blend of architectural styles and old world charm, Lyme looks very much like a film set, and fans of Austen and Fowles and the big-screen adaptations of their work flock to point their cameras and enjoy its beauty. Before the era of sea-bathing and Victorian respectability, the town was a haunt of smugglers.

Chesil Beach

In sharp contrast to Lyme's steep streets and dramatic inclines is Chesil Beach, a long shingle reef extending for 10 miles (16.1km) between

▶

Walking near Durdle Door

Abbotsbury and Portland. The beach is covered by a vast wall of shingle resulting from centuries of violent weather-influenced activity along the Devon and Dorset coastline. The novelist Ian McEwan chose the setting for his recent novel *On Chesil Beach*.

Thomas Hardy

Rural Dorset is where you can be 'far from the madding crowd'- to quote Thomas Hardy. For fans of this popular and much-admired writer there is the chance to visit two National Trust properties - the cob-and-thatch cottage in Higher Bockhampton where he was born and lived until the age of 34, and Max Gate in Dorchester, his home for 40 years and where he wrote some of his best-known works.

Walking and Cycling

For the true walker, however, there is nowhere to beat the magnificent Dorset coastline, particularly in the vicinity of Charmouth and Bridport where the domed Golden Cap stands tall and proud amid the cliffs. At 619ft it is the highest cliff on the south coast. Getting there, however, involves about 0.75 mile (1.2km) of steep walking. The Golden Cap is part of Dorset's spectacular Jurassic Coast, a World Heritage Site. This designated coastline stretches to East Devon.

The South West Coast Path, one of Britain's great walks, extends the length of the Dorset coast, from Lyme Regis to Studland Bay and Poole Harbour, and offers constant uninterrupted views of the coast and the Channel. Away from the sea there are miles of rolling downland walks which are no less impressive than the coastal stretches. The Purbeck Hills, between Weymouth and Poole Harbour, are

great for exploring on foot. Cranborne Chase, to the north of Blandford Forum and once a royal forest, is a remote, rural backwater where the walker can feel totally at home.

The National Cycle Network offers the chance to ride from Dorchester through the heart of Dorset to Lyme Regis or north to Sherborne, taking in some of the county's most picturesque villages. There is also the chance to tour the ancient hill forts of Pilsdon Pen, Coneys Castle and Lamberts Castle around Charmouth and the Marshwood Vale – among a wide choice of Dorset cycle routes.

Festivals and Events

- Among numerous live shows, exhibitions, flower festivals and craft fairs, is the Great Dorset Steam Fair in September. This famous event draws many visitors who come to look at vintage and classic vehicles. There are also heavy horse shows and rural crafts.
- Also in September is the two-day Dorset County Show which includes over 450 trade stands, exciting main ring attractions and thousands of animals.
- For something a bit more light-hearted – but perhaps a little uncomfortable - there is the annual Nettle Eating Contest in June, which attracts fans from all over Europe.

DORSET

See Walk 4 in the Walks & Cycle Rides section at the end of the guide

ALDERHOLT　　Map 5 SU11

Places to visit

Furzey Gardens, Minstead, 023 8081 2464, www.furzey-gardens.org

Breamore House and Country Museum, Breamore, 01725 512468, www.breamorehouse.com

Great for kids: Rockbourne Roman Villa, Rockbourne, 0845 603 5635, www.hants.gov.uk/rockbourne-roman-villa

►►►► 84% Hill Cottage Farm Camping and Caravan Park (SU119133)

Sandleheath Rd SP6 3EG
☎ 01425 650513　🖷 01425 652339
e-mail: hillcottagefarmcaravansite@supanet.com
dir: Take B3078 W of Fordingbridge. Turn off at Alderholt, site 0.25m on left after railway bridge

* ➡ £19-£23 ⇔ £19-£23 ▲ £13-£28

Open Mar-Nov Last arrival 19.00hrs Last departure 11.00hrs

Set within extensive grounds this rural, beautifully landscaped park offers all fully-serviced pitches set in individual hardstanding bays with mature hedges between giving adequate pitch privacy. The modern toilet block is kept immaculately clean, and there's a good range of leisure facilities. In high season there is an area available for tenting plus a rally field. A 40 acre site with 35 touring pitches, 35 hardstandings.

AA Pubs & Restaurants nearby: The Augustus John, Fordingbridge 01425 652098

Leisure: ⚙ ✎
Facilities: ⚙ ⊙ ✎ ✳ ✎ ⊙ ⚙ ➤ ⚙ ✎
Services: ⚙ ✎ ⚙ ⚙
Within 3 miles: ⚙ ✎ ⚙ ⚙
Notes: Wi-fi

BERE REGIS　　Map 4 SY89

Places to visit

Kingston Lacy, Wimborne, 01202 883402 (Mon-Fri), www.nationaltrust.org.uk

The Priests House and Garden, Wimborne, 01202 882533, www.priest-house.co.uk

Great for kids: Monkey World-Ape Rescue Centre, Wool, 01929 462537, www.monkeyworld.org

►►► 81% Rowlands Wait Touring Park

(SY842933)

Rye Hill BH20 7LP
☎ 01929 472727　🖷 01929 472275
e-mail: enquiries@rowlandswait.co.uk
web: www.rowlandswait.co.uk
dir: On approach to Bere Regis follow signs to Bovington Tank Museum. At top of Rye Hill, 0.75m from village turn right. 200yds to site

* ➡ £15-£19.50 ⇔ £15-£19.50 ▲ £13-£16

Open mid Mar-Oct (winter by arrangement) Last arrival 21.00hrs Last departure noon

This park lies in a really attractive setting overlooking Bere Regis and the Dorset countryside, set amongst undulating areas of trees and shrubs. The toilet facilities include two family rooms. Located within a few miles of the Tank Museum with its mock battles. Seasonal touring pitches are available. An 8 acre site with 71 touring pitches, 2 hardstandings.

AA Pubs & Restaurants nearby: Botany Bay Inne, Winterborne Zelston 01929 459227

Leisure: ⚙ ✎
Facilities: ⚙ ⊙ ✎ ✳ ✎ ⚙ ➤ ⚙
Services: ⚙ ✎ ⚙ ⚙ ⚙
Within 3 miles: ⚙ ✎ ⊙ ⚙ ⚙ ⚙
Notes: No open fires

BLANDFORD FORUM　　Map 4 ST80

Places to visit

Kingston Lacy, Wimborne, 01202 883402 (Mon-Fri), www.nationaltrust.org.uk

Old Wardour Castle, Tisbury, 01747 870487, www.english-heritage.org.uk

Great for kids: Monkey World-Ape Rescue Centre, Wool, 01929 462537, www.monkeyworld.org

►►►► 80% The Inside Park

(ST869046)

Down House Estate DT11 9AD
☎ 01258 453719　🖷 01258 459921
e-mail: inspark@aol.com
dir: From town, over River Stour, follow Winterborne Stickland signs. Site in 1.5m

* ➡ £14-£21 ⇔ £14-£21 ▲ £14-£21

Open Etr-Oct Last arrival 22.00hrs Last departure noon

An attractive, well-sheltered and quiet park, half a mile off a country lane in a wooded valley. Spacious pitches are divided by mature trees and shrubs, and amenities are housed in an 18th-century coach house and stables. There are some lovely woodland walks within the park and an excellent fenced play area for children. A 12 acre site with 125 touring pitches.

AA Pubs & Restaurants nearby: Crown Hotel, Blandford Forum 01258 456626

Anvil Inn, Blandford Forum 01258 453431

Leisure: ⚙ ✎
Facilities: ⚙ ⊙ ✎ ✳ ✎ ⊙ ⚙ ➤
Services: ⚙ ✎ ⚙ ⚙ ⚙
Within 3 miles: ⚙ ✎ ⚙ ⚙ ⚙
Notes: Farm trips (main season), kennels for hire

BRIDPORT

Places to visit

Forde Abbey, Chard, 01460 221290, www.fordeabbey.co.uk

Dorchester County Museum, Dorchester, 01305 262735, www.dorsetcountymuseum.org

Great for kids: Abbotsbury Swannery, Abbotsbury, 01305 871858, www.abbotsbury-tourism.co.uk

---

BRIDPORT
Map 4 SY49

87% Freshwater Beach Holiday Park (SY493892)

Burton Bradstock DT6 4PT
☎ 01308 897317 📄 01308 897336
e-mail: office@freshwaterbeach.co.uk
web: www.freshwaterbeach.co.uk
dir: *Take B3157 from Bridport towards Burton Bradstock. Site 1.5m from Crown rdbt on right*

* 🚐 £14-£37 🚑 £14-£37 ⛺ £14-£37

Open 15 Mar-10 Nov Last arrival 22.00hrs Last departure 10.00hrs

A family holiday centre sheltered by a sandbank and enjoying its own private beach. The park offers a wide variety of leisure and entertainment programmes for all the family. It is well placed at one end of the Weymouth/Bridport coast with spectacular views of Chesil Beach. There are three immaculate toilet blocks, with excellent private rooms. A 40 acre site with 500 touring pitches and 250 statics.

AA Pubs & Restaurants nearby: Anchor Inn, Bridport 01297 489215

Shave Cross Inn, Bridport 01308 868358

Riverside Restaurant, Bridport 01308 422011

Leisure: 🏊 🎠 🎯

Facilities: 🚿 📷 🍴 🪒 ⚡ 🕐 🛒 🐕

Services: 🚐 🔧 🍴 🛢 ⌀ 🚻 🍴 📮 🛒 ♻

Within 3 miles: 🚣 🎣 🏌 ⛳ 🛒 🎯 ⛱ ⛵

Notes: Families and couples only. Large TV, internet access, entertainment in high season & Bank Holidays. Wi-fi

see advert on page 181

81% West Bay Holiday Park (SY461906)

SILVER

West Bay DT6 4HB
☎ 0844 335 3756 📄 01308 421371
e-mail:
touringandcamping@parkdeanholidays.com
web: www.parkdeantouring.com
dir: *From A35 (Dorchester road), W towards Bridport, take 1st exit at 1st rdbt, 2nd exit at 2nd rdbt into West Bay, site on right*

🚐 £16.50-£37 🚑 £16.50-£37 ⛺ £13.50-£37

Open Mar-Oct Last arrival 21.00hrs Last departure 10.00hrs

Overlooking the pretty little harbour at West Bay, and close to the shingle beach, this park offers a full entertainment programme for all ages. There are children's clubs and an indoor pool with flume for all the family, and plenty of evening fun with shows and cabaret etc. The grassy touring area is terraced to enjoy the sea views and has plenty of hardstandings. The large adventure playground is very popular. A 6 acre site with 131 touring pitches, 10 hardstandings and 307 statics.

AA Pubs & Restaurants nearby: George Hotel, Bridport 01308 423187

West Bay, Bridport 01308 422157

Riverside Restaurant, Bridport 01308 422011

Leisure: 🏊 🎠 🎯

Facilities: 🐕 🚿 📷 🍴 🪒 ⚡ 🕐 🛒 🎪

Services: 🚐 🔧 🍴 🛢 ⌀ 🚻 🍴 📮 🛒 ♻

Within 3 miles: 🚣 🎣 🏌 ⛳ 🛒 🎯 ⛱ ⛵

Notes: No skateboards. Family entertainment, children's clubs. Wi-fi

see advert in preliminary section

▶▶▶▶▶ 86% Highlands End Holiday Park (SY454913)

Best of British
GOLD

Eype DT6 6AR
☎ 01308 422139 & 426947 📄 01308 425672
e-mail: holidays@wdlh.co.uk
dir: *1m W of Bridport on A35, turn south for Eype. Site signed*

* 🚐 £14.50-£26.25 🚑 £14.50-£26.25 ⛺ £12.50-£21

Open mid Mar-early Nov Last arrival 22.00hrs Last departure 11.00hrs

A well-screened site with magnificent cliff-top views over the Channel and Dorset coast, adjacent to National Trust land and overlooking Lyme Bay. The pitches are mostly sheltered by hedging and well spaced on hardstandings. The facilities are excellent. There is a mixture of statics and tourers, but the tourers enjoy the best cliff-top positions. A 9 acre site with 195 touring pitches, 45 hardstandings and 160 statics.

AA Pubs & Restaurants nearby: Anchor Inn, Bridport 01297 489215

Shave Cross Inn, Bridport 01308 868358

Riverside Restaurant, Bridport 01308 422011

Leisure: 🏊 🎠 🎯 🎣

Facilities: 🚿 📷 🍴 🪒 ⚡ 🕐 🛒 🎪

Services: 🚐 🔧 🍴 🛢 ⌀ 🚻 🍴 📮 🛒 ♻

Within 3 miles: 🚣 ⛳ 🛒 🎯

Notes: Gym, steam room, sauna, pitch & putt, tourist info. Wi-fi

see advert on opposite page

▶▶▶▶▶ 82% Bingham Grange Touring & Camping Park (SY478963)

Melplash DT6 3TT
☎ 01308 488234 📄 01308 488426
e-mail: enquiries@binghamsfarm.co.uk
dir: *From A35 at Bridport take A3066 N towards Beaminster. Site on left after 3m*

🚐 🚑 ⛺

Open Mar-Oct (rs Restaurant & bar seasonal) Last departure 11.00hrs

---

Set in a quiet rural location but only five miles from the Jurassic Coast, this adults-only park enjoys views over the west Dorset countryside. The mostly level pitches are attractively set amongst shrub beds and ornamental trees. There is an excellent restaurant with lounge bar and takeaway, and all facilities are of a high quality. The bottom section of the park has been transformed with new roads and spacious new pitch areas. A 20 acre site with 150 touring pitches, 70 hardstandings.

AA Pubs & Restaurants nearby: George Hotel, Bridport 01308 423187

West Bay, Bridport 01308 422157

Riverside Restaurant, Bridport 01308 422011

Facilities: ⌂ ⊙ ℓ ✳ ⚹ ⏰ 🚿 🐴

Services: 🔌 🗄 🚽 🍴 🛢 ⌀ 🔧 🍽 🚮 ♨

Within 3 miles: ✝ ℓ 🏪 🗄 U

Notes: Adults only. Woodland walks, woodland dog exercise trail leading to riverbanks. Wi-fi

---

CERNE ABBAS

Places to visit

Athelhampton House and Gardens, Athelhampton, 01305 848363, www.athelhampton.co.uk

Hardy's Cottage, Dorchester, 01305 262366, www.nationaltrust.org.uk

Great for kids: Maiden Castle, Dorchester, www.english-heritage.org.uk

---

CERNE ABBAS Map 4 ST60

►►► 85% Lyons Gate Caravan and Camping Park *(ST660062)*

Lyons Gate DT2 7AZ
☎ **01300 345260**
e-mail: info@lyons-gate.co.uk
dir: *Signed with direct access from A352, 3m N of Cerne Abbas*

🚐 �"' Å

Open all year Last arrival 20.00hrs Last departure 11.30hrs

A peaceful park with pitches set out around the four attractive coarse fishing lakes. It is surrounded by mature woodland, with many footpaths and bridleways. Other easily accessible attractions include the Cerne Giant carved into the hills, the old market town of Dorchester, and the superb sandy beach at Weymouth. Holiday homes are now available for sale. A 10 acre site with 90 touring pitches, 14 hardstandings.

AA Pubs & Restaurants nearby: The Piddle Inn, Piddletrenthide 01300 348468

Poachers Inn, Piddletrenthide 01300 348358

Facilities: ⌂ ⊙ ℓ ✳ ⚹ 🗄 🍴 🚿 🐴

Services: 🔌 🗄 🚽 🛢 ⌀

Within 3 miles: ⌥ ℓ 🗄 U

Notes: 🚫 4 fishing lakes on site. Wi-fi

►► 69% Giant's Head Caravan & Camping Park *(ST675029)*

Giants Head Farm, Old Sherborne Rd DT2 7TR
☎ **01300 341242**
e-mail: holidays@giantshead.co.uk
dir: *From Dorchester into town avoiding by-pass, at Top O'Town rdbt take A352 (Sherborne road), in 500yds right fork at Esso (Loder's) garage, site signed*

🚐 £9-£14 🚐 £9-£14 Å £9-£14

Open Etr-Oct (rs Etr shop & bar closed) Last arrival anytime Last departure 13.00hrs

A pleasant, though rather basic, park set in Dorset downland near the Cerne Giant (the famous landmark figure cut into the chalk) with stunning views. This is a good stopover site, ideal for tenters and backpackers on the Ridgeway route. A 4 acre site with 50 touring pitches.

AA Pubs & Restaurants nearby: Greyhound Inn, Sydling St Nicholas 01300 341303

European Inn, Piddletrenthide 01300 348308

Facilities: ⌂ ⊙ ℓ ✳ 🚿 🐴

Services: 🔌 🗄 🛢 ⌀ ♨

Within 3 miles: ℓ 🗄 🗄

Notes: 🚫 Two holiday chalets available

wdlh.co.uk
WEST DORSET LEISURE HOLIDAYS

West Bay Beach

A choice of five family run Holiday Parks on or near the Dorset Coastline

Ideally situated for a quiet country or coastal holiday in Dorset and a base to explore the 'World Heritage' coastline and Area of Outstanding Natural Beauty. Each park has its own special quality for Caravan Holiday Homes, Touring and Camping. We look forward to welcoming you to West Dorset this year.

Please contact us by email: **enquires@wdlh.co.uk** or to make a booking **bookings@wdlh.co.uk** or you can phone us on **01308 422139**

JURASSIC COAST Trust · BEST OF BRITISH · DORSET

SERVICES: 🔌 Electric hook up 🗄 Launderette 🚽 Licensed bar 🛢 Calor Gas ⌀ Camping Gaz 🚽 Toilet fluid 🍽 Café/Restaurant 🚮 Fast Food/Takeaway ♨ Battery charging
🍼 Baby care ⚓ Motorvan service point **ABBREVIATIONS:** BH/bank hols-bank holidays Etr-Easter Whit-Whitsun dep-departure fr-from hrs-hours m-mile mdnt-midnight
rdbt-roundabout rs-restricted service wk-week wknd-weekend 🚫 No credit cards 🚫 no dogs See page 7 for details of the AA Camping Card Scheme

Map 4 SY39
CHARMOUTH

Places to visit

Forde Abbey, Chard, 01460 221290, www.fordeabbey.co.uk

Dorchester County Museum, Dorchester, 01305 262735, www.dorsetcountymuseum.org

Great for kids: Abbotsbury Swannery, Abbotsbury, 01305 871858, www.abbotsbury-tourism.co.uk

PREMIER PARK

▶▶▶▶▶ **88% Wood Farm Caravan & Camping Park**

Best of British

(SY356940)

Axminster Rd DT6 6BT
☎ 01297 560697 📄 01297 561243
e-mail: holidays@woodfarm.co.uk
web: www.woodfarm.co.uk
dir: *Site entered directly off A35 rdbt, on Axminster side of Charmouth*

* 🚐 £14-£25.50 🚌 £14-£25.50 ▲ £12-£25.50

Open Etr-Oct Last arrival 19.00hrs Last departure noon

This top quality park is set amongst mature native trees with the various levels of the site falling away into a beautiful valley below. The park offers excellent facilities including family rooms and fully serviced pitches. The facilities throughout the park are spotless. At the bottom end of the park there is an excellent indoor swimming pool and leisure complex, plus the licensed, conservatory-style Offshore Café. There's a good children's play room plus tennis courts and a well-stocked, coarse-fishing lake. The park is well positioned on the Heritage Coast near Lyme Regis. Static holiday homes are also available for hire. A 13 acre site with 216 touring pitches, 175 hardstandings and 81 statics.

AA Pubs & Restaurants nearby: Pilot Boat Inn, Lyme Regis 01297 443157

Leisure: 🏊 ⚫ 🎮 🎯 📺

Facilities: 🛁 🚿 ⚡ 🅿 ❄ ♿ 🕐 🏪 🐕

Services: 🚐 🔯 🍴 🛢 🌿 📅 🍽 🚮 ⚰

Within 3 miles: ⚓ 🎣 🎬 🏌 ⚫ 🏊 🎿 🏪 🌊 ⛴

Notes: No skateboards, scooters, roller skates or bikes. Wi-fi

AA CAMPING CARD SITE

▶▶▶▶ **85% Newlands Caravan & Camping Park**

(SY374935)

SILVER

DT6 6RB
☎ 01297 560259 📄 01297 560787
e-mail: enq@newlandsholidays.co.uk
web: www.newlandsholidays.co.uk
dir: *4m W of Bridport on A35*

🚐 🚌 ▲

Open 10 Mar-4 Nov Last arrival 22.30hrs Last departure 10.00hrs

A very smart site with excellent touring facilities. The park offers a full cabaret and entertainment programme for all ages, and boasts an indoor swimming pool with spa and an outdoor pool with water slide. Set on gently sloping ground in hilly countryside near the sea. Holiday homes and lodges are available for hire or sale. A 23 acre site with 240 touring pitches, 52 hardstandings and 86 statics.

AA Pubs & Restaurants nearby: Pilot Boat Inn, Lyme Regis 01297 443157

Leisure: 🏊 ⚫ 🎮 🎯 📺

Facilities: 🛁 🚿 ⚡ 🅿 ❄ ♿ 🕐 🏪 🐕 🥾

Services: 🚐 🔯 🍴 🛢 🌿 📅 🍽 🚮 🛒

Within 3 miles: ⚓ 🎣 🎬 🏌 ⚫ 🏊 🎿 🏪 🌊 ⛴

Notes: Wi-fi

▶▶▶ **80% Manor Farm Holiday Centre** (SY368937)

DT6 6QL
☎ 01297 560226
e-mail: enq@manorfarmholidaycentre.co.uk
dir: *W on A35 to Charmouth, site 0.75m on right*

* 🚐 £13-£23 🚌 £13-£23 ▲ £13-£23

Open all year (rs End Oct-mid Mar statics only) Last arrival 20.00hrs Last departure 10.00hrs

Set just a short walk from the safe sand and shingle beach at Charmouth, this popular family park offers a good range of facilities. Children

enjoy the activity area and outdoor swimming pool (so do their parents!), and the park also offers a lively programme in the extensive bar and entertainment complex. Seasonal touring pitches are available. A 30 acre site with 400 touring pitches, 80 hardstandings and 29 statics.

AA Pubs & Restaurants nearby: Pilot Boat Inn, Lyme Regis 01297 443157

Leisure: ⚫ 🎮 🎯 **Facilities:** 🚿 ⚡ 🅿 ❄ ♿ 🕐 🏪 🐕

Services: 🚐 🔯 🍴 🛢 🌿 🍽 🚮 ⚰

Within 3 miles: ⚓ 🎣 🎬 🏌 ⚫ 🏊 🎿 🏪 🌊 ⛴

Notes: No skateboards. Wi-fi

Map 4 SY49
CHIDEOCK

Places to visit

Branscombe - The Old Bakery, Manor Mill and Forge, Branscombe, 01752 346585, www.nationaltrust.org.uk

Mapperton, Beaminster, 01308 862645, www.mapperton.com

Great for kids: Pecorama Pleasure Gardens, Beer, 01297 21542, www.peco-uk.com

AA CAMPING CARD SITE

▶▶▶▶ **82% Golden Cap Holiday Park** (SY422919)

GOLD

Seatown DT6 6JX
☎ 01308 422139 & 426947 📄 01308 425672
e-mail: holidays@wdlh.co.uk
dir: *On A35, in Chideock turn S for Seatown, site signed*

* 🚐 £14.50-£31 🚌 £14.50-£31 ▲ £14.50-£24

Open mid Mar-early Nov Last arrival 22.00hrs Last departure 11.00hrs

A grassy site, overlooking sea and beach and surrounded by National Trust parkland. This uniquely placed park slopes down to the sea, although pitches are generally level. A slight dip hides the view of the beach from the back of the park, but this area benefits from having trees, scrubs and meadows, unlike the barer areas closer to the sea which do have a spectacular outlook. This makes an ideal base for touring Dorset and Devon. An 11 acre site with 108 touring pitches, 24 hardstandings and 234 statics.

AA Pubs & Restaurants nearby: George Hotel, Bridport 01308 423187

West Bay, Bridport 01308 422157

Riverside Restaurant, Bridport 01308 422011

Leisure: 🏛
Facilities: ➡🛒⚡✳♿☺🛁🏇
Services: 🔌🚿🛒⌀🚰🔋
Within 3 miles: ♿🎣🛒🛍
Notes: Fishing lake, tourist information. Wi-fi

Places to visit

Red House Museum and Gardens, Christchurch, 01202 482860, www.hants.gov.uk/museum/redhouse

Hurst Castle, 01590 642344, www.english-heritage.org.uk

Great for kids: Oceanarium, Bournemouth, 01202 311993, www.oceanarium.co.uk

►►►► 88% Meadowbank Holidays (SZ136946)

Stour Way BH23 2PQ
☎ 01202 483597 📠 01202 483878
e-mail: enquiries@meadowbank-holidays.co.uk
web: www.meadowbank-holidays.co.uk
dir: *A31 onto A338 towards Bournemouth. Take 1st exit after 5m then left towards Christchurch on B3073. Right at 1st rdbt into St Catherine's Way/River Way. Stour Way 3rd right, site at end of road*

* 🚐 £9-£30 🚙 £9-£30

Open Mar-Oct Last arrival 21.00hrs Last departure noon

A very smart park on the banks of the River Stour, with a colourful display of hanging baskets and flower-filled tubs placed around the superb reception area. The toilet facilities are modern (at our last inspection they were undergoing refurbishment, to be completed for 2011), and there is excellent play equipment for children. Visitors can choose between the different pitch sizes, including luxury fully-serviced ones. There is also a good shop on site. Statics are available for hire. A 2 acre site with 41 touring pitches, 22 hardstandings and 180 statics.

AA Pubs & Restaurants nearby: Ship in Distress, Christchurch 01202 485123

Fisherman's Haunt, Christchurch 01202 477283

Splinters, Christchurch 01202 483454

Leisure: 🏛 🎿
Facilities: ➡➡🛒⚡☺🛁🏇
Services: 🔌🚿🛒⌀🚰🔋
Within 3 miles: ♿🎿🎣◎🛍🛍🎯
Notes: No pets, no tents. Fishing on site. Wi-fi

Places to visit

Corfe Castle, Corfe Castle, 01929 481294, www.nationaltrust.org.uk

Brownsea Island, 01202 707744, www.nationaltrust.org.uk

Great for kids: Swanage Railway, Swanage, 01929 425800, www.swanagerailway.co.uk

►►►► 79% Corfe Castle Camping & Caravanning Club Site (SY953818)

Bucknowle BH20 5PQ
☎ 01929 480280 & 0845 130 7633
dir: *From Wareham A351 towards Swanage. In 4m turn right at foot of Corfe Castle signed Church Knowle. 0.75m right to site*

🚐 £7.50-£9 🚙 £7.50-£9 ⛺ £7.50-£9

Open Mar-Oct Last arrival 20.00hrs Last departure noon

This lovely park is set in woodland near to the famous Corfe Castle. It has modern toilet and shower facilities which are spotless. Although the site is sloping, pitches are level and include 33 spacious hardstandings. The site is perfect for visiting the many attractions of the Purbeck area including Swanage and Studland, as well has having the nearby station at Corfe for the Swanage Steam Railway. A 5 acre site with 80 touring pitches.

AA Pubs & Restaurants nearby: Greyhound Inn, Corfe Castle 01929 480205

New Inn, Church Knowle 01929 480357

Leisure: 🏛🎱
Facilities: ⚡✳♿☺🛁
Services: 🔌🚿🛒⌀🔋⚙
Notes: Site gates closed between 23.00hrs-07.00hrs. Wi-fi

►► 78% Woody Hyde Camp Site
(SY974804)

Valley Rd BH20 5HT
☎ 01929 480274
e-mail: camp@woodyhyde.fsnet.co.uk
dir: *From Corfe Castle towards Swanage on A351, site approx 1m on right*

* 🚐 ⛺ £12

Open Etr-Oct

A large grassy campsite in a sheltered location for tents and motorhomes only, set into three paddocks - one is dog free. There is a well-stocked shop on site, and a regular bus service located near the site entrance. This site offers traditional camping in a great location on Purbeck. At the time of our last inspection a new shower block was under construction. A 13 acre site with 150 touring pitches.

AA Pubs & Restaurants nearby: Greyhound Inn, Corfe Castle 01929 480205

New Inn, Church Knowle 01929 480357

Facilities: ➡⚡✳🛁
Services: 🔌🛒⌀
Within 3 miles: 🛍
Notes: No noise after 23.00hrs

See Cerne Abbas

DRIMPTON — Map 4 ST40

Places to visit

Forde Abbey, Chard, 01460 221290, www.fordeabbey.co.uk

Mapperton, Beaminster, 01308 862645, www.mapperton.com

Great for kids: The Wildlife Park, Cricket St Thomas, 01460 30111, www.wild.org.uk

►►►► 78% Oathill Farm Touring and Camping Site (ST404055)

Oathill TA18 8PZ
☎ 01460 30234 📠 01460 30234
e-mail: oathillfarm@btconnect.com
dir: From Crewkerne take B3165. Site on left just after Clapton

🚐 £17.50-£22.50 🚉 £17.50-£22.50
▲ £13-£14.50

Open all year Last arrival 20.00hrs Last departure noon

This small peaceful park is located on the borders of Somerset and Devon, with the Jurassic coast of Lyme Regis, Charmouth and Bridport only a short drive away. The new modern facilities are spotless and there are hardstandings and fully-serviced pitches available. Lucy's Tea Room serves breakfast and meals. Three luxury lodges are available for hire. A 9 acre site with 13 touring pitches, 13 hardstandings and 3 statics.

AA Pubs & Restaurants nearby: Bottle Inn, Marshwood 01297 678254

Facilities: 🏕⊙🅿✳🖻🎋🛏🐕
Services: 🚽🖩🛢🔧🍽🌀🚿🍴🛒⛟♻
Within 3 miles: ⚓🎣🖻🛒🐎

Notes: No washing lines, no quad bikes, no noise after 23.00hrs. Separate recreational areas, landscaped fish ponds

EVERSHOT — Map 4 ST50

Places to visit

Minterne Gardens, Minterne Magna, 01300 341370, www.minterne.co.uk

Stoke-Sub-Hamdon Priory, Stoke-Sub-Hamdon, 01935 823289, www.nationaltrust.org.uk

Great for kids: Sherborne Castle, Sherborne, 01935 813182 (office), www.sherbornecastle.com

►►► 80% Clay Pigeon Caravan Park (ST610077)

Wardon Hill DT2 9PW
☎ 01935 83492
dir: Exit A37 onto unclassified road signed Batcombe, site on right in 150yds

🚐🚉▲

Open all year Last arrival 21.00hrs

A level, close-mown park with mature trees in a rural area. The toilet block has good facilities and is spotless. Adjacent to the site is a go-kart track and a clay pigeon shooting range, both of a very high standard. Customers have access to the adjacent Sportsman restaurant and café. A 3 acre site with 60 touring pitches, 12 hardstandings and 6 statics.

AA Pubs & Restaurants nearby: Acorn Inn, Evershot 01935 83228

Leisure: 🄰
Facilities: 🏕⊙🅿✳🖻🎋🛏🐕
Services: 🚽🖩🛢📞🍴🌀🛒⛟♻
Within 3 miles: 🖻

Notes: Dogs must be kept on leads

FERNDOWN

Places to visit

Poole Museum, Poole, 01202 262600, www.boroughofpoole.com/museums

Kingston Lacy, Wimborne, 01202 883402 (Mon-Fri), www.nationaltrust.org.uk

Great for kids: Oceanarium, Bournemouth, 01202 311993, www.oceanarium.co.uk

FERNDOWN — Map 5 SU00

AA CAMPING CARD SITE

►►► 75% St Leonards Farm Caravan & Camping Park (SU093014)

Ringwood Rd, West Moors BH22 0AQ
☎ 01202 872637
web: www.stleonardsfarm.biz
dir: From E (Ringwood): entrance directly off A31, after crossing rdbt, opposite Texaco garage. From W: U-turn at rdbt after Texaco garage, turn left into site

* 🚐 £10-£20 🚉 £10-£20 ▲ £10-£20

Open Apr-Sep Last departure 14.00hrs

A private road off the A31 leads to this well-screened park divided into paddocks, with spacious pitches. This is one of the nearest parks to Bournemouth with its many holiday amenities. A 12 acre site with 151 touring pitches.

AA Pubs & Restaurants nearby: Les Bouviers, Wimborne Minster 01202 889555

Leisure: 🄰
Facilities: 🏕⊙✳🖻🎋🅿🛏
Services: 🚽🖩🛢♻

Within 3 miles: ⚓🎣🖻🛒

Notes: No large groups. Dogs must be kept on leads. No noise after 23.00hrs. No disposable BBQs

HOLTON HEATH

Places to visit

Royal Signals Museum, Blandford Forum, 01258 482248, www.royalsignalsmuseum.com, Larmer Tree Gardens, Tollard Royal, 01725 516228, www.larmertreegardens.co.uk

Great for kids: Moors Valley Country Park, Ringwood, 01425 470721, www.moors-valley.co.uk

HOLTON HEATH — Map 4 SY99

82% Sandford Holiday Park (SY939916)

Organford Rd BH16 6JZ
☎ 0844 335 3756 📠 01202 625678
e-mail:
touringandcamping@parkdeanholidays.com
web: www.parkdeantouring.com
dir: A35 from Poole towards Dorchester, at lights onto A351 towards Wareham. Right at Holton Heath. Site 100yds on left

🚐 £16.50-£40 🚗 £16.50-£40 ▲ £13.50-£37

Open Mar-Oct (15 May-19 Sep outdoor pool open) Last arrival 22.00hrs Last departure 10.00hrs

With touring pitches set individually in 20 acres surrounded by woodland, this park offers a full range of leisure activities and entertainment for the whole family. The touring area, situated at the far end of the park, is neat and well maintained, and there are children's clubs in the daytime and nightly entertainment. A reception area with lounge, bar, café and restaurant creates an excellent and attractive entrance, with a covered area outside with tables and chairs and well-landscaped gardens. A 64 acre site with 354 touring pitches and 344 statics.

AA Pubs & Restaurants nearby: Kemps Country House, Wareham 0845 862 0315

Greyhound Inn, Corfe Castle 01929 480205

New Inn, Church Knowle 01929 480357

Leisure: 🎣🏊⛰🎱🎯🎮
Facilities: 🐾🐕⊙📻✻🔥🛁🕐🚻🗑🎯🚿
Services: 🔌🛢🍴🔥🧪T🍽🍔♨
Within 3 miles: 🎣🚴🏇🎣◎⛴🛒🗑🐕⛳

Notes: Bowling, family entertainment, crazy golf, bike hire, adventure playground, amusements. Wi-fi

see advert in preliminary section

LYME REGIS — Map 4 SY39

See also Charmouth

Places to visit

Marwood Hill Gardens, Barnstaple, 01271 342528, www.marwoodhillgarden.co.uk

Pecorama Pleasure Gardens, 01297 21542, www.peco-uk.com

Great for kids: The World of Country Life, Exmouth, 01395 274533, www.worldofcountrylife.co.uk

▶▶▶▶ 84% Shrubbery Touring Park (SY300914)

Rousdon DT7 3XW
☎ 01297 442227 📠 01297 446086
e-mail: enq@shrubberypark.co.uk
web: www.shrubberypark.co.uk
dir: 3m W of Lyme Regis on A3052 (coast road)

🚐 £10.75-£15.75 🚗 £10.75-£15.75
▲ £10.75-£15.75

Open Apr-Oct Last arrival 22.00hrs Last departure 11.00hrs

Mature trees enclose this peaceful park, which has distant views of the lovely countryside. The modern facilities are well kept, and there is plenty of space for children to play in the grounds. Spacious new hardstandings were added in 2010. This park is right on the Jurassic Coast bus route, which is popular with visitors to this area. A 10 acre site with 120 touring pitches, 10 hardstandings.

AA Pubs & Restaurants nearby: Pilot Boat Inn, Lyme Regis 01297 443157

Leisure: ⛰
Facilities: 🐕⊙📻✻🔥🛁🚿
Services: 🔌🛢🔥🧪
Within 3 miles: 🎣🚴🏇🎣◎⛴🛒🗑

Notes: No motor scooters/roller skates/skateboards, no groups (except rallies). Crazy golf

AA CAMPING CARD SITE

▶▶▶ 82% Hook Farm Caravan & Camping Park (SY323930)

Gore Ln, Uplyme DT7 3UU
☎ 01297 442801 📠 01297 442801
e-mail: information@hookfarm-uplyme.co.uk
dir: From A35, take B3165 towards Lyme Regis & Uplyme at Hunters Lodge pub. 2m turn right into Gore Lane, site 400yds on right

🚐🚗▲

Open 15 Mar-Oct (rs Low season shop closed) Last arrival 21.00hrs Last departure 11.00hrs

Set in a peaceful and very rural location, the popular farm site enjoys lovely views of Lym Valley and is just a mile from the seaside at Lyme Regis. There are modern toilet facilities and good on-site amenities. Most pitches are level due to excellent terracing - a great site for tents. A 5.5 acre site with 100 touring pitches, 4 hardstandings and 17 statics.

AA Pubs & Restaurants nearby: Pilot Boat Inn, Lyme Regis 01297 443157

Leisure: ⛰
Facilities: 🐕⊙📻✻🔥🛁🕐🗑🚿
Services: 🔌🛢🔥🧪♨
Within 3 miles: 🎣🚴🏇🎣◎⛴🛒🗑🐕⛳
Notes: No groups of 6 adults or more, no dangerous dog breeds

LYTCHETT MATRAVERS   Map 4 SY99

Places to visit

Brownsea Island, 01202 707744,
www.nationaltrust.org.uk

Poole Museum, Poole, 01202 262600,
www.boroughofpoole.com/museums

Great for kids: Swanage Railway, Swanage,
01929 425800, www.swanagerailway.co.uk

►►► 76% Huntick Farm Caravan Park (SY955947)

Huntick Rd BH16 6BB
☎ **01202 622222**
e-mail: huntickcaravans@btconnect.com
dir: *Site between Lytchett Minster & Lytchett Matravers. From A31 take A350 towards Poole. Follow Lytchett Minster signs, then Lytchett Matravers signs. Huntick Rd by Red Cow pub*

* ⚏ £13-£21 ⚏ £13-£21 ▲ £12-£25

Open Apr-Oct Last arrival 21.00hrs Last departure noon

A really attractive little park nestling in rural surroundings edged by woodland, a mile from the village amenities of Lytchett Matravers. This neat grassy park is divided into three paddocks offering a peaceful location, yet it is close to the attractions of Poole and Bournemouth. A 4 acre site with 30 touring pitches.

AA Pubs & Restaurants nearby: Coventry Arms, Corfe Mullen 01258 857284

Botany Bay Inne, Winterborne Zelston
01929 459227

Leisure: ⚏

Facilities: ⚏☺✻⚏

Services: ⚏⚏

Within 3 miles: ⚏⚏

Notes: No ball games on site - field provided

LYTCHETT MINSTER

Places to visit

Lulworth Castle and Park, West Lulworth,
0845 450 1054, www.lulworth.com

Clouds Hill, Bovington Camp, 01929 405616,
www.nationaltrust.org.uk

Great for kids: Monkey World-Ape Rescue Centre, Wool, 01929 462537,
www.monkeyworld.org

LYTCHETT MINSTER   Map 4 SY99

PREMIER PARK

►►►►► 86% South Lytchett Manor Caravan & Camping Park (SY954926)

Dorchester Rd BH16 6JB
☎ **01202 622577**
e-mail: info@southlytchettmanor.co.uk
dir: *On B3067, off A35, 1m E of Lytchett Minster, 600yds on right after village*

⚏⚏▲

Open Mar-2 Jan Last arrival 21.00hrs Last departure 11.00hrs

Situated in the grounds of a historic manor house the park has new and modern facilities, which are spotless and well maintained. A warm and friendly welcome awaits at this lovely park which is well located for visiting Poole and Bournemouth

the Jurassic X53 bus route (Exeter to Poole) has a stop just outside the park. This park continues to improve each year. A 20 acre site with 150 touring pitches, 60 hardstandings.

AA Pubs & Restaurants nearby: The Rising Sun, Poole 01202 771246

Guildhall Tavern, Poole 01202 671717

Leisure: ⚏🎣▭
Facilities: ⚏☺⚏✻⚏☺⚏⚏⚏
Services: ⚏⚏⚏⚏⚏⚏⚏
Within 3 miles: ⚏⚏⚏⚏⚏⚏⚏

Notes: No camp fires or Chinese lanterns. Internet access, 2 family bathrooms. Wi-fi

ORGANFORD

Places to visit

Tolpuddle Martyrs Museum, Tolpuddle,
01305 848237, www.tolpuddlemartyrs.org.uk

Kingston Lacy, Wimborne, 01202 883402
(Mon-Fri), www.nationaltrust.org.uk

Great for kids: Farmer Palmer's Farm Park,
Organford, 01202 622022,
www.farmerpalmers.co.uk

ORGANFORD   Map 4 SY99

AA CAMPING CARD SITE

►►►► 83% Pear Tree Holiday Park (SY938915)

Organford Rd, Holton Heath BH16 6LA
☎ **01202 622434**
e-mail: enquiries@peartreepark.co.uk
web: www.peartreepark.co.uk
dir: *From Poole take A35 towards Dorchester, onto A351 towards Wareham, at 1st lights turn right, site 300yds on left*

⚏⚏▲

Open Mar-Oct Last arrival 19.00hrs Last departure 10.00hrs

A quiet, sheltered country park with many colourful flowerbeds, and refurbished toilet facilities that offer quality and comfort. The touring area is divided into terraces with mature hedges for screening, with a separate level tenting area on the edge of woodland. The friendly atmosphere at this attractive park help to ensure a relaxing holiday. A bridle path leads into Wareham Forest. A 9 acre site with 154 touring pitches, 82 hardstandings and 40 statics.

AA Pubs & Restaurants nearby: Coventry Arms, Corfe Mullen 01258 857284

Botany Bay Inne, Winterborne Zelston
01929 459227

Leisure: ⚏
Facilities: ⚏☺⚏✻⚏☺⚏⚏⚏
Services: ⚏⚏⚏⚏⚏⚏
Within 3 miles: ⚏⚏⚏⚏☺⚏⚏

OWERMOIGNE

Places to visit

RSPB Nature Reserve Radipole Lake,
Weymouth, 01305 778313, www.rspb.org.uk

Clouds Hill, Bovington Camp, 01929 405616,
www.nationaltrust.org.uk

Great for kids: Weymouth Sea Life Adventure Park and Marine Sanctuary, Weymouth,
0871 423 2110, www.sealifeeurope.com

OWERMOIGNE
Map 4 SY78

AA CAMPING CARD SITE

▶▶▶ 77% Sandyholme Holiday Park (SY768863)

Moreton Rd DT2 8HZ
☎ 01308 422139 & 426947
e-mail: sandyholme@wdlh.co.uk
web: www.wdlh.co.uk
dir: From A352 (Wareham to Dorchester road) turn right to Owermoigne for 1m. Site on left

* ⛺ £14-£21 ⛺ £14-£21 ▲ £11.50-£17

Open 20 Mar-8 Nov (rs Etr) Last arrival 22.00hrs Last departure 11.00hrs

A pleasant site in a tree-lined rural setting within easy reach of the coast at Lulworth Cove, and handy for several seaside resorts. The facilities are very good, including a superb toilet block, and good food is available in the lounge/bar. A 6 acre site with 46 touring pitches and 52 statics.

AA Pubs & Restaurants nearby: Smugglers Inn, Osmington Mills 01305 833125

Lulworth Cove Inn, West Lulworth 01929 400333

Castle Inn, West Lulworth 01929 400311

Leisure: ⚫⚫
Facilities: ⚫⚫⚫⚫⚫⚫⚫⚫⚫
Services: ⚫⚫⚫⚫⚫⚫⚫⚫
Within 3 miles: ⚫⚫⚫

Notes: Table tennis, wildlife lake, tourist information. Wi-fi

POOLE
Map 4 SZ09

See also Lytchett Minster, Organford & Wimborne Minster

Places to visit

Compton Acres Gardens, Canford Cliffs, 01202 700778, www.comptonacres.co.uk

Brownsea Island, 01202 707744, www.nationaltrust.org.uk

Great for kids: Oceanarium, Bournemouth, 01202 311993, www.oceanarium.co.uk

 82% Rockley Park (SY982909)

Hamworthy BH15 4LZ
☎ 01202 679393 ☐ 01202 683159
e-mail: rockley-holidays@bourne-leisure.co.uk
dir: Take A31 off M27 to Poole centre, then follow signs to site

⛺⛺▲

Open mid Mar-Oct (rs mid Mar-May & Sep-Oct some facilities may be reduced) Last departure 10.00hrs

A complete holiday experience, including a wide range of day and night entertainment, and plenty of sports and leisure activities, notably watersports. There is also mooring and launching from the park. The touring area was new in 2010, with 60 fully serviced pitches and an excellent new toilet and shower block. A great base for all the family set in a good location to explore Poole or Bournemouth. A 90 acre site with 60 touring pitches, 71 hardstandings and 1077 statics.

AA Pubs & Restaurants nearby: The Rising Sun, Poole 01202 771246

Guildhall Tavern, Poole 01202 671717

Leisure: ⚫⚫⚫⚫⚫
Facilities: ⚫⚫⚫⚫⚫⚫⚫⚫⚫
Services: ⚫⚫⚫⚫⚫⚫⚫⚫⚫⚫
Within 3 miles: ⚫⚫⚫⚫⚫⚫⚫⚫

Notes: Dogs not allowed during peak periods or on touring pitches, tents only from May-Sep. Sailing school, spa. Wi-fi

see advert below

▶▶▶ 80% Beacon Hill Touring Park (SY977945)

Blandford Road North BH16 6AB
☎ 01202 631631 ☐ 01202 624388
e-mail: bookings@beaconhilltouringpark.co.uk
dir: On A350, 0.25m N of junct with A35, 3m NW of Poole

⛺⛺▲

Open Etr-end Oct (rs Low & mid season some services closed/restricted opening) Last arrival 23.00hrs Last departure 11.00hrs

continued

SERVICES: ⚫ Electric hook up ⚫ Launderette ⚫ Licensed bar ⚫ Calor Gas ⚫ Camping Gaz ⚫ Toilet fluid ⚫ Café/Restaurant ⚫ Fast Food/Takeaway ⚫ Battery charging ⚫ Baby care ⚫ Motorvan service point ABBREVIATIONS: BH/bank hols-bank holidays Etr-Easter Whit-Whitsun dep-departure fr-from hrs-hours m-mile mdnt-midnight rdbt-roundabout rs-restricted service wk-week wknd-weekend ⚫ No credit cards ⚫ no dogs See page 7 for details of the AA Camping Card Scheme

POOLE *continued*

Set in an attractive, wooded area with conservation very much in mind. There are two large ponds for coarse fishing within the grounds, and the terraced pitches, with fine views, are informally sited so that visitors can choose their favourite spot. The outdoor swimming pool and tennis court are popular during the summer period. At our last inspection we understood that the refurbishment of the facilities should be completed by 2011. A 30 acre site with 170 touring pitches, 10 hardstandings.

AA Pubs & Restaurants nearby: The Rising Sun, Poole 01202 771246

Guildhall Tavern, Poole 01202 671717

Leisure: ⚊ 🎢 ⚽ ✎ ⬜

Facilities: ⌐ ⊙ 🅿 ✳ ⚙ 🚿 🖤 🚼 🐾

Services: 🔌 🍽 🛢 🇹 🍴 🛒 🎂

Within 3 miles: ⚓ ⚓ ⚓ 🎣 🏌 ⊙ 🌊 ⛽ 🛢 ↺

Notes: Groups of young people not accepted during high season. Wi-fi

PORTESHAM
Map 4 SY68

Places to visit

Tutankhamun Exhibition, Dorchester, 01305 269571, www.tutankhamun-exhibition.co.uk

Maiden Castle, Dorchester, www.english-heritage.org.uk

Great for kids: Teddy Bear Museum, Dorchester, 01305 266040, www.teddybearmuseum.co.uk

▶▶▶▶ 78% Portesham Dairy Farm Campsite *(SY602854)*

Weymouth DT3 4HG
☎ 01305 871297
e-mail: info@porteshamdairyfarm.co.uk
dir: *From Dorchester on A35 towards Bridport. After 5m left at Winterbourne Abbas, follow Portesham signs. Through village, left at Kings Arms pub, site in 350yds on right*

* 🚐 £11-£25 🚗 £11-£25 ▲ £11-£25

Open mid Mar-Oct Last arrival 21.00hrs Last departure 16.00hrs

Located at the edge of the picturesque village of Portesham, this family run, level park is part of a small working farm in a quiet rural location. Near the site entrance is a pub where meals are served, and that has a garden for children. An 8 acre site with 90 touring pitches, 61 hardstandings.

AA Pubs & Restaurants nearby: Ilchester Arms, Abbotsbury 01305 871243

Manor Hotel, West Bexington 01308 897616

Leisure: 🎢 **Facilities:** ⌐ ⊙ 🅿 ✳ ⚙ 🖤 🚼 🐾

Services: 🔌 🛢 🔒 🍃

Within 3 miles: 🎣 🛢 🛢

Notes: No commercial vehicles. Fully serviced pitches, caravan storage, seasonal pitches

PUNCKNOWLE
Map 4 SY58

Places to visit

Dinosaur Museum, Dorchester, 01305 269880, www.thedinosaurmuseum.com

Hardy's Cottage, Dorchester, 01305 262366, www.nationaltrust.org.uk

Great for kids: Abbotsbury Swannery, Abbotsbury, 01305 871858, www.abbotsbury-tourism.co.uk

AA CAMPING CARD SITE

▶▶ 82% Home Farm Caravan and Campsite *(SY535887)*

Home Farm, Rectory Ln DT2 9BW
☎ 01308 897258
dir: *Dorchester towards Bridport on A35, left at start of dual carriageway, at hill bottom right to Litton Cheney. Through village, 2nd left to Puncknowle (Hazel Ln). Left at T-junct, left at phone box. Site 150mtrs on right. Caravan route: approach via Swyre on B3157*

🚐 🚗 ▲

Open Apr or Etr-Oct Last arrival 21.00hrs Last departure noon

A quiet site hidden away on the edge of this little hamlet. It offers sweeping views of the Dorset countryside from most pitches, and is just five miles from Abbotsbury, and one and a half miles from the South West Coastal Footpath. A really good base from which to tour this attractive area. A 6.5 acre site with 47 touring pitches.

AA Pubs & Restaurants nearby: Crown Inn, Puncknowle 01308 897711

Anchor Inn, Burton Bradstock 01308 897228

Manor Hotel, West Bexington 01308 897616

Facilities: ⌐ ⊙ 🅿 ✳ ⊙ 🖤 🚼

Services: 🔌 🛢 🍃 🛒 🎂 **Within 3 miles:** 🎣

Notes: ⊙ Dogs must be kept on leads, no cats, no wood burning fires, no skateboards. Swings

ST LEONARDS
Map 5 SU10

Places to visit

Rockbourne Roman Villa, Rockbourne, 0845 603 5635, www.hants.gov.uk/rockbourne-roman-villa

Red House Museum and Gardens, Christchurch, 01202 482860, www.hants.gov.uk/museum/redhouse

Great for kids: Moors Valley Country Park, Ringwood, 01425 470721, www.moors-valley.co.uk

PREMIER PARK

AA CAMPING CARD SITE

▶▶▶▶▶ 81% Shamba Holidays *(SU105029)*

230 Ringwood Rd BH24 2SB
☎ 01202 873302 📠 01202 873392
e-mail: enquiries@shambaholidays.co.uk
web: www.shambaholidays.co.uk
dir: *Off A31, from Poole turn left into Eastmoors Lane, 100yds past 2nd rdbt from Texaco garage. Site 0.25m on right (just past Woodman Inn)*

* 🚐 £20-£30 🚗 £20-£30 ▲ £20-£30

Open Mar-Oct (rs Low season some facilities only open at wknds) Last arrival 22.00hrs Last departure 11.00hrs

This top quality park has excellent modern facilities particularly suited to families. You can be certain of a warm welcome by the friendly staff. There is a really good indoor/outdoor heated pool, plus a tasteful bar supplying a good range of meals. The park is well located for visiting the south coast, which is just a short drive away, and also for the New Forest National Park. A 7 acre site with 150 touring pitches.

AA Pubs & Restaurants nearby: Old Beams Inn, Ibsley 01425 473387

Leisure: 🏊 ⬥ 🎡 🎣
Facilities: 🚿 🚻 ⊙ 🍴 ✳ 🛗 🕐 🖥 🐾
Services: 🔌 🖨 🚿 🛢 ⊘ 🚽 🍴 🚮 ⛽
Within 3 miles: 🌊 🖉 🖥 🛒 ⛳

Notes: No large groups, no commercial vehicles. Phone card top-up facility, playing field

see advert below

►►►► 81% Back of Beyond Touring Park *(SU103034)*

234 Ringwood Rd BH24 2SB
☎ 01202 876968 🖷 01202 876968
e-mail: melandsuepike@aol.com
web: www.backofbeyondtouringpark.co.uk
dir: *From E: on A31 over Little Chef rdbt, pass St Leonard's Hotel, at next rdbt U-turn into lane immediately left to site at end of lane. From W: on A31 pass Texaco garage & Woodsman Inn, immediately left to site*

* 🚐 £20-£23 🚙 £20-£23 ▲ £16-£23

Open Mar-Oct Last arrival 19.00hrs Last dep noon

Set well off the beaten track in natural woodland surroundings, with its own river and lake, yet close to many attractions. This tranquil park is run by keen, friendly owners, and the quality facilities are for adults only. A 28 acre site with 80 touring pitches.

AA Pubs & Restaurants nearby: Old Beams Inn, Ibsley 01425 473387

Facilities: 🚿 ⊙ 🍴 ✳ 🛗 🕐 🖥 🍴 🐾
Services: 🔌 🖨 🛢 ⊘ 🚽 🚮 ⛽
Within 3 miles: 🌊 🖉 ◎ 🖥 🛒 ⛳

Notes: Adults only. No commercial vehicles. Lake & river fishing, 9-hole pitch & putt course, boule piste

---

►►► 78% Forest Edge Touring Park *(SU104024)*

229 Ringwood Rd BH24 2SD
☎ 01590 648331 🖷 01590 645610
e-mail: holidays@shorefield.co.uk
dir: *From E: on A31 over 1st rdbt (Little Chef), pass St Leonards Hotel, left at next rdbt into Boundary Ln, site 100yds on left. From W: on A31 pass Texaco garage & Woodsman Inn, right at rdbt into Boundary Ln*

* 🚐 £12-£36 🚙 £12-£36 ▲ £10-£36

Open Feb-3 Jan (rs School & summer hols pool open) Last arrival 21.00hrs Last departure 10.00hrs

A tree-lined park set in grassland with plenty of excellent amenities for all the family, including an outdoor heated swimming pool and toddlers' pool, an adventure playground, and two launderettes. Visitors are invited to use the superb leisure club plus all amenities and entertainment at the sister site of Oakdene Forest Park, which is less than a mile away. Some pitches may experience some traffic noise from the nearby A31. A 9 acre site with 92 touring pitches and 28 statics.

AA Pubs & Restaurants nearby: Old Beams Inn, Ibsley 01425 473387

Leisure: ⬥ 🎡 🎣 **Facilities:** 🚿 ⊙ 🍴 ✳ 🕐 🖥
Services: 🔌 🖨 🛢 ⊘ 🚽
Within 3 miles: 🌊 🖉 ◎ 🖥 🛒 ⛳

Notes: Families & couples only. 1 dog & 1 car per pitch. Rallies welcome. Use of Oakdene facilities (1m)

see advert on page 209

AA CAMPING CARD SITE

►► 78% Blackmore Vale Caravan & Camping Park *(ST835233)*

Sherborne Causeway SP7 9PX
☎ 01747 851523 & 852573 🖷 01747 851671
e-mail: camping@bmvgroup.co.uk
dir: *From Shaftesbury's Ivy Cross rdbt take A30 signed Sherborne. Site 2m on right*

🚐 🚙 ▲

Open all year Last arrival 21.00hrs

A pleasant touring park with spacious pitches and well-maintained facilities. A fully-equipped gym is the latest addition to this park, and is open to visitors. Blackmore Vale, about two miles from Shaftesbury, is set behind a caravan sales showground and dealership. A 5 acre site with 26 touring pitches, 6 hardstandings.

AA Pubs & Restaurants nearby: Kings Arms Inn, Gillingham 01747 838325

Coppleridge Inn, Motcombe 01747 851980

Facilities: 🚿 ⊙ ✳ 🕐 🖥 🍴 🐾
Services: 🔌 🛢 ⊘ 🚽 🚮 ⛽
Within 3 miles: 🖉 🖥 🛒 ⛳

Notes: Caravan sales & accessories, gym

SIXPENNY HANDLEY — Map 4 ST91

Places to visit

Larmer Tree Gardens, Tollard Royal, 01725 516228, www.larmertreegardens.co.uk

Shaftesbury Abbey Museum and Garden, Shaftesbury, 01747 852910, www.shaftesburyheritage.org.uk

Great for kids: Moors Valley Country Park, Ringwood, 01425 470721, www.moors-valley.co.uk

---

Roger Almond Award for the Most Improved Campsite

▶▶▶▶ **84% Church Farm Caravan & Camping Park** (ST994173)

The Bungalow, Church Farm High St SP5 5ND
☎ 01725 552563/553005 & 07766 677525
e-mail: churchfarmcandcpark@yahoo.co.uk
dir: *1m S of Handley Hill rdbt. Turn off for Sixpenny Handley, right by school, site 300yds by church*

🚐 £7-£8.50 🚚 £7-£8.50 ▲ £7-£8.50

Open all year (rs Nov-Mar 10 vans max) Last arrival 21.00hrs Last departure 11.00hrs

A spacious, open park located within the Cranborne Chase in an Area of Outstanding Natural Beauty. There is a new facility block with good private facilities and an excellent café/restaurant. The pretty village of Sixpenny Handley with all its amenities is just 200 yards away. A 10 acre site with 35 touring pitches, 2 hardstandings and 2 statics.

AA Pubs & Restaurants nearby: Museum Inn, Farnham 01825 516261

Drovers Inn, Gussage All Saints 01258 840084

Leisure: ⚴ **Facilities:** ↖☉✳&🖻🎂🚻🖈
Services: 🚐🖅🐕‍🦺🔌⌀🕄🍽🚮🛒👕⚡🖕
Within 3 miles: 🎣🖻
Notes: Dogs must be kept on leads, quiet after 23.00hrs. Recycling facilities, caravan storage, use of fridge/freezer & microwave. Wi-fi

SWANAGE — Map 5 SZ07

Places to visit

Corfe Castle, 01929 481294, www.nationaltrust.org.uk

Brownsea Island, 01202 707744, www.nationaltrust.org.uk

Great for kids: Swanage Railway, Swanage, 01929 425800, www.swanagerailway.co.uk

---

▶▶▶▶ **83% *Ulwell Cottage Caravan Park*** (SZ019809)

GOLD

Ulwell Cottage, Ulwell BH19 3DG
☎ 01929 422823 📠 01929 421500
e-mail: enq@ulwellcottagepark.co.uk
web: www.ulwellcottagepark.co.uk
dir: *From Swanage N for 2m on unclass road towards Studland*

🚐 🚚 ▲

Open Mar-7 Jan (rs Mar-Spring BH & mid Sep-early Jan takeaway closed, shop open variable hrs) Last arrival 22.00hrs Last departure 11.00hrs

Nestling under the Purbeck Hills and surrounded by scenic walks, this park is only two miles from the beach. A family-run park that caters well for families and couples, and offers a newly refurbished toilet and shower block complete with good family rooms, all appointed to a high standard. There is a good indoor swimming pool and village inn offering a good range of meals. A 13 acre site with 77 touring pitches, 19 hardstandings and 140 statics.

AA Pubs & Restaurants nearby: Bankes Arms Hotel, Studland 01929 450225

Square and Compass, Worth Matravers 01929 439229

Leisure: 🏊🎠 **Facilities:** ↖☉✳&🖻🚻
Services: 🚐🖅🐕‍🦺🔌⌀🍽🎂
Within 3 miles: 🎣🖈🖻◎⛴🛥🖻🖻⛵
Notes: Wi-fi

see advert on opposite page

▶▶▶ **77% Herston Caravan & Camping Park** (SZ018785)

Washpond Ln BH19 3DJ
☎ 01929 422932 📠 01929 423888
e-mail: office@herstonleisure.co.uk
dir: *From Wareham on A351 towards Swanage. Washpond Ln on left just after 'Welcome to Swanage' sign*

* 🚐 £15-£35 🚚 £15-£35 ▲ £12-£50

Open all year

Set in a rural area, with extensive views of the Purbecks, this tree-lined park has many full facility pitches and quality toilet facilities. Herston Halt is within walking distance, a stop for the famous Swanage steam railway between the town centre and Corfe Castle. There are also yurts available for hire. A 10 acre site with 100 touring pitches, 71 hardstandings and 5 statics.

AA Pubs & Restaurants nearby: Bankes Arms Hotel, Studland 01929 450225

Square and Compass, Worth Matravers 01929 439229

Facilities: ↖☉🖻✳&🖻🚻🎂🖈
Services: 🚐🖅🐕‍🦺⌀🔌🍽🎂🛒👕⚡🖕
Within 3 miles: 🎣🖈🖻🖈◎⛴🛥🖻🖻⛵
Notes: No noise after 23.00hrs. Dogs to be kept on leads. Wi-fi

---

Not all campsites accept pets. It is advisable to check at the time of booking

---

LEISURE: 🏊 Indoor swimming pool 🏊 Outdoor swimming pool 🎠 Children's playground 🎾 Tennis court 🎯 Games room 📺 Separate TV room 🏌 9/18 hole golf course 🚤 Boats for hire 🎬 Cinema 🎣 Fishing ◎ Mini golf 🏄 Watersports ⛵ Stables **FACILITIES:** 🛁 Bath 🚿 Shower ☉ Electric shaver 🖻 Hairdryer ✳ Ice Pack Facility 🖻 Disabled facilities 🕽 Public telephone 🖻 Shop on site or within 200yds 🚚 Mobile shop (calls at least 5 days a week) 🍖 BBQ area 🖈 Picnic area 🖈 Dog exercise area

► 73% Acton Field Camping Site

(SY991785)

Acton Field, Langton Matravers BH19 3HS
☎ 01929 424184 & 439424 📠 01929 424184
e-mail: valmurray@hotmail.com
dir: From A351 right after Corfe Castle onto B3069 to Langton Matravers, 2nd right after village sign (bridleway)

🚐 £12 🚙 £10-£12 ⛺

Open mid Jul-early Sep (rs Apr-Oct open for organised groups) Last arrival 22.00hrs Last departure noon

An informal campsite bordered by farmland on the outskirts of Langton Matravers. There are superb views of the Purbeck Hills and towards the Isle of Wight, and a footpath leads to the coastal path. The site was once a stone quarry, and rock pegs may be required. A 7 acre site with 80 touring pitches.

AA Pubs & Restaurants nearby: Bankes Arms Hotel, Studland 01929 450225

Square and Compass, Worth Matravers 01929 439229

Facilities: 🔊⊙✳🔌
Services: 🔋
Within 3 miles: ⚓🏇🎣🅿◎🛒🏦🛍◡

Notes: 🐕 No open fires, no noise after midnight, dogs must be kept on leads. Freezer for freezer packs. Washing up facilities and chemical disposal unit

THREE LEGGED CROSS   Map 5 SU00

Places to visit

Lulworth Castle and Park, West Lulworth, 0845 450 1054, www.lulworth.com

Portland Castle, Portland, 01305 820539, www.english-heritage.org.uk

Great for kids: Monkey World-Ape Rescue Centre, Wool, 01929 462537, www.monkeyworld.org

►►►► 78% *Woolsbridge Manor Farm Caravan Park*

(SU099052)

SILVER

BH21 6RA
☎ 01202 826369 📠 01202 820603
e-mail: woolsbridge@btconnect.com
web: www.woolsbridgemanorcaravanpark.co.uk
dir: A31 West 1m past Ringwood. Take filter road signed Three Legged Cross, site 2m on right

🚐 🚙 ⛺

Open Mar-Oct Last arrival 20.00hrs Last departure 10.30hrs

A small farm site with spacious pitches on a level field. This quiet site is an excellent central base for touring the New Forest, Salisbury and the South coast, and is close to Moors Valley Country Park for outdoor family activities. Facilities are good and very clean and there are excellent family rooms available. A 6.75 acre site with 60 touring pitches.

Woolsbridge Manor Farm Caravan Park

AA Pubs & Restaurants nearby: Old Beams Inn, Ibsley 01425 473387

Woolsbridge Manor Farm Caravan Park

Leisure: 🎱
Facilities: 🔊⊙🅿✳🔌🚿◎🏦🍴🐾
Services: 🔌🛢🔋🚮🚽🔋
Within 3 miles: ⚓🎣🏦🛍◡

WAREHAM   Map 4 SY98

Places to visit

Compton Acres Gardens, Canford Cliffs, 01202 700778, www.comptonacres.co.uk

Brownsea Island, 01202 707744, www.nationaltrust.org.uk

Great for kids: Oceanarium, Bournemouth, 01202 311993, www.oceanarium.co.uk

PREMIER PARK

▶▶▶▶▶ 89%

Wareham Forest Tourist Park (SY894912)

North Trigon BH20 7NZ

☎ 01929 551393   📠 01929 558321

e-mail: holiday@warehamforest.co.uk

dir: *Telephone for directions*

* 🚐 £15.50-£30 🚙 £15.50-£30 ▲ £13.25-£26.50

Open all year (rs Off-peak season limited services) Last arrival 21.00hrs Last departure 11.00hrs

A woodland park within the tranquil Wareham Forest, with its many walks and proximity to Poole, Dorchester and the Purbeck coast. Two luxury blocks, with combined washbasin and toilets for total privacy, maintain a high standard of cleanliness. A heated outdoor swimming pool, off licence, shop and games room add to the pleasure of a stay on this top quality park. A 55 acre site with 200 touring pitches, 70 hardstandings.

AA Pubs & Restaurants nearby: Kemps Country House, Wareham 0845 862 0315

Greyhound Inn, Corfe Castle 01929 480205

New Inn, Church Knowle 01929 480357

Leisure: 🏊 🎠 🔍

Facilities: 🌂 ⊙ 🍴 ✳ 🚿 🔥 🛢 🍴 🐾 🌳

Services: 🔌 🛢 🚰 🔥 🚻 🎦 🛒 ↧

Within 3 miles: ⌦ 🎣 🎠 🍴 🛒 🎦 ⛵

Notes: Couples & families only, no group bookings. Wi-fi

▶▶▶ 84% Birchwood Tourist Park
(SY896905)

Bere Rd, Coldharbour BH20 7PA

☎ 01929 554763   📠 01929 556635

dir: *From Poole (A351) or Dorchester (A352) on N side of railway line at Wareham, follow road signed Bere Regis (unclassified). 2nd tourist park after 2.25m*

* 🚐 £12.35-£23 🚙 £12.35-£23 ▲ £10.10-£20.75

Open 13 Dec-23 Nov Last arrival 21.00hrs Last departure 11.30hrs

Set in 50 acres of parkland located within Wareham Forest, this site offers direct access into ideal areas for walking, mountain biking, and horse and pony riding. The modern facilities are in two central locations and are very clean. There is a good security barrier system. A 25 acre site with 175 touring pitches, 25 hardstandings.

AA Pubs & Restaurants nearby: Kemps Country House, Wareham 0845 862 0315

Greyhound Inn, Corfe Castle 01929 480205

New Inn, Church Knowle 01929 480357

Leisure: 🎠 🔍

Facilities: 🌂 ⊙ 🍴 ✳ 🕐 🛢 🌳

Services: 🔌 🛢 🚰 🔥 🎦 🛒 ↧

Within 3 miles: ⌦ 🎣 🎠 🍴 🛒

Notes: No generators, no groups on BH, no camp fires. Games field, bike hire, pitch & putt, paddling pool. Wi-fi

see advert below

▶▶▶ 80% East Creech Farm Campsite (SY928827)

East Creech Farm, East Creech BH20 5AP

☎ 01929 480519 & 481312   📠 01929 480519

e-mail: east.creech@virgin.net

dir: *From Wareham on A351 S towards Swanage. On bypass at 3rd rdbt take Furzebrook/Blue Pool Rd exit, approx 2m site on right*

🚐 🚙 ▲

Open Apr-Oct Last arrival 20.00hrs Last departure noon

A grassy park set in a peaceful location beneath the Purbeck Hills, with extensive views towards Poole and Brownsea Island. The park boasts a woodland play area, bright, clean toilet facilities, and a farm shop selling milk, eggs and bread. There are also three coarse fishing lakes teeming with fish. The park is close to the Norden Station on the Swanage to Norden steam railway, and is

---

LEISURE: 🏊 Indoor swimming pool   🏊 Outdoor swimming pool   🎠 Children's playground   🎾 Tennis court   🔍 Games room   📺 Separate TV room   ⛳ 9/18 hole golf course   ⛵ Boats for hire   🎬 Cinema   🎣 Fishing   ⛳ Mini golf   🏄 Watersports   🐴 Stables   **FACILITIES:** 🛁 Bath   🚿 Shower   ⊙ Electric shaver   🖤 Hairdryer   ✳ Ice Pack Facility   ♿ Disabled facilities   ☎ Public telephone   🛒 Shop on site or within 200yds   🚐 Mobile shop (calls at least 5 days a week)   🔥 BBQ area   🌳 Picnic area   🐾 Dog exercise area

well located for visiting Corfe Castle, Swanage and the Purbeck coast. A 4 acre site with 80 touring pitches.

AA Pubs & Restaurants nearby: Kemps Country House, Wareham 0845 862 0315

Greyhound Inn, Corfe Castle 01929 480205

New Inn, Church Knowle 01929 480357

Leisure: ⚑

Facilities: ⚑ ☺ ⚑ ⚑ ⚑

Services: ⚑ ⚑

Within 3 miles: ⚑ ⚑ ⚑ ⚑

Notes: ⚑ No camp fires

▶▶▶ 79% Lookout Holiday Park

(SY927858)

Stoborough BH20 5AZ
☎ 01929 552546   📠 01929 556662
e-mail: enquiries@caravan-sites.co.uk
web: www.caravan-sites.co.uk
dir: *Take A351 through Wareham, after crossing River Frome & through Stoborough, site signed on left*

* ⚑ £15-£28 ⚑ £15-£28 ▲ £11-£24

Open all year Last arrival 22.00hrs Last departure noon

Divided into two paddocks and set well back from the Swanage road, this touring park is separated from the static part of the operation. A superb children's playground and plenty of other attractions make this an ideal centre for families; it is also close to the popular attractions of the area. A 15 acre site with 150 touring pitches, 94 hardstandings and 89 statics.

AA Pubs & Restaurants nearby: Kemps Country House, Wareham 0845 862 0315

Greyhound Inn, Corfe Castle 01929 480205

New Inn, Church Knowle 01929 480357

Leisure: ⚑ ⚑

Facilities: ⚑ ☺ ⚑ ⚑ ⚑ ⚑ ⚑ ⚑

Services: ⚑ ⚑ ⚑ ⚑ ⚑ ⚑ ⚑ ⚑

Within 3 miles: ⚑ ⚑ ⚑ ⚑ ⚑ ⚑ ⚑

Notes: No pets, family park. Wi-fi

see advert below

▶▶▶ 77% Ridge Farm Camping & Caravan Park *(SY939868)*

Barnhill Rd, Ridge BH20 5BG
☎ 01929 556444
e-mail: info@ridgefarm.co.uk
web: www.ridgefarm.co.uk
dir: *From Wareham take B3075 towards Corfe Castle, cross river to Stoborough, then left to Ridge. Follow site signs for 1.5m*

* ⚑ £13.50-£16 ⚑ £13.50-£16 ▲ £13.50-£16

Open Etr-Sep Last arrival 21.00hrs Last dep noon

A quiet rural park, adjacent to a working farm and surrounded by trees and bushes. This away-from-it-all park is ideally located for touring this part of Dorset, and especially for birdwatchers, or those who enjoy walking and cycling. This site is perfect for visiting the Arne Nature Reserve. A 3.47 acre site with 60 touring pitches, 2 hardstandings.

AA Pubs & Restaurants nearby: Kemps Country House, Wareham 0845 862 0315

Greyhound Inn, Corfe Castle 01929 480205

New Inn, Church Knowle 01929 480357

Facilities: ⚑ ☺ ⚑ ⚑ ⚑ ⚑

Services: ⚑ ⚑ ⚑ ⚑ ⚑ ⚑

Within 3 miles: ⚑ ⚑ ⚑ ⚑ ⚑ ⚑ ⚑

Notes: ⚑ No dogs Jul-Aug

WEYMOUTH

Places to visit

RSPB Nature Reserve Radipole Lake, Weymouth, 01305 778313, www.rspb.org.uk

Portland Castle, Portland, 01305 820539, www.english-heritage.org.uk

Great for kids: Weymouth Sea Life Adventure Park and Marine Sanctuary, Weymouth, 0871 423 2110, www.sealifeeurope.com

---

SERVICES: ⚑ Electric hook up ⚑ Launderette ⚑ Licensed bar ⚑ Calor Gas ⚑ Camping Gaz ⚑ Toilet fluid ⚑ Café/Restaurant ⚑ Fast Food/Takeaway ⚑ Battery charging
⚑ Baby care ⚑ Motorvan service point **ABBREVIATIONS:** BH/bank hols-bank holidays Etr-Easter Whit-Whitsun dep-departure fr-from hrs-hours m-mile mdnt-midnight
rdbt-roundabout rs-restricted service wk-week wknd-weekend ⚑ No credit cards ⚑ no dogs See page 7 for details of the AA Camping Card Scheme

84% Littlesea Holiday Park (SY654783)

GOLD

Lynch Ln DT4 9DT

☎ 01305 774414   📄 01305 759186

dir: A35 onto A354 signed Weymouth. Right at 1st rdbt, 3rd exit at 2nd rdbt towards Chickerell. Left into Lynch Lane after lights. Site at far end of road

🚐 🚐 ▲

Open end Mar-end Oct (rs End Mar-May & Sep-Oct facilities may be reduced) Last arrival mdnt Last departure 10.00hrs

Just three miles from Weymouth with its lovely beaches and many attractions, Littlesea has a cheerful family atmosphere and fantastic facilities. Indoor and outdoor entertainment and activities are on offer for all the family, and the toilet facilities on the touring park are of a good quality. The touring section of this holiday complex is at the far end of the site adjacent to the South West Coast path. A 100 acre site with 124 touring pitches and 720 statics.

AA Pubs & Restaurants nearby: Old Ship Inn, Weymouth 01305 812522

Ilchester Arms, Abbotsbury 01305 871243

Perry's Restaurant, Weymouth 01305 785799

Leisure: 🎣 ⛱ 🎿 🎯

Facilities: 🚿 🅿 ⊙ 🇵 ✳ ⚕ 🕐 🛒 🍴 🎠 🐕

Services: 🔌 🗑 🖅 🔒 🧺 Ⓣ 🍴 ♿ 🚮

Within 3 miles: ⚓ 🏇 🎡 🎿 ⊙ ⛴ 🎿 ⛳ 🎢 U

Notes: No commercial vehicles, no boats, no dangerous dog breeds. Wi-fi

---

82% Seaview Holiday Park (SY707830)

Preston DT3 6DZ

☎ 01305 833037   📄 01305 833169

e-mail: katie.watson@bourne-leisure.co.uk

dir: A354 to Weymouth, signs for Preston/Wareham onto A353. Site 3m on right just after Weymouth Bay Holiday Park

🚐 🚐 ▲

Open mid Mar-Oct (rs mid Mar-May & Sep-Oct facilities may be reduced) Last arrival mdnt Last departure noon

A fun-packed holiday centre for all the family, with plenty of activities and entertainment during the day and evening. Terraced pitches are provided for caravans, and there is a separate field for tents. The park is close to Weymouth and other coastal attractions. There's a new toilet and shower block, plus fully-serviced hardstanding pitches. A 20 acre site with 87 touring pitches, 24 hardstandings and 259 statics.

AA Pubs & Restaurants nearby: Old Ship Inn, Weymouth 01305 812522

Smugglers Inn, Osmington Mills 01305 833125

Perry's Restaurant, Weymouth 01305 785799

Leisure: 🎣 ⛱ 🎿 🎯

Facilities: 🅿 ⊙ 🇵 ✳ ⚕ 🕐 🛒 🍴 🎠 🐕

Services: 🔌 🗑 🖅 🔒 🍴 ♿ 🚮

Within 3 miles: ⚓ 🏇 🎡 🎿 ⊙ ⛴ 🎿 ⛳ 🎢 U

Notes: No groups bookings under 21yrs, noise must be kept to a minimum outside complex, certain dog breeds are banned. Wi-fi

see advert below

LEISURE: 🎣 Indoor swimming pool ⛱ Outdoor swimming pool 🎠 Children's playground 🎾 Tennis court 🎯 Games room 🖵 Separate TV room ⛳ 9/18 hole golf course 🚣 Boats for hire 🎬 Cinema 🎣 Fishing ⊙ Mini golf 🎿 Watersports U Stables **FACILITIES:** 🚿 Bath 🚿 Shower ⊙ Electric shaver 🇵 Hairdryer ✳ Ice Pack Facility ⚕ Disabled facilities 🕐 Public telephone 🛒 Shop on site or within 200yds 🚚 Mobile shop (calls at least 5 days a week) 🍴 BBQ area 🎠 Picnic area 🐕 Dog exercise area

PREMIER PARK

►►►►► 84% East Fleet Farm Touring Park (SY640797)

Chickerell DT3 4DW
☎ **01305 785768**
e-mail: enquiries@eastfleet.co.uk
dir: *On B3157 (Weymouth-Bridport road), 3m from Weymouth*

* 🚐 £14-£25 🚌 £14-£25 ▲ £14-£25

Open 16 Mar-Oct Last arrival 22.00hrs Last departure 10.30hrs

Set on a working organic farm overlooking Fleet Lagoon and Chesil Beach, with a wide range of amenities and quality toilet facilities with family rooms in a Scandinavian log cabin. The friendly owners are welcoming and helpful, and their family bar serving meals and takeaway food is open from Easter, with glorious views from the patio area. There is also a good accessory shop. A 21 acre site with 400 touring pitches, 50 hardstandings.

AA Pubs & Restaurants nearby: Old Ship Inn, Weymouth 01305 812522

Ilchester Arms, Abbotsbury 01305 871243

Perry's Restaurant, Weymouth 01305 785799

Leisure: 🅰 🎣
Facilities: 🛁🖤☉🍴☀🕭🕙🖻🚻🎢🐾
Services: 🔌🖥🍴🛢🌀🚽🍽📦🏧♨
Within 3 miles: 🖈🎯🏇🐾🎣🚵🛥🛒🎢🎠

►►►► 79% Bagwell Farm Touring Park (SY627816)

Knights in the Bottom, Chickerell DT3 4EA
☎ **01305 782575** 📄 **01305 780554**
e-mail: aa@bagwellfarm.co.uk
web: www.bagwellfarm.co.uk
dir: *4m W of Weymouth on B3157 (Weymouth-Bridport), past Chickerell, turn left into site 500yds after Victoria Inn*

🚐 🚌 ▲

Open all year (rs Winter bar closed) Last arrival 21.00hrs Last departure 11.00hrs

An idyllically placed, terraced site on a hillside of a valley overlooking Chesil Beach. The park is well equipped with 25 new, fully-serviced pitches, a mini-supermarket, children's play area, pets' corner and a bar and grill serving food in high season. A 14 acre site with 320 touring pitches, 10 hardstandings.

AA Pubs & Restaurants nearby: Old Ship Inn, Weymouth 01305 812522

Perry's Restaurant, Weymouth 01305 785799

Leisure: 🅰
Facilities: 🛁🖤☉🍴☀🕭🕙🖻🚻🎢🐾
Services: 🔌🖥🍴🛢🌀🚽🍽📦🏧♨
Within 3 miles: 🖈🖥🚽 Wet suit shower, campers' shelter

Notes: Families only, dogs must be kept on leads. Wet suit shower, campers' shelter

►►► 82% Pebble Bank Caravan Park (SY659775)

Camp Rd, Wyke Regis DT4 9HF
☎ **01305 774844**
dir: *From Weymouth take Portland road. At last rdbt turn right, then 1st left to Army Tent Camp. Site opposite*

🚐 🚌 ▲

Open Etr-mid Oct (rs High season & wknds only bar open) Last arrival 21.00hrs Last departure 11.00hrs

This site, although only one and a half miles from Weymouth, is in a peaceful location overlooking Chesil Beach and the Fleet. There is a friendly little bar, which offers even better views. The toilet and shower block was completely refurbished in 2010 and is spotless. A 4 acre site with 40 touring pitches and 80 statics.

AA Pubs & Restaurants nearby: Old Ship Inn, Weymouth 01305 812522

Ilchester Arms, Abbotsbury 01305 871243

Perry's Restaurant, Weymouth 01305 785799

Leisure: 🅰
Facilities: 🖤☉🍴☀🕙
Services: 🔌🖥🍴🛢🌀📦
Within 3 miles: 🖈🎯🖈🎯🖥🚵🛒🎢🎠

►►► 80% West Fleet Holiday Farm (SY625811)

Fleet DT3 4EF
☎ **01305 782218** 📄 **01305 775396**
e-mail: aa@westfleetholidays.co.uk
web: www.westfleetholidays.co.uk
dir: *From Weymouth take B3157 towards Abbotsbury for 3m. Past Chickerell turn left at mini-rdbt to Fleet, site 1m on right*

* 🚐 🚌 ▲ £12-£21

Open Etr-Sep (rs May-Sep clubhouse & pool available) Last arrival 21.00hrs Last dep 11.00hrs

A spacious farm site with both level and sloping pitches divided into paddocks, and screened with hedging. Good views of the Dorset countryside, and a relaxing site for a family holiday with its heated outdoor pool and interesting clubhouse. A 12 acre site with 250 touring pitches.

AA Pubs & Restaurants nearby: Old Ship Inn, Weymouth 01305 812522

Ilchester Arms, Abbotsbury 01305 871243

Perry's Restaurant, Weymouth 01305 785799

Leisure: 🏊 🅰 🎣
Facilities: 🛁🖤☉☀🕭🖻
Services: 🔌🖥🍴🛢🌀🚽🍽📦🏧
Within 3 miles: 🖥🎠

Notes: Non-family groups by arrangement only, dogs must be on leads at all times & restricted to certain areas. Games field

►►► 79% Rosewall Camping (SY736820)

East Farm Dairy, Osmington Mills DT3 6HA
☎ **01305 832248**
e-mail: holidays@weymouthcamping.com
dir: *Take A353 towards Weymouth. At Osmington Mills sign (opposite garage) turn left for 0.25m, site on first right*

🚌 ▲

Open Etr-Oct (rs Apr, May & Oct shop opening times) Last arrival 22.00hrs Last departure 10.00hrs

A large, slightly sloping field with hedging and natural screening providing bays, in a peaceful setting close to the Dorset coastline and footpaths. The facilities are of a very good quality. This park offers an excellent spacious environment for tents and families. A 13 acre site with 225 touring pitches.

AA Pubs & Restaurants nearby: Old Ship Inn, Weymouth 01305 812522

Smugglers Inn, Osmington Mills 01305 833125

Perry's Restaurant, Weymouth 01305 785799

Leisure: 🅰
Facilities: 🖤☀🕭🖻
Services: 🖥🛢🌀📦
Within 3 miles: 🎯🖥🎠

Notes: Families & couples only. Riding stables & coarse fishing

WEYMOUTH *continued*

►►► 78% Sea Barn Farm *(SY625807)*

Fleet DT3 4ED
☎ **01305 782218** 🖷 **01305 775396**
e-mail: aa@seabarnfarm.co.uk
web: www.seabarnfarm.co.uk
dir: *From Weymouth take B3157 towards Abbotsbury for 3m. Past Chickerell turn left at mini-rdbt towards Fleet. Site 1m on left*

* 🚐 ▲ £11-£20

Open 15 Mar-Oct Last arrival 21.00hrs Last departure 11.00hrs

This site is set high on the Dorset coast and has spectacular views over Chesil Beach, The Fleet and Lyme Bay, and it is also on the South West coast path. Optional use of the clubhouse and swimming pool at West Fleet Holiday Farm is available. Pitches are sheltered by hedging, and there is an excellent new toilet facility block, and plenty of space for games. A 12 acre site with 250 touring pitches and 1 static.

AA Pubs & Restaurants nearby: Old Ship Inn, Weymouth 01305 812522

Ilchester Arms, Abbotsbury 01305 871243

Perry's Restaurant, Weymouth 01305 785799

Leisure: ⚑

Facilities: ⛄🐾☉ℱ✳🐕🕭🛅🎪🚻

Services: 🖭🛢🖴🖋🅃🛗

Within 3 miles: 🛴🛎🖳

Notes: Non-family groups by arrangement, dogs must be kept on leads at all times. Café, pool & clubhouse available at adjacent site from May-Sep

---

WIMBORNE MINSTER   Map 5 SZ09

Places to visit

Kingston Lacy, Wimborne, 01202 883402 (Mon-Fri), www.nationaltrust.org.uk

The Priests House Museum and Garden, Wimborne, 01202 882533, www.priest-house.co.uk

Great for kids: Moors Valley Country Park, Ringwood, 01425 470721, www.moors-valley.co.uk

---

PREMIER PARK

►►►►► 84% Wilksworth Farm Caravan Park *(SU004018)*

Cranborne Rd BH21 4HW
☎ **01202 885467** 🖷 **01202 885467**
e-mail: rayandwendy@wilksworthfarmcaravanpark.co.uk
web: www.wilksworthfarmcaravanpark.co.uk
dir: *1m N of Wimborne on B3078*

* 🚐 £16-£28 🚐 £16-£28 ▲ £16-£28

Open Apr-Oct (rs Oct no shop) Last arrival 20.00hrs Last departure 11.00hrs

A popular and attractive park peacefully set in the grounds of a listed house in the heart of rural Dorset. The spacious site has much to offer visitors, including an excellent heated swimming pool, takeaway and café, plus a games room. The modern toilet facilities contain en suite rooms and good family rooms. An 11 acre site with 85 touring pitches, 20 hardstandings and 77 statics.

AA Pubs & Restaurants nearby: Les Bouviers, Wimborne Minster 01202 889555

Coventry Arms, Corfe Mullen 01258 857284

Botany Bay Inne, Winterborne Zelston 01929 459227

Leisure: ⚏⚑🎱🎾

Facilities: ⛄🐾☉ℱ✳🐕🕭🛅🎪🚻🐕

Services: 🖭🛢🖴🖋🅃🍴🛗🚏🛴

Within 3 miles: 🛴🎬🖳🛎🖳

Notes: Max 2 dogs per pitch & they must kept on leads at all times. Paddling pool, volley ball, mini football pitch

see advert below

PREMIER PARK

►►►►► 78% Merley Court *(SZ008984)*

Merley BH21 3AA
☎ **01590 648331** 🖷 **01590 645610**
e-mail: holidays@shorefield.co.uk
dir: *Site signed on A31, Wimborne by-pass & Poole junct rdbt*

🚐 £14.50-£42.50 🚐 £14.50-£42.50 ▲ £12.50-£37

Open 6 Feb-2 Jan (rs Low season pool closed & bar, shop open limited hrs) Last arrival 21.00hrs Last departure 10.00hrs

A superb site in a quiet rural position on the edge of Wimborne, with woodland on two sides and good access roads. The park is well landscaped and offers generous individual pitches in sheltered grassland. There are plenty of amenities

---

LEISURE: 🏊 Indoor swimming pool 🏊 Outdoor swimming pool ⚑ Children's playground 🎾 Tennis court 🎱 Games room 📺 Separate TV room ⛳ 9/18 hole golf course 🚣 Boats for hire 🎬 Cinema 🎣 Fishing ⛳ Mini golf 🏄 Watersports 🐴 Stables **FACILITIES:** 🛁 Bath 🚿 Shower ☉ Electric shaver ℱ Hairdryer ✳ Ice Pack Facility 🐕 Disabled facilities ☎ Public telephone 🛒 Shop on site or within 200yds 🚐 Mobile shop (calls at least 5 days a week) 🍴 BBQ area 🌲 Picnic area 🐕 Dog exercise area

for all the family, including a heated outdoor pool, tennis court and adventure playground. This park tends to get busy in summer and therefore advance booking advised. A 20 acre site with 160 touring pitches, 50 hardstandings.

AA Pubs & Restaurants nearby: Les Bouviers, Wimborne Minster 01202 889555

Coventry Arms, Corfe Mullen 01258 857284

Botany Bay Inne, Winterborne Zelston 01929 459227

Leisure: 🏊 🎱 ♨ 🎯

Facilities: 🛁 📶 ☉ ⚕ ✳ ⚡ 🕐 🛒 🎣 ♿ 🚻

Services: 🔌 🛒 🍴 🎵 🚰 🔟 🍴 ⛽ 🚼 ⛟

Within 3 miles: ↧ ⛖ 🎯 🏖 ⛳ ◎ 🔟 🎡 ○

Notes: Families & couples only. Pet friendly. Rallies welcome. Use of facilities at Oakdene Forest Park (7m)

see advert under Hampshire

▶▶▶ **78% Springfield Touring Park**

(SY987989)

Candys Ln, Corfe Mullen BH21 3EF
☎ **01202 881719**
e-mail: john.clark18@btconnect.com
dir: *From Wimborne on Wimborne by-pass (A31) western end turn left after Caravan Sales, follow brown sign*

* 🚐 £14–£18 🚌 £14–£18 ▲ £10–£18

Open Apr-Oct Last arrival 21.00hrs Last departure 11.00hrs

A small touring park with extensive views over the Stour Valley and a quiet and friendly atmosphere. The park is maintained immaculately, and has a well-stocked shop. A 3.5 acre site with 45 touring pitches, 18 hardstandings.

AA Pubs & Restaurants nearby: Les Bouviers, Wimborne Minster 01202 889555

Coventry Arms, Corfe Mullen 01258 857284

Botany Bay Inne, Winterborne Zelston 01929 459227

Leisure: 🎱

Facilities: 📶 ☉ ⚕ ✳ ♿ 🎣

Services: 🔌 🛒 🍴 ⛟

Within 3 miles: ↧ ⛖ 🎯 🏖 ⛳ ◎ 🔟 ○

Notes: 🚫 No skateboards

▶▶▶ **76% Charris Camping & Caravan Park** (SY992988)

Candy's Ln, Corfe Mullen BH21 3EF
☎ **01202 885970**
e-mail: bookings@charris.co.uk
web: www.charris.co.uk
dir: *From E, exit Wimborne bypass (A31) W end. 300yds after Caravan Sales, follow brown sign. From W on A31, over A350 rdbt, take next turn after B3074, follow brown signs*

* 🚐 £13.75–£15.75 🚌 £13.75–£15.75 ▲ £10–£12

Open Mar-Jan Last arrival 21.00hrs Last departure 11.00hrs

A sheltered park of grassland lined with trees on the edge of the Stour Valley. The owners are friendly and welcoming, and they maintain the park facilities to a good standard. Barbecues are a popular occasional event. A 3.5 acre site with 45 touring pitches, 12 hardstandings.

AA Pubs & Restaurants nearby: Les Bouviers, Wimborne Minster 01202 889555

Coventry Arms, Corfe Mullen 01258 857284

Botany Bay Inne, Winterborne Zelston 01929 459227

Facilities: 📶 ☉ ⚕ ✳ 🕐 🎣

Services: 🔌 🛒 🍴 🎵 🚰 🔟 ⛟

Within 3 miles: ↧ ⛳ 🏖 🔟 ○

Notes: Earliest arrival time 11.00hrs. Wi-fi

Campsites in popular areas get very crowded at busy times – it is advisable to book well in advance

---

▶▶▶▶ **81% Whitemead Caravan Park** (SY841869)

East Burton Rd BH20 6HG
☎ **01929 462241** 📠 **01929 462241**
e-mail: whitemeadcp@aol.com
dir: *Signed from A352 at level crossing on Wareham side of Wool*

* 🚐 £12.50–£19.75 🚌 £12.50–£19.75
▲ £10–£17.25

Open mid Mar-Oct Last arrival 22.00hrs Last departure noon

A well laid-out site in the valley of the River Frome, close to the village of Wool, and surrounded by woodland. A shop and games room enhance the facilities here, and the spotless, modern toilets are heated, providing an excellent amenity. Only a short walk away are the shops and pubs, plus the main bus route and mainline station to Poole, Bournemouth and Weymouth. A 5 acre site with 95 touring pitches.

AA Pubs & Restaurants nearby: New Inn, Church Knowle 01929 480357

Leisure: 🎱 🎯

Facilities: 📶 ☉ ⚕ ✳ ♿ 🎣 🚻 🚿

Services: 🔌 🛒 🍴 🎵 🔟 ⛟

Within 3 miles: ↧ ⛳ 🏖 🔟 ○

Notes: Wi-fi

CO DURHAM

BARNARD CASTLE — Map 19 NZ01

Places to visit

Barnard Castle, www.english-heritage.org.uk

The Bowes Museum, Barnard Castle, 01833 690606, www.thebowesmuseum.org.uk

Great for kids: Raby Castle, Staindrop, 01833 660202, www.rabycastle.com

▶▶▶ 75% Pecknell Farm Caravan Park (NZ028178)

Lartington DL12 9DF
☎ 01833 638357

dir: *1.5m from Barnard Castle. From A66 take B6277. Site on right 1.5m from junct with A67*

🚐 £12-£16 🚙 £12-£16

Open Apr-Oct Last arrival 20.00hrs Last departure anytime

A small well laid out site on a working farm in beautiful rural meadowland, with spacious marked pitches on level ground. There are many walking opportunities directly from this friendly site. A 1.5 acre site with 20 touring pitches, 5 hardstandings.

AA Pubs & Restaurants nearby: Bridge Inn, Barnard Castle 01833 627341

Morritt Arms Hotel, Barnard Castle 01833 627232

Facilities: 🅿️⊙📶🕐

Services: 🔌🛒🚼

Within 3 miles: ↧🔎◎📷🛢️↻

Notes: 🐕 Maximum 2 dogs

BEAMISH

Places to visit

Tanfield Railway, Tanfield, 0191 388 7545, www.tanfield_railway.co.uk

Beanish Museum, Beamish, 0191 370 4000, www.beamish.org.uk

Great for kids: Diggerland, Langley Park, 0871 227 7007, www.diggerland.com

BEAMISH — Map 19 NZ25

▶▶▶ 74% Bobby Shafto Caravan Park (NZ232545)

Cranberry Plantation DH9 0RY
☎ 0191 370 1776 📄 0191 370 1783

dir: *From A693 signed Beamish to sign for Beamish Museum. Take approach road, turn right immediately before museum, left at pub to site 1m on right*

🚐 🚙 ⛺

Open Mar-Oct Last arrival 23.00hrs Last departure 11.00hrs

A tranquil rural park surrounded by trees, with very clean and well organised facilities. The suntrap touring area has plenty of attractive hanging baskets, and there is a clubhouse with bar, TV and pool. The fully serviced pitches enhance the amenities. A 9 acre site with 83 touring pitches, 30 hardstandings and 54 statics.

AA Pubs & Restaurants nearby: Beamish Park Hotel, Beamish 01207 230666

Leisure: 🎢🔎🖵

Facilities: 🅿️⊙📶✳️♿🕐📷

Services: 🔌🛒🚽🛢️🚻📶🔥

Within 3 miles: ↧🚴↺🔎🛢️↻

BLACKHALL COLLIERY — Map 19 NZ43

Places to visit

Hartlepool Maritime Experience, Hartlepool, 01429 860077, www.hartlepoolsmaritimeexperience.com

Auckland Castle, Bishop Auckland, 01388 602576, www.auckland-castle.co.uk

Great for kids: Captain Cook Birthplace Museum, Middlesbrough, 01642 311211, www.captcook-ne.co.uk

 79% Crimdon Dene (NZ477378)

Coast Rd TS27 4BN
☎ 0871 664 9737

e-mail: crimdon.dene@park-resorts.com
dir: *From A19 just S of Peterlee, take B1281 signed Blackhall. Through Castle Eden, left in 0.5m signed Blackhall. Approx 3m right at T-junct onto A1086 towards Crimdon. Site in 1m signed on left, by Seagull pub*

🚐 🚙

Open Apr-Oct Last arrival 23.00hrs Last departure 10.00hrs

A large, popular coastal holiday park, handily placed for access to Teeside, Durham and Newcastle. The park contains a full range of holiday centre facilities for both children and their parents. Touring facilities are appointed to a very good standard. Six seasonal touring pitches are available. 44 touring pitches, 44 hardstandings and 586 statics.

Leisure: 🏊‍♀️🎢🔎

Facilities: 🅿️⊙📶⊙📷🛢️📷

Services: 🔌🛒🚽🍽️🔥

Within 3 miles: ↧🎢🔎🛢️↻

Notes: No quad bikes, no tents. Wi-fi

CONSETT — Map 19 NZ15

Places to visit

Beamish Museum, Beamish, 0191 370 4000 www.beamish.org.uk

Tanfield Railway, Tanfield, 0191 388 7545, www.tanfield_railway.co.uk

Great for kids: Gibside, Rowlands Gill, 01207 541820, www.nationaltrust.org.uk/main/gibside

▶▶ 78% Byreside Caravan Site (NZ122560)

Hamsterley NE17 7RT
☎ 01207 560280 📄 01207 560280
dir: *From A694 onto B6310 & follow signs*

* 🚐 fr £11 🚙 fr £11 ⛺ £8-£12

Open all year Last arrival 22.00hrs Last departure noon

A small, secluded family-run site on a working farm, with well-maintained facilities. It is immediately adjacent to the coast to coast cycle track so makes an ideal location for walkers and cyclists. Handy for Newcastle and Durham; the Roman Wall and Northumberland National Park are within an hour's drive. A 1.5 acre site with 31 touring pitches, 29 hardstandings.

AA Pubs & Restaurants nearby: Manor House Inn, Carterway Heads 01207 255268

Facilities: ⋔ ⊙ ✳ ⌖ ♿ ⓢ ⊞ ⚲

Services: ⊞ ⓐ 🔒 Ⓣ ⛽

Within 3 miles: ⌖ 🏇 ⓢ ⓢ

Notes: No ball games on site, dogs must be kept on leads. Caravan storage

DURHAM   Map 19 NZ24

Places to visit

Crook Hall and Gardens, Durham, 0191 384 8028, www.crookhallgardens.co.uk

Oriental Museum, Durham, 0191 334 5694, www.dur.ac.uk/oriental.museum

Great for kids: Old Fulling Mill Museum of Archaeology, Durham, www.dur.ac.uk/fulling.mill

▶▶▶ 80% Strawberry Hill Farm Caravan & Camping Park (NZ337399)

Old Cassop DH6 4QA
☎ 0191 372 3457 & 372 2512
📄 0191 372 2512
e-mail: info@strawberryhf.co.uk
web: www.strawberry-hill-farm.co.uk
dir: From A1(M) junct 61 take A688 NE signed Peterlee. Right onto A181. (NB Do not use Sat Nav)

* ⊞ £15.50-£17.50 ⇔ £15.50-£17.50
▲ £15.50-£17.50

Open Mar-Dec Last arrival 20.00hrs Last departure noon

An attractive park, planted with many young trees and shrubs, and well screened from the road. The terraced pitches have superb panoramic views across lovely wooded countryside. Good toilet and laundry facilities, and a useful base for visiting Durham Castle and Cathedral, Beamish Museum and the coast. There are static caravans available for hire. A 6.5 acre site with 45 touring pitches, 10 hardstandings and 3 statics.

AA Pubs & Restaurants nearby: Victoria Inn, Durham 0191 386 5269

Bird in Hand, Trimdon 01429 880391

Bistro 21, Durham 0191 384 4354

Facilities: ⋔ ⊙ 🅿 ✳ ♿ ⓢ ⊞ ⚲

Services: ⊞ ⓢ 🔒 ⊘ Ⓣ ⛽ ⚲

Within 3 miles: ⌖ 🏇 ⓢ ⓤ

ESSEX

CANEWDON   Map 7 TQ99

Places to visit

RHS Garden Hyde Hall, Chelmsford, 01245 402006, www.rhs.org.uk

Southend Pier Museum, Southend-on-Sea, 01702 611214, www.southendpiermuseum.com

Great for kids: Southend Museum, Planetarium and Discovery Centre, www.southendmuseums.co.uk

---

AA CAMPING CARD SITE

▶▶▶ 79% Riverside Village Holiday Park (TQ929951)

Creeksea Ferry Rd, Wallasea Island SS4 2EY
☎ 01702 258297 📄 01702 258555
e-mail: riversidevillage@tiscali.co.uk
dir: M25 junct 29, A127, towards Southend-on-Sea. Take B1013 towards Rochford. Follow signs for Wallasea Island & Baltic Wharf

* ⊞ £15-£22 ⇔ £15-£22 ▲ £15-£22

Open Mar-Oct

Next to a nature reserve beside the River Crouch, this holiday park is surrounded by wetlands but only eight miles from Southend. A modern toilet block with disabled facilities is provided for tourers and there's a handsome new reception area. Several restaurants and pubs are within a short distance. A 25 acre site with 60 touring pitches and 162 statics.

Leisure: ⛰

Facilities: ⋔ ⊙ 🅿 ✳ ♿ ⓞ ⓢ ⊞ ⚲

Services: ⊞ ⓢ 🔒 Ⓣ

Within 3 miles: ⌖ 🏇 ⓢ ⓢ ⓤ

Notes: No dogs in tents. Freshwater fishing, mobile newspaper vendor Sun & BH

CLACTON-ON-SEA   Map 7 TM11

Places to visit

Harwich Redoubt Fort, Harwich, 01255 503429, www.harwich-society.com

The Beth Chatto Gardens, Colchester, 01206 822007, www.bethchatto.co.uk

Great for kids: Colchester Zoo, Colchester, 01206 331292, www.colchester-zoo.com

 ### 78% Highfield Grange
(TM173175)

London Rd CO16 9QY
☎ 0871 664 9746 📄 01255 689805
e-mail: highfield.grange@park-resorts.com
dir: A12 to Colchester, then A120 (Harwich) then A133 to Clacton-on-Sea. Site on B1441 clearly signed on left

⊞ ⇔

Open Apr-Oct Last arrival mdnt Last departure 10.00hrs

The modern leisure facilities at this attractively planned park make it an ideal base for a lively family holiday. The swimming complex with both indoor and outdoor pools and a huge water shoot is especially popular. There are fully serviced touring pitches, each with its own hardstanding, located at the heart of the park. The nearby resorts of Walton on the Naze, Frinton and Clacton all offer excellent beaches and a wide range of popular seaside attractions. A 30 acre site with 43 touring pitches, 43 hardstandings and 509 statics.

AA Pubs & Restaurants nearby: Rose & Crown, Colchester 01206 866677

Whalebone, Colchester 01206 729307

Leisure: ⌣ ⌣ ⛰ ⚫

Facilities: ⋔ ⊙ 🅿 ♿ ⓢ ⊞ ⚲

Services: ⊞ ⓢ 🖥 🔒 🍽 ⛁

Within 3 miles: ⌖ ✻ 🏇 🅿 ⓞ ⛴ ⓢ ⓢ ⓤ

Notes: No tents, fold-in campers or trailer tents. Wi-fi

CLACTON-ON-SEA *continued*

70% Martello Beach Holiday Park *(TM136128)*

Belsize Av, Jaywick CO15 2LF

☎ 0871 664 9782 & 01442 830100

e-mail: martello.beach@park-resorts.com

dir: *Telephone for directions*

Open Apr-Oct (rs BH & peak wks Entertainment available) Last arrival 21.30hrs Last dep noon

Direct access to a seven-mile long Blue Flag beach is an undoubted attraction at this holiday park. The touring area is next to the leisure complex, where an indoor and outdoor swimming pool, shops, cafés and bars and evening entertainment are all provided. Ten seasonal touring pitches are available. A 40 acre site with 100 touring pitches and 294 statics.

AA Pubs & Restaurants nearby: Rose & Crown, Colchester 01206 866677

Leisure: 🏊🏖🎢🎯 Facilities: 🚿⊙🅿✳♿🕐💲

Services: 🚗🔧🛒🍽🔥

Within 3 miles: 🚴🎣⛵🎯🎲🎳

Notes: ⊗ Kids' clubs, water sports, evening entertainment. Wi-fi

---

COLCHESTER   Map 13 TL92

Places to visit

Colchester Castle Museum, Colchester, 01206 282939, www.colchestermuseums.org.uk,

Layer Marney Tower, Layer Marney, 01206 330784, www.layermarneytower.co.uk

Great for kids: Colchester Zoo, Colchester, 01206 331292, www.colchester-zoo.com

▶▶▶▶ 85% Colchester Holiday Park *(TL971252)*

Cymbeline Way, Lexden CO3 4AG

☎ 01206 545551 📠 01206 710443

e-mail: enquiries@colchestercamping.co.uk

dir: *Follow tourist signs from A12, then A133 Colchester Central slip road*

Open all year Last arrival 20.30hrs Last departure noon

A well-designed campsite on level grassland, on the west side of Colchester near the town centre. Close to main routes to London (A12) and east coast. There is good provision for hardstandings,

and the owner's attention to detail is reflected in the neatly trimmed grass and well-cut hedges. Toilet facilities are housed in three buildings, two of which are modern and well equipped. A 12 acre site with 168 touring pitches, 44 hardstandings.

Colchester Holiday Park

AA Pubs & Restaurants nearby: Rose & Crown, Colchester 01206 866677

Whalebone, Colchester 01206 729307

Swan Inn, Chappel 01787 222353

Leisure: 🎢

Facilities: 🚿⊙🅿✳♿🕐💲🐕🎯

Services: 🚗🔧🛒🚽🛗♿

Within 3 miles: 🚴🎫🎣⛵🎯🎲🎳

Notes: No commercial vehicles. Badminton court

LEISURE: 🏊 Indoor swimming pool 🏊 Outdoor swimming pool 🎢 Children's playground 🎾 Tennis court 🎱 Games room 📺 Separate TV room ⛳ 9/18 hole golf course ⛵ Boats for hire 🎬 Cinema 🎣 Fishing ⛳ Mini golf 🏄 Watersports 🐴 Stables FACILITIES: 🛁 Bath 🚿 Shower 🔌 Electric shaver 💈 Hairdryer ✳ Ice Pack Facility ♿ Disabled facilities ☎ Public telephone 🏪 Shop on site or within 200yds 🚐 Mobile shop (calls at least 5 days a week) 🍖 BBQ area 🌲 Picnic area 🐕 Dog exercise area

MERSEA ISLAND — Map 7 TM01

Places to visit

Layer Marney, 01206 330784,
www.layermarneytower.co.uk

Beth Chatto Gardens, Colchester,
01206 822007, www.bethchatto.co.uk

Great for kids: Colchester Zoo, Colchester,
01206 331292, www.colchester-zoo.com

77% Waldegraves Holiday Park (TM033133)

CO5 8SE
☎ 01206 382898 📠 01206 385359
e-mail: holidays@waldegraves.co.uk
web: www.waldegraves.co.uk
dir: *B1025 to Mersea Island across The Strood. Left to East Mersea, 2nd turn on right, follow tourist signs to site*

* 🚐 £15-£25 🚐 £15-£25 ⛺ £15-£25

Open Mar-Nov Last arrival 22.00hrs Last departure 15.00hrs

A spacious and pleasant site, located between farmland and its own private beach on the Blackwater Estuary. Facilities include two freshwater fishing lakes, heated swimming pool, club, amusements, café and golf, and there is generally good provision for families. A 25 acre site with 60 touring pitches and 250 statics.

AA Pubs & Restaurants nearby: Peldon Rose, Peldon 01206 735248

Leisure: 🏊 ⚙ 🎣 ▢
Facilities: 🐕 ⊙ 🍴 ✳ ♿ ⊙ 🚿 🚻 🏪 ⛺
Services: 🔌 🔲 🍴 🛢 🚽 🍽 🚐 🛒
Within 3 miles: ⚓ 🎣 ◎ ⛴ 🏛 🛒

Notes: No large groups or groups of under 21s. Boating, golf. Wi-fi

see advert on opposite page

ST LAWRENCE — Map 7 TL90

Places to visit

RHS Garden Hyde Hall, Chelmsford,
01245 402006, www.rhs.org.uk

Kelvedon Hatch Secret Nuclear Bunker,
Brentwood, 01277 364883,
www.secretnuclearbunker.co.uk

Great for kids: Hadleigh Castle, Hadleigh,
01760 755161, www.english-heritage.org.uk

79% Waterside St Lawrence Bay (TL953056)

Main Rd CM0 7LY
☎ 0871 664 9794
e-mail: waterside@park-resorts.com
dir: *A12 towards Chelmsford then A414 signed Maldon. Follow B1010 & signs to Latchingdon, then signs for Mayland/Steeple/St Lawrence. Left towards St Lawrence. Site on right*

🚐 🚐 ⛺

Open Apr-Oct (rs Wknds entertainment available) Last arrival 22.00hrs Last departure 11.00hrs

Waterside occupies a scenic location overlooking the Blackwater estuary. In addition to the range of on-site leisure facilities there are opportunities for beautiful coastal walks and visits to the attractions of Southend. Tents are welcome on this expansive site, which has some touring pitches with electricity and good toilet facilities. The park has its own boat storage and slipway onto the Blackwater. Seasonal touring pitches are available. 72 touring pitches and 271 statics.

AA Pubs & Restaurants nearby: Ye Olde White Harte Hotel, Burnham-on-Crouch
01621 782106

Ferryboat Inn, North Fambridge 01621 740208

Leisure: 🏊 ⚙ 🎣 **Facilities:** 🐕 🍴 ♿ ⊙ 🚿 🚻 ⛺
Services: 🔌 🔲 🍴 🛢 🍽 🚐 🛒
Within 3 miles: 🎣 ⛴ 🏛 🛒

Notes: Wi-fi *see advert below*

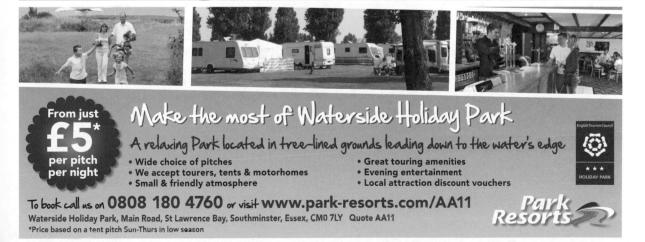

ST OSYTH — Map 7 TM11

Places to visit

Harwich Redoubt Fort, Harwich, 01255 503429, www.harwich-society.com

Colchester Castle Museum, Colchester, 01206 282939, www.colchestermuseums.org.uk

Great for kids: Colchester Zoo, Colchester, 01206 331292, www.colchester-zoo.com

79% The Orchards Holiday Park (TM125155)

CO16 8LJ

☎ 01255 820651 📠 01255 820184

e-mail: laura.hassall@bourne-leisure.co.uk

dir: From Clacton-on-Sea take B1027 towards Colchester. Left after petrol station, then straight on at x-rds in St Osyth. Follow signs to Point Clear. Park in 3m

Open end Mar-end Oct (rs mid Mar-May & Sep-Oct some facilities may be reduced) Last arrival anytime Last departure 10.00hrs

The Orchards offers much improved touring facilities with a new quality toilet block which includes two very spacious family rooms. The touring pitches are generously sized and the touring area has its own laundry and play area. There's also direct access to all the leisure, entertainment and dining outlets available on this large popular holiday park on the Essex coast. A 140 acre site with 54 touring pitches and 1000 statics.

AA Pubs & Restaurants nearby: Rose & Crown, Colchester 01206 866677

Whalebone, Colchester 01206 729307

Leisure: 🏊 🏊 🏊

Facilities: 🚿 🅿 🛗 🕐 🖥 🚽

Services: 🔌 🛢 🚽 🛁 🍴 🛒

Within 3 miles: 🎣 🎯 🎡 ⛴ 🛍 🎰 ♻

Notes: No cars by tents. Certain dog breeds are banned. Wi-fi

WALTON ON THE NAZE

Places to visit

Ipswich Museum, Ipswich, 01473 433550, www.ipswich.gov.uk

Harwich Redoubt Fort, Harwich, 01255 503429, www.harwich-society.com

WALTON ON THE NAZE — Map 7 TM22

73% Naze Marine (TM255226)

Hall Ln CO14 8HL

☎ 0871 664 9755

e-mail: naze.marine@park-resorts.com

dir: A12 to Colchester. Then A120 (Harwich road) then A133 to Weeley. Take B1033 to Walton seafront. Site on left

Open Apr-Oct Last arrival anytime Last departure 13.00hrs

With its modern indoor swimming pool, show bar, bar/restaurant and amusements, this park offers a variety of on-site attractions. The park is within easy access of the beaches and attractions of Walton on the Naze, Frinton and Clacton, and the more historic places of interest inland. Five seasonal touring pitches are available. Please note that this site does not cater for tents. A 46 acre site with 41 touring pitches and 540 statics.

Leisure: 🏊 🎡

Facilities: 🚿 🕐 ♿ 🕐 🖥 🍴

Services: 🔌 🛢 🚽 🍴 🛒

Within 3 miles: 🎣 🎯 ⛴ 🛍 🎰

Notes: Nature walk, natural meadow. Wi-fi

GLOUCESTERSHIRE

BERKELEY — Map 4 ST69

Places to visit

Edward Jenner Museum, Berkeley, 01453 810631, www.jennermuseum.com

WWT Slimbridge, Slimbridge, 01453 891900, www.wwt.org.uk

Great for kids: Berkeley Castle, Berkeley, 01453 810332, www.berkeley-castle.com

►►► 74% Hogsdown Farm Caravan & Camping Park (ST710974)

Hogsdown Farm, Lower Wick GL11 6DD

☎ 01453 810224

dir: M5 junct 14 (Falfield), take A38 towards Gloucester, turn right for site

Open all year Last arrival 21.00hrs Last departure 16.00hrs

A pleasant site with good toilet facilities, located between Bristol and Gloucester. It is well positioned for visiting Berkeley Castle and the Cotswolds, and makes an excellent overnight stop when travelling to or from the West Country. A 5 acre site with 45 touring pitches, 12 hardstandings.

Hogsdown Farm Caravan & Camping Park

AA Pubs & Restaurants nearby: Malt House, Berkeley 01453 511177

Anchor Inn, Oldbury-on-Severn 01454 413331

Leisure: 🎡

Facilities: 🚿 ❄ 🖥

Services: 🔌 🛢 🛁 🛒

Within 3 miles: 🎣 🎯 🛍 🎰

Notes: ♻ No skateboards or bicycles

CHELTENHAM — Map 10 SO92

Places to visit

Cheltenham Art Gallery and Museum, Cheltenham, 01242 237431, www.cheltenham.artgallery.museum

Holst Birthplace Museum, Cheltenham, 01242 524846, www.holstmuseum.org.uk

Great for kids: Gloucester City Museum and Art Gallery, Gloucester, 01452 396131, www.gloucester.gov.uk/citymuseum

►►► 83% Briarfields (SO899215)

Gloucester Rd GL51 0SX

☎ 01242 235324

e-mail: briarfields@hotmail.co.uk

dir: M5 junct 11, A40 towards Cheltenham. At 1st rdbt 1st left onto B4063. Site 200mtrs on left

Open all year Last arrival 19.00hrs Last departure noon

A well-designed level park, with a motel, where the facilities are modern and very clean. The park is well-positioned between Cheltenham and

Gloucester, with easy access to the Cotswolds. And, being close to junction 11 of the M5, makes a perfect overnight stopping point. A 6 acre site with 72 touring pitches, 72 hardstandings.

AA Pubs & Restaurants nearby: The Reservoir, Charlton Kings 01242 529671

The Daffodil, Cheltenham 01242 700055

Royal Well Tavern, Cheltenham 01242 221212

Facilities: ♠☉⌐&🖥

Services: ⌨🗑

Within 3 miles: ⌘⚹⊟🖉◎🖻🗑↺

Notes: No cars by tents

CIRENCESTER — Map 5 SP00

Places to visit

Corinium Museum, Cirencester, 01285 655611, www.cotswold.gov.uk/go/museum

Chedworth Roman Villa, Chedworth, 01242 890256, www.nationaltrust.org.uk/chedworth

Great for kids: Prinknash Bird and Deer Park, Cranham, 01452 812727, www.thebirdpark.com

AA CAMPING CARD SITE

►►►► 80% Mayfield Touring Park

(SP020055)

Cheltenham Rd GL7 7BH
☎ 01285 831301
e-mail: mayfield-park@cirencester.fsbusiness.co.uk
dir: From Cirencester bypass take Burford road/ A429 junct exit towards Cirencester, then follow brown signs to site (approx 3.5m)

* 🚐 £13-£20 🚛 £13-£20 ▲ £11-£18

Open all year Last arrival 20.00hrs Last departure noon

A gently sloping park on the edge of the Cotswolds, with level pitches and a warm welcome. Popular with couples and families, it offers a good licensed shop selling a wide selection of home-cooked takeaway food. Although some traffic noise can be heard at times, this lovely park makes an ideal base for visiting the Cotswolds and the many attractions of the area. A 12 acre site with 72 touring pitches, 31 hardstandings.

AA Pubs & Restaurants nearby: The Crown of Crucis, Cirencester 01285 851806

Hare & Hounds, Chedworth 01285 720288

Facilities: ♠☉⌐⚹&🕐🖻🖥⌐↿

Services: ⌨🗑🖻⌀⊤🖩

Within 3 miles: ⌘🖻🗑

Notes: Dogs only by by prior arrangement. No cycles or skateboards. Off licence

GLOUCESTER — Map 10 SO81

Places to visit

Gloucester Folk Museum, Gloucester, 01452 396868, www.gloucester.gov.uk/folkmuseum

Nature in Art, Gloucester, 01452 731422, www.nature-in-art.org.uk

Great for kids: The National Waterways Museum, Gloucester, 01452 318200, www.nwm.org.uk

►►► 71% Red Lion Caravan & Camping Park (SO849258)

Wainlode Hill, Norton GL2 9LW
☎ 01452 730251 & 731810 📄 01452 730251
dir: Exit A38 at Norton, follow road to river

🚐 🚛 ▲

Open all year Last arrival 22.00hrs Last departure 11.00hrs

An attractive meadowland park, adjacent to a traditional pub, with the River Severn just across a country lane. This is an ideal touring and fishing base. Seasonal touring pitches are available. A 13 acre site with 60 touring pitches, 10 hardstandings and 85 statics.

AA Pubs & Restaurants nearby: Queens Head, Gloucester 01452 301882

Queens Arms, Ashleworth 01452 700395 Boat Inn, Ashleworth 01452 700272

Leisure: ⌂

Facilities: ♠☉⌐⚹&🕐🖻⌐↿

Services: ⌨🗑🍴🖻⌀⊤🍽

Within 3 miles: ⌘🖉🗑↺

Notes: ◎ Freshwater fishing & private lake

NEWENT — Map 10 SO72

Places to visit

Odda's Chapel, Deerhurst, www.english-heritage.org.uk

Westbury Court Garden, Westbury in Severn, 01452 760461, www.nationaltrust.org.uk

Great for kids: The National Birds of Prey Centre, Newent, 0870 9901992, www.nbpc.co.uk

►►► 81% Pelerine Caravan and Camping (SO645183)

Ford House Rd GL18 1LQ
☎ 01531 822761
e-mail: pelerine@hotmail.com
dir: 1m from Newent

* 🚐 £18-£20 🚛 £18-£20 ▲ £18-£22

Open Mar-Nov Last arrival 22.00hrs Last departure 16.00hrs

A pleasant site divided into two areas, one of which is for adults only, with some and electric hook-ups in each area. Facilities are very good, especially for families. It is close to several vineyards, and well positioned in the north of the Forest of Dean with Tewkesbury, Cheltenham and Ross-on-Wye within easy reach. Seasonal touring pitches are available. A 5 acre site with 35 touring pitches, 2 hardstandings.

AA Pubs & Restaurants nearby: Yew Tree Inn, Clifford's Mesne 01531 820719

Penny Farthing Inn, Aston Crews 01989 750366

Facilities: ♠☉⌐⚹&🖥

Services: ⌨🗑🖻🖩

Within 3 miles: ⌘⊟🖉🖻🗑↺

Notes: ◎ Woodburners, chimineas, burning pits. Wi-fi

SLIMBRIDGE Map 4 SO70

Places to visit

Dean Forest railway, Lydney, 01594 843423 (info), www.deanforestrailway.co.uk

Berkeley Castle, Berkeley, 01453 810332, www.berkeley-castle.com

Great for kids: WWT Slimbridge, Slimbridge, 01453 891900, www.wwt.org.uk

►►►► 81% Tudor Caravan & Camping (SO728040)

Shepherds Patch GL2 7BP
☎ 01453 890483
e-mail: aa@tudorcaravanpark.co.uk
web: www.tudorcaravanpark.com
dir: From M5 junct 13/14 follow signs for WWT Wetlands Wildlife Centre-Slimbridge. Site at rear of Tudor Arms pub

* ⊞ £11.50-£19.50 ⌾ £11.50-£19.50
Å £7.50-£19.50

Open all year Last arrival 20.00hrs Last departure noon

An orchard-style park sheltered by mature trees and shrubs, set in an attractive meadow beside the Sharpness to Gloucester canal. A new facility block has been added in the more open area of the site. This tidy site offers both level grass and gravel pitches complete with electric hook-ups, and there is a separate adults-only area. The Wildfowl and Wetlands Trust at Slimbridge is close by, and there is much scope locally for birdwatching. An 8 acre site with 75 touring pitches, 48 hardstandings.

AA Pubs & Restaurants nearby: Old Passage Inn, Arlingham 01452 740547

Facilities: ↖⊙✳⚫🚿🛢🚻🚿🐕🎿
Services: ➰🛢🚐🛢🚿⊤🍽🛒⏚
Within 3 miles: 🎣🚴 🐟🛢🕽↺
Notes: ☺

GREATER MANCHESTER

LITTLEBOROUGH Map 16 SD91

Places to visit

Imperial War Museum North, Manchester, 0161 836 4000, www.iwm.org.uk

Manchester Art Gallery, Manchester, 0161 235 8888, www.manchestergalleries.org

Great for kids: Urbis, Manchester, 0161 605 8200, www.urbis.org.uk

►►► 70% Hollingworth Lake Caravan Park (SD943146)

Round House Farm, Rakewood Rd, Rakewood OL15 0AT
☎ 01706 378661 & 373919
dir: From Littleborough or Milnrow (M62 junct 21), follow 'Hollingworth Lake Country Park' signs to Fishermans Inn/The Wine Press. Take 'No Through Road' to Rakewood, then 2nd on right

⊞ £12-£16 ⌾ £12-£16 Å £8-£16

Open all year Last arrival 20.00hrs Last departure noon

A popular park adjacent to Hollingworth Lake, at the foot of the Pennines, within easy reach of many local attractions. Backpackers walking the Pennine Way are welcome at this family-run park, and there are also large rally fields. A 5 acre site with 50 touring pitches, 25 hardstandings and 53 statics.

AA Pubs & Restaurants nearby: The White House, Littleborough 01706 378456

Facilities: ↖⊙✳⚫🕒🛢🚻
Services: ➰🛢🚿🛢🚿⊤🚿⏚
Within 3 miles: ⬇🐟🚴🛢🕽↺
Notes: ☺⊗ Family groups only. Pony trekking

ROCHDALE

Places to visit

People's History Museum, Manchester, 0161 838 9190, www.phm.org.uk

Gallery of Costume, Manchester, 0161 245 7245, www.manchestergalleries.org.uk

ROCHDALE Map 16 SD81

►►► 76% Gelderwood Country Park (SD852127)

Ashworth Rd OL11 5UP
☎ 01706 364858 & 620300 🖷 01706 364858
e-mail: gelderwood@aol.com
dir: Signed midway from B6222 (Bury/Rochdale road). Turn into Ashworth Rd, continue past mill. Uphill for 800yds, site on right

* ⊞ £16-£17 ⌾ £16-£17

Open all year Last departure noon

A very rural site in a peaceful private country park with excellent facilities. All pitches have extensive views of the moor, and this is a popular base for walkers and birdwatchers. The park is for adults only - children are not allowed to visit. A 10 acre site with 34 touring pitches, 26 hardstandings.

AA Pubs & Restaurants nearby: The White House, Littleborough 01706 378456

Nutters, Rochdale 01706 650167

The Peacock Room, Rochdale 01706 368591

Facilities: ↖⊙🅿⚫🐕
Services: ➰🛢
Within 3 miles: 🚴🛢🕽↺
Notes: Adults only. ☺

HAMPSHIRE

See Walk 5 in the Walks & Cycle Rides section at the end of the guide

BRANSGORE

Places to visit

Sammy Miller Motorcycle Museum, New Milton, 01425 620777, www.sammymiller.co.uk,

Red House Museum and Gardens, Christchurch, 01202 482860, www.hants.gov.uk/museum/redhouse

Great for kids: Moors Valley Country Park, Ringwood, 01425 470721, www.moors-valley.co.uk

BRANSGORE
Map 5 SZ19

►►► 83% Harrow Wood Farm Caravan Park (SZ194978)

Harrow Wood Farm, Poplar Ln BH23 8JE
☎ 01425 672487 📄 01425 672487
e-mail: harrowwood@caravan-sites.co.uk
dir: *Exit village from S, take last turn on left. Site at end of lane*

* 🚐 £19-£25.50 🚑 £19-£25.50 ▲ £15-£21.50

Open Mar-6 Jan Last arrival 22.00hrs Last departure noon

A well laid-out and spacious site in a pleasant rural position adjoining woodland and fields. Free on-site coarse fishing is available at this peaceful park. Well located for visiting Christchurch, the New Forest National Park and the south coast. A 6 acre site with 60 touring pitches, 60 hardstandings.

AA Pubs & Restaurants nearby: Three Tuns, Bransgore 01425 672232

Facilities: 🖙 ⊙ 🅿 ⚹ ⚹ ⚹ ⚹

Services: 🔌 🔟 🍺 📶

Within 3 miles: 🎣 🏧

Notes: ⊗ No open fires. Wi-fi

see advert below

FORDINGBRIDGE
Map 5 SU11

Regional Winner – AA South East of England Campsite of the Year 2011

91% Sandy Balls Holiday Centre (SU167148)

Sandy Balls Estate Ltd, Godshill SP6 2JZ

☎ 0845 270 2248 🖷 01425 653067

e-mail: post@sandy-balls.co.uk

web: www.sandy-balls.co.uk

dir: M27 junct 1 onto B3078/B3079, W 8m to Godshill. Site 0.25m after cattle grid

🚐 🚙 Å

Open all year (rs Nov-Feb pitches reduced, no activities) Last arrival 21.00hrs Last dep 11.00hrs

A large, mostly wooded New Forest holiday complex with good provision of touring facilities on terraced, well-laid-out fields. Pitches are fully serviced with shingle bases, and groups can be sited beside the river and away from the main site. There are excellent sporting, leisure and entertainment facilities for the whole family, a new bistro and information centre, and now also four tipis and eight ready-erected tents for hire. A 120 acre site with 233 touring pitches, 233 hardstandings and 233 statics.

Leisure: 🏊 🏊 🎢 🎯

Facilities: 🚻 🍴 ⊙ 🍽 ✳ ☂ 🔥 🖈 🚿 🐕

Services: 🔌 🔊 🍴 🛢 🖉 🛒 🍽 🚻 🚐 ⚓

Within 3 miles: 🚴 🐎 🚴 🏊 🎣 U

Notes: Groups by arrangement, no gazebos.

see advert on page 207

HAMBLE-LE-RICE
Map 5 SU40

Places to visit

Royal Armouries Fort Nelson, Fareham, 01329 233734, www.royalarmouries.org,

Southampton City Art Gallery, Southampton, 023 8083 2277, www.southampton.gov.uk/art

Great for kids: Southampton Maritime Museum, Southampton, 023 8022 3941, www.southampton.gov.uk/leisure

AA CAMPING CARD SITE

▶▶▶▶ **80% Riverside Holidays** (SU481081)

21 Compass Point, Ensign Way SO31 4RA

☎ 023 8045 3220 🖷 023 8045 3611

e-mail: enquiries@riversideholidays.co.uk

web: www.riversideholidays.co.uk

dir: M27 junct 8, follow signs to Hamble B3397. Turn left into Satchell Lane, site 1m down lane on left

🚐 🚙 Å

Open Mar-Oct Last arrival 22.00hrs Last departure 11.00hrs

A small, peaceful park next to the marina, and close to the pretty village of Hamble. The park is neatly kept, and there are now two new toilet and shower blocks complete with good family rooms. A pub and restaurant are very close by. Lodges and static caravans are available for hire. A 6 acre site with 77 touring pitches and 45 statics.

Riverside Holidays

AA Pubs & Restaurants nearby: The Bugle, Hamble-le-Rice 023 8045 3000

Facilities: 🚻 🍴 ⊙ 🍽 ✳ ☂ 🚿

Services: 🔌 🔊 🛢 ⚓

Within 3 miles: 🚴 🐎 🎣 🏊 🚴 🏊 U

Notes: Bike hire, baby changing facilities

see advert below

LINWOOD

Places to visit

The New Forest Centre, Lyndhurst, 023 8028 3444, www.newforestmuseum.org.uk,

Furzey Gardens, Minstead, 023 8081 2464, www.furzey-gardens.org

Great for kids: Paultons Park, Ower, 023 8081 4442, www.paultonspark.co.uk

continued on page 210

LEISURE: 🏊 Indoor swimming pool 🏊 Outdoor swimming pool 🎢 Children's playground 🎾 Tennis court 🎯 Games room 📺 Separate TV room 🏌 9/18 hole golf course 🚣 Boats for hire 🎬 Cinema 🎣 Fishing ⛳ Mini golf 🏄 Watersports 🐴 Stables **FACILITIES:** 🛁 Bath 🚿 Shower ⊙ Electric shaver 🖈 Hairdryer ✳ Ice Pack Facility ♿ Disabled facilities 📞 Public telephone 🛒 Shop on site or within 200yds 🚐 Mobile shop (calls at least 5 days a week) 🔥 BBQ area 🌲 Picnic area 🐕 Dog exercise area

LINWOOD   Map 5 SU10

▶▶▶ 83% Red Shoot Camping Park

(SU187094)

BH24 3QT
☎ 01425 473789   📠 01425 471558
e-mail: enquiries@redshoot-campingpark.com
dir: *A31 onto A338 towards Fordingbridge & Salisbury. Right at brown signs for caravan park towards Linwood on unclassified roads, site signed*

🚐 🚌 ⚕

Open Mar-Oct Last arrival 20.30hrs Last dep 13.00hrs

Located behind the Red Shoot Inn in one of the most attractive parts of the New Forest, this park is in an ideal spot for nature lovers and walkers. It is personally supervised by friendly owners, and offers many amenities including a children's play area. There are modern and spotless facilities plus a new reception and shop. A 3.5 acre site with 130 touring pitches.

AA Pubs & Restaurants nearby: High Corner Inn, Linwood 01425 473973

Leisure: 🄰   **Facilities:** 🅁 ⊙ ℗ ✳ ⅋ ⓒ 🅢
Services: 🖭 🅶 🍴 🛢 🖉 🅃 🍽 🖇
Within 3 miles: ℗ 🐎 🅢 🅶 ∪

Notes: Quiet after 22.30hrs, dogs must be kept on leads. Family shower room

MILFORD ON SEA   Map 5 SZ29

Places to visit

Bucklers Hard Village and Maritime Museum, Bucklers Hard, 01590 616203, www.bucklershard.co.uk,

Exbury Gardens and Railway, Exbury, 023 8089 1203, www.exbury.co.uk

Great for kids: Beaulieu: National Motor Museum, Beaulieu, 01590 612345, www.beaulieu.co.uk

▶▶▶▶ 81% Lytton Lawn Touring Park *(SZ293937)*

SILVER

Lymore Ln SO41 0TX
☎ 01590 648331   📠 01590 645610
e-mail: holidays@shorefield.co.uk
dir: *From Lymington A337 to Christchurch for 2.5m to Everton. Left onto B3058 to Milford on Sea. 0.25m, left onto Lymore Lane*

* 🚐 £12-£39.50 🚌 £12-£39.50 ⚕ £12-£36

Open 6 Feb-2 Jan (rs Low season shop/reception limited hrs. No grass pitches) Last arrival 22.00hrs Last departure 10.00hrs

A pleasant well-run park with good facilities, located near the coast. The park is peaceful and quiet, but the facilities of a sister park 2.5 miles away are available to campers, including swimming pool, tennis courts, bistro and bar/carvery, and large club with family entertainment. Fully-serviced pitches provide good screening, and standard pitches are on gently-sloping grass. An 8 acre site with 136 touring pitches, 53 hardstandings.

AA Pubs & Restaurants nearby: Royal Oak, Downton 01590 642297

Leisure: 🄰 🎣   **Facilities:** 🅁 ⊙ ℗ ✳ ⅋ ⓒ 🅢 🖇
Services: 🖭 🅶 🛢 🖉 🅃 ⅃
Within 3 miles: ℗ 🐎 ◎ 🅢 🅶 ∪

Notes: Families & couples only. Rallies welcome. Free use of Shorefield Leisure Club (2.5m)

see advert on page 209

OWER   Map 5 SU31

Places to visit

The New Forest Centre, Lyndhurst, 023 8028 3444, www.newforestmuseum.org.uk

Furzey Gardens, Minstead, 023 8081 2464, www.furzey-gardens.org

Great for kids: Paultons Park, Ower, 023 8081 4442, www.paultonspark.co.uk

▶▶▶ 80% Green Pastures Farm

(SU321158)

SO51 6AJ
☎ 023 8081 4444
e-mail: enquiries@greenpasturesfarm.com
dir: *M27 junct 2. Follow Salisbury signs for 0.5m. Then follow brown tourist signs for Green Pastures. Also signed from A36 & A3090 at Ower*

* 🚐 fr £16 🚌 fr £16 ⚕ £12-£25

Open 15 Mar-Oct Last departure 11.00hrs

A pleasant site on a working farm, with good screening of trees and shrubs around the perimeter. The touring area is divided by a border of shrubs and, at times, colourful foxgloves. This peaceful location is close to the M27 and the New Forest, and is also very convenient for visiting Paultons Family Theme Park. A 5 acre site with 45 touring pitches, 2 hardstandings.

AA Pubs & Restaurants nearby: Sir John Barleycorn, Cadnam 023 8081 2236

Facilities: 🅁 ⊙ ✳ ⅋ 🅢 🖇
Services: 🖭 🅶 🛢 🖉 🅃 🖇   **Within 3 miles:** ℗ 🐎 🅢

Notes: Day kennels

RINGWOOD

See St Leonards (Dorset)

ROMSEY   Map 5 SU32

Places to visit

Sir Harold Hillier Gardens, Ampfield, 01794 369318, www.hilliergardens.org.uk

Avington Park, Avington, 01962 779260, www.avingtonpark.co.uk

Great for kids: Longdown Activity Farm, Ashurst, 023 8029 2837, www.longdownfarm.co.uk

PREMIER PARK

AA CAMPING CARD SITE

▶▶▶▶▶ 85% Hill Farm Caravan Park *(SU287238)*

Branches Ln, Sherfield English SO51 6FH
☎ 01794 340402   📠 01794 342358
e-mail: gjb@hillfarmpark.com
dir: *Signed from A27 (Salisbury to Romsey road) in Sherfield English, 4m NW of Romsey & M27 junct 2*

🚐 🚌 ⚕

Open Mar-Oct Last arrival 20.00hrs Last departure noon

A small, well-sheltered park peacefully located amidst mature trees and meadows. The two toilet blocks offer smart unisex showers as well as a fully en suite family/disabled room and plenty of privacy in the washrooms. New for 2010 - Bramleys, a good restaurant, with an outside patio, serving a wide range of snacks and meals. This attractive park is well placed for visiting Salisbury and the New Forest National Park, and the south coast is only a short drive away, making it an appealing holiday location. A 10.5 acre site with 70 touring pitches, 60 hardstandings and 6 statics.

AA Pubs & Restaurants nearby: Dukes Head, Romsey 01794 514450

Three Tuns, Romsey 01794 512639

Leisure: ⚑

Facilities: 🔦☉🄿✳🕭🖻🎪🎯🌂

Services: 🔌🖨🅱🕹🎫🍽🔋⚡

Within 3 miles: ↕🅿🖻🅱↺

Notes: ⊕ Minimum noise at all times and no noise after 23.00hrs, one unit per pitch. Unsuitable for teenagers. 9-hole pitch & putt. Wi-fi

WARSASH   Map 5 SU40

Places to visit

Explosion! Museum of Navel Firepower, Gosport, 023 9250 5600, www.explosion.org.uk

Porchester Castle, Porchester, 023 9237 8291, www.english-heritage.org.uk

Great for kids: Blue Reef Aquarium, Portsmouth, 023 9287 5222, www.bluereefaquarium.co.uk

▶▶▶ 85% Dibles Park (SU505060)

Dibles Rd SO31 9SA
☎ 01489 575232
e-mail: diblespark@btconnect.com
dir: *M27 junct 9, at rdbt 5th exit (Parkgate A27), 3rd rdbt 1st exit, 4th rdbt 2nd exit. Site 500yds on left. Or M27 junct 8, at rdbt 1st exit (Parkgate), next rdbt 3rd exit (Brook Ln), 4th rdbt 2nd exit. Site 500yds on left*

🚐 🚙

Open all year Last arrival 20.30hrs Last departure 11.00hrs

A small peaceful touring park adjacent to a private residential park. The facilities are excellent and spotlessly clean. A warm welcome awaits visitors to this well-managed park, which is very convenient for the Hamble, the Solent and the cross-channel ferries. Excellent information on local walks from the site is available. A 0.75 acre site with 14 touring pitches, 14 hardstandings and 46 statics.

AA Pubs & Restaurants nearby: The Seahorse, Gosport 023 9251 2910

Facilities: 🔦☉🄿✳🕓

Services: 🔌🖨🅱🔒

Within 3 miles: ⚓🅿⛵🖻🅱↺

Notes: Tourist information office

HEREFORDSHIRE

See Walk 6 in the Walks & Cycle Rides section at the end of the guide

EARDISLAND   Map 9 SO45

Places to visit

Berrington Hall (NT), Ashton, 01568 615721, www.nationaltrust.org.uk/main/w-berringtonhall

Hergest Croft Gardens, Kington, 01544 230160, www.hergest.co.uk

▶▶▶ 87% Arrow Bank Holiday Park (SO419588)

Nun House Farm HR6 9BG
☎ 01544 388312   🖨 01544 388312
e-mail: enquiries@arrowbankholidaypark.co.uk
dir: *From Leominster A44 towards Rhayader. Right to Eardisland, follow signs*

* 🚐 £18-£20 🚙 £18-£20 ⚊ £15-£20

Open Mar-7 Jan

This peaceful, adults-only park is set in the beautiful 'Black and White' village of Eardisland with its free exhibitions, tea rooms and heritage centre. The park is well positioned for visiting the many local attractions, as well as those further afield such as Ludlow Castle, Ross-on-Wye, Shrewsbury and Wales. The modern toilet facilities are spotlessly clean. Seasonal touring pitches are available. 45 touring pitches, 36 hardstandings.

AA Pubs & Restaurants nearby: New Inn, Pembridge 01544 388427

The Bateman Arms, Shobdon 01568 708374

Stagg Inn & Restaurant, Titley 01544 230221

Facilities: 🔦☉🄿✳🕓🌂

Services: 🔌🅱🎫

Within 3 miles: 🅿🖻🅱

Notes: Adults only. No ball games, no skateboards, no cycles in park. Wi-fi

HEREFORD

Places to visit

Cider Museum and King Offa Distillery, Hereford, 01432 354207, www.cidermuseum.co.uk

Great for kids: Goodrich Castle, Goodrich, 01600 890538, www.english-heritage.org.uk

HEREFORD   Map 10 SO53

▶ 68% *Ridge Hill Caravan and Campsite* (SO509355)

HR1 1UN
☎ 01432 351293
e-mail: ridgehill@fsmail.net
dir: *From Hereford on A49, then B4399 signed Rotherwas. At 1st rdbt follow Dinedor/Little Dewchurch signs, in 1m signed Ridge Hill/Twyford turn right, then right at phone box, 200yds, site on right*

🚐 🚙 ⚊

Open Mar-Oct Last departure noon

A simple, basic site set high on Ridge Hill a few miles south of Hereford. This peaceful site offers outstanding views over the countryside. It does not have toilets or showers, and therefore own facilities are essential, although toilet tents can be supplied on request at certain times of the year. Please do not rely on Sat Nav directions to this site - guidebook directions should be used for caravans and motorhomes. A 1.3 acre site with 5 touring pitches.

Within 3 miles: 🖽🅿🖻🅱

Notes: ⊕ Dogs must be kept on leads

LITTLE TARRINGTON   Map 10 SO64

Places to visit

Eastnor Castle, Ledbury, 01531 633160, www.eastnorcastle.com

Cider Museum and King Offa Distillery, Hereford, 01432 354207, www.cidermuseum.co.uk

▶▶▶▶ 88% Hereford Camping & Caravanning Club Site (SO625410)

The Millpond HR1 4JA
☎ 01432 890243   & 0845 130 7633
dir: *300yds off A438 on Ledbury side of Tarrington, entrance on right, 50yds before railway bridge*

🚐 £7.50-£9 🚙 £7.50-£9 ⚊ £7.50-£9

Open Mar-21 Oct Last arrival 20.00hrs Last departure noon

A much improved grassy park set beside a three-acre fishing lake in a peaceful location, and now franchised to the Camping & Caravanning Club. Well-planted trees and shrubs help to divide and screen the park, and the modern toilet block provides very good facilities. Security is excellent

continued

SERVICES: 🔌 Electric hook up 🖨 Launderette 🍺 Licensed bar 🅱 Calor Gas ⊘ Camping Gaz 🎫 Toilet fluid 🍽 Café/Restaurant 🍔 Fast Food/Takeaway ⚡ Battery charging
🚼 Baby care ⚡ Motorvan service point   **ABBREVIATIONS:** BH/bank hols-bank holidays Etr-Easter Whit-Whitsun dep-departure fr-from hrs-hours m-mile mdnt-midnight
rdbt-roundabout rs-restricted service wk-week wknd-weekend ⊕ No credit cards ⊗ no dogs   See page 7 for details of the AA Camping Card Scheme

LITTLE TARRINGTON *continued*

and Wi-fi is now available. A 4.5 acre site with 55 touring pitches.

AA Pubs & Restaurants nearby: Bunch of Carrots, Hampton Bishop 01432 870237

Crown & Anchor, Lugwardine 01432 851303

Facilities: 🅿 ✳ 🔥 🕐 🖳

Services: 🔌 🗄 🛒 🚿 🚽 ⚡

Notes: Site gates closed between 23.00hrs-07.00hrs. Wi-fi

MORETON ON LUGG   Map 10 SO54

Places to visit

The Wier Gardens (NT), Swainshill, 01981 590509, www.nationaltrust.org.uk

Brockhampton Estate (NT), Brockhampton, 01885 482077, www.nationaltrust.org.uk

►► 78% Cuckoo's Corner Campsite
(SO501456)

Cuckoo's Corner HR4 8AH
☎ 01432 760234
e-mail: cuckooscorner@gmail.com
dir: *Direct access from A49. From Hereford 2nd left after Moreton on Lugg sign. From Leominster 1st right (non gated road) after brown sign. Right just before island*

* 🚐 £12 🚐 £12 ⛺ £8-£12

Open all year Last arrival 21.00hrs Last departure 13.00hrs

This small, adults-only site is well positioned just north of Hereford, with easy access to the city. The site is in two areas, and offers hardstanding and some electric pitches. It is an ideal spot for an overnight stop or longer stay to visit the attractions of the area. There's a bus stop just outside the site and a full timetable is available from the reception office. A 3 acre site with 19 touring pitches, 15 hardstandings.

AA Pubs & Restaurants nearby: England's Gate Inn, Bodenham 01568 797286

The Wellington, Wellington 01432 830367

Facilities: 🔥 🕐 ✳ 🐕 🎯

Services: 🔌 🗄 🚚

Within 3 miles: ↧ ✎ 🖳

Notes: Adults only. 🚫 No large groups, no noise after 22.30hrs. DVD library, books & magazines. Wi-fi

PEMBRIDGE   Map 9 SO35

Places to visit

The Weir Gardens (NT), Swainshill, 01981 590509, www.nationaltrust.org.uk

Brockhampton Estate (NT), Brockhampton, 01885 482077, www.nationaltrust.org.uk

---

Regional Winner – AA Heart of England Campsite of the Year 2011

PREMIER PARK

►►►►► 86% *Townsend Touring Park* *(SO395583)*   Best of British

Townsend Farm HR6 9HB
☎ 01544 388527
e-mail: info@townsend-farm.co.uk
dir: *A44 through Pembridge. Site 40mtrs from 30mph on E side of village*

🚐 🚐 ⛺

Open Mar-mid Jan Last arrival 22.00hrs Last departure noon

This outstanding park is spaciously located on the edge of one of Herefordshire's most beautiful Black and White villages. The park offers excellent facilities, and all hardstanding pitches are fully serviced, and it has its own award-winning farm shop and butchery. It also makes an excellent base from which to explore the local area, including Ludlow Castle and Ironbridge. There's a camping pod available for hire. A 12 acre site with 60 touring pitches, 23 hardstandings.

AA Pubs & Restaurants nearby: New Inn, Pembridge 01544 388427

Stagg Inn & Restaurant, Titley 01544 230221

Leisure: 🅰 **Facilities:** 🛁 🔥 🕐 🅿 🕐 🖳 🎪 🎯 **Services:** 🔌 🗄 🛒 ⚡ **Within 3 miles:** ✎ 🖳 🗄 🔄

STANFORD BISHOP   Map 10 SO65

►►► 80% Boyce Caravan Park
(SO692528)

WR6 5UB
☎ 01886 884248   📄 01886 884187
e-mail: enquiries@boyceholidaypark.co.uk
web: www.boyceholidaypark.co.uk
dir: *From A44 take B4220. In Stanford Bishop take 1st left signed Linley Green, then 1st right down private driveway*

* 🚐 fr £18 🚐 fr £18 ⛺ fr £18

Open Feb-Dec (rs Mar-Oct tourers) Last arrival 18.00hrs Last departure noon

A friendly and peaceful park with access allowed onto the 100 acres of farmland. Coarse fishing is also available in the grounds, and there are extensive views over the Malvern and Suckley Hills. There are many walks to be enjoyed. A 10 acre site with 14 touring pitches, 3 hardstandings and 200 statics.

AA Pubs & Restaurants nearby: Three Horseshoes Inn, Little Cowarne 01885 400276

Three Crowns Inn, Ullingswick 01432 820279

Leisure: 🅰 **Facilities:** 🔥 🕐 🅿 ✳ 🔥 🕐 🎯 **Services:** 🔌 🗄 🛒 🚚 **Within 3 miles:** ✎ 🗄 🔄

Notes: Certain dog breeds are not permitted (call for details). Farm walks

SYMONDS YAT (WEST)   Map 10 SO51

Places to visit

The Nelson Museum & Local History Centre, Monmouth 01600 710630

Great for kids: Goodrich Castle, Goodrich, 01600 890538, www.english-heritage.org.uk

►►► 83% Doward Park Camp Site
(SO539167)

Great Doward HR9 6BP
☎ 01600 890438
e-mail: enquiries@dowardpark.co.uk
dir: *A40 from Monmouth towards Ross-on-Wye. In 2m exit left signed Crockers Ash, Ganarew & The Doward. Cross over A40, 1st left at T-junct, in 0.5m 1st right signed The Doward. Follow park signs up hill (NB do not follow Sat Nav for end of journey)*

🚐 ⛺

Open Mar-Oct Last arrival 20.00hrs Last dep 11.30hrs

This delightful little park is set in peaceful woodlands on the hillside above the Wye Valley. It is ideal for campers and motor homes but not caravans due to the narrow twisting approach roads. A warm welcome awaits and the facilities are kept spotless. Six seasonal touring pitches are available. A 1.5 acre site with 28 touring pitches.

AA Pubs & Restaurants nearby: Mill Race, Walford 01989 562891

Leisure: 🅰 **Facilities:** 🔥 🕐 🅿 ✳ 🔥 🖳 **Services:** 🔌 🗄 🛒 🚿 🚚 **Within 3 miles:** ↧ 🐕 ✎ ◎ 🚴 🗄 🔄

Notes: No caravans or fires, quiet after 22.00hrs, dogs must be kept on leads

---

LEISURE: 🏊 Indoor swimming pool 🏊 Outdoor swimming pool 🅰 Children's playground 🎾 Tennis court 🎱 Games room 📺 Separate TV room ⛳ 9/18 hole golf course 🚣 Boats for hire 🎬 Cinema 🎣 Fishing ⛳ Mini golf 🏄 Watersports ⛵ Stables **FACILITIES:** 🛁 Bath 🚿 Shower 🪒 Electric shaver 💨 Hairdryer ✳ Ice Pack Facility ♿ Disabled facilities ☎ Public telephone 🛒 Shop on site or within 200yds 🚐 Mobile shop (calls at least 5 days a week) 🍖 BBQ area 🌲 Picnic area 🐕 Dog exercise area

KENT

ASHFORD   Map 7 TR04

Places to visit

Leeds Castle, Maidstone, 01622 765400
www.leeds-castle.com

Great for kids: Thorpe Park, Chertsey,
0870 444 4466, www.thorpepark.com

PREMIER PARK

▶▶▶▶▶ **83% Broadhembury** *Best of British*
Caravan & Camping Park

(TR009387)

Steeds Ln, Kingsnorth TN26 1NQ
☎ 01233 620859   ▤ 01233 620918
e-mail: holidaypark@broadhembury.co.uk
web: www.broadhembury.co.uk
dir: *From M20 junct 10 take A2070. Left at 2nd rdbt signed Kingsnorth, then left at 2nd x-roads in village*

* ⚏ £18-£23 ⛺ £18-£23 ▲ £17-£23

Open all year Last arrival 22.00hrs Last departure noon

A well-run and well-maintained small family park surrounded by open pasture; it is neatly landscaped with pitches sheltered by mature hedges. There is a well-equipped campers' kitchen adjacent to the spotless toilet facilities and children will love the play areas, games room and football pitch. A new adults-only area, close to the excellent reception building, has been developed to include some popular fully serviced hardstanding pitches; this area will have its own first-class toilet block in 2011. A 10 acre site with 60 touring pitches, 24 hardstandings and 25 statics.

AA Pubs & Restaurants nearby: Wife of Bath, Ashford 01233 812232

Leisure: ⚑ ⚓ ▭
Facilities: ⚑⊙⚐✳⚕⊙▤ ⚙
Services: ⚡⚙⚑⚙⊘⊤⚏⚒
Within 3 miles: ⚗⊞⚊⊚⚏⚙∪
Notes: Sports field, campers' kitchen & appliances. Wi-fi

BELTRING   Map 6 TQ64

NEW ▶▶ 73% The Hop Farm Touring & Camping Park *(TQ674469)*

Maidstone Rd TN12 6PY
☎ 01892 838161
e-mail: touring@thehopfarm.co.uk
dir: *M20 junct 4, M25 junct 5 onto A21 S, follow brown tourist signs*

* ⚏ £12-£20 ⛺ £12-£20 ▲ £12-£20

Open Mar-Oct (rs Major Hop Farm events camping occasionally closed) Last arrival 19.00hrs Last departure 14.00hrs

Occupying a large field (for tents) and neat paddocks close to a collection of Victorian oast houses and its surrounding family attractions, which include indoor and outdoor play areas, animal farm, shire horses and restaurant, this popular touring park makes a great base for families. One paddock has good hardstanding pitches and the older-style toilet facilities are kept clean and tidy. A 16 acre site with 106 touring pitches, 25 hardstandings and 12 statics.

Facilities: ⚑⊙⚐⚕▤⚙⚒
Services: ⚡⚑⊘
Within 3 miles: ⚗⚊⚏⚙
Notes: No open fires, no large or 'same age' groups, no mini motors or quad bikes. Site campers entitled to half price entry to Hop Farm Family Park

BIRCHINGTON   Map 7 TR36

Places to visit

Reculver Towers and Roman Fort, Reculver, 01227 740676, www.english-heritage.org.uk

Great for kids: Richborough Roman Fort & Ampitheatre, Richborough, 01304 612013, www.english-heritage.org.uk

▶▶▶ **81% Quex** *Best of British SILVER*
Caravan Park *(TR321685)*

Park Rd CT7 0BL
☎ 01843 841273
e-mail: info@keatfarm.co.uk
dir: *From Birchington (A28) turn SE into Park Road to site in 1m*

* ⚏ £13-£25 ⛺ £13-£25 ▲ £13-£25

Open Mar-Nov Last arrival anytime Last departure noon

A small parkland site in a quiet and secluded woodland glade, with a very clean toilet block housed in a log cabin. This picturesque site is just one mile from the village of Birchington, while Ramsgate, Margate and Broadstairs are all within easy reach. An 11 acre site with 48 touring pitches and 145 statics.

Leisure: ⚑
Facilities: ⚑⊙⚐✳⊙▤⚒
Services: ⚡⚙⚑⊘⚙⊙⚒⚒
Within 3 miles: ⚗⚊⊞⚏⚙⊚⚏⚙∪
Notes: Wi-fi

▶▶▶ **79% Two Chimneys Caravan Park** *(TR320684)*

Shottendane Rd CT7 0HD
☎ 01843 841068 & 843157   ▤ 01843 848099
e-mail: info@twochimneys.co.uk
dir: *From A28 to Birchington Sq, right into Park Lane (B2048). Left at Manston Road (B2050) then 1st left*

* ⚏ £14.50-£29.50 ⛺ £14.50-£29.50 ▲ £14.50-£27

Open Mar-Oct (rs Mar-May & Sep-Oct shop, bar, pool & takeaway restricted) Last arrival 22.00hrs Last departure noon

An impressive entrance leads into this well-managed site, which boasts two swimming pools and a fully-licensed clubhouse. Other attractions include a tennis court and children's play area, and the immaculately clean toilet facilities fully meet the needs of this busy family park. A 40 acre site with 200 touring pitches, 5 hardstandings and 200 statics.

Leisure: ⚑⚑⚒
Facilities: ⚑⊙⚐✳⚕⊙▤
Services: ⚡⚙⚑⚙⚑⊘⊤⚏⚒⚒
Within 3 miles: ⚗⚊⊞⚏⚙⊚⚏⚙∪
Notes: ⊗ Amusement arcade

DOVER — Map 7 TR34

Places to visit

White Cliffs of Dover, Dover, 01304 202756, www.nationaltrust.org.uk

Walmer Castle and Gardens, Deal, 01304 364288, www.english-heritage.org.uk

Great for kids: Dover Castle and Secret Wartime Tunnels, Dover, 01304 211067, www.english-heritage.org.uk

►►►► 78% Hawthorn Farm Caravan Park (TR342464)

GOLD

Station Rd, Martin Mill CT15 5LA
☎ 01304 852658 & 852914 📄 01304 853417
e-mail: info@keatfarm.co.uk
dir: *Signed from A258*

* 🚐 £13-£25 🚏 £13-£25 ▲ £13-£25

Open Mar-Nov Last arrival anytime Last departure noon

This pleasant rural park set in 28 acres of beautifully-landscaped gardens is screened by young trees and hedgerows, in grounds which include woods and a rose garden. A popular night-halt to and from the cross-channel ferry port, it has decent facilities including a shop/café and new hardstanding pitches. A 28 acre site with 147 touring pitches, 15 hardstandings and 163 statics.

AA Pubs & Restaurants nearby: White Cliffs Hotel, St Margaret's at Cliffe 01304 852400

Facilities: 🅿️ ⊙ 🌂 ✳ ♿ ☺ 🅵
Services: 🔌 🖓 🛢 🧺 T 🍽 ⊕
Within 3 miles: ↨ 🕆 目 🎣 ◎ 🎣 🅵 🅵 U
Notes: Wi-fi

EASTCHURCH

Places to visit

Upnor Castle, Upnor, 01634 718742, www.english-heritage.org.uk

Historic Dockyard Chatham, Chatham, 01634 823807, www.thedockyard.co.uk

---

EASTCHURCH — Map 7 TQ97

74% Warden Springs Caravan Park (TR019722)

GOLD

Warden Point ME12 4HF
☎ 01795 880216 📄 01795 880218
dir: *From M2 junct 5 (Sheerness/Sittingbourne) follow A249 for 8m, right onto B2231 to Eastchurch. In Eastchurch left after church, follow park signs*

🚐 🚏 ▲

Open Apr-Oct (BH & peak wks Entertainment available) Last arrival 22.00hrs Last departure noon

Panoramic views from the scenic cliff-top setting can be enjoyed at their best from the touring area of this holiday park. All of the many and varied leisure activities provided by the park are included in the pitch tariff, ie the heated outdoor swimming pool, adventure playground, family entertainment and a good choice of food outlets. 66 touring pitches and 198 statics.

Leisure: 🏊 🅰
Facilities: 🅿️ ⊙ 🌂 ♿ ☺ 🅵 🅵
Services: 🖓 🍽 ⊕
Within 3 miles: 🎣 🅵 🅵 U
Notes: No cars by caravans or tents. Wi-fi

FOLKESTONE — Map 7 TR23

Places to visit

Dymchurch Martello Tower, Dymchurch, 01304 211067, www.english-heritage.org.uk

Hever Castle and Gardens, Hever, 01732 865224, www.hevercastle.co.uk

Great for kids: Port Lympne Wild Animal Park, Lympne, 0844 8424 647, www.totallywild.net

►►► 83% Little Satmar Holiday Park (TR260390)

GOLD

Winehouse Ln, Capel Le Ferne CT18 7JF
☎ 01303 251188 📄 01303 251188
e-mail: info@keatfarm.co.uk
dir: *Signed off B2011*

* 🚐 £13-£25 🚏 £13-£25 ▲ £13-£25

Open Mar-Nov Last arrival 23.00hrs Last departure 14.00hrs

A quiet, well-screened site well away from the road and statics, with clean and tidy facilities.

A useful base for visiting Dover and Folkestone, or as an overnight stop for the Channel Tunnel and ferry ports, and it's just a short walk from cliff paths with their views of the Channel, and sandy beaches below. A 5 acre site with 47 touring pitches and 75 statics.

AA Pubs & Restaurants nearby: Lighthouse Inn, Capel le Ferne 01303 223300

Leisure: 🅰
Facilities: 🅿️ ⊙ 🌂 ✳ ☺ 🅵 🅵
Services: 🔌 🖓 🛢 🧺 T 🍽 ⊕
Within 3 miles: ↨ 目 🎣 🅵 🅵 U
Notes: Wi-fi

AA CAMPING CARD SITE

►► 74% Little Switzerland Camping & Caravan Site (TR248380)

Wear Bay Rd CT19 6PS
☎ 01303 252168
e-mail: btony328@aol.com
dir: *Signed from A20 E of Folkestone. Approaching from A259 or B2011 on E outskirts of Folkestone follow signs for Wear Bay/Martello Tower, then tourist sign to site, follow signs to country park*

🚐 🚏 ▲

Open Mar-Oct Last arrival mdnt Last departure noon

Set on a narrow plateau below the white cliffs, this unusual site has sheltered camping in secluded dells and enjoys fine views across Wear Bay and the Strait of Dover. The licensed café with an alfresco area is popular; please note that the basic toilet facilities are unsuitable for disabled visitors. A 3 acre site with 32 touring pitches and 13 statics.

AA Pubs & Restaurants nearby: Lighthouse Inn, Capel le Ferne 01303 223300

Facilities: 🅿️ ⊙ ✳ ☺ ♞ 🐕
Services: 🔌 🖓 🍽 🛢 🧺 🍽 🚻 ⊕ ⊕
Within 3 miles: ↨ 🕆 目 🎣 ◎ 🎣 🅵 🅵 U
Notes: 🚭 No open fires. Wi-fi

LEYSDOWN-ON-SEA Map 7 TR07

►►► 71% Priory Hill (TR038704)

Wing Rd ME12 4QT
☎ 01795 510267 📠 01795 511503
e-mail: touringpark@prioryhill.co.uk
dir: *Take A249 signed Sheerness then B2231 to Leysdown, follow brown tourist signs*

* 🚐 £15-£27 🚐 £14-£25 ▲ £14-£25

Open Mar-Oct (rs Low season shorter opening times of pool & club) Last arrival 20.00hrs Last departure noon

A small well-maintained touring area on an established family-run holiday park close to the sea, with views of the north Kent coast. Amenities include a clubhouse and a swimming pool. The pitch price includes membership of clubhouse with live entertainment, and use of indoor swimming pool. A 1.5 acre site with 37 touring pitches.

Leisure: 🎣 🔍 🎱 ▭
Facilities: 🅿 ⊙ 🅿 ⚡ ⛎ 🕐 🖻 🖈
Services: 🚐 🖨 🍴 🛢 🍴 ⌂
Within 3 miles: 🥾 ◎ 🖻 🖻
Notes: Wi-fi

MARDEN Map 6 TQ74

PREMIER PARK

NEW ►►►►► 84%
Tanner Farm Touring Caravan & Camping Park (TQ732415)

Best of British

Tanner Farm, Goudhurst Rd TN12 9ND
☎ 01622 832399 & 831214 📠 01622 832472
e-mail: enquiries@tannerfarmpark.co.uk
dir: *From A21 or A229 on to B2079. Midway between Marden & Goudhurst*

🚐 £15-£22 🚐 £15-£22 ▲ £15-£19

Open all year Last arrival 20.00hrs Last departure noon

At the heart of a 150-acre Wealden farm, replete with oast house, this extensive, long-established touring park is peacefully tucked away down a quiet farm drive deep in unspoilt Kentish countryside, yet close to Sissinghurst Castle and within easy reach of London (Marden station 3 miles). Perfect for families, with its farm animals, two excellent play areas and recreation room (computer/TV), it offers quality toilet blocks with

privacy cubicles, a good shop, spacious hardstandings (12 fully serviced), and high levels of security and customer care. A 15 acre site with 100 touring pitches, 36 hardstandings.

Leisure: ⚡ 🔍 ▭
Facilities: 🅿 ⊙ 🅿 ⚡ ⛎ 🕐 🖻 🖈 🖈
Services: 🚐 🖨 🛢 🍴 T 🍴 ⌂
Within 3 miles: 🥾 🖻 🖻

Notes: No groups, 1 car per pitch, no commercial vehicles. MV service point, computer, room only accommodation. Wi-fi

ST NICHOLAS AT WADE Map 7 TR26

Places to visit

Reculver Towers and Roman Fort, Reculver, 01227 740676, www.english-heritage.org.uk

Great for kids: Richborough Roman Fort & Ampitheatre, Richborough, 01304 612013, www.english-heritage.org.uk

►► 76% St Nicholas Camping Site
(TR254672)

Court Rd CT7 0NH
☎ 01843 847245
dir: *Signed off A299 and A28, at W end of village near church*

* 🚐 £16-£18 🚐 £16-£18 ▲ £15-£16

Open Etr-Oct Last arrival 22.00hrs Last departure 14.00hrs

A gently-sloping field with mature hedging, on the edge of the village close to the shop. This pretty site offers upgraded facilities, including a new family/disabled room, and is conveniently located close to primary routes and the north Kent coast. A 3 acre site with 75 touring pitches.

Leisure: ⚡
Facilities: 🅿 ⊙ 🅿 ⚡ ⛎ 🖈
Services: 🚐 🛢 ⚡ T
Within 3 miles: 🥾 🖻 ∪
Notes: ◎ No music after 22.30hrs

WHITSTABLE Map 7 TR16

Places to visit

Royal Engineers Museum, Library and Archive, Gillingham, 01634 822839, www.remuseum.org.uk

Canterbury West Gate Towers, Canterbury, 01227 789576, www.canterbury-museum.co.uk

Great for kids: Howletts Wild Animal Park, Bekesbourne, 0844 8424 647, www.totallywild.net

73% Seaview Holiday Village (TR145675)

SILVER

St John's Rd CT5 2RY
☎ 01227 792246 📠 01227 792247
e-mail: info@parkholidaysuk.com
dir: *From A299 take A2990 then B2205 to Swalecliffe, site between Herne Bay & Whitstable*

* 🚐 £9-£22 🚐 £9-£22 ▲ £8-£19

Open Mar-Oct Last arrival 21.30hrs Last departure noon

A pleasant open site on the edge of Whitstable, set well away from the static area, with a smart, modern toilet block and both super and hardstanding pitches. Developments at this popular holiday centre include an excellent bar, restaurant, clubhouse (with entertainment) and games room complex, and a new outdoor swimming pool area. A 12 acre site with 171 touring pitches, 41 hardstandings and 452 statics.

AA Pubs & Restaurants nearby:
The Sportsman, Whitstable 01227 273370

Crab & Winkle Seafood Restaurant, Whitstable 01227 779377

Leisure: 🎣 ⚡ 🔍 ▭
Facilities: 🅿 ⊙ 🅿 ⚡ ⛎ 🕐 🖻 🖈 🖈
Services: 🚐 🖨 🍴 🛢 ⚡ T 🍴 ⌂ ⚡
Within 3 miles: 🥾 ⚡ 🖻 🖻 ◎ 🖻 🖻 ∪
Notes: Amusements in games room

WHITSTABLE *continued*

AA CAMPING CARD SITE

►►► 83% Homing Park

(TR095645)

Church Ln, Seasalter CT5 4BU
☎ 01227 771777 📄 01227 273512
e-mail: info@homingpark.co.uk
dir: *Exit A299 for Whitstable & Canterbury, left at brown camping-caravan sign into Church Lane. Site entrance has 2 large flag poles*

* ⛟ £18-£25 ⛺ £18-£25 ▲ £18-£25

Open Etr-Oct Last arrival 20.00hrs Last departure 11.00hrs

A small touring park close to Seasalter Beach and Whitstable, which is famous for its oysters. All pitches are generously sized and fully serviced, and most are separated by hedging and shrubs. A clubhouse and swimming pool are available on the adjacent residential park at a small cost. A 12.6 acre site with 43 touring pitches and 195 statics.

AA Pubs & Restaurants nearby: The Sportsman, Whitstable 01227 273370

Crab & Winkle Seafood Restaurant, Whitstable 01227 779377

Leisure: ⚓ ⚑ ♨ **Facilities:** ⚡☉⚐✳⚙☺
Services: ⚡🅱🍽⛽⌀🍴🚿
Within 3 miles: ⚓⊞⚡⚓🏛∪

Notes: No commercial vehicles, no tents greater than 8 berth or 5mtrs, no unaccompanied minors. Wi-fi

WROTHAM HEATH   Map 6 TQ65

►►► 76% *Gate House Wood Touring Park* *(TQ635585)*

Ford Ln TN15 7SD
☎ 01732 843062
e-mail: gatehousewood@btinternet.com
dir: *M26 junct 2a, A20 S towards Maidstone, through lights at Wrotham Heath. 1st left signed Trottiscliffe, left at next junct into Ford Ln. Site 100yds on left*

⛟ ⛺ ▲

Open Mar-Oct Last arrival 22.00hrs Last departure noon

A well-sheltered and mature site in a former quarry surrounded by tall deciduous trees and gorse banks. The well-designed facilities include reception, shop and smart toilets, and there is good

entrance security. Conveniently placed for the M20 and M25. A 3.5 acre site with 55 touring pitches.

Leisure: ⚑ **Facilities:** ⚡☉⚐✳⚙☺🅱🍽
Services: ⚡🅱🛡⌀🅃⚡ **Within 3 miles:** ⚓🏛∪
Notes: ⊘⊗ No commercial vehicles

LANCASHIRE

See Walk 7 in the Walks & Cycle Rides section at the end of the guide

See also sites under Greater Manchester & Merseyside

BLACKPOOL   Map 18 SD33

See also Lytham St Annes & Thornton

Places to visit
Blackpool Zoo, Blackpool, 01253 830830, www.blackpoolzoo.org.uk

77% Marton Mere Holiday Village

(SD347349)

Mythop Rd FY4 4XN
☎ 01253 767544 📄 01253 791252
dir: *M55 junct 4, A583 towards Blackpool. Right at Clifton Arms lights, onto Mythop Rd. Site 150yds on left*

⛟ ⛺

Open mid Mar-Oct (rs Mar-end May & Sep-Oct reduced facilities, splash zone closed) Last arrival 22.00hrs Last departure 10.00hrs

A very attractive holiday centre in an unusual setting on the edge of the mere, with plenty of birdlife to be spotted. The on-site entertainment is directed at all ages, and includes a superb show bar. There's a regular bus service into Blackpool for those who want to explore further afield. The separate touring area is well equipped with hardstandings and electric pitches, and there are good quality facilities. Seasonal touring pitches are available. A 30 acre site with 197 touring pitches, 197 hardstandings and 700 statics.

AA Pubs & Restaurants nearby: Jali Fine Indian Dining, Blackpool 01253 622223

Leisure: ⚓ ⚑ **Facilities:** 🛁⚡☉⚐✳⚙☺🐾♣
Services: ⚡🅱🍽⛽⌀🍴🚿
Within 3 miles: ⚓✤⊞⚡◎⚓🏛🅱∪

Notes: Max 2 dogs per group, certain dog breeds banned, no adult only groups, no commercial vehicles

see advert on opposite page

BOLTON-LE-SANDS   Map 18 SD46

Places to visit
Lancaster Maritime Museum, Lancaster, 01524 382264, www.lancashire.gov.uk/museums

Lancaster City Museum, Lancaster, 01524 64637, www.lancashire.gov.uk/museums

Great for kids: Lancaster Castle, Lancaster, 01524 64998, www.lancastercastle.com

AA CAMPING CARD SITE

►►► 84% Bay View Holiday Park

(SD478683)

LA5 9TN
☎ 01524 732854 & 701508 📄 01524 730612
e-mail: info@holgatesleisureparks.co.uk
dir: *W of A6, 1m N of Bolton-le-Sands*

* ⛟ £20-£23 ⛺ £20-£23 ▲ £12-£20

Open Mar-Oct (rs Mar-May shop hours restricted) Last arrival 20.00hrs Last departure 13.00hrs

At the time of our last inspection this park was being redeveloped into a high quality, family-orientated seaside destination with fully-serviced spacious all-weather pitches which have views across Morecambe Bay to the Cumbrian hills. The already completed, tastefully designed bar/restaurant is a stylish place to relax with friends. There is a wide range of activities and attractions on offer within a few miles. This makes a great place for a family holiday by the seaside. Seasonal touring pitches are available. A 10 acre site with 100 touring pitches, 100 hardstandings and 100 statics.

AA Pubs & Restaurants nearby: Longland Inn & Restaurant, Carnforth 01524 781256

Hest Bank Hotel, Hest Bank 01524 824339

Leisure: ⚑ ⚔ 🖵
Facilities: ⚡☉✳⚙☺🅱🎿✈
Services: ⚡🅱🍽🛡⌀🅃🍴🎫🛒🚿
Within 3 miles: ⚓✤⊞⚡🏛🅱
Notes: Dogs must be kept on leads. Wi-fi

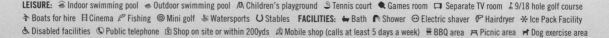

▶▶▶ 84% Sandside Caravan & Camping Park *(SD472681)*

The Shore LA5 8JS
☎ 01524 822311 📠 01524 822311
e-mail: sandside@btconnect.com
dir: *M6 junct 35, A6 through Carnforth. Right after Far Pavillion in Bolton-le-Sands, over level crossing to site*

🚐 🚏 Å

Open Mar-Oct Last arrival 20.00hrs Last departure 13.00hrs

A well-kept family park located in a pleasant spot overlooking Morecambe Bay, with distant views of the Lake District. The site is next to a West Coast railway line with a level crossing. The shop and reception are assets to this welcoming park. Booking is advisable at peak periods. A 9 acre site with 70 touring pitches, 70 hardstandings and 33 statics.

AA Pubs & Restaurants nearby: Longland Inn & Restaurant, Carnforth 01524 781256

Hest Bank Hotel, Hest Bank 01524 824339

Facilities: 🅵 ⊙ 🅿 ✳ 🅹 🖳 ↰ **Services:** 🖳 🗑 🔒
Within 3 miles: ↧ ✚ 🅷 🅿 ◎ ⇘ 🖻 🗑 ∪
Notes: 🐕

▶▶▶ 76% Red Bank Farm *(SD472681)*

LA5 8JR
☎ 01524 823196 📠 01524 824981
e-mail: mark.archer@hotmail.co.uk
dir: *Take A5105 (Morecambe road), after 200mtrs right on Shore Lane. At rail bridge turn right to site*

🚐 Å

Open Mar-Oct

A gently sloping grassy field with mature hedges, close to the sea shore and a RSPB reserve. This farm site has smart toilet facilities, a superb view across Morecambe Bay to the distant Lake District hills, and is popular with tenters. A 3 acre site with 60 touring pitches.

AA Pubs & Restaurants nearby: Longland Inn & Restaurant, Carnforth 01524 781256

Hest Bank Hotel, Hest Bank 01524 824339

Facilities: 🅵 ⊙ 🅿 ✳
Services: 🖳 🗑 🔒
Within 3 miles: ↧ ✚ 🅷 🅿 ◎ ⇘ 🖻 🗑
Notes: Dogs must be kept on leads. Pets' corner

Places to visit

Sizergh Castle and Gardens, Sizergh, 015395 60951, www.nationaltrust.org.uk

Levens Hall, Levens, 015395 60321, www.levenshall.co.uk

▶▶▶ 92% Old Hall Caravan Park *(SD533716)*

LA6 1AD
☎ 01524 733276 📠 01524 734488
e-mail: info@oldhallcaravanpark.co.uk
web: www.oldhallcaravanpark.co.uk
dir: *M6 junct 35 follow signs to Over Kellet, left onto B6254, left at village green signed Capernwray. Site 1.5m on right*

* 🚐 fr £20 🚐 fr £20

Open Mar-Oct (rs Nov-Jan owners of static vans & seasonal tourers)

A lovely secluded park set in a clearing amongst trees at the end of a half-mile long drive. This peaceful park is home to a wide variety of wildlife, and there are marked walks in the woods. The facilities are well maintained by friendly owners,

continued

CAPERNWRAY ***continued***

and booking is advisable. Seasonal touring pitches are available. A 3 acre site with 38 touring pitches, 38 hardstandings and 220 statics.

AA Pubs & Restaurants nearby: The Highwayman, Burrow 01524 273338

Lunesdale Arms, Tunstall 015242 74203

Leisure:

Facilities:

Services:

Within 3 miles:

Notes: Pets must be kept on leads, no skateboards, roller blades or roller boots. Wi-fi

COCKERHAM Map 18 SD45

Places to visit

Lancaster Maritime Museum, Lancaster, 01524 382264, www.lancashire.gov.uk/museums

Lancaster City Museum, Lancaster, 01524 64637, www.lancashire.gov.uk/museums

Great for kids: Blackpool Zoo, Blackpool, 01253 830830, www.blackpoolzoo.org.uk

►►►► 80% *Mosswood Caravan Park* *(SD456497)*

GOLD

Crimbles Ln LA2 0ES

☎ 01524 791041 01524 792444

e-mail: info@mosswood.co.uk

dir: *Approx 4m from A6/M6 junct 33, 1m W of Cockerham on A588*

Open Mar-Oct Last arrival 20.00hrs Last departure 16.00hrs

A tree-lined grassy park with sheltered, level pitches, located on peaceful Cockerham Moss. The modern toilet block is attractively clad in stained wood, and the facilities include cubicled washing facilities and a launderette. A 25 acre site with 25 touring pitches, 25 hardstandings and 143 statics.

AA Pubs & Restaurants nearby: Bay Horse Inn, Forton 01524 791204

Facilities:

Services:

Within 3 miles:

Notes: Woodland walks

CROSTON Map 15 SD41

Places to visit

Harris Museum and Art Gallery, Preston, 01772 258248, www.harrismuseum.org.uk

Great for kids: National Football Museum, Preston, 01772 908442, www.nationalfootballmuseum.com

►►► 81% Royal Umpire Caravan Park *(SD504190)*

SILVER

Southport Rd PR26 9JB

☎ 01772 600257 01704 505886

e-mail: info@royalumpire.co.uk

dir: *From Chorley take A581, 3.5m towards Croston, site on right*

* £14-£25 £14-£25 £15-£18

Open all year Last arrival 20.00hrs Last departure 16.00hrs

A pleasant level site set in open countryside, with an attractive sunken garden and seating area. Plenty of leisure opportunities include an interesting children's playground, and a large playing field. The toilets, laundry and dishwashing area are of a very good quality. An ongoing upgrade programme is underway. Seasonal touring pitches are available. A restaurant and a pub are within walking distance. A 60 acre site with 195 touring pitches, 180 hardstandings.

AA Pubs & Restaurants nearby: Farmers Arms, Heskin Green 01257 451276

Leisure: **Facilities:**

Services:

Within 3 miles:

FAR ARNSIDE Map 18 SD47

NEW ►►►► 75% Hollins Farm Camping & Caravanning *(SD450764)*

LA5 0SL

☎ 01524 701508

e-mail: reception@holgates.co.uk

dir: *M6 junct 35, A601/Carnforth. Left in 1m at rdbt to Carnforth. Right in 1m at lights signed Silverdale. Left in 1m into Sands Ln, signed Silverdale. 2.4m over auto-crossing, 0.3m to T-junct. Right, follow signs to site, approx 3m*

* £14-£22 £14-£22 £14-£30

Open 14 Mar-Oct Last arrival 20.00hrs Last departure noon

Hollins Farm is a long established park, which is under new ownership and is currently being upgraded. It has a traditional family camping feel but with facilities appointed to a high standard; most pitches offer views towards Morecambe Bay. The leisure and recreation facilities of the nearby, much larger, sister park (Silverdale Holiday Park) can be accessed by guests here. Seasonal touring pitches are available. A 30 acre site with 65 touring pitches, 5 hardstandings.

Leisure: **Facilities:**

Services: **Within 3 miles:**

Notes: No unaccompanied children

GARSTANG Map 18 SD44

Places to visit

Lancaster Maritime Museum, Lancaster, 01524 382264, www.lancashire.gov.uk/museums

Lancaster City Museum, Lancaster, 01524 64637, www.lancashire.gov.uk/museums

Great for kids: Lancaster Castle, Lancaster, 01524 64998, www.lancastercastle.com

►►►► 81% Claylands Caravan Park *(SD496485)*

Cabus PR3 1AJ

☎ 01524 791242 01524 792406

e-mail: alan@claylands.com

dir: *From M6 junct 33 S to Garstang, approx 6m pass Quattros Restaurant, signed off A6 into Weavers Lane, follow lane to end, over cattle grid*

£19-£22 £19-£22 £19-£22

Open Mar-4 Jan Last arrival 23.00hrs Last departure noon

A well-maintained site with lovely river and woodland walks and good views over the River Wyre towards the village of Scorton. This friendly park is set in delightful countryside where guests can enjoy fishing, and the atmosphere is very relaxed. The quality facilities and amenities are of a high standard, and everything is immaculately maintained. A 14 acre site with 30 touring pitches, 30 hardstandings and 68 statics.

AA Pubs & Restaurants nearby: Owd Nell's Tavern, Bilsborrow 01995 640010

Leisure: **Facilities:**

Services:

Within 3 miles:

Notes: Pets must be kept on leads, no roller blades or skateboards

►►► 76% Bridge House Marina & Caravan Park (SD483457)

Nateby Crossing Ln, Nateby PR3 0JJ
☎ 01995 603207 📄 01995 601612
e-mail: edwin@bridgehousemarina.co.uk
dir: *Exit A6 at pub & Knott End sign, immediately right into Nateby Crossing Ln, over canal bridge to site on left*

* 🚐 £15.50-£19 🚏 £15.50-£19

Open Feb-1 Jan Last arrival 22.00hrs Last departure 13.00hrs

A well-maintained site in attractive countryside by the Lancaster Canal, with good views towards the Trough of Bowland. The boatyard atmosphere is interesting, and there is a good children's playground. A 4 acre site with 30 touring pitches, 25 hardstandings and 40 statics.

AA Pubs & Restaurants nearby: Owd Nell's Tavern, Bilsborrow 01995 640010

Leisure: 🄰
Facilities: ⌂⊙🅿✳🐕🔥📷🏠🔥
Services: 🔌🔵🔴🌱🅃🔋
Within 3 miles: 🚶🎣🅿📷🔵

►►► 80% Little Orchard Caravan Park (SD399355)

Shorrocks Barn, Back Ln PR4 3HN
☎ 01253 836658
e-mail: info@littleorchardcaravanpark.com
web: www.littleorchardcaravanpark.com
dir: *M55 junct 3, A585 signed Fleetwood. Left in 0.5m opposite Ashiana Tandoori restaurant into Greenhalgh Ln in 0.75m, right at T-junct, site entrance 1st left*

* 🚐 fr £17.50 🚏 fr £17.50 🅰 fr £14.50

Open 14 Feb-1 Jan Last arrival 20.00hrs Last departure noon

Set in a quiet rural location in an orchard, this attractive park welcomes the mature visitor. The toilet facilities are to a very high standard but there is no laundry. Two excellent fisheries are within easy walking distance. The site advises that bookings should be made by phone only, not on-line. A 7 acre site with 45 touring pitches, 45 hardstandings.

Facilities: ⌂⊙🅿🔥🐕🔥
Services: 🔌🔋
Within 3 miles: 🅿📷⚓🔵📷🔵

Notes: ⊘ No cars by tents. No ball games or skateboards, no dangerous dog breeds, children must be supervised in toilets blocks. Wi-fi

►► 86% New Parkside Farm Caravan Park (SD507633)

Denny Beck, Caton Rd LA2 9HH
☎ 01524 770723
dir: *M6 junct 34, take A683 towards Caton/Kirkby Lonsdale. Site 1m on right*

🚐 £14-£17 🚏 £14-£17 🅰 £12-£14

Open Mar-Oct Last arrival 20.00hrs Last departure 16.00hrs

Peaceful, friendly grassy park on a working farm convenient for exploring the historic city of Lancaster and the delights of the Lune Valley. A 4 acre site with 40 touring pitches, 40 hardstandings and 16 statics.

AA Pubs & Restaurants nearby: Sun Hotel & Bar, Lancaster 01524 66006

The Waterwitch, Lancaster 01524 63828

Facilities: ⌂⊙🅿🔥
Services: 🔌🔴🌱
Within 3 miles: 🚶🅗🅿📷🔵

Notes: ⊘ Dogs must be kept on leads. Dish washing sink

►►► 75% *Eastham Hall Caravan Park* (SD379291)

Saltcotes Rd FY8 4LS
☎ 01253 737907 📄 01253 732559
e-mail: info@easthamhall.co.uk
web: www.easthamhall.co.uk
dir: *M55 junct 3. Straight over 3 rdbts onto B5259. Through Wrea Green & Moss Side, site 1m after level crossing*

🚐 🚏

Open Mar-Oct (rs Oct only super pitches available) Last arrival 21.00hrs Last departure noon

Secluded park with trees and hedgerows in a rural setting. The helpful owners ensure that facilities are maintained to a high standard. A 15 acre site with 160 touring pitches, 14 hardstandings and 150 statics.

AA Pubs & Restaurants nearby: Greens Bistro, St Annes-on-Sea 01253 789990

Leisure: 🄰   **Facilities:** ⌂⊙🅿🔥🐕🔥📷🏠🔥
Services: 🔌🔵🔴🌱🅃
Within 3 miles: 🚶🎣🅿⚓📷🔵📷🔵

Notes: No tents, breathable groundsheets only in awnings. Football field. Wi-fi

MIDDLETON (NEAR MORECAMBE) Map 18 SD45

▶▶▶ 66% Melbreak Caravan Park

(SD415584)

Carr Ln LA3 3LH
☎ 01524 852430
dir: *M6 junct 34 onto A683. After 6m turn left at rdbt, pass Middleton & turn right into village. Site in 0.5m*

* ⛺ fr £14.50 ⛺ fr £14.50 ▲ £12-£14

Open Mar-Oct Last arrival 22.00hrs Last dep noon

A small rural park run by a friendly owner, in open countryside south of Morecambe. It offers simple but clean facilities and ample hardstands. There's good access to historic Sunderland Point, Heysham Port for the Isle of Man ferries, and the seaside attractions of Morecambe. A 2 acre site with 10 touring pitches and 32 statics.

AA Pubs & Restaurants nearby: Sun Hotel & Bar, Lancaster 01524 66006

The Waterwitch, Lancaster 01524 63828

Facilities: ⌂⊙☂✳🖻
Services: 🔌🖽🔒🖉🍴🛒↯
Within 3 miles: ↧⌾🖻🖩 **Notes:** ⊗

MORECAMBE   Map 18 SD46

Places to visit
Leighton Hall, Nr Carnforth 01524 734474, www.leightonhall.co.uk

AA CAMPING CARD SITE

▶▶▶ 78% Venture Caravan Park

(SD436633)

Langridge Way, Westgate LA4 4TQ
☎ 01524 412986 📄 01524 422029
e-mail: mark@venturecaravanpark.co.uk
dir: *From M6 junct 34 follow Morecambe signs. At rdbt take road towards Westgate & follow site signs. 1st right after fire station*

⛺ ⛺ ▲

Open all year (rs Winter one toilet block open) Last arrival 22.00hrs Last departure noon

A large family park with good modern facilities, including a small indoor heated pool, a licensed clubhouse and a family room with children's entertainment. The site has many statics, some of which are for holiday hire, and is close to the town centre. A 17.5 acre site with 56 touring pitches, 40 hardstandings and 304 statics.

AA Pubs & Restaurants nearby: Hest Bank Hotel, Hest Bank 01524 824339

Leisure: 🏊♨🔍
Facilities: 🛁⌂⊙☂✳🖻🕒🖻
Services: 🔌🖽🖉T🍴🛒↯
Within 3 miles: ↧🖽🖉🖻🖩
Notes: Amusement arcade, off licence

Remember that prices and opening times are liable to change within the currency of this guide. It is always best to phone in advance

►►► 69% Riverside Caravan Park

(SD448615)

Lancaster Rd, Snatchems LA3 3ER
☎ 01524 844193
e-mail: info@riverside-morecambe.co.uk
dir: *M6 junct 34, follow Morecambe signs. Cross river, 1st left at rdbt. Straight on at next rdbt. 0.5m, entrance adjacent to Golden Ball pub*

* fr £15

Open Mar-Oct Last arrival 20.00hrs Last departure noon

A grassy site with views over the River Lune and Morecambe Bay. The sanitary facilities in a modern toilet block are clean and fresh. Road access is subject to tidal river flooding, and it is advisable to check tide times before crossing. Booking advisable. Holiday static caravans for hire. A 7 acre site with 50 touring pitches and 52 statics.

AA Pubs & Restaurants nearby: Hest Bank Hotel, Hest Bank 01524 824339

Leisure:

Facilities:

Services:

Within 3 miles:

Notes: No tents, no ball games, bikes, skateboards or scooters. Wi-fi

ORMSKIRK

Places to visit

Astley Hall Museum and Art Gallery, Chorley, 01257 515555, www.astleyhall.co.uk

British Commercial Vehicle Museum, Leyland, 01772 451011, www.bcvm.co.uk

Great for kids: Camelot Theme Park, Charnock Richard, 01257 452100, www.camelotthemepark.co.uk

ORMSKIRK Map 15 SD40

►►►► 79% *Abbey Farm Caravan Park* *(SD434098)*

Dark Ln L40 5TX
☎ 01695 572686 01695 572686
e-mail: abbeyfarm@yahoo.com
dir: *M6 junct 27 onto A5209 to Burscough. 4m left onto B5240. Immediate right into Hobcross Lane. Site 1.5m on right*

Open all year Last arrival 21.00hrs Last departure noon

Delightful hanging baskets and flower beds brighten this garden-like rural park which is sheltered by hedging and mature trees. Modern, very clean facilities include a family bathroom, and there are suitable pitches, close to the toilet facilities, for disabled visitors. A superb recreation field caters for children of all ages, and there is an indoor games room, large library, fishing lake and dog walk. Tents have their own area with BBQ and picnic tables. A 6 acre site with 56 touring pitches and 44 statics.

AA Pubs & Restaurants nearby: Eagle & Child, Parbold 01257 462297

Leisure:

Facilities:

Services:

Within 3 miles:

Notes: No camp fires. Off-licence, farm walk

SILVERDALE

Places to visit

Leighton Hall, Nr Carnforth 01524 734474, www.leightonhall.co.uk

Great for kids: RSPB Leighton Moss Nature Reserve, Silverdale, 01524 701601, www.rspb.org.uk

SILVERDALE Map 18 SD47

AA Campsite of the Year for England and overall winner of the AA Best Campsite of the Year 2011

PREMIER PARK

AA CAMPING CARD SITE

►►►►► 95% Silverdale Caravan Park *(SD455762)*

Middlebarrow Plain, Cove Rd LA5 0SH
☎ 01524 701508 01524 701580
e-mail: caravan@holgates.co.uk
dir: *M6 junct 35. 5m NW of Carnforth. From Carnforth centre take unclass Silverdale road & follow tourist signs after Warton*

* £30 £30 £27-£30

Open 22 Dec-7 Nov Last arrival 20.00hrs Last departure noon

A superb family holiday park set in wooded countryside next to the sea, which demonstrates high quality in all areas, and offers a wide range of leisure amenities. Its relaxing position overlooking Morecambe Bay combined with excellent touring facilities mark this park out as special. Two seasonal touring pitches are available. A 100 acre site with 80 touring pitches, 80 hardstandings and 339 statics.

AA Pubs & Restaurants nearby: Longland Inn & Restaurant, Carnforth 01524 781256

The Wheatsheaf, Beetham 015395 62123

Leisure:

Facilities:

Services:

Within 3 miles:

Notes: No unaccompanied children. Sauna, spa bath, steam room, mini-golf, gym. Wi-fi

see advert on opposite page

THORNTON

Places to visit

Blackpool Zoo, Blackpool, 01253 830830, www.blackpoolzoo.org.uk

THORNTON — Map 18 SD34

▶▶▶▶ 79% Kneps Farm Holiday Park (SD353429)

River Rd, Stanah FY5 5LR
☎ 01253 823632 ▤ 01253 863967
e-mail: enquiries@knepsfarm.co.uk
web: www.knepsfarm.co.uk
dir: Exit A585 at rdbt onto B5412 to Little Thornton. Right at mini-rdbt after school onto Stanah Road, over 2nd mini-rdbt, leading to River Road

* ⊞ £17.50-£19 ⊞ £17.50-£19 ▲ £14.50-£19

Open Mar-mid Nov (rs Apr-early Nov shop open)
Last arrival 20.00hrs Last departure noon

A quality park adjacent to the River Wyre and the Wyre Estuary Country Park, handily placed for the attractions of Blackpool and the Fylde coast. This family-run park offers an excellent toilet block with immaculate facilities, and a mixture of hard and grass pitches. The park is quietly located, but there is some noise from a nearby plastics plant. A 10 acre site with 60 touring pitches, 40 hardstandings and 60 statics.

AA Pubs & Restaurants nearby: Twelve Restaurant & Lounge Bar, Thornton 01253 821212

Leisure: ⚠ **Facilities:** ➍➐➊➋➌➍➎➏➐
Services: ➊➋➌➍➎➏➐➑
Within 3 miles: ➊➋➌➍➎➏➐

Notes: No commercial vehicles. Max 2 dogs per group, dogs are chargeable & must be kept on leads

LEICESTERSHIRE

See also Wolvey, Warwickshire

CASTLE DONINGTON

Places to visit

Twycross Zoo, Twycross, 01827 880250, www.twycrosszoo.org

National Space Centre, Leicester, 0845 605 2001, www.spacecentre.co.uk

Great for kids: Snibston Discovery Museum, Coalville, 01530 278444, www.snibston.com

CASTLE DONINGTON — Map 11 SK42

▶▶▶ 71% Donington Park Farmhouse (SK414254)

Melbourne Rd, Isley Walton DE74 2RN
☎ 01332 862409 ▤ 01332 862364
e-mail: info@parkfarmhouse.co.uk
dir: M1 junct 24, pass airport to Isley Walton, right towards Melbourne. Site 0.5m on right

* ⊞ fr £20 ⊞ fr £20 ▲ fr £12

Open Jan-23 Dec (rs Winter hardstanding only)
Last arrival 21.00hrs Last departure noon

A secluded touring site at the rear of a hotel beside Donington Park motor racing circuit, which is very popular on race days when booking is essential. Both daytime and night flights from nearby East Midlands Airport may cause disturbance. A 7 acre site with 60 touring pitches, 10 hardstandings.

AA Pubs & Restaurants nearby: Priest House on the River, Castle Donington 01332 810649

Leisure: ⚠ **Facilities:** ➍➐➊➋➌➍
Services: ➊➋➌➍➎➏➐
Within 3 miles: ➊➋➌➍➎➏

Notes: Dogs must be kept on leads. Bread & milk sold, hotel on site for bar/dining. Wi-fi

LINCOLNSHIRE

ANCASTER — Map 11 SK94

Places to visit

Belton House Park and Gardens, Belton, 01476 566116, www.nationaltrust.org.uk

Belvoir Castle, Belvoir, 01476 871002, www.belvoircastle.com

▶▶▶ 80% Woodland Waters (SK979435)

Willoughby Rd NG32 3RT
☎ 01400 230888 ▤ 01400 230888
e-mail: info@woodlandwaters.co.uk
web: www.woodlandwaters.co.uk
dir: On A153 W of x-roads with B6403

⊞ ⊞ ▲

Open all year Last arrival 21.00hrs Last dep noon

Peacefully set around five impressive fishing lakes, with a few log cabins in a separate area, this is a pleasant open park. The access road is through mature woodland, and there is an excellent heated toilet block, and a pub/club house with restaurant. A 72 acre site with 62 touring pitches, 2 hardstandings.

AA Pubs & Restaurants nearby: Bustard Inn & Restaurant, South Raceby 01529 488250
Brownlow Arms, Hough-on-the-Hill 01400 250234

Leisure: ⚠➍ **Facilities:** ➍➐➊➋➌➍➎➏➐
Services: ➊➋➌➍➎➏➐➑➒
Within 3 miles: ➊➋➌➍➎➏➐

Notes: Dogs must be kept on leads at all times

BOSTON — Map 12 TF34

Places to visit

Battle of Britain Memorial Flight Visitor Centre, Coningsby, 01522 782040, www.lincolnshire.gov.uk/bbmf

Tattershall Castle, Tattershall, 01526 342543, www.nationaltrust.org.uk

▶▶▶▶ 81% Long Acre Caravan Park (TF385535)

Station Rd, Old Leake PE22 9RF
☎ 01205 871555 ▤ 01205 871555
e-mail: lacp@btconnect.com
dir: From A16 take B1184 at Sibsey (by church) approx 1m at T-junct turn left. 1.5m, after level crossing take next right into Station Rd. Park entrance approx 0.5m on left

⊞ £15-£18 ⊞ £15-£18 ▲ £15-£18

Open Mar-Oct Last arrival 20.00hrs Last departure 11.00hrs

A small rural adults-only park in an attractive setting within easy reach of Boston, Spalding and Skegness. The park has a newly completed toilet block, which is very clean and has an appealing interior, with modern, upmarket fittings. Excellent shelter is provided by the high, mature boundary hedging. A holiday cottage is available to let. 40 touring pitches, 40 hardstandings.

Facilities: ➍➐➊➋➌➍ **Services:** ➊➋
Within 3 miles: ➊➋

Notes: Adults only. Dogs must be kept on leads at all times. Washing lines not permitted. Wi-fi

▶▶▶▶ 78% Orchard Park (TF274432)

Frampton Ln, Hubbert's Bridge PE20 3QU
☎ 01205 290328 ▤ 01205 290247
e-mail: info@orchardpark.co.uk
dir: On B1192, between A52 (Boston-Grantham) & A1121 (Boston-Sleaford)

* ⊞ £15 ⊞ £15 ▲ £7-£15

Open all year (rs Dec-Feb bar, shop & café closed)
Last arrival 22.30hrs Last departure 16.00hrs

Ideally located for exploring the unique fenlands, this rapidly-improving park has two lakes - one for fishing and the other set aside for conservation. The very attractive restaurant and bar prove popular with visitors. A 51 acre site with 87 touring pitches, 11 hardstandings and 164 statics.

Orchard Park

Leisure: 🎣

Facilities: ⬅🐴☉🅿✳🕭🕓🚻🏛🎡🚻

Services: 🔌🍴🚱🍺🇦🔧🚰🍽📦

Within 3 miles: 🚴🏇☉🚲🍴↻

Notes: Adults only. 🐕 Dogs must be kept on leads. Washing lines not permitted. Wi-fi

▶▶▶▶ **78% Pilgrims Way Caravan & Camping Park** *(TF358434)*

Church Green Rd, Fishtoft PE21 0QY
☎ 01205 366646 🖹 01205 366646
e-mail:
pilgrimsway@caravanandcampingpark.com
dir: *E from Boston on A52. In 1m, after junct with A16, at Ball House pub turn right. Follow tourist signs to site*

* 🚐 fr £15 🚐 fr £15 ⛺ £15-£17.50

Open all year Last arrival 22.00hrs Last dep noon

A peaceful and relaxing park situated in the heart of the south Lincolnshire countryside, yet only a mile from the centre of Boston. After a change of ownership a couple of years ago, the enthusiastic, hands-on owners have done a superb job in upgrading the facilities. The park offers quality toilet facilities, 22 electric hook-ups and hardstandings, and tents are welcome in a separate grassy area. A 2 acre site with 22 touring pitches, 15 hardstandings.

Leisure: ⛰ **Facilities:** 🐴☉🅿✳🕭🚻🎡

Services: 🔌🍴🚱🍺🇦

Within 3 miles: 🚴🏇🚉🍴☉🚲🍴↻

Notes: 🐕 Dogs welcome but must be on leads at all times. Tea house and sun terrace. Wi-fi

81% Thorpe Park Holiday Centre
(TA321035)

DN35 0PW
☎ 01472 813395 🖹 01472 812146
e-mail: luke.cullen@bourne-leisure.co.uk
dir: *Take unclass road off A180 at Cleethorpes, signed Humberstone & Holiday Park*

🚐 🚐 ⛺

Open mid Mar-Oct (rs mid Mar-May & Sep-Oct some facilities may be reduced) Last arrival anytime Last departure 10.00hrs

A large static site with touring facilities, including fully-serviced pitches and a new

 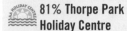

CLEETHORPES *continued*

additional toilet block, adjacent to the beach. This holiday centre offers excellent recreational and leisure activities, including an indoor pool with bar, bowling greens, crazy golf, tennis courts, and a games area. Parts of the site overlook the sea. Seasonal touring pitches are available. A 300 acre site with 134 touring pitches, 81 hardstandings and 1357 statics.

AA Pubs & Restaurants nearby: Ship Inn, Barnoldby le Beck 01472 822308

Leisure: 🏊 ⚊ 🎿 ⚊

Facilities: 🛁 🚿 ⊙ 🅿️ 🖐 🕔 🖻 🎪 🐕

Services: 🔌 🖻 🚽 🛁 🧴 🍽 ♨

Within 3 miles: 🎿 🏕 🎣 ◎ 🎿 🏪 🖻 ⛳ ↺

Notes: Max 2 dogs per group, no commercial vehicles. Pitch and putt, roller ring, fishing lakes. Wi-fi   *see advert on page 223*

GREAT CARLTON   Map 17 TF48

AA CAMPING CARD SITE

NEW ►►► 76% West End Farm

(TF418842)

Salterns Way LN11 8BF
☎ 01507 450949 & 07766 278740
e-mail: westendfarm@talktalkbusiness.net
dir: *From A157 turn towards Great Carlton at Gayton Top. Brown sign for West End Farm in 0.5m, turn right into site*

🚐 £12-£15 🚛 £12-£15 ▲ £12-£15

Open 28 Mar-2 Oct Last arrival 20.30hrs Last departure 14.00hrs

A neat and well-maintained four-acre touring park situated on the edge of the Lincolnshire Wolds. Surrounded by mature trees and bushes and well away from the busy main roads, yet connected by footpaths ideal for walking and cycling, it offers enjoyable peace and quiet close to the popular holiday resort of Mablethorpe. Good clean facilities throughout. Four seasonal touring pitches are available. A 4 acre site with 35 touring pitches.

Leisure: ⚑

Facilities: 🛁 🅿️ 🌣 🎪 🏓

Services: 🔌 🖻 🅃 🛁

Within 3 miles: 🎿 🎣 ◎ 🏪 ↺

HOLBEACH   Map 12 TF32

Places to visit

Butterfly and Wildlife Park, Spalding, www.butterflyandwildlifepark.co.uk

►►► 73% Herons Cottage Touring Park *(TF364204)*

Frostley Gate PE12 8SR
☎ 01406 540435
e-mail: simon@satleisure.co.uk
dir: *Site 4m S of Holbeach on B1165 between Sutton St James & Whaplode St Catherine*

* 🚐 £13.50 🚛 £13.50 ▲ £13.50

Open all year Last arrival 20.00hrs Last departure 11.00hrs

Under the same ownership as Heron's Mead Touring Park in Orby (see entry), this rapidly improving park is situated in the heart of the Fens beside the Little South Holland Drain, with its extremely good coarse fishing. There's excellent supervision and 18 fully-serviced pitches. A 4.5 acre site with 70 touring pitches, 50 hardstandings.

AA Pubs & Restaurants nearby: Ship Inn, Surfleet Seas End 01775 680547

Facilities: 🛁 🖐 🎪 🐕

Services: 🔌 🖻 🧴 ⊙ 🅃 🛁 🚽

Within 3 miles: 🎣 🏪 🖻

Notes: ⊘ Strictly no children under 12yrs. Phone available for warden's cottage

---

LANGWORTH

Places to visit

Lincoln Castle, Lincoln, 01522 511068, www.lincolnshire.gov.uk/lincolncastle

Usher Gallery, Lincolnshire, 01522 550990, www.thecollection.lincoln.museum

Great for kids: Museum of Lincolnshire Life, Lincolnshire, 01522 550990, www.thecollection.lincoln.museum

---

LANGWORTH   Map 17 TF07

AA CAMPING CARD SITE

NEW ►►► 78% Lakeside Caravan Park *(TF065762)*

Barlings Ln LN3 5DF
☎ 01522 753200 🖷 01522 750444
e-mail: lakesidecaravanpark@btconnect.com
dir: *Take A158 from Lincoln bypass. 4m into Langworth, right at x-rds into Barlings Lane. Site approx 0.25m on left, well signed*

* 🚐 £12-£14.50 🚛 £12-£14.50 ▲ £12-£14.50

Open all year Last arrival 21.00hrs Last departure noon

A well-maintained touring park set in 23 acres of woodlands lawns and lakes, just four miles from the Lincoln bypass, and offering an ideal base for exploring Lincoln and the surrounding countryside. It is a popular venue for campers who like fishing or just the peace and quiet of this parkland-style site. There are large open spaces and a wealth of the wildlife and, with its security gates, CCTV and on-site wardens, offers a safe, secure place to stay the night. Eight seasonal touring pitches are available. A 22 acre site with 25 touring pitches, 8 hardstandings.

AA Pubs & Restaurants nearby: Wig & Mitre, Lincoln 01522 535190

Pyewipe Inn, Lincoln 01522 528708

The Victoria, Lincoln 01522 541000

The Old Bakery, Lincoln 01522 576057

Facilities: 🛁 🌣 🖐 🎪 🐕

Services: 🔌 🔒 🚽

Within 3 miles: 🎣

Notes: Wi-fi

MABLETHORPE

Places to visit

Church Farm Museum, Skegness, 01754 76665, www.lincolnshire.gov.uk/churchfarmmuseum

Great for kids: Skegness Natureland Seal Sanctuary, Skegness, 01754 764345, www.skegnessnatureland.co.uk

---

MABLETHORPE
Map 17 TF58

80% Golden Sands Holiday Park *(TF501861)*

Quebec Rd LN12 1QJ
☎ 01507 477871 📄 01507 472066
e-mail: naomi.mcintosh@bourne-leisure.co.uk
dir: *From centre of Mablethorpe turn left on seafront road towards north end. Site on left*

Open mid Mar-Oct Last arrival anytime Last departure 10.00hrs

A large, well-equipped seaside holiday park with separate touring facilities on two sites, including a newly refurbished toilet block, additional portaloo facilities, and a much improved shop at reception. The first-floor entertainment rooms are only accessible via stairs (no lifts). A 23 acre site with 214 touring pitches, 20 hardstandings and 1500 statics.

Leisure: 🏊🏊⚠🔍
Facilities: ↝🖭☉🅿✳🕭🕒📷
Services: 🔌🍽🖭🛢🖉📅🍴🚮🛒⚙
Within 3 miles: 🚶🎠🎣◎🖼📷
Notes: Maximum of 2 dogs per group, certain dog breeds banned. Mini bowling alley, snooker/pool, indoor fun palace. Wi-fi

AA CAMPING CARD SITE

NEW ▶▶▶ 77% Kirkstead Holiday Park *(TF509835)*

North Rd, Trusthorpe LN12 2QD
☎ 01507 441483
e-mail: mark@kirkstead.co.uk
dir: *From Mablethorpe town centre take A52 S towards Sutton-on-Sea. 1m turn sharp right by phone box into North Rd. Site signed in 300yds*

* 🚐 £14-£21 🚏 £14-£21 ⚠ £10-£22
Open Mar-Nov Last arrival 22.00hrs Last departure 15.00hrs

A well-established family-run park catering for all age groups, just a few minutes' walk from Trusthorpe and the sandy beaches of Mablethorpe. The main touring area, which is serviced by good quality toilet facilities, has now been extended, with the addition of 37 fully-serviced pitches on what used to be the football pitch, and here portacabin toilets have been installed. The site is

particularly well maintained. A 12 acre site with 60 touring pitches, 3 hardstandings and 70 statics.

Leisure: ⚠🔍🖵
Facilities: ↝☉🅿✳🕭🕒🍴🎋🚻🎋
Services: 🔌🖭🍽🛒⚙
Within 3 miles: 🚶🎠🎣◎🖼📷🎢
Notes: No dogs in tents

OLD LEAKE
Map 17 TF45

Places to visit

Lincolnshire Aviation Heritage Centre, East Kirkby, 01790 763207, www.lincsaviation.co.uk

Battle of Britain Memorial Flight Visitor Centre, Coningsby, 01522 782040, www.lincolnshire.gov.uk/bbmf

▶▶▶ 71% *Alderley Campsite*

(TF415498)

Shaw Ln PE22 9LQ
☎ 01205 870121 📄 01205 870121
dir: *Just off A52, 7m NE of Boston, opposite B1184*

A pleasant, well-maintained small touring park set down a rural lane just off the A52, surrounded by the tranquillity of the Fenlands. It makes a peaceful base for exploring Boston and the Lincolnshire coast, and there are two holiday statics for hire. A 2.5 acre site with 30 touring pitches.

ORBY

Places to visit

Church Farm Museum, Skegness, 01754 76665, www.lincolnshire.gov.uk/churchfarmmuseum

Great for kids: Skegness Natureland Seal Sanctuary, Skegness, 01754 764345, www.skegnessnatureland.co.uk

ORBY
Map 17 TF46

▶▶▶▶ 80% Heron's Mead Fishing Lake & Touring Park

(TF508673)

Marsh Ln PE24 5JA
☎ 01754 811340
e-mail: mail@heronsmeadtouringpark.co.uk
dir: *From A158 (Lincoln to Skegness road) turn left at rdbt, through Orby for 0.5m*

* 🚐 £17.50 🚏 £17.50 ⚠ £15
Open Mar-1 Nov Last arrival 21.00hrs Last departure noon

A pleasant fishing and touring park with coarse fishing and an eight-acre woodland walk. The owners have made many improvements to the facilities, which prove particularly appealing to quiet couples and more elderly visitors. A 16 acre site with 50 touring pitches, 53 hardstandings and 28 statics.

Facilities: ↝☉🅿✳🕭🕒🎋🎋
Services: 🔌🖭🛢⚙ Within 3 miles: 🚶🎣🐕🖼📷🎢
Notes: No cars by caravans or tents. No ball games, no motorbikes. 2 disabled pegs for fishing, carp lake

SALTFLEET
Map 17 TF49

78% *Sunnydale*

(TF455941)

Sea Ln LN11 7RP
☎ 0871 664 9776
e-mail: sunnydale@park-resorts.com
dir: *From A16 towards Louth take B1200 through Manby & Saltfleetby. Left into Saltfleet. Sea Lane on right. Site in approx 400mtrs*

Open Mar-Oct (BH & peak wks entertainment available)

Set in a peaceful and tranquil location in the village of Saltfleet between the seaside resorts of Cleethorpes and Mablethorpe. This park offers modern leisure facilities including an indoor pool, the tavern bar with entertainment, amusements and a coarse fishing pond. There is also direct access to the huge expanse of Saltfleet beach. The touring facilities are incorporated into the leisure complex, and are modern and well cared for. 38 touring pitches and 260 statics.

Leisure: 🏊⚠ Facilities: 🕒🖼🎋
Services: 🔌🖭🍽🍴🚮
Within 3 miles: 🎣◎🐕🖼📷🎢

SALTFLEETBY ST PETER Map 17 TF48

AA CAMPING CARD SITE

►►► 83% Saltfleetby Fisheries

(TF425892)

Main Rd LN11 7SS
☎ 01507 338272
e-mail: saltfleetbyfish@btinternet.com
dir: *On B1200, 6m E of junct with A16. 3m W of A103*

* ⛺ fr £14 ⛺ fr £14 ▲ fr £14

Open Mar-Nov Last arrival 21.00hrs Last departure 10.00hrs

An excellent small site with just 12 touring pitches, each with gravel hardstanding and electric hook-up, set in a sheltered area close to two large and very popular fishing lakes. A spacious, upmarket Swedish chalet doubles as a reception and a well-furnished café with open-plan kitchen. The purpose-built toilet block is light, airy and well maintained. A 14 acre site with 12 touring pitches, 12 hardstandings and 3 statics.

AA Pubs & Restaurants nearby: Masons Arms, Louth 01507 609525

Facilities: ⌐ ⋇ & © ⓢ ⌱ ⚞
Services: ⚡ Ⓣ ⏛ ⚒
Within 3 miles: ⤢ ⌗ ⓢ ∪
Notes: Adults only. ⊛

TATTERSHALL Map 17 TF25

NEW ►►►► 77% Tattershall Lakes Country Park (TF234587)

Sleaford Rd LN4 4RL
☎ 01526 348800
e-mail: tattershall.holidays@away-resorts.com
dir: *A153 to Tattershall*

* ⛺ £3-£36 ⛺ £3-£36 ▲ £3-£36

Open late Mar-end Oct Last arrival 21.00hrs Last departure 10.00hrs

Set amongst woodlands, lakes and parkland on the edge of Tattershall in the heart of the Lincolnshire Fens, this now mature country park has been created from old gravel pits and the flat, well-drained and maintained touring area offers plenty of space for campers. There's lots to entertain the youngsters as well as the grown-ups, with good fishing on excellent lakes, and golf. The owner has positive future plans for the country park and touring site. A 400 acre site with 186 touring pitches.

WADDINGHAM Map 17 SK99

Places to visit

Gainsborough Old Hall, Gainsborough, 01427 612669, www.english-heritage.org.uk

►►► 73% Brandy Wharf Leisure Park (TF014968)

Brandy Wharf DN21 4RT
☎ 01673 818010   ▤ 01673 818010
e-mail: brandywharflp@freenetname.co.uk
dir: *From A15 onto B1205 through Waddingham. Site 3m from Waddingham*

⛺ ⛺ ▲

Open all year (rs Etr-Oct for tents) Last arrival dusk Last departure 17.00hrs

A delightful site in a very rural area on the banks of the River Ancholme, where fishing is available. The toilet block has unisex rooms with combined facilities as well as a more conventional ladies and gents with wash hand basins and toilet. All of the grassy pitches have electricity, and there's a playing and picnic area. The site attracts a lively clientele at weekends, and music around open fires is allowed until 1am. Advance booking is necessary for weekend pitches. A 5 acre site with 50 touring pitches.

AA Pubs & Restaurants nearby: The George, Kirton in Lindsey 01652 640600

Leisure: ⚑
Facilities: ⌐ ⊙ ⓟ ⋇ & ⛭ ⌱ ⚞
Services: ⚡ ⓢ ⓑ ⏛ ⏛ ⚒
Within 3 miles: ⤢ ⌗ ⓢ ∪
Notes: ⊛ No disposable BBQs on grass, no music after 01.00hrs. Fishing, boat mooring, boat launching slipway, canoe hire, pets corner

LONDON

E4 CHINGFORD Map 6 TQ39

►►► 87% Lee Valley Campsite

(TQ381970)

Sewardstone Rd, Chingford E4 7RA
☎ 020 8529 5689   ▤ 020 8559 4070
e-mail: scs@leevalleypark.org.uk
dir: *M25 junct 26, A112. Site signed*

⛺ ⛺ ▲

Open Apr-Oct Last arrival 21.00hrs Last departure noon

Overlooking King George's Reservoir and close to Epping Forest, the touring area of this popular park has been totally revamped and redesigned. It features excellent modern facilities and new hardstanding pitches including nine that are able to accommodate the larger motorhomes, and has a very peaceful atmosphere. This impressive park is maintained to a high standard and there are nine camping pods in a separate shady glade for hire. A bus calls at the site hourly to take passengers to the nearest tube station, and Enfield is easily accessible. A 12 acre site with 100 touring pitches, 20 hardstandings and 43 statics.

Leisure: ⚑
Facilities: ⌐ ⊙ ⓟ ⋇ & © ⓢ ⚞
Services: ⚡ ⓢ ⓑ ⏛ Ⓣ ⏛ ⚒
Within 3 miles: ⤢ Ⓗ ⌗ ⊙ ⓢ ⓢ ∪
Notes: Under 18s must be accompanied by an adult

N9 EDMONTON Map 6 TQ39

►►► 84% Lee Valley Camping & Caravan Park (TQ360945)

Meridian Way N9 0AR
☎ 020 8803 6900 📠 020 8884 4975
e-mail: leisurecomplex@leevalleypark.org.uk
dir: M25 junct 25, A10 S, 1st left onto A1055, approx 5m to Leisure Complex. From A406 (North Circular), N on A1010, left after 0.25m, right (Pickets Lock Ln)

* 🚐 £15-£16.40 🚑 £15-£16.40 ⛺ £15-£16.40

Open all year (rs Xmas & New Year) Last arrival 22.00hrs Last departure noon

A pleasant, open site within easy reach of London yet peacefully located close to two large reservoirs. The very good toilet facilities are beautifully kept by dedicated wardens, and the site has the advantage of being adjacent to a restaurant and bar, and a multi-screen cinema. A 4.5 acre site with 160 touring pitches, 41 hardstandings.

Leisure: 🅰
Facilities: ⌐⊙🅿✳♿🕓📵🎡🐕
Services: 🔌🅾🍴🧺⌀🎫♿
Within 3 miles: 🎣🎠🅿🎢🅾
Notes: No commercial vehicles. Cinema, golf course. Wi-fi

MERSEYSIDE

SOUTHPORT Map 15 SD31

Places to visit
The British Lawnmower Museum, Southport, 01704 501336, www.lawnmowerworld.com

Atkinson Art Gallery, Southport, 0151 934 2110, www.seftonarts.co.uk

---

AA CAMPING CARD SITE

84% Riverside Holiday Park (SD405192)

Southport New Rd PR9 8DF
☎ 01704 228886 📠 01704 505886
e-mail: reception@harrisonleisureuk.com
dir: M6 junct 27, A5209 towards Parbold/Burscough, right onto A59. Left onto A565 at lights in Tarleton. Continue to dual carriageway. At rdbt straight across, site 1m on left

🚐🚑⛺

Open 14 Feb-Jan Last arrival 17.00hrs Last departure 11.00hrs

A large, spacious park with a lively family entertainment complex for cabaret, dancing and theme nights. Children have their own club and entertainer plus games and food. A superb health and leisure centre next door is available at an extra charge. An 80 acre site with 260 touring pitches, 130 hardstandings and 355 statics.

AA Pubs & Restaurants nearby: V-Café & Sushi Bar, Southport 01704 883800

Leisure: 🅰🎣 **Facilities:** ⌐🅿♿🕓📵🐕
Services: 🔌🅾🍴🧺♿🎫🍽📶
Within 3 miles: 🎣🅿🎢🅾🎠♿
Notes: Dogs must be kept on leads & one car per pitch

►►► 85% Willowbank Holiday Home & Touring Park (SD305110)

Coastal Rd, Ainsdale PR8 3ST
☎ 01704 571566 📠 01704 571576
e-mail: info@willowbankcp.co.uk
web: www.willowbankcp.co.uk
dir: From A565 between Formby & Ainsdale exit at Woodvale lights onto coast road, site 150mtrs on left. From N: M6 junct 31, A59 towards Preston, A565, through Southport & Ainsdale, right at Woodvale lights

* 🚐 £13.20-£17.85 🚑 £13.20-£17.85

Willowbank Holiday Home & Touring Park

Open Mar-Jan Last arrival 21.00hrs Last departure noon

Set in a wooded clearing on a nature reserve next to the beautiful sand dunes, this attractive park is just off the coastal road to Southport. The immaculate toilet facilities are well equipped. An 8 acre site with 87 touring pitches, 61 hardstandings and 228 statics.

AA Pubs & Restaurants nearby: V-Café & Sushi Bar, Southport 01704 883800

Leisure: 🅰 **Facilities:** ⌐⊙🅿♿🕓🎡🐕
Services: 🔌🅾🍴⌀♿
Within 3 miles: 🎣🎠🅿🎢🎢🅾🎠♿
Notes: No dangerous dog breeds. Cannot site continental door entry units. No commercial vehicles. Baby changing facility

►►► 79% Hurlston Hall Country Caravan Park (SD398107)

Southport Rd L40 8HB
☎ 01704 841064 📠 01704 841404
e-mail: enquiries@hurlstonhallcaravanpark.co.uk
dir: On A570, 3m from Ormskirk towards Southport

🚐🚑

Open Etr-Oct Last arrival 20.30 hrs (18.30hrs at weekends) Last departure 17.00hrs

A peaceful tree-lined touring park next to a static site in attractive countryside about ten minutes' drive from Southport. The park is maturing well, with growing trees and a coarse fishing lake, and excellent on-site facilities include golf, a bistro and a well-equipped health centre. Please note that neither tents or dogs are accepted. A 5 acre site with 60 touring pitches and 68 statics.

AA Pubs & Restaurants nearby: V-Café & Sushi Bar, Southport 01704 883800

Leisure: 🏊🅰 **Facilities:** ⌐⊙🅿♿🕓
Services: 🔌🅾🍴🧺🍽 **Within 3 miles:** 🎣🅿🎢🅾
Notes: ⊗ Coarse fishing

Wells-next-the-Sea

Norfolk

Even today, with faster cars and improved road and rail systems, Norfolk still seems a separate entity, as if strangely detached from the rest of the country. There are those who would like it to stay that way. The renowned composer, actor and playwright, Noel Coward, famously described Norfolk as 'very flat' and he was right.

Top of the list of attractions is the North Norfolk Coast, designated an Area of Outstanding Natural Beauty, which has been described as a long way from anywhere, a place of traditions and ancient secrets. The coastline here represents a world of lonely beaches, vast salt marshes and extensive sand dunes stretching as far as the eye can see. It is the same today as it has always been, and is a stark reminder of how this area has been vulnerable to attack and enemy invasion.

Delightful villages

With its old harbour and quaint High Street, Wells-next-the-Sea is a popular favourite with regular

visitors to Norfolk, as is Blakeney, famous for its mudflats and medieval parish church, dedicated to the patron saint of seafarers, standing guard over the village and the estuary of the River Glaven.

Cromer is a classic example of a good old fashioned seaside resort where rather grand Victorian hotels look out to sea; the writer and actor Stephen Fry once worked as a waiter at Cromer's Hotel de Paris. A pier, such a key feature of coastal towns, completes the scene.

Farther down the coast, among a string of sleepy villages, is Happisburgh, pronounced Hazeburgh The Hill House pub here is where Sir Arthur Conan Doyle stayed at the beginning of the 20th century;

the Sherlock Holmes' story *The Adventure of the Dancing Men* (1903) is set in a Norfolk where 'on every hand enormous square-towered churches bristled up from the flat, green landscape.' Explore this corner of the county today and the scene is remarkably unchanged.

The Broads and nearby area

No visit to Norfolk is complete without a tour of the popular Broads, a network of mostly navigable rivers and lakes. Located a little inland to the south of Happisburgh, the various linked rivers, streams and man-made waterways, offer about 200 miles of highly enjoyable sailing and cruising. Away from the

▶

Cliffs at Hunstanton

Broads rural Norfolk stretches for miles. If you've the time, you could spend days exploring a network of quiet back roads and winding lanes, visiting en route a generous assortment of picturesque villages and quiet market towns, including Fakenham and Swaffham. Also well worth a look is Thetford, with its delightful Dad's Army Museum. The location filming for the much-loved BBC comedy series was completed in and around Thetford Forest, and fictional Walmington-on-Sea was in fact the town of Thetford.

Ideally, this itinerary should also include the village of Castle Acre, with its impressive monastic ruins, and, of course, Norwich, with its magnificent cathedral, one of the country's greatest examples of Norman cathedral architecture.

Walking and Cycling
The 93-mile (150km) Peddars Way and North Norfolk Coast Path is one of Britain's most popular national trails. Consisting of two paths joined together to form one continuous route, the trail begins near Thetford on the Suffolk/Norfolk border and follows ancient tracks and stretches of Roman road before reaching the coast near Hunstanton. There are also good walks around the Burnham villages, Castle Acre and the National Trust's Blickling Hall.

Hickling Broad

Barton Broad

Cycling in Norfolk offers variety and flexibility and the chance to tie it in with a bit of train travel. You can cycle beside the Bure Valley Railway on a 9-mile (14.5km) trail running from Aylsham to Wroxham and return to the start by train. Alternatively, combine an undemanding 5 miles (8km) of mostly traffic-free cycling with a trip on the North Norfolk Railway from Sheringham to Holt, starting and finishing at Kelling Heath. There is also the North Norfolk Coast Cycleway between King's Lynn and Cromer and a series of cycle trails around the Norfolk Broads.

Festivals and Events

- The Norfolk & Norwich Festival, held in May, is a celebration of creativity, innovation, jazz, comedy, dance and classical music.
- The Sandringham Game & Country Fair in September has falconry, fishing, wildfowling and archery among many other country sports and pursuits.
- The Little Vintage Lovers Fair takes place on different dates and at different venues around the county throughout the year and includes 30 stalls with the emphasis on quality vintage fashion, textiles and accessories.

NORFOLK

See Walk 8 in the Walk & Cycle Rides section at the end of the guide

BARNEY   Map 13 TF93

Places to visit

Baconsthorpe Castle, Baconsthorpe, 01799 322399, www.english-heritage.org.uk

Holkham Hall and Bygones museum, Holkham, 01328 710227, www.holkham.co.uk

Great for kids: Dinosaur Adventure Park, Lenwade, 01603 876310, www.dinosaurpark.co.uk

▶▶▶▶ **91% The Old Brick Kilns** (TG007328)

Best of British

GOLD

Little Barney Ln NR21 0NL
☎ 01328 878305   📠 01328 878948
e-mail: enquiries@old-brick-kilns.co.uk
dir: *From A148 (Fakenham-Cromer) follow brown tourist signs to Barney, left into Little Barney Lane. Site at end of lane*

* 🚐 £15-£27 🚙 £15-£27 ▲ £14.50-£23

The Old Brick Kilns

Open mid Mar-6 Jan (rs Low season bar food/takeaway selected nights only) Last arrival 21.00hrs Last departure 11.00hrs

A secluded and peaceful park approached via a quiet leafy country lane. The park is on two levels with its own boating and fishing pool and many mature trees. Excellent, well-planned toilet facilities can be found in two blocks, and there is a short dog walk. Due to a narrow access road, no arrivals are accepted until after 1pm. B&B accommodation is available and there are four self-catering holiday cottages. A 12.73 acre site with 65 touring pitches, 65 hardstandings.

AA Pubs & Restaurants nearby: Black Lion Hotel, Little Walsingham 01328 820235

Chequers Inn, Binham 01328 830297

Old Forge Seafood Restaurant, Thursford 01328 878345

Leisure: ⚡🔍🖵

Facilities: 🏳️⊙🅿️✳️⚸🕒🚿🖻💈

Services: 🔋🚽🍴🅱️🚰🧺🔵🅃🍴🛒🔽

Within 3 miles: 🖉🖼️🛒

Notes: No gazebos. Outdoor draughts, chess, family games. Wi-fi

BELTON

Places to visit

Burgh Castle, Burgh Castle, www.english-heritage.org.uk

Great for kids: Thrigby Hall Wildlife Gardens, Filby, 01493 369477, www.thrigbyhall.co.uk

LEISURE: 🏊 Indoor swimming pool 🏊 Outdoor swimming pool 🅰 Children's playground ⚞ Tennis court 🎯 Games room 🖵 Separate TV room ⛳ 9/18 hole golf course 🚣 Boats for hire 🎬 Cinema 🎣 Fishing 🏌 Mini golf 🏄 Watersports ⛎ Stables **FACILITIES:** 🛁 Bath 🚿 Shower ⊙ Electric shaver 🖙 Hairdryer ❄ Ice Pack Facility ♿ Disabled facilities 🕐 Public telephone 🏪 Shop on site or within 200yds 🚙 Mobile shop (calls at least 5 days a week) 🍖 BBQ area ⛱ Picnic area 🐕 Dog exercise area

BELTON
Map 13 TG40

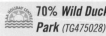 

70% *Wild Duck Holiday Park* (TG475028)
GOLD

Howards Common NR31 9NE
☎ 01493 780268 📠 01493 782308
dir: *From A47 towards Gt Yarmouth take A143 towards Beccles. Turn right at Burgh Castle, right at T-junct, left at next T-junct, site 200mtrs on right*

🚐 🚙 Å

Open mid Mar-Oct (rs mid Mar-May & Sep-Oct some facilities may be reduced) Last arrival 22.30hrs Last departure 10.00hrs

This a large holiday complex with plenty to do for all ages both indoors and out. This level grassy site has well laid-out facilities and is set in a forest with small, cleared areas for tourers. Clubs for children and teenagers, sporting activities and evening shows all add to the fun of a stay here. A 97 acre site with 120 touring pitches and 365 statics.

AA Pubs & Restaurants nearby: Fritton House, Fritton 01493 484008

Andover House, Great Yarmouth 01493 843490

Leisure: 🏊 🏊 ⛰ 🎱
Facilities: 🐕 ☉ 👶 🕐 🔥 🚻 ♨ 🎾
Services: 🔌 🖥 🍺 🛢 🍴 🍟 🚼 ♿
Within 3 miles: 🏇 🎣 🎯 🏌 ⊚ 🛍 🛒
Notes: Certain dog breeds are banned. Wi-fi
see advert on opposite page

▶▶▶▶ 87% Rose Farm Touring & Camping Park (TG488033)

Stepshort NR31 9JS
☎ 01493 780896 📠 01493 780896
dir: *Follow signs to Belton off A143, right at lane signed Stepshort, site 1st on right*

* 🚐 £15-£19 🚙 £15-£19 Å £8-£19

Open all year

A former railway line is the setting for this very peaceful site which enjoys rural views and is beautifully presented throughout. The ever-improving toilet facilities are spotlessly clean and inviting to use, and the park is brightened with many flower and herb beds. The customer care here is truly exceptional. A 10 acre site with 80 touring pitches, 15 hardstandings.

AA Pubs & Restaurants nearby: Fritton House, Fritton 01493 484008

Andover House, Great Yarmouth 01493 843490

Leisure: ⛰ 🎱 🖥
Facilities: 🐕 ☉ ⚡ 👶 🎾
Services: 🔌 🖥 🛢 🚼 ♿
Within 3 miles: 🏇 🎣 🎯 🎯 ⊚ 🛍 🛒 ⛳
Notes: No dog fouling. Wi-fi

BURGH CASTLE
Map 13 TG40

Places to visit

Burgh Castle, Burgh Castle, www.english-heritage.org.uk

Thrigby Hall Wildlife Gardens, Filby, 01493 369477, www.thrigbyhall.co.uk

Great for kids: Pettitts Animal Adventure Park, Reedham, 01493 700094, www.pettittsadventurepark.co.uk

77% Breydon Water (TG479042)
SILVER

Butt Ln NR31 9QB
☎ 0871 664 9710
e-mail: breydon.water@park-resorts.com
dir: *From Gt Yarmouth on A12 towards Lowestoft over 2 rdbts. Follow Burgh Castle sign. Right at lights signed Diss & Beccles. 1.5m, right signed Burgh Castle & Belton. At mini rdbt right onto Stepshort. Site on right*

🚐 🚙 Å

Open Apr-Oct Last arrival anytime Last departure 11.00hrs

This large park has two village areas just a short walk apart. Choose Yare Village for family fun and superb entertainment, and Bure Village as a quieter base. Although the villages are separated, guests are more than welcome to use facilities at both. Both villages have touring areas with modern, well maintained toilets, and tents are welcome. They are just a short drive from the bright lights of Yarmouth and the unique Norfolk Broads. 189 touring pitches and 327 statics.

AA Pubs & Restaurants nearby: Andover House, Great Yarmouth 01493 843490

Leisure: 🏊 🏊 ⛰ 🎱 **Facilities:** 📶 👶 🕐 🎾
Services: 🔌 🖥 🍺 🛢 🍴 🍟
Within 3 miles: 🏇 🎣 🎯 🏌 ⊚ ⛴ 🛍 🛒
Notes: Wi-fi *see advert on page 236*

CAISTER-ON-SEA
Map 13 TG51

NEW Caister Holiday Park (TG519132)
GOLD

Ormesby Rd NR30 5NQ
☎ 01493 728931
dir: *A1064 signed Caister-on-Sea. At rdbt take 2nd exit onto A149, at next rdbt take 1st exit onto Caister by-pass, at 3rd rdbt take 3rd exit which leads into Caister-on-Sea. Park is on left*

* 🚐 £15-£79 🚙 £15-£79

Open Mar-Oct Last arrival 18.00hrs Last departure 10.00hrs

An all-action holiday park located beside the beach north of the resort of Great Yarmouth, yet close to the attractions of the Norfolk Broads. The newly created touring area offers 46 fully serviced pitches and is conveniently located for all the leisure attractions, shops, cafés and bars at this popular holiday park. At the time of going to press the quality rating for this site had not been confirmed. For up-to-date information please see the AA website: theAA.com. A 138 acre site with 46 touring pitches.
see advert on page 236

CLIPPESBY

Places to visit

Fairhaven Woodland and Water Garden, South Walsham, 01603 270449, www.fairhavengarden.co.uk

Great for kids: Caister Roman Site, Caister-on-Sea, www.english-heritage.org.uk

Remember that prices and opening times are liable to change within the currency of this guide. It is always best to phone in advance

CLIPPESBY — Map 13 TG41

PREMIER PARK

AA CAMPING CARD SITE

▶▶▶▶▶ 90% Clippesby Hall (TG423147)

Hall Ln NR29 3BL
☎ 01493 367800 ▤ 01493 367809
e-mail: holidays@clippesby.com
web: www.clippesby.com
dir: From A47 follow tourist signs for The Broads. At Acle rdbt take A1064, after 2m left onto B1152, 0.5m turn left opposite village sign, site 400yds on right

* ⛺ £10.50-£26.50 ⛟ £10.50-£26.50
▲ £10.50-£26.50

Open Etr-end Oct (rs Etr-Whit some facilities restricted) Last arrival 17.30hrs Last departure 11.00hrs

A lovely country house estate with secluded pitches hidden among the trees or in sheltered sunny glades. The toilet facilities are appointed to a very good standard, providing a wide choice of cubicles. Amenities include a coffee shop with Wi-fi and wired internet access, family bar and restaurant and family golf. There are four pine lodges and 13 holiday cottages available for holiday lets. A 30 acre site with 120 touring pitches, 9 hardstandings.

AA Pubs & Restaurants nearby: Fishermans Return, Winterton-on-Sea 01493 393305

Fur & Feather Inn, Woodbastwick 01603 720003

Leisure: ⚓ 🅰 ♞ ✎
Facilities: 🛁 🚿 ⊙ 🅿 ✳ ⚡ ⏱ 🚻 🍴 🐕
Services: ⛽ 🔧 🛢 🚿 ⏱ 🚽 🍴 🛒 🐾
Within 3 miles: 🚶 🚣 🎣 ⊙ 🍴 🛒 ♻ ♨

Notes: Dogs must be kept on leads. Bicycle hire, family golf, volley ball. Wi-fi

CROMER — Map 13 TG24

Places to visit
RNLI Henry Blogg Museum, Cromer, 01263 511294, www.rnli.org.uk/henryblogg

Felbrigg Hall, Felbrigg, 01263 837444 www.nationaltrust.org.uk/main/w-felbrigghallgardenandpark

▶▶▶▶ 74% Manor Farm Caravan & Camping Site (TG198416)

East Runton NR27 9PR
☎ 01263 512858
e-mail: manor-farm@ukf.net
dir: 1m W of Cromer, exit A148 or A149 at Manor Farm sign

* ⛺ £13-£16 ⛟ £13-£16 ▲ £13-£16

Open Etr-Sep Last arrival 20.30hrs Last dep noon

A well-established family-run site on a working farm enjoying panoramic sea views. There are good modern facilities across the site, including three smart new toilet blocks that include two quality family rooms and privacy cubicles, two good play areas and a large expanse of grass for games - the park is very popular with families. A 17 acre site with 250 touring pitches.

AA Pubs & Restaurants nearby: The Wheatsheaf, West Beckham 01263 822110

Marmalade's Bisto, Sheringham 01263 822830

Frazers, Sea Marge Hotel, Overstrand 01263 579579

Leisure: 🅰 **Facilities:** 🛁 ⊙ ✳ ⚡ 🐕
Services: ⛽ 🛢 🚿 ✎ 🛒
Within 3 miles: 🚶 🍴 🎣 ♻ 🛒
Notes: 🐕 2 dog-free fields

▶▶▶ 82% Forest Park (TG233405)

Northrepps Rd NR27 0JR
☎ 01263 513290 ▤ 01263 511992
e-mail: info@forest-park.co.uk
dir: A140 from Norwich, left at T-junct signed Cromer, right signed Northrepps, right then immediate left, left at T-junct, site on right

* ⛺ fr £16.50 ⛟ fr £16.50 ▲ fr £16.50

Open 15 Mar-15 Jan Last arrival 21.00hrs Last departure 11.00hrs

Surrounded by forest, this gently sloping park offers a wide choice of pitches. Visitors have the use of a heated indoor swimming pool, and a large clubhouse with entertainment. A 100 acre site with 262 touring pitches and 420 statics.

AA Pubs & Restaurants nearby: The Wheatsheaf, West Beckham 01263 822110

Marmalade's Bisto, Sheringham 01263 822830

White Horse, Overstrand 01263 579237

Frazers, Sea Marge Hotel, Overstrand 01263 579579

Leisure: 🅰 🅰 ✎
Facilities: 🛁 ⊙ 🅿 ✳ ⚡ ⏱ 🍴 🐕
Services: ⛽ 🔧 🛢 🚿 ⏱ 🍴 🛒 🐾
Within 3 miles: 🚶 🚣 🍴 ♻ 🛒 ♨ U
Notes: Wi-fi

DOWNHAM MARKET — Map 12 TF60

▶▶▶ 82% Lakeside Caravan Park & Fisheries (TF608013)

Sluice Rd, Denver PE38 0DZ
☎ 01366 387074 & 07770 663237
▤ 01366 387074
e-mail: richesflorido@aol.com
web: www.westhallfarmholidays.co.uk
dir: Off A10 towards Denver, follow signs to Denver Windmill

⛺ ⛟ ▲

Open Mar-Oct Last arrival 21.00hrs Last departure noon

A peaceful, rapidly improving park set around four pretty fishing lakes. Several grassy touring areas are sheltered by mature hedging and trees. There is a function room, shop and laundry. A 30 acre site with 100 touring pitches and 1 static.

AA Pubs & Restaurants nearby: Hare Arms, Stow Bardolph 01366 382229

Leisure: 🅰 **Facilities:** 🛁 ⊙ 🅿 ⚡ 🛒 🐕
Services: ⛽ 🛢 🚿 ✎ ⏱ 🛒
Within 3 miles: 🚶 🚣 🍴 ♻ 🛒
Notes: Dogs must be kept on leads. Pool table. Wi-fi

Places to visit

Houghton Hall, Houghton, 01485 528569,
www.houghtonhall.com

Great for kids: Pensthorpe Nature Reserve and
Gardens, Fakenham, 01328 851465,
www.pensthorpe.co.uk

►►► 79% Fakenham Campsite

(TF907310)

Burnham Market Rd, Sculthorpe NR21 9SA
☎ **01328 856614**
e-mail: fakenham.campsite@gmail.com
dir: *From Fakenham take A148 towards King's
Lynn then B1355 Burnham Market road. Site on
right in 400yds*

* ⊞ £11.50-£18 ⊞ £11.50-£18 Å £11.50-£18

Open all year Last arrival 22.00hrs Last departure
noon

New enthusiastic owners are now running this
peaceful site that is surrounded by tranquil
countryside and which is part of a par 3, 9-hole
golf complex and driving range. The toilet
facilities are of good quality, and there is a golf
shop and licensed bar. Please note there is no
laundry. A 4 acre site with 50 touring pitches, 11
hardstandings.

AA Pubs & Restaurants nearby: White Horse Inn,
East Barsham 01328 820645

Blue Boar Inn, Great Ryburgh 01328 829212

Brisely Bell Inn & Restaurant, Brisely
01362 668686

Leisure: ⚄ **Facilities:** ⋔☀🚿🖳🎣
Services: 🔌🚽🔧 Ⓣ🍽 **Within 3 miles:** 🚶🎣🛒

►►► 78% Caravan Club M.V.C. Site

(TF926288)

Fakenham Racecourse NR21 7NY
☎ **01328 862388** 📠 **01328 855908**
e-mail: caravan@fakenhamracecourse.co.uk
dir: *From B1146, S of Fakenham follow brown
Racecourse signs (with tent & caravan symbols)
leads to site entrance*

⊞ ⊞ Å

Open all year Last arrival 21.00hrs Last departure
noon

A very well laid-out site set around the racecourse,
with a grandstand offering smart modern toilet
facilities. Tourers move to the centre of the course

on race days, and enjoy free racing, and there's a
wide range of sporting activities in the club
house. An 11.4 acre site with 120 touring pitches,
25 hardstandings.

AA Pubs & Restaurants nearby: White Horse Inn,
East Barsham 01328 820645

Blue Boar Inn, Great Ryburgh 01328 829212

Brisely Bell Inn & Restaurant, Brisely
01362 668686

Facilities: ⋔☉🚻☀🖳Ⓒ🎣🖳🎣
Services: 🔌🚽🔧🛢🔧Ⓣ🍽 🛠
Within 3 miles: 🚶🎣🛒◉🎣🛒⛳

Notes: TV aerial hook-ups, hostel accommodation
available

►► 72% Crossways Caravan & Camping Park *(TF961321)*

Crossways, Holt Rd, Little Snoring NR21 0AX
☎ **01328 878335**
e-mail: joyholland@live.co.uk
dir: *From Fakenham take A148 towards Cromer.
After 3m pass exit for Little Snoring. Site on A148
on left behind Post Office*

⊞ ⊞ Å

Open all year Last arrival 22.00hrs Last departure
noon

Set on the edge of the peaceful hamlet of Little
Snoring, this level site enjoys views across the
fields towards the North Norfolk coast some seven
miles away. Visitors can use the health suite for a
small charge, and there is a shop on site, and a
good village pub. A 2 acre site with 26 touring
pitches, 10 hardstandings and 1 static.

AA Pubs & Restaurants nearby: White Horse Inn,
East Barsham 01328 820645

Blue Boar Inn, Great Ryburgh 01328 829212

Brisely Bell Inn & Restaurant, Brisely
01362 668686

Facilities: ⋔☉☀Ⓒ🎣🖳🎣
Services: 🔌🚽🛢🔧Ⓣ
Within 3 miles: 🚶🎣🛒◉🎣🛒⛳

Notes: Dogs must be kept on leads

Places to visit

Elizabethan House Museum, Great Yarmouth,
01493 855746, www.museums.norfolk.gov.uk

Great Yarmouth Row 111 Houses & Greyfriars'
Cloister, Great Yarmouth, 01493 857900,
www.english-heritage.org.uk

Great for kids: Merrivale Model Village, Great
Yarmouth, 01493 842097,
www.merrivalemodelvillage.co.uk

87% Vauxhall Holiday Park *(TG520083)*

4 Acle New Rd NR30 1TB
☎ **01493 857231** 📠 **01493 331122**
e-mail: info@vauxhallholidays.co.uk
web: www.vauxhall-holiday-park.co.uk
dir: *On A47 approaching Great Yarmouth*

* ⊞ £16-£40 ⊞ £16-£40 Å £16-£40

Open Etr, mid May-Sep & Oct half term Last
arrival 21.00hrs Last departure 10.00hrs

A very large holiday complex with plenty of
entertainment and access to beach, river,
estuary, lake and the A47. The touring pitches
are laid out in four separate areas, each with
its own amenity block, and all arranged around
the main entertainment. A 40 acre site with 220
touring pitches and 421 statics.

AA Pubs & Restaurants nearby: Andover House,
Great Yarmouth 01493 843490

Leisure: 🏊🏖⚄🎱🎣🖥
Facilities: ⋔☉☀🚿Ⓒ🎣
Services: 🔌🚽🔧🛢🔧Ⓣ🍽🔋🍴
Within 3 miles: 🚶🎣🛒◉🎣🛒⛳

Notes: No pets. Children's pool, sauna,
solarium, fitness centre. Wi-fi

see advert on page 236

GREAT YARMOUTH *continued*

▶▶▶▶ 74% The Grange Touring Park *(TG510142)*

Yarmouth Rd, Ormesby St Margaret NR29 3QG
☎ 01493 730306 📄 01493 730188
e-mail: info@grangetouring.co.uk
dir: *From A419, 3m N of Great Yarmouth. Site at junct of A419 & B1159. Signed*

* 🚐 £10.50-£16.50 🚙 £10.50-£16.50
▲ £9.50-£16.50

Open Etr-Oct Last arrival 21.00hrs Last departure 11.00hrs

A mature, ever improving park with plenty of trees, located just one mile from the sea, within easy reach of both coastal attractions and the Norfolk Broads. The level pitches have electric hook-ups and include 13 new hardstanding pitches, and there are clean, modern toilets including three spacious new family rooms. All pitches have Wi-fi access. A 3.5 acre site with 70 touring pitches.

AA Pubs & Restaurants nearby: Andover House, Great Yarmouth 01493 843490

Leisure: 🅰️ **Facilities:** 🅽☉🅿✳♿☺🍺
Services: 🔌🗑🍺🔥∅🍴💧
Within 3 miles: ⬇☰📷◎🏧🅱🅾↻

Notes: No football, no gazebos, no open fires. Internet café at reception with facility for using own computers. Wi-fi

---

HUNSTANTON Map 12 TF64

Places to visit

Lynn Museum, King's Lynn, 01553 775001
www.museums.norfolk.gov.uk

Kings Lynn Arts Centre, King's Lynn,
01553 765565, www.kingslynnarts.co.uk

Great for kids: Hunstanton Sea Life Sanctuary,
Hunstanton, 01485 533576,
www.sealsanctuary.co.uk

87% Searles Leisure Resort *(TF671400)*

South Beach Rd PE36 5BB
☎ 01485 534211 📄 01485 533815
e-mail: bookings@searles.co.uk
web: www.searles.co.uk
dir: *A149 from King's Lynn to Hunstanton. At rdbt follow signs for South Beach. Straight on at 2nd rdbt. Site on left*

🚐 🚙 ▲

Open all year (rs 25 Dec & Feb-May limited entertainment & restaurant) Last arrival 20.45hrs Last departure 11.00hrs

A large seaside holiday complex with well-managed facilities, adjacent to sea and beach. The tourers have their own areas, including two excellent toilet blocks, and pitches are individually marked by small maturing shrubs for privacy. The bars and entertainment, restaurant, bistro and takeaway, heated indoor and outdoor pools, golf, fishing and bowling green make this park popular throughout the year. A 50 acre site with 332 touring pitches, 100 hardstandings and 460 statics.

AA Pubs & Restaurants nearby: King William IV, Hunstanton 01485 571765

Neptune Restaurant with Rooms, Hunstanton 01485 532122

Gin Trap Inn, Ringstead 01485 525264

Lifeboat Inn, Thornham 01485 512236

Leisure: 🏊🏊🅰🎱🎣
Facilities: 🛁🅽☉🅿✳♿☺🍺☰🐾
Services: 🔌🗑🍺🔥∅🍴🅃🍽💧🚿🛒
Within 3 miles: ⬇🎿☰🅿◎🏧🅱🅾↻

Notes: No dangerous dog breeds. Hire shop, beauty salon. Wi-fi

---

KING'S LYNN

See Stanhoe

NORTH WALSHAM Map 13 TG23

Places to visit

Blickling Hall, Blickling, 01263 738030,
www.nationaltrust.org.uk/blickling

Horsey Windpump, Horsey, 01263 740241,
www.nationaltrust.co.uk

▶▶▶▶ 93% Two Mills Touring Park *(TG291286)*   Best of British GOLD

Yarmouth Rd NR28 9NA
☎ 01692 405829 📄 01692 405829
e-mail: enquiries@twomills.co.uk
dir: *1m S of North Walsham on Old Yarmouth road past police station & hospital on left*

* 🚐 £15-£24 🚙 £15-£24 ▲ £15-£24

Open Mar-3 Jan Last arrival 20.30hrs Last departure noon

An intimate, beautifully presented park set in superb countryside in a peaceful, rural spot, which is also convenient for touring. A new 'Top

---

Acre' section has been incorporated into the park and features an additional 26 fully serviced pitches, offering panoramic views over the site, an immaculate new toilet block and good new planting, plus the layout of pitches and facilities is excellent. The very friendly and helpful owners keep the park in immaculate condition. Please note this park does not accept children. A 7 acre site with 81 touring pitches, 81 hardstandings.

AA Pubs & Restaurants nearby: Butchers Arms, East Ruston 01692 650237

Beechwood Hotel, North Walsham 01692 403231

Leisure: 🗔
Facilities: 🅽☉🅿✳♿☺🅱☰🐾
Services: 🔌🗑🍺∅🅃🚿
Within 3 miles: 🅿🅱🅾

Notes: Adults only. Max 2 dogs per pitch. Tourist information room & library. Wi-fi

---

ST JOHN'S FEN END Map 12 TF51

Places to visit

African Violet Centre,
Kings Lynn, 01553 828374,
www.africanvioletandgardencentre.com

Oxburgh Hall, Oxborough, 01366 328258,
www.nationaltrust.org.uk/main/w-oxburghhall

▶▶▶▶ 73% Virginia Lake Caravan Park *(TF538113)*

Smeeth Rd PE14 8JF
☎ 01945 430585 & 430167
e-mail: louise@virginialake.co.uk
dir: *From A47 E of Wisbech follow tourist signs to Terrington St John. Site on left*

🚐 🚙 ▲

Open all year Last arrival 21.00hrs Last dep noon

A well-established park beside a two-acre fishing lake with good facilities for both anglers and tourers. The toilet facilities are very good, and security is carefully observed throughout the park. A clubhouse serves a selection of meals. A 7 acre site with 100 touring pitches, 20 hardstandings.

AA Pubs & Restaurants nearby: Stuart House Hotel, Bar & Restaurant,
King's Lynn 01553 772169

Facilities: 🅽☉🅿✳♿☺🅱☰🐾
Services: 🔌🗑🍺🅃🍴💧🛒
Within 3 miles: ⬇☰🅿◎🅱🅾↻

Notes: No camp fires. Pool tables, large screen TV, fruit machines

---

SCRATBY — Map 13 TG51

Places to visit

St. Olaves Priory, St. Olaves, www.english-heritage.org.uk

Time and Tide Museum of Great Yarmouth Life, Great Yarmouth, 01493 743930, www.museums.norfolk.gov.uk

Great for kids: Caister Roman Site, Caister-on-Sea, www.english-heritage.org.uk

►►► 82% Scratby Hall Caravan Park
(TG501155)

NR29 3SR
☎ 01493 730283
e-mail: scratbyhall@aol.com
dir: 5m N of Great Yarmouth. Exit A149 onto B1159, site signed

Open Spring BH-mid Sep Last arrival 22.00hrs Last departure noon

A neatly-maintained site with a popular children's play area, well-equipped shop and outdoor swimming pool with sun terrace. The toilets are kept very clean. The beach and the Norfolk Broads are close by. A 5 acre site with 97 touring pitches.

AA Pubs & Restaurants nearby: Fishermans Return, Winterton-on-Sea 01493 393305

Nelson Head, Horsey 01493 393378

Leisure: ⚑
Facilities: ⚫☉℘✳⚫⚫⚫
Services: ⚫⚫⚫⚫⚫⚫⚫
Within 3 miles: ⚫⚫⚫⚫⚫⚫
Notes: No commercial vehicles. Food preparation room

STANHOE — Map 13 TF83

Places to visit

Norfolk Lavender, Heacham, 01485 570384, www.norfolk-lavender.co.uk

Walsingham Abbey Grounds and Shirehall Museum, Little Walsingham, 01328 820510

►►► 78% The Rickels Caravan & Camping Park (TF794355)

Bircham Rd PE31 8PU
☎ 01485 518671
dir: A148 from King's Lynn to Hillington. B1153 to Great Bircham. B1155 to x-rds, straight over, site on left

⚫⚫⚫

Open Mar-Oct Last arrival 21.00hrs Last departure 11.00hrs

Set in three acres of grassland, with sweeping country views and a pleasant, relaxing atmosphere fostered by being for adults only. The meticulously maintained grounds and facilities are part of the attraction, and the slightly sloping land has some level areas and sheltering for tents. A 3 acre site with 30 touring pitches.

AA Pubs & Restaurants nearby: Lord Nelson, Burnham Thorpe 01328 738241

The Hoste Arms, Burnham Market 01328 738777

Leisure: ⚫
Facilities: ⚫☉✳⚫
Services: ⚫⚫⚫⚫⚫
Within 3 miles: ℘⚫
Notes: Adults only. ⚫ Dogs must be on leads, no ground sheets. Field available to hire for rallies

SWAFFHAM

Places to visit

Gressenhall Farm and Workhouse, Gressenhall, 01362 860563, www.museums.norfolk.gov.uk

SWAFFHAM — Map 13 TF80

AA CAMPING CARD SITE

►►► 80% Breckland Meadows Touring Park (TF809094)

Lynn Rd PE37 7PT
☎ 01760 721246
e-mail: info@brecklandmeadows.co.uk
dir: 1m W of Swaffham on old A47

* ⚫ £11.75-£13.75 ⚫ £11.75-£13.75 ⚫ £11.50

Open all year Last arrival 21.00hrs Last departure 14.00hrs

An immaculate, well-landscaped little park on the edge of Swaffham. The impressive toilet block is well equipped, and there are hardstandings, full electricity and laundry equipment. Plentiful planting is now resulting in attractive screening. A 3 acre site with 45 touring pitches, 29 hardstandings.

AA Pubs & Restaurants nearby: Canary & Linnet, Little Fransham 01362 687027

Facilities: ⚫☉✳⚫⚫⚫⚫⚫⚫
Services: ⚫⚫⚫⚫⚫⚫⚫
Within 3 miles: ⚫⚫℘⚫⚫⚫
Notes: Adults only. ⚫ Tourist information centre, newspaper deliveries. Wi-fi

SYDERSTONE — Map 13 TF83

Places to visit

Creake Abbey, North Creake, www.english-heritage.org.uk

Great for kids: Castle Rising Castle, Castle Rising, 01553 631330, www.english-heritage.org.uk

►►► 76% The Garden Caravan Site
(TF812337)

Barmer Hall Farm PE31 8SR
☎ 01485 578220 & 578178
e-mail: nigel@gardencaravansite.co.uk
dir: Signed from B1454 at Barmer between A148 & Docking, 1m W of Syderstone

* ⚫ £15-£20 ⚫ £15-£20 ⚫

Open Mar-Nov Last arrival 21.00hrs Last departure noon

In the tranquil setting of a former walled garden beside a large farmhouse, with mature trees and shrubs, a secluded site surrounded by woodland. The site is run mainly on trust, with a daily notice indicating which pitches are available, and an honesty box for basic foods. An ideal site for the discerning camper, and well placed for touring north Norfolk. A 3.5 acre site with 30 touring pitches.

AA Pubs & Restaurants nearby: Lord Nelson, Burnham Thorpe 01328 738241

The Hoste Arms, Burnham Market 01328 738777

Facilities: ❐☉ॐ✳❦☺❒ᴴᴵ

Services: ❑▲ᴴᴵᴴ

Within 3 miles: ⓢ

Notes: ⊛ Max 2 dogs per pitch. Cold drinks, ice creams, eggs

THREE HOLES · Map 12 TF50

Places to visit

African Violet Centre,
King's Lynn, 01553 828374,
www.africanvioletandgardencentre.com

King's Lynn Art Centre,
King's Lynn, 01553 765565,
www.kingslynnarts.co.uk

►►► 77% Lode Hall Holiday Park

(TF529989)

Lode Hall, Silt Rd PE14 9JW
☎ 01354 638133 📠 01354 638133
e-mail: dick@lode-hall.co.uk
dir: From Wisbech take A1101 towards Downham Market. At Outwell continue on A1101 signed Littleport. Site signed from Three Holes. Right onto B1094 to site

🚐 🚋 Å

Open all year

Peace and tranquilly is assured at this newly-established and deeply rural park in the grounds of Lode Hall. The toilet facilities have been installed in an imaginative restoration of a former cricket pavilion and include combined toilet/wash basin cubicles and unisex showers. Please note that there are no play facilities for children. A 5 acre site with 20 touring pitches, 8 hardstandings.

AA Pubs & Restaurants nearby: Hare Arms, Stow Bardolph 01366 382229

Facilities: ❐☉✳❦❒ᴴᴵ

Services: ❑◱ᴴᴵ

Within 3 miles: ✐ⓢU

Notes: ⊛ Wi-fi

TRIMINGHAM · Map 13 TG23

Places to visit

RNLI Henry Blogg Museum, Cromer,
01263 511294, www.rnli.org.uk/henryblogg

Cromer Museum, Cromer, 01263 513543,
www.norfolk.gov.uk/tourism/museums

►►► 70% *Woodland Leisure Park*

(TG274388)

NR11 8AL
☎ 01263 579208 📠 01263 576477
e-mail: info@woodland-park.co.uk
web: www.woodland-park.co.uk
dir: 4m SE on B1159 (coast road)

🚐 🚋 Å

Open Mar-Dec Last arrival 23.00hrs Last departure noon

A secluded woodland site in an open enclosure, close to the sea but well sheltered from the winds by tall trees. Facilities include two bars, a restaurant, an indoor swimming pool, bowling green and sauna, and entertainment is provided in the clubhouse. There are holiday statics for hire and a large field is now available for tents. A 55 acre site with 20 touring pitches and 230 statics.

AA Pubs & Restaurants nearby: White Horse, Overstrand 01263 579237

Frazers, Sea Marge Hotel, Overstrand 01263 579579

Leisure: ⌘△⌂❦

Facilities: ❐☉ॐ✳❦☺ⓢ❒ᴴᴵ

Services: ❑◱ᴴᴵ▲❤❒ᴴᴵᴴ

Within 3 miles: ↓☰✐◎⤵ⓢ◱U

Notes: Wi-fi

WORTWELL · Map 13 TM28

Places to visit

Bressingham Steam Museum and Gardens,
Bressingham, 01379 686900,
www.bressingham.co.uk

Great for kids: Banham Zoo, Banham,
01953 887771, www.banhamzoo.co.uk

AA CAMPING CARD SITE

►►►► 81% Little Lakeland Caravan Park (TM279849)

IP20 0EL
☎ 01986 788646 📠 01986 788646
e-mail: information@littlelakeland.co.uk
dir: From W: exit A143 at sign for Wortwell. In village turn right 300yds past garage. From E: on A143, left onto B1062, then right. After 800yds turn left

🚐 £14.50-£19.80 🚋 £14.50-£19.80
Å £14.50-£19.80

Open 15 Mar-Oct Last arrival 22.00hrs Last departure noon

A well-kept and pretty site built round a fishing lake, and accessed by a lake-lined drive. The individual pitches are sited in hedged enclosures for complete privacy, and the purpose-built toilet facilities are excellent. Seasonal touring pitches are available. A 4.5 acre site with 38 touring pitches, 6 hardstandings and 21 statics.

AA Pubs & Restaurants nearby: Dove Restaurant with Rooms, Alburgh 01986 788315

Fox & Goose Inn, Fressingfield 01379 586247

Leisure: △

Facilities: ❐☉ॐ✳❦ⓢ

Services: ❑◱▲❤①ᴴᴵ

Within 3 miles: ↓⤳✐ⓢ

Notes: ⊛ Library. Wi-fi

NORTHUMBERLAND

BAMBURGH — Map 21 NU13

Places to visit

Chillingham Wild Cattle Park, Chillingham, 01668 215250, www.chillinghamwildcattle.com

Great for kids: Bamburgh Castle, Bamburgh, 01668 214515, www.bamburghcastle.com

►►►► 75% Waren Caravan Park (NU155343)

GOLD

Waren Mill NE70 7EE
☎ 01668 214366 📄 01668 214224
e-mail: waren@meadowhead.co.uk
dir: *2m E of town. From A1 onto B1342 signed Bamburgh. Take unclass road past Waren Mill, signed Budle*

* 🚐 £13.50-£23.50 🚙 £13.50-£23.50
🅰 £13.50-£28

Open Apr-Oct Last arrival 20.00hrs Last departure noon

Attractive seaside site with footpath access to the beach, surrounded by a slightly sloping grassy embankment giving shelter to caravans. The park offers excellent facilities including several family bathrooms. There are also wooden wigwams to rent. A 4 acre site with 180 touring pitches, 24 hardstandings and 300 statics.

AA Pubs & Restaurants nearby: Olde Ship Inn, Seahouses 01665 720200

Blue Bell Hotel, Belford 01668 213543

Grays Restaurant, Waren House Hotel, Bamburgh 01668 214581

Leisure: 🏊 🅰 🎯
Facilities: 🛁 🚿 ☉ 🖙 🕭 🕭 🕓 🛒 🍴 🚻 🐕
Services: 🖭 🖥 🖴 🍴 🛢 🗑 🅃 🍽 🛒 🛒 🐾
Within 3 miles: ↥ 🎣 ◎ 🛒 🕓
Notes: 100 acres of private heathland. Wi-fi

►►► 71% Glororum Caravan Park (NU166334)

Glororum Farm NE69 7AW
☎ 01668 214457 📄 01688 214484
dir: *Exit A1 at junct with B1341 (Purdy's Lodge). In 3.5m left onto unclass road. Site 300yds on left*

🚐 🚙

Open Mar-end Oct Last arrival 18.00hrs Last departure noon

A pleasantly situated site where tourers have their own well-established facilities. The open countryside setting affords good views of Bamburgh Castle and surrounding farmland. A 6 acre site with 100 touring pitches and 150 statics.

AA Pubs & Restaurants nearby: Olde Ship Inn, Seahouses 01665 720200

Blue Bell Hotel, Belford 01668 213543

Grays Restaurant, Waren House Hotel, Bamburgh 01668 214581

Leisure: 🅰
Facilities: 🕭 ☉ 🖙 🚿 🕓 🕭 🍴 🚻 🐕
Services: 🖭 🖥 🖴 🛢 🗑 🅃 🐾
Within 3 miles: ↥ 🎣 🐎 ⌇ 🛒 🕓
Notes: No tents, pets must be kept on leads

BELLINGHAM — Map 21 NY88

Places to visit

Wallington House and Walled Gardens, Cambo, 01670 773600, www.nationaltrust.org.uk/main

►►►► 85% Bellingham Camping & Caravanning Club Site (NY835826)

Brown Rigg NE48 2JY
☎ 01434 220175 & 0845 130 7633
dir: *From A69 take A68 N. Then B6318 to Chollerford & B6320 to Bellingham. Pass Forestry Commission land, site 0.5m S of Bellingham*

🚐 £7.50-£9 🚙 £7.50-£9 🅰 £7.50-£9

Open 11 Mar-Oct Last arrival 20.00hrs Last departure noon

A beautiful and peaceful site set in the glorious Northumberland National Park. This is a perfect base for exploring this undiscovered part of England, and it is handily placed for visiting the beautiful Northumberland coast. This is an exceptionally well-managed park that continues to improve. There are four camping pods for hire. A 5 acre site with 64 touring pitches, 64 hardstandings.

AA Pubs & Restaurants nearby: Pheasant Inn, Falstone 01434 240382

Leisure: 🅰
Facilities: 🖙 🚿 🕭 🕓 🛒 🕭
Services: 🖭 🖥 🖴 🗑 🐾
Notes: Site gates closed 23.00hrs-07.00hrs. Wi-fi

BERWICK-UPON-TWEED — Map 21 NT95

Places to visit

Berwick-upon-Tweed Barracks, Berwick-upon-Tweed, 01289 304493, www.english-heritage.org.uk

Paxton House, Gallery and Country Park, Berwick-Upon-Tweed, 01289 386291, www.paxtonhouse.com

Great for kids: Norham Castle, Norham, 01289 382329, www.english-heritage.org.uk

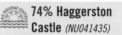 74% Haggerston Castle (NU041435)

GOLD

Beal TD15 2PA
☎ 01289 381333 📄 01289 381433
e-mail: sharon.lee@bourne-leisure.co.uk
dir: *On A1, 7m S of Berwick-upon-Tweed, site signed*

🚐 🚙

Open mid Mar-Oct (rs mid Mar-May & Sep-Oct some facilities may be reduced) Last arrival anytime Last departure 10.00hrs

A large holiday centre with a very well equipped touring park, offering comprehensive holiday activities. The entertainment complex contains amusements for the whole family, and there are several bars, an adventure playground, boating on the lake, a children's club, a 9-hole golf course, tennis courts, and various eating outlets. A 100 acre site with 150 touring pitches, 150 hardstandings and 1200 statics.

AA Pubs & Restaurants nearby: Blue Bell Hotel, Belford 01668 213543

Leisure: 🏊 🅰 🎾
Facilities: 🕭 ☉ 🚿 🕭 🛒 🚻 🐕
Services: 🖭 🖥 🖴 🛢 🅃 🍽 🛒
Within 3 miles: ↥ 🎣 ◎ 🛒 🕓
Notes: No tents. Wi-fi

see advert on opposite page

LEISURE: 🏊 Indoor swimming pool 🏊 Outdoor swimming pool 🅰 Children's playground 🎾 Tennis court 🎯 Games room 📺 Separate TV room ↥ 9/18 hole golf course 🚣 Boats for hire 🎬 Cinema 🎣 Fishing ◎ Mini golf 🏄 Watersports 🐎 Stables **FACILITIES:** 🛁 Bath 🚿 Shower ☉ Electric shaver 🖙 Hairdryer 🕭 Ice Pack Facility 🕭 Disabled facilities 🕓 Public telephone 🛒 Shop on site or within 200yds 🚐 Mobile shop (calls at least 5 days a week) 🍴 BBQ area 🚻 Picnic area 🐕 Dog exercise area

Regional Winner – AA North East of England Campsite of the Year 2011

PREMIER PARK

▶▶▶▶ **80% Ord House Country Park**

Best of British
GOLD

(NT982515)

East Ord TD15 2NS
☎ 01289 305288 📄 01289 330832
e-mail: enquiries@ordhouse.co.uk
dir: *On A1, Berwick bypass, turn off at 2nd rdbt at East Ord, follow 'Caravan' signs*

🚐 🚙 ⛺

Open all year Last arrival 23.00hrs Last dep noon

A very well run park set in the pleasant grounds of an 18th-century country house. Touring pitches are marked and well spaced, some of them fully-serviced. The very modern toilet facilities include family bath and shower suites, and first class disabled rooms. There is an outdoor leisure shop with a good range of camping and caravanning spares, as well as clothing and equipment, and an attractive licensed club selling bar meals. A 42 acre site with 79 touring pitches, 46 hardstandings and 255 statics.

AA Pubs & Restaurants nearby: Wheatsheaf at Swinton 01890 860257

Leisure: 🅰
Facilities: ➡🐾⊙♿✳️🌡️⚡🚿🍴🎣🐕
Services: 🔌🗑️🍺💧🧺🚽🍴🚚⛽
Within 3 miles: ↧≛🎿🏇🖋️⊙💰🚲
Notes: Crazy golf, table tennis. Wi-fi

▶▶ **78% Old Mill Caravan Site**

(NU055401)

West Kyloe Farm, Fenwick TD15 2PG
☎ 01289 381279 & 07971 411625
e-mail: teresamalley@westkyloe.demon.co.uk
dir: *Take B6353 off A1, 9m S of Berwick-upon-Tweed. Road signed to Lowick/Fenwick. Site 1.5m signed on left*

* 🚐 fr £15 🚙 fr £15 ⛺ fr £15

Open Etr-Oct Last arrival 19.00hrs Last departure 11.00hrs

Small, secluded site accessed through a farm complex, and overlooking a mill pond complete with resident ducks. Some pitches are in a walled garden, and the amenity block is simple but well kept. Delightful walks can be enjoyed on the 600-acre farm. Bed and breakfast accommodation and a holiday cottage are also available. A 2.5 acre site with 12 touring pitches.

AA Pubs & Restaurants nearby: Black Bull, Etal 01890 820200

Blue Bell Hotel, Belford 01668 213543

Facilities: 🐾⊙♿🐕
Services: 🔌🧺
Within 3 miles: 💰
Notes: 🚫 Dogs must be kept on leads when on site. Dish washing room

---

HEXHAM
Map 21 NY96

Places to visit

Vindolanda (Chesterholm), Bardon Mill, 01434 344277, www.vindolanda.com

Temple of Mithras, Hadrian's Wall, Carrawbrough, www.english-heritage.org.uk

Great for kids: Housesteads Roman Fort, Housesteads, 01434 344363, www.english-heritage.org.uk

---

▶▶▶ **65% Hexham Racecourse Caravan Site** *(NY919623)*

Hexham Racecourse NE46 2JP
☎ 01434 606847 & 606881 📄 01434 605814
e-mail: hexrace.caravan@uku.co.uk
dir: *From Hexham take B6305 signed Allendale/Alston. Left in 3m signed to racecourse. Site 1.5m on right*

* 🚐 £12-£15 🚙 £12-£15 ⛺ £12-£15

Open May-Sep Last arrival 20.00hrs Last dep noon

A part-level and part-sloping grassy site situated on a racecourse overlooking Hexhamshire Moors. The facilities are functional. A 4 acre site with 40 touring pitches.

AA Pubs & Restaurants nearby: Battlesteads Hotel & Restaurant, Hexham 01434 230209

Dipton Mill, Hexham 01434 606577

Leisure: 🅰🎣 **Facilities:** 🐾⊙♿✳️⊙🎣🐕
Services: 🔌🗑️🍺🧺🚚
Within 3 miles: ↧≛🎿🏇🖋️◎💰🚲

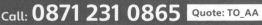

SERVICES: 🔌 Electric hook up 🧺 Launderette 🍺 Licensed bar ⛽ Calor Gas ⛽ Camping Gaz 🚽 Toilet fluid 🍴 Café/Restaurant 🍟 Fast Food/Takeaway 🔋 Battery charging 🍼 Baby care ⚙️ Motorvan service point **ABBREVIATIONS:** BH/bank hols-bank holidays Etr-Easter Whit-Whitsun dep-departure fr-from hrs-hours m-mile mdnt-midnight rdbt-roundabout rs-restricted service wk-week wknd-weekend 🚫 No credit cards 🚫 no dogs See page 7 for details of the AA Camping Card Scheme

NORTH SEATON — Map 21 NZ28

Places to visit

Woodhorn, Ashington, 01670 528080,
www.experiencewoodhorn.com

Morpeth Chantry Bagpipe Museum, Morpeth,
01670 500717, www.northumberland.gov.uk

71% Sandy Bay
(NZ302858)

NE63 9YD
☎ 0871 664 9764
e-mail: sandy.bay@park-resorts.com
dir: *From A1 at Seaton Burn take A19 signed
Tyne Tunnel. Then A189 signed Ashington,
approx 8m, at rdbt right onto B1334 towards
Newbiggin-by-the-Sea. Site on right*

Open Apr-Oct Last arrival anytime Last
departure noon

A beach-side holiday park on the outskirts of
the small village of North Seaton, within easy
reach of Newcastle. The site is handily placed
for exploring the magnificent coastline and
countryside of Northumberland, but for those
who do not wish to travel it offers the full
range of holiday centre attractions, both for
parents and children. 48 touring pitches and
396 statics.

Leisure: 🏊 🎢
Facilities: 🚿 🌂 📞 ⊙ 🖳
Services: 🚐 🖤 🍴 🛢 🍽 🚮
Within 3 miles: 🎣 🛒 🖳
Notes: Koi carp lake. Wi-fi

All the campsites in this guide are
inspected annually by a team of
experienced inspectors

NOTTINGHAMSHIRE

MANSFIELD — Map 16 SK56

Places to visit

Sherwood Forest Country Park and Visitor
Centre, Edwinstowe, 01623 823202,
www.nottinghamshire.gov.uk/sherwoodforestcp

The Tales of Robin Hood, Nottingham,
0115 948 3284, www.robinhood.uk.com

Great for kids: Vina Cooke Museum of Dolls
and Bygone Childhood, Newark-on-Trent,
01636 821364, www.vinasdolls.co.uk

AA CAMPING CARD SITE

NEW ►►► 70% Tall Trees Park Homes (SK551626)

Old Mill Ln, Forest Town NG19 0JP
☎ 01623 626503
e-mail: enquiries@jamesparkhomes.com
dir: *A60 from Mansfield towards Worksop. After
1m turn right at lights into Old Mill Lane. Site
approx 0.5m on left*

* 🚐 fr £7.50 🚐 fr £7.50 ⛺ fr £7.50

Open all year Last arrival anytime

A very pleasant park situated just on the outskirts
of Mansfield and within easy walking distance of
shops and restaurants. It is surrounded on three
sides by trees and shrubbery, and securely set at
the back of the residential park. At the time of our
inspection the small touring area was undergoing
a major redevelopment, with the addition of a new
facilities block, a fishing lake to the rear of the
site and an extra grassed area to give more space
for caravans and tents. A 3 acre site with 15
touring pitches, 15 hardstandings.

AA Pubs & Restaurants nearby: Forest Lodge,
Edwinstowe 01623 824443

Fox & Hounds, Blidworth Bottoms 01623 792383

Facilities: ♿ **Services:** 🚐
Notes: 🐕

NEWARK

See Southwell

RADCLIFFE ON TRENT — Map 11 SK63

Places to visit

Nottingham Castle Museum and Art Gallery,
Nottingham, 0115 915 3700,
www.nottingham.gov.uk/nottinghamcastle

Wollaton Hall, Gardens and Park,
Nottingham, 0115 915 3900,
www.nottingham.gov.uk/wollatonhall

Great for kids: Museum of Nottingham Life,
Nottingham, 0115 915 3640,
www.nottingham.gov.uk/nottinghamlife

►►► 75% Thornton's Holt Camping Park (SK638377)

Stragglethorpe Rd, Stragglethorpe NG12 2JZ
☎ 0115 933 2125 & 933 4204
🖷 0115 933 3318
e-mail: camping@thorntons-holt.co.uk
web: www.thorntons-holt.co.uk
dir: *Take A52, 3m E of Nottingham. Turn S at lights
towards Cropwell Bishop. Site 0.5m on left. Or A46
SE of Nottingham. N at lights. Site 2.5m on right*

* 🚐 £15-£18 🚐 £15-£18 ⛺ £12-£18

Open Apr-6 Nov Last arrival 20.00hrs Last dep noon

A well-run family site in former meadowland, with
pitches located among young trees and bushes for
a rural atmosphere and outlook. The toilets are
housed in converted farm buildings, and an indoor
swimming pool is a popular attraction. A 13 acre
site with 155 touring pitches, 35 hardstandings.

AA Pubs & Restaurants nearby: The Chesterfield,
Bingham 01949 837342

Leisure: 🏊 🎢 🎯
Facilities: 🚿 ⊙ 📞 ✳ ♿ ⊙ 🖳 🐕
Services: 🚐 🖤 🛢 🖉 🚻 🛒 🚮
Within 3 miles: 🎿 🍴 🎣 ⛳ 🛒 🖳 ⛺
Notes: Noise curfew at 22.00hrs

SOUTHWELL Map 17 SK65

Places to visit

Nottingham Industrial Museum, Nottingham, 0115 915 3900, www.wollatonhall.org.uk

Galleries of Justice, Nottingham, 0115 952 0555, www.galleriesofjustice.org.uk

►►► 76% New Hall Farm Touring Park (SK660550)

New Hall Farm, New Hall Ln NG22 8BS
☎ 01623 883041 📱 01623 883041
e-mail: enquiries@newhallfarm.co.uk
dir: From A614 at White Post Modern Farm Centre, turn E signed Southwell. Immediately after Edingley turn S into New Hall Ln to site (0.5m)

* 🚐 £10-£16 🚏 £10-£16 ⛺ £8-£16

Open Mar-Oct Last arrival 21.00hrs Last dep 13.00hrs

A park on a working stock farm with the elevated pitching area enjoying outstanding panoramic views. It is within a short drive of medieval Newark and Sherwood Forest. A log cabin viewing gantry offers a place to relax and take in the spectacular views. A 2.5 acre site with 25 touring pitches, 5 hardstandings.

AA Pubs & Restaurants nearby: Waggon & Horses, Hallam 01636 813109

Tom Browns Brasserie, Gunthorpe 0115 966 3642

Facilities: 🐕☺✳🍴🚻 **Services:** 🔌🚿🔋
Within 3 miles: 🎣🚲🛒🎯

Notes: Adults only. 🐕 Dogs must be on leads. Log cabin viewing gantry

TEVERSAL Map 16 SK46

Places to visit

Sherwood Forest Country Park and Visitor Centre, Edwinstowe, 01623 823202, www.nottinghamshire.gov.uk/sherwoodforestcp

The Tales of Robin Hood, Nottingham, 0115 948 3284, www.robinhood.uk.com

PREMIER PARK

►►►►► 85% Teversal Camping & Caravanning Club Site (SK472615)

Silverhill Ln NG17 3JJ
☎ 01623 551838
dir: M1 junct 28 onto A38 towards Mansfield. Left at lights onto B6027. At top of hill straight over at lights & left at Peacock Hotel. Right onto B6014, left at Craven Arms, site on left

* 🚐 £22-£25 🚏 £22-£25 ⛺ £22-£25

Open all year Last arrival 20.00hrs Last departure noon

A top notch park with excellent purpose-built facilities and innovative, hands-on owners. Each pitch is spacious, the excellent toilet facilities are state-of-art, and there are views of and access to the countryside and nearby Silverhill Community Woods. The attention to detail and all-round quality are truly exceptional. A 6 acre site with 126 touring pitches, 92 hardstandings and 1 static.

Leisure: 🎱
Facilities: 🐕☺🍴✳♿🕐🚿
Services: 🔌🚿🔋🚮🚽🔋♻
Within 3 miles: 🚴🎣🛒🎯

Notes: Site gates closed 23.00hrs-07.00hrs. Car hire available. Wi-fi

TUXFORD Map 17 SK77

Places to visit

Museum of Lincolnshire Life, Lincoln, 01522 528448, www.lincolnshire.gov.uk/museumoflincolnshirelife

Great for kids: Lincoln Castle, Lincoln, 01522 511068, www.lincolnshire.gov.uk/lincolncastle

AA CAMPING CARD SITE

►►► 80% Orchard Park Touring Caravan & Camping Park (SK754708)

Marnham Rd NG22 0PY
☎ 01777 870228 📱 01777 870320
e-mail: info@orchardcaravanpark.co.uk
dir: Exit A1 at Tuxford onto A6075 towards Lincoln. 0.5m, right into Marnham Rd. Site 0.75m on right

🚐 £17-£20 🚏 £17-£20 ⛺ £17-£20

Open mid Mar-Oct Last arrival mdnt Last departure 18.00hrs

A rural site set in an old fruit orchard with spacious pitches arranged in small groups separated by shrubs; many of the pitches are served with water and electricity. A network of grass pathways and picnic clearings have been created in a woodland area, and there's a superb adventure playground. A 7 acre site with 60 touring pitches, 30 hardstandings.

AA Pubs & Restaurants nearby: Mussel & Crab, Tuxford 01777 870491

Robin Hood Inn, Elkesley 01777 838259

Leisure: 🎱
Facilities: 🐕☺🍴✳♿🕐🚿🚻🚌🛫
Services: 🔌🚿🔋🚮🚽🔋
Within 3 miles: 🚲🛒🎯

Notes: Family shower room. Wi-fi

WORKSOP Map 16 SK57

Places to visit

Clumber Park, Worksop, 01909 476592, www.nationaltrust.org.uk

AA CAMPING CARD SITE

►►► 78% Riverside Caravan Park (SK582790)

Central Av S80 1ER
☎ 01909 474118
dir: From A57 E of town, take B6040 signed Town Centre at rdbt. Follow international camping sign to site

* 🚐 £16-£18 🚏 £16-£18 ⛺ £16-£18

Open all year Last arrival 18.00hrs Last departure noon

A very well maintained park within the attractive market town of Worksop and next door to the cricket and bowls club where Riverside customers are made welcome. This is an ideal park for those wishing to be within walking distance of all amenities yet also within a 10-minute car journey of the extensive Clumber Park and numerous good garden centres. The towpath of the adjacent Chesterfield Canal provides excellent walking opportunities. A 4 acre site with 60 touring pitches, 59 hardstandings.

Facilities: 🐕☺✳🚿 **Services:** 🔌🔋🚮🔋♻
Within 3 miles: 🚴🎳🚲🛒🎯

Notes: Dogs must be kept on leads, no bikes around reception or in toilet block

OXFORDSHIRE

See Walk 9 in the Walks & Cycle Rides section at the end of the book

BANBURY
Map 11 SP44

Places to visit

Banbury Museum, Banbury, 01295 753752, www.cherwell.gov.uk/banburymuseum

Great for kids: Deddington Castle, Deddington, www.english-heritage.org.uk

▶▶▶▶ 83% Barnstones Caravan & Camping Site (SP455454)

Great Bourton OX17 1QU
☎ 01295 750289
dir: *Take A423 from Banbury signed Southam. In 3m turn right signed Gt Bourton/Cropredy, site 100yds on right*

⊞ £12–£14 ⊟ £12–£14 ▲ £7–£10

Open all year

A popular, neatly laid-out site with plenty of hardstandings, some fully serviced pitches, a smart up-to-date toilet block, and excellent rally facilities. Well run by a very personable owner, this is an excellent value park. A 3 acre site with 49 touring pitches, 44 hardstandings.

AA Pubs & Restaurants nearby: Ye Olde Reindeer Inn, Banbury 01295 264031

Wykham Arms, Banbury 01295 788808

Saye and Sele Arms, Broughton 01295 263348

Leisure: ⚠
Facilities: �🅟⊙✻🅕⚙🖳🎋♂
Services: 🖳🅔🍴🖤▬🚽
Within 3 miles: 🕹⚡🅗🖉◎♨🅑🅕Ｕ
Notes: ☺

▶▶▶▶ 83% Bo Peep Farm Caravan Park (SP481348)

Bo Peep Farm, Aynho Rd, Adderbury OX17 3NP
☎ 01295 810605 🖷 01295 810605
e-mail: warden@bo-peep.co.uk
dir: *1m E of Adderbury & A4260, on B4100 (Aynho road)*

⊞ ⊟ ▲

Open Mar-Oct Last arrival 20.00hrs Last departure noon

A delightful park with good views and a spacious feel. Four well laid out camping areas including two with hardstandings and a separate tent field are all planted with maturing shrubs and trees. The two facility blocks are constructed in attractive Cotswold stone. Unusually there is a bay in which you can clean your caravan or motorhome. There are four miles of on-site walks including through woods and on the river bank. A 13 acre site with 104 touring pitches.

AA Pubs & Restaurants nearby: Ye Olde Reindeer Inn, Banbury 01295 264031

Wykham Arms, Banbury 01295 788808

Saye and Sele Arms, Broughton 01295 263348

Facilities: 🅟⊙🅕✻⚙⚙🖳🎋♂
Services: 🖳🅔🍴🖤▬🚽
Within 3 miles: 🕹🖉🅑
Notes: Wi-fi

BLETCHINGDON
Map 11 SP51

Places to visit

Rousham House, Rousham, 01869 347110, www.rousham.org

Museum of the History of Science, Oxford, 01865 277280, www.mhs.ox.ac.uk

Great for kids: Oxford Museum of Natural History, Oxford, 01865 272950, www.oum.ox.ac.uk

▶▶▶▶ 80% Diamond Farm Caravan & Camping Park (SP513170)

Islip Rd OX5 3DR
☎ 01869 350909
e-mail: warden@diamondpark.co.uk
dir: *From M40 junct 9 onto A34 S for 3m, then B4027 to Bletchingdon. Site 1m on left*

⊞ ⊟ ▲

Open all year Last arrival dusk Last departure 11.00hrs

A well-run, quiet rural site in good level surroundings, and ideal for touring the Cotswolds, situated seven miles north of Oxford in the heart of the Thames Valley. This popular park has excellent facilities, and offers a heated outdoor swimming pool and a games room for children. A 3 acre site with 37 touring pitches, 13 hardstandings.

AA Pubs & Restaurants nearby: King's Head, Woodstock 01993 812164

Feathers Hotel, Woodstock 01993 812291

Leisure: ⚌ ⚠ ⚌
Facilities: ⛟🅟⊙🅕✻⚙🅑🖳🎋
Services: 🖳🅔🍴🖤⚙🅣▬🚽
Within 3 miles: 🕹🖉🅑
Notes: ☺ Wi-fi

▶▶▶▶ 80% Greenhill Leisure Park (SP488178)

Greenhill Farm, Station Rd OX5 3BQ
☎ 01869 351600 🖷 01869 350918
e-mail: info@greenhill-leisure-park.co.uk
web: www.greenhill-leisure-park.co.uk
dir: *M40 junct 9, A34 south for 3m. Take B4027 to Bletchingdon. Site 0.5m after village on left*

⊞ £12–£15 ⊟ £12–£15 ▲ £12–£15

Open all year (rs Oct-Mar no dogs, shop & games room closed) Last arrival 21.00 hrs (20.00 hrs in winter) Last departure noon

An all-year round park set in open countryside near the village of Bletchingdon. Fishing is available in the nearby river or in the parks two well stocked lakes. Pitches are very spacious and the park is very family orientated and in keeping with the owner's theme of 'Where fun meets the countryside'. The facilities are also very good. A 7 acre site with 61 touring pitches, 25 hardstandings.

AA Pubs & Restaurants nearby: King's Head, Woodstock 01993 812164

Feathers Hotel, Woodstock 01993 812291

Leisure: ⚠ ⚌
Facilities: 🅟⊙🅕✻⚙🅑🖳♂
Services: 🖳🅔🖤⚙🅣▬
Within 3 miles: 🕹🖉🅑
Notes: No camp fires. Pets corner. Wi-fi

CHARLBURY — Map 11 SP31

Places to visit

Blenheim Palace, Woodstock, 0800 849 6500, www.blenheimpalace.com

Minister Lovell Hall and Dovecote, Minister Lovell, www.english-heritage.org.uk

Great for kids: Cogges Manor Farm Museum, Witney, 01993 772602, www.cogges.org

▶▶▶▶ 84% *Cotswold View Touring Park* (SP365210)

Enstone Rd OX7 3JH
☎ 01608 810314 📄 01608 811891
e-mail: bookings@gfwiddows.co.uk
dir: *From A44 in Enstone take B4022 towards Charlbury. Follow site signs. Site 1m from Charlbury.*

🚐 🚉 Å

Open Etr or Apr-Oct Last arrival 21.00hrs Last departure noon

A good Cotswold site, well screened and with attractive views across the countryside. The toilet facilities include fully-equipped family rooms and bathrooms, and there are spacious, sheltered pitches, some with hardstandings. Breakfasts and takeaway food are available from the shop. The site has ten camping pods available for hire. Perfect location for exploring the Cotswolds and anyone heading for the Charlbury Music Festival. A 10 acre site with 125 touring pitches.

AA Pubs & Restaurants nearby: Bull Inn, Charlbury 01608 810689

Crown Inn, Church Enstone 01608 677262

Leisure: ⚙ 🎱 🔍
Facilities: 🚿 🌂 ⊙ 🅿 ✳ ⚿ ⓒ 📶 🎂 🛒 🐾
Services: 🔌 🔟 🛢 ⚿ 🅃 🎂 ⚡
Within 3 miles: 🎣 🏵 🛢
Notes: Off licence, skittle alley, chess, boules

HENLEY-ON-THAMES

Places to visit

Greys Court, Henley-on-Thames, 01491 628529, www.nationaltrust.org.uk,

River and Rowing Museum, Henley-on-Thames, 01491 415600, www.rrm.co.uk

Great for kids: LEGOLAND Windsor, Windsor www.legoland.co.uk

HENLEY-ON-THAMES — Map 5 SU78

PREMIER PARK

AA CAMPING CARD SITE

▶▶▶▶▶ 80% Swiss Farm Touring & Camping (SU759837)

Marlow Rd RG9 2HY
☎ 01491 573419
e-mail: enquiries@swissfarmcamping.co.uk
web: www.swissfarmcamping.co.uk
dir: *On A4155, N of Henley, next left after rugby club, towards Marlow*

* 🚐 £11-£23 🚉 £11-£23 Å £11-£17.50

Open Mar-Oct Last arrival 21.00hrs Last departure noon

A conveniently-located site within a few minutes' walk of Henley, and ideal for those visiting Henley during Regatta Week. Pitches are spacious and there are fully serviced pitches available. Facilities are modern, newly refurbished and are very clean. There is a well-stocked fishing lake plus a very nice and popular outdoor pool. For those who like walking there are some lovely walks along the nearby River Thames. A 6 acre site with 140 touring pitches, 20 hardstandings and 6 statics.

AA Pubs & Restaurants nearby: Little Angel, Henley-on-Thames 01491 411008

Cherry Tree Inn, Henley-on-Thames 01491 680430

Five Horseshoes, Henley-on-Thames 01491 641282

Leisure: 🚣 ⚙
Facilities: 🌂 ⊙ 🅿 ✳ ⚿ ⓒ
Services: 🔌 🔟 🎃 🛢 ⚿ 🅃
Within 3 miles: ⚄ 🏵 🎟 🎣 🛢
Notes: No groups. No dogs during high season. Wi-fi

STANDLAKE — Map 5 SP30

Places to visit

Buscot Park, Buscot, 01367 240786, www.buscotpark.com

Great for kids: Cotswolds Wildlife Park, Burford, 01993 823006, www.cotswoldwildlifepark.co.uk

PREMIER PARK

AA CAMPING CARD SITE

▶▶▶▶▶ 95% Lincoln Farm Park Oxfordshire (SP395028)

Best of British

High St OX29 7RH
☎ 01865 300239 📄 01865 300127
e-mail: info@lincolnfarmpark.co.uk
web: www.lincolnfarmpark.co.uk
dir: *In village of Standlake off A415 between Abingdon & Witney, 5m SE of Witney*

* 🚐 £15.95-£24.95 🚉 £15.95-£24.95
Å £14.95-£24.95

Open Feb-Nov Last arrival 20.00hrs Last dep noon

An attractively landscaped park in a quiet village setting, with superb facilities and a high standard of maintenance. Family rooms, fully serviced pitches, two indoor swimming pools and a fully-equipped gym are part of the comprehensive amenities. Overall, an excellent top quality park and the perfect base for visiting the Oxfordshire area and the Cotswolds. A warm welcome is assured from the friendly staff. A 9 acre site with 90 touring pitches, 75 hardstandings.

AA Pubs & Restaurants nearby: Bear & Ragged Staff, Cumnor 01865 862329

The Vine Inn, Cumnor 01865 862567

Leisure: 🏊 ⚙ 🔍
Facilities: 🚿 🌂 ⊙ 🅿 ✳ ⚿ ⓒ 📶 🛒 🐾
Services: 🔌 🔟 🛢 ⚿ 🅃 🎂 ⚡
Within 3 miles: ⚄ 🏵 🎣 ⚓ 🛢 ⛳
Notes: No gazebos, dogs must be kept on leads, no noise after 23.00hrs. Putting green, outdoor chess. Wi-fi

UPPER HEYFORD — Map 11 SP42

AA CAMPING CARD SITE

NEW ▶▶▶ 78% Heyford Leys Camping Park (SP518256)

Camp Rd OX25 5LX
☎ 01869 232048
e-mail: heyfordleys@aol.com
dir: *M40 junct 10 take B430 towards Middleton Stoney. Right after 1.5m marked The Heyford, follow brown signs to site*

Open all year Last arrival 22.00hrs Last departure 11.00hrs

This small peaceful park near the Cherwell Valley and the village of Upper Heyford is well positioned for visiting nearby Bicester, Oxford and Banbury, as well as being about a 15-minute drive from Silverstone. The facilities are very clean and guests will be assured of a warm welcome. A small fishing lake is also available to customers. A 5 acre site with 25 touring pitches, 5 hardstandings.

Facilities: ⚫☺🅿✳🚻🐕
Services: ⚫🌀🅃🍽
Within 3 miles: 🎣✈⚓🛒🔥
Notes: No groups, no noise after 20.00hrs. Wi-fi

For full details of the pennant rating scheme see pages 10 & 11

Remember that prices and opening times are liable to change within the currency of this guide. It is always best to phone in advance

RUTLAND

GREETHAM — Map 11 SK91

Places to visit

Rutland County Museum and Visitor Centre, Oakham, 01572 758440, www.rutland.gov.uk/museum

Great for kids: Oakham Castle, Oakham, 01572 758440, www.rutland.gov.uk/castle

▶▶▶▶ 80% *Rutland Caravan & Camping* (SK925148)

Park Ln LE15 7FN
☎ 01572 813520
e-mail: info@rutlandcaravanandcamping.co.uk
dir: *From A1 onto B668 towards Greetham. Before Greetham turn right at x-rds, 2nd left to site*

Open all year

This pretty caravan park, built to a high specification and surrounded by well-planted banks, continues to improve due to the enthusiasm and vision of its owner. From the spacious reception and the innovative play area to the newly upgraded toilet block, everything is of a very high standard. The spacious grassy site is close to the Viking Way and other footpath networks, and well sited for visiting Rutland Water and the many picturesque villages in the area. A 5 acre site with 130 touring pitches, 65 hardstandings.

AA Pubs & Restaurants nearby: Ram Jam Inn, Stretton 01780 410776

Jackson Stops Inn, Stretton 01780 410237

Olive Branch, Clipsham 01780 410355

Leisure: 🄰
Facilities: ⚫☺🅿✳🅰🚻🐕
Services: ⚫🅾🔒🌀🅃🔽
Within 3 miles: 🎣✈⚓◎🛥🔥U
Notes: Wi-fi

WING — Map 11 SK80

Places to visit

Lyddingdon Bede House, Lyddingdon, 01572 822438, www.english-heritage.org.uk

Great for kids: Oakham Castle, Oakham, 01572 758440, www.rutland.gov.uk/castle

▶▶▶ 70% Wing Lakes Caravan & Camping (SK892031)

Wing Hall LE15 8RY
☎ 01572 737283 & 737090
e-mail: winghall1891@aol.com
dir: *From A1 take A47 towards Leicester, 14m, follow Morcott signs. In Morcott follow Wing signs. 2.5m, follow site signs*

Open all year Last arrival 21.00hrs Last departure noon

A deeply tranquil and rural park set in the grounds of an old manor house. The four grassy fields with attractive borders of mixed, mature deciduous trees have exceptional views across the Rutland countryside and are within one mile of Rutland Water. There's a good shop which specialises in locally sourced produce, a licensed café, and there are new high quality showers and a fully-equipped laundry. Children and tents are very welcome in a safe environment where there is space to roam. An 11 acre site with 250 touring pitches, 4 hardstandings.

AA Pubs & Restaurants nearby: Kings Arms, Wing 01572 737634

Old Pheasant, Glaston 01572 822326

Facilities: ⚫🅿✳🛒🐕
Services: ⚫🔒
Within 3 miles: 🎣✈⚓🛥◎🛒🔥U
Notes: 🚗 Farm shop, coarse fishing. Wi-fi

SHROPSHIRE

BRIDGNORTH — Map 10 SO79

Places to visit

Benthall Hall, Benthall, 01952 882159, www.nationaltrust.org.uk/main/w-benthallhall

Great for kids: Dudmaston Estate, Quatt, 01746 780866, www.nationaltrust.org.uk/main/w-dudmaston

---

PREMIER PARK

▶▶▶▶▶ 86% Stanmore Hall Touring Park (SO742923)

Stourbridge Rd WV15 6DT
☎ 01746 761761 ▤ 01746 768069
e-mail: stanmore@morris-leisure
dir: 2m E of Bridgnorth on A458

* 🚐 £19.10-£24.30 🚑 £19.10-£24.30
🏕 £19.10-£24.30

Open all year Last arrival 20.00hrs Last departure noon

An excellent park in peaceful surroundings offering outstanding facilities. The pitches, many fully serviced, are arranged around the lake close to Stanmore Hall, home of the Midland Motor Museum. Handy for touring Ironbridge and the Severn Valley Railway, while Bridgnorth itself is an attractive old market town. A 12.5 acre site with 131 touring pitches, 53 hardstandings.

AA Pubs & Restaurants nearby: Halfway House Inn, Eardington 01746 762670

Pheasant Inn, Bridgnorth 01746 762260

Leisure: ⚑
Facilities: ⋔☺🅿✳🅱☾🖨🗚🥅
Services: 🔌🅶🅰🖉🅃🖴↯
Within 3 miles: ↨✝🎠🅟🖴🅶◡
Notes: Max of 2 dogs

CRAVEN ARMS

Places to visit

Stokesay Castle, Stokesay, 01588 672544, www.english-heritage.org.uk

Great for kids: Ludlow Castle, Ludlow, 01584 873355, www.ludlowcastle.com

---

CRAVEN ARMS — Map 9 SO48

▶▶ 85% Wayside Camping and Caravan Park (SO399816)

Aston on Clun SY7 8EF
☎ 01588 660218
e-mail: waysidecamping@hotmail.com
dir: From Craven Arms on A49, W onto B4368 (Clun road) towards Clun Valley. Site approx 2m on right just before Aston-on-Clun

* 🚐 £12-£14 🚑 £12-£14 🏕 £10-£12

Open Apr-Oct

A peaceful park with lovely views, close to excellent local walks and many places of interest. The modern toilet facilities provide a good level of comfort, and there are several electric hook-ups. You are assured of a warm welcome by the helpful owner. A 2.5 acre site with 20 touring pitches, 2 hardstandings and 1 static.

AA Pubs & Restaurants nearby: Sun Inn, Corfton 01584 861239

The Plough, Winstanstow 01588 673251

Facilities: ⋔☺🅿✳🅱 **Services:** 🔌🅰🖴↯
Within 3 miles: ↨🅟🖴🅶

Notes: ⊗ Adults only on Bank Holidays. Only 1 dog per unit. Seasonal organic vegetables for sale

---

ELLESMERE

See Lyneal

HUGHLEY — Map 10 SO59

Places to visit

Old Owestry Hill Fort, Owestry, www.english-heritage.org.uk

Great for kids: Hoo Farm Animal Kingdom, Telford, 01952 677917, www.hoofarm.com

---

AA CAMPING CARD SITE

▶▶▶ 77% Mill Farm Holiday Park (SO564979)

SY5 6NT
☎ 01746 785208
e-mail: mail@millfarmcaravanpark.co.uk
dir: On unclass road off B4371 through Hughley, 3m SW of Much Wenlock, 11m SW of Church Stretton

🚐 🚑 🏕

Open Mar-Jan Last arrival 20.00hrs Last departure noon

A well-established farm site set in meadowland adjacent to river, with mature trees and bushes providing screening, and situated below Wenlock Edge. A 20 acre site with 60 touring pitches and 90 statics.

AA Pubs & Restaurants nearby: Wenlock Edge Inn, Much Wenlock 01746 785678

George & Dragon, Much Wenlock 01952 727312

Talbot inn, Much Wenlock 01952 727077

Longville Arms, Longville in the Dale 01694 771206

Facilities: ⋔☺🅿✳☾🗚🥅🖴
Services: 🔌🅶🅰🖉🖴 **Within 3 miles:** 🅟🖴◡
Notes: Site best suited for adults. Fishing, horse riding

LYNEAL (NEAR ELLESMERE) — Map 15 SJ43

Places to visit

Old Oswestry Hill Fort, Owestry, www.english-heritage.org.uk

Great for kids: Hawkstone Historic Park and Follies, Weston-Under-Redcast, 01948 841700, www.principal-hayley.co.uk

---

▶▶▶▶ 81% Fernwood Caravan Park (SJ445346)

SY12 0QF
☎ 01948 710221 ▤ 01948 710324
e-mail: enquiries@fernwoodpark.co.uk
dir: From A495 in Welshampton take B5063, over canal bridge, turn right as signed

* 🚐 £20-£25.50 🚑 £20-£25.50

Open Mar-Nov (rs Apr-Oct shop open) Last arrival 21.00hrs Last departure 17.00hrs

A peaceful park set in wooded countryside, with a screened, tree-lined touring area and coarse fishing lake. The approach is past colourful flowerbeds, and the static area which is tastefully arranged around an attractive children's playing area. There is a small child-free touring area for those wanting complete relaxation, and the park has 20 acres of woodland walks. A 26 acre site with 60 touring pitches, 8 hardstandings and 165 statics.

Leisure: ⚑
Facilities: ⋔☺🅿✳🅱☾🖨🥅
Services: 🔌🅶🅰🅃↯
Within 3 miles: ✝🅟🖴🅶

MINSTERLEY
Map 15 SJ30

Places to visit
Powis Castle and Garden, Welshpool, 01938 551920, www.nationaltrust.org.uk

Great for kids: Shrewsbury Castle and Shropshire Regimental Museum, Shrewsbury, 01743 358516, www.shrewsburymuseums.com

►► 92% The Old School Caravan Park
(SO322977)

Shelve SY5 0JQ
☎ 01588 650410 📄 01588 650410
dir: 6.5m SW of Minsterley on A488, site on left 2m after village sign for Hope

* 🚐 £15-£18.50 🚛 £15-£18.50 ▲ £15-£18.50

Open Mar-Jan Last arrival 21.00hrs Last departure 10.30hrs

Situated in the Shropshire hills with many excellent walks direct from the site, as well as being close to many cycle trails. There's also a shooting range and leisure centre within six miles. Near Snailbreach Mine, one of the most complete disused mineral mines in the country, and just a 45-minute drive from Ironbridge. This is a really beautiful small park with excellent facilities. A 1.5 acre site with 22 touring pitches, 8 hardstandings.

AA Pubs & Restaurants nearby: Sun Inn, Marton 01938 561211

Lowfield Inn, Marton 01743 891313

Facilities: 🖍⊙⚫✳⚫🚿🐕
Services: 🚐🛒
Within 3 miles: 🎣🛍️⟲
Notes: ⊘ No ball games. TV aerial connection

SHREWSBURY

Places to visit
Attingham Park, Atcham, 01743 708123, www.nationaltrust.org.uk/attinghampark

Great for kids: Wroxeter Roman City, Wroxeter, 01743 761330, www.english-heritage.org.uk

SHREWSBURY
Map 15 SJ41

PREMIER PARK

AA CAMPING CARD SITE

►►►►► 88% Beaconsfield Farm Caravan Park
(SJ522189)

Best of British

Battlefield SY4 4AA
☎ 01939 210370 & 210399 📄 01939 210349
e-mail: mail@beaconsfield-farm.co.uk
web: www.beaconsfield-farm.co.uk
dir: At Hadnall, 1.5m NE of Shrewsbury. Follow sign for Astley off A49

* 🚐 £18-£22 🚛 £21-£22

Open all year Last arrival 19.00hrs Last departure noon

A purpose-built family-run park on farmland in open countryside. This pleasant park offers quality in every area, including superior toilets, heated indoor swimming pool, luxury lodges for hire, and attractive landscaping. Fly and coarse fishing are available from the park's own fishing lake and The Bothy restaurant is excellent. Car hire is now available direct from the site, and there's a steam room, plus free Wi-fi. 12 luxury lodges are available for hire or sale plus there are seasonal touring pitches. Only adults over 21 years are accepted. A 16 acre site with 60 touring pitches, 50 hardstandings and 35 statics.

AA Pubs & Restaurants nearby: The Armoury, Shrewsbury 01743 340525

Plume of Feathers, Shrewsbury 01952 727360

Mytton & Mermaid, Shrewsbury 01743 761220

Leisure: 🏊
Facilities: 🖍⊙⚫✳⚫🚿🐕
Services: 🚐🛒🍴↯
Within 3 miles: 🎣🎣📍⊚🛍️🛒
Notes: Adults only. Wi-fi

PREMIER PARK

►►►►► 86% Oxon Hall Touring Park
(SJ455138)

Best of British

Welshpool Rd SY3 5FB
☎ 01743 340868 📄 01743 340869
e-mail: oxon@morris-leisure.co.uk
dir: Exit A5 (ring road) at junct with A458. Site shares entrance with 'Oxon Park & Ride'

🚐🚛▲

Open all year Last arrival 21.00hrs

A delightful park with quality facilities, and a choice of grass and fully-serviced pitches. A warm welcome is assured from the friendly staff. An adults-only section proves very popular, and there is an inviting patio area next to reception and the shop, overlooking a small lake. This site is ideally located for visiting Shrewsbury and the surrounding countryside, and the site also benefits from the Oxon Park & Ride, a short walk through the park. A 15 acre site with 124 touring pitches, 72 hardstandings and 42 statics.

AA Pubs & Restaurants nearby: The Armoury, Shrewsbury 01743 340525

Plume of Feathers, Shrewsbury 01952 727360

Mytton & Mermaid, Shrewsbury 01743 761220

Leisure: 🅰
Facilities: 🖍⊙⚫✳⚫🚿🛒🐕
Services: 🚐🛒🍴↯
Within 3 miles: 🎣🎣📍🛍️🛒⟲

TELFORD
Map 10 SJ60

Places to visit

Lilleshall Abbey, Lilleshall, 0121 625 6820, www.english-heritage.org.uk

Ironbridge Gorge Museums, Ironbridge, 01952 884391, www.ironbridge.org.uk

PREMIER PARK

►►►►► 79% *Severn Gorge Park*
(SJ705051)

Bridgnorth Rd, Tweedale TF7 4JB
☎ 01952 684789   ▤ 01952 587299
e-mail: info@severngorgepark.co.uk
dir: *Signed off A442, 1m S of Telford*

🚐 🚏

Open all year Last arrival 22.00hrs Last departure 18.00hrs

A very pleasant wooded site in the heart of Telford, well-screened and well-maintained. The sanitary facilities are fresh and immaculate, and landscaping of the grounds is carefully managed. Although the touring section is small, this is a really delightful park to stay on, and it is also well positioned for visiting nearby Ironbridge and its museums. A 6 acre site with 10 touring pitches, 10 hardstandings and 120 statics.

AA Pubs & Restaurants nearby: All Nations Inn, Madeley 01952 585747

New Inn, Madeley 01952 601018

Facilities: ⓝ⊙🅿☀️♿🐾
Services: 🔌🚿🔥⌀🍽️🔥⚡
Within 3 miles: 🎣🏇🐾◎🏧🎯🏊
Notes: Adults only. Well behaved dogs only

WEM
Map 15 SJ52

Places to visit

Hawkstone Historic Park and Follies, Weston-under-Redcastle, 01948 841700, www.principal-hayley.co.uk

Attingham Park, Atcham, 01743 708123, www.nationaltrust.org.uk/attinghampark

Great for kids: Shrewsbury Castle and Shropshire Regimental Museum, Shrewsbury, 01743 358516, www.shrewsburymuseums.com

AA CAMPING CARD SITE

►►► 78% Lower Lacon Caravan Park
(SJ534304)

SY4 5RP
☎ 01939 232376   ▤ 01939 233606
e-mail: info@llcp.co.uk
web: www.llcp.co.uk
dir: *Take A49 to B5065. Site 3m on right*

* 🚐 £18-£28 🚏 £18-£28 ▲ £18-£28

Open Apr-Oct (rs Nov-Mar club wknds only, toilets closed if frost) Last arrival 20.00hrs Last departure 16.00hrs

A large, spacious park with lively club facilities and an entertainments barn, set safely away from the main road. The park is particularly suited to families, with an outdoor swimming pool and farm animals. A 52 acre site with 270 touring pitches, 30 hardstandings and 50 statics.

AA Pubs & Restaurants nearby: Burlton Inn, Burlton 01939 270284

Leisure: 🏊🅰️🎣🏓
Facilities: 🍼ⓝ⊙🅿☀️♿🕐🏧🐾
Services: 🔌🚿🔥🔥⌀🍽️🍴⚡
Within 3 miles: 🎣🐾◎🏧🎯
Notes: No skateboards, no commercial vehicles Crazy golf

WENTNOR
Map 15 SO39

Places to visit

Montgomery Castle, Montgomery, 01443 336000, www.cadw.wales.gov.uk

Glansevern Hall Gardens, Berriew, 01686 640644, www.glansevern.co.uk

►►► 80% The Green Caravan Park (SO380932)

SY9 5EF
☎ 01588 650605
e-mail: karen@greencaravanpark.co.uk
dir: *1m NE of Bishop's Castle on A489. Turn right at brown tourist sign*

* 🚐 fr £13.50 🚏 fr £13.50 ▲ fr £12

Open Etr-Oct Last arrival 21.00hrs Last departure 13.00hrs

A pleasant site in a peaceful setting convenient for visiting Ludlow or Shrewsbury. Very family orientated, with good facilities. The grassy pitches are mainly level, and some hardstandings are available. A 15 acre site with 140 touring pitches, 5 hardstandings and 20 statics.

AA Pubs & Restaurants nearby: Crown Inn, Wentnor 01588 650613

Leisure: 🅰️
Facilities: ⓝ⊙🅿☀️🏧🐾
Services: 🔌🚿🔥🔥⌀🍽️🍴⚡
Within 3 miles: 🐾🏧🏊
Notes: Dogs must be kept on leads at all times

Somerset

South of Bristol and north-east of the West Country lies Somerset, that most English of counties. You tend to think of classic traditions and renowned honey traps when you think of Somerset – cricket and cider, the ancient and mysterious Glastonbury Tor and the deep gash that is Cheddar Gorge.

Somerset means 'summer pastures' – appropriate given that so much of this old county is rural and unspoiled. At its heart are the Mendip Hills, 25 miles (40km) long by 5 miles (8km) wide. Mainly of limestone over old red sandstone, and rising to just over 1,000 ft (303m) above sea level, they have a striking character and identity and are not really like any of the other Somerset hills.

Landscape of contrasts
By contrast, to the south and south-west are the Somerset Levels, a flat fenland landscape that was the setting for the Battle of Sedgemoor in 1685, while close to the rolling acres of Exmoor National

Somerset Levels

Park lie the Quantock Hills, famous for gentle slopes, heather-covered moorland stretches and red deer. From the summit, the Bristol Channel is visible where it meets the Severn Estuary; look to the east and you can see the Mendips.

The Quantocks were the haunt of several distinguished British poets. Coleridge wrote *The Ancient Mariner* and *Kubla Khan* while living in the area. Wordsworth and his sister visited on occasions and often accompanied Coleridge on his country walks.

Along the coast

Somerset's fine coastline takes a lot of beating. Various old-established seaside resorts overlook Bridgwater Bay – among them Minehead, on the edge of Exmoor National Park, and classic Weston-Super-Mare, with its striking new pier (the previous one was destroyed by fire in 2008). Fans of the classic Merchant-Ivory film production of The Remains of the Day, starring Anthony Hopkins and Emma Thompson, will recognise the Royal Pier Hotel in Birnbeck Road as one of the locations. Weston has just about everything for the holidaymaker – including Marine Parade, which runs for 2 miles (3.2km).

▶

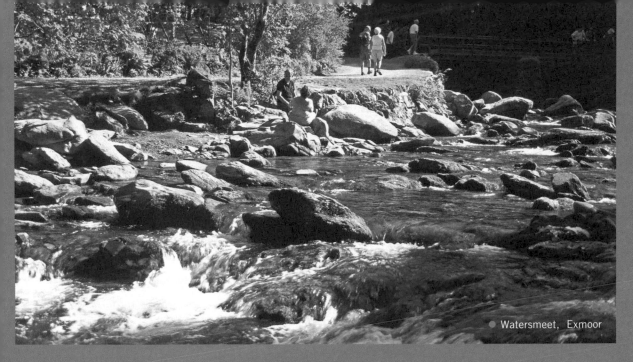
Watersmeet, Exmoor

Historic Wells

Inland – and not to be missed – is historic Wells, one of the smallest cities in the country, and with its period houses and superb cathedral, it is certainly one of the finest. Adorned with sculptures, Wells Cathedral's West Front is a masterpiece of medieval craftsmanship. Nearby are Vicar's Close, a delightful street of 14th-century houses, and the Bishop's Palace, which is 13th century and moated.

Walking and Cycling

The choice of walks in Somerset is plentiful, as is the range of cycle routes. One of the most attractive of long-distance trails is the 50-mile (80km) West Mendip Way, which runs from Weston to Frome. En route the trail visits Cheddar Gorge and Wells. The local tourist information centres throughout the county offer a varied mix of described walks and longer trails to suit all.

One of Somerset's most popular cycling trails is the delightfully named Strawberry Line which links Yatton railway station with Cheddar and runs for 9 miles (14.5km) along the course of a disused track bed. The trail is relatively easy and along the way are various picnic spots and various public artworks.

Festivals and Events

- The Cheddar Ales Beer Festival in June is a celebration of real ale with a range of beers from micro-breweries across the country.
- The Priddy Sheep Fair in mid-August is a great occasion for country lovers and farming traditions.
- Between July and September there are amazing sand sculptures down on the beach at Weston-Super-Mare.
- The Somerset in Autumn Weekend at Minehead in October is a must for steam train enthusiasts.
- The Royal Smithfield Christmas Fair at the Royal Bath and West Showground at Shepton Mallet is popular, with festive food, gift halls, cooking demonstrations and sheep shearing.

SOMERSET

See Walk 10 in the Walks & Cycle Rides section at the end of the guide

BATH — Map 4 ST76

Places to visit

Roman Baths and Pump Room, Bath, 01225 477785, www.romanbaths.co.uk

Bath Abbey, Bath, 01225 422462, www.bathabbey.org

Great for kids: The Herschel Museum of Astronomy, Bath, 01225 446865, www.bath-preservation-trust.org.uk

AA CAMPING CARD SITE

▶▶▶▶ **86% Newton Mill Holiday Park** (ST715649)

Newton Rd BA2 9JF
☎ 01225 333909
e-mail: enquiries@newtonmillpark.co.uk
dir: From Bath W on A4 to rdbt by Globe Inn, immediate left, site 1m on left

Open all year Last arrival 21.00hrs Last departure 11.00hrs

An attractive, high quality park set in a sheltered valley and surrounded by woodland, with a stream running through. It offers excellent toilet facilities with private cubicles and family rooms, and there is an appealing restaurant and bar offering a wide choice of menus throughout the year. Additional hardstandings have been put in on the top area of the park. The city of Bath is easily accessible by bus or via the Bristol to Bath cycle path. A 42 acre site with 212 touring pitches, 85 hardstandings.

AA Pubs & Restaurants nearby: Marlborough Tavern, Bath 01225 423731

King William, Bath 01225 428096 Hop Pole, Bath 01225 446327

Jamie's Italian, Bath 01225 510051

Leisure: ⋔

Facilities: ⛬ ⌂ ⊙ ☞ ✳ ⚁ ⚈ ⚄ ⚂

Services: ⚄ ⚅ ⚆ ⚇ ⚈ ⚉ Ⓣ ⚀ ⚁ ⚂ ⚃

Within 3 miles: ⚄ ⚈ ⨂ ⚂ ⚃ ⚄ ⚅

Notes: Fishing, satellite TV hook ups

BREAN — Map 4 ST25

Places to visit

King John's Hunting Lodge, Axbridge, 01934 732012, www.nationaltrust.org.uk

North Somerset Museum, Weston-Super-Mare, 01934 621028, www.n-somerset.gov.uk/museum

Great for kids: The Helicopter Museum, Weston-Super-Mare, 01934 635227, www.helicoptermuseum.co.uk

87% Warren Farm Holiday Centre (ST297564)

Brean Sands TA8 2RP
☎ 01278 751227
e-mail: enquiries@warren-farm.co.uk
dir: M5 junct 22 , B3140 through Burnham-on-Sea to Berrow & Brean. Site 1.5m past Brean Leisure Park

* ⚐ £7.50-£17 ⚑ £7.50-£17 ▲ £7.50-£17

Open Apr-Oct Last arrival 20.00hrs Last dep noon

A large family-run holiday park close to the beach, divided into several fields each with

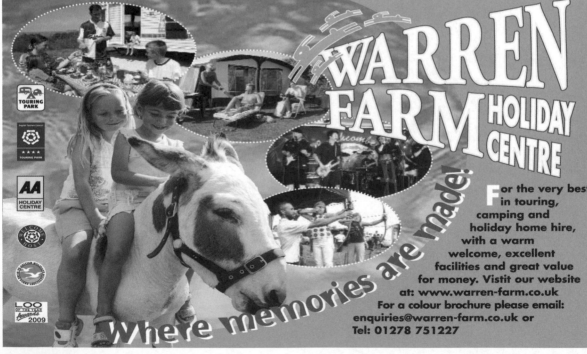

its own designated facilities. Pitches are spacious and level, and enjoy panoramic views of the Mendip Hills and Brean Down. A bar and restaurant are part of the complex, which provide entertainment for all the family, and there is also separate entertainment for children. The park has excellent modern facilities. A 100 acre site with 575 touring pitches and 400 statics.

AA Pubs & Restaurants nearby: Crossways Inn, West Huntspill 01278 783756

Leisure: 🛝 🎱 📺

Facilities: 🛁 🚿 ⊙ 💨 ❄ ♿ ☎ [$] ⛱ 🐕

Services: 🔌 🧺 🍺 🛢 ⛽ [T] 🍴 🔋 🥡 🚐

Within 3 miles: ⛳ 🎣 🎯 [$] 🐎

Notes: No commercial vehicles. Fishing lake & ponds, indoor play area. Wi-fi

see advert on opposite page

►►►► 85% Northam Farm Caravan & Touring Park *(ST299556)*

TA8 2SE
☎ 01278 751244 📠 01278 751150
e-mail: enquiries@northamfarm.co.uk
dir: *From M5 junct 22 to Burnham-on-Sea. In Brean, Northam Farm on right 0.5m past Brean Leisure Park*

* 🚃 £9.25-£24 🚌 £9.25-£24 ⛺ £9.25-£20.25

Open Mar-Oct (rs Mar & Oct shop/café/takeaway open limited hours) Last arrival 20.00hrs Last departure 10.30hrs

An attractive site a short walk from the sea and a long sandy beach. This quality park also has lots of children's play areas, and also owns the Seagull Inn about 600 yards away, which includes a restaurant and entertainment. There is a fishing lake on the site, which proves very popular. Facilities on this park are excellent following refurbishment. A DVD of the site is now available free of charge. A 30 acre site with 350 touring pitches, 252 hardstandings.

Leisure: 🛝

Facilities: 🛁 🚿 ⊙ 💨 ❄ ♿ ☎ [$] ⛱ 🐕

Services: 🔌 🧺 🛢 ⛽ [T] 🍴 🔋 🥡 🚐

Within 3 miles: ⛳ 🎣 🎯 [$] 🧺 🐎

Notes: Families & couples only, no motorcycles or commercial vehicles

see advert on the inside back cover

BRIDGETOWN — Map 3 SS93

Places to visit

Dunster Castle, Dunster, 01643 821314, www.nationaltrust.org.uk

Cleeve Abbey, Washford, 01984 640377, www.english-heritage.org.uk

►►►► 80% Exe Valley Caravan Site *(SS923333)*

Mill House TA22 9JR
☎ 01643 851432
e-mail: paul@paulmatt.fsnet.co.uk
dir: *Take A396 (Tiverton to Minehead road). Turn W in centre of Bridgetown, site 40yds on right*

* 🚃 £8.50-£14.50 🚌 £8.50-£14.50
⛺ £8.50-£17.50

Open 12 Mar-18 Oct Last arrival 22.00hrs

Set in the Exmoor National Park, this adults-only park occupies an enchanting, peaceful spot in a wooded valley alongside the River Exe. There is free fly-fishing, and an abundance of wildlife, with excellent walks directly from the park. The inn opposite serves lunchtime and evening meals. A 4 acre site with 50 touring pitches, 10 hardstandings.

AA Pubs & Restaurants nearby: Rest & Be Thankful Inn, Wheddon Cross 01643 841222

Facilities: 🚿 ⊙ 💨 ❄ ♿ ☎ [$] 🍖 ⛱ 🐕

Services: 🔌 🧺 🛢 ⛽ [T] 🔋 🚐

Within 3 miles: ⛵ 🎣 🚣 [$] 🐎

Notes: Adults only. 💳 17th-century mill, cycle hire. Wi-fi

BRIDGWATER — Map 4 ST23

Places to visit

Hestercombe Gardens, Taunton, 01823 413923, www.hestercombe.com

Coleridge Cottage, Nether Stowey, 01278 732662, www.nationaltrust.org.uk

Great for kids: Tropiquaria Animal and Adventure Park, Washford, 01984 640688, www.tropiquaria.co.uk

78% Mill Farm Caravan & Camping Park *(ST219410)*

Fiddington TA5 1JQ
☎ 01278 732286
web: www.millfarm.biz
dir: *From Bridgwater take A39 W, left at Cannington rdbt, 2m, right just beyond Apple Inn towards Fiddington. Follow camping signs*

🚃 £14-£20 🚌 £14-£20 ⛺ £14-£20

Open all year Last arrival 23.00hrs Last departure 10.00hrs

A large holiday park with plenty to interest all the family, including indoor and outdoor pools, a boating lake, a gym and horse riding. There is also a clubhouse with bar, and a full entertainment programme in the main season. Although lively and busy in the main season, the park also offers a much quieter environment at other times; out of season some activities and entertainment may not be available. A 6 acre site with 125 touring pitches.

AA Pubs & Restaurants nearby: Lemon Tree Restaurant, Walnut Tree Hotel, North Petherton 01278 662255

Leisure: 🏊 🌊 🛝 🎱 📺

Facilities: 🛁 🚿 ⊙ 💨 ❄ ♿ ☎ [$] ⛱ 🐕

Services: 🔌 🧺 🍺 🛢 ⛽ [T] 🔋 🥡

Within 3 miles: ⛳ 🎣 🎯 [$] 🧺 🐎

Notes: Canoeing, pool table, trampolines, pony rides. Wi-fi

see advert on page 256

BURNHAM-ON-SEA — Map 4 ST34

Places to visit

Glastonbury Abbey, Glastonbury, 01458 832267, www.glastonburyabbey.com

King John's Hunting Lodge, Axbridge, 01934 732012, www.nationaltrust.org.uk

Great for kids: Wookey Hole Caves and Papermill, Wookey Hole, 01749 672243, www.wookey.co.uk

82% Burnham-on-Sea Holiday Village (ST305485)

Marine Dr TA8 1LA
☎ 01278 783391 📄 01278 793776
e-mail: elaine.organ@bourne-leisure.co.uk
dir: *M5 junct 22. Left 1st rdbt onto A38 towards Highbridge. Over mini rdbt, right onto B3139 to Burnham. After Total Garage left onto Marine Drive. Park 400yds on left*

Open mid Mar-Oct (rs mid Mar-May & Sep-Oct facilities may be reduced) Last arrival anytime Last departure 10.00hrs

A large, family-orientated holiday village complex with a separate touring park containing 43 super pitches. There is a wide range of activities, including excellent indoor and outdoor pools, plus bars, restaurants and entertainment for all the family. The coarse fishing lake is very popular, and the seafront at Burnham is only half a mile away. A 94 acre site with 72 touring pitches, 44 hardstandings and 700 statics.

AA Pubs & Restaurants nearby: Crossways Inn, West Huntspill 01278 783756

Leisure: ⏺
Facilities: ⏺
Services: ⏺
Within 3 miles: ⏺
Notes: ⊗ No commercial vehicles. Wi-fi
see advert on opposite page

BURTLE — Map 4 ST34

Places to visit

Glastonbury Abbey, Glastonbury, 01458 832267, www.glastonburyabbey.com

The Bishops Palace, Wells, 01749 988111, www.bishopspalace.org.uk

Great for kids: East Somerset Railway, Cranmore, 01749 880417, www.eastsomersetrailway.com

► 75% Orchard Camping (ST397434)

Ye Olde Burtle Inn, Catcott Rd TA7 8NG
☎ 01278 722269 & 722123 📄 01278 722269
e-mail: food@theinn.eu
dir: *M5 junct 23, A39, in approx 4m left onto unclass road to Burtle, site by pub in village centre*

Open all year Last arrival anytime

A simple campsite set in an orchard at the rear of a lovely 17th-century family inn in the heart of the Somerset Levels. The restaurant offers a wide range of meals, and breakfast can be pre-ordered by campers. A shower and disabled toilet have been added and these facilities are available to campers outside pub opening hours. Free internet access and Wi-fi are available. A 0.75 acre site with 30 touring pitches.

AA Pubs & Restaurants nearby: The Burcott Inn, Wookey 01749 673874

Leisure: ⏺
Facilities: ⏺
Services: ⏺
Within 3 miles: ⏺
Notes: Bicycle & tent hire, sleeping bags & equipment

CHARD

Places to visit

Forde Abbey, Chard, 01460 221290, www.fordeabbey.co.uk

Barrington Court, Barrington, 01460 241938, www.nationaltrust.org.uk

Great for kids: The Wildlife Park, Cricket St Thomas, 01460 30111, www.wild.org.uk

CHARD — Map 4 ST30

AA CAMPING CARD SITE

►►►► 80% Alpine Grove Touring Park (ST342071)

Forton TA20 4HD
☎ 01460 63479 📄 01460 63479
e-mail: stay@alpinegrovetouringpark.com
dir: *Exit A30 between Chard & Crewkerne towards Cricket St Thomas, follow signs. Site 2m on right*

£13-£20 £13-£20 £11-£20

Open 1 wk before Etr-Sep Last arrival 21.00hrs Last departure 10.30hrs

A warm welcome awaits at this attractive, quiet wooded park with both hardstandings and grass pitches, close to Cricket St Thomas Wildlife Park. The facilities are kept spotlessly clean. Families particularly enjoy the small swimming pool and terrace in summer. Log cabins are also available for hire. This very dog-friendly site offers a dog sitting service. An 8.5 acre site with 40 touring pitches, 16 hardstandings.

AA Pubs & Restaurants nearby: George Inn, Crewkerne 01460 73650

New Inn, Ilminster 01460 52413

Leisure: ⏺
Facilities: ⏺
Services: ⏺
Within 3 miles: ⏺
Notes: No open fires, dogs must be kept on leads. Fire pits to hire. Wi-fi

CHEDDAR

Places to visit

Glastonbury Abbey, Glastonbury, 01458 832267, www.glastonburyabbey.com

The Helicopter Museum, Weston-Super-Mare, 01934 635227, www.helicoptermuseum.co.uk

Great for kids: Wookey Hole Caves and Papermill, Wookey Hole, 01749 672243, www.wookey.co.uk

CHEDDAR Map 4 ST45

AA CAMPING CARD SITE

83% Broadway House Holiday Park (ST448547)

Axbridge Rd BS27 3DB
☎ 01934 742610 📄 01934 744950
e-mail: enquiries@broadwayhousepark.co.uk
dir: From M5 junct 22 follow signs to Cheddar Gorge & Caves (8m). Site midway between Cheddar & Axbridge on A371

Open Mar-Oct (rs Mar-end May & Oct bar & pool closed, limited shop hours) Last arrival 23.00hrs Last departure noon

A well-equipped holiday park on the slopes of the Mendips with an exceptional range of activities for all ages. This is a busy and lively park in the main holiday periods, but can be quiet and peaceful off-peak. Broadway has its own competition standard BMX track, which is used for National and European Championships, plus a skateboard park and many other activities. The slightly-terraced pitches face south, and are backed by the Mendips. A 30 acre site with 388 touring pitches, 70 hardstandings and 34 statics.

AA Pubs & Restaurants nearby: Wookey Hole Inn, Wookey Hole 01749 676677

Leisure:
Facilities:
Services:
Within 3 miles:

Notes: Children to be supervised at all times Table tennis, skate park. Wi-fi

►►►► 82% Cheddar Bridge Touring Park (ST459529)

Draycott Rd BS27 3RJ
☎ 01934 743048 📄 01934 743048
e-mail: enquiries@cheddarbridge.co.uk
dir: M5 junct 22 (Burnham-on-Sea), A38 towards Cheddar & Bristol, approx 5m. Right onto A371 at Cross, follow Cheddar signs. Through Cheddar village towards Wells, site on right just before Caravan Club site

* 🚐 £10-£20 🚐 £10-£20 ⛺ £10-£20

Open Mar-Oct Last arrival 22.00hrs Last departure 11.00hrs

A peaceful adults-only park on the edge of the village of Cheddar, with the River Yeo passing attractively through its grounds. It is handy for exploring Cheddar Gorge and Wookey Hole, Wells and Bath. The toilet and shower facilities are very good. A 4 acre site with 45 touring pitches, 10 hardstandings and 4 statics.

AA Pubs & Restaurants nearby: Wookey Hole Inn, Wookey Hole 01749 676677

Facilities:
Services:
Within 3 miles:

Notes: Adults only. Quiet 23.00hrs-08.00hrs

COWSLIP GREEN

Places to visit

Clevedon Court, Clevedon, 01275 872257, www.nationaltrust.org.uk

Bristol City Museum and Art Gallery, Bristol, 0117 922 3571, www.bristol.gov.uk/museums

Great for kids: HorseWorld, Bristol, 01275 540173, www.horseworld.org.uk

COWSLIP GREEN Map 4 ST46

►►► 83% Brook Lodge Farm Camping & Caravan Park (Bristol) (ST486620)

Near Bristol, BS40 5RB
☎ 01934 862311 📄 01934 862311
e-mail: info@brooklodgefarm.com
dir: M5 junct 18 follow signs for Bristol Airport. Site 3m on left of A38 at bottom of hill. M5 junct 22 follow A38 to Churchill. Site 4m on right opposite Holiday Inn

Open Mar-Oct Last arrival 21.30hrs Last departure noon

A naturally sheltered country touring park nestling in a valley of the Mendip Hills, surrounded by trees and a historic walled garden. A friendly welcome is always assured by the family owners who are particularly keen on preserving the site's environment and are striving to achieve 'green' awards. This park is particularly well placed for visiting the Bristol Balloon Festival, held in August, plus the many country walks in the area. A 3.5 acre site with 29 touring pitches, 3 hardstandings.

AA Pubs & Restaurants nearby: Ship & Castle, Congresbury 01934 833535

White Hart Inn, Congresbury 01934 833303

Leisure:
Facilities:
Services:
Within 3 miles:

Notes: Dogs by prior arrangement. Bicycle hire & walking maps provided

CREWKERNE

See Drimpton, Dorset

CROWCOMBE
Map 3 ST13

Places to visit
Cleeve Abbey, Washford, 01984 640377, www.english-heritage.org.uk

Great for kids: Dunster Castle, Dunster, 01643 821314, www.nationaltrust.org.uk

AA CAMPING CARD SITE

▶▶▶▶ 85% *Quantock Orchard Caravan Park* (ST138357)

Flaxpool TA4 4AW
☎ 01984 618618
e-mail: member@flaxpool.freeserve.co.uk
web: www.quantock-orchard.co.uk
dir: *Take A358 from Taunton, signed Minehead & Wiliton. In 8m turn left just past Flaxpool Garage. Park immediately on left*

Open all year (rs 10 Sep-20 May swimming pool closed) Last arrival 22.00hrs Last departure noon

This small family run park is set at the foot of the beautiful Quantock Hills and makes an ideal base for touring Somerset, Exmoor and North Devon. It is also close to the West Somerset Railway. It has excellent facilities and there is a lovely heated outdoor swimming pool, plus gym and fitness centre; bike hire is also available. There are static homes for hire. A 3.5 acre site with 69 touring pitches, 30 hardstandings and 8 statics.

AA Pubs & Restaurants nearby: White Horse, Stogumber 01984 656277

Blue Ball, Triscombe 01984 618242

Rising Sun Inn, West Bagborough 01823 432575

Leisure: 🏊 🎱 🎣 ⌨
Facilities: 🚿 🅿️ ⊙ 🍴 ✳ ⚡ 🕐 🖊 🛒 🎪
Services: 🔌 🗑 🅰️ 🚿 T 🔋 🚼 ♻
Within 3 miles: 🚶 ✏️ 🎣 🛍 🎯 U

Notes: Gym & leisure suite, off-licence on site

DULVERTON
Map 3 SS92

See also East Anstey (Devon)

Places to visit
Knightshayes Court, Knightshayes Court, 01884 254665, www.nationaltrust.org.uk/knightshayes

Killerton House and Gardens, Killerton, 01392 881345, www.nationaltrust.org.uk

Great for kids: Tiverton Castle, Tiverton, 01884 253200, www.tivertoncastle.com

AA CAMPING CARD SITE

▶▶▶ 79% *Wimbleball Lake* (SS960300)

Brompton Regis TA22 9NU
☎ 01398 371257
e-mail: wimbleball@swlakestrust.org.uk
dir: *From A396 (Tiverton-Minehead road) take B3222 signed Dulverton Services, follow signs to Wimbleball Lake. Ignore 1st entry (fishing) & take 2nd entry for tea-room & camping. (NB care needed - narrow roads)*

🚐 🚌 ⛺

Open Mar-Oct Last departure 11.30hrs

A grassy site overlooking Wimbleball Lake, set high up on Exmoor National Park. The camping area is adjacent to the Visitor Centre and café, which also includes the newly refurbished camping toilets and showers. The camping field, which includes 11 electric hook-ups, is in a quiet and peaceful setting with good views of the lake, which is nationally renowned for its trout fishing, and boats can be hired with advance notice. A 1.25 acre site with 30 touring pitches, 4 hardstandings.

AA Pubs & Restaurants nearby: Masons Arms, Knowstone 01398 341231

Leisure: 🎱 **Facilities:** 🚿 ⊙ 🍴 ✳ ⚡ 🕐 🖊 🛒 🎪
Services: 🔌 🗑 🍴 **Within 3 miles:** ⛷ ✏️ 🚴 🛍 🎯 U

Notes: Dogs must be kept on leads. Watersports & activity centre, bird watching, cycling, lakeside walks

EMBOROUGH
Map 4 ST65

Places to visit
Glastonbury Abbey, Glastonbury, 01458 832267, www.glastonburyabbey.com

King John's Hunting Lodge, Axbridge, 01934 732012, www.nationaltrust.org.uk

Great for kids: East Somerset Railway, Cranmore, 01749 880417, www.eastsomersetrailway.com

AA CAMPING CARD SITE

▶▶▶ 83% Old Down Touring Park (ST628513)

Old Down House BA3 4SA
☎ 01761 232355 📠 01761 232355
e-mail: jsmallparkhomes@aol.com
dir: *A37 from Farrington Gurney through Ston Easton. In 2m left onto B3139 to Radstock. Site opposite Old Down Inn*

🚐 🚌 ⛺

Open all year Last arrival 20.00hrs Last departure noon

A small family-run site set in open parkland, surrounded by well-established trees. The excellent toilet facilities are well maintained as is every other aspect of the park. Children are welcome. A 4 acre site with 30 touring pitches, 15 hardstandings.

AA Pubs & Restaurants nearby: Moody Goose, Old Priory, Midsomer Norton 01761 416784

Facilities: 🚿 ⊙ 🍴 ✳ 🕐 🖊 🎪
Services: 🔌 🅰️ 🚿 T 🔋
Within 3 miles: 🚶 🛍 🎯 U

Notes: Dogs must be kept on leads at all times

EXFORD

Places to visit
Dunster Castle, Dunster, 01643 821314, www.nationaltrust.org.uk

West Somerset Railway, Minehead, 01643 704996, www.west-somerset-railway.co.uk

Great for kids: Exmoor Zoological Park, Blackmoor Gate, 01598 763352, www.exmoorzoo.co.uk

EXFORD   Map 3 SS83

▶▶ 84% Westermill Farm (SS825398)

TA24 7NJ
☎ 01643 831238 🖷 01643 831216
e-mail: aa@westermill.com
dir: *From Exford on Porlock road. After 0.25m left, along valley toWestermill sign on tree. Fork left*

🚐 🅰

Open all year (rs Nov-May larger toilet block & shop closed)

An idyllic site for peace and quiet, in a sheltered valley in the heart of Exmoor, which has won awards for conservation. There are four waymarked walks over the 500-acre working farm and self-catering accommodation is also available. Please note that the site should only be approached from Exford (other approaches are difficult). A 6 acre site with 60 touring pitches.

AA Pubs & Restaurants nearby: Crown Hotel, Exford 01643 831554

Facilities: 🖍☉🅿✳🕐🖻🛏
Services: 🖻🅱🖉
Within 3 miles: 🖉🖻🖻
Notes: 🐾 Shallow river for fishing/bathing

FROME

Places to visit

Stourhead, Stourhead, 01747 841152, www.nationaltrust.org.uk/main/w-stourhead

Dyrham Park, Dyrham, 0117 937 2501, www.nationaltrust.org.uk

Great for kids: Longleat Safari Park, Longleat, 01985 844400, www.longleat.co.uk

FROME   Map 4 ST74

▶▶▶ 83% Seven Acres Caravan & Camping Site (ST777444)

Seven Acres, West Woodlands BA11 5EQ
☎ 01373 464222
dir: *On B3092 approx 0.75m from rdbt with A361, Frome bypass*

🚐 🚐 🅰

Open Mar-Oct

A level meadowland site beside the shallow River Frome, with a bridge across to an adjacent field, and plenty of scope for families. The facilities are spotless. Set on the edge of the Longleat Estate with its stately home, wildlife safari park, and many other attractions. A 3 acre site with 16 touring pitches, 16 hardstandings.

AA Pubs & Restaurants nearby: Horse & Groom, Frome 01373 462802

The George at Nunney, Nunney 01373 836458

Vobster Inn, Lower Vobster 01373 812920

Leisure: 🄰 **Facilities:** 🖍☉🅿✳🇦🛏
Services: 🖻
Within 3 miles: ↓🄷🖉🖻🖻🔾
Notes: 🐾 Dogs must be kept on leads

GLASTONBURY   Map 4 ST53

Places to visit

Lytes Cary Manor, Kingsdon, 01458 224471, www.nationaltrust.org.uk/main/w-lytescarymanor

Fleet Air Arm Museum, Yeovilton, 01935 840565, www.fleetairarm.com

Great for kids: Haynes International Motor Museum, Sparkford, 01963 440804, www.haynesmotormuseum.co.uk

PREMIER PARK

▶▶▶▶▶ 94% The Old Oaks Touring Park

(ST521394)

Wick Farm, Wick BA6 8JS
☎ 01458 831437
e-mail: info@theoldoaks.co.uk
dir: *On A361 from Glastonbury towards Shepton Mallet. In 1.75m turn left at Wick sign, site on left in 1m*

🚐 £15-£26 🚐 £15-£26 🅰 £10.50-£21

Open all year (rs Low season reduced shop & reception hours) Last arrival 20.00hrs Last departure noon

An idyllic park on a working farm with panoramic views towards the Mendip Hills. Old Oaks offers sophisticated services whilst retaining a farming atmosphere, and there are some 'super' pitches as well as en suite toilet facilities. Glastonbury's two famous 1,000-year-old oak trees, Gog and Magog, are on site. This is an adult-only park, and camping cabins are available for hire. A 10 acre site with 100 touring pitches, 87 hardstandings.

AA Pubs & Restaurants nearby: Ring O'Bells, Ashcott 01458 210232

Ashcott Inn, Ashcott 01458 210282

Facilities: 🛁🖍☉🅿✳🕐🖻🛏
Services: 🖻🖻🅱🖉🇹🚮
Within 3 miles: 🖉🖻🖻
Notes: Adults only. Group or block bookings only at owners' discretion. Fishing, bicycle hire, off licence. Wi-fi

▶▶▶▶ 78% *Isle of Avalon Touring Caravan Park* (ST494397)

Godney Rd BA6 9AF
☎ 01458 833618 🖷 01458 833618
dir: *M5 junct 23, A39 to outskirts of Glastonbury, 2nd exit signed Wells at B&Q rdbt, straight over next rdbt, 1st exit at 3rd rdbt (B3151), site 200yds on right*

🚐 🚐 🅰

Open all year Last arrival 21.00hrs Last departure 11.00hrs

A popular site on the south side of this historic town and within easy walking distance of the town centre. This level park offers a quiet environment in which to stay and explore the many local attractions including the Tor, Wells, Wookey Hole and Clarks Village. An 8 acre site with 120 touring pitches, 70 hardstandings.

AA Pubs & Restaurants nearby: Ring O'Bells, Ashcott 01458 210232

Ashcott Inn, Ashcott 01458 210282

Leisure: 🄰
Facilities: 🖍☉🅿✳🕐🖻🛏
Services: 🖻🖻🅱🖉🇹🚮🞿
Within 3 miles: 🄷🖉🖻🖻🔾
Notes: Cycle hire

LEISURE: 🏊 Indoor swimming pool 🏊 Outdoor swimming pool 🄰 Children's playground 🎾 Tennis court 🎱 Games room 📺 Separate TV room ⛳ 9/18 hole golf course 🚣 Boats for hire 🎬 Cinema 🎣 Fishing ⛳ Mini golf 🏄 Watersports 🐎 Stables **FACILITIES:** 🛁 Bath 🚿 Shower ⚡ Electric shaver 🖉 Hairdryer ✳ Ice Pack Facility ♿ Disabled facilities ☎ Public telephone 🛒 Shop on site or within 200yds 🚚 Mobile shop (calls at least 5 days a week) 🍖 BBQ area 🌲 Picnic area 🐕 Dog exercise area

LANGPORT — Map 4 ST42

Places to visit

Montacute House, Montacute, 01935 823289, www.nationaltrust.org.uk

Lytes Cary Manor, Kingsdon, 01458 224471, www.nationaltrust.org.uk/main/w-lytescarymanor

Great for kids: Fleet Air Arm Museum, Yeovilton, 01935 840565, www.fleetairarm.com

▶▶▶ 75% Thorney Lakes Caravan Park (ST430237)

GOLD

Thorney Lakes, Muchelney TA10 0DW
☎ 01458 250811
e-mail: enquiries@thorneylakes.co.uk
dir: From A303 at Podimore rdbt take A372 to Langport. At Huish Episcopi Church turn left for Muchelney. In 100yds left (signed Muchelney & Crewkerne). Site 300yds after John Leach Pottery

* 🚐 £11-£16 🚐 £11-£16 ▲ £11-£16

Open Etr-Oct

A small, basic but very attractive park set in a cider apple orchard, with coarse fishing in the three well-stocked, on-site lakes. The famous John Leach pottery shop is close at hand, and The Lowland Games are held nearby in July. A 6 acre site with 36 touring pitches.

AA Pubs & Restaurants nearby: Rose & Crown, Huish Episcopi 01458 250494

Old Pound Inn, Langport 01458 250469

Devonshire Arms, Long Sutton 01458 241271

Halfway House, Pitney 01458 252513

Facilities: 🌥 ☉ ✳
Services: 🚐
Within 3 miles: ↧ 🌊 🖹
Notes: 🐕 Wi-fi

MARTOCK

Places to visit

Montacute House, Montacute, 01935 823289, www.nationaltrust.org.uk

Barrington Court, Barrington, 01460 241938, www.nationaltrust.org.uk

Great for kids: Fleet Air Arm Museum, Yeovilton, 01935 840565, www.fleetairarm.com

MARTOCK — Map 4 ST41

AA CAMPING CARD SITE

▶▶▶▶ 82% Southfork Caravan Park (ST448188)

Parrett Works TA12 6AE
☎ 01935 825661 📄 01935 825122
e-mail: southforkcaravans@btconnect.com
dir: 8m NW of Yeovil, 2m off A303. From E, take exit after Cartgate rdbt. From W, 1st exit off rdbt signed South Petherton, follow camping signs

* 🚐 £10-£21 🚐 £10-£21 ▲ £10-£18

Open all year Last arrival 22.30hrs Last departure noon

A neat, level mainly grass park in a quiet rural area, just outside the pretty village of Martock. Some excellent spacious hardstandings are now available. The facilities are always spotless and the whole site well cared for by the friendly owners, who will ensure your stay is a happy one, a fact borne out by the many repeat customers. The park is unique in that it also has a fully-approved caravan repair and servicing centre with accessory shop. There are also static caravans available for hire. A 2 acre site with 27 touring pitches, 2 hardstandings and 3 statics.

AA Pubs & Restaurants nearby: Nag's Head Inn, Martock 01935 823432

Ilchester Arms, Ilchester 01935 840220

Leisure: 🅰 **Facilities:** 🌥 ☉ 🅿 ✳ ☺ 🖹 🚻
Services: 🚐 🖸 🛢 🖉 🅃 🔋 **Within 3 miles:** ↧ 🌊 🖹
Notes: Wi-fi

MINEHEAD — Map 3 SS94

Places to visit

West Somerset Railway, Minehead, 01643 704996, www.west-somerset-railway.co.uk

Dunster Castle, Dunster, 01643 821314, www.nationaltrust.org.uk

Great for kids: Tropiquaria Animal and Adventure Park, Washford, 01984 640688, www.tropiquaria.co.uk

▶▶▶ 75% Minehead & Exmoor Caravan & Camping Park (SS950457)

Porlock Rd TA24 8SW
☎ 01643 703074
dir: 1m W of Minehead centre, take A39 towards Porlock. Site on right

🚐 🚐 ▲

Open Mar-Oct (rs Nov-Feb open certain weeks only (phone to check)) Last arrival 22.00hrs Last departure noon

A small terraced park on the edge of Exmoor, spread over five small paddocks and screened by the mature trees that surround it. The level pitches provide a comfortable space for each unit on this family-run park. There is a laundrette in nearby Minehead. Ten seasonal touring pitches are available. A 3 acre site with 50 touring pitches, 10 hardstandings.

AA Pubs & Restaurants nearby: Luttrell Arms, Dunster 01643 821555

The Smugglers, Blue Anchor 01984 640385

Leisure: 🅰
Facilities: 🌥 ☉ 🅿 ✳ 🚻 ☺ 🖭 🚻
Services: 🚐 🛢 🖉 🔋
Within 3 miles: ↧ 🖽 🌊 ◎ 🔥 🖹 🖸 ↻
Notes: 🐕 No open fires

MUCHELNEY

Places to visit

Tintinhull Garden, Tintinhull, 01935 823289, www.nationaltrust.org.uk

Munchelney Abbey, Muchelney, 01458 250664, www.english-heritage.org.uk

Great for kids: Haynes International Motor Museum, Sparkford, 01963 440804, www.haynesmotormuseum.co.uk

MUCHELNEY — Map 4 ST42

▶▶▶ 79% Muchelney Caravan & Camping Site (ST429249)

Abbey Farm TA10 0DQ
☎ 01458 250112 & 07881 524425
📠 01458 250112
dir: *From A303 at Podimore rdbt take A372 towards Langport. At church in Huish Episcopi follow Muchelney Abbey sign. In Muchelney left at village cross. Site in 50mtrs*

* 🚐 £10-£12.50 � £10-£12.50 ▲ £8-£12.50

Open all year Last arrival anytime Last departure anytime

A small, developing site situated opposite Muchelney Abbey, an English Heritage property. Quiet and peaceful, it will appeal to all lovers of the countryside, and is well positioned for visiting the Somerset Levels. The facilities are excellent and the pitch areas are maturing well. A 3 acre site with 40 touring pitches, 5 hardstandings.

AA Pubs & Restaurants nearby: Rose & Crown, Huish Episcopi 01458 250494

Old Pound Inn, Langport 01458 250469

Devonshire Arms, Long Sutton 01458 241271

Facilities: 🐕⊙✻🔥🛁🎋🎠🐾

Services: 🚐🛒🅃🚿↴ **Within 3 miles:** ⚓🎣🛒

Notes: ⊘ Dogs & cats must be kept on leads. Large covered area/barn for rallies. Bulk LPG for refillable bottles/motorhomes

OARE — Map 3 SS74

Places to visit

Watermouth Castle and Family Theme Park, Ilfracombe, 01271 863879, www.watermouthcastle.com

Marwood Hill Gardens, Barnstaple, 01271 342528, www.marwoodhillgarden.co.uk

Great for kids: Exmoor Zoological Park, Blackmoor Gate, 01598 763352, www.exmoorzoo.co.uk

▶▶▶ 75% Cloud Farm (SS794467)

EX35 6NU
☎ 01598 741278
e-mail: stay@cloudfarmcamping.co.uk
web: www.cloudfarmcamping.com
dir: *M5 junct 24/A39 towards Minehead/Porlock then Lynton. Left in 6.5m, follow signs to Oare then right & site signed*

* 🚐 fr £12 � fr £12 ▲ fr £12

Open all year

Set in the heart of Exmoor's Doone Valley, this quiet, sheltered park is arranged over four riverside fields, with modern toilet facilities. It offers a good shop and café serving all day food, including breakfasts, with a large garden for outdoor eating, and there are self-catering holiday cottages. Ten seasonal touring pitches are available. A 110 acre site with 70 touring pitches.

AA Pubs & Restaurants nearby: Rockford Inn, Brendon 01598 741214

Facilities: 🐕⊙✻🔥🛁🎋🎠🎋🎠🐾

Services: 🛒🅃🍽🚿⇄♨🚲

Within 3 miles: ⚓🎣🛒⚓🛒🅂🅂🌊

Notes: Wi-fi

PORLOCK — Map 3 SS84

Places to visit

West Somerset Railway, Minehead, 01643 704996, www.west-somerset-railway.co.uk

Dunster Castle, Dunster, 01643 821314, www.nationaltrust.org.uk

Great for kids: Tropiquaria Animal and Adventure Park, Washford, 01984 640688, www.tropiquaria.co.uk

PREMIER PARK

AA CAMPING CARD SITE

▶▶▶▶▶ 80% Porlock Caravan Park (SS882469)

GOLD

TA24 8ND
☎ 01643 862269 📠 01643 862269
e-mail: info@porlockcaravanpark.co.uk
dir: *Through village fork right signed Porlock Weir, site on right*

🚐 � ▲

Open 15 Mar-Oct Last arrival 20.00hrs Last departure 11.00hrs

A sheltered touring park, attractively laid-out in the centre of lovely countryside, on the edge of the village of Porlock. The famous Porlock Hill which starts a few hundred yards from the site, takes you to some spectacular parts of Exmoor with stunning views. The toilet facilities are superb, and there's a popular kitchen area with microwave and freezer. Holiday statics for hire. A 3 acre site with 40 touring pitches, 14 hardstandings and 55 statics.

AA Pubs & Restaurants nearby: Ship Inn, Porlock 01643 862507

The Bottom Ship, Porlock 01643 863288

Facilities: 🐕⊙🅿✻🔥🛁⊙🅂🐾

Services: 🚐🛒🍽🚲🎋

Within 3 miles: ⚓🎣🅂🐾🌊

Notes: No fires, dogs must be kept on leads. Wi-fi

▶▶▶▶ 84% Burrowhayes Farm Caravan & Camping Site & Riding Stables (SS897460)

West Luccombe TA24 8HT
☎ 01643 862463
e-mail: info@burrowhayes.co.uk
dir: *A39 from Minehead towards Porlock for 5m. Left at Red Post to Horner & West Luccombe, site 0.25m on right, immediately before humpback bridge*

* 🚐 £10-£17.50 � £10-£17.50 ▲ £10-£17.50

Open 15 Mar-Oct Last arrival 22.00hrs Last departure noon

A delightful site on the edge of Exmoor, sloping gently down to Horner Water. The farm buildings have been converted into riding stables, from where escorted rides onto the moors can be taken, and the excellent toilet facilities are housed in timber-clad buildings. There are many walks into the surrounding countryside that can be directly accessed from the site. Additional hardstandings are now available. An 8 acre site with 120 touring pitches, 10 hardstandings and 20 statics.

AA Pubs & Restaurants nearby: Ship Inn, Porlock 01643 862507

The Bottom Ship, Porlock 01643 863288

Facilities: 🐕⊙🅿✻🔥🛁⊙🅂🐾

Services: 🚐🛒🅃🚲🎋♨↴

Within 3 miles: ⚓🎣◎🅂🌊🌊

Notes: Riding stables & pony trekking on Exmoor. Wi-fi

PRIDDY — Map 4 ST55

Places to visit

Glastonbury Abbey, Glastonbury, 01458 832267, www.glastonburyabbey.com

The Helicopter Museum, Weston-Super-Mare, 01934 635227, www.helicoptermuseum.co.uk

Great for kids: Wookey Hole Caves and Papermill, Wookey Hole, 01749 672243, www.wookey.co.uk

►►►► 85% Cheddar Camping & Caravanning Club Site *(ST522519)*

Townsend BA5 3BP
☎ 01749 870241 & 0845 130 7633
dir: *From A39 take B3135 to Cheddar. After 4.5m turn left. Site 200yds on right*

🚐 £7.70-£11.10 🚙 £7.70-£11.10
⛺ £7.70-£11.10

Open Mar-15 Nov Last arrival 20.00hrs Last departure noon

A gently sloping site set high on the Mendip Hills and surrounded by trees. This excellent site offers really good facilities, which have now been upgraded with even more family rooms and private cubicles; these are spotlessly maintained. Fresh bread is baked daily and available from the well-stocked shop. The site is well positioned for visiting local attractions such as Cheddar, Wookey Hole, Wells and Glastonbury, and is popular with walkers. A 3.5 acre site with 90 touring pitches.

AA Pubs & Restaurants nearby: Wookey Hole Inn, Wookey Hole 01749 676677

The Burcott Inn, Wookey 01749 673874

Leisure: 🛝

Facilities: 🚿 ✱ ♿ ✆ [$]

Services: ⚡ 🧺 🔥 ⛽ ⤓

Notes: Site gates closed 23.00hrs-07.00hrs. Wi-fi

SHEPTON MALLET

Places to visit

Stourhead, Stourhead, 01747 841152, www.nationaltrust.org.uk/main/w-stourhead

Westwood Manor, Westwood, 01225 863374, www.nationaltrust.org.uk

Great for kids: Longleat Safari Park, Longleat, 01985 844400, www.longleat.co.uk

SHEPTON MALLET — Map 4 ST64

AA CAMPING CARD SITE

►► 95% Greenacres Camping

(ST553416)

Barrow Ln, North Wootton BA4 4HL
☎ 01749 890497
e-mail: stay@greenacres-camping.co.uk
dir: *A361 to Glastonbury. Turn at Steanbow Farm, from A39 turn at Brownes Garden Centre. Follow campsite signs & sign for North Wootton*

* 🚙 ⛺ £16

Open Apr-Sep Last arrival 21.00hrs Last departure 11.00hrs

An immaculately maintained site peacefully set within sight of Glastonbury Tor. Mainly family orientated with many thoughtful extra facilities provided, and there is plenty of space for children to play games in a very safe environment. Facilities are exceptionally clean. A 4.5 acre site with 40 touring pitches.

AA Pubs & Restaurants nearby: Bull Terrier, Croscombe 01749 343658

Leisure: 🛝 **Facilities:** 🚿 ⊙ 🚿 ✱ [$] ⛩

Services: ⚡ 🔥 ⛽ 🔋 🍼

Within 3 miles: ⛳ 日 🎣 [$] 🧺 ∪

Notes: No caravans or large motorhomes, no open fires. Free use of fridges & freezers. Book library. Wi-fi

SPARKFORD — Map 4 ST62

Places to visit

Lytes Cary Manor, Kingsdon, 01458 224471, www.nationaltrust.org.uk/main/w-lytescarymanor

Montacute House, Montacute, 01935 823289, www.nationaltrust.org.uk

►►► 83% Long Hazel Park *(ST602262)*

High St BA22 7JH
☎ 01963 440002 📠 01963 440002
e-mail: longhazelpark@hotmail.com
dir: *Exit A303 at Hazlegrove rdbt, follow signs for Sparkford. Site 400yds on left*

* 🚐 £16-£20 🚙 £16-£20 ⛺ £16-£20

Open all year Last arrival 22.00hrs Last departure 11.00hrs

A very neat, adults-only park next to the village inn in the high street. This attractive park is run by friendly owners to a very good standard. Spacious pitches, many with hardstandings. There are also luxury lodges on site for hire or purchase. A 3.5 acre site with 50 touring pitches, 30 hardstandings and 4 statics.

AA Pubs & Restaurants nearby: Sparkford Inn, Sparkford 01963 440218

Walnut Tree, West Camel 01935 851292

Queens Arms, Corton Denham 01963 220317

Facilities: 🚿 ⊙ 🚿 ✱ ♿ ✆ [$] ⛩

Services: ⚡ 🧺 🔥 ⛽ [T] 🔋 ⤓

Within 3 miles: ⛳ 🎣 [$]

Notes: Adults only. Dogs must be kept on leads & exercised off site. Picnic tables available. Wi-fi

TAUNTON — Map 4 ST22

Places to visit

Hestercombe Gardens, Taunton, 01823 413923, www.hestercombe.com

Barrington Court, Barrington, 01460 241938, www.nationaltrust.org.uk

Great for kids: Sunnycroft, Wellington, 01952 242884, www.nationaltrust.org.uk/sunnycroft

►►►► 84% Cornish Farm Touring Park *(ST235217)*

Shoreditch TA3 7BS
☎ 01823 327746 📠 01823 354946
e-mail: info@cornishfarm.com
web: www.cornishfarm.com
dir: *M5 junct 25 towards Taunton. Left at lights. 3rd left into Ilminster Rd (follow Corfe signs). Right at rdbt, left at next. Right at T-junct, left into Killams Dr, 2nd left into Killams Ave. Over motorway bridge. Site on left, take 2nd entrance*

🚐 🚙 ⛺

Open all year Last arrival anytime Last departure 11.30hrs

This smart park provides really top quality facilities throughout. Although only two miles from

continued

SERVICES: ⚡ Electric hook up 🧺 Launderette 🍺 Licensed bar 🔥 Calor Gas ⛽ Camping Gaz [T] Toilet fluid 🍴 Café/Restaurant 🍔 Fast Food/Takeaway 🔋 Battery charging 🍼 Baby care ⤓ Motorvan service point **ABBREVIATIONS:** BH/bank hols-bank holidays Etr-Easter Whit-Whitsun dep-departure fr-from hrs-hours m-mile mdnt-midnight rdbt-roundabout rs-restricted service wk-week wknd-weekend 🚫💳 No credit cards 🚫🐕 no dogs See page 7 for details of the AA Camping Card Scheme

TAUNTON *continued*

Taunton, it is set in open countryside and is a very convenient base for visiting the many attractions of the area such as Clarks Village, Glastonbury and Cheddar Gorge. A 3.5 acre site with 50 touring pitches, 25 hardstandings.

AA Pubs & Restaurants nearby: Queens Arms, Pitminster 01823 421529

Hatch Inn, Hatch Beauchamp 01823 480245

Willow Tree Restaurant, Taunton 01823 352835

Facilities: ⌂◉♥♿⌂

Services: ⊞⛽Ⓣ♻

Within 3 miles: ⚓⊞◎🛒⛽∪

Notes: Wi-fi

▶▶▶ **81% Ashe Farm Camping & Caravan Site** (ST279229)

Thornfalcon TA3 5NW
☎ 01823 443764
e-mail: info@ashefarm.co.uk
dir: *M5 junct 25, A358 E for 2.5m. Right at Nags Head pub. Site 0.25m on right*

* ⛺ £10-£13 ⛞ £10-£13 ▲ £10-£12

Open Apr-Oct Last arrival 22.00hrs Last dep noon

A well-screened site surrounded by mature trees and shrubs, with two large touring fields. A modern facilities block includes toilets and showers plus a separate laundry room. Not far from the bustling market town of Taunton, and handy for both south and north coasts. A 7 acre site with 30 touring pitches, 11 hardstandings.

AA Pubs & Restaurants nearby: Queens Arms, Pitminster 01823 421529

Hatch Inn, Hatch Beauchamp 01823 480245

Willow Tree Restaurant, Taunton 01823 352835

Leisure: ⚠ ⚉ **Facilities:** ⌂◉♥❄♿🐾
Services: ⊞⛽ **Within 3 miles:** ⚓⊞♿🛒⛽∪
Notes: ⊛ Baby changing facilities

▶▶▶ **81%** *Holly Bush Park* (ST220162)

Culmhead TA3 7EA
☎ 01823 421515
e-mail: info@hollybushpark.com
web: www.hollybushpark.com
dir: *M5 junct 25 towards Taunton. At 1st lights left signed Corfe/Taunton Racecourse. 3.5m past Corfe on B3170 right at x-rds at top of hill on unclass road towards Wellington. Right at next junct, site 150yds on left*

⛺ ⛞ ▲

Open all year Last arrival 21.00hrs Last dep 11.00hrs

An immaculate little park set in an orchard in attractive countryside, high on the Blackdown Hills, with easy access to Wellington and Taunton. The friendly owners are welcoming and keen to help, and keep the facilities in good order. A 2 acre site with 40 touring pitches, 7 hardstandings.

AA Pubs & Restaurants nearby: Queens Arms, Pitminster 01823 421529

Hatch Inn, Hatch Beauchamp 01823 480245

Willow Tree Restaurant, Taunton 01823 352835

Facilities: ⌂◉♥❄🕓🛒🚿
Services: ⊞⛽♻⛽Ⓣ🛒
Within 3 miles: ⚓♿🛒⛽∪ **Notes:** Wi-fi

WATCHET   Map 3 ST04

Places to visit

West Somerset Railway, Minehead, 01643 704996, www.west-somerset-railway.co.uk

Dunster Castle, Dunster, 01643 821314, www.nationaltrust.org.uk

Great for kids: Tropiquaria Animal and Adventure Park, Washford, 01984 640688, www.tropiquaria.co.uk

▶▶▶ **85% Home Farm Holiday Centre** (ST106432)

St Audries Bay TA4 4DP
☎ 01984 632487   🖷 01984 634687
e-mail: dib@homefarmholidaycentre.co.uk
dir: *Follow A39 towards Minehead, right onto B3191 at West Quantoxhead after St Audries garage, then right in 0.25m*

* ⛺ £12-£25 ⛞ £12-£25 ▲ £12-£25

Open all year (rs mid Nov-Etr shop & bar closed) Last arrival dusk Last departure noon

In a hidden valley beneath the Quantock Hills, this park overlooks its own private beach. The

atmosphere is friendly and quiet, and there are lovely sea views from the level pitches. Flowerbeds, woodland walks, and a Koi carp pond all enhance this very attractive site, along with a lovely indoor swimming pool and a beer garden. A 45 acre site with 40 touring pitches, 35 hardstandings and 230 statics.

AA Pubs & Restaurants nearby: The Smugglers, Blue Anchor 01984 640385

Leisure: ⚉⚠ **Facilities:** ⌂◉♥❄♿🕓🛒🐾
Services: ⊞⛽🍴🏠♻Ⓣ
Within 3 miles: ♿🛒⛽

Notes: No cars by caravans or tents

WELLINGTON   Map 3 ST12

Places to visit

Sunnycroft, Wellington, 01952 242884, www.nationaltrust.org.uk/sunnycroft

Hestercombe Gardens, Taunton, 01823 413923, www.hestercombe.com

Great for kids: Diggerland, Collompton, 0871 227 7007, www.diggerland.com

▶▶▶▶ **81% Greenacres Touring Park** (ST156001)

Haywards Ln, Chelston TA21 9PH
☎ 01823 652844
e-mail: enquiries@wellington.co.uk
dir: *M5 junct 26, right at rdbt signed Wellington, approx 1.5m. At Chelston rdbt, take 1st left, signed A38 West Buckland Rd. In 500mtrs follow sign for site*

⛺ ⛞

Open Apr-end Sep Last arrival 20.00hrs Last departure 11.00hrs

This attractively landscaped adults-only park is situated close to the Somerset/Devon border in a peaceful setting with great views of the Blackdown and Quantock Hills. It is in a very convenient location for overnight stays, being just one and half miles from the M5. It is also close to a local bus route. It has excellent facilities, which are spotlessly clean and well maintained. A 2.5 acre site with 40 touring pitches, 30 hardstandings.

AA Pubs & Restaurants nearby: White Horse Inn, Bradford-on-Tone 01823 461239

Facilities: ⌂◉♥♿⌂ **Services:** ⊞
Within 3 miles: ⚓⊞♿🛒⛽∪
Notes: Adults only. ⊛ No RVs.

▶▶▶ 78% Gamlins Farm Caravan Park (ST083195)

Gamlins Farm House, Greenham TA21 0LZ
☎ 01823 672859 & 07967 683738
📄 01823 673391
e-mail: nataliehowe@hotmail.com
dir: M5 junct 26, A38 towards Tiverton & Exeter. 5m, right for Greenham, site 1m on right

* 🚐 £8-£12 🚐 £8-£12 ▲ £6-£12

Open Mar-Oct

A well-planned site in a secluded position with panoramic views. The friendly owners keep the toilet facilities to a good standard of cleanliness. A 3 acre site with 25 touring pitches, 6 hardstandings and 3 statics.

AA Pubs & Restaurants nearby: White Horse Inn, Bradford-on-Tone 01823 461239

Leisure: 🎣
Facilities: 🐾⊙♿⚘🚿🎡
Services: 🔌🔓
Within 3 miles: ⚓🏇🎯🛒🎣U

Notes: 🐕 Dogs must be kept on leads, no loud noise after 22.00hrs. Free coarse fishing on site

▶▶▶▶ 81% Wells Holiday Park (ST531459)

Haybridge BA5 1AJ
☎ 01749 676869
e-mail: jason@wellsholidaypark.co.uk
dir: A38 then follow signs for Axbridge, Cheddar & Wells

🚐 🚐 ▲

Open all year Last arrival 20.00hrs Last dep noon

This well established holiday park has been completely upgraded with new toilet facilities, plus many hardstandings, all with electricity. A restful park set in countryside on the outskirts of Wells, it is within easy walking distance of the city, with its spectacular cathedral and Bishop's Palace. Cheddar Gorge and Caves, Bath, Bristol, Weston-Super-Mare, Wookey Hole and Glastonbury are all within easy driving distance. Holiday cottages are available for hire. A 7.5 acre site with 72 touring pitches, 54 hardstandings.

AA Pubs & Restaurants nearby: City Arms, Wells 01749 673916

Fountains Inn & Boxer's Restaurant, Wells 01749 672317

Goodfellows, Wells 01749 673866 The Old Spot, Wells 01749 689099

Facilities: 🐾⊙♿🚿♿🛒🚻
Services: 🔌🔓📞🚽🛒🚮
Within 3 miles: ⚓🏇🎯🛒🎣U   Notes: Wi-fi
see advert below

SERVICES: 🔌 Electric hook up 🔓 Launderette 🍺 Licensed bar 🔥 Calor Gas ⚗ Camping Gaz 🚽 Toilet fluid 🍴 Café/Restaurant 🍟 Fast Food/Takeaway 🔋 Battery charging 🚼 Baby care ⚙ Motorvan service point ABBREVIATIONS: BH/bank hols-bank holidays Etr-Easter Whit-Whitsun dep-departure fr-from hrs-hours m-mile mdnt-midnight rdbt-roundabout rs-restricted service wk-week wknd-weekend 🚫 No credit cards 🚫 no dogs See page 7 for details of the AA Camping Card Scheme

WELLS *continued*

▶▶ 84% Homestead Park *(ST532474)*

Wookey Hole BA5 1BW
☎ 01749 673022　📄 01749 673022
e-mail: homesteadpark@onetel.com
dir: *0.5m NW off A371. (NB weight limit on bridge into touring area now 1 tonne)*

Open Etr-Sep Last arrival 20.00hrs Last dep noon

This attractive, small site for tents only is set on a wooded hillside and meadowland with access to the river and Wookey Hole. This park is for adults only and the statics are residential caravans. Please note that this site only accepts tents. A 2 acre site with 30 touring pitches and 28 statics.

AA Pubs & Restaurants nearby: City Arms, Wells 01749 673916

Goodfellows, Wells 01749 673866 The Old Spot, Wells 01749 689099

Facilities: ⌐⊙☞☀①🖳　**Services:** 🔒⌀⊞
Within 3 miles: ↕🎏☞🖳🛍U

Notes: Adults only. 🐾

▶▶▶ 81% West End Farm Caravan & Camping Park *(ST354600)*

Locking BS24 8RH
☎ 01934 822529　📄 01934 822529
e-mail: robin@westendfarm.org
dir: *M5 junct 21 onto A370. Follow International Helicopter Museum signs. Right at rdbt, follow signs to site*

🚐🚕Å

Open all year Last arrival 21.00hrs Last departure noon

A spacious and well laid out park bordered by hedges, with good landscaping, and well kept facilities. It is handily located next to a helicopter museum, and offers good access to Weston-Super-Mare and the Mendips. A 10 acre site with 75 touring pitches and 11 statics.

AA Pubs & Restaurants nearby: The Cove, Weston-Super-Mare 01934 418217

Leisure: 🅰🎣　**Facilities:** ⌐⊙☀🕭🛍🐕
Services: 🚽🛢🔒⌀
Within 3 miles: ↕🎏🎏☞◎🛥🛍🛍U

Notes: 🐾

▶▶▶ 80% Country View Holiday Park *(ST335647)*

Sand Rd, Sand Bay BS22 9UJ
☎ 01934 627595
e-mail: info@cvhp.co.uk
dir: *M5 junct 21, A370 towards Weston-Super-Mare. Immediately into left lane, follow Kewstoke/ Sand Bay signs. Straight over 3 rdbts onto Lower Norton Ln. At Sand Bay right into Sand Rd, site on right*

* 🚐 £10-£25　🚕 £10-£25　Å £10-£25

Open Mar-Jan Last arrival 20.00hrs Last dep noon

A pleasant open site in a rural area a few hundred yards from Sandy Bay and beach. The park is also well placed for energetic walks along the coast at either end of the beach and is only a short drive away from Weston-Super-Mare. The facilities are excellent and well maintained. An 8 acre site with 120 touring pitches, 90 hardstandings and 65 statics.

AA Pubs & Restaurants nearby: The Cove, Weston-Super-Mare 01934 418217

Leisure: 🏊🅰🎣　**Facilities:** ⌐⊙☞☀🕭①🛍
Services: 🚽🛢🖳🚽①
Within 3 miles: ↕🎏🎏☞◎🛥🛍🛍U

▶▶▶ 78% Halse Farm Caravan & Camping Park *(SS894344)*

TA24 7JL
☎ 01643 851259　📄 01643 851592
e-mail: enquiries@halsefarm.co.uk
web: www.halsefarm.co.uk
dir: *Signed from A396 at Bridgetown. In Winsford turn left, bear left past pub. 1m up hill, entrance on left immediately after cattle grid*

* 🚐 £12-£14　🚕 £12-£14　Å £12-£14

Open 22 Mar-Oct Last arrival 22.00hrs Last departure noon

A peaceful little site on Exmoor overlooking a wooded valley with glorious views. This moorland site is quite remote, but it provides good modern toilet facilities which are kept immaculately clean. This is a good base for exploring the Exmoor National Park. A 3 acre site with 44 touring pitches.

AA Pubs & Restaurants nearby: Crown Hotel, Exford 01643 831554

Leisure: 🅰
Facilities: ⌐⊙☞☀🕭①🐕
Services: 🚽🛢🔒⌀
Within 3 miles: ☞🛍U

WIVELISCOMBE
Map 3 ST02

PREMIER PARK

▶▶▶▶ 84%
Waterrow Touring Park

(ST053251)

TA4 2AZ
☎ 01984 623464
e-mail: waterrowpark@yahoo.co.uk
dir: *From M5 junct 25 take A358 (signed Minehead) around Taunton, then B3227 through Wiveliscombe. Site after 3m at Waterrow, 0.25m past Rock Inn*

🚐 £15-£24 🚗 £15-£24 ▲ £15-£21

Open all year Last arrival 19.00hrs Last dep 11.30hrs

This really delightful park for adults only has spotless facilities and plenty of spacious hardstandings. The River Tone runs along a valley beneath the park, accessed by steps to a nature area created by the owners, where fly-fishing is permitted. Painting workshops and other activities are available, and the local pub is a short walk away. A 6 acre site with 45 touring pitches, 38 hardstandings and 1 static.

AA Pubs & Restaurants nearby: White Hart, Wiveliscombe 01984 623344

Rock Inn, Waterrow 01984 623293

Three Horseshoes, Langley Marsh 01984 623763

Facilities: 🌀⊙🅿✳♿🕭🚻🅿🚼
Services: 🔌🖲🔒🅃🔋⛽ **Within 3 miles:** 🖉🏧🖲
Notes: Adults only. No gazebos. Watercolour painting. Wi-fi

YEOVIL
Map 4 ST51
Places to visit
Montacute House, Montacute, 01935 823289, www.nationaltrust.org.uk

Lytes Cary Manor, Kingsdon, 01458 224471, www.nationaltrust.org.uk

Great for kids: Fleet Air Arm Museum, Yeovilton, 01935 840565, www.fleetairarm.com

▶▶ 80% Halfway Caravan & Camping
Park *(ST530195)*

Trees Cottage, Halfway, Ilchester Rd BA22 8RE
☎ 01935 840342
e-mail: halfwaycaravanpark@earthlink.net
web: www.halfwaycaravanpark.com
dir: *On A37 between Ilchester & Yeovil*

🚐 £10-£12.50 🚗 £10-£12.50 ▲ £7-£15

Open Mar-Oct Last arrival 19.00hrs Last departure noon

An attractive little park near the Somerset and Dorset border, and next to the Halfway House pub and restaurant, which also has excellent AA-graded accommodation. It overlooks a fishing lake and is surrounded by attractive countryside, with free fishing for people staying at the park. Dogs are welcome here. A 2 acre site with 20 touring pitches, 10 hardstandings.

AA Pubs & Restaurants nearby: Masons Arms, Yeovil 01935 862591

Helyar Arms, East Coker 01935 862332

Facilities: 🚻🌀 **Services:** 🔌🍽
Within 3 miles: 🖈🎡🖉🏧🖲
Notes: ⊗ No group parties

STAFFORDSHIRE

ALTON
Map 10 SK04
Places to visit
Kedleston Hall, Kedleston Hall, 01332 842191, www.nationaltrust.org.uk

Sudbury Hall and Museum of Childhood, Sudbury, 01283 585305, www.nationaltrust.org.uk

Great for kids: Alton Towers, Alton, 08705 204060 www.altontowers.com

▶▶▶▶ 85% The Star Caravan
& Camping Park *(SK066456)*

Star Rd, Cotton ST10 3DW
☎ 01538 702219
dir: *From N: M1 junct 28, (or from S: M1 junct 23a) follow Alton Towers signs. With Alton Towers main gate on right, follow for 0.75m to x-rds in Cotton. Take B5417, past Ye Old Star Inn, to site*

🚐 £17-£20 🚗 £12-£22 ▲ £12-£30

Open Mar-Nov Last arrival 20.00hrs Last departure 11.00hrs

With its close proximity to Alton Towers, this park is a natural favourite with families visiting the popular attraction. Grounds and buildings are beautifully designed and maintained, and there is an excellent children's playground as well as a football field for working off steam. Seasonal touring pitches are available. A 48 acre site with 120 touring pitches, 30 hardstandings and 65 statics.

AA Pubs & Restaurants nearby: Bulls Head Inn, Alton 01538 702307

Leisure: 🅰 **Facilities:** 🚿🌀⊙🅿✳♿🕭🚻🅿🚼
Services: 🔌🖲🔒🖉🚼⛽
Within 3 miles: 🖈🖉🎡🏧🖲🚻

Notes: Families and couples only. Football field for children, 5-acre dog walk, wildlife meadow. Wi-fi

CHEADLE
Map 10 SK04
Places to visit
Wedgwood Visitor Centre, Stoke-on-Trent, 01782 282986, www.wedgwoodvisitorcentre.com

The Potteries Museum and Art Gallery, Stoke-on-Trent, 01782 232323, www.stoke.gov.uk/museums

Great for kids: Alton Towers, Alton, 08705 204060 www.altontowers.com

Etruria Industrial Museum, Stoke-on-Trent, 01782 233144, www.stoke.gov.uk/museums

▶▶▶▶ 76% Quarry Walk Park
(SK045405)

Coppice Ln, Croxden Common, Freehay ST10 1RQ
☎ 01538 723412
e-mail: quarry@quarrywalkpark.co.uk
dir: *From A522 (Uttoxeter-Cheadle road) turn at Crown Inn at Mabberley signed Freehay. In 1m at rdbt by Queen pub turn to Great Gate. Site signed on right in 1.25m*

*🚐 £21.50 🚗 £21.50 ▲ £12-£20

Open all year Last arrival 18.00hrs Last dep 11.00hrs

A pleasant park, close to Alton Towers, developed in an old quarry with well-screened pitches, all with water and electricity, and mature trees and shrubs, which enhance the peaceful ambience of the park. There are seven glades of varying sizes used exclusively for tents, one with ten electric hook-ups. There are several camping pods and, when completed, there will be 18 timber lodges for hire, each with its own hot tub. Expect good toilet facilities, which include two family rooms in the reception building. A 46 acre site with 40 touring pitches, 40 hardstandings.

AA Pubs & Restaurants nearby: The Queens at Freehay, Cheadle 01538 722383

Leisure: 🅰 **Facilities:** 🌀⊙🅿♿🚻🅿🚼
Services: 🔌🖲🔒🖉🚼
Within 3 miles: 🖈🖉🎡🏧🖲🚻

Suffolk

Suffolk's superb Heritage Coast is the jewel in the county's crown. The beaches, often windswept and completely deserted, run for miles, with the waves of the North Sea breaking beside them in timeless fashion. But it is an ecologically fragile coastline with much of it claimed by the sea over the years. The poet, George Crabbe, perfectly summed up the fate of this area when he wrote: *'The ocean roar whose greedy waves devour the lessening shore.'*

With its huge skies and sense of space and solitude, Suffolk's crumbling, time-ravaged coastline is highly evocative and wonderfully atmospheric. This is where rivers wind lazily to the sea and 18th-century smugglers hid from the excise men.

Suffolk's coast

Between Felixstowe and Lowestoft the coast offers something for everyone. For example, Orford Ness is a unique visitor attraction where ecology meets military history. This internationally important nature reserve - home to many breeding birds, including the avocet – was once the setting for a highly secret military testing site. These days, Orford Ness is managed by the National Trust.

Aldeburgh is all about the arts and in particular the Aldeburgh Music Festival. Benjamin Britten lived at nearby Snape and wrote *Peter Grimes* here.

▶

Aldeburgh

Flatford Mill, East Bergholt

The Suffolk coast is where both the sea and the natural landscape have influenced generations of writers, artists and musicians. The charm of Southwold, further north, is undimmed and reminiscent of a fashionable, genteel seaside resort from a bygone era.

Inland towns and villages

But there is much more to Suffolk than its scenic coastline. Far away to the west lies Newmarket and the world of horseracing. Apart from its equine associations, the town boasts some handsome buildings and memorable views. Palace House in Palace Street was the home of Charles II while the High Street is the setting for the National Horseracing Museum, illustrating how this great sporting tradition has evolved over the last 400 years.

Bury St Edmunds, Sudbury and Ipswich also feature prominently on the tourist trail and the county's smaller towns offer a wealth of attractions, too. With their picturesque, timber-framed houses, Lavenham, Kersey and Debenham are a reminder of Suffolk's key role in the wool industry and the vast wealth it yielded for the merchants.

Constable's legacy

It was the artist John Constable who really put Suffolk's delightful countryside on the map. Son of a wealthy miller, Constable spent much of his early life sketching in the vicinity of Dedham Vale. Situated on the River Stour at Flatford, Constable's mill is now a major tourist attraction in the area but a close look at the surroundings confirms rural Suffolk is little changed since the family lived here. Constable himself maintained that the Suffolk countryside 'made me a painter and I am grateful.'

Walking and Cycling

With 3,300 miles of rights of way, walkers in the county have plenty of choice. There are many publicised trails and waymarked routes, including the Angles Way which runs along Norfolk and Suffolk's boundary in the glorious Waveney Valley. Hard to beat is the county's famous Suffolk Coast Path which runs for 50 miles (80km) between Felixstowe and Lowestoft and is the best way to explore Suffolk's dramatic eastern extremity.

The county offers plenty of potential for cycling, too. There is the Heart of Suffolk Cycle Route, which extends for 78 miles (125km), while the National Byway, a 4,000-mile (6,436km) cycle route around Britain takes in part of Suffolk and is a highly enjoyable way to tour the county.

Festivals and events

- The popular Aldeburgh Literary Festival takes place in March.
- The Alde Valley Spring Festival is staged in April and May with a 4-week celebration of food, farming, landscape and the arts. The venue is Great Glemham near Saxmundham.
- There is the Lattitude Music Festival at Southwold in July and the two-day Lowestoft Seafront Airshow in August, with over four hours of breathtaking precision flying displays.
- The 3-day Christmas Fayre at Bury St Edmunds showcases the ancient town and in recent years has attracted 70,000 visitors.

SUFFOLK

BUCKLESHAM   Map 13 TM24

Places to visit

Ipswich Museum, Ipswich, 01473 433550, www.ipswich.gov.uk

Christchurch Mansion, Ipswich, 01473 433554, www.ipswich.gov.uk

▶▶▶▶ 84% Westwood Caravan Park

(TM253411)

Old Felixstowe Rd IP10 0BN
☎ **01473 659637** 📄 **01473 659637**
e-mail: info@westwoodcaravanpark.co.uk
dir: From A14 junct 58 (SE of Ipswich) follow signs for Bucklesham. Site SE of Bucklesham near Kembroke Hall

* 🚐 £15-£20 🚗 £15-£20 ▲ £15-£20

Open Mar-15 Jan Last arrival 19.00hrs Last departure 13.00hrs

This site is in the heart of rural Suffolk in an idyllic, peaceful setting. All buildings are of traditional Suffolk style, and the toilet facilities are of outstanding quality. There is also a spacious room for disabled visitors, and plenty of space for children to play. A 5 acre site with 100 touring pitches.

AA Pubs & Restaurants nearby: Ship Inn, Levington 01473 659573

Mariners, Ipswich 01473 289748

The Eaterie at Salthouse Harbour Hotel, Ipswich 01473 226789

Leisure: 🄰
Facilities: 🄼☉✳🄳🄶🎋 🕈
Services: 🔌🗑🚽🖉🅃
Within 3 miles: ⚓🚣🎌🖉🅱🖻
Notes: No unruly behaviour. Wi-fi

BUNGAY   Map 13 TM38

▶▶▶ 68% Outney Meadow Caravan Park *(TM333905)*

Outney Meadow NR35 1HG
☎ **01986 892338** 📄 **01986 896627**
e-mail: c.r.hancy@ukgateway.net
dir: At Bungay, site signed from rdbt junction of A143 & A144

🚐🚗▲

Open Mar-Oct Last arrival 21.00hrs Last departure 16.00hrs

Three pleasant grassy areas beside the River Waveney, with screened pitches. The central toilet block offers good modern facilities, especially in the ladies, and is open at all times. The views from the site across the wide flood plain could be straight out of a Constable painting. Canoeing and boating, coarse fishing and cycling are all available here. A 6 acre site with 45 touring pitches, 5 hardstandings and 30 statics.

Outney Meadow Caravan Park

AA Pubs & Restaurants nearby: Earsham Street Café, Bungay 01986 893103

Wicked at St Peter's Hall, St Peter South Elmham 01986 782288

Facilities: 🄼☉🄿✳🄳 🕈
Services: 🔌🗑🚿🖉🅃🎋
Within 3 miles: ⚓🚣🖉🚣🅱🖻
Notes: 🐕 Dogs must be kept on leads. Boat, canoe & bike hire

BURY ST EDMUNDS   Map 13 TL86

Places to visit

Moyse Hall Museum, Bury St Edmunds, 01284 706183, www.moyseshall.org

Ickworth House, Park and Gardens, Horringer, 01284 735270, www.nationaltrust.org.uk/ickworth

Great for kids: National Horse Racing Museum and Tours, Newmarket, 01638 667333 www.nhrm.co.uk

▶▶▶▶ 85% Dell Touring Park

(TL928640)

Beyton Rd, Thurston IP31 3RB
☎ **01359 270121**
e-mail: thedellcaravanpark@btinternet.com
dir: Signed from A14 at Beyton/Thurston (4m E of Bury St Edmunds) & from A143 at Barton/Thurston

* 🚐 £12-£17 🚗 £12-£17 ▲ £10-£30

Open all year Last arrival 21.00hrs Last dep noon

A small site with enthusiastic owners that has been developed to a high specification with more improvements planned. Set in a quiet spot with lots of mature trees, the quality purpose-built toilet facilities include family rooms, dishwashing and laundry. This is an ideal base for exploring this picturesque area. A 6 acre site with 60 touring pitches, 12 hardstandings.

Dell Touring Park

AA Pubs & Restaurants nearby: Old Cannon Brewery, Bury St Edmunds 01284 768769

Linden Tree, Bury St Edmunds 01284 754600

Maison Bleue, Bury St Edmunds 01284 760623

Leaping Hare Restaurant & Country Store, Bury St Edmunds 01359 250287

Facilities: 🛁🄼☉🄿✳🄳🎋 🕈
Services: 🔌🗑🚿🖉🚣 **Within 3 miles:** 🖉🖻
Notes: 🐕 No footballs

DUNWICH   Map 13 TM47

▶▶ 71% *Haw Wood Farm Caravan Park* *(TM421717)*

Hinton IP17 3QT
☎ **01986 784248**
dir: Exit A12, 1.5m N of Darsham level crossing at Little Chef. Site 0.5m on right

🚐🚗▲

Open Mar-14 Jan Last arrival 21.00hrs Last dep noon

An unpretentious family-orientated park set in two large fields surrounded by low hedges. The toilets are clean and functional, and there is plenty of space for children to play. An 8 acre site with 65 touring pitches and 25 statics.

AA Pubs & Restaurants nearby: Westleton Crown, Westleton 01728 648777

Ship Inn, Dunwich 01728 648219

Queen's Head, Halesworth 01986 784214

Leisure: 🄰   **Facilities:** 🄼☉✳🄳 🕈
Services: 🔌🗑🖉🅃 **Within 3 miles:** ⚓🖉🅱🎡
Notes: 🐕

FELIXSTOWE
Map 13 TM33

Places to visit

Ipswich Museum, Ipswich, 01473 433550, www.ipswich.gov.uk

Christchurch Mansion, Ipswich, 01473 433554, www.ipswich.gov.uk

►►► 75% *Peewit Caravan Park* (TM290338)

Walton Av IP11 2HB
☎ **01394 284511**
dir: *Signed from A14 in Felixstowe, 100mtrs past Dock Gate 1, 1st on left*

Open Apr or Etr-Oct Last arrival 21.00hrs Last departure 11.00hrs

A grass touring area fringed by trees, with well-maintained grounds and a colourful floral display. This handy urban site is not overlooked by houses, and the toilet facilities are clean and well cared for, with upgraded showers in 2010. A function room contains a TV and library. The beach is a few minutes away by car. A 13 acre site with 45 touring pitches, 4 hardstandings and 200 statics.

AA Pubs & Restaurants nearby: Ship Inn, Levington 01473 659573

Leisure: ⚙ **Facilities:** 🚿⊙🅿✳♿☺🐕
Services: 🔌🗑🛢🔋
Within 3 miles: ↧⚑🎣🎿⊚♒🛒🛍

Notes: ⊗ Only foam footballs are permitted. Boules area, bowling green, adventure trail

HOLLESLEY
Map 13 TM34

Places to visit

Woodbridge Tide Mill, Woodbridge, 01728 746959, www.tidemill.org.uk

Sutton Hoo, Woodbridge, 01394 389700, www.nationaltrust.org.uk/suttonhoo

Great for kids: Orford Castle, Orford, 01394 450472, www.english-heritage.org.uk

►►► 85% Run Cottage Touring Park
(TM350440)

Alderton Rd IP12 3RQ
☎ **01394 411309**
e-mail: info@run-cottage.co.uk
dir: *From A12 (Ipswich-Saxmundham) onto A1152 at Melton. 1.5m, right at rdbt onto B1083. 0.75m, left to Hollesley. In Hollesley right into The Street, through village, down hill, over bridge, site 100yds on left*

* 🚐 £16 🚌 ▲ £14

Open all year Last arrival 20.00hrs Last departure 11.00hrs

Located in the peaceful village of Hollesley on the Suffolk coast, this landscaped park is set behind the owners' house. The generously-sized pitches are serviced by a well-appointed and immaculately maintained toilet block. This site is handy for the National Trust's Sutton Hoo, and also by travelling a little further north, the coastal centre and beach at Dunwich Heath, and the RSPB bird reserve at Minsmere. A 2.5 acre site with 20 touring pitches, 6 hardstandings.

AA Pubs & Restaurants nearby: The Crown, Woodbridge 01394 384242

Seckford Hall Hotel, Woodbridge 01394 385678

Facilities: 🚿⊙✳♿🛢🚻 **Services:** 🔌🔋
Within 3 miles: ↧🎣🛒🛍⚑
Notes: No groundsheets, ball games or cycles

IPSWICH
Map 13 TM14

Places to visit

Ipswich Museum, Ipswich, 01473 433550, www.ipswich.gov.uk

Christchurch Mansion, Ipswich, 01473 433554, www.ipswich.gov.uk

►►► 77% Low House Touring Caravan Centre (TM227425)

Bucklesham Rd, Foxhall IP10 0AU
☎ **01473 659437 & 07710 378029**
📠 **01473 659880**
e-mail: low.house@btinternet.com
dir: *From A14 (south ring road) take slip road to A1156 signed East Ipswich. Right in 1m, right again in 0.5m. Site on left*

* 🚐 fr £14 🚌 fr £14 ▲ fr £20

Open all year Last arrival anytime Last departure 14.00hrs

A secluded site surrounded by hundreds of mature trees. Buildings have been hand-crafted by the owner in stained timber, and there is a children's play area, and a collection of caged rabbits, bantams and guinea fowl. Tents are accepted only if there is space available. A 3.5 acre site with 30 touring pitches.

AA Pubs & Restaurants nearby: Mariners, Ipswich 01473 289748

The Eaterie at Salthouse Harbour Hotel, Ipswich 01473 226789

Ship Inn, Levington 01473 659573

Leisure: ⚙
Facilities: 🚿⊙🅿✳🚻
Services: 🔌🗑🛢🔋
Within 3 miles: ↧🎣⊚🛒🛍⚑
Notes: ⊗ Dogs must be kept on leads

KESSINGLAND
Map 13 TM58

Places to visit

East Anglia Transport Museum, Lowestoft, 01502 518459, www.eatm.org.uk

Maritime Museum, Lowestoft, 01502 561963, www.lowestoftmaritimemuseum.org.uk

Great for kids: Pleasurewood Hills, Lowestoft, 01502 586000 (admin), www.pleasurewoodhills.com

71% Kessingland Beach Holiday Park (TM535852)

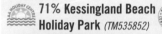

Beach Rd NR33 7RN
☎ **01502 740636** 📠 **01502 740907**
e-mail: holidaysales.kessinglandbeach@park-resorts.com
dir: *From Lowestoft take A12 S. At Kessingland take 3rd exit at rdbt towards beach. Through village. At beach follow road to right. In 400yds fork left for park*

Open Apr-Oct Last arrival mdnt Last departure 10.00hrs

A large holiday centre with direct access onto the beach, and a variety of leisure facilities. The touring area is tucked away from the statics, and served by a clean and functional toilet block. A fish and chip shop and Boat House Restaurant are popular features. A 69 acre site with 90 touring pitches and 95 statics.

AA Pubs & Restaurants nearby: Swan Inn, Barnby 01502 476646

Leisure: 🏊🎿⚙🎱🎯🎮
Facilities: 🚿⊙🅿✳♿☺🛢🚻
Services: 🔌🗑🍴🍽🍔♨
Within 3 miles: ↧🎣🎿⚑🛒🛍
Notes: Kids' clubs, entertainment, mini ten-pin bowling, archery. Wi-fi

---

KESSINGLAND *continued*

AA CAMPING CARD SITE

►►►► **86% Heathland Beach Caravan Park** *(TM533877)*

London Rd NR33 7PJ
☎ 01502 740337 📠 01502 742355
e-mail: heathlandbeach@btinternet.com
web: www.heathlandbeach.co.uk
dir: *1m N of Kessingland off A12 onto B1437*

Open Apr-Oct Last arrival 21.00hrs Last departure 11.00hrs

A well-run and maintained park offering superb toilet facilities. The park is set in meadowland, with level grass pitches, and mature trees and bushes. There is direct access to the sea and beach, and good provisions for families on site with a heated swimming pool and three play areas. A 5 acre site with 63 touring pitches and 200 statics.

AA Pubs & Restaurants nearby: Swan Inn, Barnby 01502 476646

Leisure: 🏊 🎠 🎾

Facilities: 🚿 ⛱ 🍴 ⚡ 💇 🕐 🛒 🍴 🔨 🐕

Services: 🅿 🔧 🍴 💧 ♻ Ⓣ

Within 3 miles: 🎣 ✈ 🎪 ⛳ 🍴 🛒 🐕 ♻

Notes: One dog only per unit. Freshwater & sea fishing. Wi-fi

---

LEISTON — Map 13 TM46

Places to visit

Long Shop Museum, Leiston, 01728 832189, www.longshopmuseum.co.uk

Leiston Abbey, Leiston, 01728 831354, www.leistonabbey.co.uk

Great for kids: Easton Farm Park, Easton, 01728 746475, www.eastonfarmpark.co.uk

AA CAMPING CARD SITE

►►► **86% Cakes & Ale** *(TM432637)*

Abbey Ln, Theberton IP16 4TE
☎ 01728 831655
e-mail: cakesandalepark@gmail.com
web: www.cakesandale.net
dir: *From Saxmundham E on B1119. 3m follow minor road over level crossing, turn right, in 0.5m straight on at x-rds, entrance 0.5m on left*

* 🚐 £17-£26 🚙 £17-£26 ⛺ £17-£26

Open Apr-Oct (rs Low season club, shop & reception limited hours) Last arrival 20.00hrs Last departure 13.00hrs

A large, well spread out and beautifully maintained site with many trees and bushes on a former Second World War airfield. The spacious touring area includes plenty of hardstandings and super pitches, and there is a good bar and a well-maintained toilet block, which has now been extended to house ladies' showers, a fully-serviced family/disabled room and a washing-up room. Wi-fi access is available on site. A 45 acre site

---

with 50 touring pitches, 50 hardstandings and 200 statics.

AA Pubs & Restaurants nearby: 152 Aldeburgh, Aldeburgh 01728 454594

Mill Inn, Aldeburgh 01728 452563

Regatta Restaurant, Aldeburgh 01728 452011

Leisure: 🎠 🎾

Facilities: 🚿 ⛱ ⊙ ⛱ ⚡ 🕐 🛒 🐕

Services: 🅿 🔧 🍴 💧 ♻ ⚡

Within 3 miles: 🎣 ✈ 🎪 ⛳ 🛒 🐕 ♻

Notes: No group bookings, no noise between 21.00hrs-08.00hrs. 5-acre recreation ground, practise range/net, volleyball court, boules rink, football nets. Wi-fi

see advert below

LOWESTOFT

See Kessingland

SAXMUNDHAM

Places to visit

Long Shop Museum, Leiston, 01728 832189, www.longshopmuseum.co.uk

Leiston Abbey, Leiston, 01728 831354, www.leistonabbey.co.uk

Great for kids: Museum of East Anglian Life, Stowmarket 01449 612229 www.eastanglianlife.org.uk

---

LEISURE: 🏊 Indoor swimming pool 🏊 Outdoor swimming pool 🎠 Children's playground 🎾 Tennis court 🎱 Games room 📺 Separate TV room ⛳ 9/18 hole golf course 🚣 Boats for hire 🎬 Cinema 🎣 Fishing ⛳ Mini golf 🏄 Watersports ♞ Stables **FACILITIES:** 🛁 Bath 🚿 Shower ⊙ Electric shaver ⚡ Hairdryer ✳ Ice Pack Facility 💇 Disabled facilities 🕐 Public telephone 🛒 Shop on site or within 200yds 🚚 Mobile shop (calls at least 5 days a week) 🍴 BBQ area 🌲 Picnic area 🐕 Dog exercise area

SAXMUNDHAM
Map 13 TM36

►►►► 81% Carlton Meres Country Park *(TM372637)*

Rendham Rd, Carlton IP17 2QP
☎ 01728 603344 ▤ 01728 652015
e-mail: enquiries@carlton-meres.co.uk
dir: *From A12 , W of Saxmundham, take B1119 towards Framlingham. Site signed from A12*

* 🚐 £25 🚙 £25

Open Etr-Oct Last arrival 17.00hrs Last departure 10.00hrs

With two large fishing lakes, a new modern fitness suite, a beauty saloon, new sauna and steam rooms, tennis court, a bar, and a heated outdoor swimming pool, Carlton Meres offers a wealth of leisure facilities, and all for the exclusive use for those staying on the site (holiday statics and lodges for hire). There is a modern heated toilet block and excellent security. This site is well-placed for all the Suffolk coast attractions. A 52 acre site with 96 touring pitches, 56 hardstandings.

AA Pubs & Restaurants nearby: 153 Aldeburgh, Aldeburgh 01728 454594

Mill Inn, Aldeburgh 01728 452563

Regatta Restaurant, Aldeburgh 01728 452011

Crown Inn, Great Glemham 01728 663693

Leisure: 🏊 ⚑ 🎣

Facilities: 📶 ✳ �& 🚼

Services: 🔌 🗑 🍺 🐕 🍴 🍟

Within 3 miles: 🚶 ⛳ 🎯 ⚓ 🛒 💷 🎣 ↻

Notes: No tents. Wi-fi

To find out more about the AA Camping Card and reduced camping fees see page 7

►►► 80% Whitearch Touring Caravan Park *(TM379610)*

Main Rd, Benhall IP17 1NA
☎ 01728 604646 & 603773
dir: *At junct of A12 & B1121*

* 🚐 fr £15.50 🚙 fr £15.50 ⛺ fr £13

Open Apr-Oct Last arrival 20.00hrs

A small, maturing park set around an attractive coarse-fishing lake, with good quality, imaginatively refurbished toilet facilities and secluded pitches tucked away among trees and shrubs. The park is popular with anglers; there is some traffic noise from the adjacent A12. A 14.5 acre site with 50 touring pitches, 50 hardstandings.

AA Pubs & Restaurants nearby: 153 Aldeburgh, Aldeburgh 01728 454594

Mill Inn, Aldeburgh 01728 452563

Regatta Restaurant, Aldeburgh 01728 452011

Crown Inn, Great Glemham 01728 663693

Leisure: 🎣

Facilities: 📶 ⊙ ⚑ ✳ �& 🕒 🗑 🚻 🚼

Services: 🔌 🗑 🍺 🌿 **Within 3 miles:** ⛳ 💷 🛒

Notes: 🚫 No cars by caravans. No bicycles

►► 82% *Marsh Farm Caravan Site* *(TM385608)*

Sternfield IP17 1HW
☎ 01728 602168
dir: *A12 onto A1094 (Aldeburgh road), at Snape x-roads left signed Sternfield, follow signs to site*

🚐 🚙 ⛺

Open all year Last arrival 21.00hrs Last departure 17.00hrs

A very pretty site overlooking reed-fringed lakes which offer excellent coarse fishing. The facilities are very well maintained, and the park is a truly peaceful haven. A 30 acre site with 45 touring pitches.

AA Pubs & Restaurants nearby: 153 Aldeburgh, Aldeburgh 01728 454594

Mill Inn, Aldeburgh 01728 452563

Regatta Restaurant, Aldeburgh 01728 452011

Crown Inn, Great Glemham 01728 663693

Facilities: 📶 ✳ 🗑 🚻 🚼

Services: 🔌 ⛽ **Within 3 miles:** 🚶 🎯 ⚓ 🛒 ↻

Notes: 🚫 Dogs must be kept on leads

SUDBURY
Map 13 TL84

Places to visit

Melford Hall, Long Melford, 01787 379228, www.nationaltrust.org.uk/melford

Kentwell Hall, Long Melford, 01787 310207, www.kentwell.co.uk

Great for kids: Colne Valley Railway and Museum, Castle Hedingham, 01787 461174, www.colnevalleyrailway.co.uk

►►► 75% Willowmere Caravan Park *(TL886388)*

Bures Rd, Little Cornard CO10 0NN
☎ 01787 375559 & 310422 ▤ 01787 375559
e-mail: awillowmere@aol.com
dir: *1.5m S of Sudbury on B1508 (Bures road)*

🚐 £11.50 🚙 £11.50 ⛺ £11.50

Open Etr-Oct Last arrival anytime Last departure noon

A pleasant little site in a quiet location tucked away beyond a tiny residential static area, offering spotless facilities. A 3 acre site with 40 touring pitches and 9 statics.

AA Pubs & Restaurants nearby: Scutchers Restaurant, Long Melford 01787 310200

White Hart, Great Yeldham 01787 237250

Bell Inn, Great Hadingham 01787 460350

Facilities: 📶 ⊙ ✳ �& 🕒

Services: 🔌 🗑 🍺

Within 3 miles: 🚶 ⛳ ◎ 🛒 💷 ↻

Notes: 🚫 Fishing

WOODBRIDGE

Places to visit

Sutton Hoo, Woodbridge, 01394 389700, www.nationaltrust.org.uk/suttonhoo

Orford Castle, Orford, 01394 450472, www.english-heritage.org.uk

Great for kids: Easton Farm Park, Easton, 01728 746475, www.eastonfarmpark.co.uk

WOODBRIDGE Map 13 TM24

PREMIER PARK

AA CAMPING CARD SITE

▶▶▶▶▶ **92% Moon & Sixpence**
(TM263454)

Newbourn Rd, Waldringfield IP12 4PP
☎ **01473 736650** 🖷 **01473 736270**
e-mail: info@moonandsixpence.eu
web: www.moonandsixpence.eu
dir: *Follow caravan & Moon & Sixpence signs from A12 Ipswich (east bypass). 1.5m, left at x-roads*

* 🚐 £18-£30 🚐 £18-£30 ▲ £18-£30

Open Apr-Oct (rs Low season club, shop, reception open limited hours) Last arrival 20.00hrs Last departure noon

A well-planned site, with tourers occupying a sheltered valley position around an attractive boating lake with a sandy beach. Toilet facilities are housed in a smart Norwegian-style cabin, and there is a laundry and dishwashing area. Leisure facilities include two tennis courts, a bowling green, fishing, boating and a games room. There is an adult-only area, and a strict 'no groups and no noise after 9pm' policy. A 5 acre site with 65 touring pitches and 225 statics.

AA Pubs & Restaurants nearby: The Crown, Woodbridge 01394 384242

Seckford Hall Hotel, Woodbridge 01394 385678

Leisure: 🅰 🏊 🔍
Facilities: 🚿 🕭 ⊙ ℙ ⚹ 🚽 🎪 🐕
Services: 🖳 🔋 🍽 🛢 ⌀ 🍴 🛒 🗑
Within 3 miles: ↕ 🄷 🖋 🚴 🛒 🗑

Notes: No group bookings or commercial vehicles, quiet 21.00hrs-08.00hrs. Cycle trail, 10-acre sports area & 9-hole golf. Wi-fi

see advert below

▶▶ **85% Moat Barn Touring Caravan Park** (TM269530)

Dallinghoo Rd, Bredfield IP13 6BD
☎ **01473 737520**
dir: *Exit A12 at Bredfield, 1st right at village pump. Through village, 1m site on left*

* 🚐 fr £15 🚐 fr £15 ▲ fr £15

Open Mar-15 Jan Last arrival 22.00hrs Last departure noon

An attractive small park set in idyllic Suffolk countryside, perfectly located for touring the heritage coastline and for visiting the National Trust's Sutton Hoo. The modern toilet block is well equipped and maintained. There are now ten tent pitches and the park is located on the popular Hull to Harwich cycle route. Cycle hire is available, but there are no facilities for children. A 2 acre site with 25 touring pitches.

AA Pubs & Restaurants nearby: The Crown, Woodbridge 01394 384242

Seckford Hall Hotel, Woodbridge 01394 385678

Facilities: 🕭 ⊙ ℙ 🗑
Services: 🖳
Within 3 miles: ↕ 🖋 🛒 🗑 ↻

Notes: Adults only. No ball games, breathable groundsheets only, dogs must be kept on leads

LEISURE: 🅰 Indoor swimming pool 🏊 Outdoor swimming pool 🅰 Children's playground 🎾 Tennis court 🎱 Games room 📺 Separate TV room ↕ 9/18 hole golf course 🚣 Boats for hire 🎬 Cinema 🎣 Fishing ◎ Mini golf 🏄 Watersports ↻ Stables **FACILITIES:** 🚿 Bath 🕭 Shower ⊙ Electric shaver ℙ Hairdryer ⚹ Ice Pack Facility ♿ Disabled facilities ☏ Public telephone 🏪 Shop on site or within 200yds 🛒 Mobile shop (calls at least 5 days a week) 🍖 BBQ area 🌲 Picnic area 🐕 Dog exercise area

SERVICES: ⚡ Electric hook up ⬛ Launderette 🍺 Licensed bar 🔵 Calor Gas ⬗ Camping Gaz Ⓣ Toilet fluid 🍽 Café/Restaurant 🍟 Fast Food/Takeaway ⚡ Battery charging
🍼 Baby care ⬇ Motorvan service point **ABBREVIATIONS:** BH/bank hols-bank holidays Etr-Easter Whit-Whitsun dep-departure fr-from hrs-hours m-mile mdnt-midnight
rdbt-roundabout rs-restricted service wk-week wknd-weekend Ⓝ No credit cards Ⓝ no dogs See page 7 for details of the AA Camping Card Scheme

Sussex

Sussex, deriving its name from 'South Saxons' is divided into two - East and West - but the name is so quintessentially English that we tend to think of it as one entity. Mention its name anywhere in the world and for those who are familiar with 'Sussex by the sea', images of rolling hills, historic towns and villages and miles of spectacular chalky cliffs immediately spring to mind. Perhaps it is the bare South Downs with which Sussex is most closely associated.

This swathe of breezy downland represents some of the finest walking in southern England. Now a National Park, the South Downs provide country-loving locals and scores of visitors with a perfect natural playground. As well as walkers and cyclists, you'll find kite flyers, model aircraft enthusiasts and hang gliders.

View from Fulking Escarpment, South Downs Way

Beaches and cliffs

The coast is one of the county's gems. At its western end lies sprawling Chichester harbour, with its meandering channels, creeks and sleepy inlets, and on the horizon is the imposing outline of the cathedral, small but beautiful. To the east are the seaside towns of Worthing, Brighton, Eastbourne, Bexhill and Hastings. Here, the South Downs sweep down towards the sea with two famous landmarks, Birling Gap and Beachy Head, demonstrating how nature and the elements have shaped the land over time.

The heart of the county

Inland is Arundel, with its rows of elegant Georgian and Victorian buildings standing in the shadow of the great castle, ancestral home of the Dukes of Norfolk, and the magnificent French Gothic-style Roman Catholic cathedral. Mid Sussex is the setting for a chain of attractive, typically English towns, including Midhurst, Petworth, Pulborough, Billingshurst, Uckfield and Haywards Heath.

There are grand country houses, too. Parham, built during the reign of Henry VIII, was one of the first stately homes to open its doors to the public, while the National Trust's Petworth House, in 2,000

▶

Bodiam Castle

● Brighton

acres of parkland, retains the 13th-century chapel of an earlier mansion and has a fine art collection including works by Rembrandt and Van Dyck.

Walking and Cycling

In terms of walking, this county is spoilt for choice. Glancing at the map reveals innumerable paths and bridleways, while there are many more demanding and adventurous long-distance paths – a perfect way to get to the heart of rural East and West Sussex. The Sussex Border Path meanders along the boundary between the two counties; the Monarch's Way broadly follows Charles II's escape route in 1651; the most famous of all of them, the South Downs Way, follows hill paths and clifftop tracks all the way from Winchester to Eastbourne; the West Sussex Literary Trail links Horsham with Chichester and recalls many literary figures associated with this area – Shelley, Tennyson and Wilde among them.

East and West Sussex offer exciting cycle rides through the High Weald, along the South Downs Way and via coastal routes between Worthing and Rye. Brighton to Hastings via Polegate is part of the Downs and Weald Cycle Route. There is also the Forest Way through East Grinstead to Groombridge and the Cuckoo Trail from Heathfield to Eastbourne. For glorious coastal views and stiff sea breezes, the

very easy ride between Chichester and West Wittering is recommended. You can vary the return by taking the Itchenor Ferry to Bosham.

Festivals and Events

- March is the month for the Pioneer Motorcycle Run from Epsom Downs to Brighton. All the participating motorcycles are pre 1915 and the event offers a fascinating insight into the early history of these machines – 300 of which are on display.
- During April there is A Taste of Sussex Fine Food Fair at the Weald and Downland Open Air Museum near Chichester.
- The 15th-century moated Herstmonceux Castle hosts England's Medieval Festival on August Bank Holiday weekend, complete with minstrels, magicians, lords, ladies and serfs.
- Goodwood is the venue for the Motor Circuit Revival Meeting in September. This is when fast cars and track legends celebrate the golden age of British motor sport from the 1940s and '50s.
- The same month – September – sees Uckfield Bonfire and Carnival Society's Annual Carnival with fancy dress and a torchlight procession.

SUSSEX, EAST

See Walk 11 in the Walks & Cycle Rides section at the end of the guide

BATTLE
Map 7 TQ71

Places to visit

1066 Story in Hastings Castle, Hastings St. Leonards, 01424 781111, www.discoverhastings.co.uk/hastings-castle-1066/

Blue Reef Aquarium, Hastings St. Leonards, 01424 718776, www.bluereefaquarium.co.uk

Great for kids: Smugglers Adventure, Hastings St. Leonards, 01424 422964, www.discoverhastings.co.uk

▶▶▶ 79% Brakes Coppice Park
(TQ765134)

Forewood Ln TN33 9AB
☎ 01424 830322
e-mail: brakesco@btinternet.com
web: www.brakescoppicepark.co.uk
dir: *From Battle on A2100 towards Hastings. After 2m turn right for Crowhurst. Site 1m on left*

* 🚐 £14-£18 🚗 £14-£18 ▲ £14-£18

Open Mar-Oct Last arrival 21.00hrs Last departure noon

A secluded farm site in a sunny meadow deep in woodland with a small stream and a coarse fishing lake. The toilet block has been revamped and modernised with quality fittings and there's a new washing-up area and a good fully-serviced family/disabled room. Hardstanding pitches are neatly laid out on a terrace, and tents are pitched on grass edged by woodland. A peaceful base for exploring Battle and the south coast. A 3 acre site with 30 touring pitches, 10 hardstandings.

AA Pubs & Restaurants nearby: Ash Tree Inn, Ashburnham Place 01424 892104 Wild Mushroom Restaurant, Westfield 01424 751137

Leisure: ⚑ **Facilities:** 🚿⊙�☀⚑🕐🕭🛗🎋🐾
Services: 🚊🛢🍴⊘🛎🚼
Within 3 miles: ⚓🏌🛍🛎♻

Notes: No fires, footballs or kite flying & dogs must be kept on leads

▶▶▶ 71% Senlac Wood Holiday Park
(TQ722153)

Catsfield Rd, Catsfield TN33 9LN
☎ 01424 773969
e-mail: senlacwood@xlninternet.co.uk
dir: *From Battle take A271, left on B2204 signed Bexhill. Site on left*

* 🚐 £13-£15 🚗 £13-£15 ▲ £13-£15

Open Mar-Oct Last arrival 22.00hrs Last dep noon

An improving woodland site with many secluded bays with hardstanding pitches, and two peaceful grassy glades for tents. The functional toilet facilities are clean, and the site is ideal for anyone looking for seclusion and shade. Well placed for visiting nearby Battle and the south coast beaches. A 20 acre site with 35 touring pitches, 16 hardstandings.

AA Pubs & Restaurants nearby: Ash Tree Inn, Ashburnham Place 01424 892104

Wild Mushroom Restaurant, Westfield 01424 751137

Leisure: ⚑🎣
Facilities: 🚿⊙�☀🕐🛗🎋🐾
Services: 🚊🛢🍴🛎🚼
Within 3 miles: ⚓🏌🛍🛎♻

Notes: No camp fires

BEXHILL
Map 6 TQ70

PREMIER PARK

NEW ▶▶▶▶▶ 85% Kloofs Caravan Park (TQ709091)

Sandhurst Ln TN39 4RG
☎ 01424 842839
e-mail: camping@kloofs.com
dir: *NE of Bexhill. For detailed directions contact the site*

🚐 £23-£31 🚗 £23-£31 ▲ £23-£31

Open all year Last arrival anytime Last departure 11.00hrs

Hidden away down a quiet lane, just inland from Bexhill and the coast, Kloofs is a friendly, family-run park surrounded by farmland and oak woodlands, with views extending to the South Downs from hilltop pitches. Lovingly developed by the owners over the past 15 years, the site is well landscaped and thoughtfully laid out, with excellent hardstandings (some large enough for RVs), colourful flower beds, and spacious pitches, each with mini patio, bench and barbeque stand. Spotless, upmarket toilet facilities include a family shower room and a unisex block with privacy cubicles, a dog shower, and a drying room. A 3 acre site with 50 touring pitches.

CAMBER
Map 7 TQ91

Places to visit

Rye Castle Museum, Rye, 01797 226728, www.ryemuseum.co.uk

Lamb House, Rye, 01580 762334, www.nationaltrust.org.uk/main/w-lambhouse

Great for kids: 1066 Story in Hastings Castle, Hastings St Leonards 01424 781111 www.discoverhastings.co.uk/hastings-castle-1066/

66% Camber Sands
(TQ972184)

New Lydd Rd TN31 7RT
☎ 0871 664 9719
e-mail: camber.sands@park-resorts.com
dir: *M20 junct 10 (Ashford International Station), A2070 signed Brenzett. Follow Hastings & Rye signs on A259. 1m before Rye, left signed Camber. Site in 3m*

🚐 🚗 ▲

Open Apr-Oct Last arrival anytime Last departure 10.00hrs

Located opposite Camber's vast sandy beach, this large holiday centre offers a good range of leisure and entertainment facilities. The touring area is positioned close to the reception and entrance, and is served by a clean and functional toilet block. A 110 acre site with 40 touring pitches, 6 hardstandings and 921 statics.

AA Pubs & Restaurants nearby: Mermaid Inn, Rye 01797 223065

Globe Inn, Rye 01797 227918 Ypres Castle, Rye 01797 223248

George in Rye, Rye 01797 222114

Leisure: 🏊⚑🎱🎣
Facilities: 🚿⊙🛗🕐🛎🎋
Services: 🚊🛢🍴🍽️🛒
Within 3 miles: ⚓🏌◎🚣🛍🛎

Notes: Quiet between 23.00hrs-7.00hrs. Wi-fi

LEISURE: 🏊 Indoor swimming pool 🏊 Outdoor swimming pool ⚑ Children's playground 🎾 Tennis court 🎱 Games room 📺 Separate TV room ⚑ 9/18 hole golf course ⛵ Boats for hire 🎬 Cinema 🎣 Fishing ◎ Mini golf 🚣 Watersports ♻ Stables **FACILITIES:** 🛁 Bath 🚿 Shower ⊙ Electric shaver 🖥 Hairdryer ☀ Ice Pack Facility 🛗 Disabled facilities 🕐 Public telephone 🛍 Shop on site or within 200yds 🚚 Mobile shop (calls at least 5 days a week) 🍴 BBQ area 🎋 Picnic area 🐾 Dog exercise area

FURNER'S GREEN
Map 6 TQ42

Places to visit

Sheffield Park Garden, Sheffield Park, 01825 790231, www.nationaltrust.org.uk/main/w-sheffieldparkgarden

Nymans, Handcross, 01444 405250, www.nationaltrust.org.uk/main/w-nymansgarden2

►► 81% Heaven Farm (TQ403264)

TN22 3RG
☎ **01825 790226** 📄 **01825 790881**
e-mail: heavenfarmleisure@btinternet.com
dir: *On A275 between Lewes & East Grinstead, 1m N of Sheffield Park Gardens*

🚐 🚌 Å

Open Apr-Oct Last arrival 21.00hrs Last departure noon

A delightful, small, rural site on a popular farm complex incorporating a farm museum, craft shop, organic farm shop, tea room and nature trail. Good clean toilet facilities are housed in well-converted outbuildings. Ashdown Forest, the Bluebell Railway and Sheffield Park Garden are nearby. A 1.5 acre site with 25 touring pitches, 2 hardstandings.

AA Pubs & Restaurants nearby: Coach & Horses, Danehill 01825 740369

Griffin Inn, Fletchling 01825 722890

Facilities: 🅿 ⊙ 🅫 🅐 🅗 🖉 🎋 ⋔
Services: 🖭 🆃 🍽 🛒 ↴
Within 3 miles: 🖍 🏌 🖆 ∪

Notes: ⊛ The site prefers no children between 6-18yrs. Fishing

HEATHFIELD

Places to visit

Pashley Manor Garden's, Ticehurst, 01580 200888, www.pashleymanorgardens.com

The Truggery, Herstmonceux, 01323 832314, www.truggery.co.uk

Great for kids: Bentley Wildfowl and Motor Museum, Halland, 01825 840573, www.bentley.org.uk

HEATHFIELD
Map 6 TQ52

►► 77% Greenviews Caravan Park
(TQ605223)

Burwash Rd, Broad Oak TN21 8RT
☎ **01435 863531** 📄 **01435 863531**
dir: *Through Heathfield on A265 for 1m. Site on left after Broad Oak sign*

🚐 🚌 Å

Open Apr-Oct (rs Apr & Oct bookings only, subject to weather) Last arrival 22.00hrs Last departure 10.30hrs

A small touring area adjoining a residential park, with a smart clubhouse. The facility block includes a room for disabled visitors. The owners always offer a friendly welcome, and they take pride in the lovely flower beds which adorn the park. A 3 acre site with 10 touring pitches and 51 statics.

AA Pubs & Restaurants nearby: The Middle House, Mayfield 01435 872146

Best Beech Inn, Wadhurst 01892 782046

Facilities: 🅫 ⊙ 🅐 🅗 🕒
Services: 🖭 🆃 🍽 🅐 🖉
Within 3 miles: 🖆
Notes: ⊛ ⊗

PEVENSEY BAY

Places to visit

How We Lived Then Museum of Shops and Social History, Eastbourne, 01323 737143, www.how-we-lived-then.co.uk

Alfriston Clergy House, Alfriston, 01323 870001, www.nationaltrust.org.uk/main/w-alfristonclergyhouse

Great for kids: The Observatory Science Centre, Herstmonceux, 01323 832731, www.the-observatory.org

PEVENSEY BAY
Map 6 TQ60

AA CAMPING CARD SITE

►►► 83% Bay View Park
(TQ648028)

Old Martello Rd BN24 6DX
☎ **01323 768688** 📄 **01323 769637**
e-mail: holidays@bay-view.co.uk
web: www.bay-view.co.uk
dir: *Signed from A259 W of Pevensey Bay. On sea side of A259 along private road towards beach*

🚐 🚌 Å

Open Mar-Oct Last arrival 20.00hrs Last departure noon

A pleasant well-run site just yards from the beach, in an area east of Eastbourne town centre known as 'The Crumbles'. The level grassy site is very well maintained and the new toilet facilities feature fully-serviced cubicles. A 6 acre site with 94 touring pitches, 10 hardstandings and 8 statics.

AA Pubs & Restaurants nearby: Lamb Inn, Wartling 01323 832116

Leisure: 🅐
Facilities: 🅫 ⊙ 🅟 ✳ 🅐 🕒 🖆
Services: 🖭 🅐 🅐 🆃 🍽 🛒 🎋
Within 3 miles: 🖍 🖯 🏌 ◎ 🍴 🖆 🖆

Notes: Families & couples only, no commercial vehicles. 9-hole golf course. Wi-fi

SUSSEX, WEST

ARUNDEL   Map 6 TQ00

Places to visit

Arundel Castle, Arundel, 01903 882173, www.arundelcastle.org

Harbour Park, Littlehampton, 01903 721200, www.harbourpark.com

Great for kids: Look and Sea! Visitor Centre, Littlehampton, 01903 718984, www.lookandsea.co.uk

AA CAMPING CARD SITE

▶▶ **78% Ship & Anchor Marina** (TQ002040)

GOLD

Station Rd, Ford BN18 0BJ
☎ 01243 551262   📠 01243 555256
e-mail: enquiries@shipandanchormarina.co.uk
dir: *From A27 at Arundel take road S signed Ford. Site 2m on left after level crossing*

* 🚐 £12.50-£18.50 🚙 £12.50-£18.50
🏕 £12.50-£18.50

Open Mar-Oct Last arrival 21.00hrs Last departure noon

A neat and tidy site with dated but spotlessly clean toilet facilities enjoying a pleasant position beside the Ship & Anchor pub and the tidal River Arun. There are good walks from the site to Arundel and the coast. A 12 acre site with 120 touring pitches, 11 hardstandings.

AA Pubs & Restaurants nearby: The Townhouse, Arundel 01903 883847

George & Dragon, Burpham 01903 883131

The Spur, Slindon 01243 814216

Leisure: ⚴

Facilities: ⚭ 🐾 ⊙ 🌡 ⚿ ♿ 🕐 🖭 🐕

Services: 🔌 🚿 🔒 🚮 T 🍽 🎫

Within 3 miles: ↧ ⇵ ✎ ◉ 🚤 🛒 🎣 ∪

Notes: 🚫 No music audible to others. River fishing from site

BARNS GREEN

Places to visit

Parham House and Gardens, Pulborough, 01903 744888, www.parhaminsussex.co.uk

Great for kids: Bignor Roman Villa and Museum, Bignor, 01798 869259, www.bignorromanvilla.co.uk

BARNS GREEN   Map 6 TQ12

AA CAMPING CARD SITE

▶▶▶▶ **82% Sumners Ponds Fishery & Campsite** (TQ125268)

GOLD

Chapel Rd RH13 0PR
☎ 01403 732539
e-mail: sumnersponds@dsl.co.uk
dir: *From A272 at Coolham x-rds, N towards Barns Green. In 1.5m take 1st left at small x-rds. 1m, over level crossing. Site on left just after right bend*

* 🚐 £17-£21 🚙 £17-£21 🏕 £17-£21

Open all year Last arrival 20.00hrs Last departure noon

Diversification towards high quality camping continues apace at this working farm set in attractive surroundings on the edge of the quiet village of Barns Green. There are now three touring areas; one is under development and will include camping pods, and another, which will have a new toilet block for 2011, has excellent pitches on the banks of one of the well-stocked fishing lakes. A woodland walk has direct access to miles of footpaths. Horsham and Brighton are within easy reach. Seasonal touring pitches are available. A 40 acre site with 85 touring pitches, 45 hardstandings.

AA Pubs & Restaurants nearby: Cricketers Arms, Wisborough Green 01403 700369

Black Horse Inn, Nuthurst 01403 891272

White Horse, Maplehurst 01403 891208

Leisure: ⚴

Facilities: 🐾 ⊙ 🌡 ⚿ ♿ 🖭 🎋 🐕

Services: 🔌 🚿 🚮 T 🍽 🛒 🎫

Within 3 miles: ↧ ✎ 🚤 🛒 🎣 ∪

Notes: Only one car per pitch. Cycling paths, cycle racks. Wi-fi

BILLINGSHURST

Places to visit

Borde Hill Garden, Haywards Heath, 01444 450326, www.bordehill.co.uk

Petworth House and Park, Petworth, 01798 342207 & 343929, www.nationaltrust.org.uk/main/w-petworthhouse

BILLINGSHURST   Map 6 TQ02

▶▶ **72% Limeburners Arms Camp Site** (TQ072255)

Lordings Rd, Newbridge RH14 9JA
☎ 01403 782311
e-mail: chippy.sawyer@virgin.net
dir: *From A29 take A272 towards Petworth for 1m, left onto B2133. Site 300yds on left*

🚐 🚙 🏕

Open Apr-Oct Last arrival 22.00hrs Last departure 14.00hrs

A secluded site in rural West Sussex, at the rear of the Limeburners Arms public house, and surrounded by fields. It makes a pleasant base for touring the South Downs and the Arun Valley. The toilets are basic but very clean. A 2.75 acre site with 40 touring pitches.

AA Pubs & Restaurants nearby: Cricketers Arms, Wisborough Green 01403 700369

Black Horse Inn, Nuthurst 01403 891272

White Horse, Maplehurst 01403 891208

Leisure: ⚴

Facilities: 🐾 ⊙ ⚿ 🕐

Services: 🔌 🍽 🛒 🎫 ⚒

Within 3 miles: ↧ 🛒 ∪

BIRDHAM

Places to visit

Chichester Cathedral, Chichester, 01243 782595, www.chichestercathedral.org.uk

Pallant House Gallery, Chichester, 01243 774557 www.pallant.org.uk

Great for kids: Mechanical Music and Doll Collection, Chichester 01243 372646

BIRDHAM   Map 5 SU80

► 72% Tawny Touring Park (SZ818991)

Tawny Nurseries, Bell Ln PO20 7HY
☎ **01243 512168**
e-mail: tawny@pobox.co.uk
dir: *From A27 at Stockbridge rdbt take A286 towards The Witterings. 5m to mini rdbt in Birdham. 1st exit onto B2198. Site 300mtrs on left*

* 🚐 £12.50-£15 🚌 £12.50-£15

Open all year Last arrival 21.00hrs Last departure 19.00hrs

A small site for the self-contained tourer only, on a landscaped field adjacent to the owners' nurseries. There are six hardstanding pitches for American RVs but no toilet facilities. The beach is just one mile away. A 4.5 acre site with 30 touring pitches, 7 hardstandings.

AA Pubs & Restaurants nearby: Crab & Lobster, Sidlesham 01243 641233

Facilities: 🖻 🕁

Services: 🖳 🔒 T 🖳

Within 3 miles: ↨ ⚴ ⯑ ⌖ ◎ ⛴ 🖻 🖸 ∪

Notes: Dogs must be kept on leads

CHICHESTER   Map 5 SU80

Places to visit

Chichester Cathedral, Chichester, 01243 782595, www.chichestercathedral.org.uk

Pallant House Gallery, Chichester, 01243 774557, www.pallant.org.uk

Great for kids: Mechanical Music and Doll Collection, Chichester 01243 372646

►►► 81% Ellscott Park (SU829995)

Sidlesham Ln, Birdham PO20 7QL
☎ **01243 512003** 📄 01243 512003
e-mail: camping@ellscottpark.co.uk
dir: *Take A286 (Chichester/Wittering road) for approx 4m, left at Butterfly Farm sign, site 500yds right*

🚐 🚌 Å

Open Apr-3rd wk in Oct Last arrival daylight Last departure variable

A well-kept park set in meadowland behind the owners' nursery and van storage area. The park attracts a peace-loving clientele, and is handy for the beach, Chichester, Goodwood House and Races, walking on the South Downs, and other local attractions. Home-grown produce is for sale. A 2.5 acre site with 50 touring pitches.

AA Pubs & Restaurants nearby: Crab & Lobster, Sidlesham 01243 641233

Leisure: ⚑

Facilities: 🖭 ⊙ ⚹ 🕁 🖳 🕁

Services: 🖳 🔒 ⌀ T 🖳

Within 3 miles: ↨ ⚴ ⯑ ⛴ 🖻 🖸 ∪

Notes: 🐾

DIAL POST   Map 6 TQ11

Places to visit

Bignor Roman Villa and Museum, Bignor, 01798 869259, www.bignorromanvilla.co.uk

Great for kids: Amberley Working Museum, Amberley, 01798 831370, www.amberleymuseum.co.uk

AA CAMPING CARD SITE

►►►► 88% Honeybridge Park

(TQ152183)

Honeybridge Ln RH13 8NX
☎ **01403 710923** 📄 01403 712815
e-mail: enquiries@honeybridgepark.co.uk
dir: *10m S of Horsham, just off A24 at Dial Post. Behind Old Barn Nursery*

* 🚐 £17.40-£23.40 🚌 £17.40-£23.40
Å £14.40-£23.40

Open all year Last arrival 19.00hrs Last departure noon

An attractive and very popular park on gently-sloping ground surrounded by hedgerows and mature trees. A comprehensive amenities building houses upmarket toilet facilities including luxury family and disabled rooms, as well as a laundry, shop and off-licence. There are plenty of hardstandings and electric hook-ups, and an excellent children's play area. Seasonal touring pitches are available. A 15 acre site with 130 touring pitches, 70 hardstandings and 20 statics.

AA Pubs & Restaurants nearby: Countryman Inn, Shipley 01403 741383

George & Dragon, Shipley 01403 741320

Queens Head, West Chiltington 01798 812244

Leisure: ⚑ ⚴ ▭

Facilities: 🖴 🖭 ⊙ ⯑ ⚹ 🕁 🖻 🖳 🕁

Services: 🖳 🔒 ⌀ T 🖳

Within 3 miles: ⯑ ⛴ 🖻 🖸 ∪

Notes: Dogs must be kept on leads, no open fires. Fridges available

HENFIELD   Map 6 TQ21

NEW ⛺ Blacklands Campsite (TQ231180)

Blacklands Farm, Wheatsheaf Rd BN5 9AT
☎ **01273 493528**
e-mail: info@blacklandsfarm.co.uk
dir: *A23/B2118/B2116 toward Henfield. Site approx 4m on right*

* 🚐 £10-£20 🚌 £10-£20 Å £10-£20

Open Mar-Jan Last arrival 20.00hrs Last departure noon

Plans are afoot to improve and develop this secluded campsite, tucked away off the B2116, east of Henfield, and well placed for visiting Brighton and exploring the South Downs National Park. Currently there are adequate portaloo facilities, but there are plans to build a new toilet block, upgrade the children's play area, and generally improve the appearance of the park. At the time of going to press the rating for this park had not been confirmed. Please see the AA website for up-to-date information. theAA.com
A 5 acre site with 75 touring pitches.

Leisure: ⚑

Facilities: 🖭 ⚹ 🖻 🖳 🕁 🕁

Services: 🖳

Within 3 miles: ↨ ⯑ 🖻 🖸 ∪

Notes: 🐾 No camp fires, no commercial vehicles

HORSHAM

See Barns Green & Dial Post

SELSEY   Map 5 SZ89

Places to visit

Chichester Cathedral, Chichester, 01243 782595, www.chichestercathedral.org.uk

Pallant House Gallery, Chichester, 01243 774557, www.pallant.org.uk

Great for kids: Mechanical Music and Doll Collection, Chichester, 01243 372646

79% Warner Farm Touring Park *(SZ845939)*

Warner Ln, Selsey PO20 9EL
☎ 01243 604499
e-mail: touring@bunnleisure.co.uk
web: www.warnerfarm.co.uk
dir: *From B2145 in Selsey turn right into School Lane & follow signs*

⚕ £21-£47.50 ⚕ £21-£47.50 ▲ £19-£37

Open Mar-Oct Last arrival 17.30hrs Last departure 10.00hrs

A well-screened touring site with newly refurbished toilet facilities that adjoins the three static parks under the same ownership. A courtesy bus runs around the complex to entertainment areas and supermarkets. The park backs onto open grassland, and the leisure facilities with bar, amusements and bowling alley, and swimming pool/sauna complex are also accessible to tourers. A 10 acre site with 250 touring pitches, 60 hardstandings and 1500 statics.

AA Pubs & Restaurants nearby: Crab & Lobster, Sidlesham 01243 641233

Leisure: 🌊⚓♨🎱☎📺
Facilities: 🔥⊙🅿✳♿🕐🚿🍴🚻
Services: 🔌🍽🍕🛒🚰🕐🍽🚮🚽
Within 3 miles: ♨🚴🎣◎♨🛒🎯
Notes: Wi-fi

see advert below

TYNE & WEAR

SOUTH SHIELDS   Map 21 NZ36

Places to visit

Arbeia Roman Fort and Museum, South Shields, 0191 456 1369, www.twmuseums.org.uk/arbeia

Tynemouth Priory and Castle, Tynemouth, 0191 257 1090, www.english-heritage.org.uk

Great for kids: Blue Reef Aquarium, Tynemouth, 0191 258 1031, www.bluereefaquarium.co.uk

▶▶▶ **69% Lizard Lane Caravan & Camping Site** *(NZ399648)*

Lizard Ln NE34 7AB
☎ 0191 454 4982   📠 0191 455 4466
e-mail: info@littlehavenhotel.com
dir: *2m S of town centre on A183 (Sunderland road)*

* ⚕ £12.75-£25 ⚕ £12.75-£25

Open Feb-28 Jan Last arrival anytime Last departure 11.00hrs

A park which is undergoing an extensive upgrade, and the toilet block has now been completed to a high standard. The majority of pitches enjoy sea views, and the park is convenient for the attractions of both South Shields and Sunderland. A 2 acre site with 45 touring pitches and 70 statics.

Facilities: 🔥⊙🅿✳🕐🚻 **Services:** 🔌🍽🚰🛒
Within 3 miles: ♨🚴🎣♨🛒🎯
Notes: 9-hole putting green

LEISURE: 🌊 Indoor swimming pool 🏊 Outdoor swimming pool 🎪 Children's playground 🎾 Tennis court 🎱 Games room 📺 Separate TV room ⛳ 9/18 hole golf course 🚣 Boats for hire 🎬 Cinema 🎣 Fishing ◎ Mini golf 🏄 Watersports ⛴ Stables **FACILITIES:** 🛁 Bath 🚿 Shower ⊙ Electric shaver 🅿 Hairdryer ✳ Ice Pack Facility ♿ Disabled facilities ☎ Public telephone 🏪 Shop on site or within 200yds 🚚 Mobile shop (calls at least 5 days a week) 🍴 BBQ area 🏞 Picnic area 🐕 Dog exercise area

WARWICKSHIRE

ASTON CANTLOW — Map 10 SP16

Places to visit

Mary Arden's House, Wilmcote, 01789 293455, www.shakespeare.org.uk

Charlecote Park, Charlecote, 01789 470277, www.nationaltrust.org.uk/main/w-charlecotepark

Great for kids: Warwick Castle, Warwick, 0870 442 2000, www.warwick-castle.com

►►► 78% Island Meadow Caravan Park *(SP137596)*

GOLD

The Mill House B95 6JP
☎ 01789 488273 📠 01789 488273
e-mail: holiday@islandmeadowcaravanpark.co.uk
dir: *From A46 or A3400 for Aston Cantlow. Site 0.25m W off Mill Lane*

* 🚐 fr £18.50 🚌 fr £18.50 ⛺ £14-£20

Open Mar-Oct Last arrival 21.00hrs Last departure noon

A small well-kept site bordered by the River Alne on one side and its mill stream on the other. Mature willows line the banks, and this is a very pleasant place to relax and unwind. There are six holiday statics for hire. A 7 acre site with 24 touring pitches, 14 hardstandings and 56 statics.

AA Pubs & Restaurants nearby: The Stag, Red Hill 01789 764634

Blue Boar Inn, Temple Grafton 01789 750010

Facilities: 🚿 ☉ 💨 ❄ ♿ ✆ [S]

Services: 🔌 🧺 🔥 ⛽ [T] 🔋

Within 3 miles: ⛳ 🎣 ◎ [S]

Notes: Free fishing for visitors

HARBURY

Places to visit

Warwick Castle, Warwick, 0870 442 2000, www.warwick-castle.com,

Farnborough Hall, Farnborough, 01295 690002, www.nationaltrust.org.uk

Great for kids: Stratford Butterfly Farm, Stratford, 01789 299288, www.butterflyfarm.co.uk

HARBURY — Map 11 SP35

►►►► 86% Harbury Fields *(SP352604)*

Harbury Fields Farm CV33 9JN
☎ 01926 612457
e-mail: rdavis@harburyfields.co.uk
dir: *M40 junct 12 onto B4451 (signed Kenton/Gaydon). 0.75m, right signed Lightborne. 4m, right at rdbt onto B4455 (signed Harbury). 3rd right by petrol station, site in 700yds (by two cottages)*

* 🚐 £13-£19 🚌 £13-£19

Open 2 Jan-19 Dec Last arrival 21.30hrs Last departure noon

This developing park is in a peaceful farm setting with lovely countryside views. All pitches have hardstandings with electric and the facilities are spotless. It is well positioned for visiting Warwick and Leamington Spa as well as the exhibition centres at NEC Birmingham, and the National Agricultural Centre at Stoneleigh Park. A 3 acre site with 32 touring pitches, 31 hardstandings.

AA Pubs & Restaurants nearby: Duck on the Pond, Long Itchington 01926 815876

Facilities: 🚿 ☉ ♿ ✆ 🐕

Services: 🔌 🧺 Ψ

Within 3 miles: ⛳ [S]

Notes: 🚫💳

KINGSBURY — Map 10 SP29

Places to visit

Sarehole Mill, Birmingham, 0121 777 6612, www.bmag.org.uk

Museum of the Jewellery Quarter, Birmingham, 0121 554 3598, www.bmag.org.uk

► 70% Tame View Caravan Site *(SP209979)*

Cliff B78 2DR
☎ 01827 873853
dir: *400yds off A51 (Tamworth-Kingsbury road), 1m N of Kingsbury opposite pub. Signed Cliff Hall Lane*

🚐 🚌 ⛺

Open all year Last arrival 23.00hrs Last departure 23.00hrs

A secluded spot overlooking the Tame Valley and river, sheltered by high hedges. Sanitary facilities are minimal but clean on this small park. The site is popular with many return visitors who like a peaceful basic site. A 5 acre site with 5 touring pitches.

AA Pubs & Restaurants nearby: Chapel House Restaurant with Rooms, Atherstone 01827 718949

Facilities: ❄ [S] 🪑 🐕

Services: 🔋

Within 3 miles: ⛳ ⛵ 🏋 🎣 ◎ 🏊 [S] 🧺 🐴

Notes: 🚫💳 Fishing

RUGBY — Map 11 SP57

Places to visit

The Webb Ellis Rugby Football Museum, Rugby, 01788 567777, www.webb-ellis.co.uk

Coventry Transport Museum, Coventry, 024 7623 4270, www.transport-museum.com

Great for kids: Lunt Roman Fort, Coventry, 024 7629 4734 www.theherbert.org

►► 69% Lodge Farm Campsite *(SP476748)*

Bilton Ln, Long Lawford CV23 9DU
☎ 01788 560193
e-mail: adrian@lodgefarm.com
web: www.lodgefarm.com
dir: *From Rugby take A428 (Lawford road), towards Coventry, 1.5m. At Sheaf & Sickle pub left into Bilton Ln, site 500yds*

🚐 🚌 ⛺

Open Etr-Nov Last arrival 22.00hrs

A small, simple farm site set behind the friendly owner's home and self-catering cottages, with converted stables housing the toilet facilities. Rugby is only a short drive away, and the site is tucked well away from the main road. Wi-fi is now available. A 2.5 acre site with 35 touring pitches, 3 hardstandings and 10 statics.

AA Pubs & Restaurants nearby: Bell Inn, Monks Kirby 01788 832352

Golden Lion, Easenhall 01788 832265 Old Smithy, Church Lawford 02476 542333

Facilities: 🚿 ☉ ❄ ♿ 🔥 🐕

Services: 🔌 🔥 🔋

Within 3 miles: ⛳ ⛵ 🏋 🎣 ◎ 🏊 [S] 🧺 🐴

Notes: Wi-fi

WOLVEY — Map 11 SP48

Places to visit

Arbury Hall, Nuneaton, 024 7638 2804

Jaguar Daimler Heritage Centre, Coventry, 024 7620 3322, www.jdht.com

Great for kids: Lunt Roman Fort, Coventry, 024 7629 4734, www.theherbert.org

►►► 76% Wolvey Villa Farm Caravan & Camping Site *(SP428869)*

LE10 3HF

☎ 01455 220493 & 220630

dir: M6 junct 2, B4065 follow Wolvey signs. Or M69 junct 1 & follow Wolvey signs

🚐 fr £15 🚌 fr £15 ▲ fr £15

Open all year Last arrival 22.00hrs Last departure noon

A level grass site surrounded by trees and shrubs, on the borders of Warwickshire and Leicestershire. This quiet country site has its own popular fishing lake, and is convenient for visiting the cities of Coventry and Leicester. A 7 acre site with 110 touring pitches, 24 hardstandings.

AA Pubs & Restaurants nearby: Bell Inn, Monks Kirby 01788 832352

The Pheasant, Withybrook 01455 220480

Leisure: 🔍 ▢

Facilities: ⋔ ⊙ ℱ ✳ ⅍ ⊙ 🖨 ✈

Services: 🚐 🗑 🔒 ⌀ ⊤ 🖴

Within 3 miles: ↧ ⵌ ℐ 🖨 🗑 ∪

Notes: ⊘ No twin axles. Putting green, off licence

WEST MIDLANDS

MERIDEN — Map 10 SP28

Places to visit

Blakesley Hall, Birmingham, 0121 464 2193, www.bmag.org.uk

Aston Hall, Birmingham, 0121 464 2193, www.bmag.org.uk

►►►► 88% Somers Wood Caravan Park

(SP225824)

Somers Rd CV7 7PL

☎ 01676 522978 📄 01676 522978

e-mail: enquiries@somerswood.co.uk

dir: M42 junct 6, A45 signed Coventry. Keep left (do not take flyover). Then right onto A452 signed Meriden/Leamington. At next rdbt left onto B4102, Hampton Lane. Site in 0.5m on left

🚐 🚌

Open all year Last arrival variable Last departure variable

A peaceful adults-only park set in the heart of England with spotless facilities. The park is well positioned for visiting the National Exhibition Centre (NEC), the NEC Arena and National Indoor Arena (NIA), and Birmingham is only 12 miles away. The park also makes an ideal touring base for Warwick, Coventry and Stratford-upon-Avon just 22 miles away. Please note that tents are not accepted. A 4 acre site with 48 touring pitches, 48 hardstandings.

AA Pubs & Restaurants nearby: White Lion, Hampton-in-Arden 01675 442833

Facilities: ⋔ ⊙ ℱ ✳ ⅍ ⊙

Services: 🚐 🔒 ⊤ 🖴

Within 3 miles: ↧ ℐ 🗑 ∪

Notes: Adults only. Laundry service available. Wi-fi

LEISURE: 🏊 Indoor swimming pool 🏊 Outdoor swimming pool ⛹ Children's playground 🎾 Tennis court 🔍 Games room ▢ Separate TV room ↧ 9/18 hole golf course ⛵ Boats for hire 🎬 Cinema ℱ Fishing ⊙ Mini golf 🏄 Watersports ∪ Stables **FACILITIES:** 🛁 Bath 🚿 Shower ⊙ Electric shaver ℱ Hairdryer ✳ Ice Pack Facility ⅍ Disabled facilities ⊙ Public telephone 🖨 Shop on site or within 200yds 🚚 Mobile shop (calls at least 5 days a week) 🍖 BBQ area 🌲 Picnic area ✈ Dog exercise area

SERVICES: ⚡ Electric hook up ⊚ Launderette ⏛ Licensed bar 🛢 Calor Gas ⌀ Camping Gaz ⊤ Toilet fluid ⦿ Café/Restaurant 🍔 Fast Food/Takeaway 🔋 Battery charging
🍼 Baby care ⚱ Motorvan service point **ABBREVIATIONS:** BH/bank hols-bank holidays Etr-Easter Whit-Whitsun dep-departure fr-from hrs-hours m-mile mdnt-midnight
dbt-roundabout rs-restricted service wk-week wknd-weekend ⊗ No credit cards ⊗ no dogs See page 7 for details of the AA Camping Card Scheme

Cowes Harbour

Isle of Wight

Generations of visitors to the Isle of Wight consistently say the same thing, that to go there is akin to stepping back to the 1950s and '60s. The pace of life is still gentle and unhurried and the place continues to exude that familiar salty tang of the sea we all remember from childhood, when bucket and spade holidays were an integral part of growing up. Small and intimate – just 23 miles by 13 miles – the Isle of Wight is just the place to get away-from-it-all.

Being an island, it has a unique and distinctive identity. With its mild climate, long hours of sunshine and exuberant architecture, the Isle of Wight has something of a continental flavour. In the summer the place understandably gets very busy, especially during Cowes week in August – a key date in the country's sporting calendar. Elsewhere, seaside towns such as Ventnor, Shanklin and Sandown are popular during the season for their many and varied attractions.

Variety is the key on this delightful and much-loved holiday island. Queen Victoria made the place fashionable and popular when she and Prince Albert chose it as the setting for their summer home, Osborne House, and the island has never looked back. In recent years the steady increase in tourism has ushered in many new visitor attractions to meet the demands of the late 20th and early

● Godshill

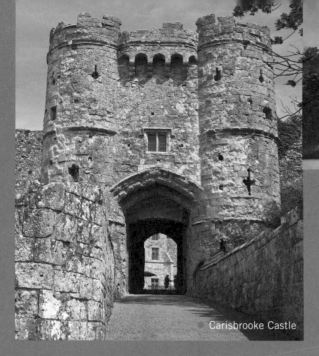
● Carisbrooke Castle

21st centuries, but there are still the perennial old favourites. The Needles, the iconic series of chalk stacks, is a classic example, and just about everyone who has visited over the years can recall buying tubes of sand from nearby Alum Bay – a multi-coloured mix of white quartz, red iron oxide and yellow limonite.

Walking and Cycling

Despite the large numbers of summer visitors, there are still plenty of places on the island where you can be alone and savour its tranquillity. The 65-mile Isle of Wight Coast Path allows walkers to appreciate the natural beauty and diversity of its coastal scenery. Much of the path in the southern half of the island is a relatively undemanding walk over sweeping chalk downs, and beyond Freshwater Bay the coast is often remote and essentially uninhabited. Completing the whole trail or just part of it is the ideal way to discover the island's coastline without the aggravation. Mostly, the route is over cliff-top paths, tracks, sea walls and esplanades. Nearly 40 miles of it is beside the coast, though the inland stretches are never far from the sea. However, beware of erosion and expect to find the path diverted in places. The Isle of Wight's hinterland may lack the sea views but the scenery is no less appealing. Here walkers can explore a vast and well publicised network of paths that reach the very heart of the island. In all, the Isle of Wight has more than 500 miles of public rights of way and more than half the island is recognised as an Area of Outstanding Natural Beauty.

For cyclists there is also a good deal of choice. The Round the Island Cycle Route runs for 49 miles and takes advantage of quiet roads and lanes. There are starting points at Yarmouth, Cowes and Ryde and the route is waymarked with official Cycle Route blue signs.

Festivals and Events

Among a host of festivals and events held on the Isle of Wight throughout the year are:-

• The Real Ale Festival in May
• The Isle of Wight Walking Festival in May and the Isle of Wight Weekend Walking Festival held in October
• The Cycling Festival in September
• The Garlic Festival in August

For more information visit www.islandbreaks.co.uk

WIGHT, ISLE OF

See Cycle Ride 4 in the Walks & Cycle Rides section at the end of the guide

BEMBRIDGE

See Whitecliff Bay

COWES
Map 5 SZ49

Places to visit

Osborne House, Osborne House, 01983 200022, www.english-heritage.org.uk

Bembridge Windmill, Bembridge, 01983 873945, www.nationaltrust.org.uk/isleofwight

Great for kids: Robin Hill Country Park, Arreton, 01983 527352, www.robin-hill.com

84% Thorness Bay Holiday Park (SZ448928)

Thorness PO31 8NJ
☎ 01983 523109 🖷 01983 822213
e-mail:
holidaysales.thornessbay@park-resorts.com
dir: On A3054 towards Yarmouth, 1st right after BMW garage, signed Thorness Bay

🚐 🚌 ⚊

Open Apr-1 Nov Last arrival anytime Last departure 10.00hrs

Splendid views of The Solent can be enjoyed from this rural park located just outside Cowes. A footpath leads directly to the coast, while on site there is an all-weather sports court, entertainment clubs for children, and cabaret shows, and a bar for all the family. There are 23 serviced pitches, in the separate touring area, with TV boosters. Eight seasonal touring pitches are available. A 148 acre site with 124 touring pitches, 21 hardstandings and 560 statics.

AA Pubs & Restaurants nearby: The Folly, Cowes 01983 297171

Leisure: 🏊 ⚙

Facilities: 🌂 ⊙ ☞ ✳ ⚕ ⚙ 🚻 🚿

Services: 🚐 🖥 🍽 📶 ⚊ 🔌 T 🍴 🛒 🛍 ♻

Within 3 miles: 🚻 ⚑ 🏊 📮 🛒

Notes: Kids' clubs, evening entertainment, water slide. Wi-fi

---

FRESHWATER
Map 5 SZ38

Places to visit

Coleman's Farm Park, Porchfield, 01983 522831, www.colemansfarmpark.co.uk

Dimbola Lodge Museum, Freshwater, 01983 756814, www.dimbola.co.uk

Great for kids: Blackgang Chine Fantasy Park, Blackgang, 01983 730330 www.blackgangchine.com

▶▶▶▶ **82% Heathfield Farm Camping** (SZ335879)

GOLD

Heathfield Rd PO40 9SH
☎ 01983 407822
e-mail: web@heathfieldcamping.co.uk
dir: 2m W from Yarmouth ferry port on A3054, left to Heathfield Rd, entrance 200yds on right

🚐 🚌 ⚊

Open May-Sep Last arrival 20.00hrs Last departure 11.00hrs

A very good quality park with friendly and welcoming staff. There are lovely views across the Solent to Hurst Castle. The upgraded toilet facilities, amenities and grounds are very well maintained, and this park is now amongst the best on the island. A 10 acre site with 60 touring pitches.

AA Pubs & Restaurants nearby: Red Lion, Freshwater 01983 754925

Facilities: 🌂 ⊙ ☞ ✳ ⚕ ⚙ 🚻 🚿

Services: 🚐 🖥 ♻ ⚊

Within 3 miles: 🚻 ⚑ 🏊 📮 ⊙ 🛒 🛍 U

Notes: Family camping only. Separate playing field for ball games etc. Wi-fi

---

NEWBRIDGE
Map 5 SZ48

Places to visit

Newtown Old Town Hall, Newtown, 01983 531785, www.nationaltrust.org.uk/isleofwight

Brighstone Shop and Museum, Brighstone, 01983 740689, www.nationaltrust.org.uk/isleofwight

Great for kids: Yarmouth Castle, Yarmouth, 01983 760678, www.english-heritage.org.uk

---

PREMIER PARK

▶▶▶▶▶ **91%**
Orchards Holiday Caravan Park (SZ411881)

Best of British
GOLD

Main Rd PO41 0TS
☎ 01983 531331 ⚊ 531350 🖷 01983 531666
e-mail: info@orchards-holiday-park.co.uk
web: www.orchards-holiday-park.co.uk
dir: 4m E of Yarmouth
6m W of Newport on B3401. Take A3054 from Yarmouth, after 3m turn right at Horse & Groom Inn. Follow signs to Newbridge. Entrance opposite Post Office

* 🚐 £16-£30 🚌 £16-£30 ⚊ £16-£30

Open 11 Feb-2 Jan (rs Mar-Oct takeaway, shop, outdoor pool open) Last arrival 23.00hrs Last departure 11.00hrs

A really excellent, well-managed park set in a peaceful village location amid downs and meadowland, with glorious downland views. Pitches are terraced and offer a good provision of hardstandings, including water serviced pitches. There is a new high quality facility centre offering excellent spacious showers and family rooms, plus there is access for disabled visitors to all site facilities and disabled toilets. The park has indoor and outdoor swimming pools, a shop, takeaway and licensed coffee shop. A 15 acre site with 171 touring pitches, 74 hardstandings and 65 statics.

continued

AA Pubs & Restaurants nearby: New Inn, Shalfleet 01983 531314

Leisure: 🏊🎣🎱🎯🖥

Facilities: 🚿🚻⊙🅿✕🔥🛗🖥🔥🚻

Services: 🔌🗑🔋⊘🅃🍽🚰🚮🐾↯

Within 3 miles: ⚓🥾🔥🛒

Notes: No cycling. Petanque, table tennis room, poolside café. Wi-fi

---

Places to visit

Carisbrooke Castle, Carisbrooke, 01983 522107, www.english-heritage.org.uk

Osborne House, Osborne House, 01983 200022, www.english-heritage.org.uk

►► 80% Riverside Paddock Camp Site *(SZ503911)*

Dodnor Ln PO30 5TE
☎ 01983 821367
e-mail: p.herbert928@btinternet.com
dir: *From Newport take dual carriageway towards Cowes. At 1st rdbt take 3rd exit, immediately left at next rdbt. Follow until road meets National Cycle Route. Site on left*

🚐🚚⚑

Open all year

Although fairly close to Newport this quiet campsite offers a really peaceful environment and has direct access to the national cycle route from Newport to Cowes.The Medina River with its riverside walks is also nearby. The park has good hardstandings many with electric plus spotless facilities. The location of the park makes it perfect for people who like to walk or ride their bikes. An 8 acre site with 28 touring pitches, 18 hardstandings.

AA Pubs & Restaurants nearby: White Lion, Arreton 01983 528479

Facilities: ⊙✕🔥

Services: 🔌

Within 3 miles: ⚓🔥🛒🔥🛒⟲

Notes: Adults only. ⊗ 18 pitches available for motorvans/caravans & 10 pitches for tents

---

►►► 76% Seaview Holidays Camping Park *(SZ622911)*

PO34 5AQ
☎ 01983 612330   📠 01983 613511
dir: *From Ryde take A3055 then left on B3330 to Seaview. Site next to Wishing Well pub*

🚐🚚⚑

Open May-26 Sep Last arrival 23.00hrs Last departure 11.00hrs

A secluded spacious site in quiet rural surroundings close to the sea, on slightly sloping ground with some level areas. The village is within easy walking distance, and there is a walkway through to the coast from the bottom of the site. A 9 acre site with 150 touring pitches.

AA Pubs & Restaurants nearby: Boathouse, Seaview 01983 810616

Seaview Hotel & Restaurant, Seaview 01983 612711

Leisure: 🎱🎯🖥

Facilities: 🚿⊙🅿✕🕐🛗🔥

Services: 🔌🗑🔋⊘🚰

Within 3 miles: ⚓🥾🔥🛒◎🔥🛒⟲

Notes: No pets, no unaccompanied children

Places to visit

Nunwell House and Gardens, Brading, 01983 407240

Bembridge Windmill, Bembridge, 01983 873945, www.nationaltrust.org.uk/isleofwight

Great for kids: Robin Hill Country Park, Arreton, 01983 527352, www.robin-hill.com

---

►►►►► 87% Whitefield Forest Touring Park *(SZ604893)*

Brading Rd PO33 1QL
☎ 01983 617069
e-mail: pat&louise@whitefieldforest.co.uk
web: www.whitefieldforest.co.uk
dir: *From Ryde follow A3055 towards Brading, after Tesco rdbt site 0.5m on left*

🚐🚚⚑

Open Etr-Oct Last arrival 21.00hrs Last departure 11.00hrs

This park is beautifully laid out in Whitefield Forest, and offers a wide variety of pitches, all of which have electricity. It offers excellent modern facilities, which are spotlessly clean. The park takes great care in retaining the natural beauty of the forest, and is a haven for wildlife, including the red squirrel, which may be seen on the park's nature walk. A 23 acre site with 80 touring pitches, 20 hardstandings.

AA Pubs & Restaurants nearby: The St Helens, Ryde 01983 872303

Boathouse, Seaview 01983 810616

Leisure: 🎱

Facilities: 🚿⊙🅿✕🛗🔥

Services: 🔌🗑🔋⊘🅃🚰↯

Within 3 miles: ⚓🥾🔥🛒🔥🛒

Notes: Wi-fi

RYDE *continued*

▶▶▶ 83% *Roebeck Camping and Caravan Park* (SZ581903)

Gatehouse Rd, Upton Cross PO33 4BP
☎ 01983 611475 & 07930 992080
e-mail: info@roebeck-farm.co.uk
dir: *Right from Fishbourne ferry terminal. At lights left onto A3054 towards Ryde. In outskirts straight on at 'All Through Traffic' sign. At end of Pellhurst Rd right in Upton Rd. Site 50yds beyond mini-rdbt*

Open Apr-Nov

A quiet park in a country setting on the outskirts of Ryde offering very nice facilities, especially for campers, including a new dishwashing/kitchen cabin. The unique, ready-erected tipis, which are available for hire, add to the ambience of the site. There is also an excellent fishing lake. A 4 acre site with 37 touring pitches.

AA Pubs & Restaurants nearby: The St Helens, Ryde 01983 872303

Boathouse, Seaview 01983 810616

Facilities: 🌐🥊🍴🚿🚽🪑🐴🐕
Services: 🔌🔋
Within 3 miles: ↕️🚴🎣🎯◎🏊🍴🎰🏊⛳
Notes: Wi-fi

ST HELENS

Places to visit

Brading, the Experience, Brading, 01983 407286, www.bradingtheexperience.co.uk

Great for kids: Lilliput Antique Doll and Toy Museum, Brading, 01983 407231, www.lilliputmuseum.org.uk

---

ST HELENS   Map 5 SZ68

85% Nodes Point Holiday Park (SZ636897)

Nodes Rd PO33 1YA
☎ 01983 872401 📠 01983 874696
e-mail: gm.nodespoint@park-resorts.com
dir: *From Ryde take B3330 signed Seaview/Puckpool. At junct for Puckpool bear right. 1m past Road Side Inn in Nettlestone, site on left*

🚐🚙⛺

Open Apr-Oct Last arrival 21.00hrs Last departure 10.00hrs

A well-equipped holiday centre on an elevated position overlooking Bembridge Bay with direct access to the beach. The touring area is mostly sloping with some terraces. Activities are organised for youngsters, and there is entertainment for the whole family. Buses pass the main entrance road. The touring area has very well appointed, ready-erected tents for hire. Four seasonal touring pitches are available. A 16 acre site with 150 touring pitches, 4 hardstandings and 195 statics.

AA Pubs & Restaurants nearby: Windmill Inn, Bembridge 01983 872875

Leisure: 🏊🎢 **Notes:** Wi-fi
Facilities: 🚿🌐🥊🍴🚿🐴🐕🚻🍴🍴🐕
Services: 🔌🔋🚿🛢🔫🍴🍺
Within 3 miles: ↕️🚴🎣🎯◎🏊🍴🎰🏊⛳

see advert on opposite page

SANDOWN   Map 5 SZ58

Places to visit

Nunwell House and Gardens, Brading, 01983 407240

Bembridge Windmill, Bembridge, 01983 873945, www.nationaltrust.org.uk/isleofwight

Great for kids: Dinosaur Isle, Sandown, 01983 404344, www.dinosaurisle.com

---

▶▶▶▶ 78% Old Barn Touring Park (SZ573833)

Cheverton Farm, Newport Rd, Apse Heath PO36 9PJ
☎ 01983 866414 📠 01983 865988
e-mail: oldbarn@weltinet.com
dir: *On A3056 from Newport, site on left after Apse Heath rdbt*

* 🚐 £14-£18 🚙 £14-£18 ⛺ £14-£18

Open May-Sep Last arrival 21.00hrs Last departure noon

A terraced site with good quality facilities, bordering onto open farmland. The spacious pitches are secluded and fully serviced, and there is a decent, modern toilet block. A 5 acre site with 60 touring pitches, 9 hardstandings.

AA Pubs & Restaurants nearby: Windmill Inn, Bembridge 01983 872875

Leisure: 🎢🎣🖥
Facilities: 🌐◎🥊🚿🐕🚻
Services: 🔌🛢🔫🍴🛢🍴🍺
Within 3 miles: ↕️🚴🎣🎯◎🏊🍴🎰🏊⛳

▶ 78% Queenbower Dairy Caravan Park (SZ567846)

Alverstone Rd, Queenbower PO36 0NZ
☎ 01983 403840 📠 01983 409671
e-mail: queenbowerdairy@aol.com
dir: *3m N of Sandown off A3056 turn right towards Alverstone Rd, site 1m on left*

* 🚐 £6-£9 🚙 £6-£9 ⛺ £6-£9

Open May-Oct

A small site with basic amenities that will appeal to campers keen to escape the crowds and the busy larger sites. The enthusiastic owners keep the facilities very clean. A 2.5 acre site with 20 touring pitches.

AA Pubs & Restaurants nearby: Windmill Inn, Bembridge 01983 872875

Facilities: 🚿🛢
Services: 🔌🍴
Within 3 miles: ↕️🚴🎣🎯◎🏊🍴🎰🏊
Notes: 🐕 Dogs must be exercised off site

SHANKLIN   Map 5 SZ58

Places to visit

Shanklin Chine, Shanklin, 01983 866432, www.shanklinchine.co.uk

Ventnor Botanic Gerdens, Ventnor, 01983 855397, www.botanic.co.uk

Great for kids: Dinosaur Isle, Sandown, 01983 404344, www.dinosaurisle.com

---

83% Lower Hyde Holiday Park (SZ575819)

Landguard Rd PO37 7LL
☎ 01983 866131 📠 01983 862532
e-mail:
holidaysales.lowerhyde@park-resorts.com
dir: *From Fishbourne ferry terminal follow A3055 to Shanklin. Site signed just past lake*

⛺ 🚐 ⛺

Open Apr-Oct Last arrival anytime Last departure 10.00hrs

A popular holiday park on the outskirts of Shanklin, close to the sandy beaches. There is an outdoor swimming pool and plenty of organised activities for youngsters of all ages. In the evening there is a choice of family entertainment. The touring facilities are located in a quiet area away from the main complex, with good views over the downs. Six seasonal touring pitches are available. A 65 acre site with 148 touring pitches, 25 hardstandings and 313 statics.

AA Pubs & Restaurants nearby: Bonchurch Inn, Bonchurch 01983 852611

The Taverners, Godshill 01983 840707

Leisure: 🏊 ⛱ 🎬 ♨ 🎱 🎮

Facilities: 🚿 ⊙ 🅿 ✳ 🚻 🕐 🛒

Services: 🔌 🚿 🍺 🛢 🧴 🍽 🍟

Within 3 miles: ⌗ 🎣 ♨ 🅿 ⊙ 🚣 🛒 🎯 🐴

Notes: No cars by caravans. Water flume, evening entertainment, kids' club. Wi-fi

---

▶▶▶ 79% Ninham Country Holidays (SZ573825)

Ninham PO37 7PL
☎ 01983 864243 & 866040 📠 01983 868881
e-mail: office@ninham-holidays.co.uk
dir: *Signed off A3056 (Newport to Sandown road)*

⛺ 🚐 ⛺

Open May day BH-15 Sep (end May-early Sep outdoor pool heated)

Enjoying a lofty rural position with fine country views, this delightful, spacious park occupies two separate, well-maintained areas in a country park setting near the sea and beach. There's a good outdoor swimming pool. A 12 acre site with 98 touring pitches, 4 hardstandings.

AA Pubs & Restaurants nearby: Bonchurch Inn, Bonchurch 01983 852611

The Taverners, Godshill 01983 840707

Leisure: 🏊 ⛱ 🔍 **Facilities:** 🚿 ⊙ ✳ 🕐 🛒

Services: 🔌 🚿 🧴 🚙

Within 3 miles: ⌗ 🎣 🅿 ⊙ 🚣 🛒 🎯 🐴

Notes: ⊗ Swimming pool & coarse fishing rules apply. Dish wash areas, all-service pitches. Late night/arrival area available. Wi-fi

---

TOTLAND BAY

Places to visit

Dimbola Lodge Museum, Freshwater, 01983 756814, www.dimbola.co.uk

Great for kids: Yarmouth Castle, Yarmouth, 01983 760678, www.english-heritage.org.uk

---

TOTLAND BAY   Map 5 SZ38

▶▶▶ 75% Stoats Farm Caravan & Camping (SZ324865)

PO39 0HE
☎ 01983 755258 & 753416
e-mail: david@stoats-farm.co.uk
dir: *On Alum Bay road, 1.5m from Freshwater & 0.75m from Totland*

⛺ £10.50-£12.50 🚐 £10.50-£12.50 ⛺ £9.50-£10.50

Open Apr-Oct

A friendly, personally run site in a quiet country setting close to Alum Bay, Tennyson Down and The Needles. It has good laundry and shower facilities, and the shop, although small, is well stocked. Popular with families, walkers and cyclists, it makes the perfect base for campers wishing to explore this part of the island. A 10 acre site with 100 touring pitches.

AA Pubs & Restaurants nearby: Red Lion, Freshwater 01983 754925

Facilities: 🚿 ⊙ ✳ 🚻 🕐 🛒 🐕 🍴

Services: 🔌 🚿 🧴 🔋 🚙

Within 3 miles: ⌗ 🎣 🅿 ⊙ 🚣 🛒 🐴

Notes: No loud noise after 23.00hrs, no camp fires. Campers' fridge available

---

SERVICES: 🔌 Electric hook up 🚿 Launderette 🍺 Licensed bar 🛢 Calor Gas 🧴 Camping Gaz 🚽 Toilet fluid 🍽 Café/Restaurant 🍟 Fast Food/Takeaway 🔋 Battery charging 🍼 Baby care 🚙 Motorvan service point **ABBREVIATIONS:** BH/bank hols-bank holidays Etr-Easter Whit-Whitsun dep-departure fr-from hrs-hours m-mile mdnt-midnight rdbt-roundabout rs-restricted service wk-week wknd-weekend ⊗ No credit cards 🐕 no dogs See page 7 for details of the AA Camping Card Scheme

WHITECLIFF BAY — Map 5 SZ68

83% Whitecliff Bay Holiday Park (SZ637862)

Hillway Rd, Bembridge PO35 5PL
☎ 01983 872671 📠 01983 872941
e-mail: holiday@whitecliff-bay.com
dir: *1m S of Bembridge, signed off B3395 in village*

Open Mar-Oct Last arrival 21.00hrs Last departure 10.30hrs

A large seaside complex on two sites, with camping on one and self-catering chalets and statics on the other. There is an indoor pool with flume and spa pool, and an outdoor pool with a kiddies' pool, a family entertainment club, and plenty of traditional on-site activities including crazy golf, a soft play area and table tennis, plus a restaurant and a choice of bars the facilities have been refurbished. A Canvas Village has been introduced with 12 ready-erected tents for hire. There is easy access to Whitecliff beach. Dogs are welcome. A 49 acre site with 400 touring pitches, 50 hardstandings and 227 statics.

AA Pubs & Restaurants nearby: Windmill Inn, Bembridge 01983 872875

Leisure: 🏊⚓️🎢🎣📺
Facilities: 🛁🚿⚡️🅿️✂️♿️🕐🛒🍽️🔥🚮🐕
Services: 🔌🚿🚽🔧🅿️🚰🍽️🚛🛒🚿⛽️
Within 3 miles: ⛳️🚴🏇🎣💰🐟🛒🎡⛵
Notes: Adults & families only

see advert below

WOOTTON BRIDGE — Map 5 SZ59

Places to visit

Osborne House, Osborne House, 01983 200022, www.english-heritage.org.uk

Bembridge Windmill, Bembridge, 01983 873945, www.nationaltrust.org.uk/isleofwight

Great for kids: Robin Hill Country Park, Arreton, 01983 527352, www.robin-hill.com

▶▶▶ 81% Kite Hill Farm Caravan & Camping Park (SZ549906)

Firestone Copse Rd PO33 4LE
☎ 01983 882543 & 883261 📠 01983 883883
e-mail: welcome@kitehillfarm.co.uk
dir: *Signed off A3054 at Wootton Bridge, between Ryde & Newport*

Open all year Last arrival anytime Last departure anytime

The park, on a gently sloping field, is tucked away behind the owners' farm, just a short walk from the village and attractive river estuary. The newly refurbished facilities are very clean. This park provides a nice relaxing atmosphere to stay on the island. A 12.5 acre site with 50 touring pitches, 10 hardstandings.

Kite Hill Farm Caravan & Camping Park

AA Pubs & Restaurants nearby: The Folly, Cowes 01983 297171

The St Helens, Ryde 01983 872303

Leisure: 🎢
Facilities: 🚿⚡️✂️♿️🐕🔥
Services: 🔌🚿🔧🚛
Within 3 miles: ⛳️🎡💰🛒🎡⛵
Notes: 🐕 Dogs must be kept on leads at all times (owners must clean up after pets)

WROXALL — Map 5 SZ57

Places to visit

Appuldurcombe House, Wroxall, 01983 852484, www.english-heritage.org.uk

Great for kids: Blackgang Chine Fantasy Park, Blackgang, 01983 730330 www.blackgangchine.com

NEW ▶▶▶▶ 83% Appuldurcombe Gardens Holiday Park (SZ546804)

Appuldurcombe Rd PO38 3EP
☎ 01983 852597 📠 01983 856225
e-mail: info@appuldurcombegardens.co.uk
dir: *From Newport take A3020 towards Shanklin & Ventnor. Through Rookley & Godshill. Right at Whiteley Bank rdbt towards Wroxall village, then follow brown signs*

* 🚐 £12.30-£21.20 🚉 £12.30-£21.20 ▲ £9.30-£18

Open Mar-Oct Last arrival 21.00hrs Last departure 11.00hrs

This well-appointed park is set in a unique setting fairly close to the town of Ventnor. It has modern and spotless facilities plus a very tasteful lounge bar and function room. There is an excellent, screened outdoor pool and paddling pool plus café and shop. Static caravans and apartments are also available for hire. The site is close to cycle routes and is only 150 yards from the bus stop making it perfect for those with a motorhome or those not wanting to take the car out. A 14 acre site with 100 touring pitches, 2 hardstandings.

AA Pubs & Restaurants nearby: Spyglass Inn, Ventnor 01983 855338

Pond Café, Ventnor 01983 855666

Leisure: 🏊 🎱 ⚓
Facilities: 🛁 📶 ☉ 🅿 ✱ 🔥 🛒 🌰 🚻 🍴
Services: 🔌 🛢 🍸 🔥 🖉 🚽 🍽 🚰 🏭
Within 3 miles: 🚶 🎣 🚲 🅿 ◎ ⛴ 🏌 🛒 ↺
Notes: No skate boards. Wi-fi

YARMOUTH

See Newbridge

WILTSHIRE

CALNE — Map 4 ST97

Places to visit

Avebury Manor and Garden, Avebury, 01672 539250, www.nationaltrust.org.uk

Bowood House and Gardens, Calne, 01249 812102, www.bowood.org

Great for kids: Alexander Keiller Museum, Avebury, 01672 539250, www.nationaltrust.org.uk

▶▶▶ 70% Blackland Lakes Holiday & Leisure Centre (ST973687)

Stockley Ln SN11 0NQ
☎ 01249 810943 📠 01249 811346
e-mail: blacklandlakes.bookings@btconnect.com
web: www.blacklandlakes.co.uk
dir: *From Calne take A4 E for 1.5m, right at camp sign. Site 1m on left*

* 🚐 £12-£15.50 🚉 £12-£15.50 ▲ £9-£15.50

Open all year (rs 30 Oct-1 Mar pre-paid bookings only) Last arrival 22.00hrs Last departure noon

A rural site surrounded by the North and West Downs. The park is divided into several paddocks separated by hedges, trees and fences, and there are two well-stocked carp fisheries for the angling enthusiast. There are some excellent walks close by, and the interesting market town of Devizes is just a few miles away. A 15 acre site with 180 touring pitches, 25 hardstandings.

AA Pubs & Restaurants nearby: Red Lion Inn, Lacock 01249 730456

George Inn, Lacock 01249 730263 Rising Sun, Lacock 01249 730363

Leisure: ⚓
Facilities: 📶 ☉ 🅿 ✱ ♿ 🔥 🛒 🚻 🍴
Services: 🔌 🛢 🔥 🖉 🚽 🚰 ↯
Within 3 miles: 🚶 🅿 🛒 🏌 ↺
Notes: Wildfowl sanctuary, bike trail

LACOCK

Places to visit

Lacock Abbey, Fox Talbot Museum and Village, Locock, 01249 730459, www.nationaltrust.org.uk/lacock

Corsham Court, Corsham, 01249 701610, www.corsham-court.co.uk

LACOCK — Map 4 ST96

▶▶▶ 87% Piccadilly Caravan Park (ST913683)

Folly Lane West SN15 2LP
☎ 01249 730260 📠 01249 730260
e-mail: piccadillylacock@aol.com
dir: *4m S of Chippenham just past Lacock. Exit A350 signed Gastard. Site 300yds on left*

🚐 £16-£18 🚉 £16-£18 ▲ £16-£21.50

Open Etr/Apr-Oct Last arrival 21.00hrs Last departure noon

A peaceful, pleasant site, well established and beautifully laid-out, close to the village of Lacock. Facilities and grounds are immaculately kept, and there is very good screening. A new section of the park was being developed at the time of our last inspection in order to provide spacious pitches, especially for tents. A 2.5 acre site with 41 touring pitches, 12 hardstandings.

AA Pubs & Restaurants nearby: Red Lion Inn, Lacock 01249 730456

George Inn, Lacock 01249 730263 Rising Sun, Lacock 01249 730363

Leisure: ⚓
Facilities: 📶 ☉ 🅿 ✱ ☉ 🍴
Services: 🔌 🛢 🔥 🖉 🚰
Within 3 miles: 🚶 🎣 🅿 🛒 🏌 ↺
Notes: 🚫

LANDFORD

Places to visit

Furzey Gardens, Minstead, 023 8081 2464, www.furzey-gardens.org

Mottisfont Abbey and Gardens, Mottisfont, 01794 340757, www.nationaltrust.org.uk/mottisfontabbey

Great for kids: Paulton's Park, Ower, 023 8081 4442, www.paultonspark.co.uk

LANDFORD   Map 5 SU21

►►► 74% Greenhill Farm Caravan & Camping Park (SU266183)

Greenhill Farm, New Rd SP5 2AZ
☎ 01794 324117
e-mail: info@greenhillholidays.co.uk
dir: *M27 junct 2, A36 towards Salisbury, approx 3m after Hants/Wilts border, (Shoe Inn pub on right, BP garage on left) take next left into New Rd, signed Nomansland, 0.75m on left*

* ⌂ £15-£23 ⌂ £15-£23 ▲ £12-£23

Open all year Last arrival 21.30hrs Last dep 11.00hrs

A tranquil, well-landscaped park hidden away in unspoilt countryside on the edge of the New Forest. Pitches overlooking the fishing lake include hardstandings and are for adults only. The other section of the park is for families and includes a new play area and games room. Well placed for visiting Paulton's Park. A 13 acre site with 160 touring pitches, 40 hardstandings.

AA Pubs & Restaurants nearby: Woodfalls Inn, Woodfalls 01725 513222

Royal Oak, Fritham 023 8081 2606

Leisure: ⚴ ⚔ **Facilities:** ⚘ ✳ ☺ ⚑ ⚙
Services: ⚡ ⚙ ⚗ ⚗ Ⓣ ⚙ ⚙
Within 3 miles: ⚗ ⚗ ◎ ⚙ ⚙ ∪
Notes: Dogs must be on leads. Disposable BBQs

MARSTON MEYSEY   Map 5 SU19

Places to visit

Lydiard Park, Lydiard Park, 01793 770401, www.lydiardpark.org.uk

Buscot Park, Buscot, 01367 240786, www.buscotpark.com

Great for kids: STEAM - Museum of the Great Western Railway, Swindon, 01793 466646, www.swindon.gov.uk/steam

AA CAMPING CARD SITE

►► 77% *Second Chance Touring Park* (SU140960)

SN6 6SZ
☎ 01285 810675 & 810939
e-mail: secondchancepark@hotmail.co.uk
dir: *A419 from Cirencester towards Swindon, exit at Latton junct. Through Latton, left at next mini-rdbt, towards Fairford. Follow signs to site. From*

M4 junct 15, A419 towards Fairford, right after Marston Meysey

⌂ ⌂ ▲

Open Mar-Nov Last arrival 21.00hrs Last departure 13.30hrs

An attractive and much improved quiet site located near the source of the Thames, and well positioned for those wishing to visit the nearby Cotswold Water Park. A 1.75 acre site with 22 touring pitches, 10 hardstandings and 4 statics.

AA Pubs & Restaurants nearby: Masons Arms, Meysey Hampton 01285 850164

Jolly Tarr, Hannington 01793 762245

Facilities: ⚘ ◎ ✳ ⚑
Services: ⚡ ⚙
Within 3 miles: ⚗ ⚗ ⚙
Notes: ⚫ ⚫ No loud music or parties. Fishing, access for canoes

ORCHESTON   Map 5 SU04

Places to visit

Heale Gardens, Middle Woodford, 01722 782504

Stonehenge, Stonehenge, 0870 333 1181, www.english-heritage.org.uk

Great for kids: Ludgershall Castle and Cross, Ludgershall, www.english-heritage.org.uk

►►► 78% Stonehenge Touring Park (SU061456)

SP3 4SH
☎ 01980 620304
e-mail: stay@stonehengetouringpark.com
dir: *From A360 towards Devizes turn right, follow lane, site at bottom of village on right*

⌂ £9-£15 ⌂ £9-£15 ▲ £9-£26

Open all year Last arrival 21.00hrs Last departure 11.00hrs

A quiet site adjacent to the small village of Orcheston near the centre of Salisbury Plain and four miles from Stonehenge. There's an excellent on-site shop. A 2 acre site with 30 touring pitches, 12 hardstandings.

Leisure: ⚴
Facilities: ⚘ ◎ ⚑ ✳ ☺ ⚙ ⚙
Services: ⚡ ⚙ ⚗ ⚗ Ⓣ ⚙
Within 3 miles: ⚙ ⚙
Notes: Wi-fi with access charge

SALISBURY   Map 5 SU12

Places to visit

Salisbury and South Wiltshire Museum, Salisbury, 01722 332151, www.salisburymuseum.org.uk

Salisbury Cathedral, Salisbury, 01722 555120, www.salisburycathedral.org.uk

Great for kids: The Medieval Hall, Salisbury, 01722 412472, www.medieval-hall.co.uk

►►►► 84% Coombe Touring Park (SU099282)

Race Plain, Netherhampton SP2 8PN
☎ 01722 328451 ▤ 01722 328451
e-mail: enquiries@coombecaravanpark.co.uk
dir: *Exit A36 onto A3094, 2m SW, site adjacent to Salisbury racecourse*

⌂ ⌂ ▲

Open 3 Jan-20 Dec (rs Oct-May shop closed) Last arrival 21.00hrs Last departure noon

A very neat and attractive site adjacent to the racecourse with views over the downs. The park is well landscaped with shrubs and maturing trees, and the very colourful beds are stocked from the owner's greenhouse. A comfortable park with a superb luxury toilet block, and four static holiday homes for hire. A 3 acre site with 50 touring pitches and 4 statics.

AA Pubs & Restaurants nearby: Haunch of Venison, Salisbury 01722 411313

Wig & Quill, Salisbury 01722 335665

Facilities: ⚘ ◎ ⚑ ✳ ⚘ ☺ ⚙
Services: ⚡ ⚙ ⚗ ⚗ Ⓣ ⚙ ⚙
Within 3 miles: ⚗ ⚙ ⚙ ∪
Notes: ⚫ No disposable BBQs or fires, no mini motorbikes. Children's bathroom

►►► 74% Alderbury Caravan & Camping Park *(SU197259)*

Southampton Rd, Whaddon SP5 3HB
☎ 01722 710125
e-mail: alderbury@aol.com
dir: *Just off A36, 3m from Salisbury, opposite The Three Crowns*

Open all year Last arrival 21.00hrs Last departure 12.30hrs

A pleasant, attractive park set in the village of Whaddon not far from Salisbury. The small site is well maintained by friendly owners, and is ideally positioned near the A36 for overnight stops to and from the Southampton ferry terminals. A 1.5 acre site with 39 touring pitches, 12 hardstandings and 1 static.

AA Pubs & Restaurants nearby: Green Dragon, Alderbury 01722 710263

Facilities:

Services:

Within 3 miles:

Notes: No open fires. Microwave, electric kettle, small fridge available

TROWBRIDGE — Map 4 ST85

Places to visit

Great Chalfield Manor & Garden, Bradford-upon-Avon, 01225 782239, www.nationaltrust.org.uk

The Courts Garden, Holt, 01225 782875, www.nationaltrust.org.uk

Great for kids: Longleat, Longleat, 01985 844400, www.longleat.co.uk

►► 73% Stowford Manor Farm *(ST810577)*

Stowford, Wingfield BA14 9LH
☎ 01225 752253
e-mail: stowford1@supanet.com
dir: *From Trowbridge take A366 W towards Radstock. Site on left in 3m*

* £14-£16 £14-£16 £12-£14

Open Etr-Oct

A very simple farm site set on the banks of the River Frome behind the farm courtyard. The owners are friendly and relaxed, and the park enjoys a similarly comfortable ambience. The Village Pump Folk Festival is held at the end of July each year on the site. A 1.5 acre site with 15 touring pitches.

AA Pubs & Restaurants nearby: Red or White, Trowbridge 01225 781666

George Inn, Norton St Philip 01373 834224

Facilities:

Services:

Within 3 miles:

Notes: No open fires. Fishing, boating, swimming in river

WESTBURY — Map 4 ST85

Places to visit

Great Chalfield Manor & Garden, Bradford-upon-Avon, 01225 782239, www.nationaltrust.org.uk

The Courts Garden, Holt, 01225 782875, www.nationaltrust.org.uk

AA CAMPING CARD SITE

►►►► 81% Brokerswood Country Park *(ST836523)*

GOLD

Brokerswood BA13 4EH
☎ 01373 822238 01373 858474
e-mail: info@brokerswood.co.uk
web: www.brokerswoodcountrypark.co.uk
dir: *M4 junct 17, S on A350. Right at Yarnbrook to Rising Sun pub at North Bradley, left at rdbt. Left on bend approaching Southwick, 2.5m, site on right*

* £11-£29 £11-£29 £11-£29

Open all year Last arrival 21.30hrs Last departure 11.00hrs

A popular park on the edge of an 80-acre woodland park with nature trails and fishing lakes. An adventure playground offers plenty of fun for all ages, and there is a miniature railway, an indoor play centre, and a café. There are high quality toilet facilities and fully-equipped, ready-erected tents are now available for hire. A 5 acre site with 69 touring pitches, 21 hardstandings.

AA Pubs & Restaurants nearby: Full Moon, Rudge 01373 830936

Bell Inn, Great Cheverell 01380 813277

Leisure:

Facilities:

Services:

Within 3 miles:

Notes: Families only

WORCESTERSHIRE

HONEYBOURNE — Map 10 SP14

Places to visit

Kiftsgate Court Garden, Mickleton, 01386 438777, www.kiftsgate.co.uk

Hidcote Manor Garden, Mickleton, 01386 438333, www.nationaltrust.org.uk/hidcote

Great for kids: Anne Hathaway's Cottage, Shottery, 01789 292100, www.shakespeare.org.uk

►►►► 85% Ranch Caravan Park *(SP113444)*

Station Rd WR11 7PR
☎ 01386 830744 📄 01386 833503
e-mail: enquiries@ranch.co.uk
dir: *Through village x-rds towards Bidford, site 400mtrs on left*

* 🚐 £20-£25.50 🚐

Open Mar-Nov (rs Mar-May & Sep-Nov swimming pool closed, shorter club hours) Last arrival 20.00hrs Last departure noon

An attractive and well-run park set amidst farmland in the Vale of Evesham and landscaped with trees and bushes. Tourers have their own excellent facilities in two locations, and the use of an outdoor heated swimming pool in peak season. There is also a licensed club serving meals. A 12 acre site with 120 touring pitches, 43 hardstandings and 218 statics.

AA Pubs & Restaurants nearby: Fleece Inn, Bretforton 01386 831173

Ebrington Arms, Ebrington 01386 593223

Leisure: 🏊 ⛺ 🎱 ▭

Facilities: 🚿 ⊙ 📷 ✳ 🕐 🛁 🛗

Services: 🚐 🛢 🔧 🛎 🧺 🇹 🍴 🚮 🛒 ↧

Within 3 miles: 🏌 🛍 🛢 🐴

Notes: No unaccompanied minors, no tents. Gym & sauna (chargeable)

see advert below

WORCESTER

Places to visit

The City Museum and Art Gallery, Worcester, 01905 25371, www.worcestercitymuseums.org.uk

The Greyfriars, Worcester, 01905 23571, www.nationaltrust.org.uk

Great for kids: West Midland Safari & Leisure Park, Bewdley, 01299 402114, www.wmsp.co.uk

WORCESTER — Map 10 SO85

►►► 83% Peachley Leisure Touring Park *(SO807576)*

Peachley Ln, Lower Broadheath WR2 6QX
☎ 01905 641309 📄 01905 641854
e-mail: info@peachleyleisure.com
dir: *M5 junct 7, A44 (Worcester ring road) towards Leominster. Exit at sign for Elgar's Birthplace Museum. Pass museum, at x-roads turn right. In 0.75m at T-junct turn left. Park signed on right*

🚐 🚐 ⛺

Open all year Last arrival 21.30hrs Last departure noon

The park is set in its own area in the grounds of Peachley Farm. It has new facilities, and all hardstanding and fully-serviced pitches. There is also a fishing lake, and a really excellent quad bike course. The park provides a peaceful haven, and is an excellent base from which to explore the area, which includes the Elgar Museum. Seasonal touring pitches are available. An 8 acre site with 82 touring pitches, 82 hardstandings.

AA Pubs & Restaurants nearby: The Talbot, Knightwick 01886 821235

Bear & Ragged Staff, Bransford 01886 833399

Facilities: 🚿 ⊙ ✳ 🛁 🐴

Services: 🚐 🛢 🍴

Within 3 miles: 🎣 🎌 🏌 ⛵ 🛍 🛢 🐴

Notes: No skateboards, no riding of motorbikes or scooters. Quad bike trekking, fishing

LEISURE: 🏊 Indoor swimming pool 🏊 Outdoor swimming pool ⛰ Children's playground 🎾 Tennis court 🎱 Games room ▭ Separate TV room 🏌 9/18 hole golf course 🚣 Boats for hire 🎬 Cinema 🎣 Fishing ◎ Mini golf 🏄 Watersports ⛴ Stables **FACILITIES:** 🛁 Bath 🚿 Shower ⊙ Electric shaver 🖤 Hairdryer ✳ Ice Pack Facility 🦽 Disabled facilities 📞 Public telephone 🛒 Shop on site or within 200yds 🚚 Mobile shop (calls at least 5 days a week) 🍴 BBQ area 🌲 Picnic area 🐕 Dog exercise area

SERVICES: ⊞ Electric hook up ⊟ Launderette ⊡ Licensed bar 🛢 Calor Gas ⊘ Camping Gaz Ⓣ Toilet fluid ⓘ⌂ Café/Restaurant 🍟 Fast Food/Takeaway 🔋 Battery charging
⤴ Baby care ⤶ Motorvan service point **ABBREVIATIONS:** BH/bank hols-bank holidays Etr-Easter Whit-Whitsun dep-departure fr-from hrs-hours m-mile mdnt-midnight
rdbt-roundabout rs-restricted service wk-week wknd-weekend ⊗ No credit cards ⊗ no dogs See page 7 for details of the AA Camping Card Scheme

Swaledale

Yorkshire

There is nowhere in the British Isles quite like Yorkshire. By far the largest county, and with such scenic and cultural diversity, it is almost a country within a country. For sheer scale, size and grandeur, there is nowhere to beat it.

Much of it in the spectacular Pennines, Yorkshire is a land of castles, grand houses, splendid rivers, tumbling becks and historic market towns. But it is the natural, unrivalled beauty of the Yorkshire Dales and the North York Moors that captures the heart and leaves a lasting impression. Surely no-one could fail to be charmed by the majestic landscapes of these two much-loved National Parks.

The Dales

Wherever you venture in the Yorkshire Dales, stunning scenery awaits you; remote emerald green valleys, limestone scars and timeless villages of charming stone cottages. The Dales, beautifully represented in the books of James Herriot, are characterised and complemented by their rivers – the Wharfe, Ribble, Ure, Nidd and Swale among them.

Touring this glorious region reveals the broad sweep of Wensleydale, the delights of Arkengarthdale and the charming little villages of Swaledale. There is also the spectacular limestone country of the western Dales – the land of the Three Peaks. Perhaps here, more than anywhere

▶

Rievaulx Abbey

else in the area, there is a true sense of space and freedom. This is adventure country – a place of endless views and wild summits.

The Moors

To the east lies another sprawling landscape – the North York Moors. This is where the purple of the heather gives way to the grey expanse of the North Sea. Covering 554 square miles (1,436km) and acknowledged as an internationally important site for upland breeding birds, the North York Moors National Park is a vast, intricately-woven tapestry of heather moorland, narrow valleys, rolling dales, broad-leaved woodland and extensive conifer forests. Few places in Britain offer such variety and breadth of terrain.

● Clevedon Hills from Great Ayrton

Extending for 36 miles (58km), the North Yorkshire and Cleveland Heritage Coast forms the Park's eastern boundary. The popular holiday resorts of Whitby and Scarborough are the two largest settlements on this stretch of coastline, which is rich in fossils and minerals and protected for its outstanding natural beauty and historic interest.

Towards the south

To the south of the North York Moors is the beautiful city of York, its history stretching back 2,000 years. At its heart stands the minster, constructed between 1220 and 1470 and the largest medieval church in northern Europe. There is so much to see and do in this ancient, vibrant city that you can easily lose track of time.

Farther south, despite the relics of the county's industrial heritage, is Yorkshire's magical *Last of the Summer Wine* country. The BBC's long-running and much-loved comedy series, *Last of the Summer Wine*, ran for 37 years and was filmed in and around the town of Holmfirth, near Huddersfield.

Staithes from Cowbar Nab

Walking and Cycling

Not surprisingly, Yorkshire offers a myriad of circular walks and long-distance trails throughout the county. For the more ambitious walker there is the Pennine Way, which runs through Yorkshire from top to bottom, from the Scottish Borders as far south as Derbyshire. The 81-mile (130km) Dales Way, another popular route, is a perfect way to explore the magnificent scenery of Wharfedale, Ribblesdale and Dentdale, while the 50-mile (80km) Calderdale Way offers a fascinating insight into the Pennine heartland of industrial West Yorkshire.

Yorkshire also boasts a great choice of cycle routes. You can cycle to York on the track bed of the former King's Cross to Edinburgh railway line, or ride along a 20-mile (32.2km) stretch of the former Whitby to Scarborough line, looping around Robin Hood's Bay. There are also cycle routes through the Yorkshire Wolds, Dalby Forest in the North York Moors National Park and around Castle Howard, the magnificent estate near Malton where Evelyn Waugh's *Brideshead Revisited* was filmed.

Events and festivals

- The long established Jorvik Festival is held in York in February and lasts eight days. The festival celebrates Viking heritage with various lectures, arts and crafts and river events.
- Easter Monday is the date for Ossett's Coal Carrying Championships where competitors carry a sack of coal through the streets.
- November sees the three-day Northern Antiques Fair at Harrogate. This event includes various indoor stalls, as well as displays of glass and ceramics.
- The Yorkshire Dales has numerous events and festivals throughout the year, including the Masham Arts Festival in October, the Lunesdale Agricultural Show in August and the Grassington Festival of Music & Arts in June.

YORKSHIRE, EAST RIDING OF

BRANDESBURTON — Map 17 TA14

Places to visit

The Guildhall, Beverley, 01482 392783, www.eastriding.gov.uk/museums

Burton Constable Hall, Sproatley, 01964 562400, www.burtonconstable.com

Great for kids: 'Streetlife' Hull Museum of Transport, Kingston-upon-Hull, 01482 613902, www.hullcc.gov.uk

▶▶▶ 80% *Dacre Lakeside Park*

(TA118468)

YO25 8RT
☎ 0800 1804556 📠 01964 544040
e-mail: dacrepark@btconnect.com
dir: *Off A165 bypass, midway between Beverley & Hornsea*

Open Mar-Oct Last arrival 21.00hrs Last departure noon

A large lake popular with watersports enthusiasts is the focal point of this grassy site, which has a refurbished toilet block and three camping pods. The clubhouse offers indoor activities there's a fish and chip shop, a pub and a Chinese takeaway in the village, which is within walking distance. The six-acre lake is used for windsurfing, sailing, kayaking, canoeing and fishing. An 8 acre site with 120 touring pitches.

AA Pubs & Restaurants nearby: White Horse Inn, Beverley 01482 861973

Leisure: 🏊 🎣 **Facilities:** 🚿☉🅿✳♿🅗🖤
Services: 🔌🅗🚽🔒🧹🚰🛒
Within 3 miles: ⚓♨🖉🛝🅗↺
Notes: Windsurfing, fishing, canoeing, sailing & bowling

BRIDLINGTON — Map 17 TA16

See also Rudston

Places to visit

Sewerby Hall and Gardens, Bridlington, 01262 673769, www.sewerby-hall.co.uk

Hornsea Museum, Hornsea, 01964 533443, www.hornseamuseum.com

Great for kids: Flamingo Land, Kirby Misperton, 01653 668287, www.flamingoland.co.uk

▶▶▶ 80% *Fir Tree Caravan Park*

(TA195702)

Jewison Ln, Sewerby YO16 6YG
☎ 01262 676442
e-mail: info@flowerofmay.com
dir: *1.5m from centre of Bridlington. Turn left off B1255 at Marton Corner. Site 600yds on left*

🚐

Open Mar-Oct (rs Early & late season bar & entertainment restrictions) Last arrival dusk Last departure noon

Fir Tree Park has a well laid out touring area with its own facilities within a large, mainly static park. It has an excellent swimming pool complex, and the adjacent bar-cum-conservatory serves

meals. There is also a family bar, games room and outdoor children's play area. A 22 acre site with 45 touring pitches, 45 hardstandings and 400 statics.

AA Pubs & Restaurants nearby: Seabirds Inn, Flamborough 01262 850242

Old Star Inn, Kilham 01262 420619

Leisure: 🏊♿🎣
Facilities: 🚿☉✳♿🅗🖤
Services: 🔌🅗🚽🔒🚰
Within 3 miles: ⚓♨🇭🖉◎🛝🅗↺
Notes: Dogs accepted by prior arrangement only. Wi-fi

KINGSTON UPON HULL

See Sproatley

RUDSTON — Map 17 TA06

Places to visit

Sewerby Hall and Gardens, Bridlington, 01262 673769, www.sewerby-hall.co.uk

▶▶▶ 86% *Thorpe Hall Caravan & Camping Site*

(TA108677)

Thorpe Hall YO25 4JE
☎ 01262 420393 & 420574 📠 01262 420588
e-mail: caravansite@thorpehall.co.uk
dir: *5m from Bridlington on B1253*

* 🚐 £15-£29 🚐 £15-£29 ⛺ £11-£25

Open Mar-Oct (rs Limited opening hours reception & shop) Last arrival 22.00hrs Last departure noon

LEISURE: 🏊 Indoor swimming pool 🏊 Outdoor swimming pool 🎢 Children's playground 🎾 Tennis court 🎯 Games room 📺 Separate TV room ⛳ 9/18 hole golf course ⚓ Boats for hire 🎬 Cinema 🎣 Fishing ◎ Mini golf 🏄 Watersports ↺ Stables **FACILITIES:** 🛁 Bath 🚿 Shower ☉ Electric shaver 🖉 Hairdryer ✳ Ice Pack Facility ♿ Disabled facilities 🕭 Public telephone 🛒 Shop on site or within 200yds 🚐 Mobile shop (calls at least 5 days a week) 🍖 BBQ area 🌲 Picnic area 🐕 Dog exercise area

A delightful, peaceful small park within the walled gardens of Thorpe Hall yet within a few miles of the bustling seaside resort of Bridlington. The site offers a games field, its own coarse fishery, pitch and putt, and a games and TV lounge, and there are numerous walks locally. There is a refurbished amenity block. A 4.5 acre site with 90 touring pitches.

Thorpe Hall Caravan & Camping Site

AA Pubs & Restaurants nearby: Old Star Inn, Kilham 01262 420619

Leisure: ⚙ ⚉ ▢

Facilities: ⚙ ↑ ⊙ ⌒ ✻ ⚉ ☺ ☖ ⚁ ⚌

Services: ⚂ ⚄ 🛢 ⌀ ⊤ ⚌

Within 3 miles: ⚿ ⚁ ☖ ∪

Notes: Well behaved dogs only, no ball games (field provided). Golf practice area (4.5 acres). Wi-fi

see advert on opposite page

SKIPSEA — Map 17 TA15

Places to visit

Hornsea Museum, Hornsea, 01964 533443, www.hornseamuseum.com

Sewerby Hall and Gardens, Bridlington, 01262 673769, www.sewerby-hall.co.uk

84% Low Skirlington Leisure Park (TA188528)

YO25 8SY
☎ 01262 468213 & 468466 📠 01262 468105
e-mail: info@skirlington.com
dir: *From M62 towards Beverley then Hornsea. Between Skipsea & Hornsea on B1242*

🚐 🚙

Open Mar-Oct

A large well-run seaside park set close to the beach in partly-sloping meadowland with young trees and shrubs. The site has five toilet blocks, a supermarket and an amusement arcade, with occasional entertainment in the clubhouse.

The wide range of family amenities includes an indoor heated swimming pool complex with sauna, jacuzzi and sunbeds. A 10-pin bowling alley and indoor play area for children are added attractions. A 24 acre site with 285 touring pitches, 15 hardstandings and 450 statics.

Leisure: ⚙ ⚙ ⚉ ▢

Facilities: ⚙ ↑ ⊙ ⌒ ✻ ⚉ ☺ ☖ ⚁ ⚌

Services: ⚂ ⚄ 🛢 ⌀ ⊤ ⚌ ⚌

Within 3 miles: ⚿ ⚁ ⌒ ◎ ⚌ ☖ ∪

Notes: Putting green

SPROATLEY — Map 17 TA13

Places to visit

Burton Constable Hall, Sproatley, 01964 562400, www.burtonconstable.com

Maritime Museum, Kingston-upon-Hull, 01482 613902, www.hullcc.gov.uk

Great for kids: The Deep, Kingston-upon-Hull, 01482 381000, www.thedeep.co.uk

►►►► 80% Burton Constable Holiday Park & Arboretum (TA186357)

Old Lodges HU11 4LN
☎ 01964 562508 📠 01964 563420
e-mail: info@burtonconstable.co.uk
dir: *Off A165 onto B1238 to Sproatley. Follow signs to site*

* 🚐 £15-£27 🚙 £15-£27 ▲ £15-£26

Open Mar-Jan (rs Mar-Oct tourers/tents) Last arrival 22.00hrs Last departure 14.00hrs

A very attractive parkland site overlooking the fishing lakes, in the grounds of Burton Constable Hall. The toilet facilities are kept very clean, and the Lakeside Club provides a focus for relaxing in the evening. Children will enjoy the extensive adventure playground. A 90 acre site with 140 touring pitches, 14 hardstandings and 342 statics.

Leisure: ⚙ ⚉

Facilities: ↑ ⊙ ⌒ ⚉ ☺ ☖ ⚁ ⚌

Services: ⚂ ⚄ 🛢 ⌀ ⊤ ⚌ ⚌

Within 3 miles: ⚿ ⌒ ☖ ∪

Notes: Dogs must be kept on leads, no skateboards/rollerblades. Two 10-acre fishing lakes, snooker table

WITHERNSEA — Map 17 TA32

Places to visit

Wilberforce House, Kingston-upon-Hull, 01482 613902, www.hullcc.gov.uk

Maister House, Kingston-upon-Hull, 01482 324114, www.nationaltrust.org.uk

Great for kids: The Deep, Kingston-upon-Hull, 01482 381000, www.thedeep.co.uk

76% Withernsea Sands (TA335289)

Waxholme Rd HU19 2BS
☎ 0871 664 9803
e-mail: withernsea.sands@park-resorts.com
dir: *M62 junct 38, A63 through Hull. At end of dual carriageway, turn right onto A1033, follow Withernsea signs. Through village, left at mini-rdbt onto B1242. Next right at lighthouse. Site 0.5m on left*

🚐 🚙 ▲

Open Apr-Oct (rs BH & peak wknds entertainment & sports available) Last arrival 22.00hrs Last departure noon

Touring is very much at the heart of this holiday park's operation, with 100 all-electric pitches and additional space for tents. The owners, Park Resorts, are in the process of upgrading the facilities and attractions, and the leisure complex with its futuristic design is especially impressive. 115 touring pitches and 400 statics.

Leisure: ⚙ ⚙ ⚉

Facilities: ⚙ ↑ ⊙ ⌒ ⚉ ☺ ⚁ ⚌

Services: ⚂ ⚄ 🛢 ⌀ ⊤ ⚌

Within 3 miles: ⚿ ⌒ ☖ ∪

Notes: Extension leads/utilities from reception. Wi-fi

YORKSHIRE, NORTH

See Cycle Ride 5 and Walks 12 & 13 in the Walks and Cycle Rides section at the end of the guide

ACASTER MALBIS   Map 16 SE54

Places to visit

Yorkshire Museum, York, 01904 551800, www.york.gov.uk

York Art Gallery, York, 01904 687687, www.york.trust.museum

Great for kids: Jorvik Viking Centre, York, 01904 615505, www.jorvik-viking-centre.com

▶▶▶ **77% Moor End Farm** *(SE589457)*

YO23 2UQ
☎ **01904 706727 & 07860 405872**
e-mail: moorendfarm@acaster99.fsnet.co.uk
dir: *Follow signs to Acaster Malbis from A64/A1237 junct at Copmanthorpe*

🚐 🚑 ⛺

Open Etr or Apr-Oct Last arrival 22.00hrs Last departure 12.00hrs

A very pleasant farm site with modernised facilities including a heated family/disabled shower room. A riverboat pickup to York is 150 yards from the site entrance, and the village inn and restaurant are a short stroll away. A good place to hire a boat or simply watch the boats go by. A 1 acre site with 10 touring pitches and 7 statics.

AA Pubs & Restaurants nearby: Ye Old Sun Inn, Colton 01904 744261

Leisure: 🅰

Facilities: 🚿⊙☝✳🔥🚻

Services: 🚐🗑📥

Within 3 miles: ↨⚡🎣🖊🏪🛒

Notes: 🐕 Dogs must be kept on leads. Use of fridge, freezer, microwave & pot wash sink

ALLERSTON   Map 19 SE88

Places to visit

Scarborough Castle, Scarborough, 01723 372451, www.english-heritage.org.uk

Pickering Castle, Pickering, 01751 474989, www.english-heritage.org.uk

Great for kids: Sea Life and Marine Sanctuary, Scarborough, 01723 376125, www.sealife.co.uk

PREMIER PARK

▶▶▶▶▶ **79% Vale of Pickering Caravan Park**
(SE879808)

Carr House Farm YO18 7PQ
☎ **01723 859280**   🖨 **01723 850060**
e-mail: tony@valeofpickering.co.uk
dir: *On B1415, 1.75m off A170 (Pickering-Scarborough road)*

🚐 🚑 ⛺

Open 5 Mar-3 Jan (rs Mar) Last arrival 21.00hrs Last departure 11.30hrs

A well-maintained, spacious family park with excellent facilities including a well-stocked shop and immaculate toilet facilities. Younger children will enjoy the attractive play area, while the large ball sports area will attract older ones. The park is set in open countryside bounded by hedges, has manicured grassland and stunning seasonal floral displays, and is handy for the North Yorkshire Moors and the attractions of Scarborough. A woodland walk was created in 2010. A 13 acre site with 120 touring pitches, 80 hardstandings.

AA Pubs & Restaurants nearby:
New Inn, Thornton le Dale 01751 474226

Coachman Inn, Snainton 01723 859231

Cayley Arms, Brompton-by-Sawdon 01723 859372

Leisure: 🅰   **Facilities:** 🚿⊙☝✳🔥🚻🛁🚻
Services: 🚐🗑📥🚿🚽📥
Within 3 miles: ↨🖊◎🏪🛒⛵
Notes: Microwave available

ALNE   Map 19 SE46

Places to visit

Castle Howard, Malton, 01653 648333, www.castlehoward.co.uk

Sutton Park, Sutton-on-the-Forest, 01347 810249, www.statelyhome.co.uk

Great for kids: National Railway Museum, York, 01904 621261, www.nrm.org.uk

▶▶▶▶ **80% Alders Caravan Park**
(SE497654)

Home Farm YO61 1RY
☎ **01347 838722**   🖨 **01347 838722**
e-mail: enquiries@homefarmalne.co.uk
dir: *From A19 exit at Alne sign, in 1.5m turn left at T-junct, 0.5m site on left in village centre*

* 🚐 £16-£17.50 🚑 £16-£17.50 ⛺ £16

Open Mar-Oct Last arrival 21.00hrs Last departure 14.00hrs

A tastefully developed park on a working farm with screened pitches laid out in horseshoe-shaped areas. This well designed park offers excellent toilet facilities including a bathroom and fully-serviced washing and toilet cubicles. A woodland area and a water meadow are pleasant places to walk. A 12 acre site with 87 touring pitches, 6 hardstandings.

AA Pubs & Restaurants nearby: Black Bull Inn, Boroughbridge 01423 322413

The Dining Room Restaurant, Boroughbridge 01423 326426

Facilities: 🛁🚿⊙☝✳🔥🚻🛒🚻
Services: 🚐🗑📥📥
Within 3 miles: ↨🖊🏪🛒
Notes: Max 2 dogs per pitch. Summer house. Bread, eggs, milk & other farm produce for sale

BISHOP MONKTON

Places to visit

Newby Hall and Gardens, Newby Hall and Gardens, 01423 322583, www.newbyhall.com

Fountains Abbey and Studley Royal, Ripon, 01765 608888, www.fountainsabbey.org.uk

Great for kids: Stump Cross Caverns, Pateley Bridge, 01756 752780, www.stumpcrosscaverns.co.uk

BISHOP MONKTON   Map 19 SE36

▶▶▶ 70% Church Farm Caravan Park (SE328660)

Knaresborough Rd HG3 3QQ
☎ 01765 677668 & 07932 158924
📠 01765 677668
e-mail: churchfarmcaravans@uwclub.net
dir: *Turn E off A61. At x-rds turn right. Site approx 500mtrs on right*

🚐 🚐 Å

Open Mar-Oct Last arrival 22.30hrs Last departure 15.30hrs

A very pleasant rural site on a working farm, on the edge of the attractive village of Bishop Monkton with its well-stocked shop and pubs. Whilst very much a place to relax, there are many attractions close by including Fountains Abbey, Newby Hall, Ripon and Harrogate. A 4 acre site with 45 touring pitches, 3 hardstandings and 3 statics.

AA Pubs & Restaurants nearby: Black Bull Inn, Boroughbridge 01423 322413

The Dining Room Restaurant, Boroughbridge 01423 326426

Facilities: 📻 ☉ ⁂ 🕭 🖻
Services: 🚭 🚟 ↯
Within 3 miles: ↯ 🖉 🖻 🖯 ∪
Notes: ⊛ No ball games, pets must be kept on leads

BOLTON ABBEY   Map 19 SE05

Places to visit

RHS Garden Harlow Carr, Harrogate, 01423 565418, www.rhs.org.uk/harlowcarr

Parcevall Hall Gardens, 01756 720311, www.parcevallhallgardens.co.uk

Great for kids: Stump Cross Caverns, Pateley Bridge, 01756 752780, www.stumpcrosscaverns.co.uk

▶▶▶ 83% Howgill Lodge

(SD065593)

Barden BD23 6DJ
☎ 01756 720655
e-mail: info@howgill-lodge.co.uk
dir: *From Bolton Abbey take B6160 signed Burnsall. In 3m at Barden Tower turn right signed Appletreewick. 1.5m at phone box turn right into lane to site*

* 🚐 fr £17 🚐 Å fr £17

Open mid Mar-Oct Last arrival 20.00hrs Last departure noon

A beautifully-maintained and secluded site offering panoramic views of Wharfedale. The spacious hardstanding pitches are mainly terraced, and there is a separate tenting area with numerous picnic tables. There are three toilet facilities spread throughout the site, with the main block newly refurbished to a high standard including private, cubicled wash facilities. There is also a well stocked shop. A 4 acre site with 40 touring pitches, 20 hardstandings.

AA Pubs & Restaurants nearby: The Fleece, Addingham 01943 830491

Craven Arms, Appletreewick 01756 720270

Facilities: 📻 ☉ 🅿 ⁂ ⊙ 🖻 ⊐
Services: 🚭 🖻 🖉 T 🚟
Within 3 miles: 🖉 🖻 🖯
Notes: Wi-fi

CONSTABLE BURTON   Map 19 SE19

Places to visit

Middleham Castle, Middleham, 01969 623899, www.english-heritage.org.uk

Great for kids: Bedale Museum, Bedale, 01677 423797

▶▶▶▶ 80% Constable Burton Hall Caravan Park (SE158907)

DL8 5LJ
☎ 01677 450428
e-mail: caravanpark@constableburton.com
dir: *Off A684*

🚐 🚐

Open Apr-Oct Last arrival 20.00hrs Last departure noon

A pretty site in the former deer park of the adjoining Constable Burton Hall, screened from the road by the deer park walls and surrounded by mature trees in a quiet rural location. The laundry is housed in a converted 18th-century deer barn, there is a pub and restaurant opposite, and seasonal pitches are available. A 10 acre site with 120 touring pitches.

AA Pubs & Restaurants nearby: Old Horn Inn, Spennithorne 01969 622370

Sandpiper Inn, Leyburn 01969 622206

White Swan, Middleham 01969 622093

Black Swan, Middleham 01969 622221

Wensleydale Heifer West Witton 01969 622322

Facilities: 📻 ☉ 🅿 ⁂ 🕭 ⊐
Services: 🚭 🖻 🖴 🚟
Within 3 miles: ↯ 🖻
Notes: No tents or commercial vehicles. Dogs must be kept on leads. No games

EASINGWOLD   Map 19 SE56

Places to visit

Byland Abbey, Coxwold, 01347 868614, www.english-heritage.org.uk

The York Brewery Co. Ltd, York, 01904 621162, www.yorkbrew.co.uk

Great for kids: Falconry UK - Birds of Prey Visitor Centre, Thirsk, 01845 587522, www.falconrycentre.co.uk

▶▶▶ 68% *Folly Garth* (SE543687)

Green Ln YO61 3ES
☎ 01347 821150
dir: *From Easingwold take Stillington road for 1.5m, site on right*

🚐 🚐 Å

Open Feb-Dec

A small country site tucked away at the end of a lane, just one and a half miles from the Georgian market town of Easingwold. Facilities include a well-equipped kitchen and a fully-carpeted lounge with table and chairs, opening onto a decking area. The toilets are appointed to a good standard. A 3 acre site with 20 touring pitches.

AA Pubs & Restaurants nearby: Blackwell Ox Inn, Sutton-on-the-Forest 01347 810328

Rose & Crown, Sutton-on-the-Forest 01347 811333

Facilities: 📻
Services: 🚭

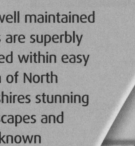

FILEY
Map 17 TA18

Places to visit

Scarborough Castle, Scarborough, 01723 372451, www.english-heritage.org.uk

Sea Life and Marine Sanctuary, Scarborough, 01723 376125, www.sealife.co.uk

89% Flower of May Holiday Park (TA085835)

Lebberston Cliff YO11 3NU
☎ 01723 584311 📠 01723 585716
e-mail: info@flowerofmay.com
dir: Signed off A165 on Scarborough side of Filey

* 🚐 £18-£24 🚚 £18-£24 ▲ £14-£24

Open Etr-Oct (rs Early & late season restricted opening in café, shop & bars) Last arrival dusk Last departure noon

A well-run, high quality family holiday park with top class facilities. This large landscaped park offers a full range of recreational activities, with plenty to occupy everyone. Grass and hard pitches are available, all on level ground, and arranged in avenues screened by shrubs. Seasonal touring pitches are available. A 13 acre site with 300 touring pitches, 250 hardstandings and 193 statics.

AA Pubs & Restaurants nearby: Cayley Arms, Brompton-by-Sawdon 01723 859372

Leisure: 🏊 ⛰ 🎱 🖵
Facilities: 🌂 ☉ ✳ ❤ ⚴ ☺ 🖻 🐕 🚿
Services: 🔌 🖩 🍴 🛢 ⌀ 🚽 🍽 🎣 🍟
Within 3 miles: ⚡ 🎣 ⛳ ✎ 🎡 ◎ 🚣 🏪 🖻 U

Notes: 1 dog per pitch by arrangement only. Squash, bowling, 9-hole golf, basketball court, skate park. Wi-fi

see advert on opposite page

80% Primrose Valley Holiday Park (TA123778)

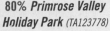

YO14 9RF
☎ 01723 513771 & 0870 405 0126
📠 01723 513777
e-mail: lisa.mcewan@bourne-leisure.co.uk
dir: Signed off A165 (Scarborough-Bridlington road), 3m S of Filey

🚐 🚚

Open mid Mar-Oct Last arrival anytime Last departure 10.00hrs

A large all-action holiday centre with a wide range of sports and leisure activities to suit everyone from morning until late in the evening. The touring area is completely separate from the main park with its own high quality amenity block. All touring pitches are fully-serviced hardstandings with grassed awning strips. A 160 acre site with 50 touring pitches, 50 hardstandings and 1514 statics.

AA Pubs & Restaurants nearby: Cayley Arms, Brompton-by-Sawdon 01723 859372

Leisure: 🏊 ⛱ ⛰ ⛳ 🔍
Facilities: 🚿 🌂 ❤ ⚴ ☺ 🖻 🚿 🐕
Services: 🔌 🖩 🍴 🛢 ⌀ 🍽 🎣 🍟
Within 3 miles: ⚡ 🎣 ⛳ ◎ 🖻 🚣

Notes: Maximum of 2 dogs per group, certain dog breeds banned. Wi-fi

75% Blue Dolphin Holiday Park (TA095829)

Gristhorpe Bay YO14 9PU
☎ 01723 515155 📠 01723 512059
dir: Site off A165, 2m N of Filey

🚐 🚚 ▲

Open mid Mar-Oct (rs mid Mar-May & Sep-Oct some facilities may be reduced) Last arrival mdnt Last departure 10.00hrs

There are great cliff-top views to be enjoyed from this fun-filled holiday centre with an extensive and separate touring area. The emphasis is on non-stop entertainment, with organised sports and clubs, all-weather leisure facilities, heated swimming pools and plenty of well-planned amusements. Pitches are mainly on level or gently-sloping grass plus some fully-serviced hardstandings, the toilet facilities have now been upgraded the beach is just two miles away. An 85 acre site with 343 touring pitches, 21 hardstandings and 600 statics.

AA Pubs & Restaurants nearby: Cayley Arms, Brompton-by-Sawdon 01723 859372

Leisure: 🏊 ⛱ ⛰
Facilities: 🌂 ☉ ✳ ❤ ⚴ ☺ 🖻 🚿 🐕 🚿
Services: 🔌 🖩 🍴 🛢 ⌀ 🚽 🍽 🎣 🍟
Within 3 miles: ⚡ ◎ 🖻 🚣

Notes: Dogs must be kept on leads, max 2 dogs per group, certain dog breeds banned. Multi-sports court, kids' clubs, entertainment. Wi-fi

see advert on page 314

74% Reighton Sands Holiday Park (TA142769)

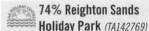

Reighton Gap YO14 9SH
☎ 01723 890476 📠 01723 891043
e-mail: jon.cussins@bourne-leisure.co.uk
dir: On A165, 5m S of Filey at Reighton Gap, signed

🚐 £10-£40 🚚 £10-£40 ▲ £6-£20

Open mid Mar-Oct (rs mid Mar-May & Sep-Oct some facilities may be reduced) Last arrival 22.00hrs Last departure 10.00hrs

A large, lively holiday centre with a wide range of entertainment and all-weather leisure facilities, located just a 10-minute walk from a long sandy beach. There are good all-weather pitches and a large tenting field. The site is particularly geared towards families with young children. A 229 acre site with 83 touring pitches, 83 hardstandings and 800 statics.

AA Pubs & Restaurants nearby: Cayley Arms, Brompton-by-Sawdon 01723 859372

Leisure: 🏊 ⛰ 🔍
Facilities: 🚿 🌂 ☉ ⛳ ❤ ☺ 🖻 🚿 🐕 🚿
Services: 🔌 🖩 🍴 🚽 🍽 🍟 🎣 🚿
Within 3 miles: ⚡ 🎣 ✎ ◎ 🖻 🚣 U

Notes: Indoor play area. Wi-fi

see advert on page 315

FILEY *continued*

▶▶▶▶ 86% Lebberston
Touring Park *(TA077824)*

Filey Rd YO11 3PE
☎ 01723 585723
e-mail: info@lebberstontouring.co.uk
dir: *Off A165 (Filey to Scarborough road). Site signed*

🚐 £15-£25 🚐 £15-£25

Open Mar-Oct Last arrival 20.00hrs Last departure 11.00hrs

A peaceful family park in a gently-sloping rural area, where the quality facilities are maintained to a high standard of cleanliness. The keen owners are friendly and helpful, and create a relaxing atmosphere. A natural area offers views of the surrounding countryside through the shrubbery. Please note that this park does not accept tents. A 7.5 acre site with 125 touring pitches, 25 hardstandings.

AA Pubs & Restaurants nearby: Cayley Arms, Brompton-by-Sawdon 01723 859372

Facilities: 🛁🚿🎣⊙♿🚿✻🔥🖙🚻

Services: 🔌🖙🅿🗑🚽🅃

Within 3 miles: ⚓🎣🕮◉♨🅱🅑🅾∪

Notes: Dogs must be kept on short leads. Wi-fi

▶▶▶ 78% Centenary Way Camping & Caravan Park *(TA115798)*

Muston Grange YO14 0HU
☎ 01723 516415 & 512313
dir: *Just off A1039 near A165 junct towards Bridlington*

* 🚐 £10-£16 🚐 £10-£16 ▲ £7-£14

Open Mar-Oct Last arrival 21.00hrs Last departure noon

A well set-out family-owned park, with footpath access to nearby beach. Close to the seaside resort of Filey, and caravan pitches enjoy views over open countryside. A 3 acre site with 75 touring pitches, 25 hardstandings.

AA Pubs & Restaurants nearby: Cayley Arms, Brompton-by-Sawdon 01723 859372

Leisure: 🅐

Facilities: 🎣⊙✻♿🖙🚻

Services: 🔌🖙�

Within 3 miles: ⚓🎣🕮◉🅱🅾

Notes: ⊘ No group bookings in peak period, no 9-12 berth tents, no gazebos

▶▶▶ 76% Filey Brigg Touring Caravan & Country Park *(TA115812)*

North Cliff YO14 9ET
☎ 01723 513852
e-mail: fileybrigg@scarborough.gov.uk
dir: *0.5m from Filey town centre on coast road from Scarborough, A165*

🚐 🚐 ▲

Open Etr-2 Jan Last arrival 18.00hrs Last departure noon

A municipal park overlooking Filey Brigg with splendid views along the coast, and set in a country park. The beach is just a short walk

LEISURE: 🏊 Indoor swimming pool 🏊 Outdoor swimming pool 🅐 Children's playground 🎾 Tennis court 🎯 Games room 📺 Separate TV room ⛳ 9/18 hole golf course 🚣 Boats for hire 🎬 Cinema 🎣 Fishing ◉ Mini golf 🏄 Watersports ∪ Stables **FACILITIES:** 🛁 Bath 🚿 Shower ⊙ Electric shaver 🖙 Hairdryer ✻ Ice Pack Facility ♿ Disabled facilities 🕾 Public telephone 🅱 Shop on site or within 200yds 🅐 Mobile shop (calls at least 5 days a week) 🍖 BBQ area 🍴 Picnic area 🐾 Dog exercise area

away, as is the resort of Filey. There is a new, good quality amenity block, and 50 all-weather pitches are available. The electric hook-ups and the amenity blocks have now been upgraded. A 9 acre site with 158 touring pitches, 82 hardstandings.

AA Pubs & Restaurants nearby: Cayley Arms, Brompton-by-Sawdon 01723 859372

Leisure: 🛝

Facilities: 🚿 ⊙ ✱ ♿ ☎ [S] 🐕

Services: 🔌 🧺 [T] 🍴 🍟

Within 3 miles: ⛳ ⛵ 🎣 ◎ [S] 🧺 🐴

►►► 75% Crow's Nest Caravan Park

(TA094826)

Gristhorpe YO14 9PS

☎ 01723 582206 📠 01723 582206

e-mail: enquires@crowsnestcaravanpark.com

dir: *5m S of Scarborough & 2m N of Filey. On seaward side of A165, signed off rdbt, near petrol station*

🚐 🚗 ⛺

Open Mar-Oct Last departure noon

A beautifully situated park on the coast between Scarborough and Filey, with excellent panoramic views. This large and mainly static park offers lively entertainment, and two bars. The touring caravan area is near the entertainment complex, whilst the tenting pitches are at the top of the site. A 20 acre site with 49 touring pitches, 49 hardstandings and 217 statics.

AA Pubs & Restaurants nearby: Cayley Arms, Brompton-by-Sawdon 01723 859372

Leisure: 🏊 🛝 🎱

Facilities: 🚿 ⊙ ✱ ☎ [S] 🐕

Services: 🔌 🧺 🍷 ⛽ 🔥 [T] 🍟

Within 3 miles: ⛳ 🎣 ◎ ⛵ [S] 🧺 🐴

Notes: Free entertainment in bar. Wi-fi

see advert below

HARROGATE — Map 19 SE35

Places to visit

RHS Garden Harlow Carr, Harrogate, 01423 565418, www.rhs.org.uk/harlowcarr

The Royal Pump Room Museum, Harrogate, 01423 556188, www.harrogate.gov.uk/museums

Great for kids: Stump Cross Caverns, Pateley Bridge, 01756 752780, www.stumpcrosscaverns.co.uk

PREMIER PARK

▶▶▶▶▶ 80% Rudding Holiday Park (SE333531)

GOLD

Follifoot HG3 1JH
☎ 01423 870439 📠 01423 870859
e-mail: holiday-park@ruddingpark.com
web: www.ruddingpark.co.uk/caravans-camping/index.php
dir: From A1 take A59 to A658 signed Bradford. 4.5m then right, follow signs

* ⊞ £17-£35 ⊞ £22-£39 Å £17-£35

Open Mar-Jan (rs Nov-Jan shop & Deer House Pub - limited opening) Last arrival 22.30hrs Last departure 14.00hrs

A spacious park set in the stunning 200 acres of mature parkland and walled gardens of Rudding Park. The setting has been tastefully enhanced with terraced pitches and dry-stone walls. A separate area houses super pitches where all services are supplied including a picnic table and TV connection, and there are excellent toilets. An 18-hole golf course, a 6-hole short course, driving range, golf academy, heated outdoor swimming pool, the Deer House Pub, and a children's play area complete the amenities. Seasonal touring pitches are available. A 55 acre site with 109 touring pitches, 20 hardstandings and 57 statics.

AA Pubs & Restaurants nearby: van Zeller, Harrogate 01423 508762

Boars Head Hotel, Harrogate 01423 771888

General Tarleton, Knaresborough 01423 340284

Leisure: ⊚ ⋔ ⚲
Facilities: ⇤ ⋔ ☉ ⚑ ⚿ ⚒ ⚠ ⌚ 📦 ⛱ ⚞
Services: ⊕ ⛽ ⚡ 🛢 ⚗ ⓣ ⑩ 🛄 ⚑ ⚑ ⚑
Within 3 miles: ↧ ⌗ ⌒ 🛒 ⓡ ∪

Notes: Under 18s must be accompanied by an adult, outside swimming pool open summer only. Wi-fi

PREMIER PARK

▶▶▶▶▶ 73% Ripley Caravan Park (SE289610)

GOLD

Knaresborough Rd, Ripley HG3 3AU
☎ 01423 770050 📠 01423 770050
e-mail: ripleycaravanpark@talk21.com
web: www.ripleycaravanpark.com
dir: 3m N of Harrogate on A61. Right at rdbt onto B6165 signed Knaresborough. Site 300yds left

* ⊞ £14-£16.50 ⊞ £14-£16.50 Å £14-£16.50

Open Etr-Oct Last arrival 21.00hrs Last departure noon

A well-run rural site in attractive meadowland which has been landscaped with mature tree plantings. The resident owners lovingly maintain the facilities, and there is a heated swimming pool and sauna, a games room, and a covered playroom for small children. An 18 acre site with 100 touring pitches, 35 hardstandings and 50 statics.

AA Pubs & Restaurants nearby: van Zeller, Harrogate 01423 508762

Boars Head Hotel, Harrogate 01423 771888

Malt Shovel Inn, Brearton 01423 862929

General Tarleton, Knaresborough 01423 340284

Leisure: ⊚ ⋔ ⚲
Facilities: ⋔ ☉ ⚑ ⚿ ⚒ ⓒ 📦 ⚞
Services: ⊕ ⛽ 🛢 ⚗ ⓣ ⛱ ⚑
Within 3 miles: ↧ ⚔ ⌗ ⌒ ◎ 🛒 ⓡ ∪

Notes: Family camping only, dogs must be kept on leads, BBQs must be off ground, no skateboards. Nursery playroom, football, TV (games room), sauna

▶▶▶▶ 77% High Moor Farm Park (SE242560)

Skipton Rd HG3 2LT
☎ 01423 563637 & 564955 📠 01423 529449
e-mail: highmoorfarmpark@btconnect.com
dir: 4m W of Harrogate on A59 towards Skipton

⊞ £20-£22 ⊞ £20-£22

Open Etr or Apr-Oct Last arrival 23.30hrs Last departure 15.00hrs

An excellent site with very good facilities, set beside a small wood and surrounded by thorn hedges. The numerous touring pitches are located in meadowland fields, each area with its own toilet block. A large heated indoor swimming pool, games room, 9-hole golf course, full-sized crown bowling green, and a bar serving meals and snacks are all popular. Please note that this park does not accept tents. A 15 acre site with 320 touring pitches, 51 hardstandings and 158 statics.

AA Pubs & Restaurants nearby: van Zeller, Harrogate 01423 508762

Boars Head Hotel, Harrogate 01423 771888

General Tarleton, Knaresborough 01423 340284

Leisure: ⊚ ⋔ ⚲
Facilities: ⇤ ⋔ ☉ ⚑ ⚿ ⚒ ⓒ 📦 ⚞ ⚞
Services: ⊕ ⛽ ⚡ 🛢 ⚗ ⓣ ⑩ 🛄 ⛱
Within 3 miles: ↧ ⌗ ⌒ 🛒 ⓡ ∪

Notes: Coarse fishing

▶▶▶ 76% Bilton Park (SE317577)

Village Farm, Bilton Ln HG1 4DH
☎ 01423 863121
e-mail: welcome@biltonpark.co.uk
dir: Turn E off A59 at Skipton Inn into Bilton Lane. Site approx 1m

⊞ fr £16 ⊞ fr £16 Å fr £16

Open Apr-Oct

An established family-owned park in open countryside yet only two miles from the shops and tearooms of Harrogate. The spacious grass pitches are complemented by a well-appointed toilet block with private facilities. The Nidd Gorge is right on the doorstep. A 4 acre site with 50 touring pitches.

Bilton Park

AA Pubs & Restaurants nearby: van Zeller, Harrogate 01423 508762

Boars Head Hotel, Harrogate 01423 771888

Malt Shovel Inn, Brearton 01423 862929

General Tarleton, Knaresborough 01423 340284

Leisure: ⚙ **Facilities:** ⚙⚙⚙⚙⚙⚙

Services: ⚙⚙⚙⚙⚙

Within 3 miles: ⚙⚙⚙⚙⚙⚙

Notes: ⚙

►►► 64% Shaws Trailer Park

(SE325557)

Knaresborough Rd HG2 7NE
☎ 01423 884432   📄 01423 883622
dir: *On A59 1m from town centre. 0.5m SW of Starbeck railway crossing, by Johnsons dry cleaners*

⚙⚙⚙

Open all year Last arrival 20.00hrs Last departure 14.00hrs

A long-established site just a mile from the centre of Harrogate. The all-weather pitches are arranged around a carefully kept grass area, and the toilets are basic but functional and clean. The entrance is on the bus route to Harrogate. An 11 acre site with 60 touring pitches, 24 hardstandings and 146 statics.

AA Pubs & Restaurants nearby: van Zeller, Harrogate 01423 508762

Boars Head Hotel, Harrogate 01423 771888

Malt Shovel Inn, Brearton 01423 862929

General Tarleton, Knaresborough 01423 340284

Facilities: ⚙⚙⚙⚙⚙ **Services:** ⚙⚙⚙

Within 3 miles: ⚙⚙⚙⚙⚙⚙

Notes: Adults only. ⚙

HAWES   Map 18 SD88

Places to visit

Dales Countryside Museum and National Park Centre, Hawes, 01969 666210, www.yorkshiredales.org.uk

►► 86% Bainbridge Ings Caravan & Camping Site *(SD879895)*

DL8 3NU
☎ 01969 667354
e-mail: janet@bainbridge-ings.co.uk
dir: *Approaching Hawes from Bainbridge on A684, left at Gayle sign, site 300yds on left*

* ⚙ £16-£18 ⚙ £13-£16 ⚙ £13

Open Apr-Oct Last arrival 22.00hrs Last departure noon

A quiet, well-organised site in open countryside close to Hawes in the heart of Upper Wensleydale, popular with ramblers. Pitches are sited around the perimeter of several fields, each bounded by traditional stone walls. A 5 acre site with 70 touring pitches, 8 hardstandings and 15 statics.

AA Pubs & Restaurants nearby: Moorcock Inn, Hawes 01969 667488

Kings Arms, Askrigg 01969 650817

Facilities: ⚙⚙⚙⚙⚙

Services: ⚙⚙⚙⚙⚙

Within 3 miles: ⚙⚙⚙

Notes: ⚙ No noise after 23.00hrs

HELMSLEY

Places to visit

Duncombe Park, Helmsley, 01439 778625, www.duncombepark.com

Helmsley Castle, Helmsley, 01439 770442, www.english-heritage.org.uk

Great for kids: Flamingo Land Theme Park and Zoo, Kirby Misperton, 01653 668287, www.flamingoland.co.uk

---

HELMSLEY   Map 19 SE68

PREMIER PARK

►►►►► 78% Golden Square Touring Caravan Park *(SE604797)*

Oswaldkirk YO62 5YQ
☎ 01439 788269   📄 01439 788236
e-mail: reception@goldensquarecaravanpark.com
dir: *From Thirsk A19 towards York turn left onto Caravan Route to Helmsley (1m out of Ampleforth village). From York B1363, turn off B1257 to Ampleforth, 0.5m on right*

* ⚙ £15-£18 ⚙ £15-£18 ⚙ £15-£18

Open Mar-Oct Last arrival 21.00hrs Last departure noon

An excellent, popular and spacious site with very good facilities. This friendly, immaculately maintained park is set in a quiet rural situation with lovely views over the North York Moors. Terraced on three levels and surrounded by mature trees, it caters particularly for families, with excellent play areas and space for ball games. Country walks and mountain bike trails start here and a new and attractive holiday home development is underway. Seasonal touring pitches are available. A 12 acre site with 129 touring pitches, 10 hardstandings and 10 statics.

AA Pubs & Restaurants nearby: Crown Inn, Helmsley 01439 770297

The Star Inn, Harome 01439 770397

Leisure: ⚙⚙

Facilities: ⚙⚙⚙⚙⚙⚙⚙⚙⚙⚙⚙

Services: ⚙⚙⚙⚙⚙⚙⚙⚙

Within 3 miles: ⚙⚙⚙⚙⚙

Notes: ⚙ No skateboards or fires. Microwave available

HELMSLEY *continued*

►►► 75% Foxholme Caravan Park

(SE658828)

Harome YO62 5JG
☎ **01439 771904**
dir: *A170 from Helmsley towards Scarborough, right signed Harome, left at church, through village, follow signs*

🚐 £20 🚏 £20 ⛺ £20

Open Etr-Oct Last arrival 23.00hrs Last departure noon

A quiet park set in secluded wooded countryside, with well-shaded pitches in individual clearings divided by mature trees. The facilities are well maintained, and the site is ideal as a touring base or a place to relax. Please note that caravans are prohibited on the A170 at Sutton Bank between Thirsk and Helmsley. A 6 acre site with 60 touring pitches.

AA Pubs & Restaurants nearby: Crown Inn, Helmsley 01439 770297

The Star Inn, Harome 01439 770397

Facilities: 🛁 🚿 ⊙ 🌡 ✳ ⛭ 🕐 🏪 🐕

Services: 🔌 🔟 🛢 🧴 🚽 🛒 ⬇

Within 3 miles: ⚓ 🏪 🎣 ↺   **Notes:** Adults only. 🐕

HIGH BENTHAM   Map 18 SD66

Places to visit

Lancaster Maritime Museum, Lancaster, 01524 382264, www.lancashire.gov.uk/museums

Lancaster City Museum, Lancaster, 01524 64637, www.lancashire.gov.uk/museums

Great for kids: Lancaster Castle, Lancaster, 01524 64998, www.lancastercastle.com

PREMIER PARK

►►►►► 80% Riverside Caravan Park *(SD665688)*

Best of British   GOLD

LA2 7FJ
☎ **015242 61272**   🖶 **015242 62835**
e-mail: info@riversidecaravanpark.co.uk
dir: *Off B6480, signed from High Bentham town centre*

* 🚐 £18.75-£24.25 🚏 £18.75-£24.25

Open Mar-16 Dec (rs 28 Dec-2 Jan) Last arrival 20.00hrs Last departure noon

A well-managed riverside park developed to a high standard, with level grass pitches set in avenues separated by trees, and there are excellent facilities for children, who are made to feel as important as the adults! It has an excellent, modern amenity block, including a new family bathroom, and an excellent shop, laundry and information room. The superb games room and adventure playground are hugely popular, and the market town of High Bentham is close by. Please note that this site does not accept tents. A 12 acre site with 61 touring pitches, 27 hardstandings and 206 statics.

AA Pubs & Restaurants nearby: The Traddock, Austwick 015242 51224

Game Cock Inn, Austwick 015242 51226

New Inn, Clapham 01524 251203

Leisure: 🎠 🕹

Facilities: 🌡 ⊙ 🌡 & 🕐 🏪 🐕

Services: 🔌 🔟 🛢 🧴 🔟 🛒 ⬇

Within 3 miles: ⚓ 🎣 🏪 ↺

Notes: Permits for private fishing (chargeable). Wi-fi

► 81% Lowther Hill Caravan Park

(SD696695)

LA2 7AN
☎ **015242 61657**
web: www.caravancampingsites.co.uk/northyorkshire/lowtherhill.htm
dir: *From A65 at Clapham onto B6480 signed Bentham. 3m to site on right*

🚐 £16.50-£17.50 🚏 £16.50-£17.50 ⛺ fr £10

Open Mar-Nov Last arrival 21.00hrs Last departure 14.00hrs

A simple site with stunning panoramic views from every pitch. Peace reigns on this little park, though the tourist villages of Ingleton, Clapham and Settle are not far away. All pitches have electricity, and there is a heated toilet/washroom and new dishwashing facilities. A 1 acre site with 9 touring pitches, 4 hardstandings.

AA Pubs & Restaurants nearby: The Traddock, Austwick 015242 51224

Game Cock Inn, Austwick 015242 51226

New Inn, Clapham 01524 251203

Facilities: 🌡 &

Services: 🔌

Within 3 miles: ⚓ 🎣 🏪 🔟

Notes: 🐕 Dogs must be kept on leads, payment on arrival. Utensil washing facilities for campers

HINDERWELL   Map 19 NZ71

Places to visit

Whitby Abbey, Whitby, 01947 603568, www.english-heritage.org.uk

RNLI Zetland Museum, Redcar, 01642 494311

Great for kids: Saltburn Smugglers Heritage Centre, Saltburn-by-the-Sea, 01287 625252, www.redcar-cleveland.gov.uk

►►► 77% Serenity Touring and Camping Park *(NZ792167)*

26A High St TS13 5JH
☎ **01947 841122**
e-mail: patandni@aol.com
web: www.serenitycaravanpark.co.uk
dir: *Off A174 in Hinderwell*

* 🚐 £14.50-£16 🚏 £14.50-£16 ⛺ fr £6.50

Open Mar-Oct Last arrival 21.00hrs Last departure noon

A charming park mainly for adults, being developed by enthusiastic owners. It lies behind the village of Hinderwell with its two pubs and store, and is handy for backpackers on the Cleveland Way. The sandy Runswick Bay and old fishing port of Staithes are close by, whilst Whitby is a short drive away. A 5.5 acre site with 20 touring pitches, 3 hardstandings.

AA Pubs & Restaurants nearby: Magpie Café, Whitby 01947 602058

Facilities: 🌡 ⊙ 🌡 ✳ 🏪 🐕

Services: 🔌 🔟 🛢 🧴 🛒 ⬇

Within 3 miles: 🎣 🏪 ↺

Notes: 🐕 Mainly adult site, no ball games, kites or frisbees

HUNMANBY — Map 17 TA07

Places to visit

Sewerby Hall and Gardens, Bridlington, 01262 673769, www.sewerby-hall.co.uk

Scarborough Castle, Scarborough, 01723 372451, www.english-heritage.org.uk

Great for kids: Sea Life and Marine Sanctuary, Scarborough, 01723 376125, www.sealife.co.uk

▶▶▶▶ 76% Orchard Farm Holiday Village (TA105779)

Stonegate YO14 0PU
☎ 01723 891582 📠 01723 891582
e-mail: sharon.dugdale@virgin.net
dir: *A165 from Scarborough towards Bridlington. Turn right signed Hunmanby, site on right just after rail bridge*

🚐 £12-£18 🚗 £12-£18 ▲ £12-£18

Open Mar-Oct (rs Off peak some facilities restricted) Last arrival 23.00hrs Last departure 11.00hrs

Pitches are arranged around a large coarse fishing lake at this grassy park. The young owners are keen and friendly, and offer a wide range of amenities including an indoor heated swimming pool and a licensed bar. A 14 acre site with 91 touring pitches, 34 hardstandings and 46 statics.

AA Pubs & Restaurants nearby: Star Country Inn, Weaverthorpe 01944 738273

Leisure: 🏊 🅰 🎣 ▢
Facilities: 🏳 ⊙ 🇵 ✳ ⚿ 🕔 🖻 🎇 🛒 🖈
Services: 🔌 🔵 🗑 💧 🔥 🎁 🚰
Within 3 miles: ⌇ 🎣 ◎ 🏊 🚲 🖼
Notes: ⊛ Fishing lake, minature railway

HUTTON-LE-HOLE — Map 19 SE79

Places to visit

Nunnington Hall, Nunnington, 01439 748283, www.nationaltrust.org.uk

Rievaulx Abbey, Rievaulx, 01439 798228, www.english-heritage.org.uk

Great for kids: Pickering Castle, Pickering, 01751 474989, www.english-heritage.org.uk

▶▶▶▶ 78% Hutton-le-Hole Caravan Park (SE705895)

Westfield Lodge YO62 6UG
☎ 01751 417261 📠 01751 417876
e-mail: rwstrickland@farmersweekly.net
dir: *From A170 onto Hutton-le-Hole road, N for approx 2m, over cattle grid, 500yds left into Park Drive, signed into site*

🚐 fr £14 🚗 fr £14 ▲ fr £11.50

Open Etr-Oct Last arrival 21.00hrs Last departure noon

A small high quality park on a working farm in the North York Moors National Park. The purpose-built toilet block offers en suite family rooms, and there is a choice of hard-standing or grass pitches within a well-tended area surrounded by hedges and shrubs. The village facilities are a 10-minute walk away. Please note that caravans are prohibited from the A170 at Sutton Bank between Thirsk and Helmsley. A 5 acre site with 38 touring pitches, 6 hardstandings.

AA Pubs & Restaurants nearby: Plough Inn, Fadmoor 01751 431515

Black Smiths Arms, Lastingham 01751 417247

Facilities: 🏳 ⊙ 🇵 ✳ ⚿ 🕔 🛒 🖈
Services: 🔌 🎁 💧 🔥 🚰
Within 3 miles: ⌇ ◎ 🖼 U
Notes: Farm walks

KNARESBOROUGH

Places to visit

RHS Garden Harlow Carr, Harrogate, 01423 565418, www.rhs.org.uk/harlowcarr

The Royal Pump Room Museum, Harrogate, 01423 556188, www.harrogate.gov.uk/museums

Great or kids: Knaresborough Castle and Museum, Knaresborough, 01423 556188, www.harrogate.gov.uk/museums

KNARESBOROUGH — Map 19 SE35

▶▶▶ 74% Kingfisher Caravan Park (SE343603)

Low Moor Ln, Farnham HG5 9JB
☎ 01423 869411 📠 01423 869411
dir: *From Knaresborough take A6055. After 1m turn left towards Farnham & left again in village signed Scotton. Site 1m on left*

* 🚐 £13-£17 🚗 £13-£17 ▲ £13-£17

Open Mar-Oct Last arrival 21.00hrs Last departure 16.00hrs

A large grassy site with open spaces set in a wooded area in rural countryside. Whilst Harrogate, Fountains Abbey and York are within easy reach, anglers will want to take advantage of on-site coarse and fly fishing lakes. The park has a separate flat tenting field with electric hook-ups available. A 14 acre site with 35 touring pitches and 80 statics.

AA Pubs & Restaurants nearby: General Tarleton, Knaresborough 01423 340284

Leisure: 🅰
Facilities: 🏳 ⊙ 🇵 ✳ ⚿ 🕔 🖻 🎇 🛒 🖈
Services: 🔌 🔵 🔥 ⊘
Within 3 miles: ⌇ 🥾 🎣 🖼 ◎ U
Notes: ⊛ Pets must be kept on leads & under strict adult control, no football

MARKINGTON — Map 19 SE26

Places to visit

Fountains Abbey and Studley Royal, Ripon, 01765 608888, www.fountainsabbey.org.uk

Norton Conyers, Ripon, 01765 640333

Great for kids: Stump Cross Caverns, Pateley Bridge, 01756 752780, www.stumpcrosscaverns.co.uk

▶▶▶ 77% Yorkshire Hussar Inn Holiday Caravan Park (SE288650)

High St HG3 3NR
☎ 01765 677327 & 677715
e-mail: yorkshirehussar@yahoo.co.uk
dir: *Between Harrogate & Ripon (A61) turn W at Wormald Green, 1m into Markington, turn left past Post Office into High Street*

* 🚐 £15-£20 🚗 £15-£20 ▲ £10-£20

Open Etr-Oct Last arrival 20.00hrs Last departure noon

continued

MARKINGTON *continued*

A terraced site behind the village inn with well-kept grass. This pleasant site offers spacious pitches with some hardstandings and electricity, and there are a few holiday statics for hire. Although the pub does not provide food, an alternative food pub is available within walking distance. A 5 acre site with 20 touring pitches, 2 hardstandings and 73 statics.

AA Pubs & Restaurants nearby: Sawley Arms, Sawley 01765 620642

Leisure: ⚑

Facilities: ⬛☉♟✳♿

Services: ⬛⛽⛽☎🛒

Within 3 miles: ✎☖⬛↺

Notes: ⊕ Dogs must be kept on leads. Paddling pool

MASHAM   Map 19 SE28

Places to visit

Theakston Brewery and Visitor Centre, Marsham, 01765 680000, www.theakstons.co.uk

Norton Conyers, Ripon, 01765 640333

Great for kids: Lightwater Valley Theme Park, North Stainley, 0871 720 0011, www.lightwatervalley.co.uk

►►► 78% Old Station Holiday Park (SE232812)

Old Station Yard, Low Burton HG4 4DF
☎ 01765 689569   🖷 01765 689569
e-mail: oldstation@tiscali.co.uk
dir: *Exit A1 onto B6267 signed Masham & Thirsk. In 8m left onto A6108. In 100yds left into site*

* 🚐 £15-£18.50 🚉 £15-£18.50 ▲ fr £14

Open Mar-Nov Last arrival 20.00hrs Last departure noon

An interesting site on a former station. The enthusiastic and caring family owners have maintained the railway theme in creating a park with high quality facilities. The small town of Masham with its Theakston and Black Sheep breweries are within easy walking distance of the park. The reception/café in a carefully restored wagon shed provides a range of meals using local produce. A 3.75 acre site with 50 touring pitches and 12 statics.

AA Pubs & Restaurants nearby: Kings Head Hotel, Masham 01765 689295

Black Sheep Brewery, Masham 01765 680101

Vennell's, Masham 01765 689000

Facilities: ⬛☉♟✳♿☉⬛🎋🅿

Services: ⬛⛽🔒☎🍴🛒🚮♻

Within 3 miles: ✎☖⬛↺

Notes: No fast cycling around site, no campfires. Wi-fi

NABURN   Map 16 SE54

Places to visit

Clifford's Tower, York, 01904 646940, www.english-heritage.org.uk

Fairfax House, York, 01904 655543, www.fairfaxhouse.co.uk

Great for kids: Jorvik Viking Centre, York, 01904 615505, www.jorvik-viking-centre.com

►►►► 78% Naburn Lock Caravan Park (SE596446)

Y019 4RU
☎ 01904 728697   🖷 01904 728697
e-mail: wilks@naburnlock.co.uk
dir: *From A64 (McArthur Glen designer outlet) take A19 N, turn left signed Naburn on B1222, site on right 0.5m past village*

🚐 🚉 ▲

Open Mar-6 Nov Last arrival 20.00hrs Last departure 13.00hrs

A family park where the enthusiastic owners are steadily improving its quality. The mainly grass pitches are arranged in small groups separated by mature hedges. The park is close to the River Ouse, and the river towpath provides excellent walking and cycling opportunities. The river bus to nearby York leaves from a jetty beside the park. A 7 acre site with 100 touring pitches, 12 hardstandings.

AA Pubs & Restaurants nearby: Blue Bell, York 01904 654904

Lysander Arms, York 01904 640845

Facilities: ⬛☉♟✳♿⬛🎋🅿

Services: ⬛⛽🔒⚡☎🛒♻

Within 3 miles: ✎⬛⬛↺

Notes: Adults-only section. River fishing

NETHERBY   Map 16 SE34

Places to visit

Abbey House Museum, Leeds, 0113 230 5492, www.leeds.gov.uk

Royal Armouries Museum, Leeds, 0113 220 1866, www.royalarmouries.org

►►►► 80% Maustin Caravan Park (SE332470)

Kearby with Netherby LS22 4DA
☎ 0113 288 6234
e-mail: info@maustin.co.uk
dir: *From A61 (Leeds-Harrogate road) follow signs for Kirkby Overblow. Right towards Kearby, pass farm buildings to x-rds. Right to site*

🚐 🚉 ▲

Open Mar-28 Jan

A secluded park for adults only, with pitches set around a well-tended grassed area. Adjacent to the pitching area, the amenity block offers a high standard of facilities. The charming Stables Restaurant with its cosy bar and patio is open at weekends and bank holidays, and the park has its own flat bowling green where competitions are held throughout the season. An 8 acre site with 25 touring pitches and 70 statics.

AA Pubs & Restaurants nearby: Windmill Inn, Linton 01937 582209

Facilities: ⬛☉♟✳

Services: ⬛⛽🔒☎🍴

Within 3 miles: ✎☖⬛↺

Notes: Adults only. Wi-fi

NORTHALLERTON

Places to visit

Mount Grace Priory, Osmotherly, 01609 883494, www.english-heritage.org.uk

Theakston Brewery and Visitor Centre, Marsham, 01765 680000, www.theakstons.co.uk

Great for kids: Falconry UK - Birds of Prey Visitor Centre, Thirsk, 01845 587522, www.falconrycentre.co.uk

NORTHALLERTON — Map 19 SE39

AA CAMPING CARD SITE

▶▶▶▶ 78% Otterington Park *(SE378882)*

Station Farm, South Otterington DL7 9JB
☎ 01609 780656
e-mail: info@otteringtonpark.com
dir: *Turn W from A168 midway between Northallerton & Thirsk, signed South Otterington. Site on right just before South Otterington*

* 🚐 £16-£20 🚚 £16-£20

Open Mar-Oct Last arrival 21.00hrs Last departure 13.00hrs

A high quality park on a working farm with open outlooks across the Vale of York. Newly extended to include another paddock with 22 hardstanding pitches and three camping pods, it enjoys a peaceful location with a lovely nature walk and on-site fishing, which is very popular. Young children will enjoy the play area. Toilet facilities are very good. The attractions of Northallerton and Thirsk are a few minutes' drive away. A 6 acre site with 62 touring pitches, 62 hardstandings.

Leisure: 🅰
Facilities: 🛁📶☉🅿✳⚡🕐🚰🖼🎪🐕
Services: 🔌🗑🛢🔋
Within 3 miles: 🚶🎣📶🐕🛒🗑
Notes: Hot tub, fitness equipment. Wi-fi

NORTH STANLEY

Places to visit

Norton Conyers, Ripon, 01765 640333

Falconry UK - Birds of Prey Visitor Centre, Thirsk, 01845 587522, www.falconrycentre.co.uk

Great for kids: Lightwater Valley Theme Park, North Stanley, 0871 720 0011, www.lightwatervalley.co.uk

NORTH STANLEY — Map 19 SE27

▶▶▶▶ 76% Sleningford Watermill Caravan Camping Park *(SE280783)*

HG4 3HQ
☎ 01765 635201
web: www.sleningfordwatermill.co.uk
dir: *Adjacent to A6108. 5m N of Ripon & 1m N of North Stanley*

🚐🚚⛺

Open Etr & Apr-Oct Last arrival 21.00hrs Last departure 12.30hrs

The old watermill and the River Ure make an attractive setting for this touring park which is laid out in two areas. Pitches are placed in meadowland and close to mature woodland, and the park has two enthusiastic managers. This is a popular place with canoeists. A 14 acre site with 40 touring pitches, 9 hardstandings.

AA Pubs & Restaurants nearby: Bruce Arms, West Tanfield 01677 470325

Kings Head Hotel, Masham 01765 689295

Black Sheep Brewery, Masham 01765 680101

Vennell's, Masham 01765 689000

Facilities: 📶☉✳⚡🗑🐕
Services: 🔌🗑🛢🍴🔋🚰
Within 3 miles: 🚶🎣📶🚵🗑
Notes: Youth groups by prior arrangement only booked through organisations or associations. Off-licence, fly fishing, outdoor activities, canoe sales, hire & tuition

OSMOTHERLEY

Places to visit

Mount Grace Priory, Osmotherly, 01609 883494, www.english-heritage.org.uk

Guisborough Priory, Guisborough, 01287 633801, www.english-heritage.org.uk

Great for kids: Falconry UK - Birds of Prey Visitor Centre, Thirsk, 01845 587522, www.falconrycentre.co.uk

OSMOTHERLEY — Map 19 SE49

PREMIER PARK

▶▶▶▶▶ 77% Cote Ghyll Caravan & Camping Park *(SE459979)*

DL6 3AH
☎ 01609 883425
e-mail: hills@coteghyll.com
dir: *Exit A19 dual carriageway at A684 (Northallerton junct). Follow signs to Osmotherley. Left in village centre. Site entrance 0.5m on right*

🚐🚚⛺

Open Mar-Oct Last arrival 22.00hrs Last departure noon

A quiet, peaceful site in a pleasant valley on the edge of moors, close to the village. The park is divided into terraces bordered by woodland, and the extra well-appointed amenity block is a welcome addition to this attractive park. Mature trees, shrubs and an abundance of fresh seasonal floral displays create a relaxing and peaceful atmosphere and the whole park is immaculately maintained. Major investment has delivered high standards in landscaping and facilities. There are pubs and shops nearby and holiday statics for hire. A 7 acre site with 77 touring pitches, 22 hardstandings and 18 statics.

AA Pubs & Restaurants nearby: Golden Lion, Osmotherley 01609 883526

Queen Catherine, Osmotherley 01609 883209

Leisure: 🅰
Facilities: 🛁📶☉🅿✳⚡🕐🗑🖼🎪
Services: 🔌🗑🛢🍴📶🔋🚰🛒
Within 3 miles: 📶🗑🛒🎣
Notes: Family park, dogs must be kept on leads at all times. Tourist information, laundry. Wi-fi

PICKERING

Places to visit

Pickering Castle, Pickering, 01751 474989, www.english-heritage.org.uk

North Yorkshire Moors Railway, Pickering, 01751 472508, www.northyorkshiremoorsrailway.com

Great for kids: Flamingo Land Theme Park and Zoo, Kirby Misperton, 01653 668287, www.flamingoland.co.uk

PICKERING
Map 19 SE78

▶▶▶▶ 77% Wayside Holiday Park
(SE764859)

Wrelton YO18 8PG
☎ 01751 472608 📠 01751 472608
e-mail: wrelton@waysideholidaypark.co.uk
web: www.waysideparks.co.uk
dir: 2.5m W of Pickering off A170, follow signs at Wrelton

🚐 £20 🚙 £20

Open Etr-end Oct Last arrival 22.00hrs Last departure noon

Located in the village of Wrelton, this well-maintained mainly seasonal touring and holiday home park is divided into small paddocks by mature hedging. Major investment in 2010 resulted in the complete refurbishment of the amenity block, which now has smart, modern facilities. The village pub and restaurant are within a few minutes' walk of the park. Please note that caravans are prohibited from the A170 at Sutton Bank between Thirsk and Helmsley. A 10 acre site with 40 touring pitches, 5 hardstandings and 122 statics.

AA Pubs & Restaurants nearby: Fox & Hounds Country Inn, Pickering 01751 431577

White Swan Inn, Pickering 01751 472288

Fox & Rabbit Inn, Lockton 01751 460213

Leisure: 🅐
Facilities: 🌢⊙♟♿☀️🐕
Services: 🔌🅗🛢🚿🚽🖀
Within 3 miles: ↨🚶🎣🏧🛒🎠
Notes: Dogs must be kept on leads

RICHMOND
Map 19 NZ10

Places to visit

Green Howards Museum, Richmond, 01748 826561, www.greenhowards.org.uk

Bolton Castle, Castle Bolton, 01969 623981, www.boltoncastle.co.uk

Great for kids: Richmond Castle, Richmond, 01748 822493, www.english-heritage.org.uk

▶▶▶▶ 77% Brompton Caravan Park
(NZ199002)

Brompton-on-Swale DL10 7EZ
☎ 01748 824629 📠 01748 826383
e-mail: brompton.caravanpark@btinternet.com
dir: Exit A1 signed Catterick. Take B6271 to Brompton-on-Swale, site 1m on left

* 🚐 £18-£22 🚙 £18-£22 ⛺ £18

Open mid Mar-Oct Last arrival 21.00hrs Last departure noon

An attractive and well-managed family park where pitches have an open outlook across the River Swale. There is a good children's playground, an excellent family recreation room, a takeaway food service, and fishing is available on the river. Newly converted holiday apartments are also available. A 14 acre site with 177 touring pitches, 2 hardstandings and 22 statics.

AA Pubs & Restaurants nearby: Charles Bathurst Inn, Near Reeth 01748 884567

Leisure: 🅐🔍
Facilities: 🌢⊙♟✳♿☀️🖀🚿🐕
Services: 🔌🅗🛢🚿🚽🖀
Within 3 miles: ↨🚶🎣◎🏧🛒🎠
Notes: No gazebos, no motor or electric cars or scooters, quiet at midnight

▶▶▶ 76% Swale View Caravan Park (NZ134013)

SILVER

Reeth Rd DL10 4SF
☎ 01748 823106 📠 01748 823106
e-mail: swaleview@teesdaleonline.co.uk
dir: 3m W of Richmond on A6108 (Reeth to Leyburn road)

🚐🚙

Open Mar-15 Jan Last arrival 21.00hrs Last departure noon

Shaded by trees and overlooking the River Swale is this attractive, mainly grassy site, which has a number of attractive holiday homes and seasonal tourers. The facilities continue to be improved by enthusiastic owners and the park now offers facilities for 30 tourers, all with electric and hardstandings. It is a short distance from Richmond, and well situated for exploring Swaledale and Wensleydale. A 13 acre site with 30 touring pitches, 50 hardstandings and 100 statics.

AA Pubs & Restaurants nearby: Charles Bathurst Inn, Near Reeth 01748 884567

Leisure: 🅐🖵
Facilities: 🌢⊙♟♿☀️🖀🚿🐕
Services: 🔌🅗🛢🚿🚽🖀🛒
Within 3 miles: ↨🚶🎣🏧🛒🎠
Notes: 1 dog per pitch. Wi-fi

RIPON
Map 19 SE37

See also North Stainley

Places to visit

Fountains Abbey and Studley Royal, Ripon, 01765 608888, www.fountainsabbey.org.uk

Norton Conyers, Ripon, 01765 640333

Great for kids: Falconry UK - Birds of Prey Visitor Centre, Thirsk, 01845 587522, www.falconrycentre.co.uk

▶▶▶▶ 78% Riverside Meadows Country Caravan Park (SE317726)

Ure Bank Top HG4 1JD
☎ 01765 602964 📠 01765 604045
e-mail: info@flowerofmay.com
dir: On A61 at N end of bridge out of Ripon, W along river (do not cross river). Site 400yds, signed

* 🚐 £18-£25 🚙 £18-£25 ⛺ £14-£25

Open Etr-Oct (rs Low-mid season bar open wknds only) Last arrival dusk Last departure noon

LEISURE: 🅢 Indoor swimming pool 🅢 Outdoor swimming pool 🅐 Children's playground 🅢 Tennis court 🔍 Games room 🖵 Separate TV room ↧ 9/18 hole golf course
✦ Boats for hire 🅗 Cinema 🎣 Fishing ◎ Mini golf 🅢 Watersports 🎠 Stables **FACILITIES:** 🛁 Bath 🌢 Shower ⊙ Electric shaver ♟ Hairdryer ✳ Ice Pack Facility
♿ Disabled facilities 🕾 Public telephone 🅗 Shop on site or within 200yds 🛒 Mobile shop (calls at least 5 days a week) 🖀 BBQ area 🥧 Picnic area 🐕 Dog exercise area

This pleasant, well-maintained site stands on high ground overlooking the River Ure, one mile from the town centre. The site has an excellent club with family room and quiet lounge. There is no access to the river from the site. Seasonal touring pitches are available. A 28 acre site with 80 touring pitches and 269 statics.

AA Pubs & Restaurants nearby: Sawley Arms, Sawley 01765 620642

Leisure: ⚑ ⚔ ▢

Facilities: ⬟☉✳⚒⚙☺⚙☴⌇

Services: ⚑⚙⚏⚏⚒⚙⏹⚏

Within 3 miles: ⚓✻☰⚏⚏⚏⚙↻

Notes: Dogs by arrangement only. Wi-fi

ROBIN HOOD'S BAY

See also Whitby

Places to visit

Whitby Abbey, Whitby, 01947 603568, www.english-heritage.org.uk

Scarborough Castle, Scarborough, 01723 372451, www.english-heritage.org.uk

Great for **Great for kids:** Sea Life and Marine Sanctuary, Scarborough, 01723 376125, www.sealife.co.uk

---

| ROBIN HOOD'S BAY | Map 19 NZ90 |

▶▶▶▶ **78% Middlewood Farm Holiday Park** *(NZ945045)*

Middlewood Ln, Fylingthorpe YO22 4UF
☎ 01947 880414 📠 01947 880871
e-mail: info@middlewoodfarm.com
dir: *From A171 towards Robin Hood's Bay & into Fylingthorpe. Site signed from A171*

* ⚏ £14-£25 ⚏ £14-£25 ▲ £12-£24

Open Mar-Oct Last arrival 20.00hrs Last dep noon

A peaceful, friendly family park enjoying panoramic views of Robin Hood's Bay in a picturesque fishing village. The park has two toilet blocks with private facilities. The village pub is a five-minute walk away, and the beach is a ten-minute walk. A 7 acre site with 100 touring pitches, 19 hardstandings and 30 statics.

AA Pubs & Restaurants nearby: Laurel Inn, Robin Hood's Bay 01947 880400

Magpie Café, Whitby 01947 602058

Leisure: ⚑ **Facilities:** ⛟⬟☉⌇✳⚒⚙☴⌇

Services: ⚑⚙⚏⚏⚏⚏⚏⚏

Within 3 miles: ⚓✻⚏⚏⚏↻

Notes: Dogs must be kept on leads at all times, dangerous breeds are not accepted, no radios or noise after 22.00hrs. Pot wash sinks. Wi-fi

see advert below

▶▶▶▶ **77% Grouse Hill Caravan Park** *(NZ928002)*

Flask Bungalow Farm, Fylingdales YO22 4QH
☎ 01947 880543 & 880560 📠 01947 880543
e-mail: info@grousehill.co.uk
dir: *Off A171 (Whitby-Scarborough road), entered via loop road at Flask Inn*

⚏ ⚏ ▲

Open Mar-Oct (rs Etr-May shop & reception restricted) Last arrival 21.00hrs Last dep noon

A spacious family park on a south-facing slope, with many terraced pitches overlooking the North Yorkshire Moors National Park. Major investment in recent years has greatly improved the touring areas and amenities, in particular one of the toilet blocks, which has a superb fully-serviced shower room and a private bathroom. An ideal base for walking and touring. A 14 acre site with 175 touring pitches, 30 hardstandings.

AA Pubs & Restaurants nearby: Laurel Inn, Robin Hood's Bay 01947 880400

Magpie Café, Whitby 01947 602058

Leisure: ⚑⚔ **Facilities:** ⬟☉⌇✳⚒⚙☺⚙☴⌇
Services: ⚑⚙⚏⚏⏹⚏ **Within 3 miles:** ⚓⚏⚏↻

Notes: Dogs must be kept on leads at all times. Fish & chip van on Saturdays from 20.15hrs

see advert on page 324

SERVICES. ⚑ Electric hook up ⚙ Launderette ⚏ Licensed bar ⚏ Calor Gas ⚏ Camping Gaz ⏹ Toilet fluid ⏹ Café/Restaurant ⚏ Fast Food/Takeaway ⚏ Battery charging ⚏ Baby care ⚏ Motorvan service point   **ABBREVIATIONS:** BH/bank hols-bank holidays Etr-Easter Whit-Whitsun dep-departure fr-from hrs-hours m-mile mdnt-midnight rdbt-roundabout rs-restricted service wk-week wknd-weekend ⊗ No credit cards ⊗ no dogs See page 7 for details of the AA Camping Card Scheme

ROSEDALE ABBEY
Map 19 SE79

Places to visit

Pickering Castle, Pickering, 01751 474989, www.english-heritage.org.uk

North Yorkshire Moors Railway, Pickering, 01751 472508, www.northyorkshiremoorsrailway.com

Great for kids: Flamingo Land Theme Park and Zoo, Kirby Misperton, 01653 668287, www.flamingoland.co.uk

▶▶▶▶ 74% Rosedale Caravan & Camping Park (SE725958)

YO18 8SA
☎ 01751 417272
e-mail: info@flowerofmay.com
dir: From Pickering take A170 towards Sinnington for 2.25m. At Wrelton turn right onto unclass road signed Cropton & Rosedale, 7m. Site on left in village

* ⊕ £18-£25 ⊕ £18-£25 ▲ £14-£25

Open Mar-Oct Last arrival dusk Last departure noon

Set in a sheltered valley in the centre of the North Yorkshire Moors National Park, and divided into separate areas for tents, tourers and statics. A very popular park, with well-tended grounds, and close to the pretty village of Rosedale Abbey. Two toilet blocks offer private, combined facilities. A 10 acre site with 100 touring pitches and 35 statics.

AA Pubs & Restaurants nearby: Black Smiths Arms, Lastingham 01751 417247

New Inn, Cropton 01751 417330

Leisure: ⋔
Facilities: ⌐⊙☀&⊙☖ா ⊨
Services: ⊕⊠🔒⌀T⌷
Within 3 miles: ⌄⌀🔒⊙U

Notes: Dogs by arrangement only

SCARBOROUGH
Map 17 TA08

See also Filey & Wykeham

Places to visit

Scarborough Castle, Scarborough, 01723 372451, www.english-heritage.org.uk

Pickering Castle, Pickering, 01751 474989, www.english-heritage.org.uk

Great for kids: Sea Life and Marine Sanctuary, Scarborough, 01723 376125, www.sealife.co.uk

PREMIER PARK

▶▶▶▶▶ 75% Jacobs Mount Caravan Park (TA021868)

Jacobs Mount, Stepney Rd YO12 5NL
☎ 01723 361178 📠 01723 361178
e-mail: jacobsmount@yahoo.co.uk
dir: Direct access from A170

⊕ £13-£21 ⊕ £13-£21 ▲ £13-£21

Open Mar-Nov (rs Mar-May & Oct limited hours at shop/bar) Last arrival 22.00hrs Last dep noon

An elevated family-run park surrounded by woodland and open countryside, yet only two miles from the beach. Touring pitches are terraced gravel stands with individual services. The Jacobs Tavern serves a wide range of appetising meals and snacks, and there is a separate well-equipped games room for teenagers. An 18 acre site with 156 touring pitches, 131 hardstandings and 60 statics.

Jacobs Mount Caravan Park

AA Pubs & Restaurants nearby: Cayley Arms, Brompton-by-Sawdon 01723 859372

Anvil Inn, Sawdon 01723 859896

Leisure: ⋔ ◄ ⊒
Facilities: ⊨⌐⊙℘☀&⊙☖ா⊨
Services: ⊕⊠🔒⌀T⊚⌷⊞ ▾⌄
Within 3 miles: ⌄⊹☰℘◎≥🔒⊙U

Notes: Pets must be kept on leads. Food preparation area

LEISURE: 🏊 Indoor swimming pool 🏊 Outdoor swimming pool ⋔ Children's playground ⛳ Tennis court ◄ Games room ⊒ Separate TV room ⌄ 9/18 hole golf course ⊹ Boats for hire ⌂ Cinema ℘ Fishing ◎ Mini golf ≥ Watersports U Stables **FACILITIES:** ⊨ Bath ⌐ Shower ⊙ Electric shaver ℘ Hairdryer ☀ Ice Pack Facility & Disabled facilities ⊙ Public telephone 🔒 Shop on site or within 200yds ⌀ Mobile shop (calls at least 5 days a week) ☰ BBQ area ா Picnic area ⊨ Dog exercise area

AA CAMPING CARD SITE

►►►► 77% Scalby Close Park

(TA020925)

Burniston Rd YO13 0DA
☎ 01723 365908
e-mail: info@scalbyclosepark.co.uk
web: www.scalbyclosepark.co.uk
dir: *2m N of Scarborough on A615 coast road, 1m from junct with A171*

* 🚐 £17-£25 🚌

Open Mar-Oct Last arrival 22.00hrs Last departure noon

An attractive park with enthusiastic owners who have carried out many improvements. The site has a shower block, a laundry and fully-serviced pitches, and the landscaping is also very good. This is an ideal base from which to explore the nearby coast and countryside. Seasonal touring pitches are available. A 3 acre site with 42 touring pitches, 42 hardstandings and 5 statics.

AA Pubs & Restaurants nearby: Cayley Arms, Brompton-by-Sawdon 01723 859372

Anvil Inn, Sawdon 01723 859896

Facilities: 🚿 ⊙ 💨 ❄ ♿ ☎ [$]

Services: ⚡ 🧺 🔥 ⛽ [T] 🔋 ⬇

Within 3 miles: ⛳ ⛵ 🏸 🎣 [$] 🧺 U **Notes:** 💳

AA CAMPING CARD SITE

►►► 78% Killerby Old Hall *(TA063829)*

Killerby YO11 3TW
☎ 01723 583799 📠 01723 581608
e-mail: killerbyhall@btconnect.com
dir: *Direct access via B1261 at Killerby, near Cayton*

🚐 🚌

Open 14 Feb-4 Jan Last arrival 20.00hrs Last departure noon

A small secluded park, well sheltered by mature trees and shrubs, located at the rear of the old hall. Use of the small indoor swimming pool is shared by visitors to the hall's holiday accommodation. There is a children's play area. A 2 acre site with 20 touring pitches, 20 hardstandings.

AA Pubs & Restaurants nearby: Cayley Arms, Brompton-by-Sawdon 01723 859372

Anvil Inn, Sawdon 01723 859896

Leisure: 🏊 🛝 🎾

Facilities: 🚿 ⊙ 💨 🪑 🐕

Services: ⚡ 🧺

Within 3 miles: ⛳ 🎣 ◎ 🏄 [$] 🧺 U

SCOTCH CORNER Map 19 NZ20

Places to visit

Green Howards Museum, Richmond, 01748 826561, www.greenhowards.org.uk

Bolton Castle, Castle Bolton, 01969 623981, www.boltoncastle.co.uk

Great for kids: Raby Castle, Staindrop, 01833 660202, www.rabycastle.com

►►► 74% Scotch Corner Caravan Park *(NZ210054)*

DL10 6NS
☎ 01748 822530 📠 01748 822530
e-mail: marshallleisure@aol.com
dir: *From Scotch Corner junct of A1 & A66 take A6108 towards Richmond. 250mtrs then cross central reservation, return 200mtrs to site entrance*

🚐 🚌 ⛺

Open Etr-Oct Last arrival 22.30hrs Last departure noon

A well-maintained site with good facilities, ideally situated as a stopover, and an equally good location for touring. The Vintage Hotel, which serves food, can be accessed from the rear of the site. A 7 acre site with 96 touring pitches, 4 hardstandings.

AA Pubs & Restaurants nearby: Black Bull Inn, Moulton 01325 377289

Hack & Spade, Whashton 01748 823721

Facilities: 🚿 ⊙ 💨 ❄ ♿ [$] ♨ 🪑 🐕

Services: ⚡ 🧺 🍷 🔥 ⛽ [T] 🍴 🔋 ⬇

Within 3 miles: ⛳ 🎣 [$] 🧺 U

Notes: 💳 Recreation area for children

SELBY Map 16 SE63

Places to visit

York Castle Museum, York, 01904 687687, www.yorkcastlemuseum.org.uk

Micklegate Bar Museum, York, 01904 615505, www.micklegatebar.com

Great for kids: DIG, York, 01904 615505, www.digyork.co.uk

►►► 79% The Ranch Caravan Park

(SE664337)

Cliffe Common YO8 6EF
☎ 01757 638984 📠 01757 630089
e-mail: contact@theranchcaravanpark.co.uk
dir: *Exit A63 at Cliffe signed Skipwith. Site 1m N on left*

🚐 fr £15 🚌 fr £15 ⛺ fr £15

Open 5 Feb-5 Jan Last arrival 20.00hrs Last departure noon

A compact, sheltered park in open countryside offering excellent amenities. The enthusiastic and welcoming family owners have created a country club feel, with a tasteful bar serving food at weekends. There are timber lodge holiday homes for sale. A 7 acre site with 50 touring pitches, 50 hardstandings.

Leisure: 🛝

Facilities: 🚿 ⊙ 💨 ❄ ♿ ☎ 🪑 🐕

Services: ⚡ 🧺 🍷 🔥 ⛽ [T] 🍴 👶 ⬇

Within 3 miles: 🎣 [$] 🧺

Notes: No ball games, no campfires, no hanging of washing from trees. Wi-fi

SERVICES: ⚡ Electric hook up 🧺 Launderette 🍷 Licensed bar 🔥 Calor Gas ⛽ Camping Gaz [T] Toilet fluid 🍴 Café/Restaurant 🍔 Fast Food/Takeaway 🔋 Battery charging 👶 Baby care ⬇ Motorvan service point **ABBREVIATIONS:** BH/bank hols-bank holidays Etr-Easter Whit-Whitsun dep-departure fr-from hrs-hours m-mile mdnt-midnight rdbt-roundabout rs-restricted service wk-week wknd-weekend 💳 No credit cards 🚫 no dogs See page 7 for details of the AA Camping Card Scheme

SLINGSBY Map 19 SE67

Places to visit

Nunnington Hall, Nunnington, 01439 748283, www.nationaltrust.org.uk

Castle Howard, Malton, 01653 648333, www.castlehoward.co.uk

►►►► 77% Robin Hood Caravan & Camping Park *(SE701748)*

Green Dyke Ln YO62 4AP
☎ 01653 628391 📠 01653 628392
e-mail: info@robinhoodcaravanpark.co.uk
dir: *On edge of Slingsby. Access off B1257 (Malton-Helmsley road)*

* 🚐 £15-£25 🚌 £15-£25 ⛺ £15-£20

Open Mar-Oct Last arrival 18.00hrs Last dep noon

A pleasant, well-maintained grassy park, in a good position for touring North Yorkshire. Situated on the edge of the village of Slingsby, the park has hardstandings and electricity for every pitch. A 2 acre site with 32 touring pitches, 22 hardstandings and 35 statics.

AA Pubs & Restaurants nearby: Worsley Arms Hotel, Hovingham 01653 628234

Malt Shovel, Hovingham 01653 628264

Royal Oak Inn, Nunnington 01439 748271

Leisure: 🛝

Facilities: 🚿 ⊙ 💨 ❄ ♿ 📞 🏪 🍖 🐕

Services: 🔌 🫧 🛢 🔥 [T] 🍴 👶

Within 3 miles: 🎣 🏪 🐎

Notes: Caravan hire, off-licence

see advert below

SNAINTON Map 17 SE98

Places to visit

Scarborough Castle, Scarborough, 01723 372451, www.english-heritage.org.uk

Pickering Castle, Pickering, 01751 474989, www.english-heritage.org.uk

Great for kids: Sea Life and Marine Sanctuary, Scarborough, 01723 376125, www.sealife.co.uk

►►►► 82% Jasmine Caravan Park *(SE928813)*

Cross Ln YO13 9BE
☎ 01723 859240
e-mail: enquiries@jasminepark.co.uk
dir: *Turn S off A170 in Snainton, then follow signs*

* 🚐 £18-£30 🚌 £18-£30 ⛺ £18-£30

Open Mar-Oct Last arrival 22.00hrs Last departure noon

A peaceful and beautifully-presented park on the edge of a pretty village, and sheltered by high hedges. The toilet block with individual wash cubicles is maintained to a very high standard and there is a new and enlarged shop. This picturesque park lies midway between Pickering and Scarborough on the southern edge of the North Yorkshire Moors. Seasonal touring pitches are available. Please note there is no motorhome service point. A 5 acre site with 94 touring pitches, 10 hardstandings and 16 statics.

AA Pubs & Restaurants nearby: Coachman Inn, Snainton 01723 859231

New Inn, Thornton le Dale 01751 474226

Cayley Arms, Brompton-by-Sawdon 01723 859372

Facilities: 🛁 🚿 ⊙ 💨 ❄ ♿ 📞 🏪 🧺

Services: 🔌 🫧 🛢 🔥 [T]

Within 3 miles: ⛳ 🎣 ◎ 🏪 🫧 🐎

Notes: Dogs must be kept on leads. Baby changing unit. Wi-fi

STAINFORTH

Places to visit

Brodsworth Hall and Gardens, Doncaster, 01302 722598, www.english-heritage.org.uk

Doncaster Museum and Art Gallery, Doncaster, 01302 734293, www.doncaster.gov.uk/museums

Great for kids: The Yorkshire Waterways Museum, Goole, 01405 768730, www.waterwaysmuseum.org.uk

STAINFORTH
Map 18 SD86

▶▶▶▶ 78% Knight Stainforth Hall Caravan & Campsite (SD816672)

BD24 0DP

☎ 01729 822200 ▤ 01729 823387

e-mail: info@knightstainforth.co.uk

dir: *From W, on A65 take B6480 for Settle, left before swimming pool signed Little Stainforth. From E, through Settle on B6480, over bridge to swimming pool, then turn right*

* ➡ £14-£20 ⇌ £14-£20 ⛺ £14-£20

Open Mar-Oct Last arrival 22.00hrs Last dep noon

Located near Settle and the River Ribble in the Yorkshire Dales National Park, this well-maintained family site is sheltered by mature woodland. It is an ideal base for walking or touring in the beautiful surrounding areas. The toilet block is appointed to a very high standard. A 6 acre site with 100 touring pitches, 30 hardstandings and 60 statics.

AA Pubs & Restaurants nearby: Black Horse Hotel, Giggleswick 01729 822506

Game Cock Inn, Austwick 015242 51226

The Traddock, Austwick 015242 51224

New Inn, Clapham 01524 251203

Leisure: ⚑ ⚉ ▢

Facilities: ⏏ ⊙ ⏢ ✳ ⛭ ⓒ 🏠 ⏢ ⇥ ⏱

Services: �🔌 ⌷ ⛽ ⌂ Ⓣ ⛽ ⏫

Within 3 miles: ⌘ ⏢ ⛽ ⏢ ↺

Notes: No groups of unaccompanied minors. Fishing. Wi-fi

STILLINGFLEET
Map 16 SE54

Places to visit

Merchant Adventurers' Hall, York, 01904 654818, www.theyorkcompany.co.uk

Guildhall, York, 01904 613161, www.york.gov.uk

Great for kids: National Railway Museum, York, 01904 621261, www.nrm.org.uk

▶▶▶ 69% Home Farm Caravan & Camping (SE595427)

Moreby YO19 6HN

☎ 01904 728263 ▤ 01904 720059

e-mail: home_farm@hotmail.co.uk

dir: *6m from York on B1222, 1.5m N of Stillingfleet*

➡ ⇌ ⛺

Open Feb-Dec Last arrival 22.00hrs

A traditional meadowland site on a working farm bordered by parkland on one side and the River Ouse on another. Facilities are in converted farm buildings, and the family owners extend a friendly welcome to tourers. An excellent site for relaxing and unwinding in, yet only a short distance from the attractions of York. There are four log cabins for holiday hire. A 5 acre site with 25 touring pitches and 2 statics.

Facilities: ⏏ ⊙ ⏢ ✳ ⓒ ⇥

Services: �🔌 ⌷ ⛽ ⌂ Ⓣ ⇥

Within 3 miles: ⛽ ↺

Notes: ⊗ Dogs must be kept on leads

SUTTON-ON-THE-FOREST
Map 19 SE56

Places to visit

Sutton Park, Sutton-on-the-Forest, 01347 810249, www.statelyhome.co.uk

Treasurers' House, York, 01904 624247, www.nationaltrust.org.uk

Great for kids: Jorvik Viking Centre, York, 01904 615505, www.jorvik-viking-centre.com

PREMIER PARK

▶▶▶▶▶ 80% Goosewood Caravan Park (SE595636)

YO61 1ET

☎ 01347 810829 ▤ 01347 811498

e-mail: enquiries@goosewood.co.uk

dir: *From A1237 take B1363. After 5m turn right. Take right turn after 0.5m & site on right*

* ➡ £18-£25 ⇌ £18-£25

Open Mar-2 Jan Last arrival dusk Last departure noon

A relaxing and immaculately maintained park with its own lake and seasonal fishing, set in attractive woodland just six miles north of York. Mature shrubs and stunning seasonal floral displays at the entrance create an excellent first impression and the well located toilet facilities are kept spotlessly clean. The generous patio pitches are randomly spaced throughout the site, providing optimum privacy, and there's a good adventure play area for younger children, with a recreation barn for teenagers, plus a health spa. Seasonal touring pitches are available. A 20 acre site with 100 touring pitches, 75 hardstandings and 35 statics.

AA Pubs & Restaurants nearby: Blackwell Ox Inn, Sutton-on-the-Forest 01347 810328

Rose & Crown, Sutton-on-the-Forest 01347 811333

Leisure: ⚑ ⚉ ▢

Facilities: ⏏ ⊙ ⏢ ✳ ⛭ ⓒ 🏠 ⏢ ⇥ ⏱

Services: �🔌 ⌷ ⛽ Ⓣ ⇥ ⏫

Within 3 miles: ⌘ ⏢ ⛽ ⏢ ⌷

Notes: Dogs by arrangement only. Wi-fi

THIRSK
Map 19 SE48

Places to visit

Monk Park Farm Visitor Centre, Thirsk, 01845 597730, www.monkparkfarm.co.uk

Norton Conyers, Ripon, 01765 640333

Great for kids: Falconry UK - Birds of Prey Visitor Centre, Thirsk, 01845 587522, www.falconrycentre.co.uk

AA CAMPING CARD SITE

▶▶▶▶ 79% Hillside Caravan Park (SE447889)

Canvas Farm, Moor Rd, Knayton YO7 4BR

☎ 01845 537349 & 07711 643652

e-mail: info@hillsidecaravanpark.co.uk

dir: *From Thirsk take A19 north. Left at Knayton sign. In 0.25m right (crossing bridge over A19), through village. Site on left in approx 1.5m*

* ➡ £17-£27 ⇌ £17-£27

Open 4 Feb-4 Jan Last arrival 21.00hrs Last departure noon

A high quality, spacious park with first-class facilities, set in open countryside. It is an excellent base for walkers and for those wishing to explore the Thirsk area. Please note that the park does not accept tents. A 5 acre site with 35 touring pitches, 35 hardstandings.

AA Pubs & Restaurants nearby: Black Swan, Oldstead (AA Pub of the Year for England 2010-11) 01347 868387

Bagby Inn, Bagby 01845 597315

Leisure: ⚑

Facilities: ⏏ ⊙ ⏢ ⛭ ⇥ ⇥

Services: �🔌 ⌷ ⛽ ⇥

Within 3 miles: ⌘ ⏢ ⛽ ↺

Notes: ⊗ Wi-fi

THIRSK *continued*

►►► 76% Thirkleby Hall Caravan Park *(SE472794)*

Thirkleby YO7 3AR
☎ 01845 501360 & 07799 641815
e-mail: greenwood.parks@virgin.net
web: www.greenwoodparks.com
dir: *3m S of Thirsk on A19. Turn E through arched gatehouse into site*

* ⚕ £20-£21 ⛺ £20-£21 ▲ £12-£20

Open Mar-Oct Last arrival 20.00hrs Last departure 14.30hrs

A long-established site in the grounds of the old hall, with statics in wooded areas around a fishing lake and tourers based on slightly sloping grassy pitches. Recent investment has included a new quality amenities block and laundry for the 2010 season. This well-screened park has superb views of the Hambledon Hills. A 53 acre site with 50 touring pitches, 3 hardstandings and 185 statics.

AA Pubs & Restaurants nearby: Black Swan, Oldstead (AA Pub of the Year for England 2010-11) 01347 868387

Bagby Inn, Bagby 01845 597315

Leisure: ⚴

Facilities: ⚊⊙℘✳⚄☴⚹

Services: ⚄⚄⚋⚋⚋

Within 3 miles: ⚴⚄⚋⚄⚄

Notes: ⊛ Dogs must be kept on leads 12-acre woods, large recreation field

►►► 64% Sowerby Caravan Park *(SE437801)*

Sowerby YO7 3AG
☎ 01845 522753 ▤ 01845 574520
e-mail: sowerbycaravans@btconnect.com
dir: *From A19 approx 3m S of Thirsk, turn W for Sowerby. Turn right at junct. Site 1m on left*

* ⚕ £10.50-£12 ⛺ £10.50-£12

Open Mar-Oct Last arrival 22.00hrs

A grassy site beside a tree-lined river bank, with basic but functional toilet facilities. Tourers enjoy a separate grassed area with an open outlook, away from the statics. A 1 acre site with 25 touring pitches, 5 hardstandings and 85 statics.

AA Pubs & Restaurants nearby: Black Swan, Oldstead (AA Pub of the Year for England 2010-11) 01347 868387

Bagby Inn, Bagby 01845 597315

Leisure: ⚴ ⚴

Facilities: ⚊⊙✳⚄☴⚹

Services: ⚄⚄⚋⚋⚋⚋

Within 3 miles: ⚄⚄⚄⚄

Notes: ⊛

TOLLERTON   Map 19 SE56

Places to visit

The York Brewery Co. Ltd, York, 01904 621162, www.yorkbrew.co.uk

Yorkshire Museum, York, 01904 551800, www.york.gov.uk

Great for kids: Jorvik Viking Centre, York, 01904 615505, www.jorvik-viking-centre.com

►►►► 74% Tollerton Holiday Park *(SE513643)*

Station Rd YO61 1RD
☎ 01347 838313 ▤ 01347 838313
e-mail: greenwood.parks@virgin.net
dir: *From York take A19 towards Thirsk. At Cross Lanes left towards Tollerton. 1m to Chinese restaurant just before rail bridge. Site entrance through restaurant car park*

⚕ £20.50-£21.50 ⛺ ▲ £13-£20.50

Open Mar-Oct Last arrival 20.00hrs Last departure 15.00hrs

Set in open countryside within a few minutes walk of Tollerton and just a short drive from the Park &

Ride for York, this small park has seen major improvements in 2010. There's a new amenities block of real quality, which includes a family bathroom and laundry, and six new hardstandings have been installed. There is little disturbance from the East Coast mainline which passes near to the park. A 5 acre site with 50 touring pitches, 6 hardstandings and 75 statics.

Tollerton Holiday Park

AA Pubs & Restaurants nearby: Blackwell Ox Inn, Sutton-on-the-Forest 01347 810328

Rose & Crown, Sutton-on-the-Forest 01347 811333

Leisure: ⚴

Facilities: ⚊⊙℘⚄⊙⚹⚹

Services: ⚄⚄⚋⚋⚋⚋⚋

Within 3 miles: ⚴⚄⚄⚄

Notes: ⊛ No groups, dogs must be kept on leads. Small fishing lake, large recreation field

TOWTHORPE

Places to visit

Malton Museum, Malton, 01653 695136, www.maltonmuseum.co.uk

Wolds Way Lavender, Malton, 01944 758641, www.woldswaylavender.co.uk

Great for kids: Eden Camp Modern History Theme Museum, Malton, 01653 697777, www.edencamp.co.uk

---

TOWTHORPE
Map 19 SE65

AA CAMPING CARD SITE

▶▶▶▶ **77% York Touring Caravan Site** (SE648584)

Greystones Farm, Towthorpe Moor Ln YO32 9ST
☎ 01904 499275 📄 01904 499271
e-mail: info@yorkcaravansite.co.uk
web: www.yorkcaravansite.co.uk
dir: Exit A64 at turn for Strensall/Haxby, site 1.5m on left

🚐 £16-£21 🚚 £16-£21 ▲ £15-£18

Open all year Last arrival 21.00hrs Last departure noon

This purpose-built golf complex and caravan park is situated just over five miles from York. There is a 9-hole golf course, driving range and golf shop with a coffee bar/café. The generous sized, level pitches are set within well-manicured grassland with a backdrop of trees and shrubs. A 6 acre site with 44 touring pitches, 12 hardstandings.

AA Pubs & Restaurants nearby: Blackwell Ox Inn, Sutton-on-the-Forest 01347 810328

Rose & Crown, Sutton-on-the-Forest 01347 811333

Facilities: 🅿️☉📶✳️♿🕭🔥🐕🏕️
Services: 🔌🗑️🍴🔋
Within 3 miles: ✈️🎣◎🎿🏠

WEST KNAPTON
Map 19 SE87

Places to visit
Pickering Castle, Pickering, 01751 474989, www.english-heritage.org.uk

North Yorkshire Moors Railway, Pickering, 01751 472508, www.northyorkshiremoorsrailway.com

Great for kids: Eden Camp Modern History Theme Museum, Malton, 01653 697777, www.edencamp.co.uk

▶▶▶▶ **78% Wolds Way Caravan and Camping** (SE896743)

West Farm YO17 8JE
☎ 01944 728463 & 728180
e-mail: knapton.wold.farms@farming.co.uk
dir: Signed between Rillington & West Heslerton on A64 (Malton to Scarborough road). Site 1.5m

* 🚐 £11.50-£20 🚚 £11.50-£20 ▲ £11-£20

Open Mar-Oct Last arrival 22.30hrs Last departure 19.00hrs

A park on a working farm in a peaceful, high position on the Yorkshire Wolds, with magnificent views over the Vale of Pickering. This is an excellent walking area, with the Wolds Way passing the entrance to the park. A pleasant one and a half mile path leads to a lavender farm, with its first-class coffee shop. A 7.5 acre site with 70 touring pitches, 5 hardstandings.

AA Pubs & Restaurants nearby: Coachman Inn, Snainton 01723 859231

New Inn, Thornton le Dale 01751 474226

Cayley Arms, Brompton-by-Sawdon 01723 859372

Leisure: ⛰️
Facilities: 🚿🅿️☉✳️♿🔥🚻🍴🏕️🐕
Services: 🔌🗑️🛢️🚿🚽🔋
Within 3 miles: 🎿🏠
Notes: Free use of microwave, toaster & TV. Drinks machine

WHITBY
Map 19 NZ81

See also Robin Hood's Bay

Places to visit
Whitby Abbey, Whitby, 01947 603568, www.english-heritage.org.uk

Scarborough Castle, Scarborough, 01723 372451, www.english-heritage.org.uk

Great for kids: Sea Life and Marine Sanctuary, Scarborough, 01723 376125, www.sealife.co.uk

▶▶▶▶ **76% Ladycross Plantation Caravan Park**
(NZ821080)

Egton YO21 1UA
☎ 01947 895502
e-mail: enquiries@ladycrossplantation.co.uk
dir: On unclassified road (signed) off A171 (Whitby-Teesside road)

* 🚐 £16.10-£19.20 🚚 £16.10-£19.20 ▲ £16.10-£19.20

Open end Mar-Oct Last arrival 20.30hrs Last departure noon

A unique forest setting creates an away-from-it-all feeling at this peaceful touring park, which is under enthusiastic new ownership. Pitches are sited in small groups in clearings around an amenities block, while an additional fully refurbished toilet block offers excellent facilities. The site is well placed for Whitby and the Moors. Children will enjoy exploring the woodland around the site. A 12 acre site with 130 touring pitches, 18 hardstandings.

AA Pubs & Restaurants nearby: Wheatsheaf Inn, Egton 01947 895271

Horseshoe Hotel, Egton Bridge 01947 895245

Magpie Café, Whitby 01947 602058

Facilities: 🅿️☉📶✳️♿🕭🔥🐕
Services: 🔌🗑️🛢️🚿🚽🔋⬇️
Within 3 miles: ✈️🎣◎🎿🏠

WYKEHAM — Map 17 SE98

Places to visit

Scarborough Castle, Scarborough, 01723 372451, www.english-heritage.org.uk

Pickering Castle, Pickering, 01751 474989, www.english-heritage.org.uk

Great for kids: Sea Life and Marine Sanctuary, Scarborough, 01723 376125, www.sealife.co.uk

PREMIER PARK

AA CAMPING CARD SITE

▶▶▶▶▶ **80% St Helens Caravan Park** (SE967836)

YO13 9QD
☎ 01723 862771 📠 01723 866613
e-mail: caravans@wykeham.co.uk
dir: On A170 in village, 150yds on left beyond Downe Arms Hotel towards Scarborough

* ⛺ £15-£22 🚐 £15-£22 ▲ £11-£20

Open 15 Feb-15 Jan (rs Nov-Jan shop/laundry closed) Last arrival 22.00hrs Last departure 17.00hrs

Set on the edge of the North York Moors National Park this delightfully landscaped park is immaculately maintained and thoughtfully laid out with top quality facilities and a high level of customer care. The site is divided into terraces with tree-screening creating smaller areas, including an adults' zone. A cycle route leads through the surrounding Wykeham Estate, and there is a short pathway to the adjoining Downe Arms country pub. A 25 acre site with 250 touring pitches, 10 hardstandings.

AA Pubs & Restaurants nearby: Coachman Inn, Snainton 01723 859231

New Inn, Thornton le Dale 01751 474226

Cayley Arms, Brompton-by-Sawdon 01723 859372

Leisure: ⚉

Facilities: ⬥⬧⬤⬥✳⬥⬤⬥⬥⬥⬥

Services: ⬤⬤⬤⬤⬤⬤⬤⬤⬤⬤

Within 3 miles: ⬥⬥⬥⬤⬥⬥⬤⬤

Notes: Caravan storage. Wi-fi

see advert below

The quality percentage score for all parks ranges from 50%-100%

All the campsites in this guide are inspected annually by a team of experienced inspectors

YORKSHIRE, SOUTH

WORSBROUGH — Map 16 SE30

Places to visit

Monk Bretton Priory, Barnsley, www.english-heritage.org.uk

Millenium Gallery, Sheffield, 0114 278 2600, www.museums-sheffield.org.uk

Great for kids: Magna Science Adventure Centre, Rotherham, 01709 720002, www.visitmagna.co.uk

▶▶ **74% Greensprings Touring Park** (SE330020)

Rockley Abbey Farm, Rockley Ln S75 3DS
☎ 01226 288298 📠 01226 288298
dir: M1 junct 36, A61 to Barnsley. Left after 0.25m signed Pilley. Site 1m at bottom of hill

⛺ 🚐 ▲

Open Apr-Oct Last arrival 21.00hrs Last departure noon

A secluded and attractive farm site set amidst woods and farmland, with access to the river and several good local walks. There are two touring areas, one gently sloping. Although not far from the M1, there is almost no traffic noise, and this site is convenient for exploring the area's industrial heritage, as well as the Peak District. Seasonal touring pitches are available. A 4 acre site with 65 touring pitches, 5 hardstandings.

Facilities: ⬥⬤✳⬥ **Services:** ⬤⬤

Within 3 miles: ⬥⬥⬥⬥⬤⬤ **Notes:** ⬤

LEISURE: 🏊 Indoor swimming pool 🏊 Outdoor swimming pool ⚉ Children's playground 🎾 Tennis court 🎯 Games room 📺 Separate TV room ⛳ 9/18 hole golf course 🚣 Boats for hire 🎬 Cinema 🎣 Fishing ⛳ Mini golf 🏄 Watersports ♘ Stables **FACILITIES:** 🛁 Bath 🚿 Shower ⊙ Electric shaver 💇 Hairdryer ✳ Ice Pack Facility ♿ Disabled facilities ☎ Public telephone 🛒 Shop on site or within 200yds 🚚 Mobile shop (calls at least 5 days a week) 🍖 BBQ area 🏞 Picnic area 🐕 Dog exercise area

YORKSHIRE, WEST

BARDSEY   Map 16 SE34

Places to visit

Bramham Park, Bramham, 01937 846000,
www.bramhampark.co.uk

Thackray Museum, Leeds, 0113 244 4343,
www.thackraymuseum.org

Great for kids: Leeds Industrial Museum at
Armley Mills, Leeds, 0113 263 7861,
www.leeds.gov.uk/armleymills

▶▶▶ 85% Moor Lodge Park *(SE352423)*

Blackmoor Ln LS17 9DZ
☎ 01937 572424 📄 01937 572424
e-mail: rodatmlcp@aol.com
dir: *From A1(M) take A659 (S of Wetherby) signed
Otley. Left onto A58 towards Leeds for 5m. Right
after Bracken Fox pub (Ling Lane), right at x-rds,
1m. Site on right*

🚐 £15 🚌 £15 ▲ £15

Open all year Last arrival 20.00hrs Last departure
noon

A well-kept site in a peaceful and beautiful
setting, close to Harewood House and only 25
minutes' drive from York and the Dales; the centre
of Leeds is just 15 minutes away. The touring area
is for adults only. A 7 acre site with 12 touring
pitches and 60 statics.

AA Pubs & Restaurants nearby: Windmill Inn,
Linton 01937 582209

Facilities: 🅿️⊙℗✳️⊙🍴🎪

Services: 🔌🚿🛢️🧺🛒

Within 3 miles: 🎣℗◎🏧⛴️∪

Notes: Adults only

▶▶▶ 81% Glenfield Caravan Park

(SE351421)

120 Blackmoor Ln LS17 9DZ
☎ 01937 574657 📄 01937 579529
e-mail: glenfieldcp@aol.com
web: www.ukparks.co.uk/glenfield/
dir: *From A58 at Bardsey into Church Ln, past
church, up hill. 0.5m, site on left*

* 🚐 fr £14 🚌 ▲ £10-£20

Open all year Last arrival 21.00hrs Last dep noon

A quiet family-owned rural site in a well-screened,
tree-lined meadow. The site has an excellent toilet
block complete with family room. A convenient
touring base for Leeds and the surrounding area.
Discounted golf and food are both available at the
local golf club. A 4 acre site with 30 touring
pitches, 30 hardstandings and 1 static.

AA Pubs & Restaurants nearby: Windmill Inn,
Linton 01937 582209

Facilities: 🅿️⊙℗✳️⊙🍴🎪

Services: 🔌🚿🛢️🔋🛒

Within 3 miles: 🎣🚴℗◎🏧∪

Notes: ⊗ Children must be supervised. Dogs
must be kept on leads

HORSFORTH   Map 19 SE23

Places to visit

Cartwright Hall and Art Gallery, Bradford,
01274 431212, www.bradfordmuseums.org

National Media Museum,
Bradford, 01274 202030,
www.nationalmediamuseum.org.uk

▶▶▶ 78% St Helena's
Caravan Park *(SE240421)*

GOLD

Otley Old Rd LS18 5HZ
☎ 0113 284 1142
dir: *From A658 follow signs for Leeds/Bradford
Airport. Then follow site signs*

* 🚐 £15-£20 🚌 £15-£20 ▲

Open Apr-Oct Last arrival 19.30hrs Last dep 14.00hrs

A well-maintained parkland setting surrounded by
woodland yet within easy reach of Leeds with its
excellent shopping and cultural opportunities,
Ilkley, and the attractive Wharfedale town of Otley.
Some visitors may just want to relax in this
adults-only park's spacious and pleasant
surroundings. A 25 acre site with 60 touring
pitches and 40 statics.

Facilities: 🖥️🅿️⊙℗✳️⊙🍴🎪

Services: 🔌🚿🚻 **Within 3 miles:** 🎣℗🏧⛴️

Notes: Adults only

CHANNEL ISLANDS

GUERNSEY

CASTEL   Map 24

Places to visit

Sausmarez Manor, St. Martin, 01481 235571,
www.sausmarezmanor.co.uk

Fort Grey Shipwreck Museum, Rocquaine Bay,
01481 265036, www.museum.gov.gg

▶▶▶▶ 82% *Fauxquets Valley
Campsite*

GY5 7QL
☎ 01481 236951 & 07781 413333
e-mail: info@fauxquets.co.uk
dir: *Off pier. 2nd exit off rdbt. Top of hill left onto
Queens Rd. Continue for 2m. Turn right onto Candie
Rd. Opposite sign for German Occupation Museum*

▲

Open mid Jun-Aug

A beautiful, quiet farm site in a hidden valley
close to the sea. The friendly and helpful owners,
who understand campers' needs, offer good
quality facilities and amenities, including
upgraded toilets, an outdoor swimming pool, bar/
restaurant, a nature trail and sports areas.
Additional spacious pitches were added in 2010.
Fully equipped tents for hire. A 3 acre site with
120 touring pitches.

AA Pubs & Restaurants nearby: Fleur du Jardin,
Castel 01481 257996

Hotel Hogue du Pommier, Castel 01481 256531

Cobo Bay Restaurant, Castel 01481 257102

Leisure: 🏊🎱🏸🎯

Facilities: 🅿️⊙℗✳️⊙🍴🎪

Services: 🔌🚿🚻🛢️🍴🍴🔋🍽️🍴🛒🚿

Within 3 miles: 🎣🐴℗◎🏧⛴️∪

Notes: Birdwatching

ST SAMPSON — Map 24

Places to visit

Sausmarez Manor, St. Martin, 01481 235571, www.sausmarezmanor.co.uk

Castle Cornet, St. Peter Port, 01481 721657, www.museums.gov.gg

►►► 82% *Le Vaugrat Camp Site*

Route de Vaugrat GY2 4TA
☎ 01481 257468 📠 01481 251841
e-mail: enquiries@vaugratcampsite.com
web: www.vaugratcampsite.com
dir: *From main coast road on NW of island, site signed at Port Grat Bay into Route de Vaugrat, near Peninsula Hotel*

⚹

Open May-mid Sep

Overlooking the sea and set within the grounds of a lovely 17th-century house, this level grassy park is backed by woodland, and is close to the lovely sandy beaches of Port Grat and Grand Havre. It is run by a welcoming family who pride themselves on creating magnificent floral displays. The facilities here are excellent. A 6 acre site with 150 touring pitches.

AA Pubs & Restaurants nearby: The Admiral de Saumarez, St Peter Port 01481 721431

Governor's, St Peter Port 01481 738623

The Absolute End, St Peter Port 01481 723822

Mora Restaurant & Grill, St Peter Port 01481 715053

Leisure: 🅰️ 🖵
Facilities: ➊ ☉ 🅿️ ✳️ ♿ ⏱ 🛁 🍴 🎪
Services: 🔌 🗑 🛢 ⌀ 🎁
Within 3 miles: ✈ 🎬 ⚡ ◉ ⛵ 🏬 🔵 U
Notes: No animals

VALE — Map 24

Places to visit

Rousse Tower, Vale, 01489 726518, www.museums.gov.gg

Guernsey Museum and Art Gallery, St. Peters Port, 01481 726518, www.museums.gov.gg

Great for kids: Castle Cornet, St. Peter Port, 01481 721657, www.museums.gov.gg

►►► 81% *La Bailloterie Camping & Leisure*

Bailloterie Ln GY3 5HA
☎ 01481 243636 & 07781 103420
📠 01481 243225
e-mail: info@campinginguernsey.com
dir: *3m N of St Peter Port, take Vale road to Crossways, turn right into Rue du Braye. Site 1st left at sign*

⚹

Open 15 May-15 Sep Last arrival 23.00hrs

A pretty rural site with one large touring field and a few small, well-screened paddocks. This delightful site has been in the same family ownership for over 30 years, and offers good facilities in converted outbuildings. There are also fully-equipped tents for hire. A 12 acre site with 100 touring pitches.

AA Pubs & Restaurants nearby: The Admiral de Saumarez, St Peter Port 01481 721431

Governor's, St Peter Port 01481 738623

The Absolute End, St Peter Port 01481 723822

Mora Restaurant & Grill, St Peter Port 01481 715053

Leisure: 🅰️ 🎱 🖵
Facilities: ➊ ☉ 🅿️ ✳️ ♿ 🛁 🍴 🎪 🐕
Services: 🔌 🗑 🛢 ⌀ 🍴 🎁 🛍 🚽
Within 3 miles: ✈ 🚤 🎬 ⚡ ◉ ⛵ 🏬 🔵 U
Notes: Dogs by arrangement only. Volleyball net, boules pitch

HERM

HERM — Map 24

►►► 80% **Seagull Campsite**

GY1 3HR
☎ 01481 750000 📠 01481 700334
e-mail: reservations@herm.com
dir: *Please telephone for directions*

✱ ⚹ £13.20

Open May-Sep Last arrival 17.00hrs Last departure 17.30hrs

An away-from-it-all location on the idyllic tiny island of Herm. The well-maintained grassy site offers stunning views over the sea and surrounding islands, and all pitches are level, with some in individually terraced bays. Tents are available for hire. Herm is traffic free, so parking must be arranged with Trident Travel at St Peter Port, Guernsey, on 01481 721379, or ask when booking. Campers should check in at the information office on the quay. 50 touring pitches.

AA Pubs & Restaurants nearby: White House Hotel, Herm 01481 722159

Facilities: ✳️ 🛍 🎪
Within 3 miles: ⚡ 🏬 🔵
Notes: ⊗ Groceries can be delivered

JERSEY

ST MARTIN

Places to visit

Mont Orgueil Castle, Gorey, 01534 853292, www.jerseyheritage.org

Maritime Museum and Occupation Tapestry Gallery, St. Helier, 01534 811043, www.jerseyheritage.org

Great for kids: Elizabeth Castle, St. Helier, 01534 723971, www.jerseyheritage.org

ST MARTIN
Map 24

PREMIER PARK

AA CAMPING CARD SITE

▶▶▶▶▶ 80% *Beuvelande Camp Site*

Beuvelande JE3 6EZ
☎ 01534 853575 📠 01534 857788
e-mail: info@campingjersey.com
web: www.campingjersey.com
dir: *Take A6 from St Helier to St Martin & follow signs to site before St Martins Church*

⚕

Open Apr-Sep (rs Apr-May & Sep pool & restaurant closed, shop hours limited)

A well-established site with excellent toilet facilities, accessed via narrow lanes in peaceful countryside close to St Martin. An attractive bar/restaurant is the focal point of the park, especially in the evenings, and there is a small swimming pool and playground. Motorhomes and towed caravans will be met at the ferry and escorted to the site if requested when booking. A 6 acre site with 150 touring pitches and 75 statics.

AA Pubs & Restaurants nearby: Royal Hotel, St Martin 01534 856289

Leisure: ⚑ ⚑ ⚔ ▢
Facilities: ⚑ ☉ ✳ ♿ ☺ ⓕ ✚
Services: ⚡ ⓕ ⚔ ⓐ ⵁ ⓣ ⓞ ⓔ ⵖ
Within 3 miles: ⵚ ⵢ ⵗ ⵈ ⓕ ⓕ ⵣ

▶▶▶▶ 85% Rozel Camping Park

Summerville Farm JE3 6AX
☎ 01534 855200 📠 01534 856127
e-mail: rozelcampingpark@jerseymail.co.uk
web: www.rozelcamping.co.uk
dir: *Take A6 from St Helier through Five Oaks to St Martins Church, turn right onto A38 towards Rozel, site on right*

* ⚡ £17.20-£19.20 ⚑ £17.20-£19.20
⚕ £17.20-£19.20

Open May-mid Sep Last departure noon

Customers can be sure of a warm welcome at this delightful family run park. Set in the north east of the island, it offers large spacious pitches, many with electric, for tents, caravans and motorhomes. The lovely Rozel Bay is just a short distance away and spectacular views of the French coast can be seen from one of the four fields on the park. The

site also offers excellent facilities including a swimming pool. Motorhomes and caravans will be met at the ferry and escorted to the park by arrangement when booking. Dogs are accepted all season. A 4 acre site with 100 touring pitches and 20 statics.

AA Pubs & Restaurants nearby: Royal Hotel, St Martin 01534 856289

Leisure: ⚑ ⚑ ⚔ ▢
Facilities: ⚑ ☉ ⓕ ✳ ♿ ☺ ⓕ
Services: ⚡ ⓕ ⚔ ⓐ ⵁ ⵢ ⵖ ⵗ
Within 3 miles: ⵚ ⵢ ⵗ ⵈ ⓕ ⓕ ⵣ
Notes: Mini golf. Wi-fi

ST OUEN
Map 24

Places to visit

Kemp Tower Visitor Centre, St. Ouen, 01534 483651, www.eco-active.je

Greve De Lecq Barracks, La Greve De Lecq, 01534 483193, www.nationaltrustjersey.org.je

Great for kids: The Channel Islands Military Centre, St. Ouen, 07797 732072

▶▶▶▶ 79% Bleu Soleil Campsite

La Route de Vinchelez, Leoville JE3 2DB
☎ 01534 481007 📠 01534 481525
e-mail: info@bleusoleilcamping.com
web: www.bleusoleilcamping.com
dir: *From St Helier ferry port take A2 towards St Aubin, right onto A12 passing airport to Leoville. Site on right of La Route de Vinchelez*

⚑ ⚕

Open all year Last arrival 23.00hrs Last departure 10.00hrs

A compact tent park set in the north-west corner of the island and surrounded by beautiful countryside. Greve-de-Lacq beach is close by, and the golden beaches at St Ouen's Bay and St Brelade's Bay are only a short drive away. There are 45 ready-erected tents and six family tipis for hire. A 1.5 acre site with 55 touring pitches, 8 hardstandings and 45 statics.

AA Pubs & Restaurants nearby: Old Court House Inn, St Aubin 01534 746433

The Boat House, St Aubin 01534 744226

Salty Dog Bar & Bistro, St Aubin 01534 742760

Leisure: ⚑ ⚑ ⚔ ▢
Facilities: ⚑ ☉ ⓕ ✳ ☺ ⓕ
Services: ⚡ ⓕ ⚔ ⓐ ⵁ ⓣ ⓞ ⵖ
Within 3 miles: ⵚ ⵢ ⵗ ⵈ ⓕ ⓕ ⵣ
Notes: No noise after 22.00hrs, owners must clean up after dogs. Hot tub. Wi-fi

ISLE OF MAN

KIRK MICHAEL
Map 24 SC39

Places to visit

Peel Castle, Peel, 01624 648000, www.storyofmann.com

House of Manannan, Peel, 01624 648000, www.storyofmann.com

Great for kids: Carraghs Wildlife Park, Ballaugh, 01624 897323, www.gov.im/wildlife

▶▶▶ 76% Glen Wyllin Campsite

(SC302901)

IM6 1AL
☎ 01624 878231 & 878836 📠 01624 878836
e-mail: michaelcommissioners@manx.net
dir: *From Douglas take A1 to Ballacraine, right at lights onto A3 to Kirk Michael. Left onto A4 signed Peel. Site 100yds on right*

⚑ ⚕

Open mid Apr-mid Sep Last departure noon

Set in a beautiful wooded glen with bridges over a pretty stream dividing the camping areas. A gently-sloping tarmac road gives direct access to a good beach. Hire tents are available. A 9 acre site with 90 touring pitches and 18 statics.

AA Pubs & Restaurants nearby: The Creek Inn, Peel 01624 842216

Leisure: ⚑ ▢
Facilities: ⚑ ☉ ⓕ ✳ ♿ ☺ ⓕ ⵗ ⵣ ✚
Services: ⚡ ⓕ ⚔ ⓐ ⓞ ⵖ ⵗ
Within 3 miles: ⓕ ⓕ ⓕ ⵣ
Notes: No excess noise after midnight, dogs must be kept under control & on leads. Wi-fi

Scotland

Timintoul, Cairngorms National Park

Scotland

It is virtually impossible to distil the spirit and essence of Scotland in a few short sentences. It is a country with a particular kind of beauty and something very special to offer. Around half the size of England but with barely one fifth of its population, the statistics alone are enough to make you want to rush there and savour its solitude and sense of space.

The Borders, maybe the most obvious place to begin a tour of Scotland, was for so long one of Britain's most bitterly contested frontiers. The border has survived the years of lawlessness, battle and bloodshed, though few crossing it today would probably give its long and turbulent history a second thought. Making up 1,800 square miles of dense forest, rolling hills and broad sweeps of open heather, this region includes some of the most spectacular scenery anywhere in the country. Next door is Dumfries & Galloway, where just across the English/Scottish border is Gretna Green, famous for the 'anvil marriages' of eloping couples.

Glen Liu near Braemar

Travelling north and miles of open moorland and swathes of forest stretch to the Ayrshire coast where there are views towards the islands of Bute and Arran.

The country's two great cities, Glasgow and Edinburgh, include innumerable historic sites, popular landmarks and innovative visitor attractions. To the north lies a landscape of tranquil lochs, fishing rivers, wooded glens and the cities of Perth and Dundee. There's also the superb scenery of the Trossachs, Loch Lomond and Stirling, which, with its wonderful castle perched on a rocky crag, is Scotland's heritage capital.

Further north

The country's prominent north-east shoulder is the setting for the mountain landscape of the Cairngorms and the Grampians, while Aberdeenshire and the Moray coast enjoy a pleasantly mild, dry climate with plenty of sunshine. Here, the River Spey, one of Scotland's great rivers and a mecca for salmon anglers, winds between lush pastures to the North Sea. Various famous distilleries can be found along its banks, some offering visitors the chance to sample a wee dram!

The remote far north is further from many parts of England than a good many European

▶

Walking and Cycling

There are numerous excellent walks in Scotland. Among the best is the 95-mile (152km) West Highland Way, Scotland's first long-distance path. The trail runs from Glasgow to Fort William. The Southern Upland Way and St Cuthbert's Way explore the best of the Scottish Borders, which is also the northerly terminus for the 250-mile (402km) Pennine Way.

Scotland's majestic landscapes are perfect for exploring by bike. There are scores of popular routes and trails – among them a ride through Dumfries & Galloway to Drumlanrig Castle and the museum where blacksmith, Kirkpatrick MacMillan, invented the bicycle. Alternatively, there's the chance to get away from the city and head for the coast along disused railway lines; perhaps the route from Edinburgh to Cramond, with good views of the Firth of Forth.

destinations. Names such as Pentland Firth, Sutherland, Caithness and Ross and Cromarty spring to mind, as does Cape Wrath, Britain's most northerly outpost. The stunning coast is known for its spectacular sea cliffs and deserted beaches – the haunt of some of the rarest mammals.

Highlands and Islands

The beauty of the Western Highlands and the islands has to be seen to be believed. It is, without question, one of Europe's wildest and most spectacular regions, evoking a truly breathtaking sense of adventure. There are a great many islands, as a glance at the map will reveal – Skye, Mull, Iona, Coll, Jura and Islay to name but a few; all have their own individual character and identity. The two most northerly island groups are Orkney and the Shetlands, which, incredibly, are closer to the Arctic Circle than London.

Festivals and Events

- The Viking Festival is staged at Largs on the Ayrshire coast on August Bank Holiday. This is where the last Viking invasion of Britain took place in 1263. There are birds of prey displays, battle re-enactments, fireworks and the ritual burning of a longship.
- Also in August is the internationally famous Edinburgh Military Tattoo, which draws numerous visitors and participants from many parts of the world.
- The Highland Games, another classic fixture in the Scottish calendar, run from May onwards; the most famous being the Braemar gathering in September.

ABERDEENSHIRE

ABOYNE
Map 23 NO59

Places to visit

Alford Valley Castle. Alford, 019755 64236, www.alfordvalleyrailway.org.uk

Crathes Castle Gardens and Estate, Crathes, 0844 4932166, www.nts.org.uk

Great for kids: Craigievar Castle, Alford, 0844 493 2174, www.nts.org.uk

▶▶▶ **71% Aboyne Loch Caravan Park** (NO538998)

AB34 5BR
☎ 013398 86244 & 82589 📠 013398 82589
dir: On A93, 1m E of Aboyne

* 🚐 fr £17 🚏 fr £17 ▲ fr £12

Open 31 Mar-Oct Last arrival 20.00hrs Last departure 11.00hrs

An attractively sited caravan park set amidst woodland on the shores of the lovely Aboyne Loch in scenic Deeside. The facilities are modern and immaculately maintained, and amenities include boat-launching, boating and fishing. An ideally situated park for touring Royal Deeside and the Aberdeenshire uplands. A 6 acre site with 20 touring pitches, 25 hardstandings and 120 statics.

AA Pubs & Restaurants nearby: Milton Restaurant, Crathes 01330 844566

Banchory Lodge Hotel, Banchory 01330 822625

Leisure: 🄰 🔍
Facilities: 🄽⊙🅿✳🅰⊙🅱🎿📮
Services: 🅿🖸🔒⊘🆃⬇
Within 3 miles: ⬇🎣🅿⊙🎿🅱🖸⟳
Notes: 🄳 Coarse & pike fishing, boats for hire

FORDOUN

Places to visit

Edzell Castle and Garden, Edzell, 01356 648631, www.historic-scotland.gov.uk

House of Dun, Montrose, 0844 493 2144, www.nts.org.uk

FORDOUN
Map 23 NO77

▶▶▶ **74% Brownmuir Caravan Park** (NO740772)

AB30 1SJ
☎ 01561 320786 📠 01561 320786
e-mail: brownmuircaravanpark@talk21.com
web: www.brownmuircaravanpark.co.uk
dir: From N: A90 take B966 signed Fettercairn, site 1.5m on left. From S: A90, exit 4m N of Laurencekirk signed Fordoun, site 1m on right

* 🚐 £13.50-£15 🚏 £13.50-£15 ▲ £8-£15

Open Apr-Oct Last arrival 23.00hrs Last departure noon

A mainly static site set in a rural location with level pitches and good touring facilities. The area is ideal for cyclists, walkers and golfers, as well as those wanting to visit Aberdeen, Banchory, Ballater, Balmoral, Glamis and Dundee. Seven seasonal touring pitches are available. A 7 acre site with 11 touring pitches, 7 hardstandings and 49 statics.

AA Pubs & Restaurants nearby: Tolbooth Restaurant, Stonehaven 01569 762287

Carron Art Deco Restaurant, Stonehaven 01569 760460

Leisure: 🄰
Facilities: 🄽⊙🅿✳🅰⊙🎿📮
Services: 🅿🖸🔒
Within 3 miles: ⬇🅿🖸
Notes: 🄳

HUNTLY

Places to visit

Leith Hall, Garden and Estate, Rhynie, 0844 493 2175, www.nts.org.uk

Glenfiddich Distillery, Dufftown, 01340 820373, www.glenfiddich.com

Great for kids: Archaeolink Prehistory Park, Oyne, 01464 851500, www.archaeolink.co.uk

HUNTLY
Map 23 NJ53

PREMIER PARK

AA CAMPING CARD SITE

▶▶▶▶▶ **82% Huntly Castle Caravan Park** (NJ525405)

The Meadow AB54 4UJ
☎ 01466 794999
e-mail: enquiries@huntlycastle.co.uk
web: www.huntlycastle.co.uk
dir: From Aberdeen on A96 to Huntly. 0.75m after rdbt (on outskirts of Huntly) right towards town centre, left into Riverside Drive

* 🚐 £16.75-£20.50 🚏 £16.75-£20.50
▲ £12-£16.50

Open Apr-Oct (rs Wknds & school hols indoor activity centre open) Last arrival 20.00hrs Last departure noon

A quality parkland site within striking distance of the Speyside Malt Whisky Trail, the beautiful Moray coast, and the Cairngorm Mountains. The park provides exceptional toilet facilities, and there are some fully serviced pitches. The indoor activity centre provides a wide range of games; the attractive town of Huntly is only a five-minute walk away, with its ruined castle plus a wide variety of restaurants and shops. A 15 acre site with 90 touring pitches, 46 hardstandings and 40 statics.

Leisure: 🄰 🔍
Facilities: 🄽⊙🅿✳🅰⊙🎿📮
Services: 🅿🖸🔒🆃⬇⬇
Within 3 miles: ⬇🅿🖸🖸
Notes: Indoor activity centre, indoor children's play area, snooker table. Wi-fi

KINTORE

Places to visit

Pitmedden Garden, Pitmedden, 0844 493 2177, www.nts.org.uk

Tolquhon Castle, Pitmedden, 01651 851286, www.historic-scotland.gov.uk

Great for kids: Castle Fraser, Kenmay, 0844 493 2164, www.nts.org.uk

KINTORE
Map 23 NJ71

▶▶▶ 78% Hillhead Caravan Park
(NJ777163)

AB51 0YX
☎ **01467 632809 & 0870 413 0870**
🖹 **01467 633173**
e-mail: enquiries@hillheadcaravan.co.uk
dir: *1m from village & A96 (Aberdeen-Inverness road). From A96 follow signs to site on B994, then unclass road*

* 🚐 £15-£17 🚌 £15-£17 ▲ £11-£14

Open all year Last arrival 21.00hrs Last departure 13.00hrs

A peaceful site in the River Don Valley, with pitches well screened by shrubs and trees, and laid out around a small central area containing a children's play space. The enthusiastic owners are constantly improving the facilities, and the park is very well maintained. A 1.5 acre site with 29 touring pitches, 14 hardstandings.

AA Pubs & Restaurants nearby: Old Blackfriars, Aberdeen 01224 581922

Leisure: ⚏
Facilities: ⚹⊙℗⚹⚹⚭⚟🍴🎃🎃
Services: 🚐🖷🔋⌀🏧🖳
Within 3 miles: 🚲🖉🏧🖷
Notes: Caravan storage, accessories shop

MACDUFF

Places to visit
House, Banff, 01261 818181, www.historic-scotland.gov.uk

Banff Museum, Banff, 01771 622807, www.aberdeenshire.gov.uk/museums

MACDUFF
Map 23 NJ76

▶▶ 65% Wester Bonnyton Farm Site
(NJ741638)

Gamrie AB45 3EP
☎ **01261 832470** 🖹 **01261 831853**
e-mail: westerbonnyton@fsmail.net
dir: *From A98 (1m S of Macduff) take B9031 signed Rosehearty. Site 1.25m on right*

* 🚐 £10-£15 🚌 £10-£15 ▲ £7-£15

Open Mar-Oct

A spacious farm site in a screened meadow, with level touring pitches enjoying views across Moray Firth. The site is continually improving, and offers some electric hook-ups and a laundry. An 8 acre site with 10 touring pitches, 5 hardstandings and 50 statics.

Leisure: ⚏🔍
Facilities: ⚹⊙℗⚟🍴🎃🎃
Services: 🚐🖷🔋🖳
Within 3 miles: 🚲🖉🖉🏧🖷
Notes: Children's playbarn. Wi-fi

NORTH WATER BRIDGE
Map 23 NO66

▶▶▶ 75% Dovecot Caravan Park
(NO648663)

GOLD

AB30 1QL
☎ **01674 840630** 🖹 **01674 840630**
e-mail: adele@dovecotcaravanpark.co.uk
dir: *Take A90, 5m S of Laurencekirk. At Edzell Woods sign turn left. Site 500yds on left*

* 🚐 £12.50-£13.50 🚌 £12.50-£13.50 ▲ £9-£15

Open Apr-Oct Last arrival 20.00hrs Last departure noon

A level grassy site in a country area close to the A90, with mature trees screening one side and the River North Esk on the other. The immaculate toilet facilities make this a handy overnight stop in a good touring area. A 6 acre site with 25 touring pitches, 8 hardstandings and 44 statics.

Leisure: ⚏🔍
Facilities: ⚹⊙℗⚹⚹⚭🎃
Services: 🚐🔋🖳🖳
Within 3 miles: 🏧
Notes: Wi-fi

ST CYRUS
Map 23 NO76

Places to visit
House of Dun, Montrose, 0844 493 2144, www.nts.org.uk

Pictavia Visitor Centre, Brechin, 01356 626241, www.pictavia.org.uk

Great for kids: Brechin Town House Museum, Brechin, 01356 625536, www.angus.gov.uk/history/museum

▶▶▶▶ 79% East Bowstrips Caravan Park *(NO745654)*

DD10 0DE
☎ **01674 850328** 🖹 **01674 850328**
e-mail: tully@bowstrips.freeserve.co.uk
web: www.caravancampingsites.co.uk/aberdeenshire/eastbowstrips.htm
dir: *From S on A92 (coast road) into St Cyrus. Pass hotel on left. 1st left then 2nd right signed*

🚐🚌▲

Open Etr or Apr-Oct Last arrival 20.00hrs Last departure noon

A quiet, rural site close to a seaside village, with modernised facilities and a particular welcome for disabled visitors. The park is surrounded by farmland on the edge of a village, with extensive views. Touring pitches are sited on rising ground amongst attractive landscaping. A 4 acre site with 32 touring pitches, 22 hardstandings and 17 statics.

Leisure: ⚏
Facilities: ⚹⊙℗⚹⚹⚭⚟🎃🎃
Services: 🚐🖷🔋
Within 3 miles: 🖉🏧
Notes: If camping - no dogs allowed, if touring - dogs must be kept on short leads at all times. Separate garden with boule pitch

ANGUS

MONIFIETH   Map 21 NO43

Places to visit

Barry Mill, Barry, 0844 493 2140,
www.nts.org.uk

HM Frigate 'Unicorn', Dundee, 01382 200900,
www.frigateunicorn.org

Great for kids: Discovery Point and RRS
Discovery, Dundee, 01382 309060,
www.rrsdiscovery.com

►►►► 79% Riverview Caravan Park (NO502322)

Best of British

Marine Dr DD5 4NN
☎ 01382 535471   📠 01382 811525
e-mail: info@riverview.co.uk
web: www.riverview.co.uk
dir: *From Dundee on A930 follow signs to
Monifieth, past supermarket, right signed golf
course, left under rail bridge. Site signed on left*

🚐 🚏

Open Apr-Oct Last arrival 22.00hrs Last departure
12.30hrs

A well-landscaped seaside site with individual
hedged pitches, and direct access to the beach.
The modernised toilet block has excellent facilities
which are immaculately maintained. Amenities
include a multi-gym, sauna and steam rooms. A
5.5 acre site with 40 touring pitches, 40
hardstandings and 46 statics.

AA Pubs & Restaurants nearby: Royal Arch Bar,
Broughty Ferry, 01382 779741

Dalhousie Restaurant at Carnoustie Golf Hotel,
Carnoustie 01241 411999

Leisure: ⚙ 🔍
Facilities: 🚿 ☉ 🅿 ✳ ♿ ⏱ 🍴 🚻 🐕
Services: 🔌 🚽 🛢 T 🚮 ⚡
Within 3 miles: ⛳ ⛺ 🎣 ◎ 🚤 🏬 🚽 ⛵

ARGYLL & BUTE

CARRADALE   Map 20 NR83

►►► 81% Carradale Bay Caravan Park (NR815385)

PA28 6QG
☎ 01583 431665
e-mail: info@carradalebay.com
dir: *A83 from Tarbert towards Campbeltown, left
onto B842 (Carradale road), right onto B879. Site
0.5m*

🚐 🚏 ⛺

Open Apr-Sep Last arrival 22.00hrs Last departure
noon

A beautiful, natural site on the sea's edge with
superb views over Kilbrannan Sound to the Isle of
Arran. Pitches are landscaped into small bays
broken up by shrubs and bushes, and backed by
dunes close to the long sandy beach. Toilet
facilities have now been refurbished to a very high
standard. Lodges and static caravans for holiday
hire. An 8 acre site with 75 touring pitches and 12
statics.

AA Pubs & Restaurants nearby: Dunvalanree,
Carradale 01583 431226

Facilities: 🚿 ☉ 🅿 ✳ ♿ ⏱ 🍴 🐕
Services: 🔌 🚽 🛢
Within 3 miles: ⛳ ⛺ 🎣 🚤 🏬 🚽 ⛵

GLENDARUEL   Map 20 NR98

Places to visit

Benmore Botanic Gardens, Benmore,
01369 706261, www.rbge.org.uk

►►► 77% *Glendaruel Caravan Park* (NR005865)

PA22 3AB
☎ 01369 820267   📠 01369 820367
e-mail: mail@glendaruelcaravanpark.com
web: www.glendaruelcaravanpark.com
dir: *A83 onto A815 to Strachur, 13m to site on
A886. By ferry from Gourock to Dunoon then B836,
then A886 for approx 4m N. (NB this route not
recommended for towing vehicles - 1:5 uphill
gradient on B836)*

🚐 🚏 ⛺

Open Apr-Oct Last arrival 22.00hrs Last departure
noon

A very pleasant, well-established site in the
beautiful Victorian gardens of Glendaruel House.

The level grass and hardstanding pitches are set
in 23 acres of wooded parkland in a valley
surrounded by mountains, with many rare
specimen trees. The owners are hospitable and
friendly. Static caravans are available for hire. A 3
acre site with 25 touring pitches, 15
hardstandings and 33 statics.

AA Pubs & Restaurants nearby: Kilfinan Hotel
Bar, Kilfinan 01700 821201

Leisure: ⚙ 🔍
Facilities: 🚿 ☉ 🅿 ✳ ⏱ 🍴 🚻 🐕
Services: 🔌 🚽 🛢 🧹 T 🚮
Within 3 miles: 🎣 🏬 🚽
Notes: Dogs must be kept on leads at all times.
Sea trout & salmon fishing, woodland walks, 24-
hour emergency phone available. Wi-fi

MACHRIHANISH   Map 20 NR62

►►►► 74% Machrihanish Caravan Park (NR647208)

East Trodigal PA28 6PT
☎ 01586 810366
e-mail: mail@campkintyre.co.uk
dir: *A82 from Glasgow to Tarbet, A83 to Inveraray,
then to Campbeltown. Take B843 to Machrihanish.
Site 300yds before village on right*

🚐 🚏 ⛺

Open Mar-Oct & Dec Last arrival 22.00hrs Last
departure 11.30hrs

Machrihanish is an open and breezy coastal site
close to the Mull of Kintyre and a glorious three
mile sandy beach. There is a campers' room,
static caravans and four wooden wigwams for hire
and great sea views to the isles of Jura and Islay.
The park is adjacent to a fine links golf course,
and Campbeltown, with its shops and restaurants,
is five miles away. Seven seasonal touring pitches
are available. An 8 acre site with 90 touring
pitches, 12 hardstandings and 5 statics.

Leisure: ▭
Facilities: 🚿 ☉ 🅿 ✳ ♿ ⏱ 🍴 🚻 🐕
Services: 🔌 🚽 🛢 T
Within 3 miles: ⛳ ⛺ 🎣 ◎ 🚤 🚽
Notes: No campfires, 10mph speed limit. Crazy
golf & fishing on site

LEISURE: 🏊 Indoor swimming pool 🏊 Outdoor swimming pool ⚙ Children's playground 🎾 Tennis court 🔍 Games room ▭ Separate TV room ⛳ 9/18 hole golf course
🚤 Boats for hire 🎬 Cinema 🎣 Fishing ◎ Mini golf 🏄 Watersports ⛵ Stables **FACILITIES:** 🛁 Bath 🚿 Shower ☉ Electric shaver 🅿 Hairdryer ✳ Ice Pack Facility
♿ Disabled facilities 📞 Public telephone 🏬 Shop on site or within 200yds 🚚 Mobile shop (calls at least 5 days a week) 🍴 BBQ area 🚻 Picnic area 🐕 Dog exercise area

OBAN   Map 20 NM82

Places to visit

Dunstaffnage Castle and Chapel, Oban,
01631 562465, www.historic-scotland.gov.uk

Bonawie Historic Iron Furnace, Taynuilt,
01866 822432, www.historic-scotland.gov.uk

►►► 78% Oban Caravan & Camping Park (NM831277)

Gallanachmore Farm, Gallanach Rd PA34 4QH
☎ 01631 562425
e-mail: info@obancaravanpark.com
dir: From Oban centre follow signs for Mull Ferry.
Take turn past terminal signed Gallanach. 2m
to site

🚐 🚌 ⛺

Open Etr/Apr-Oct Last arrival 23.00hrs Last
departure noon

A tourist park in an attractive location close to sea
and ferries. This family park is a popular base for
walking, sea-based activities and for those who
just want to enjoy the peace and tranquillity.
There are self-catering holiday lodges for hire. A
15 acre site with 150 touring pitches, 35
hardstandings and 12 statics.

AA Pubs & Restaurants nearby: Coast, Oban
01631 569900

Leisure: 🅰 🎣
Facilities: 🅵⊙🅿✳🕒🏧🎪🐴
Services: 🖭🅾🔋🍴🕒Ⓣ🚼🛒
Within 3 miles: 🚴🎣🎡🐴🏊🍴🕒Ⓤ

Notes: No commercial vehicles. Indoor kitchen for
tent campers

DUMFRIES & GALLOWAY

ANNAN   Map 21 NY16

Places to visit

Ruthwell Cross, Ruthwell, 0131 550 7612,
www.historic-scotland.gov.uk

Great for kids: Caerlaverock Castle,
Caerlaverock, 01387 770244,
www.historic-scotland.gov.uk

►► 70% Galabank Caravan & Camping Group (NY192676)

North St DG12 5DQ
☎ 01461 203539 & 204108
dir: Enter site via North Street

🚐 🚌 ⛺

Open Apr-early Sep Last departure noon

A tidy, well-maintained grassy little park with
spotless facilities close to the centre of town but
with pleasant rural views, and skirted by River
Annan. A 1 acre site with 30 touring pitches.

AA Pubs & Restaurants nearby: Smiths of Gretna
Green, Gretna 01461 337007

Facilities: 🅵🅿🏧🎪
Services: 🖭
Within 3 miles: 🚴🎡🍴🏧

Notes: Dogs must be kept on leads. Social
club adjacent

BARGRENNAN   Map 20 NX37

►►► 77% Glentrool Holiday Park (NX350769)

DG8 6RN
☎ 01671 840280   📠 01671 840342
e-mail: enquiries@glentroolholidaypark.co.uk
dir: Exit Newton Stewart on A714 towards Girvan,
right at Bargrennan towards Glentrool. Site on left
before village

🚐 🚌 ⛺

Open Mar-Oct Last arrival 21.00hrs Last
departure noon

A small park close to the village of Glentrool, and
bordered by the Galloway Forest Park. Both the
touring and static area with vans for hire are
immaculately presented and the amenity block is
clean and freshly painted. The on-site shop is well
stocked. A 6.75 acre site with 14 touring pitches,
12 hardstandings and 26 statics.

AA Pubs & Restaurants nearby: Creebridge House
Hotel, Newton Stewart 01671 402121

Galloway Arms Hotel, Newton Stewart
01671 402653

Kirroughtree House, Minnigaff, Newton Stewart
01671 402141

Leisure: 🅰
Facilities: 🅵⊙🅿✳🕒🏧
Services: 🖭🅾🔋🚼
Notes: No cars by tents. No ball games, no
groups

BRIGHOUSE BAY   Map 20 NX64

PREMIER PARK

►►►►► 93%

Brighouse Bay Holiday
Park (NX628453)

DG6 4TS
☎ 01557 870267   📠 01557 870319
e-mail: info@brighouse-bay.co.uk
dir: Off B727 (Kirkcudbright to Borgue) or take
A755 (Kirkcudbright) off A75 2m W of Twynholm.
Site signed

🚐 🚌 ⛺

Open all year (rs Nov-Mar leisure club closed
2 days each week) Last arrival 21.30hrs Last
departure 11.30hrs

This top class park has a country club feel and
enjoys a marvellous coastal setting adjacent to
the beach and with superb sea views. Pitches
have been imaginatively sculpted into the
meadowland, with stone walls and hedges
blending in with the site's mature trees. These
features, together with the large range of leisure
activities, make this an excellent park for families
who enjoy an active holiday. Many of the facilities
are at an extra charge. A range of self-catering
units is available for hire. A 30 acre site with 190
touring pitches, 100 hardstandings and 120
statics.

Leisure: 🏊 🅰 🎣
Facilities: 🚿🅵⊙🅿✳🕒🏧🎪🐴
Services: 🖭🅾🍺🔋🍴Ⓣ🍽🚼🛒🚐🛒
Within 3 miles: 🚴🎣🍴◎🏊🏧🕒Ⓤ

Notes: No motorised scooters, jet skis or private
quad bikes. Mini golf, 18-hole golf, riding, fishing,
quad bikes. Wi-fi

SERVICES: 🖭 Electric hook up 🅾 Launderette 🍺 Licensed bar 🔋 Calor Gas 🕒 Camping Gaz Ⓣ Toilet fluid 🍽 Café/Restaurant 🍴 Fast Food/Takeaway 🚐 Battery charging
🚼 Baby care 🛒 Motorvan service point ABBREVIATIONS: BH/bank hols-bank holidays Etr-Easter Whit-Whitsun dep-departure fr-from hrs-hours m-mile mdnt-midnight
rdbt-roundabout rs-restricted service wk-week wknd-weekend 🚫 No credit cards ⊗ no dogs See page 7 for details of the AA Camping Card Scheme

CREETOWN Map 20 NX46

Places to visit

Cardoness Castle, Cardoness Castle, 01557 814427, www.historic-scotland.gov.uk

Great for kids: Creetown Gem Rock Museum, Creetown, 01671 820357, www.gemrock.net

PREMIER PARK

▶▶▶▶▶ 84% Castle Cary Holiday Park (NX475576)

DG8 7DQ
☎ 01671 820264 📄 01671 820670
e-mail: enquiries@castlecarypark.f9.co.uk
web: www.castlecary-caravans.com
dir: *Signed with direct access off A75, 0.5m S of village*

* 🚐 £14.25-£17.80 � £14.25-£17.80
🅰 £14.25-£17.80

Open all year (rs Oct-Mar reception/shop, no heated outdoor pool) Last arrival anytime Last departure noon

This attractive site in the grounds of Cassencarie House is sheltered by woodlands, and faces south towards Wigtown Bay. The park is in a secluded location with beautiful landscaping and excellent facilities. The bar/restaurant is housed in part of an old castle, and enjoys extensive views over the River Cree estuary. A 12 acre site with 50 touring pitches, 50 hardstandings and 26 statics.

AA Pubs & Restaurants nearby: Creebridge House Hotel, Newton Stewart 01671 402121

Galloway Arms Hotel, Newton Stewart 01671 402653

Kirroughtree House, Minnigaff, Newton Stewart 01671 402141

Cally Palace Hotel, Gatehouse-of-Fleet 01557 814341

Leisure: 🔊🏊♨️🔍📺
Facilities: 🚿📶⊙📍✳️🖤⏰🍴🎱🔥🐾♿
Services: 🔌🔟🍽️🛢️🚿📶🍴🛒🚻
Within 3 miles: 🎣📍◎🐕🎱

Notes: Dogs must be kept on leads at all times. Bike hire, crazy golf, coarse fishing, full size football pitch. Wi-fi

see advert in preliminary section

CROCKETFORD

Places to visit

Drumcoltran Tower, Drumcoltran Tower, www.historic-scotland.gov.uk

Sweetheart Abbey, New Abbey, 01387 850397, www.historic-scotland.gov.uk

Great for kids: Threave Castle, Castle Douglas, 07711 223101, www.historic-scotland.gov.uk

CROCKETFORD Map 21 NX87

AA CAMPING CARD SITE

▶▶▶▶ 84% The Park of Brandedleys (NX830725)

DG2 8RG
☎ 01387 266700 📄 01556 690681
e-mail: brandedleys@holgates.com
web: www.holgates.com
dir: *In village on A75, from Dumfries towards Stranraer site on left along minor road, entrance 200yds on right*

🚐 £18.50-£25.50 � £18.50-£25.50
🅰 £18.50-£25.50

Open all year (rs Nov-Mar bar/restaurant open Fri-Sun afternoon) Last arrival 22.00hrs Last dep noon

A well-maintained site in an elevated position off the A75, with fine views of Auchenreoch Loch and beyond. This comfortable park offers a wide range of amenities, including a fine games room and a tastefully-designed bar with adjoining bistro. There are attractive holiday homes for sale and hire on this park, which is well placed for enjoying walking, fishing, sailing and golf. A 24 acre site with 45 touring pitches, 40 hardstandings and 52 statics.

Leisure: 🔊♨️❄️🔍
Facilities: 🚿⊙📍✳️🖤⏰🍴🎱🔥🐾♿
Services: 🔌🔟🍽️🛢️🚿📶🍴🛒🚻🚗
Within 3 miles: 🎣📍⛳🎱⛵

Notes: Guidelines issued on arrival. Badminton court

see advert below

pitch perfect.

The Park of BRANDEDLEYS

Set in beautiful Dumfries & Galloway, the Park is perfect for exploring the surrounding area, the Solway Coast or just take time out to relax and unwind.

Restaurant and bar, indoor pool, sauna and tennis courts.

Touring and camping pitches plus holiday homes and lodges to hire or buy.

The Park of Brandedleys, Crocketford DG2 8RG
Telephone. 01387 266 700

visit us online at
www.brandedleys.co.uk

LEISURE: 🔊 Indoor swimming pool 🏊 Outdoor swimming pool 🎠 Children's playground 🎾 Tennis court 🔍 Games room 📺 Separate TV room ⛳ 9/18 hole golf course 🚣 Boats for hire 🎬 Cinema 🎣 Fishing ⛳ Mini golf 🏄 Watersports 🐎 Stables **FACILITIES:** 🛁 Bath 🚿 Shower ⊙ Electric shaver 🖤 Hairdryer ✳️ Ice Pack Facility ♿ Disabled facilities ☎ Public telephone 🏪 Shop on site or within 200yds 🚐 Mobile shop (calls at least 5 days a week) 🔥 BBQ area 🌲 Picnic area 🐾 Dog exercise area

DALBEATTIE — Map 21 NX86

Places to visit

Threave Garden and Estate, Castle Douglas, 08449 4932245, www.nts.org.uk

Orchardtown Tower, Palnackie, www.historic-scotland.gov.uk

▶▶▶▶ 79% Glenearly Caravan Park

(NX838628)

DG5 4NE
☎ 01556 611393 📄 01556 612058
e-mail: glenearlycaravan@btconnect.com
dir: From Dumfries take A711 towards Dalbeattie. Site entrance after Edingham Farm on right (200yds before boundary sign)

* 🚐 £13.50-£15.50 🚗 £13.50-£15.50 🅰 £13.50-£15.50

Open all year Last arrival 19.00hrs Last departure noon

An excellent small park set in open countryside with panoramic views of Long Fell, Maidenpap and Dalbeattie Forest. The park is located in 84 beautiful acres of farmland which visitors are invited to enjoy. The attention to detail here is of the highest standard and this is most notable in the presentation of the amenity block. Static holiday caravans for hire. A 10 acre site with 39 touring pitches, 33 hardstandings and 74 statics.

Leisure: 🄰 🔍
Facilities: 🌂 ☺ ⚹ ⚹ 🌡 🕒 🚿
Services: 🔌 🕹 🍴 🔋
Within 3 miles: 🎣 ⛳ 🛒 ◎ 🕹 🕹 ↻
Notes: ⊛ No commercial vehicles, dogs must be kept on leads

DUMFRIES

See Shawhead

ECCLEFECHAN

Places to visit

Robert Burns House, Dumfries, 01387 255297, www.dumgal.gov.uk/museums

Old Bridge House Museum, Dumfries, 01387 256904, www.dumgal.gov.uk/museums

Great for kids: Dumfries Museum and Camera Obscura, Dumfries, 01387 253374, www.dumgal.gov.uk/museums

---

ECCLEFECHAN — Map 21 NY17

PREMIER PARK

▶▶▶▶▶ 77% Hoddom Castle Caravan Park (NY154729)

Hoddom DG11 1AS
☎ 01576 300251 📄 01576 300757
e-mail: hoddomcastle@aol.com
dir: M74 junct 19, follow signs to site. From A75 W of Annan take B723 for 5m, follow signs to site

* 🚐 £14-£21 🚗 £14-£21 🅰 £11-£18

Open Etr or Apr-Oct (rs Early season cafeteria closed) Last arrival 21.00hrs Last departure 14.00hrs

The peaceful, well-equipped park can be found on the banks of the River Annan, and offers a good mix of grassy and hard pitches, beautifully landscaped and blending into the surroundings. There are signed nature trails, maintained by the park's countryside ranger, a 9-hole golf course, trout and salmon fishing, and plenty of activity ideas for children. A 28 acre site with 200 touring pitches, 150 hardstandings and 54 statics.

Leisure: 🄰 ⚞ 🔍
Facilities: 🚿 🌂 ☺ 🅿 ⚹ 🌡 🕒 🚿 🍴 🔋 🚻 🚼
Services: 🔌 🕹 🍴 🔋 ⊘ 🚽 🍴 🚚 ↯
Within 3 miles: 🎣 ⛳ ◎ 🕹 🕹
Notes: No electric scooters, no gazebos, no fires. Visitor centre

---

GATEHOUSE OF FLEET — Map 20 NX55

Places to visit

MacLellan's Castle, Kirkcudbright, 01557 331856, www.historic-scotland.gov.uk

Great for kids: Galloway Wildlife Conservation Park, Kirkcudbright, 01557 331645, www.gallowaywildlife.co.uk

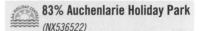

83% Auchenlarie Holiday Park

(NX536522)

DG7 2EX
☎ 01556 506200 & 206201 📄 01556 206220
e-mail: enquiries@auchenlarie.co.uk
web: www.auchenlarie.co.uk
dir: Direct access off A75, 5m W of Gatehouse of Fleet

* 🚐 £17-£30 🚗 £17-£30 🅰 £15-£28

Open Mar-Oct Last arrival 20.00hrs Last departure noon

A well-organised family park set on cliffs overlooking Wigtown Bay, with its own sandy beach. The tenting area, in sloping grass surrounded by mature trees, has its own sanitary facilities, while the marked caravan pitches are in paddocks, with open views and the provision of high quality toilets. The leisure centre includes swimming pool, gym, solarium and sports hall. The park also has an extensive selection of holiday homes for hire. A 32 acre site with 49 touring pitches, 49 hardstandings and 350 statics.

AA Pubs & Restaurants nearby: Cally Palace Hotel, Gatehouse-of-Fleet 01557 814341

Leisure: 🏊 🄰 ⚞ 🔍
Facilities: 🚿 🌂 ☺ 🅿 ⚹ 🌡 🕒 🍴 🔋 🚻 🚼
Services: 🔌 🕹 🍴 🔋 ⊘ 🚽 🍴 🚚 🚚
Within 3 miles: 🎣 ⛳ ◎ 🕹 🕹 ↻
Notes: Baby changing facilities, internet café, crazy golf. Wi-fi

---

GATEHOUSE OF FLEET *continued*

AA CAMPING CARD SITE

►►►► 77% Anwoth Caravan Site

(NX595563)

DG7 2JU
☎ 01557 814333 & 840251 ▤ 01557 814333
e-mail: enquiries@auchenlarie.co.uk
dir: *From A75 into Gatehouse of Fleet, site on right towards Stranraer. Signed from town centre*

＊ ⌂ £15-£25 ⇔ £15-£25 Å £15-£25

Open Mar-Oct Last arrival 20.00hrs Last departure noon

A very high quality park in a peaceful sheltered setting within easy walking distance of the village, ideally placed for exploring the scenic hills, valleys and coastline. Grass, hardstanding and fully serviced pitches are available and guests may use the leisure facilities at the sister site, Auchenlarie Holiday Park. Seasonal touring pitches are available. A 2 acre site with 28 touring pitches, 13 hardstandings and 44 statics.

AA Pubs & Restaurants nearby: Cally Palace Hotel, Gatehouse-of-Fleet 01557 814341

Facilities: ⌂ ↑ ⊙ ℗ ✳ ⅃ ⊙ 🖥 ⊞

Services: ⊞ 🖥 🛢 ⊘

Within 3 miles: ↓ ⌀ 🖥 🖥 **Notes:** Wi-fi

GRETNA	Map 21 NY36

Places to visit

Carlisle Cathedral, Carlisle, 01228 535169, www.carlislecathedral.org.uk

Tullie House Museum and Art Gallery, Carlisle, 01228 618718, www.tulliehouse.co.uk

Great for kids: Carlisle Castle, Carlisle, 01228 591992, www.english-heritage.org.uk

►►►► 74% King Robert the Bruce's Cave Caravan & Camping Park

(NY266705)

Cove Estate, Kirkpatrick Fleming DG11 3AT
☎ 01461 800285 & 07779 138694
▤ 01461 800269
e-mail: enquiries@brucescave.co.uk
web: www.brucescave.co.uk
dir: *Exit A74(M) junct 21 for Kirkpatrick Fleming, follow N through village, pass Station Inn, left at Bruce's Court. Over rail crossing to site*

⌂ ⇔ Å

King Robert the Bruce's Cave Caravan & Camping Park

Open Apr-Nov (rs Nov shop closed, water restriction) Last arrival 22.00hrs Last departure 16.00hrs

The lovely wooded grounds of an old castle and mansion are the setting for this pleasant park. The mature woodland is a haven for wildlife, and there is a riverside walk to Robert the Bruce's Cave. A toilet block with en suite facilities is of special appeal to families. An 80 acre site with 75 touring pitches, 60 hardstandings and 35 statics.

AA Pubs & Restaurants nearby: Smiths of Gretna Green, Gretna 01461 337007

Leisure: ⋀ ⚲ ⊡

Facilities: ⌘ ↑ ⊙ ℗ ✳ ⅃ ⊙ 🖥 ⊞ 🖥 ⋈

Services: ⊞ 🖥 🛢 ⊘ ⊤ ⌷ 🍽 ⛟ ⤵

Within 3 miles: ↓ ⌀ 🖥 🖥 U

Notes: Dogs must be kept on leads. BMX bike hire, coarse fishing, first aid available

---

►►►► 73% Braids Caravan Park

(NY313674)

Annan Rd DG16 5DQ
☎ 01461 337409
e-mail: enquiries@thebraidscaravanpark.co.uk
dir: *On B721, 0.5m from village on right, towards Annan*

⌂ ⇔

Open all year Last arrival 21.00hrs (20.00hrs winter) Last departure noon

A very well-maintained park conveniently located on the outskirts of Gretna village. Within walking distance is Gretna Gateway Outlet Village and nearby is Gretna Green with the World Famous Old Blacksmith's Shop, which became famous for the 'anvil marriages' of run-away couples seeking a clandestine union. It is also a convenient stop-over for people travelling to and from both the north of Scotland and Northern Ireland. The park has first-class toilet facilities and generous-sized all-weather pitches. A 6 acre site with 93 touring pitches, 29 hardstandings.

AA Pubs & Restaurants nearby: Smiths of Gretna Green, Gretna 01461 337007

Facilities: ↑ ⊙ ℗ ✳ ⅃ ⊙

Services: ⊞ 🖥 🛢 ⊘ ⊤ ⤵

Within 3 miles: 🖥

Notes: No skateboards, dogs must be kept on leads at all times

KIPPFORD	Map 21 NX85

Places to visit

Orchardtown Tower, Palnackie, www.historic-scotland.gov.uk

AA CAMPING CARD SITE

►►► 79% Kippford Holiday Park (NX844564)

DG5 4LF
☎ 01556 620636 ▤ 01556 620607
e-mail: info@kippfordholidaypark.co.uk
dir: *From Dumfries take A711 to Dalbeattie, left onto A710 (Solway coast road) for 3.5m. Park 200yds beyond Kippford turn on right*

⌂ ⇔ Å

Open all year Last arrival 21.30hrs Last departure noon

An attractively landscaped park set in hilly countryside close to the Urr Water estuary and a sand/shingle beach, and with spectacular views. The level touring pitches are on grassed hardstands with private garden areas, and many are fully serviced, and there are attractive lodges for hire. The Doon Hill and woodland walks separate the park from the lovely village of Kippford. An 18 acre site with 45 touring pitches, 22 hardstandings and 119 statics.

AA Pubs & Restaurants nearby: Balcary Bay Hotel, Auchencairn 01556 640217

Kippford Holiday Park

Leisure: ⚓ 🔍
Facilities: 🐾⊙📶✳🕭🕐🖭🎣🎾🐕
Services: 🔌🅿🛢🧴🚼♿
Within 3 miles: ⚓🎣◎🎣🅿🛢U

Notes: No camp fires. Golf, fly fishing, nature walk, cycle hire. Wi-fi

---

KIRKCUDBRIGHT   Map 20 NX65

Places to visit
Stewartry Museum, Kirkcudbright, 01557 331643, www.dumgal.gov.uk/museums

Tolbooth Art Centre, Kirkcudbright, 01557 331556, www.dumgal.gov.uk/museums

Great for kids: Broughton House and Garden, Kirkcudbright, 0844 493 2246, www.nts.org.uk

▶▶▶▶ **82% Seaward Caravan Park**
(NX662494)

Dhoon Bay DG6 4TJ
☎ 01557 870267 & 331079   📠 01557 870319
e-mail: aa@seaward-park.co.uk
dir: *2m SW off B727 (Borgue road)*

* 🚐 £17.20-£22.80 � £17.20-£22.80 ▲ £12.90-£18.50

Open Mar-Oct (rs Mar-mid May & mid Sep-Oct swimming pool closed) Last arrival 21.30hrs Last departure 11.30hrs

A very attractive elevated park with outstanding views over Kirkcudbright Bay which forms part of the Dee Estuary. Access to a sandy cove with rock pools is just across the road. Facilities are well organised and neatly kept, and the park offers a very peaceful atmosphere. The leisure facilities at the other Gillespie parks are available to visitors to Seaward Caravan Park. An 8 acre site with 26 touring pitches, 20 hardstandings and 54 statics.

AA Pubs & Restaurants nearby: Selkirk Arms Hotel, Kirkcudbright 01557 330402

Leisure: ⚓ ⚓ 🔍
Facilities: 🛏🐾⊙📶✳🕭🕐🖭🎣🎾
Services: 🔌🅿🛢🧴🚼🖭
Within 3 miles: ⚓🎣◎🅿🛢U

Notes: No motorised scooters or bikes (except disabled vehicles), pets must be kept on leads. Pitch & putt, volley ball, badminton, table tennis

---

KIRKGUNZEON   Map 21 NX86

Places to visit
Robert Burns Centre, Dumfries, 01387 264808, www.dumgal.gov.uk/museums

National Museum of Costume Scotland, New Abbey, 01387 850260, www.historic-scotland.gov.uk

Great for kids: Burns Mausoleum, Dumfries, 01387 255297, www.dumgal.gov.uk/museums

---

AA CAMPING CARD SITE

▶▶▶ **70% Mossband Caravan Park**
(NX872665)

Mossband DG2 8JP
☎ 01387 760505
e-mail: mossbandcp@btconnect.com
dir: *Adjacent to A711 to Dalbeattie, 1.5m E of Kirkgunzeon*

🚐 £14-£16 � £14-£16 ▲ £7.50-£9.50

Open Mar-Oct Last arrival 21.00hrs Last departure 11.00hrs

A level park on the site of an old railway station, set in a peaceful rural location with good views. The new and experienced owners are already making a difference having refreshed some of the dated facilities. A 3 acre site with 25 touring pitches, 3 hardstandings and 12 statics.

Facilities: 🐾⊙✳
Services: 🔌🅿🛢🖭
Within 3 miles: ⚓🎣
Notes: ⊗

LANGHOLM

Places to visit
Hermitage Castle, Hermitage, 01387 376222, www.historic-scotland.gov.uk

---

LANGHOLM   Map 21 NY38

▶▶▶ **75% Ewes Water Caravan & Camping Park** (NY365855)

Milntown DG13 0DH
☎ 013873 80386   📠 013873 81670
e-mail: aeneasmn@aol.com
dir: *Directly off A7 approx 0.5m N of Langholm. Site in Langholm Rugby Club*

🚐 £12-£16 � £12-£14 ▲ £6-£9

Open Apr-Sep Last departure noon

On the banks of the River Esk, this is a very attractive park in a sheltered wooded valley close to an unspoilt Borders town. A 2 acre site with 24 touring pitches.

Facilities: 🐾⊙✳🕭🕐🖭🎣🎾
Services: 🔌🛢🧴🖭   **Within 3 miles:** ⚓🎣🛢
Notes: ⊗ Large playing area

LOCKERBIE

See Ecclefechan

NEWTON STEWART   Map 20 NX46

▶▶▶ **67% Creebridge Caravan Park**
(NX415656)

Minnigaff DG8 6AJ
☎ 01671 402324 & 402432   📠 01671 402324
e-mail: john_sharples@btconnect.com
dir: *0.25m E of Newton Stewart at Minnigaff on bypass, signed off A75*

* 🚐 £14-£16 � £14-£16 ▲ £13-£15

Open all year (rs Mar only one toilet block open) Last arrival 20.00hrs Last departure 10.00hrs

A small family-owned site a short walk from the town's amenities. The site is surrounded by mature trees, and the toilet facilities are clean and functional. A 5.5 acre site with 36 touring pitches, 12 hardstandings and 50 statics.

AA Pubs & Restaurants nearby: Creebridge House Hotel, Newton Stewart 01671 402121

Galloway Arms Hotel, Newton Stewart 01671 402653

Kirroughtree House, Minnigaff, Newton Stewart 01671 402141

Leisure: ⚓ **Facilities:** 🐾⊙📶✳🕭🕐🖭🎣🎾🐕
Services: 🔌🅿🛢🧴🖭
Within 3 miles: ⚓🅱🎣🎣🛢🛢U
Notes: ⊗ Security street lighting

PALNACKIE — Map 21 NX85

Places to visit

Orchardtown Tower, Palnackie,
www.historic-scotland.gov.uk

►►► 79% *Barlochan Caravan Park*

(NX819572)

DG7 1PF
☎ 01556 600256 & 01557 870267
🖷 01557 870319
e-mail: aa@barlochan.co.uk
dir: *On A711, N of Palnackie, signed*

🚐 🚙 🛆

Open Apr-Oct Last arrival 21.30hrs Last dep 11.30hrs

A small terraced park with quiet landscaped pitches in a level area backed by rhododendron bushes. There are spectacular views over the River Urr estuary, and the park has its own coarse fishing loch nearby. The amenity block has been upgraded to include combined wash facilities. The leisure facilities at Brighouse Bay are available to visitors. A 9 acre site with 20 touring pitches, 3 hardstandings and 65 statics.

AA Pubs & Restaurants nearby: Balcary Bay Hotel, Auchencairn 01556 640217

Leisure: 🏊 🎠 🎱 🖳
Facilities: 🕭 ⊙ 🍴 ✳ 🕐 ⊙ 🖻 🚻 🐕
Services: 🚐 🖥 🔒 🚿 🚽 🎠
Within 3 miles: 🎣 🏌 ◎ 🖻 🖻 **Notes:** Pitch & putt

PARTON — Map 20 NX67

Places to visit

The Rum Story, Whitehaven, 01946 592933,
www.rumstory.co.uk

The Beacon, Whitehaven, 01946 592302,
www.thebeacon-whitehaven.co.uk

►►► 77% Loch Ken Holiday Park *(NX687702)*

DG7 3NE
☎ 01644 470282
e-mail: penny@lochkenholidaypark.co.uk
web: www.lochkenholidaypark.co.uk
dir: *On A713, N of Parton*

* 🚐 £17-£20 🚙 £17-£20 🛆 £12-£16

Open Mar-mid Nov (rs Mar/Apr (ex Etr) & late Sep-Nov restricted shop hours) Last departure noon

Much improved following a huge injection of energy, enthusiasm and commitment from the hands-on Bryson family, this busy and popular park, with a natural emphasis on water activities, is set on the eastern shores of Loch Ken, with superb views. It is in a peaceful and beautiful spot opposite the RSPB reserve, with direct access to the loch for fishing and boat launching. The park offers a variety of watersports, as well as farm visits and nature trails. Static caravans for hire. A 7 acre site with 52 touring pitches, 4 hardstandings and 35 statics.

Leisure: 🎠 **Facilities:** 🕭 ⊙ 🍴 ✳ 🕐 ⊙ 🖻 🚻 🐕
Services: 🚐 🖥 🔒 🚿 🚽 🎠
Within 3 miles: 🎣 🏊 🏌 🏊 🖻 🖻
Notes: Bike, boat & canoe hire, fishing on loch

PORT WILLIAM — Map 20 NX34

Places to visit

Glenluce Abbey, Glenluce, 01581 300541,
www.historic-scotland.gov.uk

►►► 76% Kings Green Caravan Site

(NX340430)

South St DG8 9SG
☎ 01988 700489
dir: *Direct access from A747 at junct with B7085, towards Whithorn*

🚐 🚙 🛆

Open Etr, May & Jul-Aug Last arrival 20.00hrs Last departure noon

Set beside the unspoilt village with all its amenities and the attractive harbour, this level grassy park is community owned and run. Approached via the coast road, the park has views reaching as far as the Isle of Man. A 3 acre site with 30 touring pitches.

AA Pubs & Restaurants nearby: Steam Packet Inn, Isle of Whithorn 01988 500334

Facilities: 🕭 ⊙ 🍴 🕐 ⊙ 🖻 🚻 🐕
Services: 🚐 🖥 **Within 3 miles:** 🎣 🏌 🏊 🖻
Notes: ◎ No golf or fireworks on site. Free book lending

SANDHEAD — Map 20 NX04

Places to visit

Glenwhan Gardens, Stranraer, 01581 400222,
www.glenwhangardens.co.uk

Great for kids: Castle Kennedy and Gardens, Stranraer, 01776 702024,
www.castlekennedygardens.co.uk

►►►► 76% Sands of Luce Holiday Park *(NX103510)*

Sands of Luce DG9 9JN
☎ 01776 830456 🖷 01776 830477
e-mail: info@sandsofluceholidaypark.co.uk
web: www.sandsofluceholidaypark.co.uk
dir: *From S & E: left from A75 onto B7084 signed Drummore. Site signed at junct with A716. From N: A77 through Stranraer towards Portpatrick, 2m, follow A716 signed Drummore, site signed in 5m*

🚐 £18-£22 🚙 £18-£22 🛆 £15-£20

Open Mar-Jan Last arrival 20.00hrs Last departure noon

This is a large, well managed park with a balance of static and touring caravans and enjoys a stunning position with direct access to a sandy beach and with views across Luce Bay. It has its own boat storage area and boasts an excellent static hire fleet and a tastefully decorated well-managed club. A 30 acre site with 100 touring pitches and 190 statics.

AA Pubs & Restaurants nearby: Knockinaam Lodge, Portpatrick 01776 810471

Crown Hotel, Portpatrick 01776 810261

Leisure: 🎠 🎱
Facilities: 🕭 ⊙ 🍴 ✳ 🕐 ⊙ 🖻 🚻 🐕
Services: 🚐 🖥 🚿 🍴 🍺
Within 3 miles: 🏊 🏌 🏊 🖻 🖻 ∪
Notes: Dogs must be kept on leads & dog fouling must be cleared up by owners. No quad bikes. Boat launching, play park. Wi-fi

---

SANDYHILLS — Map 21 NX85

Places to visit

Threave Garden and Estate, Castle Douglas, 08449 4932245, www.nts.org.uk

Orchardtown Tower, Palnackie, www.historic-scotland.gov.uk

Great for kids: Threave Castle, Castle Douglas, 07711 223101, www.historic-scotland.gov.uk

►►► 80% *Sandyhills Bay Leisure Park* (NX892552)

DG5 4NY
☎ 01557 870267 & 01387 780257
📠 01557 870319
e-mail: info@sandyhills-bay.co.uk
dir: *On A710, 7m from Dalbeattie, 6.5m from Kirkbean*

🚐 🚙 Å

Open Apr-Oct Last arrival 21.30hrs Last departure 11.30hrs

A well-maintained park in a superb location beside a beach, and close to many attractive villages. The level, grassy site is sheltered by woodland, and the south-facing Sandyhills Bay and beach are a treasure trove for all the family, with their caves and rock pools. The leisure facilities at Brighouse Bay are available to visitors here. Two camping pods are available for hire. A 6 acre site with 26 touring pitches and 34 statics.

AA Pubs & Restaurants nearby: Cavens, Kirkbean 01387 880234

Leisure: 🄰

Facilities: 🄰☉🄿✳☉🛁🛒🕶

Services: 🄰🄰🄰🄰🄰🄰🄰🄰🄰🄰

Within 3 miles: 🄰🄰🄰🄰🄰

SHAWHEAD

Places to visit

Robert Burns House, Dumfries, 01387 255297, www.dumgal.gov.uk/museums

Old Bridge House Museum, Dumfries, 01387 256904, www.dumgal.gov.uk/museums

SHAWHEAD — Map 21 NX87

►►► 79% Barnsoul Farm

(NX876778)

GOLD

DG2 9SQ
☎ 01387 730249 & 730453 📠 01387 730453
e-mail: barnsouldg@aol.com
web: www.barnsoulfarm.co.uk
dir: *Exit A75 between Dumfries & Crocketford at site sign onto unclass road signed Shawhead. Right at T-junct, immediate left. Site 1m on left, follow Barnsoul signs*

* 🚐 £14-£18 🚙 £14-£25 Å £14-£18

Open Apr-Oct Last arrival 23.00hrs Last departure noon

A very spacious, peaceful and scenic farm site with views across open countryside in all directions. Set in 250 acres of woodland, parkland and farmland, and an ideal centre for touring the surrounding unspoilt countryside. It offers excellent kitchen facilities and a dining area for lightweight campers. There are wigwam mountain bothies for hire and seasonal touring pitches are available. A 100 acre site with 55 touring pitches, 12 hardstandings and 11 statics.

Leisure: 🄰🖵

Facilities: 🄰☉🄿✳☉☉🛒🕶

Services: 🄰🄰🄰🄰🄰

Within 3 miles: 🄰🄰🄰🄰🄰

Notes: ⊘ No unbooked groups, no loud noise after 23.00hrs. 2-axle caravans must pre-book. Fishing on site

SOUTHERNESS — Map 21 NX95

81% Southerness Holiday Village (NX976545)

GOLD

Off Sandy Ln DG2 8AZ
☎ 0844 335 3756 📠 01387 880429
e-mail:
touringandcamping@parkdeanholidays.com
web: www.parkdeantouring.com
dir: *From S: A75 from Gretna to Dumfries. From N: A74, exit at A701 to Dumfries. Take A710 (coast road), approx 16m, site easily visible*

🚐 £15.50-£34 🚙 £15.50-£34 Å £13.50-£30

Open Mar-Oct Last arrival 21.00hrs Last departure 10.00hrs

There are stunning views across the Solway Firth from this holiday park at the foot of the Galloway Hills. A sandy beach on the Solway Firth is accessible directly from the park. The emphasis is on family entertainment, and facilities include an indoor pool, show bar, coast bar and kitchen. A very well organised park with excellent all-weather, fully-serviced pitches available. A 50 acre site with 100 touring pitches, 60 hardstandings and 611 statics.

AA Pubs & Restaurants nearby: Cavens, Kirkbean 01387 880234

Leisure: 🏊🄰🎣

Facilities: 🄰☉🄿✳☉🕐🛁🛒

Services: 🄰🄰🄰🄰🄰🄰🄰🄰🄰

Within 3 miles: 🄰🄰🄰🄰🄰

Notes: Amusements centre, live entertainment, children's clubs. Wi-fi

see advert in preliminary section

STRANRAER
Map 20 NX06

Places to visit

Ardwell House Gardens, Ardwell, 01776 860227

AA CAMPING CARD SITE

▶▶▶▶ **77% Aird Donald Caravan Park** *(NX075605)*

London Rd DG9 8RN
☎ **01776 702025**
e-mail: enquiries@aird-donald.co.uk
dir: *From A75 left on entering Stranraer (signed). Opposite school, site 300yds*

🚐 £15-£17 🚐 £15-£17 ▲ £13-£15

Open all year Last departure 16.00hrs

A spacious touring site, mainly grass but with tarmac hardstanding area, with pitches large enough to accommodate a car and caravan overnight without unhitching. On the fringe of town screened by mature shrubs and trees. Ideal stopover en route to Northern Irish ferry ports. A 12 acre site with 100 touring pitches, 30 hardstandings.

AA Pubs & Restaurants nearby: Knockinaam Lodge, Portpatrick 01776 810471

Crown Hotel, Portpatrick 01776 810261

Leisure: 🅰
Facilities: 🚿☺🅿♿🐕
Services: 🚽🔋🎣🖤🚮
Within 3 miles: 🚶🏊🎡🎣🛒🎮🎯
Notes: ⊛ Tents Apr-Sep

WIGTOWN
Map 20 NX45

▶▶▶ **85% Drumroamin Farm Camping & Touring Site** *(NX444512)*

1 South Balfern DG8 9DB
☎ **01988 840613** & 07752 471456
e-mail: enquiry@drumroamin.co.uk
dir: *A75 towards Newton Stewart, onto A714 for Wigtown. Left on B7005 through Bladnock, A746 through Kirkinner. Take B7004 signed Garlieston, 2nd left opposite Kilsture Forest, site 0.75m at end of lane*

🚐 £15 🚐 £15 ▲ £13

Open all year Last arrival 21.00hrs Last departure noon

An open, spacious park in a quiet spot a mile from the main road, and close to Wigtown Bay. A superb toilet block offers spacious showers, and there's a lounge/games room and plenty of room for children to play. A 5 acre site with 48 touring pitches and 3 statics.

AA Pubs & Restaurants nearby: Creebridge House Hotel, Newton Stewart 01671 402121

Galloway Arms Hotel, Newton Stewart 01671 402653

Kirroughtree House, Minnigaff, Newton Stewart 01671 402141

Leisure: 🅰🔍
Facilities: 🚿☺🅿✳♿🎯🐕
Services: 🚽🔋🖤🚮
Within 3 miles: 🚶🎣🛒
Notes: No fires. Ball games area

EAST LOTHIAN

ABERLADY
Map 21 NT47

Places to visit

Dirleton Castle and Gardens, Dirleton, 01620 850330, www.historic-scotland.gov.uk

Hailes Castle, East Linton, www.historic-scotland.gov.uk

Great for kids: Myreton Motor Museum, Aberlady, 01875 870288

▶▶ **70% Aberlady Caravan Park** *(NT482797)*

Haddington Rd EH32 0PZ
☎ **01875 870666** 🖷 01875 870666
dir: *Off A6137 at Aberlady. 0.25m turn right, site on right*

🚐 🚐 ▲

Open Mar-Oct Last arrival 22.00hrs Last departure noon

A small, simple campsite in pleasantly wooded surroundings, with a delightful outlook towards the Lammermuir Hills. It offers level pitches in a well-maintained meadow with electric hook-ups, and is within easy reach of Edinburgh and the East Lothian coast. A 4.5 acre site with 15 touring pitches, 4 hardstandings.

AA Pubs & Restaurants nearby: La Potinière, Gullane 01620 843214

Macdonald Marine Hotel & Spa, North Berwick 0870 400 8129

Leisure: 🅰 **Facilities:** 🚿☺🅿✳🐕🎯
Services: 🚽🔋🎣🖤🚮
Within 3 miles: 🚶🎣☺🏊🛒🎮
Notes: ⊛ No ball games, no loud music. Wi-fi

DUNBAR
Map 21 NT67

Places to visit

Preston Mill and Phantassie Doocot, East Linton, 0844 493 2128, www.nts.org.uk

Great for kids: Tantallon Castle, North Berwick, 01620 892727, www.historic-scotland.gov.uk

PREMIER PARK

▶▶▶▶▶ **88% *Thurston Manor Holiday Home Park*** *(NT712745)*

Innerwick EH42 1SA
☎ **01368 840643** 🖷 01368 840261
e-mail: mail@thurstonmanor.co.uk
dir: *4m S of Dunbar, signed off A1*

🚐 🚐 ▲

Open Mar-8 Jan (rs 1-22 Dec site open wknds only) Last arrival 23.00hrs Last departure noon

A pleasant park set in 250 acres of unspoilt countryside. The touring and static areas of this large park are in separate areas. The main touring area occupies an open, level position, and the toilet facilities are modern and exceptionally well maintained. The park boasts a well-stocked fishing loch, a heated indoor swimming pool, steam room, sauna, jacuzzi, mini-gym and fitness room and seasonal entertainment. A superb new family toilet block opened in 2010. A 250 acre site with 100 touring pitches, 45 hardstandings and 500 statics.

AA Pubs & Restaurants nearby: Macdonald Marine Hotel & Spa, North Berwick 0870 400 8129

Leisure: 🏊🅰🔍🖵
Facilities: 🚿☺🅿✳♿☺🐕🎯
Services: 🚽🔋🍺🎣🖤🍽️🛒🎪🚮
Within 3 miles: 🎣☺🎮
Notes: Wi-fi

see advert on opposite page

▶▶▶ 74% *Belhaven Bay Caravan & Camping Park*

(NT661781)

Belhaven Bay EH42 1TS
☎ 01368 865956 📠 01368 865022
e-mail: belhaven@meadowhead.co.uk
dir: *From A1 onto A1087 towards Dunbar. Site (1m) in John Muir Park*

Open Mar-13 Oct Last arrival 20.00hrs Last departure noon

Small, well-maintained park in a sheltered location and within walking distance of the beach. This is an excellent spot for seabird watching, and there is a good rail connection with Edinburgh from Dunbar. A new children's play area and additional electric hook-ups were added in 2010. A 40 acre site with 52 touring pitches, 11 hardstandings and 64 statics.

AA Pubs & Restaurants nearby: Macdonald Marine Hotel & Spa, North Berwick 0870 400 8129

Leisure: ⚙
Facilities: ⚙⊙🅿✳♿🕐🖥🎯🚿🚻
Services: ⚡🛒🅃♨
Within 3 miles: ⚙🅿◎♨🐕🛒🅱U

Notes: Dogs must be kept on leads at all times. Internet café. Wi-fi

---

LONGNIDDRY   Map 21 NT47

Places to visit
Crichton Castle, Crichton, 01875 320017, www.historic-scotland.gov.uk

 66% *Seton Sands Holiday Village*

(NT420759)

EH32 0QF
☎ 01875 813333 📠 01875 813531
e-mail: lee.mckay@bourne-leisure.co.uk
dir: *A1 to A198 exit, then B6371 to Cockenzie. Right onto B1348. Site 1m on right*

Open mid Mar-Oct (rs mid Mar-May & Sep-Oct some facilities may be reduced) Last arrival 22.00hrs Last departure 10.00hrs

A well-equipped holiday centre with plenty of organised entertainment, clubs and bars, restaurants, and sports and leisure facilities. A multi-sports court, heated swimming pool, and various play areas ensure that there is plenty to do, and there is lots to see and do in and around Edinburgh which is nearby. The good touring facilities are separate from the large static areas. A 1.75 acre site with 38 touring pitches and 635 statics.

AA Pubs & Restaurants nearby: La Potinière, Gullane 01620 843214

Leisure: ⚙⚙🏊   **Facilities:** ⚙⊙🅿♿🅱
Services: ⚡🛒🅃🚽🍽♨🛒
Within 3 miles: ⚙🅱🛒U

Notes: Dogs not allowed at peak periods, but at other times max 2 dogs per pitch, certain dog breeds banned. Wi-fi

---

MUSSELBURGH   Map 21 NT37

Places to visit
Dalmeny House, South Queensferry, 0131 331 1888, www.dalmeny.co.uk

Lauriston Castle, Edinburgh, 0131 336 2060, www.cac.org.uk

▶▶▶▶ 81% **Drum Mohr Caravan Park** *(NT373734)*

Levenhall EH21 8JS
☎ 0131 665 6867 📠 0131 653 6859
e-mail: admin@drummohr.org
web: www.drummohr.org
dir: *Exit A1 at A199 junct through Wallyford, at rdbt onto B1361 signed Prestonpans. 1st left, site 400yds*

⚙ £18-£21 ⚙ £18-£21 ▲ £18-£21

Open all year (rs Winter arrivals by arrangement) Last arrival 17.00hrs Last departure noon

This attractive park is sheltered by mature trees on all sides, and carefully landscaped within. The park is divided into separate areas by mature hedging and planting of trees and ornamental shrubs. Pitches are generous in size, and there are

continued

MUSSELBURGH *continued*

a number of fully serviced pitches plus first-class amenities. There are five new bothys for hire and seasonal touring pitches are available. A 9 acre site with 120 touring pitches, 50 hardstandings and 12 statics.

AA Pubs & Restaurants nearby: The Kitchen, Leith, Edinburgh 0131 555 1755

Plumed Horse, Leith 0131 554 5556

The Vintners Rooms, Leith 0131 554 6767

Leisure: ⚙ **Facilities:** 🚿⊙🅿✳🐕🅾🛁🚻🪑 **Services:** 🔌🔳🛢🚰🕥🅃🚮🛒⚡ **Within 3 miles:** 🎣🏊🛎🖥

Notes: Max of 2 dogs per pitch, dogs must be kept on leads. Freshly baked bread & croissants, tea & coffee in high season. Wi-fi

---

FIFE

LUNDIN LINKS   Map 21 NO40

Places to visit

Kellie Castle and Gardens, Kellie Castle and Gardens, 0844 493 2184, www.nts.org.uk

▶▶▶ **82% Woodland Gardens Caravan & Camping Site** *(NO418031)*

Blindwell Rd KY8 5QG
☎ 01333 360319
e-mail: enquiries@woodland-gardens.co.uk
dir: *Off A915 (coast road) at Largo at E end of Lundin Links, turn N off A915, 0.5m signed*

* 🚐 £15-£18 🚐 £15-£18 🛆 £12-£18

Open Apr-Oct Last arrival 21.00hrs Last dep noon

A secluded and sheltered little jewel of a site in a small orchard under the hill called Largo Law. This very attractive site is family owned and run to an immaculate standard, and pitches are grouped in twos and threes by low hedging and gorse. Six seasonal touring pitches are available. A 1 acre site with 20 touring pitches, 6 hardstandings and 5 statics.

AA Pubs & Restaurants nearby: Crusoe Hotel, Lower Largo 01333 320759

Inn at Lathones, Largoward 01334 840494

The Orangery at Balbirnie House, Markinch 01592 610066

Leisure: 🎱🛝 **Facilities:** 🚿⊙🅿✳🎣🐕 **Services:** 🔌🛢🚿🚰 **Within 3 miles:** 🎣🏊🛎🖥U

Notes: Adults only 🐾

ST ANDREWS   Map 21 NO51

Places to visit

Castle and Visitor Centre, St. Andrews, 01334 477196

British Golf Museum, St. Andrews, 01334 460046, www.britishgolfmuseum.co.uk

Great for kids: St. Andrews Aquarium, St. Andrews, 01334 474786, www.standrewsaquarium.co.uk

---

PREMIER PARK

▶▶▶▶▶ **91% Craigtoun Meadows Holiday Park** *(NO482150)*

Mount Melville KY16 8PQ
☎ 01334 475959   🖷 01334 476424
e-mail: craigtoun@aol.com
web: www.craigtounmeadows.co.uk
dir: *M90 junct 8, A91 to St Andrews. Just after Guardbridge right for Strathkinness. At 2nd x-rds left for Craigtoun*

* 🚐 £21-£27.50 🚐 £21-£27.50 🛆 £18

Open 15 Mar-Oct (rs Mar-Etr & Sep-Oct no shop & restaurant open shorter hours) Last arrival 21.00hrs Last departure 11.00hrs

An attractive site set unobtrusively in mature woodlands, with large pitches in spacious hedged paddocks. All pitches are fully serviced, and there are also some patio pitches and a summerhouse containing picnic tables and chairs. The modern toilet block provides cubicled en suite facilities as well as spacious showers, baths, disabled facilities and baby changing areas. The licensed restaurant and coffee shop are popular, and there is a takeaway, a launderette, and indoor and outdoor games areas. Located near the sea and sandy beaches. Three seasonal touring pitches are available. A 32 acre site with 57 touring pitches, 57 hardstandings and 166 statics.

AA Pubs & Restaurants nearby: Jigger Inn, St Andrews 01334 474371

Inn at Lathones, Largoward 01334 840494

Leisure: 🎱🎣
Facilities: 🛁🚿⊙🅿🎣🅾🚻🍴🅿
Services: 🔌🛢🍴🚰🛒🚮⚡
Within 3 miles: 🎣🏇🖥⊙🏊🛎🖥U

Notes: No groups of unaccompanied minors, no pets. Putting green, football pitch

---

HIGHLAND

ARISAIG   Map 22 NM68

▶▶▶▶ **77% Camusdarach Campsite** *(NM664916)*

Camusdarach PH39 4NT
☎ 01687 450221
e-mail: asimpson@camusdarach.com
dir: *On B8008, 4m N of Arisaig. Exit A830 at Arisaig, follow coast road*

* 🚐 £19 🚐 £19 🛆 £14

Open 15 Mar-15 Oct Last arrival 21.00hrs Last departure 18.00hrs

A very attractive, quiet and secluded park with direct access to a silver beach. The striking scenery and coastal setting are certainly part of the appeal here, and the superbly designed and equipped toilet block is a pleasure to use. The site is four miles from the Arisaig ferry, and six miles from the Mallaig ferry to the Isle of Skye. There are new hardstandings and the site has Wi-fi. A 2.8 acre site with 42 touring pitches, 6 hardstandings.

AA Pubs & Restaurants nearby: Cnoc-na-Faire, Arisaig 01687 450249

Facilities: 🚿⊙🅿✳🐕 **Services:** 🔌🛢🚰🕥⚡ **Within 3 miles:** 🎣🏊🖥🖥

Notes: Baby changing facilities. Wi-fi

BALMACARA   Map 22 NG82

Places to visit

Balmacara Estate and Lochalsh Woodland Garden, Balmacara, 0844 493 2233, www.nts.org.uk

▶▶▶ **76% Reraig Caravan Site** *(NG815272)*

IV40 8DH
☎ 01599 566215
e-mail: warden@reraig.com
dir: *On A87 3.5m E of Kyle, 2m W of junct with A890*

* 🚐 £14.30 🚐 £14.30 🛆 £12.50

Open May-Sep Last arrival 22.00hrs Last departure noon

Set on level, grassy ground surrounded by trees, the site is located on the saltwater Sound of Sleet, and looks south towards Loch Alsh and Skye. Very nicely organised with a high standard of maintenance, and handy for the bridge crossing to the Isle of Skye. A 2 acre site with 45 touring pitches, 34 hardstandings.

AA Pubs & Restaurants nearby: Waterside Seafood Restaurant, Kyle of Lochalsh 01599 534813

Plockton Inn & Seafood Restaurant, Plockton 01599 544222

Facilities: ⚑ ⊙ ☏ 🖳   **Services:** 🖳 ⬇

Within 3 miles: 🖳

Notes: No awnings Jul & Aug. Only small tents permitted. Ramp access to block

CORPACH   Map 22 NN07

Places to visit

West Highland Museum, Fort William, 01397 702169, www.westhighlandmuseum.org.uk

---

AA Campsite of the Year for Scotland 2011

PREMIER PARK

▶▶▶▶▶ 85% Linnhe Lochside Holidays *(NN074771)*

GOLD

PH33 7NL

☎ 01397 772376 🖷 01397 772007

e-mail: relax@linnhe-lochside-holidays.co.uk

dir: On A830, 1m W of Corpach

🖳 🚐 Å

Open Etr-Oct Last arrival 21.00hrs Last dep 11.00hrs

An excellently maintained site in a beautiful setting on the shores of Loch Eil, with Ben Nevis to the east and the mountains and Sunart to the west. The owners have worked in harmony with nature to produce an idyllic environment, where the highest standards of design and maintenance are evident. A 5.5 acre site with 85 touring pitches, 63 hardstandings and 20 statics.

AA Pubs & Restaurants nearby: Lime Tree Hotel & Restaurant, Fort William 01397 701806

Leisure: ⚠ **Facilities:** ⬅ ⚑ ⊙ ☏ ✳ ⚿ ⊙ 🖳 🖳 🎾 ⚑

Services: 🖳 ⊞ 🛢 ⌀ T ⚏ ⬇

Within 3 miles: ⬇ ✎ ⊙ 🖳

Notes: No cars by tents. Slipway, free fishing

DORNOCH   Map 23 NH78

Places to visit

Dunrobin Castle, Golspie, 01408 633177, www.dunrobincastle.co.uk

77% Grannie's Heilan Hame Holiday Park

(NH818924)

SILVER

Embo IV25 3QD

☎ 0844 335 3756 🖷 01862 810368

e-mail: touringandcamping@parkdeanholidays.com

web: www.parkdeantouring.com

dir: A949 to Dornoch, left in square. Follow Embo signs

🖳 £14.50-£31 🚐 £14.50-£31 Å £12.50-£27

Open Mar-Oct Last arrival 21.00hrs Last departure 10.00hrs

A holiday park on the Highland coast, with a wide range of leisure facilities, including indoor swimming pool with sauna and solarium, spa bath, separate play areas, crazy golf, tennis courts and very much more. The sanitary facilities are clean and well maintained, and there is a family pub and entertainment. A 60 acre site with 160 touring pitches and 262 statics.

AA Pubs & Restaurants nearby: Dornach Castle Hotel, Dornoch 01862 810216

Leisure: ⚑ ⚠ ⚽ ⚲

Facilities: ⚑ ⊙ ☏ ✳ ⚿ ⊙ 🖳 🐎

Services: 🖳 ⊞ 🍴 🛢 ⌀ T ⏝ ⚏ 🍔

Within 3 miles: ⬇ ✎ ⊙ 🖳 ⊞

Notes: Children's clubs, mini ten-pin bowling, family entertainment, sauna & solarium. Wi-fi

see advert in preliminary section

DUROR   Map 22 NM95

NEW ▶▶▶ 78% Achindarroch Touring Park *(NM997554)*

PA38 4BS

☎ 01631 740329 & 07739 554813

e-mail: stay@achindarrochtp.co.uk

dir: A82 onto A828 at Ballachulish Bridge then towards Oban for 5.2m. In Duror site on left, signed

🖳 🚐 Å

Open Mar-Oct & 15 Dec-15 Jan Last departure 11.00hrs

A long established, well-laid out park which is being up-graded to a high standard by an enthusiastic and friendly family team. There is a well-appointed heated toilet block and spacious all-weather pitches. The park is well placed for visits to the attractions of Oban, Fort William and Glencoe. A wide variety of outdoor sports is available in the area. Five seasonal touring pitches are available. A 5 acre site with 40 touring pitches, 21 hardstandings.

Facilities: ⚑ ⊙ ☏ ⚿ ⚑ ⚑

Services: 🖳 ⊞ 🛢 ⌀ ⚏ ⬇

Within 3 miles: ✎ 🖳 ∪

Notes: Groups by appointment only. Campers' kitchen, freezer, toaster, kettle, microwave. Wi-fi

---

FORT WILLIAM

Places to visit

West Highland Museum, Fort William, 01397 702169, www.westhighlandmuseum.org.uk

Great for kids: Inverlochy Castle, Fort William, www.historic-scotland.gov.uk

---

FORT WILLIAM   Map 22 NN17

See also Corpach

▶▶▶▶ **85%** *Glen Nevis Caravan & Camping Park*

(NN124722)

Glen Nevis PH33 6SX
☎ **01397 702191** ▤ **01397 703904**
e-mail: holidays@glen-nevis.co.uk
web: www.glen-nevis.co.uk
dir: *On northern outskirts of Fort William follow A82 to mini-rdbt. Exit for Glen Nevis. Site 2.5m on right*

🚐 🚙 ⛺

Open 13 Mar-9 Nov (rs Mar & mid Oct-Nov limited shop & restaurant facilities) Last arrival 22.00hrs Last departure noon

A tasteful site with well-screened enclosures, at the foot of Ben Nevis in the midst of some of the most spectacular Highland scenery; an ideal area for walking and touring. The park boasts a restaurant which offers a high standard of cooking and provides good value for money. A 30 acre site with 380 touring pitches, 150 hardstandings and 30 statics.

AA Pubs & Restaurants nearby: Inverlochy Castle Hotel, Fort William 01397 702177

Moorings Hotel, Fort William 01397 772797

Lime Tree Hotel & Restaurant, Fort William 01397 701806

Leisure: 🅰

Facilities: 🅵 ⊙ 🅵 ✳ ⅄ 🅾 🅱 🎋 🐕 🐾

Services: 🚐 🅾 🍴 🅱 🖉 🅃 🍽 🎋 🖤 ⑊

Within 3 miles: ⅃ 🎋 🖉 🅱 🅾

Notes: Quiet 23.00hrs-08.00hrs

see advert below

GAIRLOCH   Map 22 NG87

Places to visit

Gairloch Heritage Museum, Gairloch, 01445 712287, www.gairlochheritagemuseum.org

Inverewe Garden, Poolewe, 0844 493 2225, www.nts.org.uk

AA CAMPING CARD SITE

▶▶▶ **78%** *Gairloch Caravan Park*

(NG798773)

Strath IV21 2BX
☎ **01445 712373**
e-mail: info@gairlochcaravanpark.com
dir: *From A832 take B8021 signed Melvaig towards Strath. In 0.5m turn right, just after Millcroft Hotel. Immediately right again*

🚐 🚙 ⛺

Open Etr-Oct Last arrival 21.00hrs Last dep noon

A clean, well-maintained site on flat coastal grassland close to Loch Gairloch. The owners and managers are hard working and well organised and continued investment in recent years has seen significant improvements around the park, including new hardstandings, good shrub and flower planting, better attention to detail, and the building of a new bunkhouse that provides accommodation for families. Six seasonal touring pitches are available. A 6 acre site with 70 touring pitches, 13 hardstandings.

AA Pubs & Restaurants nearby: Old Inn, Gairloch 01445 712006

Badachro Inn, Badachro 01445 741255

Facilities: 🅵 ⊙ 🅵 ✳ ⑊ 🅾

Services: 🚐 🅾 🅃 🎋

Within 3 miles: ⅃ 🖉 ⊚ 🖤 🅱 🅾 ∪

Notes: Dogs must be kept on leads at all times. 4 bed bunkhouse with kitchen facilities. Wi-fi

GLENCOE

Places to visit

Glencoe and Dalness, Glencoe, 0844 493 2222, www.nts.org.uk

Great for kids: Glencoe and North Lorn Folk Museum, Glencoe, 01855 811664, www.glencoefolkmuseum.com

LEISURE: 🖥 Indoor swimming pool 🏊 Outdoor swimming pool 🅰 Children's playground 🎾 Tennis court 🎮 Games room 📺 Separate TV room ⛳ 9/18 hole golf course 🚣 Boats for hire ⌗ Cinema 🎣 Fishing ⊚ Mini golf 🏄 Watersports ∪ Stables **FACILITIES:** 🛁 Bath 🅵 Shower ⊙ Electric shaver 🖉 Hairdryer ✳ Ice Pack Facility 🅾 Disabled facilities 🕓 Public telephone 🅱 Shop on site or within 200yds 🚚 Mobile shop (calls at least 5 days a week) 🍴 BBQ area 🌲 Picnic area 🐾 Dog exercise area

GLENCOE
Map 22 NN15

►►►► 79% Invercoe Caravan & Camping Park *(NN098594)*

PH49 4HP
☎ 01855 811210 🖹 01855 811210
e-mail: holidays@invercoe.co.uk
web: www.invercoe.co.uk
dir: *Exit A82 at Glencoe Hotel onto B863 for 0.25m*

* 🚐 fr £20 🚏 fr £20 ▲ fr £20

Open all year Last departure noon

A level grass site set on the shore of Loch Leven, with excellent mountain views. The area is ideal for both walking and climbing, and also offers a choice of several freshwater and saltwater lochs. Convenient for the good shopping in Fort William. A 5 acre site with 60 touring pitches and 4 statics.

AA Pubs & Restaurants nearby: Loch Leven Hotel, North Balluchulish 01855 821236

The Restaurant at Onich Hotel, Onich 01855 821214

Leisure: 🅰 **Facilities:** 🌣⊙℗✳🕭🕒🖢🐕🚻
Services: 🔌🗑🛢🖉⊤🎇🖢
Within 3 miles: ⬆🌣🖉🖥🗑
Notes: No large group bookings

JOHN O'GROATS
Map 23 ND37

Places to visit
The Castle and Gardens of Mey, Thurso, 01847 851473, www.castleofmey.org.uk

►►► 76% John O'Groats Caravan Site *(ND382733)*

KW1 4YR
☎ 01955 611329 & 07762 336359
e-mail: info@johnogroatscampsite.co.uk
dir: *At end of A99*

* 🚐 £15-£17 🚏 £15-£17 ▲ £11-£17

Open Apr-Sep Last arrival 22.00hrs Last departure 11.00hrs

An attractive site in an open position above the seashore and looking out towards the Orkney Islands. Nearby is the passenger ferry that makes day trips to the Orkneys, and there are grey seals to watch, and sea angling can be organised by the site owners. A 4 acre site with 90 touring pitches, 30 hardstandings.

Facilities: 🌣⊙℗✳🕭🕒🖢
Services: 🔌🗑🛢🖉🎇🖢
Within 3 miles: 🖉🖥🗑 **Notes:** 🐕

LAIRG
Map 23 NC50

►►► 70% *Dunroamin Caravan and Camping Park* *(NC585062)*

Main St IV27 4AR
☎ 01549 402447 🖹 01549 402784
e-mail: enquiries@lairgcaravanpark.co.uk
dir: *300mtrs from centre of Lairg on S side of A839*

🚐🚏▲

Open Apr-Oct Last arrival 21.00hrs Last dep noon

An attractive little park with clean and functional facilities, adjacent to a licensed restaurant. The park is close to the lower end of Loch Shin, and a short distance from the town. A 4 acre site with 40 touring pitches, 8 hardstandings and 9 statics.

Facilities: 🌣⊙℗✳🕒🖢
Services: 🔌🗑🛢🖉⊤🎇🖢🍴
Within 3 miles: ✳🖉🖥🗑
Notes: No vehicles to be driven on site between 21.00hrs-07.00hrs

►►► 63% Woodend Caravan & Camping Site *(NC551127)*

Achnairn IV27 4DN
☎ 01549 402248 🖹 01549 402248
dir: *4m N of Lairg off A836 onto A838, signed at Achnairn*

🚐🚏▲

Open Apr-Sep Last arrival 23.00hrs

A clean, simple site set in hilly moors and woodland with access to Loch Shin. The area is popular with fishing and boating enthusiasts, and there is a choice of golf courses within 30 miles. A spacious campers' kitchen is a useful amenity. A 4 acre site with 55 touring pitches.

Leisure: 🅰 **Facilities:** 🌣⊙℗✳
Services: 🔌🗑 **Within 3 miles:** ✳🖉🗑
Notes: 🐕

NAIRN
Map 23 NH85

Places to visit
Sueno's Stone, Forres, 01667 460232, www.historic-scotland.gov.uk

Dallas Dhu Distillery, Forres, 01309 676548, www.historic-scotland.gov.uk

Great for kids: Brodie Castle, Brodie Castle, 0844 493 2156, www.nts.org.uk

74% Nairn Lochloy Holiday Park *(NH895574)*

East Beach IV12 5DE
☎ 0844 335 3756 🖹 01667 454721
e-mail: touringandcamping@parkdeanholidays.com
web: www.parkdeantouring.com
dir: *In Nairn, just off Fast Beach. On entering Nairn follow road until Bridgemill Direct shop, turn left before shop & follow signs to park*

🚐 £16.50-£35.50 🚏 £16.50-£35.50
▲ £13.50-£31.50

Open Mar-Oct Last arrival 21.00hrs Last departure 10.00hrs

A small touring site situated within a popular holiday park with a wide range of leisure facilities including heated pool, sauna, spa bath, children's play-area and clubs, crazy golf, amusements, bars, restaurant and mini supermarket. A small, well-maintained toilet block exclusively serves the touring area where all pitches have electricity. Handily placed in the centre of Nairn, only minutes from the beach and within striking distance of Inverness and the Highlands. A 15 acre site with 13 touring pitches and 280 statics.

AA Pubs & Restaurants nearby: Cawdor Tavern, Cawdor 01667 404777

Leisure: 🏊🅰🎯 **Facilities:** 🖢🌣⊙℗🕭🕒🖢
Services: 🔌🗑🍺🖉🍴🖢
Within 3 miles: ⬆🖉◎🌣🖥🗑🅾
Notes: Family entertainment. Wi-fi
see advert in preliminary section

ULLAPOOL — Map 22 NH19

▶▶▶ 70% Broomfield Holiday Park

(NH123939)

West Shore St IV26 2UT
☎ 01854 612020 & 612664 📠 01854 613151
e-mail: sross@broomfieldhp.com
web: www.broomfieldhp.com
dir: *Take 2nd right past harbour*

* 🚐 £16-£17 � £15-£16 ▲ £8-£16

Open Etr/Apr-Sep Last departure noon

Set right on the water's edge of Loch Broom and the open sea, with lovely views of the Summer Isles. The clean, well maintained and managed park is close to the harbour and town centre with their restaurants, bars and shops. A 12 acre site with 140 touring pitches.

AA Pubs & Restaurants nearby: The Ceilidh Place, Ullapool 01854 612103

Leisure: ⋀

Facilities: ⋔☉✳⌖👌🖻🖻🎠

Services: 🚐🖥📥⚡

Within 3 miles: 🎣🌐🖻🖥

Notes: Pets must be kept on leads, no noise at night

MORAY

ABERLOUR — Map 23 NJ24

Places to visit

Balvenie Castle, Dufftown, 01340 820121, www.historic-scotland.gov.uk

AA CAMPING CARD SITE

▶▶▶ 78% Aberlour Gardens Caravan Park

(NJ282434)

AB38 9LD
☎ 01340 871586 📠 01340 871586
e-mail: info@aberlourgardens.co.uk
dir: *Midway between Aberlour & Craigellachie on A95 turn onto unclass road. Site signed. (NB vehicles over 10' 6" use A941 Dufftown to Craigellachie road where park is signed)*

🚐 £16.60-£20.75 � £16.60-£20.75
▲ £13.15-£20.75

Open Mar-27 Dec Last arrival 19.00hrs Last departure noon

This attractive parkland site is set in the five-acre walled garden of the Victorian Aberlour House, surrounded by the full range of spectacular scenery from the Cairngorm National Park, through pine clad glens, to the famous Moray coastline; the park is also well placed for the world renowned Speyside Malt Whiskey Trail. It offers a small, well-appointed toilet block, laundry and small licensed shop. A 5 acre site with 34 touring pitches, 16 hardstandings and 32 statics.

AA Pubs & Restaurants nearby: Craigellachie Hotel, Craigellachie 01340 881204

Archiestown Hotel, Archiestown 01340 810218

Leisure: ⋀ **Facilities:** ⋔☉ℱ✳⌖👌⏰🖻

Services: 🚐🖥🚰⚡Ⓣ⚡

Within 3 miles: 🎣🌐🖻🖥

Notes: Pets must be kept on leads, no ball games, max 5mph speed limit, no noise after 23.00hrs. Wi-fi

---

ALVES — Map 23 NJ16

Places to visit

Pluscarden Abbey, Elgin, 01343 890257, www.pluscardenabbey.org

Elgin Museum, Elgin, 01343 543675, www.elginmuseum.org.uk

Great for kids: Duffus Castle, Duffus, 01667 460232, www.historic-scotland.gov.uk

▶▶▶ 68% *North Alves Caravan Park*

(NJ122633)

IV30 8XD
☎ 01343 850223
dir: *1m W of A96, halfway between Elgin & Forres. Site signed on right*

🚐 � ▲

Open Apr-Oct Last arrival 23.00hrs Last departure noon

A quiet rural site in attractive rolling countryside within three miles of a good beach. The site is on a former farm, and the stone buildings are quite unspoilt. A 10 acre site with 45 touring pitches and 45 statics.

Leisure: ⋀⚊⌗

Facilities: ⋔☉ℱ✳⏰🖻🎠

Services: 🚐🖥🚰⚡Ⓣ📥

Within 3 miles: 🎣⛳🎋ℱ🖥⛴

CULLEN — Map 23 NJ56

▶▶▶ 83% Cullen Bay Holiday Park

(NJ516674)

Logie Head AB56 4TW
☎ 01542 840766
e-mail: enquiries@cullenbay.co.uk
web: www.cullenbayholidaypark.co.uk
dir: *From Portsoy on A98 into Cullen, 1st right into Seafield Street, site at end of road*

* 🚐 £15.80-£19.20 � £15.80-£19.20

Open Apr-Oct Last arrival 21.30hrs Last departure noon

A cliff top site with fine views over the small Scottish fishing port of Cullen. The site is well maintained, and offers a modern and well appointed toilet block with full disabled facilities and a good laundry. It is well placed for accessing the north-east coastline with its small and picturesque fishing ports and dolphin colonies offshore and is but a short distance from the Speyside Malt Whisky Trail. Please note that tents

---

are no longer accepted. A 4 acre site with 12 touring pitches, 7 hardstandings and 40 statics.

AA Pubs & Restaurants nearby: Cullen Bay Hotel, Cullen 01542 840432

Facilities:

Services:

Within 3 miles:

Notes: Wi-fi

FOCHABERS Map 23 NJ35

Places to visit

Strathisla Distillery, Keith, 01542 783044, www.chivas.com

Glengrant Distillery, Rothes, 01340 832118, www.glengrant.com

►►► 76% Burnside Caravan Park

(NJ350580)

IV32 7ET

☎ 01343 820511 01343 820511

e-mail: burnside7et@googlemail.com

dir: *0.5m E of town off A96*

* fr £20 fr £20 £10-£30

Open Mar-Nov Last departure noon

Attractive site in a tree-lined, sheltered valley with a footpath to the village. Owned by the garden centre on the opposite side of the A96, it has seen significant investment and improvements following serious flood damage. New, fully serviced pitches have been created and there is a new camping area for 20 tents, all with water and electricity. A 5 acre site with 51 touring pitches, 36 hardstandings and 101 statics.

AA Pubs & Restaurants nearby: Gordon Arms Hotel, Fochabers 01343 820508

Leisure:

Facilities:

Services:

Within 3 miles:

Notes: Jacuzzi & sauna. Wi-fi

LOSSIEMOUTH Map 23 NJ27

Places to visit

Elgin Cathedral, Elgin, 01343 547171, www.historic-scotland.gov.uk

►►►► 75% Silver Sands Leisure Park *(NJ205710)*

Covesea, West Beach IV31 6SP

☎ 01343 813262 01343 815205

e-mail: enquiries@silver-sands.co.uk

dir: *From Lossiemouth follow B9040, 2m W to site*

* £15-£24 £15-£24 £11.50-£20

Open 15 Feb-15 Jan (rs 15 Feb-Jun & Oct-15 Jan shops & entertainment restricted) Last arrival 22.00hrs Last departure noon

A large holiday park with entertainment during the peak season, set on the links beside the shore of the Moray Firth. Touring campers and caravans are catered for in three areas: one offers de-luxe, fully-serviced facilities, while the others are either unserviced or include electric hook-ups and water. There's a well-stocked shop, a clubroom and bar, and takeaway food outlet. A 60 acre site with 140 touring pitches, 30 hardstandings and 200 statics.

Leisure:

Facilities:

Services:

Within 3 miles:

Notes: Over 14yrs only in bar. Children's entertainment

Not all campsites accept pets. It is advisable to check at the time of booking

NORTH AYRSHIRE

SALTCOATS Map 20 NS24

Places to visit

North Ayrshire Museum, Saltcoats, 01294 464174, www.north-ayrshire.gov.uk/museums

Kelburn Castle and Country Centre, Largs, 01475 568685, www.kelburnstate.com

Great for kids: Scottish Maritime Museum, Irvine, 01294 278283, www.scottishmaritimemuseum.org

73% Sandylands

(NS258412)

James Miller Crescent, Auchenharvie Park KA21 5JN

☎ 0871 664 9767

e-mail: sandylands@park-resorts.com

dir: *From Glasgow take M77 & A77 to Kilmarnock, A71 towards Irvine. Follow signs for Ardrossan. Take A78 follow Stevenston signs. Through Stevenston, past Auchenharvie Leisure Centre, 1st left follow signs to site on left*

Open Apr-Oct Last arrival mdnt Last departure noon

Sandylands is an all action holiday centre with plenty of on-site leisure and recreational activities for the whole family. Off park, there is a links golf course adjacent, and trips to the Isle of Arran from the nearby Ardrossan. 20 touring pitches, 20 hardstandings and 438 statics.

Leisure:

Facilities:

Services:

Within 3 miles:

Notes: Wi-fi

NORTH LANARKSHIRE

MOTHERWELL   Map 21 NS75

Places to visit

Motherwell Heritage Centre, Motherwell, 01698 251000, www.northlan.gov.uk

Bothwell Castle, Bothwell, 01698 816894, www.historic-scotland.gov.uk

Great for kids: National Museum of Rural Life in Scotland, East Kilbride, 0131 225 7534, www.nms.ac.uk/rural

▶▶▶ **76% Strathclyde Country Park Caravan Site** (*NS717585*)

366 Hamilton Rd ML1 3ED
☎ **01698 402060** 📠 **01698 252925**
e-mail: strathclydepark@northlan.gov.uk
dir: *From M74 junct 5, direct access to site*

** 🚐 fr £11.20 🚙 fr £11.20 ▲ £5-£9.50

Open Apr-Oct Last arrival 22.30hrs Last departure noon

An attractive landscaped site situated in a country park amidst woodland and meadowland with lots of attractions. A large grass area caters for 150 tents, while 100 well-screened pitches, with electrics and some hardstandings, are also available. 150 touring pitches.

Leisure: 🅰

Facilities: 🌣⊙📻&🕐📷🖐🏻🐕🖐

Services: 🚐🗄🔋🖊🍴🎡

Within 3 miles: ↥⚡🎯🕳️/◎⛵🅿🛒🛍U

Notes: Site rules available on request by post

see advert below

PERTH & KINROSS

BLAIR ATHOLL

Places to visit

Blair Castle, Blair Atholl, 01796 481207, www.blair-castle.co.uk

Killiecrankie Visitor Centre, Killiecrankie, 0844 493 2194, www.nts.org.uk

BLAIR ATHOLL   Map 23 NN86

PREMIER PARK

▶▶▶▶▶ 81% *River Tilt Caravan Park* (*NN875653*)

PH18 5TE
☎ **01796 481467** 📠 **01796 481511**
e-mail: stuart@rivertilt.co.uk
dir: *7m N of Pitlochry on A9, take B8079 to Blair Atholl & site at rear of Tilt Hotel*

🚐🚙▲

Open 16 Mar-12 Nov Last arrival 21.00hrs Last departure noon

An attractive park with magnificent views of the surrounding mountains, idyllically set in hilly woodland country on the banks of the River Tilt, next to the golf course. Fully-serviced pitches are available, and the park boasts its own bistro and restaurant. There is also a leisure complex with heated indoor swimming pool, sun lounge area, spa pool and multi-gym, all available for an extra charge; outdoors there is a short tennis court. The toilet facilities are very good. A 2 acre site with 30 touring pitches and 69 statics.

AA Pubs & Restaurants nearby: Killiecrankie House Hotel, Killicrankie 01796 473220

Moulin Hotel, Pitlochry 01796 472196

Leisure: 🏊♨

Facilities: 🌣⊙📻✳🕐📷🖐

Services: 🚐🗄🍽🔋🖊🍴

Within 3 miles: ↥/◎🅿🛒🛍U

Notes: Sauna, solarium, steam room

PREMIER PARK

▶▶▶▶▶ 80% Blair Castle Caravan Park (NN874656)

PH18 5SR
☎ 01796 481263 📠 01796 481587
e-mail: mail@blaircastlecaravanpark.co.uk
dir: *From A9 junct with B8079 at Aldclune, then NE to Blair Atholl. Site on right after crossing bridge in village*

🚐 £16-£19 🚙 £16-£19 ▲ £16-£19

Open Mar-Nov Last arrival 21.30hrs Last departure noon

An attractive site set in impressive seclusion within the Atholl estate, surrounded by mature woodland and the River Tilt. Although a large park, the various groups of pitches are located throughout the extensive parkland, and each has its own sanitary block with all-cubicled facilities of a very high standard. There is a choice of grass pitches, hardstandings, or fully-serviced pitches. This park is particularly suitable for the larger type of motorhome. A 32 acre site with 248 touring pitches and 109 statics.

AA Pubs & Restaurants nearby: Killiecrankie House Hotel, Killicrankie 01796 473220

Moulin Hotel, Pitlochry 01796 472196

Leisure: ⚑ 🎣
Facilities: ⌂ ⌂ ⊙ ℘ ✻ ⚑ ⊙ 🖻 ⩗ ⚐
Services: ⚡ 🖥 ⛽ 🍴 T ⇌ ⚒
Within 3 miles: ⌂ ℘ ⊚ 🖻 🖥 ⛴

Notes: Family park, no noise after 23.00hrs. Internet gallery with broadband access. Wi-fi

---

Places to visit
The Ell Shop and Little Houses, Dunkeld, 0844 4932192, www.nts.org.uk
Castle Menzies, Weem, 01887 820982, www.menzies.org

▶▶▶ 78% Inver Mill Farm Caravan Park (NO015422)

Inver PH8 0JR
☎ 01350 727477 📠 01350 727477
e-mail: invermill@talk21.com
dir: *A9 onto A822 then immediately right to Inver*

🚐 🚙 ▲

Open end Mar-Oct Last arrival 22.00hrs Last departure noon

A peaceful park on level former farmland, located on the banks of the River Braan and surrounded by mature trees and hills. The active resident owners keep the park in very good condition. A 5 acre site with 65 touring pitches.

Facilities: ⌂ ⊙ ℘ ✻ ⚑ ⊙
Services: ⚡ 🖥 ⛽ ⚒ ⇌
Within 3 miles: ⌂ ℘ 🖻 🖥
Notes: ⊛

▶ 67% Kilvrecht Campsite (NN623567)

PH16 5QA
☎ 01350 727284 📠 01350 727811
e-mail: tay.fd@forestry.gsi.gov.uk
dir: *3m along S shore of Loch Rannoch. Approach via unclass road along Loch, with Forestry Commission signs*

* 🚐 fr £6 🚙 fr £6 ▲ fr £6

Open Apr-Oct Last arrival 22.00hrs Last departure 10.00hrs

Set in a remote and beautiful spot in a large forest clearing, about three-quarters of a mile from Loch Rannoch shore. This small and basic

---

campsite has no hot water, but the few facilities are very well maintained. A 17 acre site with 60 touring pitches.

AA Pubs & Restaurants nearby: Dunalistair Hotel, Kinloch Rannoch 01882 632323

Facilities: ⚿ ⩗
Within 3 miles: ⚄ ℘ 🖻
Notes: ⊛ No fires

Places to visit
Edradour Distillery, Pitlochry, 01796 472095, www.edradour.co.uk

Great for kids: Scottish Hydro Electric Visitor Centre, Dam and Fish Pass, Pitlochry, 01796 473152

▶▶▶▶ 80% Milton of Fonab Caravan Site (NN945573)

Bridge Rd PH16 5NA
☎ 01796 472882 📠 01796 474363
e-mail: info@fonab.co.uk
dir: *0.5m S of town off A924*

* 🚐 £16-£19 🚙 £16-£19 ▲ £16

Open Apr-Oct Last arrival 21.00hrs Last departure 13.00hrs

Set on the banks of the River Tummel, with extensive views down the river valley to the mountains, this park is close to the centre of Pitlochry, adjacent to the Pitlochry Festival Theatre. The sanitary facilities are exceptionally good, with most contained in combined shower/wash basin and toilet cubicles. A 15 acre site with 154 touring pitches and 36 statics.

AA Pubs & Restaurants nearby: Moulin Hotel, Pitlochry 01796 472196

Killiecrankie House Hotel, Killicrankie 01796 473220

Facilities: ⌂ ⌂ ⊙ ℘ ✻ ⚑ ⊙ 🖻 ⩗
Services: ⚡ 🖥 ⛽ ⚒
Within 3 miles: ⌂ ⚄ ℘ ⊚ 🖻 🖥

Notes: ⊛ Couples & families only, no motor cycles. Free trout fishing. Wi-fi

---

PITLOCHRY *continued*

▶▶▶▶ 74% *Faskally Caravan Park*

(NN916603)

PH16 5LA
☎ 01796 472007 📄 01796 473896
e-mail: info@faskally.co.uk
dir: *1.5m N of Pitlochry on B8019*

🚐 🚙 ⛺

Open 15 Mar-Oct Last arrival 23.00hrs

A large park attractively divided into sections by mature trees, set in gently-sloping meadowland beside the tree-lined River Garry. The excellent amenities include a leisure complex with heated indoor swimming pool, spa, sauna and steam room, bar, restaurant and indoor amusements. The park is close to, but unaffected by, the A9. A 27 acre site with 300 touring pitches and 130 statics.

AA Pubs & Restaurants nearby: Moulin Hotel, Pitlochry 01796 472196

Leisure: 🏊 🎠 🎯 **Facilities:** ↖ ⊙ ☂ ✳ ♿ 🕐 🛒
Services: 🔌 🛢 💷 🍴 🚿 T 🍽
Within 3 miles: 🎣 🚴 🏌 🛒 ⛴ ⛵ U
Notes: Dogs must be kept on leads

see advert below

AA CAMPING CARD SITE

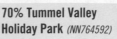 **70% Tummel Valley Holiday Park** *(NN764592)*

PH16 5SA
☎ 0844 335 3756 📄 01882 634302
e-mail: touringandcamping@parkdeanholidays.com
web: www.parkdeantouring.com
dir: *From Perth take A9 N to bypass Pitlochry. 3m after Pitlochry take B8019 signed Tummel Bridge. Site 11m on left*

🚐 🚙

Open Mar-Oct Last arrival 21.00hrs Last departure 10.00hrs

A well-developed site amongst mature forest in an attractive valley, beside the famous bridge on the banks of the River Tummel. Play areas and the bar are sited alongside the river, and there is an indoor pool, children's clubs and live family entertainment. This is an ideal base in which to relax. Please note that this park does not accept tents or trailer tents. A 55 acre site with 34 touring pitches, 34 hardstandings and 159 statics.

AA Pubs & Restaurants nearby: Dunalistair Hotel, Kinloch Rannoch 01882 632323

Moulin Hotel, Pitlochry 01796 472196

Leisure: 🏊 🎠 🎯
Facilities: ↖ ↖ ⊙ ☂ ✳ ♿ 🕐 🛒 ⛲ 🍴
Services: 🔌 🛢 💷 🍴 🍽 ⛲
Within 3 miles: 🚴 ◎ 💷 🛒
Notes: Sports courts, sauna, solarium, toddlers' pool, amusements, rod hire. Wi-fi

see advert in preliminary section

SCOTTISH BORDERS

Places to visit

Manderston, Duns, 01361 883450, www.manderston.co.uk

Great for kids: Eyemouth Museum, Eyemouth, 018907 50678

72% Eyemouth

(NT941646)

Fort Rd TD14 5BE
☎ 0871 664 9740
e-mail: eyemouth@park-resorts.com
dir: *From A1, approx 6m N of Berwick-upon-Tweed take A1107 to Eyemouth. On entering town, site signed. Right after petrol station, left at bottom of hill into Fort Rd*

🚐 🚙

LEISURE: 🏊 Indoor swimming pool 🏊 Outdoor swimming pool 🎠 Children's playground 🎾 Tennis court 🎯 Games room 📺 Separate TV room ⛳ 9/18 hole golf course 🚣 Boats for hire 🎬 Cinema 🎣 Fishing ◎ Mini golf 🏄 Watersports U Stables **FACILITIES:** 🛁 Bath 🚿 Shower ⊙ Electric shaver ☂ Hairdryer ✳ Ice Pack Facility ♿ Disabled facilities 🕐 Public telephone 🛒 Shop on site or within 200yds 🚚 Mobile shop (calls at least 5 days a week) ⛲ BBQ area 🍴 Picnic area 🐕 Dog exercise area

Open Apr-Oct (BH & peak wknds entertainment available) Last arrival mdnt Last departure 11.00hrs

A cliff-top holiday park on the outskirts of the small fishing village of Eyemouth, within easy reach of Edinburgh and Newcastle. The site is handily placed for exploring the beautiful Scottish Borders, and the magnificent coastline and countryside of north Northumberland. A 22 acre site with 17 touring pitches, 7 hardstandings and 242 statics.

Leisure: 🅰️ 🎣
Facilities: 🎣🚻🕐🍴
Services: 🔌🚿🍺🔥🍽️🥤
Within 3 miles: 🎣🚲🏇🎣🎡🚿
Notes: Wi-fi

►►►► 78% Springwood Caravan Park *(NT720334)*

GOLD

TD5 8LS
☎ **01573 224596** 📠 **01573 224033**
e-mail: admin@springwood.biz
dir: *1m E of Kelso on A699, signed Newton St Boswells*
🚐 fr £20 🚏 fr £20

Open 21 Mar-13 Oct Last arrival 23.00hrs Last departure noon

Set in a secluded position on the banks of the tree-lined River Teviot, this well-maintained site enjoys a pleasant and spacious spot in which to relax. It offers a high standard of modern toilet facilities which are mainly contained in cubicled units. Floors Castle and the historic town of Kelso are close by. A 2 acre site with 20 touring pitches, 20 hardstandings and 212 statics.

AA Pubs & Restaurants nearby: Roxburghe Hotel & Golf Course, Kelso 01573 450331

Leisure: 🅰️ 🎣
Facilities: 🎣☺🍴✳️🐕🕐🍴
Services: 🔌🚿🍺🥤
Within 3 miles: 🎣🚲🎡🍴🚿
Notes: Dogs must be kept on leads

►►► 75% Thirlestane Castle Caravan & Camping Site *(NT536473)*

Thirlestane Castle TD2 6RU
☎ **01578 718884** & **07976 231032**
e-mail: thirlestanepark@btconnect.com
dir: *Signed off A68 & A697, just S of Lauder*

* 🚐 £14-£17 🚏 £14-£17 ⛺ £14-£17

Open Apr-1 Oct Last arrival 20.30hrs Last departure noon

Set in the grounds of the impressive Thirlestane Castle, with mainly level grassy pitches. The park and facilities are kept in sparkling condition. A 5 acre site with 60 touring pitches, 17 hardstandings and 24 statics.

AA Pubs & Restaurants nearby: Black Bull, Lauder 01578 722208

Facilities: 🎣☺✳️🕐🍴
Services: 🔌🚿🥤
Within 3 miles: 🎣🚲🍴🚿
Notes: 🚫

►►►► 78% Crossburn Caravan Park *(NT248417)*

Edinburgh Rd EH45 8ED
☎ **01721 720501** 📠 **01721 720501**
e-mail: enquiries@crossburncaravans.co.uk
web: www.crossburncaravans.co.uk
dir: *0.5m N of Peebles on A703*

* 🚐 £20-£22 🚏 £20-£22 ⛺ £18-£20

Open Apr-Oct Last arrival 21.00hrs Last departure 14.00hrs

A peaceful site in a relatively quiet location, despite the proximity of the main road which partly borders the site, as does the Eddleston Water. There are lovely views, and the park is well stocked with trees, flowers and shrubs. Facilities are maintained to a high standard, and fully-serviced pitches are available. A large caravan dealership is on the same site. A 6 acre site with 45 touring pitches, 15 hardstandings and 85 statics.

AA Pubs & Restaurants nearby: Cringletie House, Peebles 01721 725750

Renwicks at Macdonald Cardrona Hotel, Peebles 0844 879 9024

Leisure: 🅰️ 🎣
Facilities: 🍼🎣☺✳️🐕🍴🍴
Services: 🔌🚿🍺🚿🍽️🥤
Within 3 miles: 🎣🚲🍴🚿
Notes: Dogs must be kept on leads

SOUTH AYRSHIRE

AYR
Map 20 NS32

Places to visit

The National Wallace Monument Tower, Stirling, 01786 472140, www.nationalwallacemonument.com

Great for kids: Culzean Castle and Country Park, Culzean Castle, 0844 493 2149, www.nts.org.uk

▶▶▶ **75% Craig Tara Holiday Park** (NS300184)

GOLD

KA7 4LB
☎ 01292 265141 📠 01292 445206
e-mail: donna.moulton@bourne-leisure.co.uk
dir: Take A77 towards Stranraer, then 2nd right after Bankfield rdbt. Follow signs to A719 & to park

🚐 🚏

Open mid Mar-Oct (rs mid Mar-May & Sep-Oct some facilities may be limited) Last arrival 20.00hrs Last departure 10.00hrs

A large, well-maintained holiday centre with on-site entertainment and sporting facilities to suit all ages. The touring area is set apart from the main complex at the entrance to the park, and campers can use all the facilities, including water world, soft play areas, sports zone, show bars, and supermarket with in-house bakery. There is a bus service to Ayr. A 213 acre site with 38 touring pitches, 38 hardstandings and 1100 statics.

AA Pubs & Restaurants nearby: Fouters, Ayr 01292 261391

Fairfield House Hotel, Ayr 01292 267461

Western House Hotel, Ayr 0870 055 5510

Leisure: 🏊 🅰
Facilities: 🚿 ☉ ♿ ⏰ 🏪 🍴
Services: 🔌 🚿 🛢 🍴 ⛽ 🚮
Within 3 miles: ⛳ 🎣 🎯 🎬 🏪 🍴 ⛺

Notes: Max 2 dogs per pitch, certain dog breeds banned. Access to beach from park. Wi-fi

BARRHILL
Map 20 NX28

▶▶▶▶ **78% Barrhill Holiday Park**
(NX216835)

KA26 0PZ
☎ 01465 821355 📠 01465 821355
e-mail: barrhill@surfree.co.uk
dir: On A714 (Newton Stewart to Girvan road). 1m N of Barrhill

🚐 🚏 ⛺

Open Mar-Jan

A small, friendly park in a tranquil rural location, screened from the A714 by trees. The park is terraced and well landscaped, and a high quality amenity block includes disabled facilities. A 6 acre site with 30 touring pitches, 30 hardstandings and 39 statics.

Leisure: 🅰 **Facilities:** 🚿 ☉ 🅿 ❄ ♿ ⏰ 🏪 🐕
Services: 🔌 🚿 🛢 🍴 T **Within 3 miles:** 🎣 🏪
Notes: 🐕

COYLTON
Map 20 NS41

▶▶▶ **78% Sundrum Castle Holiday Park** (NS405208)

GOLD

KA6 5JH
☎ 0844 335 3756 📠 01292 570065
e-mail: touringandcamping@parkdeanholidays.com
web: www.parkdeantouring.com
dir: Just off A70, 4m E of Ayr near Coylton
🚐 £16.50-£29 🚏 £16.50-£29 ⛺ £14.50-£31

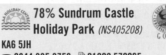

Open Mar-Oct Last arrival 21.00hrs Last departure 10.00hrs

A large family holiday park in rolling countryside, with plenty of on-site entertainment, and just a 10-minute drive from the centre of Ayr. Leisure facilities include an indoor swimming pool complex with flume, crazy golf, clubs for young children and teenagers. The touring pitch areas and amenity block have been upgraded to a high standard. A 30 acre site with 45 touring pitches, 30 hardstandings and 250 statics.

AA Pubs & Restaurants nearby: Browne's at Enterkine, Annbank 01292 520580

Leisure: 🏊 🅰 🎯 📺 **Facilities:** 🚿 ☉ 🅿 ♿ ⏰ 🏪
Services: 🔌 🚿 🍴 🛢 🚮 🍴 🏪
Within 3 miles: ⛳ 🎣 🎬 🏪 🍴 ⛺

Notes: No cars by tents. Adventure play area, nature trail. Wi-fi
see advert in preliminary section

SOUTH LANARKSHIRE

ABINGTON
Map 21 NS92

Places to visit

Moat Park Heritage Centre, Biggar, 01899 221050, www.biggarmuseumtrust.co.uk

Great for kids: National Museum of Rural Life Scotland, East Kilbride, 0131 225 7534, www.nms.ac.uk/rural

▶▶▶ **78% Mount View Caravan Park**
(NS935235)

ML12 6RW
☎ 01864 502808
e-mail: info@mountviewcaravanpark.co.uk
dir: M74 junct 13, A702 S into Abington. Left into Station Rd, over river & railway. Site on right

🚐 🚏 ⛺

Open Mar-Oct

A delightfully maturing family park, surrounded by the Southern Uplands and handily located between Carlisle and Glasgow. It is an excellent stopover site for those travelling between Scotland and the south, and the West Coast Railway passes beside the park. A 5.5 acre site with 51 touring pitches, 51 hardstandings and 20 statics.

Leisure: 🅰 **Facilities:** 🚿 ☉ 🅿 ♿ 🍴
Services: 🔌 🚿 🛢 **Within 3 miles:** 🎣 🏪 🍴

Notes: No cars by tents. Dogs must be kept on leads & walked outside the park. 5mph speed limit. Emergency phone

STIRLING

ABERFOYLE

Places to visit

Inchmahome Priory, Port of Mentieth, 01877 385294, www.historic-scotland.gov.uk

Great for kids: Blair Drummond Safari and Leisure Park, Blair Drummond, 01786 841456, www.blairdrummond.com

---

ABERFOYLE Map 20 NN50

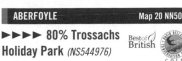

▶▶▶▶ 80% Trossachs Holiday Park *(NS544976)*

FK8 3SA

☎ 01877 382614 📠 01877 382732

e-mail: info@trossachsholidays.co.uk

web: www.trossachsholidays.co.uk

dir: *Access on E side of A81, 1m S of junct A821 & 3m S of Aberfoyle*

* 🚐 £15-£21 🚐 £15-£21 ▲ £14.50-£20.50

Open Mar-Oct Last arrival 21.00hrs Last departure noon

An imaginatively designed terraced site offering a high degree of quality all round, with fine views across Flanders Moss. All touring pitches are fully serviced with water, waste, electricity and TV aerial, and customer care is a main priority. Set grounds within the Queen Elizabeth Forest Park, with plenty of opportunities for cycling off-road on mountain bikes, which can be hired or purchased on site. There are self-catering units including lodges for rental. A 40 acre site with 66 touring pitches, 46 hardstandings and 84 statics.

Leisure: 🅿 🔦 ◨

Facilities: 🔦☉℗⚒☉ⓢ🏧✈

Services: 🔌ⓢ🔋⊤🍴☕

Within 3 miles: ↨↿🎣ⓢⓢ↺

Notes: Groups by prior arrangement only. Wi-fi

see advert below

SERVICES: 🔌 Electric hook up 🅢 Launderette 🍸 Licensed bar 🅐 Calor Gas 🅐 Camping Gaz ⊤ Toilet fluid 🍴 Café/Restaurant 🍟 Fast Food/Takeaway 🔋 Battery charging 🍼 Baby care ♿ Motorvan service point **ABBREVIATIONS:** BH/bank hols-bank holidays Etr-Easter Whit-Whitsun dep-departure fr-from hrs-hours m-mile mdnt-midnight rdbt-roundabout rs-restricted service wk-week wknd-weekend 🚫 No credit cards 🚫 no dogs See page 7 for details of the AA Camping Card Scheme

AUCHENBOWIE — Map 21 NS78

Places to visit

Stirling Old Town Jail, Stirling, 01786 450050, www.oldtownjail.com

Stirling Smith Art Gallery and Museum, Stirling, 01786 471917, www.smithartgallery.demon.co.uk

Great for kids: Stirling Castle, Stirling, 01786 450000, www.stirlingcastle.gov.uk

►►► 69% Auchenbowie Caravan & Camping Site (NS795880)

FK7 8HE
☎ 01324 823999   📠 01324 822950
dir: 0.5m S of M9/M80 junct 9. Right off A872 for 0.5m, signed

* 🚐 £12-£15 🚛 £12-£15 ▲ £9-£12

Open Apr-Oct Last departure noon

A pleasant little site in a rural location, with mainly level grassy pitches. The friendly warden creates a relaxed atmosphere, and given its position close to the junction of the M9 and M80, this is a handy stopover spot for tourers. A 3.5 acre site with 60 touring pitches and 12 statics.

Leisure: 🅰
Facilities: 🍴☉📮☉🚻
Services: 🚐🔒💧🌀
Within 3 miles: ⅃🎬🎣📅🛒U

see advert on page 363

BLAIRLOGIE — Map 21 NS89

Places to visit

Alloa Tower, Alloa Tower, 0844 493 2129, www.nts.org.uk

The Regimental Museum of the Argyll and Sutherland Highlanders, Stirling, 01786 475165, www.argylls.co.uk

►►►► 85% Witches Craig Caravan & Camping Park (NS821968)

GOLD

FK9 5PX
☎ 01786 474947
e-mail: info@witchescraig.co.uk
dir: 3m NE of Stirling on A91 (Hillfoots to St Andrews road)

* 🚐 £16-£20 🚛 £16-£20 ▲ £15-£19

Open Apr-Oct Last arrival 20.00hrs Last dep noon

In an attractive setting with direct access to the lower slopes of the dramatic Ochil Hills, this is a well-maintained family-run park. It is in the centre of 'Braveheart' country, with easy access to historical sites and many popular attractions. A 5 acre site with 60 touring pitches, 26 hardstandings.

Leisure: 🅰
Facilities: 🍴☉📮☀☉🚻🚻
Services: 🚐🔒💧🌀🅃🚻⚡
Within 3 miles: ⅃🎬🎣📅🛒U

Notes: Food preparation area, baby bath & changing area

CALLANDER — Map 20 NN60

Places to visit

Doune Castle, Doune, 01786 841742, www.historic-scotland.gov.uk

Great for kids: Blair Drummond Safari and Leisure Park, Blair Drummond, 01786 841456, www.blairdrummond.com

►►►► 80% Gart Caravan Park (NN643070)

The Gart FK17 8LE
☎ 01877 330002   📠 01877 330002
e-mail: enquiries@theholidaypark.co.uk
dir: 1m E of Callander on A84

* 🚐 £21 🚛 £21

Open Etr or Apr-15 Oct Last arrival 22.00hrs Last departure 11.30hrs

A very well maintained spacious parkland site within easy walking distance of Callander. The on-site play area for children is excellent, whilst free fishing is available on a private stretch of the River Teith. A wide range of leisure activities is available within the locality. A 26 acre site with 128 touring pitches and 66 statics.

AA Pubs & Restaurants nearby: Roman Camp Country House Hotel, Callander 01877 330003

Callander Meadows, Callander 01877 330181

Leisure: 🅰
Facilities: 🍴☉☀☉🚻
Services: 🚐🔒💧⚡
Within 3 miles: ⅃🎣📅🛒U

Notes: No commercial vehicles

LUIB — Map 20 NN42

Places to visit

Balmacara Estate and Lochalsh Woodland Garden, Balmacara, 0844 493 2233, www.nts.org.uk

►►►► 79% Glendochart Holiday Park (NN477278)

FK20 8QT
☎ 01567 820637   📠 01567 820024
e-mail: info@glendochart-caravanpark.co.uk
dir: On A85 (Oban to Stirling road), midway between Killin & Crianlarich

* 🚐 £16-£17.50 🚛 £16-£17.50 ▲ £11-£14

Open Mar-Nov Last arrival 21.00hrs Last dep noon

A small, well maintained park on a hillside in Glendochart, with imaginative landscaping and glorious mountain and hill views. The site is well located for trout and salmon fishing, and ideal for walking. A 15 acre site with 35 touring pitches, 28 hardstandings and 60 statics.

Facilities: 🍴☉📮☀☉🚻🚻
Services: 🚐🔒💧🌀 **Within 3 miles:** 🎣

STIRLING

See Auchenbowie & Blairlogie

STRATHYRE — Map 20 NN51

►►► 73% Immervoulin Caravan and Camping Park (NN560164)

FK18 8NJ
☎ 01877 384285   📠 01877 384390
dir: Off A84, approx 1m S of Strathyre

🚐▲

Open Mar-Oct Last arrival 22.00hrs

A family run park on open meadowland next to the River Balvaig, where fishing, canoeing and other water sports can be enjoyed. A riverside walk leads to Loch Lubnaig, and the village of Strathyre offers restaurants. The park has a newly built, well-appointed amenity block. A 5 acre site with 50 touring pitches.

AA Pubs & Restaurants nearby: Creagan House, Strathyre 01877 384638

Roman Camp Country House Hotel, Callander 01877 330003

Callander Meadows, Callander 01877 330181

Facilities: 🍴☉📮☀☉🚻🚻
Services: 🚐🔒💧🌀🅃🚻⚡ **Within 3 miles:** 🎣📅

WEST DUNBARTONSHIRE

BALLOCH
Map 20 NS38

Places to visit

Finlaystone Country Estate, Langbank, 01475 540505, www.finlaystone.co.uk

The Tall Ship at Glasgow Harbour, Glasgow, 0141 222 2513, www.thetallship.com

AA CAMPING CARD SITE

►►►► 80% Lomond Woods Holiday Park (NS383816)

Old Luss Rd G83 8QP
☎ 01389 755000 📠 01389 755563
e-mail: lomondwoods@holiday-parks.co.uk
web: www.holiday-parks.co.uk
dir: *From A82, 17m N of Glasgow, take A811 (Stirling to Balloch road). Left at 1st rdbt, follow holiday park signs, 150yds on left*

* 🚐 £18-£22 🚏

Open all year Last arrival 20.00hrs Last departure noon

A mature park with well-laid out pitches and self-catering lodges screened by trees and shrubs, surrounded by woodland and hills. The park is within walking distance of Loch Lomond Shores, a leisure and retail complex, which is the main gateway to Scotland's first National Park. Amenities include the Loch Lomond Aquarium, an Interactive Exhibition, and loch cruises. Seasonal touring pitches are available. Please note that this park does not accept tents. A 13 acre site with 100 touring pitches, 100 hardstandings and 35 statics.

AA Pubs & Restaurants nearby: Cameron Grill 01389 755565 & Martin Wishart Loch Lomond 01389 722504 - both at Cameron House Hotel, Balloch

Leisure: 🅰 🎣 ▢
Facilities: 🚿 📷 ☉ 🅿 ✳ ♿ 🖊 🚻 🖈
Services: 🔌 🔲 🛢 🚻 ➡ ♿
Within 3 miles: ↨ ⚓ 🎣 ⛷ 🔲 🔲 ↻
Notes: No jet skis. Wi-fi

WEST LOTHIAN

EAST CALDER
Map 21 NT06

Places to visit

Suntrap Garden, Gogar, 0131 339 7283, www.suntrap-garden.org.uk

Malleny Garden, Balerno, 0844 493 2123, www.nts.org.uk

►►► 85% Linwater Caravan Park (NT104696)

West Clifton EH53 0HT
☎ 0131 333 3326 📠 0131 333 1952
e-mail: linwater@supanet.com
dir: *M9 junct 1, signed from B7030 or from Wilkieston on A71*

🚐 £13-£18 🚏 £13-£18 ⛺ £11-£16

Open late Mar-late Oct Last arrival 21.00hrs. Last departure noon

A farmland park in a peaceful rural area within easy reach of Edinburgh. The very good facilities are housed in a Scandinavian-style building, and are well maintained by resident owners, who are genuinely caring hosts and nothing is too much trouble to ensure campers are enjoying themselves. There are three 'timber tents' for hire and nearby are plenty of pleasant woodland walks. A 5 acre site with 60 touring pitches, 18 hardstandings.

AA Pubs & Restaurants nearby: Bridge Inn, Ratho 0131 333 1320

Leisure: 🅰
Facilities: 🚿 ☉ 🅿 ✳ ♿ ⓘ 🖈
Services: 🔌 🔲 🛢 ⌀ 🔲 ➡
Within 3 miles: ↨ 🎣 🔲 🔲
Notes: Wi-fi

LINLITHGOW
Map 21 NS97

Places to visit

Linlithgow Palace, Linlithgow, 01506 842896, www.historic-scotland.gov.uk

House of the Binns, Linlithgow, 0844 493 2127, www.nts.org.uk

Great for kids: Blackness Castle, Linlithgow, 01506 834807, www.historic-scotland.gov.uk

►►►► 80% Beecraigs Caravan & Camping Site (NT006746)

Beecraigs Country Park, The Park Centre EH49 6PL
☎ 01506 844516 📠 01506 846256
e-mail: mail@beecraigs.com
web: www.beecraigs.com
dir: *From Linlithgow on A803 or from Bathgate on B792, follow signs to country park. Reception either at restaurant or park centre*

* 🚐 £14.50-£16.80 🚏 £14.50-£16.80 ⛺ £12.70-£20.85

Open all year (rs 25-26 Dec, 1-2 Jan no new arrivals) Last arrival 21.00hrs Last departure noon

A wildlife enthusiast's paradise where even the timber facility buildings are in keeping with the environment. Beecraigs is situated peacefully in the open countryside of the Bathgate Hills. Small bays with natural shading offer intimate pitches, and there's a restaurant serving lunch and evening meals. The smart toilet block on the main park includes en suite facilities, and there is a new luxury toilet block for tenters. A 6 acre site with 36 touring pitches, 36 hardstandings.

AA Pubs & Restaurants nearby: The Chop & Ale House, Champany Inn, Linlithgow 01506 834532

Leisure: 🅰
Facilities: 🚻 🚿 ☉ 🅿 ✳ ♿ ⓘ 🚻 🖈
Services: 🔌 🔲 🛢 🔲 🍽
Within 3 miles: ↨ 🎣 ⛷ 🔲 🔲 ↻
Notes: No cars by tents. No ball games near caravans, no noise after 22.00hrs. Children's bath, country park facilities

SCOTTISH ISLANDS

ISLE OF ARRAN

LOCHRANZA · Map 20 NR25

►►► 79% Lochranza Caravan & Camping Site (NR942500)

KA27 8HL
☎ 01770 830273 & 07733 611083
e-mail: office@lochgolf.demon.co.uk
dir: On A841 at N of island, beside Kintyre ferry & 14m N of Brodick for ferry to Ardrossan

* ➡ £15-£16 ⇌ £15-£16 ▲ £8-£16

Open Mar-30 Oct Last arrival 22.00hrs Last departure 16.00hrs

A well-established park acquired by new, enthusiastic and knowledgeable owners who are steadily enhancing the park. There is an 18-hole golf course adjacent to the park and a restaurant near the park entrance whilst Arran Distillery and a hotel are close by. A wide variety of outdoor activities are easily accessible from the park. A 2.2 acre site with 60 touring pitches, 10 hardstandings.

AA Pubs & Restaurants nearby: Kilmichael Country House Hotel, Brodick 01770 302219

Facilities: ⋔☉℘✳🕭🖻🚻🐾
Services: 🖭🖸🔋🖉🅃🍽🛒🔥
Within 3 miles: 🌡✎🚤🖀🖸
Notes: No fires. Putting green

ISLE OF MULL

CRAIGNURE · Map 20 NM73

Places to visit

Mull and West Highland Narrow Gauge Railway, Craignure, 01680 812494 (in season), www.mullrail.co.uk

►►►► 76% Shieling Holidays

(NM724369)

PA65 6AY
☎ 01680 812496
e-mail: sales@shielingholidays.co.uk
web: www.shielingholidays.co.uk
dir: From ferry left onto A849 to Iona. 400mtrs left at church, follow site signs towards sea

* ➡ £15.50-£18 ⇌ £15.50-£18 ▲ £14.50-£16.50

Open 12 Mar-1 Nov Last arrival 22.00hrs Last departure noon

A lovely site on the water's edge with spectacular views, and less than one mile from the ferry landing. Hardstandings and service points are provided for motorhomes, and there are astro-turf pitches for tents. The park also offers unique, en suite cottage tents for hire and bunkhouse accommodation for families. A 7 acre site with 90 touring pitches, 30 hardstandings and 15 statics.

Leisure: 🄰🕭🖳
Facilities: ⋔⋔☉℘✳🕭🕓🚻🖀🐾
Services: 🖭🖸🔋🖉🅃🛒
Within 3 miles: 🌡✎🖸🖸
Notes: Bikes available. Wi-fi

ISLE OF SKYE

EDINBANE · Map 22 NG35

►►►► 80% Skye Camping & Caravanning Club Site (NG345527)

Borve, Arnisort IV51 9PS
☎ 01470 582230 📠 01470 582230
e-mail: skye.site@thefriendlyclub.co.uk
dir: Approx 12m from Portree on A850 (Dunvegan road). Site by loch shore

* ➡ £18.60-£24.80 ⇌ £18.60-£24.80 ▲ £18.60-£24.80

Open Apr-Oct Last arrival 22.00hrs Last departure noon

The Club site on Skye stands out for its stunning waterside location and glorious views, the generous pitch density, the overall range of facilities, and the impressive ongoing improvements under enthusiastic franchisee owners. Layout maximises the beauty of the scenery and genuine customer care is very evident with an excellent tourist information room and campers' shelter being just two examples. The new amenities block (opened in 2010) has that definite 'wow' factor with smart modern fittings, including excellent showers and the generously proportioned disabled room and family bathroom. There are several wooden camping pods for hire. A 7 acre site with 105 touring pitches, 36 hardstandings.

AA Pubs & Restaurants nearby: Stein Inn, Stein 01470 592362

Loch Bay Seafood Restaurant, Stein 01470 592235

Three Chimneys Restaurant, Colbost 01470 511258

Facilities: ⋔☉℘✳🕭🕓🖻🚻🐾
Services: 🖭🖸🔋🖉🅃🛒🔥
Within 3 miles: ✎🖸🖸
Notes: Dogs must be kept under control & exercised off site. Car hire. Wi-fi

STAFFIN · Map 22 NG46

►►► 75% Staffin Camping & Caravanning (NG492670)

IV51 9JX
☎ 01470 562213 📠 01470 562213
e-mail: staffincampsite@btinternet.com
dir: On A855, 16m N of Portree. Turn right before 40mph signs

➡ ⇌ ▲

Open Apr-Oct Last arrival 22.00hrs Last departure 11.00hrs

A large sloping grassy site with level hardstandings for motor homes and caravans, close to the village of Staffin. The toilet block is appointed to a very good standard and the park now has a laundry. Mountain bikes are available for hire. A 2.5 acre site with 50 touring pitches, 18 hardstandings.

AA Pubs & Restaurants nearby: The Glenview, Staffin 01470 562248

Flodigarry Country House Hotel, Staffin 01470 552203

Facilities: ⋔☉℘✳🕭🖻🚻🖀🐾
Services: 🖭🖸🔋🖉🛒
Within 3 miles: 🚤✎🖸🖸
Notes: 🐾 No music after 22.00hrs. Picnic tables, kitchen area, bike hire

SERVICES: ⚡ Electric hook up 🖳 Launderette 🍷 Licensed bar 🛢 Calor Gas ⌀ Camping Gaz 🅃 Toilet fluid 🍽 Café/Restaurant 🍟 Fast Food/Takeaway 🔋 Battery charging
🍼 Baby care ⚙ Motorvan service point **ABBREVIATIONS:** BH/bank hols-bank holidays Etr-Easter Whit-Whitsun dep-departure fr-from hrs-hours m-mile mdnt-midnight
rdbt-roundabout rs-restricted service wk-week wknd-weekend 🚫 No credit cards ⊗ no dogs See page 7 for details of the AA Camping Card Scheme

Wales

Ffrancon Valley

Wales

Wales may be small but it certainly packs a punch. Its scenery is a matchless mix of magnificent mountains, rolling green hills and craggy coastlines. But it is not just the landscape that makes such a strong impression - Wales is renowned for its prominent position in the world of culture and the arts.

This is a land of ancient myths and traditions, of male voice choirs, exceptionally gifted singers and leading actors of stage and screen. Richard Burton hailed from the valleys in south Wales, Anthony Hopkins originates from Port Talbot and Tom Jones, born Thomas Jones Woodward, comes from Pontypridd. One man who is inextricably linked to Wales is the poet Dylan Thomas. Born in Swansea in 1914, he lived at the Boat House in Laugharne, on the Taf and Tywi estuaries, overlooking Carmarthen Bay. He is buried in the local churchyard.

The valleys

East of here are the old industrial valleys of the Rhondda, once a byword for hardship and poverty and the grime of the local coal and iron workings, it has been transformed into now a very different place. Also vastly altered and improved by the passage of time are the great cities of Swansea and Cardiff, the latter symbolising New Labour's 'Cool Britannia' philosophy with its café culture and Docklands-style apartments.

▶

● Tenby Harbour

Going west and north

Tenby in west Wales still retains the charm of a typical seaside resort while the Pembrokeshire coast, overlooking Cardigan Bay, is one of the country's scenic treasures. Lower Fishguard has a connection with Dylan Thomas. In 1971, less than 20 years after his death, some of the theatre's greatest names – Richard Burton and Peter O'Toole among them – descended on this picturesque village to film *Under Milk Wood*, which Thomas originally wrote as a radio play.

Farther north is Harlech Castle, built by Edward I around 1283, with the peaks of Snowdonia in the distance. The formidable Caernarfon Castle, the setting for the investiture of the Prince of Wales in 1969, stands in the north-west corner of the country. Both castles are part of a string of massive strongholds built by Edward to establish a united Britain.

The mountains

With its many attractions and miles of natural beauty, the coast of Wales is an obvious draw for its many visitors but ultimately it is the country's spectacular hinterland that people make for. Snowdonia, with its towering summits and craggy peaks, is probably top of the list of adventure destinations. Heading back south reveals still more scenic landscapes – the remote country of the

Conwy Castle

terrain. Try the Taff Trail, which runs north from Cardiff to Caerphilly and includes three castles en route; it's a fairly easy trail, quite flat and largely free of traffic.

For something completely different, cycle from Swansea to Mumbles, enjoying memorable views of the Gower Peninsula.

Welsh Borders and the stunning scenery of the dramatic Brecon Beacons among them.

Walking and Cycling

With mile upon mile of natural beauty, it's hardly surprising that Wales offers so much potential for walking. There's the Cistercian Way, which circles the country by incorporating its Cistercian abbeys; the Glyndwr's Way, named after the 15th-century warrior statesman; and the Pembrokeshire Coast Path, which is a great way to explore the Pembrokeshire National Park.

Cycling is understandably very popular here but be prepared for some tough ascents and dramatic

Festivals and Events

- May is the month for the Royal Welsh Smallholder & Garden Festival, held on the Royal Welsh Showground at Llanelwedd. The event features all manner of farming and horticultural activities.
- The August Bank Holiday weekend sees the Summer Harp Festival at the National Botanic Garden of Wales at Llanarthne in Carmarthenshire. There are concerts, talks and workshops.
- The Abergavenny Food Festival takes place in September with more than 80 events, including masterclasses, tutored tastings, talks and debates.

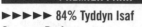

ANGLESEY, ISLE OF

DULAS

Map 14 SH48

PREMIER PARK

▶▶▶▶▶ 84% Tyddyn Isaf
Caravan Park (SH486873)
GOLD

Lligwy Bay LL70 9PQ
☎ **01248 410203** & 410667 ▤ 01248 410667
e-mail: mail@tyddynisaf.co.uk
dir: *Take A5025 through Benllech to Moelfre rdbt, left towards Amlwch to Brynrefail village. Turn right opposite craft shop. Site 0.5m down lane on right*

* ⊞ £18-£26 ⊞ £18-£26 Å £18-£26

Open Mar-Oct (rs Mar-Jul & Sep-Oct bar & shop opening limited) Last arrival 21.30hrs Last departure 11.00hrs

A beautifully situated, very spacious family park on rising ground adjacent to a sandy beach, with magnificent views overlooking Lligwy Bay. A private footpath leads direct to the beach and there is an excellent nature trail around the park. There are very good toilet facilities, including a new additional block with under-floor heating and excellent unisex privacy cubicles, a well-stocked shop, and café/bar serving meals, which are best enjoyed on the terrace with its magnificent coast and sea views. Seasonal touring pitches are available. A 16 acre site with 30 touring pitches, 50 hardstandings and 56 statics.

AA Pubs & Restaurants nearby: The Ship Inn, Red Wharf Bay 01248 852568

Ye Olde Bulls Head Inn, Beaumaris 01248 810329

Leisure: ⚑▢ **Facilities:** ⚹⊙℗✻&⊙圓⊞Ħ
Services: ⚑圓☜▯⚚⊘▯℩▢⛟▦⛛
Within 3 miles: ⚴⚹⚟圓⛎

Notes: ⊛ Dogs must be kept on leads, no groups, maximum 3 units together. Baby changing unit. Wi-fi

LLANBEDRGOCH

Map 14 SH58

Places to visit

Bryn Celli Ddu Burial Chamber, Bryncelli Ddu, 01443 336000, www.cadw.wales.gov.uk

Great for kids: Anglesey Sea Zoo, Brynsiencyn, 01248 430411, www.angleseyseazoo.co.uk

▶▶▶ 78% Ty Newydd Leisure Park
(SH507811)

LL76 8TZ
☎ **01248 450677** ▤ 01248 450312
e-mail: mike@tynewydd.com
web: www.tynewydd.com
dir: *A5025 from Brittania Bridge. Through Pentraeth, bear left at layby. Site 0.75m on right*

⊞ ⊞ Å

Open Mar-Oct (rs Mar-Whit & mid Sep-Oct club wknds only, outdoor pool closed) Last arrival 23.30hrs Last departure 10.00hrs

Ty Newydd Leisure Park

A low-density park with good facilities, including clean and tidy toilets, a newly refurbished restaurant, good swimming pool facilities, a new games room, and a well equipped playground for children. The park is close to Benllech Bay, and is set in four acres of lovely countryside. A 4 acre site with 48 touring pitches, 15 hardstandings and 62 statics.

AA Pubs & Restaurants nearby: The Ship Inn, Red Wharf Bay 01248 852568

Ye Olde Bulls Head Inn, Beaumaris 01248 810329

Bishopsgate House Hotel, Beaumaris 01248 810302

Leisure: ⛱⚑⚑❋
Facilities: ⚹⊙℗&⊙Ħ Ħ
Services: ⚑圓☜▯⚚⊘▯℩▢
Within 3 miles: ⚴⚟⛱圓圓⛎
Notes: Jacuzzi. Wi-fi

see advert below

LEISURE: ⛱ Indoor swimming pool ⚑ Outdoor swimming pool Å Children's playground ⚑ Tennis court ❋ Games room ▢ Separate TV room ⚴ 9/18 hole golf course ⚑ Boats for hire ▤ Cinema ⚟ Fishing ⊙ Mini golf ⚑ Watersports ⛎ Stables **FACILITIES:** ⛴ Bath ⚹ Shower ⊙ Electric shaver ℗ Hairdryer ✻ Ice Pack Facility & Disabled facilities ⚙ Public telephone 圓 Shop on site or within 200yds ⚚ Mobile shop (calls at least 5 days a week) ▦ BBQ area Ħ Picnic area Ħ Dog exercise area

MARIAN-GLAS Map 14 SH58

Places to visit

Bryn Celli Ddu Burial Chamber, Bryncelli Ddu, 01443 336000, www.cadw.wales.gov.uk

PREMIER PARK

►►►►► 92% Home Farm Caravan Park

Best of British GOLD

(SH498850)

LL73 8PH

01248 410614 **01248 410900**

e-mail: enq@homefarm-anglesey.co.uk

web: www.homefarm-anglesey.co.uk

dir: *On A5025, 2m N of Benllech. Site 300mtrs beyond church*

Open Apr-Oct Last arrival 21.00hrs Last departure noon

A first-class park, run with passion and enthusiasm, set in an elevated and secluded position sheltered by trees, with good planting and landscaping. The peaceful rural setting affords views of farmland, the sea, and the mountains of Snowdonia. The modern toilet blocks are spotlessly clean and well maintained, and there are excellent play facilities for children both indoors and out. New improvements include a super visitors' parking area, a stunning water feature and a children's play area with top-notch equipment. The area is blessed with sandy beaches, and local pubs and shops cater for everyday needs. A 6 acre site with 98 touring pitches, 21 hardstandings and 84 statics.

AA Pubs & Restaurants nearby: The Ship Inn, Red Wharf Bay 01248 852568

Ye Olde Bulls Head Inn, Beaumaris 01248 810329

Bishopsgate House Hotel, Beaumaris 01248 810302

Leisure:

Facilities:

Services:

Within 3 miles:

Notes: No roller blades, skateboards or scooters. Indoor adventure playground

PENTRAETH Map 14 SH57

Places to visit

Bryn Celli Ddu Burial Chamber, Bryncelli Ddu, 01443 336000, www.cadw.wales.gov.uk

Plas Newydd, Plas Newydd, 01248 714795, www.nationaltrust.org.uk/main/plasnewydd

►►► 78% Rhos Caravan Park

(SH517794)

Rhos Farm LL75 8DZ

01248 450214 **01248 450214**

e-mail: rhosfarm@googlemail.com

web: www.rhoscaravanpark.co.uk

dir: *Site on A5025, 1m N of Pentraeth*

£11.50-£13.50 £11.50-£13.50 £11.50-£13.50

Open Etr-Oct Last arrival 22.00hrs Last departure 16.00hrs

A warm welcome awaits families at this spacious park on level, grassy ground with easy access to the main road to Amlwch. A 200-acre working farm that has two play areas and farm animals to keep children amused, with good beaches, pubs, restaurants and shops nearby. The two toilet blocks are kept to a good standard by enthusiastic owners, who are constantly improving the facilities. A 15 acre site with 98 touring pitches and 66 statics.

AA Pubs & Restaurants nearby: The Ship Inn, Red Wharf Bay 01248 852568

Ye Olde Bulls Head Inn, Beaumaris 01248 810329

Bishopsgate House Hotel, Beaumaris 01248 810302

Leisure:

Facilities:

Services:

Within 3 miles:

Notes:

RHOS LLIGWY Map 14 SH48

►►► 68% Ty'n Rhos Caravan Park

(SH495867)

Lligwy Bay, Moelfre LL72 8NL

01248 852417 **01248 853417**

e-mail: robert@bodafonpark.co.uk

dir: *Take A5025 from Benllech to Moelfre rdbt, right to T-junct in Moelfre. Left, then approx 2m to site, pass x-roads leading to beach, site 50mtrs on right*

* £17-£25 £17-£25 £12-£20

Open Mar-Oct Last arrival 21.00hrs Last departure noon

A family park close to the beautiful beach at Lligwy Bay, and cliff walks along the Heritage Coast. Historic Din Lligwy, and the shops at picturesque Moelfre are nearby. Please note that guests should register at Bodafon Caravan Park in Benllech where detailed directions will be given and pitches allocated. Seasonal touring pitches are available. A 10 acre site with 50 touring pitches, 50 hardstandings and 80 statics.

AA Pubs & Restaurants nearby: The Ship Inn, Red Wharf Bay 01248 852568

Ye Olde Bulls Head Inn, Beaumaris 01248 810329

Bishopsgate House Hotel, Beaumaris 01248 810302

Facilities:

Services:

Within 3 miles:

RHOSNEIGR — Map 14 SH37

►►► 77% Ty Hen *(SH327738)*

Station Rd LL64 5QZ
☎ 01407 810331 📠 01407 810331
e-mail: info@tyhen.com
web: www.tyhen.com
dir: *From A55 exit 5 follow signs to Rhosneigr, at clock turn right. Entrance 50mtrs before Rhosneigr railway station*

Open mid Mar-Oct Last arrival 21.00hrs Last departure noon

Attractive seaside position near a large fishing lake and riding stables, in lovely countryside. A smart toilet block offers a welcome amenity at this popular family park, where friendly owners are always on hand. The park is close to RAF Valley, which is great for plane spotters, but expect some aircraft noise during the day. A 7.5 acre site with 38 touring pitches, 5 hardstandings and 42 statics.

AA Pubs & Restaurants nearby: Ye Olde Bulls Head Inn, Beaumaris 01248 810329

Bishopsgate House Hotel, Beaumaris 01248 810302

Leisure: ⬤ ⛰ 🔍
Facilities: 🚿⊙🅿✳♿🕐🚻
Services: 🚡🅱🔋🛒🚮
Within 3 miles: ⚓🖉🚤🏬🛍

Notes: 1 motor vehicle per pitch, dogs must be kept on leads, children must not be out after 22.00hrs. Fishing, family room, walks. Wi-fi

BRIDGEND

PORTHCAWL — Map 9 SS87

Places to visit
Newcastle, Bridgend, 01443 336000, www.cadw.wales.gov.uk

Coity Castle, Coity, 01443 336000, www.cadw.wales.gov.uk

►► 72% Brodawel Camping & Caravan Park *(SS816789)*

Moor Ln, Nottage CF36 3EJ
☎ 01656 783231
dir: *M4 junct 37, A4229 towards Porthcawl. Site on right off A4229*

* 🚐 £15-£20 🚙 £15-£20 ⛺ £13-£20

Open Apr-Sep Last arrival 19.00hrs Last departure 11.00hrs

A family run park catering mainly for families, on the edge of the village of Nottage. It is very convenient for Porthcawl and the Glamorgan Heritage Coast, each is within a five-minute drive. A 4 acre site with 100 touring pitches.

AA Pubs & Restaurants nearby: Prince of Wales Inn, Kenfig 01656 740356

Leisure: ⛰ 🔍
Facilities: 🚿⊙✳♿🕐🅱🚻🏓
Services: 🚡🅱🔋🌿🅃
Within 3 miles: ⚓🎣🎬🖉◎🚤🏬🛍🎡
Notes: 🐕

CARMARTHENSHIRE

HARFORD — Map 8 SN64

►►► 83% Springwater Lakes *(SN637430)*

SA19 8DT
☎ 01558 650788
dir: *4m E of Lampeter on A482, entrance well signed on right*

* 🚐 fr £19 🚙 fr £19 ⛺ fr £19

Open Mar-Oct Last arrival 20.00hrs Last departure 11.00hrs

In a rural setting overlooked by the Cambrian Mountains, this park is adjoined on each side by four spring-fed and well-stocked fishing lakes. All pitches have hardstandings, electricity and TV hook-ups, and there is a small and very clean toilet block and a shop. There are plans for more hardstanding pitches and two wooden cabins for 2011. A 20 acre site with 20 touring pitches, 20 hardstandings.

AA Pubs & Restaurants nearby: Brunant Arms, Caio, Llanwrda 01558 650483

Facilities: 🚿⊙✳♿🕐🏓🏓
Services: 🚡🅱🔋🛒
Within 3 miles: 🖉🏬🎡

Notes: 🐕 Dogs must be kept on leads at all times, children must be supervised around lakes, no cycling on site, no ball games. 4 fishing lakes, bait & tackle shop

LLANDOVERY — Map 9 SN73

Places to visit
Dolaucothi Gold Mines, Pumsaint, 01558 650177, www.nationaltrust.org.uk/ main/w-dolaucothigoldmines

►►►► 89% Erwlon Caravan & Camping Park *(SN776343)*

Brecon Rd SA20 0RD
☎ 01550 721021 📠 720332
e-mail: peter@erwlon.co.uk
dir: *0.5m E of Llandovery on A40*

Open all year Last arrival anytime Last departure noon

A long-established, family-run site set beside a brook in the Brecon Beacons foothills. The town of Llandovery and the hills overlooking the Towy Valley are a short walk away. The superb, Scandinavian-style facilities block has cubicled washrooms, family and disabled rooms and is an impressive feature; ongoing improvements include a campers' kitchen. An 8 acre site with 75 touring pitches, 15 hardstandings.

AA Pubs & Restaurants nearby: Brunant Arms, Caio, Llanwrda 01558 650483

Leisure: ⛰
Facilities: 🚿⊙🅿✳♿🕐🅱🚻🏓🏓
Services: 🚡🅱🔋🌿🛒🚮
Within 3 miles: 🖉🏬🛍🎡

Notes: 🐕 Quiet after 22.30hrs. Fishing, bicycle storage & hire. Wi-fi

▶▶ 72% Llandovery Caravan Park

(SN762342)

Church Bank SA20 0DT
☎ 01550 721993 & 07970 650 606
e-mail: drovers.rfc@btinternet.com
dir: *A40 from Carmarthen, over rail crossing, past junct with A483 (Builth Wells). Turn right for Llangadog, past church, 1st right signed Rugby Club & Camping*

🚐 🚌 ▲

Open all year Last arrival 20.00hrs Last departure 20.00hrs

A level, spacious and developing small site adjacent to the Rugby Club on the outskirts of Llandovery. Toilets facilities are adequate but there are plans to upgrade and improve the facilities. Seasonal touring pitches are available. An 8 acre site with 100 touring pitches, 32 hardstandings.

AA Pubs & Restaurants nearby: Brunant Arms, Caio, Llanwrda 01558 650483

Leisure: 🎱 🖥
Facilities: 🚿 ⚿ 🎠 🐕
Services: 🔌 🛒 🚽 🔋
Within 3 miles: 🚴 🎣 🍴 🛒 🎯 ⛳
Notes: ⊗ Dogs must be kept on leads. Dishwashing area

LLANGADOG

Places to visit

Dinefwr Park and Castle, Llandeilo, 01558 823902, www.nationaltrust.org.uk/main/w-dinefwrpark

Carreg Cennen Castle, Carreg Cennen Castle, 01558 822291, www.cadw.wales.gov.uk

---

LLANGADOG   Map 9 SN72

▶▶▶ 76% Abermarlais Caravan Park

(SN695298)

SA19 9NG
☎ 01550 777868 & 777797
dir: *On A40 midway between Llandovery & Llandeilo, 1.5m NW of Llangadog*

* 🚐 £10-£12 🚌 £10-£12 ▲ £10-£12

Open 15 Mar-15 Nov (rs Mar & Nov 1 toilet block, water point no hot water) Last arrival 23.00hrs Last departure noon

An attractive, well-run site with a welcoming atmosphere. This part-level, part-sloping park is in a wooded valley on the edge of the Brecon Beacons National Park, beside the River Marlais. A 17 acre site with 88 touring pitches, 2 hardstandings

AA Pubs & Restaurants nearby: Brunant Arms, Caio, Llanwrda 01558 650483

Leisure: 🎱
Facilities: 🚿 ☺ ✳ ⚿ ⏱ 🛒 🐕
Services: 🔌 🛒 🚽 🔋
Within 3 miles: 🎣 🛒 ⛳

Notes: Dogs must be kept on leads, no open fires, quiet from 23.00hrs-08.00hrs. Volleyball, badminton court, softball tennis net

LLANWRDA

See Harford

NEWCASTLE EMLYN

Places to visit

Cilgerran Castle, Cilgerran, 01239 621339, www.cadw.wales.gov.uk

Castell Henllys Iron Age Fort, Crymych, 01239 891319, www.castellhenllys.com

Great for kids: Felinwynt Rainforest Centre, Felinwynt, 01239 810882 www.butterflycentre.co.uk

---

NEWCASTLE EMLYN   Map 8 SN34

PREMIER PARK

▶▶▶▶▶ 84% Cenarth Falls Holiday Park *(SN265421)*

Best of British

Cenarth SA38 9JS
☎ 01239 710345 🖨 01239 710344
e-mail: enquiries@cenarth-holipark.co.uk
dir: *Off A484 on outskirts of Cenarth towards Cardigan*

🚐 £15-£26 🚌 £15-£26 ▲ £15-£26

Open Mar-16 Dec Last arrival 20.00hrs Last departure 11.00hrs

A high quality park with excellent facilities, close to the village of Cenarth where the River Teifi (famous for its salmon and sea trout) cascades through the Cenarth Falls Gorge. A well-landscaped park with an indoor heated swimming pool and fitness suite, and a restaurant and bar. A 2 acre site with 30 touring pitches, 30 hardstandings and 89 statics.

AA Pubs & Restaurants nearby: Nags Head Inn, Abercych 01239 841200

Pendre Inn, Cilgerran 01239 614223

Webley Waterfront Inn & Hotel, St Dogmaels 01239 612085

Leisure: 🏊 🎿 🎱 🎣
Facilities: 🚿 ☺ 🅿 ✳ ⚿ ⏱
Services: 🔌 🖥 🚽 🔋 ⚿ 🍴 🔋 ⚙
Within 3 miles: 🚌 🎣 ⛷ 🛒 🖥

Notes: No dogs from 15 Jul-2 Sep. Pool table, health & leisure complex

---

SERVICES: 🔌 Electric hook up   🖥 Launderette   🍴 Licensed bar   🛢 Calor Gas   ⚿ Camping Gaz   ⊤ Toilet fluid   🍴 Café/Restaurant   🍟 Fast Food/Takeaway   🔋 Battery charging
🍼 Baby care   ⚙ Motorvan service point   **ABBREVIATIONS:** BH/bank hols-bank holidays   Etr-Easter   Whit-Whitsun   dep-departure   fr-from   hrs-hours   m-mile   mdnt-midnight
rdbt-roundabout   rs-restricted service   wk-week   wknd-weekend   ⊗ No credit cards   ⊗ no dogs   See page 7 for details of the AA Camping Card Scheme

NEWCASTLE EMLYN *continued*

►►► 85% Argoed Meadow Caravan and Camping Site *(SN268415)*

Argoed Farm SA38 9JL
☎ 01239 710690
dir: *From Newcastle Emlyn on A484 towards Cenarth, take B4332. Site 300yds on right*

🚐 🚙 ⛺

Open all year Last arrival anytime Last dep noon

Pleasant open meadowland on the banks of the River Teifi, very close to Cenarth Falls gorge, this site has a modern toilet block which adds to the general appeal of this mainly adults-only park. A 3 acre site with 30 touring pitches, 5 hardstandings.

AA Pubs & Restaurants nearby: Nags Head Inn, Abercych 01239 841200

Pendre Inn, Cilgerran 01239 614223

Webley Waterfront Inn & Hotel, St Dogmaels 01239 612085

Facilities: 🚿 🪒 💨 ❄ ♿ 📞 🏪 🍖 🐕

Services: ⚡ 🫧 🛢 🍃 🔋 👶

Within 3 miles: 🎬 🎣 🏪 🚚 🐴

Notes: ⊜ Dogs must be kept on leads, no bikes or skateboards

►►► 80% Moelfryn Caravan & Camping Park *(SN321370)*

Ty-Cefn, Pant-y-Bwlch SA38 9JE
☎ 01559 371231
e-mail: moelfryn@moelfryncaravanpark.co.uk
dir: *A484 from Carmarthen towards Cynwyl Elfed. Pass Blue Bell Inn on right, 200yds take left fork onto B4333 towards Hermon. In 7m brown sign on left. Turn left, site on right*

* 🚐 £12-£15 🚙 £12-£15 ⛺ £10-£13

Open Mar-10 Jan Last arrival 22.00hrs Last dep noon

A small, beautifully maintained, family-run park in a glorious elevated location overlooking the valley of the River Teifi. Pitches are level and spacious, and well screened by hedging and mature trees. Facilities are spotlessly clean and tidy, and the playing field is well away from the touring area. Home-cooked meals can be ordered and Sunday breakfast delivered to the tent/caravan door. A 3 acre site with 25 touring pitches, 13 hardstandings.

AA Pubs & Restaurants nearby: Nags Head Inn, Abercych 01239 841200

Pendre Inn, Cilgerran 01239 614223

Webley Waterfront Inn & Hotel, St Dogmaels 01239 612085

Leisure: 🛝 **Facilities:** 🚿 🪒 💨 ❄ 🏪 🍖

Services: ⚡ 🫧 🛢 🔋 🍟

Within 3 miles: ⛳ ⛵ 🎬 🎣 🏄 🏪 🚚 🐴

Notes: Games to be played in designated area only. Caravan storage. Wi-fi

►►► 74% Afon Teifi Caravan & Camping Park *(SN338405)*

Pentrecagal SA38 9HT
☎ 01559 370532
e-mail: afonteifi@btinternet.com
dir: *Signed off A484, 2m E of Newcastle Emlyn*

🚐 🚙 ⛺

Open Apr-Oct Last arrival 23.00hrs

Set on the banks of the River Teifi, a famous salmon and sea trout river, this park is secluded with good views. Family owned and run, and only two miles from the market town of Newcastle Emlyn. A 6 acre site with 110 touring pitches, 22 hardstandings and 10 statics.

AA Pubs & Restaurants nearby: Nags Head Inn, Abercych 01239 841200

Pendre Inn, Cilgerran 01239 614223

Webley Waterfront Inn & Hotel, St Dogmaels 01239 612085

Leisure: 🛝 🎱

Facilities: 🛁 🚿 🪒 💨 ❄ ♿ 📞 🏪 🍖 🧺 🐕

Services: ⚡ 🫧 🛢 🍃 [T] 🔋

Within 3 miles: ⛳ 🎣 🏄 🏪 🚚 🐴

Notes: ⊜ 15 acres of woodland, fields & walks, ball area

CEREDIGION

ABERAERON Map 8 SN46

Places to visit

Llanerchaeron, Aberaeron, 01545 570200, www.nationaltrust.org.uk

AA CAMPING CARD SITE

►►► 85% Aeron Coast Caravan Park *(SN460631)*

North Rd SA46 0JF
☎ 01545 570349 📠 01545 571289
e-mail: enquiries@aeroncoast.co.uk
web: www.aeroncoast.co.uk
dir: *On A487 (coast road) on N edge of Aberaeron, signed. Filling station at entrance*

🚐 £15-£25 🚙 £15-£25 ⛺ £15-£25

Open Mar-Oct Last arrival 23.00hrs Last departure 11.00hrs

A well-managed family holiday park on the edge of the attractive resort of Aberaeron, with direct access to the beach. The spacious pitches are all level. On-site facilities include an extensive outdoor pool complex, a multi-activity outdoor sports area, an indoor children's play area, a small lounge bar which serves food, a games room and an entertainment suite. A 22 acre site with 100 touring pitches, 23 hardstandings and 200 statics.

AA Pubs & Restaurants nearby: Harbourmaster, Aberaeron 01545 570755

Ty Mawr Mansion, Aberaeron 01570 470033

Leisure: 🌊 🛝 🎾 🎱 📺

Facilities: 🚿 🪒 ❄ ♿ 📞 🏪

Services: ⚡ 🫧 🍷 🛢 🍃 [T] 🍽 🔋 🍟 🚰

Within 3 miles: 🎣 🏄 🏪 🐴

Notes: Families only, no motorcycles

ABERYSTWYTH | Map 8 SN58

Places to visit

The National Library of Wales, Aberystwyth 01970 632800, www.llgc.org.uk

AA CAMPING CARD SITE

►►► 79% Ocean View Caravan Park

(SN592842)

North Beach, Clarach Bay SY23 3DT
☎ **01970 828425 & 623361**
e-mail: enquiries@oceanviewholidays.com
dir: *Exit A487 in Bow Street. Straight on at next x-roads. Site 2nd on right*

* 🚐 £15.50-£19.50 🚐 £15.50-£19.50
Å £12.50-£15

Open Mar-Oct Last arrival 20.00hrs Last departure noon

In a sheltered valley on gently sloping ground, with wonderful views of both the sea and the countryside. The beach of Clarach Bay is just 200 yards away, and this welcoming park is ideal for all the family. Seasonal touring pitches are available. A 9 acre site with 24 touring pitches, 15 hardstandings and 56 statics.

AA Pubs & Restaurants nearby: New Cross Inn, New Cross 01974 261526

Facilities: 🐕 ⊙ ☂ ✳ 🔥 🎪 🚿

Services: 🔌 🅢 🔋

Within 3 miles: ↧ 🎣 🖋 ◎ ⛵ 🅢 🅢 ↻

BETTWS EVAN | Map 8 SN34

Places to visit

Pentre Ifan Burial Chamber, Newport, 01443 336000, www.cadw.wales.gov.uk

Tredegar House and Park, Newport, 01633 815880, www.newport.gov.uk

►►► 80% Pilbach Holiday Park

(SN306476)

SA44 5RT
☎ **0845 050 8176**
e-mail: info@barkersleisure.com
web: www.barkersleisure.com
dir: *S on A487, turn left onto B4333*

🚐 🚐 Å

Open Mar-Oct (rs Mar-Spring BH & Oct swimming pool closed) Last arrival 22.00hrs Last departure noon

Pilbach Holiday Park is set in secluded countryside, with two separate paddocks and pitches clearly marked in the grass, close to nearby seaside resorts. It has a heated outdoor swimming pool, and entertainment in the club two or three times a week in high season. A 15 acre site with 65 touring pitches, 10 hardstandings and 70 statics.

AA Pubs & Restaurants nearby: Nags Head Inn, Abercych 01239 841200

Pendre Inn, Cilgerran 01239 614223

Leisure: 🏊 🎿 🎣

Facilities: 🐕 ⊙ ☂ 🕐 🅢 🔥 🎪

Services: 🔌 🅢 🍺 🍽 🍴

Within 3 miles: ↧ 🎣 🖋 ⛵ 🅢 🅢 ↻

Notes: Bike/skateboard parks

BORTH | Map 14 SN69

Places to visit

The National Library of Wales, Aberystwyth; 01970 632800, www.llgc.org.uk

73% Brynowen Holiday Park *(SN608893)*

SY24 5LS
☎ **01970 871366** 📠 **01970 871125**
e-mail: brynowen@park-resorts.com
dir: *Signed off B4353, S of Borth*

🚐 🚐

Open Apr-Oct Last arrival mdnt Last departure noon

Enjoying spectacular views across Cardigan Bay and the Cambrian Mountains, a small touring park in a large and well-equipped holiday centre. The well-run park offers a wide range of organised activities and entertainment for all the family from morning until late in the evening. A long sandy beach is a few minutes' drive away. Four seasonal touring pitches are available. A 52 acre site with 16 touring pitches, 16 hardstandings and 480 statics.

Leisure: 🏊 🎿 🎣

Facilities: 🐕 ⊙ ♿ 🕐 🅢 🎪

Services: 🔌 🅢 🍺 🥫 🍽 🍴

Within 3 miles: ↧ 🅢 🅢

Notes: Kids' clubs, mini ten-pin bowling, Wi-fi

LLANON | Map 8 SN56

Places to visit

The National Library of Wales, Aberystwyth; 01970 632800, www.llgc.org.uk

►►► 75% *Woodlands Caravan Park* (SN509668)

SY23 5LX
☎ **01974 202342 & 202454** 📠 **01974 202342**
dir: *Through Llanon, exit A487 at international sign, site 280yds right*

🚐 🚐 Å

Open Apr-Oct Last arrival 21.30hrs Last departure noon

A well maintained, mainly grass site surrounded by mature trees and shrubs near woods and meadowland, adjacent to the sea and a stony beach. The park is half a mile from the village. A 4 acre site with 40 touring pitches, 10 hardstandings and 54 statics.

AA Pubs & Restaurants nearby: Harbourmaster, Aberaeron 01545 570755

Ty Mawr Mansion, Aberaeron 01570 470033

Facilities: 🐕 ⊙ ☂ ✳ 🅢

Services: 🔌 🅢 🍺 🔋

Within 3 miles: ↧ 🖋 ◎ 🅢 🅢

Notes: ⊗

CONWY

See Walk 14 in the Walks & Cycle Rides section at the end of the guide

BETWS-YN-RHOS
Map 14 SH97

Places to visit

Denbigh Castle, Denbigh, 01745 813385, www.cadw.wales.gov.uk

▶▶▶▶ 79% Hunters Hamlet Caravan Park (SH928736)

Sirior Goch Farm LL22 8PL
☎ 01745 832237 & 07721 552106
e-mail: huntershamlet@aol.com
web: www.huntershamlet.co.uk
dir: From A55 W'bound, A547 into Abergele. At 2nd lights turn left by George & Dragon pub, onto A548. 2.75m right at x-rds onto B5381. Site 0.5m on left

🚐 £17-£22 🚐 £17-£22

Open 21 Mar-Oct Last arrival 22.00hrs Last departure noon

A quiet working farm park next to the owners' Georgian farmhouse. Pitches are in two grassy paddocks with pleasant views, and the beach is three miles away. The very good toilets, including unisex bathrooms, are kept in spotless condition. A 2 acre site with 23 touring pitches, 23 hardstandings.

AA Pubs & Restaurants nearby: Wheatsheaf Inn, Betws-Yn-Rhos 01492 680218

Leisure: ⚑

Facilities: 🛁 🌂 ☉ 🌡 ✳ ♿

Services: 🔌 🔄 🛢 🖤

Within 3 miles: ↕ 🐾 🎣 🖩

Notes: No tents, no football, dogs must not be left unattended. Baby bath & changing facilities. Wi-fi

AA CAMPING CARD SITE

▶▶▶▶ 77% Plas Farm Caravan Park
(SH897744)

LL22 8AU
☎ 01492 680254 & 07831 482176
e-mail: info@plasfarmcaravanpark.co.uk
dir: A547 Abergele, right Rhyd y Foel Rd, 3m then left signed B5381, 1st farm on right

🚐 £16-£24 🚐 £20-£24 ⛺ £10-£25

Open Mar-Oct Last departure 11.00hrs

A small, quiet caravan park on a working farm, surrounded by rolling countryside and farmland. The park continues to improve, with plans in place for an additional 20 pitches. It is an ideal holiday location for both families and couples, with its modern facilities, fully-serviced pitches, and well-equipped children's play area, as well as spacious fields to roam through. Close to Bodnant Gardens and glorious beaches. A 10 acre site with 40 touring pitches, 40 hardstandings.

Plas Farm Caravan Park

AA Pubs & Restaurants nearby: Wheatsheaf Inn, Betws-Yn-Rhos 01492 680218

Leisure: ⚑

Facilities: 🌂 ☉ 🌡 ✳ ♿ ☏ 🖩 🎪 🐾

Services: 🔌 🔄 🛢 T 🖤 ⛽ 🖤

Within 3 miles: ↕ 🖩 🎣 🖩

Notes: Bike hire, dog kennels. Wi-fi

LLANDDULAS
Map 14 SH97

Places to visit

Great Orme Bronze Age Copper Mine, Llandudno, 01492 870447, www.greatormemines.info

Bodelwyddan Castle, Bodelwyddan, 01745 584060, www.bodelwyddan-castle.co.uk

PREMIER PARK

▶▶▶▶▶ 83% Bron-Y-Wendon Caravan Park (SH903785)

Wern Rd LL22 8HG
☎ 01492 512903 📄 01492 512903
e-mail: stay@northwales-holidays.co.uk
dir: Take A55 W. Turn right at sign for Llanddulas A547 junct 23, then sharp right. 200yds, under A55 bridge. Park on left

* 🚐 £19-£22 🚐 £19-£22

Open all year Last arrival anytime Last departure 11.00hrs

A top quality site in a stunning location, with panoramic sea views from every pitch and excellent purpose-built toilet facilities. Pitch density is excellent, offering a high degree of privacy, and the grounds are beautifully landscaped and immaculately maintained. Staff are helpful and friendly, and everything from landscaping to maintenance has a stamp of excellence. An ideal seaside base for touring Snowdonia and visiting Colwyn Bay, Llandudno and Conwy. An 8 acre site with 130 touring pitches, 85 hardstandings.

AA Pubs & Restaurants nearby: Pen-y-Bryn, Colwyn Bay 01492 533360

Leisure: 🔍

Facilities: 🌂 ☉ 🌡 ✳ ♿ ☏ 🖩 🎪

Services: 🔌 🔄 🛢 🖤

Within 3 miles: ↕ 🐾 🎣 🖩 🖩 U

Notes: Tourist information, heated shower blocks, internet access. Wi-fi

LLANRWST
Map 14 SH86

Places to visit

Gwydyr Uchaf Chapel, Llanrwst, 01492 640578, www.cadw.wales.gov.uk

Dolwyddelan Castle, Dolwyddelan, 01690 750366, www.cadw.wales.gov.uk

Great for kids: Conwy Valley Railway Museum, Betws-Y-Coed, 01690 710568, www.conwyrailwaymuseum.co.uk

PREMIER PARK

▶▶▶▶▶ 85% Bron Derw Touring Caravan Park (SH798628)

LL26 0YT
☎ 01492 640494 📄 01492 640494
e-mail: bronderw@aol.com
web: www.bronderw-wales.co.uk
dir: From A55 take A470 for Betwys-y-Coed & Llanwrst. In Llanwrst left into Parry Rd signed Llanddoged. Left at T-junct, site signed at 1st farm entrance on right

* 🚐 £16-£18 🚐 £16-£18

Open Mar-Oct Last arrival 22.00hrs Last departure 11.00hrs

Surrounded by hills and beautifully landscaped from what was once a dairy farm, Bron Derw has been built to a very high standard and is now fully matured, with stunning flora and fauna displays. All pitches are fully serviced, and there is a heated, stone-built toilet block with excellent and immaculately maintained facilities. The tiled utility room, set in a modern conservatory alongside the facility block, houses a washing machine, tumble dryer and sinks for washing up and vegetable preparation. CCTV security cameras cover the whole park. A 2.5 acre site with 20 touring pitches, 20 hardstandings.

Bron Derw Touring Caravan Park

AA Pubs & Restaurants nearby: White Horse Inn, Capel Garmon, Betws-Y-Coed 01690 710271

Facilities:

Services:

Within 3 miles:

Notes: Children must be supervised, no bikes, scooters or skateboards, dogs must be kept on short leads

►►►► 80% Bodnant Caravan Park

(SH805609)

Nebo Rd LL26 0SD
01492 640248
e-mail: ermin@bodnant-caravan-park.co.uk
dir: *S in Llanrwst, exit A470 opposite Birmingham garage onto B5427 signed Nebo. Site 300yds on right, opposite leisure centre*

£12.50-£17.50 £12.50-£17.50
£12.50-£15.50

Open Mar-end Oct Last arrival 21.00hrs Last departure 11.00hrs

This well maintained and stunningly attractive park is filled with flower beds, and the landscape includes shrubberies and trees. The statics are unobtrusively sited and the quality toilet blocks are spotlessly clean. All caravan pitches are multi-service, and the tent pitches serviced. There is a separate playing field and rally field. There are lots of farm animals on the park to keep children entertained, and Victorian farming implements are on display around the touring fields. A 5 acre site with 54 touring pitches, 20 hardstandings and 2 statics.

AA Pubs & Restaurants nearby: White Horse Inn, Capel Garmon, Betws-Y-Coed 01690 710271

Facilities:

Services:

Within 3 miles:

Notes: Main gates locked 23.00hrs-08.00hrs, quiet after 23.00hrs

TAL-Y-BONT (NEAR CONWY) Map 14 SH76

Places to visit

Bodnant Garden, Tal-Y-Cafn, 01492 650460, www.bodnant-garden.co.uk

Great for kids: Smallest House, Conwy, 01492 593484

► 89% Tynterfyn Touring Caravan Park *(SH768695)*

LL32 8YX
01492 660525
dir: *5m S of Conwy on B5106, signed Tal-y-Bont, 1st on left*

* fr £13 fr £13.50 fr £7

Open Mar-Oct (rs 28 days in year tent pitches only) Last arrival 22.00hrs Last departure noon

A quiet, secluded little park set in the beautiful Conwy Valley, and run by family owners. The grounds are tended with care, and the older-style toilet facilities sparkle. There is lots of room for children and dogs to run around. A 2 acre site with 15 touring pitches, 4 hardstandings.

Leisure:

Facilities:

Services:

Within 3 miles:

Notes:

TOWYN (NEAR ABERGELE)   Map 14 SH97

Places to visit

Rhuddlan Castle, Rhuddlan, 01745 590777, www.cadw.wales.gov.uk

Great for kids: Welsh Mountain Zoo, Colwyn Bay, 01492 532938, www.welshmountainzoo.org

73% Ty Mawr Holiday Park (SH965792)

Towyn Rd LL22 9HG
☎ 01745 832079   📠 01745 827454
e-mail: admin.tymawr@parkresorts.com
dir: On A548, 0.25m W of Towyn

🚐 🚐 Å

Open Apr-Oct (rs Apr (excluding Etr)) Last arrival mdnt Last departure 10.00hrs

A very large coastal holiday park with extensive leisure facilities including sports and recreational amenities, and club and eating outlets. The toilet facilities in The Warren have been refurbished to a high standard. Ideally located for both Rhyl's attractions and the nearby historical site of Rhuddlan Castle. Seasonal touring pitches are available. An 18 acre site with 406 touring pitches and 464 statics.

AA Pubs & Restaurants nearby: Kinmel Arms, Abergele 01745 832207

Barratt's at Ty'n Rhyl, Rhyl 01745 344138

Leisure: 🏊 ⚑ 🎱
Facilities: 🚿 ⊙ ♿ 🕐 🖈 🍴 🪁
Services: 🔌 🖨 🍴🍽 🍺
Within 3 miles: 🎣 🎪 🎣 ◎ 🖮 🖳 ∪

Notes: Free evening entertainment, kids' club. Wi-fi

see advert on page 381

DENBIGHSHIRE

CORWEN   Map 15 SJ04

See also Llandrillo

Places to visit

Rug Chapel, Corwen, 01490 412025, www.cadw.wales.gov.uk

Ewe-Phoria Sheepdog Centre, Corwen, 01490 460369, www.ewe-phoria.co.uk

►► 70% Llawr-Betws Farm Caravan Park (SJ016424)

LL21 0HD
☎ 01490 460224 & 460296
dir: 3m W of Corwen off A494 (Bala road)

＊ 🚐 fr £10 🚐 fr £10 Å fr £8

Open Mar-Oct Last arrival 23.00hrs Last departure noon

A quiet grassy park with mature trees and gently sloping pitches. The friendly owners keep the facilities in good condition. A 12.5 acre site with 35 touring pitches and 68 statics.

AA Pubs & Restaurants nearby: The Corn Mill, Llangollen 01978 869555

Leisure: ⚑ 🎱
Facilities: 🚿 ⊙ ✳ 🕐 🖈 🪁
Services: 🔌 🖨 🍴 🪧 🖳 🍺
Within 3 miles: 🎣 🖮 🖳
Notes: ⊛ Fishing

LLANDRILLO   Map 15 SJ03

Places to visit

Chirk Castle, Chirk, 01691 777701, www.nationaltrust.org.uk/main/w-chirkcastle

Rug Chapel, Corwen, 01490 412025, www.cadw.wales.gov.uk

►►► 77% Hendwr Country Park (SJ042386)

LL21 0SN
☎ 01490 440210
dir: From Corwen (A5) take B4401 for 4m. Right at Hendwr sign. Site 0.5m on right down wooded driveway. Or follow brown signs from A5 at Corwen

＊ 🚐 £18-£20 🚐 £18-£20 Å £18-£20

Open Apr-Oct Last arrival 22.00hrs Last departure 16.00hrs

Set in parkland at the end of a tree-lined lane, Hendwr (it means 'old tower') has a stream meandering through its grounds, and all around is the stunning Snowdonia mountain range. The toilet facilities are good. Self-catering holiday lodges and 29 seasonal touring pitches are available. An 11 acre site with 40 touring pitches, 3 hardstandings and 80 statics.

Facilities: 🚿 ⊙ ✳ 🕐 🖈 🪁
Services: 🔌 🖨 🍴 🪧 🖳 🍺
Within 3 miles: 🎣 🖳
Notes: ⊛ Dogs must be kept on leads at all times. Wet weather camping facilities

LLANGOLLEN   Map 15 SJ24

Places to visit

Plas Newydd, Llangollen, 01978 861314, www.denbighshire.gov.uk

Valle Crucis Abbey, Llangollen, 01978 860326, www.cadw.wales.gov.uk

Great for kids: Llangollen Railway, Llangollen, 01978 860979, www.llangollen-railway.co.uk

►► 76% Ty-Ucha Caravan Park (SJ232415)

Maesmawr Rd LL20 7PP
☎ 01978 860677
dir: 1m E of Llangollen. Signed 250yds off A5

＊ 🚐 £11-£15 🚐 £10-£14

Open Etr-Oct Last arrival 22.00hrs Last departure 13.00hrs

A very spacious site in beautiful unspoilt surroundings, with a small stream on site, and superb views. Ideal for country and mountain walking, and handily placed near the A5. Pitch density is excellent, facilities are clean and well maintained, and there is a games room with table tennis. Please note that this site does not accept tents. A 4 acre site with 40 touring pitches.

AA Pubs & Restaurants nearby: The Corn Mill, Llangollen 01978 869555

Leisure: 🎱
Facilities: 🚿 ⊙
Services: 🔌
Within 3 miles: 🎣 🍴 🖮 🎣 🖳 🖳 ∪
Notes: ⊛

LEISURE: 🏊 Indoor swimming pool 🏊 Outdoor swimming pool ⚑ Children's playground 🎾 Tennis court 🎱 Games room 📺 Separate TV room 🏌 9/18 hole golf course 🚣 Boats for hire 🎬 Cinema 🎣 Fishing ◎ Mini golf 🏄 Watersports ∪ Stables **FACILITIES:** 🛁 Bath 🚿 Shower ⊙ Electric shaver 🖈 Hairdryer ✳ Ice Pack Facility ♿ Disabled facilities 🕐 Public telephone 🖮 Shop on site or within 200yds 🚚 Mobile shop (calls at least 5 days a week) 🍺 BBQ area 🪁 Picnic area 🪁 Dog exercise area

PRESTATYN
Map 15 SJ08

Places to visit

Basingswerk Abbey, Holywell, 01443 336000, www.cadw.wales.gov.uk

Great for kids: Rhuddlan Castle, Rhuddlan, 01745 590777, www.cadw.wales.gov.uk

75% Presthaven Sands
(SJ091842)

Gronant LL19 9TT
☎ 01745 856471   ▤ 01745 886646
dir: *A548 from Prestatyn towards Gronant. Site signed. (NB For Sat Nav use LL19 9ST)*

Open mid Mar-Oct (rs mid Mar-May & Sep-Oct facilities may be reduced) Last arrival 20.00hrs Last departure 10.00hrs

Set beside two miles of superb sandy beaches and dunes, this large holiday centre offers extensive leisure and sports facilities and lively entertainment for all the family. The leisure complex houses clubs, swimming pools, restaurants, shops, launderette and pub, and the touring area is separate from the much larger static section. A 21 acre site with 34 touring pitches and 1052 statics.

AA Pubs & Restaurants nearby: Nant Hall Restaurant & Bar, Prestatyn 01745 886766

Leisure: 🏊 🎣 🎠
Facilities: 🚿 ⊙ ♿ ⊙ 🖻
Services: 🔌 🔥 🍴 🍔 🔋 ⚕
Within 3 miles: 🏇 🅿 ⊙ 🖻 🖥 ∪

Notes: Dogs must be kept on a lead at all times, certain dog breeds banned. Kids' clubs. Wi-fi

RHUALLT

Places to visit

Rhuddlan Castle, Rhuddlan, 01745 590777, www.cadw.wales.gov.uk

Bodelwyddan Castle, Bodelwyddan, 01745 584060, www.bodelwyddan-castle.co.uk

Great for kids: Denbigh Castle, Denbigh, 01745 813385, www.cadw.wales.gov.uk

RHUALLT
Map 15 SJ07

AA CAMPING CARD SITE

▶▶▶▶ 89% Penisar Mynydd Caravan Park *(SJ093770)*

Caerwys Rd LL17 0TY
☎ 01745 582227   ▤ 01745 582227
e-mail: contact@penisarmynydd.co.uk
web: www.penisarmynydd.co.uk
dir: *From Llandudno 1st left at top of Rhuallt Hill (junct 29). From Chester take junct 29, follow Dyserth signs, site 500yds on right*

Open Mar-15 Jan Last arrival 21.00hrs Last departure 21.00hrs

A very tranquil, attractively laid-out park set in three grassy paddocks with superb facilities block including a disabled room and dishwashing area. The majority of pitches are super pitches. Everything is immaculately maintained, and the amenities of the seaside resort of Rhyl are close by. A 6.6 acre site with 75 touring pitches, 75 hardstandings.

AA Pubs & Restaurants nearby: Plough Inn, St Asaph 01745 585080

The Oriel, St Asaph 01745 582716

Facilities: 🚿 ⊙ ✳ ♿ ⊙ 🖻 🎪 🐾
Services: 🔌 🖻 🍔 🔋 ⚕
Within 3 miles: 🏇 🅿 ⊙ 🖻 🖥 ∪
Notes: No cycling, dogs must be on kept on leads except in dog walk area. Large playing field, rally area

RUABON
Map 15 SJ34

Places to visit

Plas Newydd, Llangollen, 01978 861314, www.denbighshire.gov.uk

Valle Crucis Abbey, Llangollen, 01978 860326, www.cadw.wales.gov.uk

Great for kids: Horse Drawn Boats Centre, Llangollen, 01978 860702, www.horsedrawnboats.co.uk

▶▶▶ 72% James' Caravan Park
(SJ300434)

LL14 6DW
☎ 01978 820148   ▤ 01978 820148
e-mail: ray@carastay.demon.co.uk
dir: *Approach on A483 South, at rdbt with A539, turn right (signed Llangollen) over dual carriageway bridge, site 500yds on left*

Open all year Last arrival 21.00hrs Last departure 11.00hrs

A well-landscaped park on a former farm, with modern heated toilet facilities. Old farm buildings house a collection of restored original farm machinery, and the village shop, four pubs, takeaway and launderette are a 10-minute walk away. A 6 acre site with 40 touring pitches, 4 hardstandings.

AA Pubs & Restaurants nearby: The Corn Mill, Llangollen 01978 869555

Facilities: 🚿 ⊙ 🅿 ✳ ♿ ⊙ 🐾
Services: 🔌 🖻 🍔 🔋   **Within 3 miles:** 🏇 🖻 🖥
Notes: Chest freezer available

GWYNEDD

ABERSOCH
Map 14 SH32

Places to visit

Plas Yn Rhiw, Plas Yn Rhiw, 01758 780219, www.nationaltrust.org.uk

Penarth Fawr, Penarth Fawr, 01443 336000, www.cadw.wales.gov.uk

Great for kids: Criccieth Castle, Criccieth, 01766 522227, www.cadw.wales.gov.uk

▶▶▶▶ 80% Beach View Caravan Park *(SH316262)*

Bwlchtocyn LL53 7BT
☎ 01758 712956
dir: *Through Abersoch & Sarn Bach. Over x-rds, next left signed Porthtocyn Hotel. Pass chapel to another Porthocyn Hotel sign. Turn left, site on left*

Open mid Mar-mid Oct Last arrival 19.00hrs Last departure 11.00hrs

A compact family park run by a very enthusiastic owner who makes continual improvements. Just a six-minute walk from the beach, the site's immaculately maintained grounds, good hardstanding pitches (mostly seasonal) and excellent facilities are matched by great sea and country views. Seasonal touring pitches are available. A 4 acre site with 47 touring pitches.

AA Pubs & Restaurants nearby: Porth Tocyn Hotel, Abersoch 01758 713303

Bae Abermaw, Abersoch 01341 280550

Neigwl Hotel, Abersoch 01758 712363

Facilities: 🚿 ⊙ 🅿 🐾   **Services:** 🔌 🖻 🍔 🌊
Within 3 miles: 🏇 🎣 🅿 🖻 🖥 ∪
Notes: 🚫

ABERSOCH *continued*

▶▶▶▶ 78% Deucoch Touring & Camping Park *(SH301269)*

Sarn Bach LL53 7LD
☎ 01758 713293 & 07740 281770
📠 01758 713293
e-mail: info@deucoch.com
dir: *From Abersoch take Sarn Bach road, at x-rds turn right, site on right in 800yds*

🚐 🚙 Å

Open Mar-Oct Last arrival 22.00hrs Last departure 11.00hrs

A sheltered site with sweeping views of Cardigan Bay and the mountains, just a mile from Abersoch and a long sandy beach. The facilities block is well maintained, and this site is of special interest to watersports enthusiasts and those touring the Llyn Peninsula. A 5 acre site with 70 touring pitches, 10 hardstandings.

AA Pubs & Restaurants nearby: Porth Tocyn Hotel, Abersoch 01758 713303

Bae Abermaw, Abersoch 01341 280550

Neigwl Hotel, Abersoch 01758 712363

Leisure: 🄰 🔍
Facilities: 🚿☉☏✳♿🛎🚻
Services: 🔌🗑🛢⛽
Within 3 miles: ⌛🎣🏊⛵🏰🎯U
Notes: 🐕 Families only

▶▶▶ 82% Tyn-y-Mur Touring & Camping *(SH304290)*

GOLD

Lon Garmon LL53 7UL
☎ 01758 712328
e-mail: info@tyn-y-mur.co.uk
dir: *From Pwllheli into Abersoch on A499, sharp right at Land & Sea Garage. Site approx 0.5m on left*

🚐 £25 🚙 £25 Å £18-£25

Open May-Oct Last departure 11.00hrs

A family-only park in a glorious hill-top location overlooking a lush valley and with views extending across Abersoch to the mountains beyond Cardigan Bay. Good, clean modernised toilet facilities and spacious tent pitches in a level grassy field. The beach at Abersoch is just a short walk away and the park offers boat storage facilities. Seasonal touring pitches are available. A 22 acre site with 50 touring pitches, 37 hardstandings.

AA Pubs & Restaurants nearby: Porth Tocyn Hotel, Abersoch 01758 713303

Bae Abermaw, Abersoch 01341 280550

Neigwl Hotel, Abersoch 01758 712363

Leisure: 🄰
Facilities: 🚿☉☏✳♿🛎🚻
Services: 🔌🗑🛢🚮⛽
Within 3 miles: ⌛🎣🏊⛵🏰🎯U
Notes: 🐕 No open fires, use of motorcycles prohibited, no noisy activity after 23.00hrs, 1 dog per unit

▶▶▶ 79% Bryn Bach Caravan & Camping Site *(SH315258)*

Tyddyn Talgoch Uchaf, Bwlchtocyn LL53 7BT
☎ 01758 712285
e-mail: brynbach@abersochcamping.co.uk
dir: *From Abersoch take Sarn Bach road for approx 1m, left at sign for Bwlchtocyn. Site approx 1m on left*

* 🚐 £18-£22 🚙 £18-£22 Å £10-£25

Open Mar-Oct Last arrival 22.00hrs Last departure 11.00hrs

This well-run, elevated park overlooks Abersoch Bay, with lovely sea views towards the Snowdonia mountain range. Pitches are well laid out in sheltered paddocks, with well-placed modern facilities. Fishing, watersports, golf and beach access are all nearby. A 4 acre site with 30 touring pitches, 1 hardstanding and 2 statics.

AA Pubs & Restaurants nearby: Porth Tocyn Hotel, Abersoch 01758 713303

Bae Abermaw, Abersoch 01341 280550

Neigwl Hotel, Abersoch 01758 712363

Leisure: 🄰
Facilities: 🚿☉☏✳♿🚻🚻
Services: 🔌🗑🛢🚮⛽
Within 3 miles: ⌛🎣🏊⛵🏰🎯U
Notes: Families & couples only. Private shortcut to beach, boat storage

▶▶▶ 69% Rhydolion *(SH283276)*

Rhydolion, Llangian LL53 7LR
☎ 01758 712342
e-mail: enquiries@rhydolion.co.uk
dir: *From A499 take unclassified road to Llangian for 1m, turn left, through Llangian. Site 1.5m after road fork towards Hell's Mouth/Porth Neigwl*

* 🚐 £15-£25 Å fr £12

Open Mar-Oct Last arrival 22.00hrs Last departure noon

A peaceful small site with good views, on a working farm close to the long sandy surfers beach at Hell's Mouth. The simple, newly revamped toilet facilities are kept to a high standard by the friendly owners, and nearby Abersoch is a mecca for boat owners and water sports enthusiasts. A 1.5 acre site with 28 touring pitches.

AA Pubs & Restaurants nearby: Porth Tocyn Hotel, Abersoch 01758 713303

Bae Abermaw, Abersoch 01341 280550

Neigwl Hotel, Abersoch 01758 712363

Leisure: 🄰 **Facilities:** 🚿☉✳🐕
Services: 🔌🗑🛢
Within 3 miles: ⌛🎣🏊⛵🏰🎯U
Notes: 🐕 Families and couples only, dogs by arrangement only. 3 fridge freezers

---

BALA   Map 14 SH93

Places to visit
Bala Lake Railway, Llanuwchllyn, 01678 540666, www.bala-lake-railway.co.uk
Rug Chapel, Corwen, 01490 412025, www.cadw.wales.gov.uk

Great for kids: Ewe-Phoria Sheepdog Centre, Corwen, 01490 460369, www.ewe-phoria.co.uk

---

AA CAMPING CARD SITE

▶▶▶▶ 80% Pen-y-Bont Touring Park *(SH932350)*

Llangynog Rd LL23 7PH
☎ 01678 520549 📠 01678 520006
e-mail: penybont-bala@btconnect.com
dir: *From A494 take B4391. Site 0.75m on right*

🚐 🚙 Å

Open Mar-Oct Last arrival 21.00hrs Last dep noon

A family run attractively landscaped park in a woodland country setting. Set close to Bala Lake and the River Dee, with plenty of opportunities for

---

LEISURE: 🏊 Indoor swimming pool 🏊 Outdoor swimming pool 🄰 Children's playground 🎾 Tennis court 🔍 Games room 📺 Separate TV room ⛳ 9/18 hole golf course ⛵ Boats for hire 🎬 Cinema 🎣 Fishing 🏌 Mini golf 🏊 Watersports U Stables **FACILITIES:** 🛁 Bath 🚿 Shower ☉ Electric shaver 📮 Hairdryer ✳ Ice Pack Facility ♿ Disabled facilities ☏ Public telephone 🛒 Shop on site or within 200yds 🚚 Mobile shop (calls at least 5 days a week) 🍖 BBQ area 🌲 Picnic area 🐕 Dog exercise area

water sports including kayaking and white water rafting. The park offers good facilities including Wi-fi and a new motorhome service point, and many pitches have water and electricity. Around the park are superb large wood carvings of birds and mythical creatures depicting local legends. A 7 acre site with 95 touring pitches, 59 hardstandings.

Facilities: 🌳⊙🅿☀☕🕭🚿🚻🎣🚭

Services: 🔌🗑🔋🚿🚰🚹

Within 3 miles: 🚶🚉🎯🎣🚴🍴🛒🔋

Notes: No camp fires, BBQs must be kept off ground, quiet after 22.30hrs. Wi-fi

---

▶▶▶▶ 79% Tyn Cornel Camping & Caravan Park (SH895400)

Frongoch LL23 7NU
☎ 01678 520759   📠 01678 520759
e-mail: tyncornel@mail.com
dir: From Bala take A4212 (Porthmadog road) for 4m. Site on left before National Whitewater Centre

* 🚐 £14-£18 🚙 £14-£18 ⛺ £14-£18

Open Etr-Oct Last arrival 20.00hrs (22.00hrs on Fri) Last departure noon

A delightful riverside park with mountain views, popular with those seeking a base for river kayaks and canoes, with access to the nearby White Water Centre and riverside walk with tearoom. The helpful, resident owners keep the modern facilities, including a laundry and dishwashing room, very clean. A 10 acre site with 67 touring pitches, 10 hardstandings.

Facilities: 🌳⊙🅿☀☕🕭🚿🚻🎣🚭

Services: 🔌🗑🔋🚿

Within 3 miles: 🚶🚉🎯🎣🚴🍴🛒🔋

Notes: Quiet after 23.00hrs, no cycling, no camp fires or wood burning. Fridge, freezer & tumble dryer. Wi-fi

BANGOR   Map 14 SH57

▶▶ 68% Treborth Hall Farm Caravan Park (SH554707)

The Old Barn, Treborth Hall Farm LL57 2RX
☎ 01248 364399   📠 01248 364333
e-mail: enquiries@treborthleisure.co.uk
dir: A55 junct 9, 1st left at rdbt, straight over 2nd rdbt, site approx 800yds on left

🚐 🚙 ⛺

Open Etr-end Oct Last arrival 22.30hrs Last departure 10.30hrs

Set in eight acres of beautiful parkland with its own trout fishing lake and golf course, this park offers serviced pitches in a sheltered, walled orchard. Tents have a separate grass area, and there is a good clean toilet block. This is a useful base for families, with easy access for the Menai Straits, Anglesey beaches, Snowdon and the Lleyn peninsula. Seasonal touring pitches are available. An 8 acre site with 34 touring pitches, 34 hardstandings and 4 statics.

Leisure: 🌊

Facilities: 🌳⊙🚿🚻

Services: 🔌

Within 3 miles: 🚶🎣⊚🛒🔋

Notes: Dogs must be kept on leads

BARMOUTH   Map 14 SH61

PREMIER PARK

▶▶▶▶▶ 90% Trawsdir Touring Caravans & Camping Park (SH596198)

Best of British

Llanaber LL42 1RR
☎ 01341 280611 & 280999   📠 01341 280740
e-mail: enquiries@barmouthholidays.co.uk
web: www.barmouthholidays.co.uk
dir: 3m N of Barmouth on A496, just past Wayside pub on right

* 🚐 £24-£31 🚙 £24-£31 ⛺ £16-£26

Open Mar-Jan Last arrival 20.00hrs Last departure noon

Well run by enthusiastic wardens, this quality park enjoys spectacular views to the sea and hills, and is very accessible to motor traffic. The facilities are appointed to a very high standard, and include spacious cubicles containing showers and washbasins, individual showers, smart toilets with sensor-operated flush, and under-floor heating. Tents and caravans have their own designated areas divided by dry-stone walls, and the site is very convenient for large recreational vehicles. There is an excellent new children's play area, plus glorious seasonal floral displays and an illuminated dog walk that leads directly to the nearby pub! There are also luxury holiday lodges for hire. A 15 acre site with 70 touring pitches, 70 hardstandings.

AA Pubs & Restaurants nearby: Bae Abermawr, Barmouth 01341 280550

Leisure: 🌊

Facilities: 🌳⊙🅿☀🕭🚿🚻🎣🚭

Services: 🔌🗑🔋🚿🚰🚹

Within 3 miles: 🎣🛒🔋

Notes: Families & couples only. Milk/bread etc available from reception. Wi-fi

BARMOUTH *continued*

PREMIER PARK

AA CAMPING CARD SITE

▶▶▶▶ 82% Hendre Mynach
Touring Caravan & Camping Park

(SH605170)

Llanaber Rd LL42 1YR
☎ 01341 280262 ▤ 01341 280586
e-mail: mynach@lineone.net
web: www.hendremynach.co.uk
dir: *0.75m N of Barmouth on A496*

🚐 🚑 🅰

Open Mar-9 Jan (rs Nov-Jan shop closed) Last
arrival 22.00hrs Last departure noon

A lovely site with enthusiastic new owners and
immaculate facilities, just off the A496 and near
the railway, with almost direct access to the
promenade and beach. Caravanners should not be
put off by the steep descent, as park staff are
always on hand if needed. Spacious pitches have
TV and satellite hook-up as well as water and
electricity. A small café serves light meals and
takeaways. Seasonal touring pitches are
available. A 10 acre site with 240 touring pitches,
75 hardstandings and 1 static.

AA Pubs & Restaurants nearby: Bae Abermawr,
Barmouth 01341 280550

Leisure: 🅰 Facilities: 🐾⊙🅿✳🕭🕓🅱🏇
Services: 🖳🖩🅰🖉🅃🍽🛒🖐
Within 3 miles: 🖩🖉🅱🖩U
Notes: 50 TV hook ups. Wi-fi

BETWS GARMON   Map 14 SH55

Places to visit

Snowdon Mountain Railway, Llanberis,
01286 870223, www.snowdonrailway.co.uk

Great for kids: Dolbadarn Castle, Llanberis,
01443 336000, www.cadw.wales.gov.uk

▶▶▶▶ 79% Bryn Gloch Caravan &
Camping Park *(SH534574)*

LL54 7YY
☎ 01286 650216
e-mail: eurig@bryngloch.co.uk
web: www.bryngloch.co.uk
dir: *On A4085, 5m SE of Caernarfon*

🚐 £15-£25 🚑 £15-£25 🅰 £15-£25

Open all year Last arrival 23.00hrs Last departure
17.00hrs

An excellent family-run site with immaculate
modern facilities, and all level pitches in
beautiful surroundings. The park offers the best
of two worlds, with its bustling holiday
atmosphere and the peaceful natural
surroundings. The 28 acres of level fields are
separated by mature hedges and trees,
guaranteeing sufficient space for families
wishing to spread themselves out. There are
static holiday caravans for hire and plenty of
walks in the area. A 28 acre site with 160 touring
pitches, 60 hardstandings and 17 statics.

AA Pubs & Restaurants nearby: Snowdonia Parc
Brewpub, Waunfawr 01286 650409

Leisure: 🅰🔍🖵
Facilities: 🛁🐾⊙🅿✳🕭🕓🅱🏇🏇
Services: 🖳🖩🅰🖉🅃🛒🖐
Within 3 miles: 🖩🖉🅱🖩U
Notes: Family bathroom, mother & baby room. Wi-fi
see advert below

CAERNARFON   Map 14 SH46

See also Dinas Dinlle & Llandwrog

Places to visit

Segontium Roman Museum, Caernarfon,
01286 675625, www.segontium.org.uk

Welsh Highland Railway, Caernarfon,
01286 677018, www.festrail.co.uk

Great for kids: Caernarfon Castle, Caernarfon,
01286 677617, www.cadw.wales.gov.uk

▶▶▶ 85% Riverside Camping

(SH505630)

Seiont Nurseries, Pont Rug LL55 2BB
☎ 01286 678781 ▤ 01286 677223
e-mail: brenda@riversidecamping.co.uk
web: www.riversidecamping.co.uk
dir: *2m from Caernarfon on right of A4086
towards Llanberis, also signed Seiont Nurseries*

* 🚐 £12-£19 🚑 £12-£19 🅰 £12-£19

Open Etr-end Oct Last arrival anytime Last
departure noon

Set in the grounds of a large garden centre beside
the small River Seiont, this park is approached by
an impressive tree-lined drive. Immaculately
maintained by the owners, there are good grassy

LEISURE: 🏊 Indoor swimming pool 🏊 Outdoor swimming pool 🅰 Children's playground 🎾 Tennis court 🔴 Games room 🖵 Separate TV room ⛳ 9/18 hole golf course 🚤 Boats for hire 🎭 Cinema 🎣 Fishing ⊙ Mini golf 🏄 Watersports U Stables FACILITIES: 🛁 Bath 🐾 Shower ⊙ Electric shaver 🅿 Hairdryer ✳ Ice Pack Facility 🕭 Disabled facilities 🕓 Public telephone 🅱 Shop on site or within 200yds 🖉 Mobile shop (calls at least 5 days a week) 🍽 BBQ area 🏞 Picnic area 🏇 Dog exercise area

riverside tent pitches, clean and tidy toilet facilities and an excellent café/restaurant. A haven of peace close to Caernarfon, Snowdonia and some great walking opportunities. A 4.5 acre site with 60 touring pitches, 8 hardstandings.

AA Pubs & Restaurants nearby: Seiont Manor Hotel, Llanrug 01286 673366

Rhiwafallen Restaurant with Rooms, Llandwrog 01286 830172

Leisure: 𝌆

Facilities: 🐾☉🅿✳♿🎒🚿

Services: 🔌🖴🍽🔋♨

Within 3 miles: ↨✈🏌🛶🏦🖴↻

Notes: ⊘ No fires, no loud music, dogs must be kept on leads. Family shower room & baby changing facilities. Wi-fi

►►► 80% Plas Gwyn Caravan & Camping Park

(SH520633)

Llanrug LL55 2AQ
☎ 01286 672619
e-mail: info@plasgwyn.co.uk
web: www.plasgwyn.co.uk
dir: A4086, 3m E of Caernarfon, site on right. Between River Seiont & Llanryg village

* 🚐 £15-£18 🚙 £15-£18 ⛺ £9-£16

Open Mar-Oct Last arrival 22.00hrs Last departure 11.30hrs

A secluded park in an ideal location for visiting the glorious nearby beaches, historic Caernarfon, the Snowdonia attractions, and for walking. The site is set within the grounds of Plas Gwyn House, a Georgian property with colonial additions, and the friendly owners are gradually upgrading the park. There are four fully serviced pitches, a wooden camping pod, five static caravans for hire and eight seasonal touring pitches. A 3 acre site with 30 touring pitches, 8 hardstandings and 18 statics.

AA Pubs & Restaurants nearby: Seiont Manor Hotel, Llanrug 01286 673366

Rhiwafallen Restaurant with Rooms, Llandwrog 01286 830172

Facilities: 🐾☉🅿✳🎒🚿🐕

Services: 🔌🖴🛢⌀🅃♨↯

Within 3 miles: ↨✈🏌🛶🏦🖴↻

Notes: Wi-fi

►►► 77% Cwm Cadnant Valley

(SH487628)

Cwm Cadnant Valley, Llanberis Rd LL55 2DF
☎ 01286 673196   📠 01286 675941
e-mail: aa@cwmcadnant.co.uk
web: www.cwmcadnant.co.uk
dir: On outskirts of Caernarfon on A4086 towards Llanberis, next to fire station

* 🚐 £12-£18 🚙 £12-£18 ⛺ £9-£15

Open 14 Mar-3 Nov Last arrival 22.00hrs Last departure 11.00hrs

Set in an attractive wooded valley with a stream is this terraced site with secluded pitches, a good camping area for backpackers and clean, modernised toilet facilities. It is located on the outskirts of Caernarfon in a rural location, close to the main Caernarfon-Llanberis road and just a 10-minute walk from the castle and town centre. A 4.5 acre site with 60 touring pitches.

AA Pubs & Restaurants nearby: Seiont Manor Hotel, Llanrug 01286 673366

Rhiwafallen Restaurant with Rooms, Llandwrog 01286 830172

Leisure: 𝌆   **Facilities:** 🐾☉🅿✳♿🕔🅗🎌

Services: 🔌🖴🛢⌀🅃♨

Within 3 miles: ↨✈🏌🛶🏦🖴↻

Notes: Family room with baby changing facilities. Wi-fi

NEW ►►► 74% Ty'n yr Onnen Caravan Park (SH533588)

Waunfawr LL55 4AX
☎ 01286 650281   📠 01286 650043
dir: At Waunfawr on A4085, onto unclass road opposite church. Site signed

🚐 🚙 ⛺

Open Etr-Oct (rs Etr & May Day BH open if weather permitting) Last arrival 20.00hrs Last dep noon

A gently sloping site on a 200-acre sheep farm set in magnificent surroundings close to Snowdon and enjoying stunning mountain views. This secluded

park is well equipped and has quality toilet facilities. Access is via a very narrow, unclassified road, which would be a challenge for the larger unit or the faint hearted. A 3.5 acre site with 20 touring pitches.

Leisure: 𝌆🎣🖳

Facilities: 🐾🐾☉🅿✳♿🕔🅗🚿🎌🐕

Services: 🔌🖴🛢⌀🅃♨

Within 3 miles: ↨✈🏌🛶🏦🖴↻

Notes: No music after 22.00hrs. Fishing & nature park

CRICCIETH   Map 14 SH43

Places to visit

Criccieth Castle, Criccieth, 01766 522227, www.cadw.wales.gov.uk

Portmeirion, Portmerion, 01766 770000, www.portmeirion-village.com

Great for kids: Ffestiniog Railway, Porthmadog, 01766 516000, www.festrail.co.uk

---

►►►► 81% Eisteddfa (SH518394)

Eisteddfa Lodge, Pentrefelin LL52 0PT
☎ 01766 522696
e-mail: eisteddfa@criccieth.co.uk
dir: From Porthmadog take A497 towards Criccieth. After approx 3.5m, through Pentrefelin, site signed 1st right after Plas Gwyn Nursing Home

🚐 🚙 ⛺

Open Mar-Oct Last arrival 22.30hrs Last departure 11.00hrs

A quiet, secluded park on elevated ground, sheltered by the Snowdonia Mountains and with lovely views of Cardigan Bay; Criccieth is nearby. The owners are carefully improving the park whilst preserving its unspoilt beauty, and are keen to welcome families, who will appreciate the cubicled facilities. There's a field and play area, woodland walks, a tipi, six superb new slate-based hardstandings, three static holiday caravans for hire, and a three-acre coarse fishing lake adjacent to the park. An 11 acre site with 100 touring pitches, 17 hardstandings.

AA Pubs & Restaurants nearby: Bron Eifion Country House Hotel, Criccieth 01766 522385

Plas Bodegroes, Pwllheli 01758 612363

Leisure: 𝌆🎣   **Facilities:** 🐾☉🅿✳♿🎌🐕

Services: 🔌🖴🛢⌀♨

Within 3 miles: ↨✈🏌🛶🏦◎🖴↻

Notes: Football pitch, baby bath

CRICCIETH *continued*

►► 82% Llwyn-Bugeilydd Caravan & Camping Site *(SH498398)*

LL52 0PN
☎ 01766 522235
dir: *From Porthmadog on A497, 1m N of Criccieth on B4411. Site 1st on right. From A55 take A487 through Caernarfon. After Bryncir right onto B4411, site on left in 3.5m*

⚏ ⚏ Å

Open Mar-Oct Last arrival anytime Last departure 11.00hrs

A quiet rural site with sea and Snowdon mountain views, and well tended grass pitches. The toilets are kept very clean, and the resident owner is always on hand. A 6 acre site with 45 touring pitches, 2 hardstandings.

AA Pubs & Restaurants nearby: Bron Eifion Country House Hotel, Criccieth 01766 522385

Plas Bodegroes, Pwllheli 01758 612363

Leisure: ⚑

Facilities: ⚏ ☺ ⚏ ✳ ✚

Services: ⚏ ⚏

Within 3 miles: ⚏ ⚏ ⚏ ⚏ ⚏ ⚏ ⚏ ⚏ ⚏ ⚏ ⚏ U

Notes: ⚏ No skateboards

► 64% Tyddyn Morthwyl Camping & Caravan Site *(SH491399)*

LL52 0NF
☎ 01766 522115
e-mail: trumper@henstabl147freeserve.co.uk
dir: *1.5m N of Criccieth on B4411. Sign at entrance*

* ⚏ £10 ⚏ £10 Å £10

Open Etr-Oct (rs Mar & Oct) Last departure 14.00hrs

A simple and very quiet sheltered site on a farm with level grass pitches in three fields, which offer plenty of space. The simple facilities include some electric hook-ups, basic yet clean toilets, lovely surrounding walks, bunkhouse accommodation, and Criccieth and the sea are close by. At the remarkable age of 99, owner Mrs Trumper must be our oldest campsite operator. A 10 acre site with 40 touring pitches and 22 statics.

AA Pubs & Restaurants nearby: Bron Eifion Country House Hotel, Criccieth 01766 522385

Plas Bodegroes, Pwllheli 01758 612363

Facilities: ⚏ ☺ ⚏ ⚏

Services: ⚏ ⚏

Within 3 miles: ⚏ ⚏ ⚏ ⚏ ⚏ U

Notes: ⚏ Dogs must be kept on leads at all times, rallies welcome

---

DINAS DINLLE   Map 14 SH45

Places to visit

Snowdon Mountain Railway, Llanberis, 01286 870223, www.snowdonrailway.co.uk

St Cybi's Well, Llangybi, 01443 336000, www.cadw.wales.gov.uk

Great for kids: Dolbadarn Castle, Llanberis, 01443 336000, www.cadw.wales.gov.uk

---

►►►► 85% Dinlle Caravan Park *(SH438568)*

LL54 5TW
☎ 01286 830324   ▤ 01286 831526
e-mail: enq@thornleyleisure.co.uk
dir: *S on A499 turn right at sign for Caernarfon Airport. 2m W of Dinas Dinlle coast*

* ⚏ £9-£21 ⚏ £9-£21 Å £9-£21

Open Mar-Oct Last arrival 23.00hrs Last departure noon

A very accessible, well-kept grassy site, adjacent to sandy beach, with good views to Snowdonia.

The park is situated in acres of flat grassland, with plenty of room for even the largest groups. A lounge bar and family room are comfortable places in which to relax, and children are well provided for with an exciting adventure playground. The beach road gives access to the golf club, a nature reserve, and to Air World at Caernarfon Airport. The new man-made dune offers campers additional protection from sea breezes. A 20 acre site with 175 touring pitches, 20 hardstandings and 167 statics.

AA Pubs & Restaurants nearby: Rhiwafallen Restaurant with Rooms, Llandwrog 01286 830172

Leisure: 🏊 🎨 🔍

Facilities: 🚿 ⊙ 🅿 ✳ ♿ 🕐

Services: 🔌 🗄 🎁 🛒 🍴 🚽

Within 3 miles: 📍 🎣 🅱 ↻

Notes: No skateboards. Wi-fi

see advert on opposite page

Places to visit

Cymer Abbey, Cymer Abbey, 01443 336000, www.cadw.wales.gov.uk

Great for kids: Harlech Castle, Harlech, 01766 780552, www.cadw.wales.gov.uk

►►► 78% Murmur-yr-Afon Touring Park (SH586236)

LL44 2BE
☎ 01341 247353 📠 01341 247353
e-mail: murmuryrafon1@btinternet.com
dir: *On A496 N of village*

🔌 🚐 ⚠

Open Mar-Oct Last arrival 22.00hrs Last departure 11.00hrs

A pleasant family-run park alongside a wooded stream on the edge of the village, and handy for large sandy beaches. Expect good, clean facilities, and lovely views of rolling hills and mountains. A 6 acre site with 77 touring pitches, 37 hardstandings.

AA Pubs & Restaurants nearby: Victoria Inn, Llanbedr 01341 241213

Leisure: 🎨

Facilities: 🚿 ⊙ 🅿 ✳ ♿ 🕐 🗄 🍴 ⛺

Services: 🔌 🗄 ⛽

Within 3 miles: 📍 🅱 🅱

Notes: 🚫

Places to visit

Sygun Copper Mine, Beddgelert, 01766 890595, www.syguncoppermine.co.uk

Great for kids: Caernarfon Castle, Caernarfon, 01286 677617, www.cadw.wales.gov.uk

AA CAMPING CARD SITE

►►►► 77% White Tower Caravan Park (SH453582)

LL54 5UH
☎ 01286 830649 & 07802 562785
📠 01286 830649
e-mail: whitetower@supanet.com
web: www.whitetowerpark.co.uk
dir: *1.5m from village on Tai'r Eglwys road. From Caernarfon take A487 (Porthmadog road). Cross rdbt, 1st right. Site 3m on right*

🔌 £18-£25 🚐 £18-£25 ⚠ £18-£25

Open Mar-10 Jan (rs Mar-mid May & Sep-Oct bar open wknds only) Last arrival 23.00hrs Last departure noon

There are lovely views of Snowdonia from this park located just two miles from the nearest beach at Dinas Dinlle. A well-maintained toilet block has key access, and the hardstanding pitches have water and electricity. Popular amenities include an outdoor heated swimming pool, a lounge bar with family room, and a games and TV room. Seasonal touring pitches are available. A 6 acre site with 104 touring pitches, 80 hardstandings and 54 statics.

AA Pubs & Restaurants nearby: Rhiwafallen Restaurant with Rooms, Llandwrog 01286 830172

Leisure: 🏊 🎨 🔍 📺

Facilities: 🚿 ⊙ 🅿 ✳ ♿ 🕐

Services: 🔌 🗄 🎁 🛒 🍴 ⛺

Within 3 miles: 📍 🎣 🅱 🅱 ↻

Places to visit

Plas Yn Rhiw, Plas Yn Rhiw, 01758 780219, www.nationaltrust.org.uk

Penarth Fawr, Penarth Fawr, 01443 336000, www.cadw.wales.gov.uk

AA CAMPING CARD SITE

►►► 70% Tanrallt Farm (SH296288)

Tanrallt LL53 7LN
☎ 01758 713527
e-mail: www.abersoch-holiday.co.uk
dir: *A499 to Abersoch, right up hill, follow signs for Llangian. Site in village on left*

🔌 🚐 ⚠

Open Etr-end Oct Last arrival 21.30hrs Last departure 10.30hrs

Tanrallt Farm site is in a secluded valley on a working farm. Friendly owners make their guests feel welcome, providing a BBQ area, very clean and serviceable toilets, a laundry room with washer, dryer, spin dryer, ironing board and iron plus a drying area for wet clothing. There are also three bunk rooms and a kitchen. A 1.5 acre site with 12 touring pitches, 12 hardstandings.

AA Pubs & Restaurants nearby: Porth Tocyn Hotel, Abersoch 01758 713303

Bae Abermaw, Abersoch 01341 280550

Neigwl Hotel, Abersoch 01758 712363

Facilities: 🚿 ✳ ♿ 🗄 🍴 🎨

Services: 🔌 🗄 ⛺ 🚽

Within 3 miles: 🅱 🎣 📍 ⊙ 🅱 🅱 ↻

Notes: 🚫 Families & couples only. No noise after 23.00hrs

LLANRUG
Map 14 SH56

Places to visit

Segontium Roman Museum, Caernarfon, 01286 675625, www.segontium.org.uk

Dolbadarn Castle, Llanberis, 01443 336000, www.cadw.wales.gov.uk

Great for kids: Greenwood Forest Park, Y Felinheli, 01248 670076, www.greenwoodforestpark.co.uk

▶▶▶▶ **83% Llys Derwen Caravan & Camping Site** *(SH539629)*

Ffordd Bryngwyn LL55 4RD
☎ **01286 673322**
e-mail: llysderwen@aol.com
dir: *From A55 junct 13 (Caernarfon) take A4086 to Llanberis, through Llanrug, turn right at pub, site 60yds on right*

* 🚐 £12-£14 🚐 £12-£14 ▲ fr £7

Open Mar-Oct Last departure noon

A pleasant, beautifully maintained small site set in woodland within easy reach of Caernarfon, Snowdon, Anglesey and the Lleyn Peninsula. Visitors can expect a warm welcome from enthusiastic, hands-on owners, who keep the toilet facilities spotlessly clean. A 5 acre site with 20 touring pitches and 2 statics.

AA Pubs & Restaurants nearby: Seiont Manor Hotel, Llanrug 01286 673366

Facilities: 🅿️⊙✳️♿🚿📶 **Services:** 🚐🗄️🛁
Within 3 miles: 🚶✚𝒫⛵🎣🏇🎯🦌↺
Notes: 🐕 No open fires

PONT-RUG

See Caernarfon

PORTHMADOG
Map 14 SH53

Places to visit

Inigo Jones Slateworks, Groeslon, 01286 830242, www.inigojones.co.uk

Great for kids: Ffestiniog Railway, Porthmadog, 01766 516000, www.festrail.co.uk

 **76% Greenacres**
(SH539374)

Black Rock Sands, Morfa Bychan LL49 9YF
☎ **01766 512781** 📄 **01766 512781**
e-mail: lizzy.sayer@bourne-leisure.co.uk
dir: *From Porthmadog High Street follow Black Rock Sands signs between The Factory Shop & Post Office. Park 2m on left at end of Morfa Bychan*

🚐🚐

Open mid Mar-Oct (rs mid Mar-May & Sep-Oct some facilities may be reduced) Last arrival anytime Last departure 10.00hrs

A quality holiday park on level ground just a short walk from Black Rock Sands, and set against a backdrop of Snowdonia National Park. All touring pitches are on hardstandings surrounded by closely-mown grass, and near the entertainment complex. A full programme of entertainment, organised clubs, indoor and outdoor sports and leisure, pubs, shows and cabarets all add to a holiday here. A bowling alley and a large shop/bakery are useful amenities. A 121 acre site with 52 touring pitches, 52 hardstandings and 370 statics.

AA Pubs & Restaurants nearby: Royal Sportsman Hotel, Porthmadog 01766 512015

Hotel Portmeirion, Portmeirion Village, Penrhyndeudraeth 01766 770000

Castell Deudraeth, Portmeirion Village 01766 772400

Leisure: 🏊🎬🎣
Facilities: 🅿️⊙𝒫♿🚿🛁📶
Services: 🚐🗄️🍽️🍺🛒
Within 3 miles: 🚶🎬𝒫🎯🛒🍺↺
Notes: Certain dog breeds banned
see advert below

PWLLHELI

Places to visit

Penarth Fawr, Penart Fawr, 01443 336000, www.cadw.wales.gov.uk

Plas Yn Rhiw, Plas Yn Rhiw, 01758 780219, www.nationaltrust.org.uk

Great for kids: Criccieth Castle, Criccieth, 01766 522227, www.cadw.wales.gov.uk

---

LEISURE: 🏊 Indoor swimming pool 🏊 Outdoor swimming pool ⋀ Children's playground 🎾 Tennis court ● Games room ⬜ Separate TV room 🏌 9/18 hole golf course ⛵ Boats for hire 🎬 Cinema 𝒫 Fishing ◉ Mini golf 🏄 Watersports ↺ Stables **FACILITIES:** 🛁 Bath 🚿 Shower ⊙ Electric shaver 𝒫 Hairdryer ✳️ Ice Pack Facility ♿ Disabled facilities 🕐 Public telephone 🛒 Shop on site or within 200yds 🚐 Mobile shop (calls at least 5 days a week) 🍽 BBQ area ⋈ Picnic area 🐕 Dog exercise area

PWLLHELI
Map 14 SH33

68% Hafan Y Mor Holiday Park *(SH431368)*

LL53 6HJ
☎ 0871 231 0887 📠 01766 810379
dir: *From Caernarfon A499 to Pwllheli. A497 to Porthmadog. Park on right, approx 3m from Pwllheli. Or from Telford, A5, A494 to Bala. Right for Porthmadog. Left at rdbt in Porthmadog signed Criccieth & Pwllheli. Park on left 3m from Criccieth*

Open 20 Mar-2 Nov (rs Mar-May & Sep-Oct reduced facilities) Last arrival 21.00hrs Last departure 10.00hrs

Set between the seaside towns of Pwllheli and Criccieth on the sheltered Llyn Peninsula, this is an all action caravan park with direct beach access. Facilities include an indoor splash pool with flumes and bubble pools, wave rider, aqua jet racer and boating lake. A 500 acre site with 73 touring pitches and 800 statics.

AA Pubs & Restaurants nearby: Plas Bodegroes, Pwllheli 01758 612363

Leisure: ⛱ 🏊
Facilities: 📶 🅿 ♿ 🕐 🚿
Services: 🔌 🗄 🚽 🛢 🍽 🔋
Within 3 miles: ↕ ⚓ 🎣 ⛳ ☕ 🎢
Notes: Wi-fi

see advert below

►►► 72% Abererch Sands Holiday Centre *(SH403359)*

LL53 6PJ
☎ 01758 612327 📠 01758 701556
e-mail: enquiries@abererch-sands.co.uk
dir: *On A497 (Porthmadog to Pwllheli road), 1m from Pwllheli*

Open Mar-Oct Last arrival 21.00hrs Last departure 21.00hrs

Glorious views of Snowdonia and Cardigan Bay can be enjoyed from this very secure, family-run site adjacent to a railway station and a four-mile stretch of sandy beach. A large heated indoor swimming pool, snooker room, pool room, fitness centre and children's play area make this an ideal holiday venue. An 85 acre site with 70 touring pitches, 70 hardstandings and 90 statics.

AA Pubs & Restaurants nearby: Plas Bodegroes, Pwllheli 01758 612363

Leisure: ⛱ 🏊 🎣
Facilities: 📶 ☀ ♿ 🕐 🚿 🚻
Services: 🔌 🗄 🛢 🚽 🛒 ↯
Within 3 miles: ↕ 🚴 ⚓ ⛳ ☕ 🎢
Notes: Wi-fi

TALSARNAU Map 14 SH63

Places to visit

Portmeirion, Portmerion, 01766 770000, www.portmeirion-village.com

Harlech Castle, Harlech, 01766 780552, www.cadw.wales.gov.uk

Great for kids: Ffestiniog Railway, Porthmadog, 01766 516000, www.festrail.co.uk

AA CAMPING CARD SITE

►►►► 82% Barcdy Touring Caravan & Camping Park

(SH620375)

LL47 6YG

☎ 01766 770736

e-mail: anwen@barcdy.co.uk

dir: *From Maentwrog take A496 for Harlech. Site 4m on left*

* 🚐 £22-£28 🚌 £22-£28 ⛺ £16-£22

Open Apr-Sep Last arrival 21.00hrs Last departure noon

A quiet picturesque park on the edge of the Vale of Ffestiniog near the Dwryd estuary. Two touring areas serve the park, one near the park entrance, and the other with improved and more secluded terraced pitches beside a narrow valley. The tent area is secluded and peaceful, and the toilet facilities are clean and tidy. Footpaths through adjacent woodland lead to small lakes and an established nature trail. A 12 acre site with 80 touring pitches, 40 hardstandings and 30 statics.

AA Pubs & Restaurants nearby: Hotel Portmeirion, Portmeirion Village, Penrhyndeudraeth 01766 770000

Castell Deudraeth, Portmeirion Village 01766 772400

Facilities: 🚿 ⊙ 💨 ✻ ⛱ **Services:** 🔌 🧺 🔥 🍃

Within 3 miles: ⛳ 🎣 [$] Ω

Notes: 🚫🐕 No noisy parties. Wi-fi

TAL-Y-BONT Map 14 SH52

Places to visit

Cymer Abbey, Cymer Abbey, 01443 336000, www.cadw.wales.gov.uk

Great for kids: Fairbourne Railway, Fairbourne, 01341 250362, www.fairbournerailway.com

PREMIER PARK

AA CAMPING CARD SITE

NEW ►►►►► 86% Islawrffordd Caravan Park *(SH584215)*

LL43 2AQ

☎ 01341 247269

e-mail: jane@islawrffordd.co.uk

dir: *On sea side of main A496 coast road, 4m N of Barmouth, 6m S of Harlech*

🚐 🚌 ⛺

Open Mar-1 Nov Last arrival 20.00hrs Last departure noon

Situated on the coast between Barmouth and Harlech, and within the Snowdonia National Park, with clear views of Cardigan Bay, the Lleyn Peninsula and the Snowdonia and Cader Idris mountain ranges, this excellent, family-run and family-friendly park has seen considerable investment since opening around five years ago. Fully matured, the touring area boasts fully serviced pitches, a superb new toilet block with under-floor heating and top-quality fittings, and the park has private access to miles of sandy beach. Plans include refurbishing the restaurant, bar and games room. A 25 acre site with 120 touring pitches, 25 hardstandings.

AA Pubs & Restaurants nearby: Victoria Inn, Llanbedr 01341 241213

Leisure: 🏊 ⛺ 🎱 🎮

Facilities: 🚿 ⊙ 💨 ✻ ♿ 📞 [$]

Services: 🔌 🧺 🍷 🔥 🍃 [T] 🍴 🔋 🥡 👶 ⛽

Within 3 miles: ⛳ 🎣 ◎ 🏄 [$] 🧺 Ω

Notes: Strictly families & couples only, no groups. Wi-fi

see advert on opposite page

TYWYN Map 14 SH50

Places to visit

Talyllyn Railway, Tywyn, 01654 710472, www.talyllyn.co.uk

Castell-y-Bere, Llanfihangel-y-Pennant, 01443 336000, www.cadw.wales.gov.uk

Great for kids: King Arthur's Labyrinth, Machynlleth, 01654 761584, www.kingarthurslabyrinth.com

►►►► 81% Ynysymaengwyn Caravan Park *(SH602021)*

LL36 9RY

☎ 01654 710684 📠 01654 710684

e-mail: rita@ynysy.co.uk

dir: *On A493, 1m N of Tywyn, towards Dolgellau*

🚐 🚌 ⛺

Open Etr or Apr-Oct Last arrival 23.00hrs Last departure noon

A lovely park set in the wooded grounds of a former manor house, with designated nature trails through 13 acres of wildlife-rich woodland, scenic river walks, fishing and a sandy beach nearby. The attractive stone amenity block is clean and well kept, and this smart municipal park is ideal for families. A 4 acre site with 80 touring pitches and 115 statics.

Leisure: ⛺

Facilities: 🚿 ⊙ 💨 ✻ ♿ 📞 [$] ⛱ 🐕

Services: 🔌 🧺 🔥 🍃 🔋

Within 3 miles: ⛳ 🏨 🎣 ◎ 🏄 [$] 🧺 Ω

Notes: 🚫💳 Dogs must be kept on leads at all times

SERVICES: 🔌 Electric hook up 🧺 Launderette 🍷 Licensed bar 🔥 Calor Gas 🍃 Camping Gaz [T] Toilet fluid 🍴 Café/Restaurant 🥡 Fast Food/Takeaway 🔋 Battery charging 👶 Baby care ⛽ Motorvan service point **ABBREVIATIONS:** BH/bank hols-bank holidays Etr-Easter Whit-Whitsun dep-departure fr-from hrs-hours m-mile mdnt-midnight rdbt-roundabout rs-restricted service wk-week wknd-weekend 🚫💳 No credit cards 🚫🐕 no dogs See page 7 for details of the AA Camping Card Scheme

MONMOUTHSHIRE

ABERGAVENNY   Map 9 SO21

Places to visit

White Castle, White Castle, 01600 780380, www.cadw.wales.gov.uk

Hen Gwrt, Llantilio Crosseny, 01443 336000, www.cadw.wales.gov.uk

Great for kids: Raglan Castle, Raglan, 01291 690228, www.cadw.wales.gov.uk

►►► 79% Pyscodlyn Farm Caravan & Camping Site (SO266155)

Llanwenarth Citra NP7 7ER
☎ 01873 853271 & 07816 447942
e-mail: pyscodlyn.farm@virgin.net
dir: From Abergavenny take A40 (Brecon road), site 1.5m from entrance of Nevill Hall Hospital, on left 50yds past phone box

♥♥♨

Open Apr-Oct

With its outstanding views of the mountains, this quiet park in the Brecon Beacons National Park makes a pleasant venue for country lovers. The Sugarloaf Mountain and the River Usk are within easy walking distance and, despite being a working farm, dogs are welcome. Please note that credit cards are not taken on this site. A 4.5 acre site with 60 touring pitches and 6 statics.

AA Pubs & Restaurants nearby: Angel Hotel, Abergavenny 01873 857121

Llansantffraed Court Hotel, Llanvihangel Gobion, Abergavenny 01873 840678

Facilities: ♠⊙✳♿✿
Services: ♥♨♠♫
Within 3 miles: ♨♫♪◎♨♻
Notes: ♨

DINGESTOW

Places to visit

Raglan Castle, Raglan, 01291 690228, www.cadw.wales.gov.uk

Tintern Abbey, Tintern Parva, 01291 689251, www.cadw.wales.gov.uk

Great for kids: The Nelson Museum and Local History Centre, Monmouth, 01600 710630

DINGESTOW   Map 9 SO41

►►► 80% Bridge Caravan Park & Camping Site (SO459104)

Bridge Farm NP25 4DY
☎ 01600 740241 📄 01600 740241
e-mail: info@bridgecaravanpark.co.uk
dir: Signed from Raglan. Off A449 (S Wales-Midlands road)

* ♥ £13-£15 ♥ £13-£15 ♨ £13-£14.50

Open Etr-Oct Last arrival 22.00hrs Last departure 16.00hrs

The River Trothy runs along the edge of this quiet village park, which has been owned by the same family for many years. Touring pitches are both grass and hardstanding, and there is a backdrop of woodland. The quality facilities are enhanced by good laundry equipment. A 4 acre site with 94 touring pitches, 15 hardstandings.

AA Pubs & Restaurants nearby: Beaufort Arms Coaching Inn & Brasserie, Raglan 01291 690412

Facilities: ♠⊙♫✳♿☾♨♫
Services: ♥♨♠♫Ⓣ♫♻
Within 3 miles: ♨♫♪◎♨♻♻
Notes: ♨ Fishing

USK

Places to visit

Caerleon Roman Baths, Caerleon, 01663 422518, www.cadw.wales.gov.uk

Big Pit National Coal Museum, Cwmbran, 01495 790311, www.museumwales.ac.uk

Great for kids: Greenmeadow Community Farm, Cwmbran, 01633 647662, www.greenmeadowcommunityfarm.org.uk

---

USK   Map 9 SO30

PREMIER PARK

►►►►► 82% Pont Kemys Caravan & Camping Park (SO348058)

Chainbridge NP7 9DS
☎ 01873 880688 📄 01873 880270
e-mail: info@pontkemys.com
web: www.pontkemys.com
dir: On B4598 (Usk to Abergavenny road), 300yds N of Chainbridge, 4m from Usk

* ♥ £17-£19 ♥ £17-£19 ♨ £15-£17

Open Mar-Oct Last arrival 21.00hrs Last departure noon

A peaceful park next to the River Usk, offering an excellent standard of toilet facilities with family rooms. A section of the park has fully serviced pitches. The park is in a rural area with mature trees and country views, and attracts quiet visitors who enjoy the many attractions of this area. An 8 acre site with 65 touring pitches, 29 hardstandings.

AA Pubs & Restaurants nearby: Raglan Arms, Llandenny 01291 690800

Nags Head Inn, Usk 01291 672820

Three Salmons Hotel, Usk 01291 672133

Leisure: ▭
Facilities: ♠⊙♫✳♿☾♨♫
Services: ♥♨♠♫Ⓣ♫♻
Within 3 miles: ♨♫♪♨
Notes: Dogs must be kept on leads at all times. Mother & baby room, kitchen facilities for groups

---

PEMBROKESHIRE

See Walk 15 in the Walks & Cycle Rides section at the end of the guide

BROAD HAVEN — Map 8 SM81

Places to visit

Pembroke Castle, Pembroke, 01646 681510, www.pembrokecastle.co.uk

Llawhaden Castle, Llawhaden, 01443 336000, www.cadw.wales.gov.uk

Great for kids: Scolton Manor Museum and Country Park, Scolton, 01437 731328 (Museum)

▶▶▶ 84% Creampots Touring Caravan & Camping Park (SM882131)

Broadway SA62 3TU
☎ 01437 701770
dir: From Haverfordwest take B4341 to Broadway. Turn left, follow brown tourist signs to site

* ⌂ £14.75-£19.75 ⌂ £14.75-£19.75
▲ £13.50-£16.95

Open Mar-Jan Last arrival 21.00hrs Last departure noon

Set just outside the Pembrokeshire National Park, this quiet site is just one and a half miles from a safe sandy beach at Broad Haven, and the coastal footpath. The park is well laid out and carefully maintained, and the toilet block offers a good standard of facilities. The owners welcome families. An 8 acre site with 71 touring pitches, 12 hardstandings and 1 static.

AA Pubs & Restaurants nearby: Swan Inn, Little Haven 01437 781880

Facilities: ⋔ ⊙ ℙ ⋇ ⅋

Services: ⌂ ⓢ ⌂ ⊘ ⌂

Within 3 miles: ⤳ ⵌ ℙ ⤳ ⓐ ⓢ ∪

▶▶▶ 76% South Cockett Caravan & Camping Park (SM878136)

South Cockett SA62 3TU
☎ 01437 781296 & 781760 ▤ 01437 781296
e-mail: esmejames@hotmail.co.uk
dir: From Haverfordwest take B4341 to Broad Haven, at Broadway turn left, site 300yds

* ⌂ £13.65-£16 ⌂ £13.65-£16 ▲ £12.75-£14.75

Open Etr-Oct Last arrival 22.30hrs

A small park on a working farm, with touring areas divided into neat paddocks by high, well-trimmed hedges. Good toilet facilities, and in a convenient location for the lovely beach at nearby Broad Haven. A 6 acre site with 73 touring pitches.

AA Pubs & Restaurants nearby: Swan Inn, Little Haven 01437 781880

Facilities: ⋔ ⊙ ⋇ ⓒ

Services: ⌂ ⓢ ⌂ ⊘ ⌂

Within 3 miles: ⤳ ℙ ⤳ ⓐ ⓢ ∪

Notes: ⓐ

FISHGUARD — Map 8 SM93

Places to visit

Pentre Ifan Burial Chamber, Newport, 01443 336000, www.cadw.wales.gov.uk

Tredegar House and Park, Newport, 01633 815880, www.newport.gov.uk

Great for kids: OceanLab, Fishguard, 01348 874737, www.ocean-lab.co.uk

▶▶▶ 87% Fishguard Bay Caravan & Camping Park (SM984383)

Garn Gelli SA65 9ET
☎ 01348 811415 ▤ 01348 811425
e-mail: enquiries@fishguardbay.com
web: www.fishguardbay.com
dir: If approaching Fishguard from Cardigan on A487 ignore Sat Nav to turn right. Turn at sign to campsite. (Single track road with grass in places)

* ⌂ £16-£20 ⌂ £16-£20 ▲ £15-£23

Open Mar-9 Jan Last arrival after noon Last departure noon

Set high up on cliffs with outstanding views of Fishguard Bay, and the Pembrokeshire Coastal Path running right through the centre. The park is extremely well kept, with three good toilet blocks, a common room with TV, a lounge/library, decent laundry, and well-stocked shop. A 5 acre site with

50 touring pitches, 4 hardstandings and 50 statics.

AA Pubs & Restaurants nearby: Sloop Inn, Porthgain 01348 831449

The Shed, Porthgain 01348 831518

Salutation Inn, Felindre Farchog 01239 820564

Leisure: ⋀ ⚼ ▯

Facilities: ⋔ ⊙ ℙ ⋇ ⅋ ⓒ ⓐ ⌂

Services: ⌂ ⓢ ⌂ ⊘ ⓣ ⌂

Within 3 miles: ⤳ ⵌ ℙ ⤳ ⓐ ⓢ ∪

Notes: Wi-fi

▶▶▶ 75% Gwaun Vale Touring Park (SM977356)

Llanychaer SA65 9TA
☎ 01348 874000
e-mail: margaret.harries@talk21.com
dir: From Fishguard take B4313. Site 1.5m on right

* ⌂ £17-£20 ⌂ £17-£20 ▲ £15-£23

Open Apr-Oct Last arrival anytime Last departure 11.00hrs

Located at the opening of the beautiful Gwaun Valley, this well-kept park is set on the hillside with pitches tiered on two levels. There are lovely views of the surrounding countryside, and good facilities. A 1.6 acre site with 29 touring pitches, 5 hardstandings and 1 static.

AA Pubs & Restaurants nearby: Sloop Inn, Porthgain 01348 831449

The Shed, Porthgain 01348 831518

Salutation Inn, Felindre Farchog 01239 820564

Leisure: ⋀

Facilities: ⋔ ⊙ ℙ ⋇ ⓒ ⓐ ⌂ ⌂

Services: ⌂ ⓢ ⌂ ⊘

Within 3 miles: ⤳ ⵌ ℙ ⓐ ⓢ ∪

Notes: ⓐ Dogs must be kept on leads, no skateboards. Guidebooks available

HASGUARD CROSS — Map 8 SM80

Places to visit

Pembroke Castle, Pembroke, 01646 681510, www.pembrokecastle.co.uk

►►► 82% Hasguard Cross Caravan Park (SM850108)

SA62 3SL
☎ 01437 781443 🖷 01437 781443
e-mail: hasguard@aol.com
dir: From Haverfordwest take B4327 towards Dale. In 7m right at x-rds. Site 1st right

Open all year (rs Aug tent field for 28 days) Last arrival 21.00hrs Last departure 10.00hrs

A very clean, efficient and well-run site in the Pembrokeshire National Park, just one and a half miles from the sea and beach at Little Haven, and with views of the surrounding hills. The toilet and shower facilities are immaculately clean, and there is a licensed bar (evenings only) serving a good choice of food. A 4.5 acre site with 12 touring pitches and 42 statics.

AA Pubs & Restaurants nearby: Swan Inn, Little Haven 01437 781880

Facilities: 🅵⊙🅿✳️♿🅾️🅿️🚿🐕
Services: 🅴🅾️🅿️🅰️🅾️🍴🚮
Within 3 miles: 🚶🚣🎣🛒🅾️🅾️⛳
Notes: Football field

AA CAMPING CARD SITE

►►► 82% Redlands Touring Caravan & Camping Park (SM853109)

SA62 3SJ
☎ 01437 781300
e-mail: info@redlandscamping.co.uk
dir: From Haverfordwest take B4327 towards Dale. Site 7m on right

* 🚐 £17.70-£22.95 🚙 £17.70-£22.95
🏕 £13.25-£20.75

Open Mar-Dec Last arrival 21.00hrs Last departure 11.30hrs

A family owned and run park set in five acres of level grassland with tree-lined borders, close to many sandy beaches and the famous coastal footpath. This site is the ideal spot for exploring the Pembrokeshire National Park. Seasonal touring pitches are available. A 6 acre site with 60 touring pitches, 32 hardstandings.

AA Pubs & Restaurants nearby: Swan Inn, Little Haven 01437 781880

Facilities: 🅵⊙🅿✳️♿🅾️🅿️🚿🚮
Services: 🅴🅾️🅿️🅰️🅾️🍴🚮
Within 3 miles: 🚶🚣🎣🛒🅾️🅾️⛳

Notes: ⊗ No commercial vans or minibuses. Use of freezers, extra large tent pitches

HAVERFORDWEST — Map 8 SM91

Places to visit

Llawhaden Castle, Llawhaden, 01443 336000, www.cadw.wales.gov.uk

Carew Castle and Tidal Mill, Carew, 01646 651782, www.carewcastle.com

Great for kids: Oakwood Theme Park, Narberth, 01834 861889, www.oakwoodthemepark.co.uk

►► 79% Nolton Cross Caravan Park (SM879177)

Nolton SA62 3NP
☎ 01437 710701 🖷 01437 710329
e-mail: info@noltoncross-holidays.co.uk
web: www. noltoncross-holidays.co.uk
dir: 1m off A487 (Haverfordwest to St David's road) at Simpson Cross, towards Nolton & Broadhaven

* 🚐 £7.25-£13.75 🚙 £7.25-£13.75
🏕 £7.25-£13.75

Open Mar-Dec Last arrival 22.00hrs Last departure noon

High grassy banks surround the touring area of this park next to the owners' working farm. It is located on open ground above the sea and St Bride's Bay (within one and a half miles), and there is a coarse fishing lake close by - equipment for hire and reduced permit rates for campers are available. A 4 acre site with 15 touring pitches and 30 statics.

AA Pubs & Restaurants nearby: Swan Inn, Little Haven 01437 781880

Leisure: 🅰
Facilities: 🅵⊙✳️🅾️🅿️🚿
Services: 🅴🅾️🅰️🅿️🅾️
Within 3 miles: 🎣🛒🅾️🅾️⛳
Notes: No youth groups

LITTLE HAVEN

See Hasguard Cross

ROSEBUSH — Map 8 SN02

Places to visit

Cilgerran Castle, Cilgerran, 01239 621339, www.cadw.wales.gov.uk

OceanLab, Fishguard, 01348 874737, www.ocean-lab.co.uk

►► 71% Rosebush Caravan Park (SN073293)

Rhoslwyn SA66 7QT
☎ 01437 532206 & 07831 223166
🖷 01437 532206
dir: From A40, near Narberth, take B4313, between Haverfordwest & Cardigan take B4329, site 1m

Open 14 Mar-Oct Last arrival 23.00hrs Last departure noon

A most attractive park with a large ornamental lake at its centre and good landscaping. Set off the main tourist track, it offers lovely views of the Presely Hills which can be reached by a scenic walk. Rosebush is a quiet village with a handy pub, and the park owner also runs the village shop. Please note that due to the deep lake on site, children are not accepted. A 12 acre site with 65 touring pitches and 15 statics.

AA Pubs & Restaurants nearby: Tafarn Sinc, Rosebush 01437 532214

Facilities: 🅵⊙🅿✳️🅾️🚿🚮
Services: 🅴🅰️🅿️
Within 3 miles: 🎣🅾️
Notes: Adults only ⊗

ST DAVID'S

Places to visit

St. David's Bishop's Palace, St. David's, 01437 720517, www.cadw.wales.gov.uk

St David's Cathedral, St. David's, 01437 720202, www.stdavidscathedral.org.uk

Great for kids: Oakwood Theme Park, Narberth, 01834 861889, www.oakwoodthemepark.co.uk

ST DAVID'S Map 8 SM72

►►►► 87% Caerfai Bay Caravan & Tent Park *(SM759244)*

Caerfai Bay SA62 6QT
☎ 01437 720274 📠 01437 720577
e-mail: info@caerfaibay.co.uk
web: www.caerfaibay.co.uk
dir: *At St David's exit A487 at Visitor Centre/Grove Hotel. Follow signs for Caerfai Bay. Right at end of road*

🚐 🚙 ⛺

Open Mar-mid Nov Last arrival 21.00hrs Last departure 11.00hrs

Magnificent coastal scenery and an outlook over St Bride's Bay can be enjoyed from this delightful site, located just 300 yards from a bathing beach. The facilities include four en suite family rooms, which are a huge asset to the park, and ongoing improvements include a second, solar-heated wet suit shower room, six extra hardstanding pitches, upgraded roadways, and modernised water points. There is an excellent on-site farm shop. A 10 acre site with 106 touring pitches, 23 hardstandings and 34 statics.

AA Pubs & Restaurants nearby: Cwtch, St David's 01437 720491

Sloop Inn, Porthgain 01348 831449

The Shed, Porthgain 01348 831518

Cambrian Inn, Solva 01437 721210

Facilities: 🚿 ⊙ 💨 ✳ ♿ ☎ 🏪 🐕

Services: 🔌 🧺 🛢 🔥 🔋 👶 ⚓

Within 3 miles: ⛳ ⛵ 🎣 🏄 🏪 🧺

Notes: No dogs in tent field mid Jul-Aug, no skateboards or rollerblades. Family washrooms

►►► 80% Hendre Eynon Camping & Caravan Site *(SM771284)*

SA62 6DB
☎ 01437 720474 📠 01437 720474
dir: *Take A487 (Fishguard road) from St David's, fork left at rugby club signed Llanrhian. Site 2m on right (NB do no take turn to Whitesands)*

* 🚐 £14-£18 🚙 £14-£18 ⛺ £14-£18

Open Apr-Sep Last arrival 21.00hrs Last dep noon

A peaceful country site on a working farm, with a modern toilet block including family rooms. Within easy reach of many lovely sandy beaches, and two miles from the cathedral city of St David's. A 7 acre site with 50 touring pitches.

AA Pubs & Restaurants nearby: Cwtch, St David's 01437 720491

Sloop Inn, Porthgain 01348 831449

The Shed, Porthgain 01348 831518

Cambrian Inn, Solva 01437 721210

Facilities: 🚿 ⊙ ✳ ♿ ☎ 🐕 **Services:** 🔌 🧺 🛢 🔥 🔋

Within 3 miles: ⛳ ⛵ 🎣 🏄 🏪 🧺 🐎

Notes: 💳 Maximum 2 dogs per unit

AA CAMPING CARD SITE

►► 77% Tretio Caravan & Camping Park *(SM787292)*

SA62 6DE
☎ 01437 781600 📠 01437 781594
e-mail: info@tretio.com
dir: *From St David's take A487 towards Fishguard, keep left at Rugby Football Club, straight on 3m. Site signed, turn left to site*

🚐 🚙 ⛺

Open Mar-Oct Last arrival 20.00hrs Last dep 10.00hrs

An attractive site in a very rural spot with distant country views, and beautiful local beaches. A mobile shop calls daily at peak periods, and the tiny cathedral city of St David's is only three miles away. A 6.5 acre site with 10 touring pitches and 30 statics.

AA Pubs & Restaurants nearby: Cwtch, St David's 01437 720491

Sloop Inn, Porthgain 01348 831449

The Shed, Porthgain 01348 831518

Leisure: 🛝 **Facilities:** 🚿 ⊙ 💨 ✳ ♿ 🏪 ♨ 🐕

Services: 🔌 🛢 🔥 [T] 🔋

Within 3 miles: ⛳ ⛵ 🎣 ◎ 🏄 🏪 🧺

Notes: Dogs kept on leads at all times. Pitch & putt, ball games area

TENBY Map 8 SN10

Places to visit

Tudor Merchants House, Tenby, 01834 842279, www.nationaltrust.org.ukmain-w-tudormerchantshouse

Tenby Museum and Art Gallery, Tenby, 01834 842809, www.tenbymuseum.org.uk

Great for kids: Colby Woodland Garden, Amroth, 01834 811885, www.nationaltrust.org.uk/main

85% *Kiln Park Holiday Centre* *(SN119002)*

Marsh Rd SA70 7RB
☎ 01834 844121 📠 01834 845159
e-mail: sue.james@bourne-leisure.co.uk
dir: *Follow A477/A478 to Tenby for 6m, then follow signs to Penally, site 0.5m on left*

🚐 🚙 ⛺

Open mid Mar-Oct (rs mid Mar-May & Sep-Oct some facilities may be reduced) Last arrival 22.00hrs Last departure 10.00hrs

A large holiday complex complete with leisure and sports facilities, and lots of entertainment for all the family. There are bars and cafés, and plenty of security. This touring, camping and static site is on the outskirts of town, with a short walk through dunes to the sandy beach. The well-equipped toilet block is very clean. A 103 acre site with 193 touring pitches and 703 statics.

AA Pubs & Restaurants nearby: Stackpole Inn, Stackpole 01646 672324

New Inn, Amroth 01834 812368

Leisure: 🏊 🏊 🛝 🎭

Facilities: 🚿 💨 ✳ ♿ ☎ 🏪 ♨ 🐕

Services: 🔌 🧺 🍷 🛢 🔥 🍴 🍔 👶

Within 3 miles: ⛳ ⛵ 🏋 🎣 ◎ 🏄 🏪 🧺 🐎

Notes: No dogs Jul & Aug, certain dog breeds banned. Entertainment complex, bowling & putting green. Wi-fi

see advert on page 398

SERVICES: 🔌 Electric hook up 🧺 Launderette 🍷 Licensed bar 🛢 Calor Gas 🔥 Camping Gaz [T] Toilet fluid 🍴 Café/Restaurant 🍔 Fast Food/Takeaway 🔋 Battery charging 👶 Baby care ⚓ Motorvan service point **ABBREVIATIONS:** BH/bank hols-bank holidays Etr-Easter Whit-Whitsun dep-departure fr-from hrs-hours m-mile mdnt-midnight rdbt-roundabout rs-restricted service wk-week wknd-weekend 💳 No credit cards 🚫 no dogs See page 7 for details of the AA Camping Card Scheme

LEISURE: Indoor swimming pool Outdoor swimming pool Children's playground Tennis court Games room Separate TV room 9/18 hole golf course Boats for hire Cinema Fishing Mini golf Watersports Stables FACILITIES: Bath Shower Electric shaver Hairdryer Ice Pack Facility Disabled facilities Public telephone Shop on site or within 200yds Mobile shop (calls at least 5 days a week) BBQ area Picnic area Dog exercise area

TENBY *continued*

►►►► 83% Trefalun Park *(SN093027)*

Devonshire Dr, St Florence SA70 8RD
☎ **01646 651514** 📠 **01646 651746**
e-mail: trefalun@aol.com
dir: 1.5m NW of St Florence & 0.5m N of B4318

* 🚐 £13-£23.50 🚛 £13-£23.50 ▲ £11-£20.50

Open Etr-Oct Last arrival 19.00hrs Last departure noon

Set within 12 acres of sheltered, well-kept grounds, this quiet country park offers well-maintained level grass pitches separated by bushes and trees, with plenty of space to relax in. Children can feed the park's friendly pets. Plenty of activities are available at the nearby Heatherton Country Sports Park, including go-karting, indoor bowls, golf and bumper boating. Seasonal touring pitches are available. A 12 acre site with 00 touring pitches, 54 hardstandings and 10 statics.

AA Pubs & Restaurants nearby: Stackpole Inn, Stackpole 01646 672324

New Inn, Amroth 01834 812368

Leisure: 🅰

Facilities: 🎣☉🅿✳🕭🅲🅐🌂🚂

Services: 🔌🅾🍴🅐🖉🅃🍴🔋

Within 3 miles: 🕹🎣🎿🅿🅟◎🎣🅐🅾

Notes: No motorised scooters
see advert on opposite page

►►►► 80% Well Park Caravan & Camping Site *(SN128028)*

SA70 8TL
☎ **01834 842179** 📠 **01834 842179**
e-mail: enquiries@wellparkcaravans.co.uk
dir: Off A478 on right approx 1.5m before Tenby

🚐🚛▲

Open Mar-Oct (rs Mar-mid Jun & mid Sep-Oct bar, launderette, baby room may be closed) Last arrival 22.00hrs Last departure 11.00hrs

An attractive, well-maintained park with good landscaping from trees, ornamental shrubs, and attractive flower borders. The amenities include a launderette and indoor dishwashing, games room with table tennis, and an enclosed play area. Tenby is just a 15-minute walk away or can be reached via a traffic-free cycle track. A 10 acre site with 100 touring pitches, 16 hardstandings and 42 statics.

AA Pubs & Restaurants nearby: Stackpole Inn, Stackpole 01646 672324

New Inn, Amroth 01834 812368

Leisure: 🅰🎣☐

Facilities: 🎣☉🅿✳🕭🅲🅐🌂🚂

Services: 🔌🅾🍴🅐🖉🍴🔋

Within 3 miles: 🕹🎣🎿🅿🅟◎🎣🅐🅾🌀

Notes: ⊛ Family parties only. TV hook-ups

AA CAMPING CARD SITE

►►► 75% Wood Park Caravans

(SN128025)

New Hedges SA70 8TL
☎ **0845 129 8314 & 129 8344 (winter)**
e-mail: info@woodpark.co.uk
dir: At rdbt 2m N of Tenby follow A478 towards Tenby, then take 2nd right & right again

🚐 £14-£26 🚛 £14-£26 ▲ £13-£25

Open Spring BH-Sep (rs May & mid-end Sep laundrette & games room may not be open) Last arrival 22.00hrs Last departure 10.00hrs

Situated in beautiful countryside between the popular seaside resorts of Tenby and Saundersfoot, and with Waterwynch Bay just a 15-minute walk away, this peaceful site provides a spacious and relaxing atmosphere for holidays. The slightly sloping touring area is partly divided by shrubs into three paddocks. Ten seasonal touring pitches are available. A 10 acre site with 60 touring pitches, 40 hardstandings and 90 statics.

AA Pubs & Restaurants nearby: Stackpole Inn, Stackpole 01646 672324

New Inn, Amroth 01834 812368

Leisure: 🅰🎣

Facilities: 🎣☉🅿✳🅐

Services: 🔌🅾🍴🅐🖉🔋

Within 3 miles: 🕹🎣🎿🅿🅟◎🎣🅐🅾🌀

Notes: ⊛ Only 1 car per unit, only small dogs accepted, no dogs Jul-Aug & BHs. No groups

---

POWYS

BRECON Map 9 SO02

Places to visit

Brecknock Museum and Art Gallery, Brecon, 01874 624121, www.powys.gov.uk/breconmuseum

Regimental Museum of the Royal Welsh, Brecon, 01874 613310, www.rrw.org.uk

---

PREMIER PARK

►►►►► 88% Pencelli Castle Caravan & Camping Park

(SO096248)

Pencelli LD3 7LX
☎ **01874 665451**
e-mail: pencelli@tiscali.co.uk
dir: Exit A40 2m E of Brecon onto B4558, follow signs to Pencelli

🚐🚛▲

Open 30 Dec-3 Dec (rs 30 Oct-Etr shop closed) Last arrival 22.00hrs Last departure noon

Lying in the heart of the Brecon Beacons National Park, this charming park offers peace, beautiful scenery and high quality facilities. The park is bordered by the Brecon and Monmouth Canal. Attention to detail is superb, and the well-equipped heated toilets with en suite cubicles are matched by a drying room for clothes and boots, full laundry, and shop. A 10 acre site with 80 touring pitches, 40 hardstandings.

AA Pubs & Restaurants nearby: Felin Fach Griffin, Felin Fach 01874 620111

White Swan Inn, Llanfrynach 01874 665276

Old Ford Inn, Llanhamlach 01874 665391

Leisure: 🅰

Facilities: 🎣☉🅿✳🕭🅲🅐🌂🚂

Services: 🔌🅾🅐🖉🅃🍴🔋

Within 3 miles: 🎿🅿🅟🅐🅾🌀

Notes: No radios, music or campfires, assistance dogs only. Bike hire. Wi-fi

---

BRECON *continued*

▶▶▶▶ 82% *Bishops Meadow Caravan Park* (SO060300)

Bishops Meadow, Hay Rd LD3 9SW
☎ 01874 610000 🖹 01874 622090
e-mail: enquiries@bishops-meadow.co.uk
dir: *From A470 (just N of Brecon) take B4602. Site on right*

🚐 🚙 Å

Open Mar-Oct

A family site with most pitches enjoying spectacular views of the Brecon Beacons. The site has its own outdoor swimming pool, and next door to the park is an all-day restaurant with a lounge bar open in the evenings. Facilities include two good quality amenity blocks. Brecon is just under two miles from the park. A 3.5 acre site with 82 touring pitches, 24 hardstandings.

AA Pubs & Restaurants nearby: Felin Fach Griffin, Felin Fach 01874 620111

Usk Inn, Talybont-on-Usk 01874 676251

Star Inn, Talybont-on-Usk 01874 676635

Leisure: 🏊 🎠 **Facilities:** 🚿 🎠 ⊙ ⚡ 🔌 🕐 🐕 🎋
Services: 🖭 🍴 🔧 ⊘ T 🍽 🎒 🛒 ✈
Within 3 miles: ↧ 🏇 🎠 🎣 🏧 🖭 ∪

AA CAMPING CARD SITE

▶▶▶ 80% Anchorage Caravan Park
(SO142351)

LD3 0LD
☎ 01874 711246 & 711230 🖹 01874 711711
dir: *8m NE of Brecon in village centre*

🚐 fr £12 🚙 fr £12 Å fr £12

Open all year (rs Nov-Mar TV room closed) Last arrival 23.00hrs Last departure 18.00hrs

A well-maintained site with a choice of south-facing, sloping grass pitches and superb views of the Black Mountains, or a more sheltered lower area with a number of excellent super pitches. There are new toilet facilities and the site is a

short distance from the water sports centre at Llangorse Lake. An 8 acre site with 110 touring pitches, 8 hardstandings and 101 statics.

Anchorage Caravan Park

AA Pubs & Restaurants nearby: Castle Inn, Talgarth 01874 711353

Old Black Lion, Hay-on-Wye 01497 820841

Kilverts Inn, Hay-on-Wye 01497 821042

Leisure: 🎠 🖵
Facilities: 🎠 ⊙ ⚡ ✳ ⚡ 🕐 🐕 ✈
Services: 🖭 🍴 🔧 ⊘ T 🛒 ✈
Within 3 miles: 🎣 🖭 🖭 ∪

Notes: ⊘ Family shower & toilet room, post office, hairdresser

---

BUILTH WELLS   Map 9 SO05

▶▶▶ 78% Fforest Fields Caravan & Camping Park
(SO100535)

GOLD

Hundred House LD1 5RT
☎ 01982 570406
e-mail: office@fforestfields.co.uk
web: www.fforestfields.co.uk
dir: *From town follow New Radnor signs on A481. 4m to signed entrance on right, 0.5m before Hundred House village*

🚐 fr £12.50 🚙 fr £12.50 Å fr £12.50

Open Etr & Apr-Oct Last arrival 21.00hrs Last departure 18.00hrs

A sheltered park in a hidden valley with wonderful views and plenty of wildlife. Set in unspoilt

countryside, this is a peaceful park with delightful hill walks beginning on site. The historic town of Builth Wells and the Royal Welsh Showground are only four miles away, and there are plenty of outdoor activities in the vicinity. A 12 acre site with 60 touring pitches, 17 hardstandings.

AA Pubs & Restaurants nearby: Laughing Dog, Howey 01597 822406

Facilities: 🎠 ⊙ ⚡ ✳ 🕐 🖭 🎒 ✈
Services: 🖭 🍴 🔧 🛒 ✈
Within 3 miles: ↧ 🏇 🎣 🖭 🖭

Notes: ⊘ No loud music or revelry. Bread, dairy produce & cured bacon available. Wi-fi

---

▶▶▶ 79% Mellington Hall Caravan Park (SO252934)

Mellington SY15 6HX
☎ 01588 620011 🖹 01588 620011
e-mail: info@mellingtonhallcaravanpark.co.uk
web: www.mellingtonhallcaravanpark.co.uk
dir: *Exit A489 1.5m W of Churchstoke onto B4385 to Mellington*

＊ 🚐 fr £20 🚙 fr £20 Å £5-£15

Open all year Last arrival 20.00hrs

A small touring park set a mile down a wooded private drive in the grounds of Mellington Hall Hotel. The 270 acres of park and farmland guarantee peace and seclusion, and there is plenty of wildlife and thousands of rare trees. The Offa's Dyke footpath runs through the grounds, and this park is ideal for walking, cycling and fishing. The hotel has an attractive bistro. A 4 acre site with 40 touring pitches, 40 hardstandings and 95 statics.

AA Pubs & Restaurants nearby: Dragon Hotel, Montgomery 01686 668359

Lion Hotel, Berriew 01686 640452

Leisure: 🎠 **Facilities:** 🎠 ⊙ ⚡ 🕐 🖭 ✈
Services: 🖭 🍴 🔧 🍴
Within 3 miles: 🎣 🖭 🖭 ∪

Notes: ⊘ No cars by caravans or tents. Hiking maps available

CRICKHOWELL — Map 9 SO21

Places to visit

Tretower Court and Castle, Tretower, 01874 730279, www.cadw.wales.gov.uk

Big Pit National Coal Museum, Cwmbran, 01495 790311, www.museumwales.ac.uk

►►► 77% Riverside Caravan & Camping Park (SO215184)

New Rd NP8 1AY
☎ **01873 810397**
dir: On A4077, well signed from A40

⬛ fr £15 ⬛ fr £15 ⬛ fr £12

Open Mar-Oct Last arrival 22.00hrs

A very well tended adults-only park in delightful countryside on the edge of the small country town of Crickhowell. The adjacent riverside park is an excellent facility for all, including dog walkers. Crickhowell has numerous specialist shops including a first-class delicatessen. Within a few minutes' walk of the park are several friendly pubs with good restaurants. A 3.5 acre site with 35 touring pitches and 20 statics.

AA Pubs & Restaurants nearby: Bear Hotel, Crickhowell 01873 810408

Nantyffin Cider Mill Inn, Crickhowell 01873 810775

Facilities: ⬛⬛⬛⬛ **Services:** ⬛⬛⬛
Within 3 miles: ⬛⬛⬛⬛

Notes: Adults only. ⬛ No hangliders or paragliders. Large canopied area for drying clothes, cooking & socialising

LLANDRINDOD WELLS — Map 9 SO06

Places to visit

The Judges Lodgings, Presteigne, 01544 260650, www.judgeslodging.org.uk

AA CAMPING CARD SITE

►►► 81% Disserth Caravan & Camping Park (SO035583)

Disserth, Howey LD1 6NL
☎ **01597 860277**
e-mail: disserthcaravan@btconnect.com
dir: 1m off A483, between Howey & Newbridge-on-Wye, by church. Follow brown signs from A483 or A470

⬛ £14-£16 ⬛ £14-£16 ⬛ £7-£20

Open Mar-Oct Last arrival 22.00hrs Last departure noon

A delightfully secluded and predominantly adult park nestling in a beautiful valley on the banks of the River Ithon, a tributary of the River Wye. This little park is next to a 13th-century church, and has a small bar open at weekends and busy periods. The chalet toilet block offers spacious, combined cubicles. A 4 acre site with 30 touring pitches, 6 hardstandings and 25 statics.

AA Pubs & Restaurants nearby: Laughing Dog, Howey 01597 822406

Bell Country Inn, Llanyre 01597 823959

Facilities: ⬛⬛⬛⬛⬛⬛⬛⬛⬛
Services: ⬛⬛⬛⬛⬛⬛⬛
Within 3 miles: ⬛⬛⬛⬛⬛⬛
Notes: ⬛ Private trout fishing

►► 82% Dalmore Camping & Caravanning Park (SO045568)

Howey LD1 5RG
☎ **01597 822483** ⬛ **01597 822483**
dir: 3m S of Llandrindod Wells off A483. 4m N of Builth Wells, at top of hill

* ⬛ £8-£11 ⬛ £8-£11 ⬛ £8-£11

Open Mar-Oct Last arrival 22.00hrs Last departure noon

An intimate and well laid out adults-only park. Pitches are attractively terraced to ensure that all enjoy the wonderful views from this splendidly landscaped little park. Six seasonal touring pitches available. Please note, dogs are not allowed. A 3 acre site with 20 touring pitches, 12 hardstandings and 20 statics.

AA Pubs & Restaurants nearby: Laughing Dog, Howey 01597 822406

Bell Country Inn, Llanyre 01597 823959

Facilities: ⬛⬛⬛⬛⬛⬛
Services: ⬛⬛⬛⬛⬛
Within 3 miles: ⬛⬛⬛⬛⬛⬛⬛
Notes: Adults only. ⬛ ⬛ Gates closed 23.00hrs-07.00hrs, no ball games

LLANGORS — Map 9 SO12

Places to visit

Llanthony Priory, Llanthony, 01443 336000, www.cadw.wales.gov.uk

Great for kids: Tretower Court and Castle, Tretower, 01874 730279, www.cadw.wales.gov.uk

►►► 72% Lakeside Caravan Park (SO128272)

LD3 7TR
☎ **01874 658226**
e-mail: holidays@llangorselake.co.uk
dir: Exit A40 at Bwlch onto B4560 towards Talgarth. Site signed towards lake in Llangors centre

⬛⬛⬛

Open Etr or Apr-Oct (rs Mar-May & Oct clubhouse, restaurant, shop limited) Last arrival 21.30hrs Last departure 10.00hrs

Next to Llangors common and lake this attractive park has launching and mooring facilities and is an ideal centre for water sports enthusiasts. Popular with families, and offering a clubhouse/bar, with a well-stocked shop and café/takeaway next door. Boats, bikes and windsurfing equipment can be hired on site. A 2 acre site with 40 touring pitches, 8 hardstandings and 72 statics.

AA Pubs & Restaurants nearby: Usk Inn, Talybont-on-Usk 01874 676251

Star Inn, Talybont-on-Usk 01874 676635

Leisure: ⬛⬛
Facilities: ⬛⬛⬛⬛⬛⬛⬛⬛
Services: ⬛⬛⬛⬛⬛⬛⬛⬛
Within 3 miles: ⬛⬛⬛⬛⬛⬛
Notes: No pets in hire caravans, no open fires. Fishing from boats

MIDDLETOWN   Map 15 SJ31

Places to visit

Powis Castle and Garden, Welshpool, 01938 551920, www.nationaltrust.org.uk

Great for kids: Old Oswestry Hill Fort, Oswestry, www.english-heritage.org.uk

AA CAMPING CARD SITE

▶▶▶ **79% Bank Farm Caravan Park**

(SJ293123)

SY21 8EJ
☎ **01938 570526**
e-mail: bankfarmcaravans@yahoo.co.uk
dir: *13m W of Shrewsbury, 5m E of Welshpool on A458*

Open Mar-Oct Last arrival 20.00hrs

An attractive park on a small farm, maintained to a high standard. There are two touring areas, one on either side of the A458, and each with its own amenity block, and immediate access to hills, mountains and woodland. A pub serving good food, and a large play area are nearby. A 2 acre site with 40 touring pitches and 33 statics.

AA Pubs & Restaurants nearby: Old Hand & Diamond Inn, Coedway 01743 884379

Leisure: ⚙ 🔍
Facilities: 🚿 ☺ ✻ 🚿 🚻 🅿
Services: 🚐 🔯 🛢 📥
Within 3 miles: ⚓ 🌳 🏧
Notes: ☺ Coarse fishing pool, jacuzzi, snooker room

PRESTEIGNE

Places to visit

The Judges Lodgings, Presteigne, 01544 260650, www.judgeslodging.org.uk

Great for kids: Croft Castle and Parkland (NT), Yarpole, 01568 780246, www.nationaltrust.org.uk/main/w-croftcastle

PRESTEIGNE   Map 9 SO36

▶▶▶ **72% Rockbridge Park** *(SO294654)*

LD8 2NF
☎ **01547 560300**   🖶 **01547 560300**
e-mail: dustinrockbridge@hotmail.com
dir: *1m W of Presteigne off B4356*

Open Apr-Oct Last arrival 21.30hrs Last departure noon

A pretty little park set in meadowland with trees and shrubs along the banks of the River Lugg. A bridge across the stream gives good access to nearby footpaths. Facilities are very well maintained, and the owner is friendly and helpful. Please note, dogs are not allowed on site. A 3 acre site with 35 touring pitches and 30 statics.

AA Pubs & Restaurants nearby: Bateman Arms, Shobden 01568 708374

Milebrook House Hotel, Knighton 01547 528632

Facilities: 🚿 ☺ ✻ 🚻 🅿
Services: 🚐 🔯 📥
Within 3 miles: 🌳 🌿 🏧
Notes: 🐕 🚫 Fishing

RHAYADER   Map 9 SN96

Places to visit

Blaenavon Ironworks, Blaenavon, 01495 792615, www.cadw.wales.gov.uk

White Castle, White Castle, 01600 780380, www.cadw.wales.gov.uk

Great for kids: Raglan Castle, Raglan, 01291 690228, www.cadw.wales.gov.uk

▶▶▶ **75% Wyeside Caravan & Camping Park** *(SO967690)*

Llangurig Rd LD6 5LB
☎ **01597 810183**
e-mail: info@wyesidecamping.co.uk
dir: *400mtrs N of Rhayader town centre on A470*

Open Feb-Nov Last arrival 22.30hrs Last departure noon

With direct access from the A470, the park sits on the banks of the River Wye. Situated just 400 metres from the centre of the market town of Rhayader, and next to a recreation park with tennis courts, bowling green and children's playground. There are good riverside walks from here, though the river is fast flowing and unfenced, and care is especially needed when walking with children. A 6 acre site with 140 touring pitches, 22 hardstandings and 39 statics.

AA Pubs & Restaurants nearby: Bell Country Inn, Llanyre 01597 823959

Facilities: 🚿 ☺ 🅿 ✻ 🚻 🕐
Services: 🚐 🔯 🛢 🌿 T 📥
Within 3 miles: 🌳 🎣 ⚓ 🏧 🌿 U
Notes: Wi-fi

SWANSEA

PONTARDDULAIS   Map 8 SN50

Places to visit

The National Botanic Garden of Wales, Llanarthne, 01558 668768, www.gardenofwales.org.uk

Glynn Vivian Art Gallery, Swansea, 01792 516900, www.glynnviviangallery.org

Great for kids: Plantasia, Swansea, 01792 474555, www.plantasia.org

▶▶▶▶ **86% River View Touring Park** *(SN578086)*

The Dingle, Llanedi SA4 0FH
☎ **01269 844876**
e-mail: info@riverviewtouringpark.com
web: www.riverviewtouringpark.com
dir: *From M4 junct 49 take A483 signed Llandeilo. 0.5m, 1st left after lay-by, follow lane to site*

* 🚐 £14-£18 🚙 £14-£18 ▲ £14-£18

Open Mar-late Nov Last arrival 20.00hrs Last departure noon

This peaceful park is set on one lower and two upper levels in a sheltered valley with an abundance of wild flowers and wildlife. The River Gwili flows around the bottom of the park in which fishing for brown trout is possible. The excellent toilet facilities are an added bonus. This park is ideally situated for visiting the beaches of South Wales, The Black Mountains and the Brecon Beacons. A 6 acre site with 60 touring pitches, 39 hardstandings.

Facilities: 🚿 ☺ 🅿 ✻ 🚻 🏧 🅿
Services: 🚐 🔯 🛢 🌿 T
Within 3 miles: 🌳 🎪 🌿 🏧 🔯 U
Notes: Dogs must be kept on leads. Outdoor activities organised, tourist information

---

LEISURE: 🏊 Indoor swimming pool   🏊 Outdoor swimming pool   ⚙ Children's playground   🎾 Tennis court   🔍 Games room   📺 Separate TV room   ⛳ 9/18 hole golf course   ⛵ Boats for hire   🎬 Cinema   🎣 Fishing   ⛳ Mini golf   🏄 Watersports   U Stables   **FACILITIES:** 🛁 Bath   🚿 Shower   ☺ Electric shaver   🅿 Hairdryer   ✻ Ice Pack Facility   ♿ Disabled facilities   🕐 Public telephone   🏧 Shop on site or within 200yds   🚚 Mobile shop (calls at least 5 days a week)   🍖 BBQ area   🚻 Picnic area   🅿 Dog exercise area

PORT EINON
Map 8 SS48

Places to visit

Weobley Castle, Llanrhidian, 01792 390012, www.cadw.wales.gov.uk

Gower Heritage Centre, Swansea, 01792 371206, www.gowerheritagecentre.co.uk

Great for kids: Oxwich Castle, Oxwich, 01792 390359, www.cadw.wales.gov.uk

▶▶▶ 81% Carreglwyd Camping & Caravan Park (SS465863)

SA3 1NL

☎ 01792 390795 ◻ 01792 390796
dir: A4118 to Port Einon, site adjacent to beach

▢▢▲

Open Mar-Dec Last arrival 18.00hrs Last departure 15.00hrs

Set in an unrivalled location alongside the safe sandy beach of Port Einon on the Gower Peninsula, this popular park is an ideal family holiday spot. Close to an attractive village with pubs and shops, most pitches offer sea views. The sloping ground has been partly terraced, and facilities are excellent. A 12 acre site with 150 touring pitches.

AA Pubs & Restaurants nearby: Fairyhill, Reynoldston 01792 390139

King Arthur Hotel, Reynoldston 01792 390775

Facilities: ▢▢▢▢▢▢▢
Services: ▢▢▢▢▢▢▢▢
Within 3 miles: ▢▢▢▢
Notes: Dogs must be kept on leads at all times

RHOSSILI

Places to visit

Weobley Castle, Llanrhidian, 01792 390012, www.cadw.wales.gov.uk

Gower Heritage Centre, Swansea, 01792 371206, www.gowerheritagecentre.co.uk

Great for kids: Oxwich Castle, Oxwich, 01792 390359, www.cadw.wales.gov.uk

RHOSSILI
Map 8 SS48

▶▶▶ 82% Pitton Cross Caravan & Camping Park (SS434877)

SA3 1PH

☎ 01792 390593 ◻ 01792 391010
e-mail: admin@pittoncross.co.uk
web: www.pittoncross.co.uk
dir: 2m W of Scurlage on B4247

* ▢ £16-£23.50 ▢ £16-£23.50 ▲ £9-£30

Open all year (rs Nov-Apr no bread, milk or papers) Last arrival 20.00hrs Last departure 11.00hrs

Surrounded by farmland close to sandy Menslade Bay, which is within walking distance across the fields, this grassy park is divided by hedging into paddocks. Nearby Rhossili Beach is popular with surfers. Performance kites are sold, and instruction in flying is given. A 6 acre site with 100 touring pitches, 21 hardstandings.

AA Pubs & Restaurants nearby: Fairyhill, Reynoldston 01792 390139

King Arthur Hotel, Reynoldston 01792 390775

Kings Head, Llangennith 01792 386212

Leisure: ▢
Facilities: ▢▢▢▢▢▢▢▢▢
Services: ▢▢▢▢▢
Within 3 miles: ▢▢▢▢
Notes: Dogs must be kept on leads, quiet at all times, charcoal BBQs must be off ground. Motor caravan, baby bath available

SWANSEA
Map 9 SS69

Places to visit

Swansea Museum, Swansea, 01792 653763, www.swanseaheritage.net

Glynn Vivain Art Gallery, Swansea, 01792 516900, www.glynnviviangallery.org

Great for kids: Plantasia, Swansea, 01792 474555, www.plantasia.org

77% Riverside Caravan Park (SS679991)

Ynys Forgan Farm, Morriston SA6 6QL
☎ 01792 775587 ◻ 01792 795751
e-mail: reception@riversideswansea.com
dir: Exit M4 junct 45 towards Swansea. Left into private road signed to site

▢▢▲

Open all year (rs Winter months pool & club closed) Last arrival mdnt Last departure noon

A large and busy park close to the M4 but in a quiet location beside the River Taw. This friendly, family orientated park has a licensed club and bar with a full high-season entertainment programme. There is a choice of eating outlets with the clubhouse restaurant, takeaway or chip shop. The park has a good indoor pool. A 5 acre site with 90 touring pitches and 256 statics.

AA Pubs & Restaurants nearby: Hanson at the Chelsea Restaurant, Swansea 01792 464068

Leisure: ▢▢▢▢
Facilities: ▢▢▢▢▢▢▢▢▢
Services: ▢▢▢▢▢▢▢▢
Within 3 miles: ▢▢▢▢▢▢▢
Notes: Dogs by arrangement only (no aggressive dog breeds permitted). Fishing on site by arrangement. Wi-fi

VALE OF GLAMORGAN

LLANTWIT MAJOR   Map 9 SS96

Places to visit

Old Beaupre Castle, St. Hilary, 01443 336000, www.cadw.wales.gov.uk

Great for kids: Ogmore Castle, Ogmore, 01443 336000, www.cadw.wales.gov.uk

►►► 83% Acorn Camping & Caravan Site *(SS973678)*

Ham Lane South CF61 1RP
☎ **01446 794024**
e-mail: info@acorncamping.co.uk
dir: *B4265 to Llantwit Major, follow camping signs. Approach site through Ham Manor residential park*

Open Feb-8 Dec Last arrival 21.00hrs Last departure 11.00hrs

A peaceful country site in level meadowland, with some individual pitches divided by hedges and shrubs. It is about one mile from the beach, which can be reached via a cliff top walk, and the same distance from the historic town of Llantwit Major. An internet station and a full-size snooker table are useful amenities. A 5.5 acre site with 90 touring pitches, 10 hardstandings and 15 statics.

AA Pubs & Restaurants nearby: Illtud's 216, Llantwit Major 01446 793800

Plough & Harrow, Monknash 01656 890209

Blue Anchor Inn, East Aberthaw 01446 750329

Leisure:
Facilities:
Services:
Within 3 miles:
Notes: No noise 23.00hrs-07.00hrs. Wi-fi

WREXHAM

EYTON   Map 15 SJ34

AA CAMPING CARD SITE

►►►►► 91% The Plassey Leisure Park

Best of British GOLD

(SJ353452)

The Plassey LL13 0SP
☎ **01978 780277** 🖷 **01978 780019**
e-mail: enquiries@plassey.com
web: www.plassey.com
dir: *From A483 at Bangor-on-Dee exit onto B5426 for 2.5m. Site entrance signed on left*

£13.50-£24.50 £13.50-£24.50 £13.50-£24.50

Open Feb-Nov Last arrival 20.30hrs Last dep noon

A lovely park set in several hundred acres of quiet farm and meadowland in the Dee Valley. The superb toilet facilities include individual cubicles for total privacy and security, while the Edwardian farm buildings have been converted into a restaurant, coffee shop, beauty studio, and various craft outlets. There is plenty here to entertain the whole family, from scenic walks and swimming pool to free fishing, and use of the 9-hole golf course. Seasonal touring pitches are available. A 10 acre site with 90 touring pitches, 45 hardstandings and 15 statics.

AA Pubs & Restaurants nearby: Hanmer Arms, Hanmer 01948 830532

Leisure: **Facilities:**
Services:
Within 3 miles:
Notes: No footballs, bikes or skateboards, dogs must be kept on leads. Badminton & table tennis. Wi-fi

see advert on opposite page

SERVICES: ⚡ Electric hook up 🌀 Launderette 🍺 Licensed bar 🔵 Calor Gas 🔶 Camping Gaz 🚽 Toilet fluid 🍽️ Café/Restaurant 🍔 Fast Food/Takeaway 🔋 Battery charging 🍼 Baby care 🚐 Motorvan service point **ABBREVIATIONS:** BH/bank hols-bank holidays Etr-Easter Whit-Whitsun dep-departure fr-from hrs-hours m-mile mdnt-midnight rdbt-roundabout rs-restricted service wk-week wknd-weekend ⊗ No credit cards ⊗ no dogs See page 7 for details of the AA Camping Card Scheme

Ireland

Co Donegal

ANTRIM
Map 1 D5

Places to visit

Antrim Round Tower, Antrim, 028 9023 5000, www.ehsni.gov.uk

Bonamargy Friary, Ballycastle, 028 9023 5000, www.ehsni.gov.uk

Great for kids: Belfast Zoological Gardens, Belfast, 028 9077 6277, www.belfastzoo.co.uk

▶▶▶ 83% Six Mile Water Caravan Park (J137870)

Lough Rd BT41 4DG
☎ 028 9446 4963 & 9446 3113
e-mail: sixmilewater@antrim.gov.uk
web: www.antrim.gov.uk/caravanpark
dir: *1m from town centre, follow Antrim Forum/ Loughshore Park signs. On Dublin road take Lough road (pass Antrim Forum on right). Site at end of road on right*

* ⛺ £18-£20 ⛺ £18-£20 ▲ £15-£18

Open Mar-Oct Last arrival 21.45hrs Last departure noon

A pretty tree-lined site in a large municipal park, within walking distance of Antrim and the Antrim Forum leisure complex yet very much in the countryside. The modern toilet block is well equipped, and other facilities include a laundry and electric hook-ups. New for 2010 - 37 hardstanding caravan pitches on a new plot of land, which also has space for 30 tents. As with the existing pitches they have been precisely set on generous plots. A 9.61 acre site with 67 touring pitches, 37 hardstandings.

AA Pubs & Restaurants nearby: Galgorm Resort & Spa, Ballymena 028 2588 1001

Leisure: ⚄ ▭
Facilities: ⚄⊙☂⚄⚄⚄⚄⚄
Services: ⚄⚄⚄⚄⚄
Within 3 miles: ⚄⚄⚄⚄⚄⚄
Notes: Max stay 14 nights, no noise between 22.00hrs-08.00hrs, dogs must be under control & on leads. Watersports, angling stands & launching facilities

BALLYCASTLE
Map 1 D6

Places to visit

Bonamargy Friary, Ballycastle, 028 9023 5000, www.ehsni.gov.uk

Great for kids: Dunluce Castle, Portballintrae, 028 2073 1938, www.ehsni.gov.uk

▶▶▶ 71% Watertop Farm (D115407)

188 Cushendall Rd BT54 6RN
☎ 028 2076 2576
e-mail: watertopfarm@aol.com
dir: *Off A2 from Ballycastle towards Cushendall. Opposite Ballypatrick forest*

* ⛺ £18 ⛺ £18 ▲ £10

Open Etr-Oct (rs Etr-Jun & Sep-Oct farm activities not available)

Located on a family hill sheep farm set in the glens of Antrim, the farm offers a range of activities and attractions including pony trekking, boating, pedal go-karts, farm tours, tea room and lots more. The touring facilities consist of three individual sections, two reserved for caravans and the other for tents. The toilets are housed in a converted traditional Irish cottage, and the attached small rural museum serves as a night time social area. A 0.5 acre site with 14 touring pitches, 9 hardstandings.

AA Pubs & Restaurants nearby: Frances Anne Restaurant, Londonderry Arms Hotel, Carnlough 028 2888 5255

Leisure: ⚄ ⚄
Facilities: ⚄⊙☀⚄⚄⚄
Services: ⚄⚄Ⓣ⚄⚄⚄
Within 3 miles: ⚄⚄⚄⚄⚄⚄⚄
Notes: ⊘ No camp fires, no BBQ trays on grass. Small cottage/museum for campers/caravanners to sit in at night

BALLYMONEY
Map 1 C6

Places to visit

Leslie Hill Open Farm, Ballymoney, 028 2766 6803, www.lesliehillopenfarm.co.uk

Bonamargy Friary, Ballycastle, 028 9023 5000, www.ehsni.gov.uk

Great for kids: Dunluce Castle, Portballintrae, 028 2073 1938, www.ehsni.gov.uk

▶▶▶▶ 78% Drumaheglis Marina & Caravan Park (C901254)

36 Glenstall Rd BT53 7QN
☎ 028 2766 0280 & 2766 0227
🖶 028 2766 0222
e-mail: drumaheglis@ballymoney.gov.uk
dir: *Signed off A26, approx 1.5m from Ballymoney towards Coleraine. Also accessed from B66, S of Ballymoney*

* ⛺ £19-£20 ⛺ £19-£20 ▲ £14

Open 17 Mar-Oct Last arrival 20.00hrs Last departure 13.00hrs

Exceptionally well-designed and laid out park beside the Lower Bann River, with very spacious pitches and two quality toilet blocks. Ideal base for touring Antrim and for watersports enthusiasts. A 16 acre site with 55 touring pitches, 55 hardstandings.

Leisure: ⚄
Facilities: ⚄⊙☂☀⚄⚄⚄⚄⚄
Services: ⚄⚄⚄⚄
Within 3 miles: ⚄⚄⚄⚄⚄
Notes: Dogs must be kept on leads. Marina berths, table tennis & volleyball. Wi-fi

BUSHMILLS

Places to visit

Old Bushmills Distillery, Bushmills, 028 2073 1521, www.bushmills.com

Great for kids: Belfast Zoological Gardens, Belfast, 028 9077 6277, www.belfastzoo.co.uk

BUSHMILLS
Map 1 C6

PREMIER PARK

AA CAMPING CARD SITE

▶▶▶▶▶ 87% Ballyness
Caravan Park *(C944393)*

40 Castlecatt Rd BT57 8TN
☎ 028 2073 2393 📄 028 2073 2713
e-mail: info@ballynesscaravanpark.com
web: www.ballynesscaravanpark.com
dir: *0.5m S of Bushmills on B66, follow signs*

✻ 🚐 £20 🚌 £20 ▲

Open 17 Mar-Oct Last arrival 21.00hrs Last
departure noon

A quality park with superb toilet and other
facilities, on farmland beside St Columb's Rill, the
stream that supplies the famous nearby
Bushmills distillery. The friendly owners built this
park with the discerning camper in mind, and they
continue to improve it to ever higher standards.
There is a pleasant walk around several ponds,
and the park is peacefully located close to the
beautiful north Antrim coast. A 16 acre site with

48 touring pitches, 48 hardstandings and 65
statics.

AA Pubs & Restaurants nearby: Bushmills Inn
Hotel, Bushmills 028 2073 3000

Leisure: 🅰

Facilities: 🛁 🍴 ☉ 🍽 ✳ ఉ 🕒 🖥 🚻

Services: 🔌 🖥 🛢 ⊘ 🚽 🎠 ⌄

Within 3 miles: 🚶 🖉 🛒

Notes: No skateboards or roller blades. Family
room with bath, library, internet access. Wi-fi

CUSHENDUN
Map 1 D6

Places to visit

Bonamargy Friary, Ballycastle, 028 9023 5000,
www.ehsni.gov.uk

Antrim Round Tower, Antrim, 028 9023 5000,
www.ehsni.gov.uk

Great for kids: Giant's Causeway Centre,
Giant's Causeway, 028 2073 1855,
www.northantrim.com

▶▶▶ 77% *Cushendun Caravan Park*
(D256332)

14 Glendun Rd BT44 0PX
☎ 028 2176 1254 📄 028 2076 2515
e-mail: cushenduncp@moyle-council.org
dir: *From A2 take B92 for 1m towards Glenarm,
clearly signed*

🚐 🚌 ▲

Open Apr-Sep Last arrival 22.00hrs Last departure
12.30hrs

A pretty little grassy park surrounded by trees,
with separate secluded areas offering some
privacy, and static vans discreetly interspersed
with tourers. The beautiful north Antrim coast is a
short drive away through scenic countryside. A 3
acre site with 12 touring pitches and 64 statics.

AA Pubs & Restaurants nearby: Frances Anne
Restaurant, Londonderry Arms Hotel, Carnlough
028 2888 5255

Leisure: 🎣 ⌐

Facilities: 🍴 ☉ ఉ 🕒 🖥

Services: 🔌 🖥 ⌄

Within 3 miles: 🚶 ✚ 🖉 ◎ 🖥 ∪

Notes: Dogs must be kept on leads at all times

BELFAST

DUNDONALD

Places to visit

Mount Stewart House and Gardens,
Newtownards, 028 4278 8387,
www.nationaltrust.org.uk

Giant's Ring, Belfast, 028 9023 5000,
www.ehsni.gov.uk

Great for kids: Belfast Zoological Gardens,
Belfast, 028 9077 6277, www.belfastzoo.co.uk

SERVICES: 🔌 Electric hook up 🖥 Launderette 🍺 Licensed bar 🛢 Calor Gas ⊘ Camping Gaz 🚽 Toilet fluid 🍽 Café/Restaurant 🍟 Fast Food/Takeaway 🎠 Battery charging 🍼 Baby care ⌄ Motorvan service point ABBREVIATIONS: BH/bank hols-bank holidays Etr-Easter Whit-Whitsun dep-departure fr-from hrs-hours m-mile mdnt-midnight rdbt-roundabout rs-restricted service wk-week wknd-weekend ⊛ No credit cards ⊗ no dogs See page 7 for details of the AA Camping Card Scheme

DUNDONALD — Map 1 D5

►►► 73% Dundonald Touring Caravan Park (J410731)

111 Old Dundonald Rd BT16 1XT
☎ 028 9080 9123 & 9080 9129
📄 028 9048 9604
e-mail: sales@castlereagh.gov.uk
dir: From Belfast city centre follow M3 & A20 to City Airport. Then A20 to Newtownards & follow signs to Dundonald & Ulster Hospital. At hospital right at sign for Dundonald Ice Bowl. Follow to end, turn right. (Ice Bowl on left)

* 🚐 £22 🚏 £6-£22 ▲ £14-£16

Open 17 Mar-Oct (rs Nov-Mar Aire de Service restricted to motorhomes) Last arrival 23.00hrs Last departure noon

A purpose-built park in a quiet corner of Dundonald Leisure Park on the outskirts of Belfast. This peaceful park is ideally located for touring County Down and exploring the capital. In the winter it offers an 'Aire de Service' for motorhomes. A 1.5 acre site with 22 touring pitches, 22 hardstandings.

AA Pubs & Restaurants nearby: Clandeboye Lodge Hotel, Clandeboye 028 9185 2500

Facilities: 🚿☉♿⚕✕♿☕🚻🅿️
Services: 🚐🖨🍴🛒⛽
Within 3 miles: ⛴🏕🎣◎🖨🅿️♨️

Notes: No commercial vehicles, dogs must be kept on leads. Bowling, indoor play area, olympic ice rink (additional charges applicable). Wi-fi

see advert on page 409

CO FERMANAGH

BELCOO — Map 1 C5

PREMIER PARK

NEW ►►►►► 82% Rushin House Caravan Park (H835047)

Holywell BT93 5DY
☎ 028 6638 6519
e-mail: enquiries@rushinhousecaravanpark.com
dir: From Enniskillen take A4 W for 13m to Belcoo. Right onto B52 towards Garrison for 1m. Site signed

🚐 £22 🚏 £22 ▲ £12-£20

Open mid Mar-Oct Last arrival 21.00hrs Last departure 13.00hrs

This park occupies a scenic location overlooking Lough MacNean, close to the picturesque village of Belcoo, and is the product of meticulous planning and execution over the past four years. There are 24 very generous, fully-serviced pitches standing on a terrace overlooking the lough, with additional tenting pitches below; all are accessed by excellent wide tarmac roads. Play facilities include a lovely well-equipped play area and a hard surface and fenced five-a-side football pitch. There is a slipway providing boat access to the lough and, of course, fishing. Excellent toilet facilities are housed in a purpose-built structure and include a family room, with two more rooms planned for 2011. A 4 acre site with 24 touring pitches, 24 hardstandings.

Leisure: ⛰🎱🖥
Facilities: 🚿☉♿✕♿☕🚻🅿️
Services: 🚐🖨⛽🛒🚿⛽
Within 3 miles: ⛴🏕🎣♨️🖨🅿️
Notes: No cars by tents. Dogs on leads. Wi-fi

IRVINESTOWN — Map 1 C5

Places to visit

Castle Coole, Enniskillen, 028 6632 2690, www.nationaltrust.org.uk

Great for kids: Castle Balfour, Lisnaskea, 028 9023 5000, www.ehsni.gov.uk

►►►► 84% Castle Archdale Caravan Park & Camping Site (H176588)

Lisnarick BT94 1PP
☎ 028 6862 1333 📄 028 6862 1176
e-mail: info@castlearchdale.com
dir: Site off B82 (Enniskillen to Kesh road). 10m from Enniskillen

* 🚐 £20-£25 🚏 £20-£25 ▲ £15-£20

Open Apr-Oct (rs Apr-Jun & Sep-Oct shop, restaurant & bar open wknds only) Last departure noon

On the shores of Lower Loch Erne amidst very scenic countryside, this site is ideal for watersports enthusiasts with its marina and launching facilities. Other amenities available on the site include pony trekking, pedal go-karting, cycle hire and coarse fishing. The toilet facilities are very good. An 11 acre site with 158 touring pitches, 110 hardstandings and 139 statics.

AA Pubs & Restaurants nearby: Catalina Restaurant, Lough Erne Resort, Enniskillen 028 6632 3230

Leisure: ⛰
Facilities: 🚿☉✕♿☕🖨🚻🅿️
Services: 🚐🖨🍴🛒⛽🚿🍴🍴🛒⛽
Within 3 miles: ⛴🏕🎣♨️🖨🅿️
Notes: No open fires, dogs must be kept on leads

LISNASKEA — Map 1 C5

Places to visit

Castle Balfour, Lisnaskea, 028 9023 5000, www.ehsni.gov.uk

Florence Court, Enniskillen, 028 6634 8249, www.nationaltrust.org.uk

Great for kids: Castle Coole, Enniskillen, 028 6632 2690, www.nationaltrust.org.uk

►►► 81% Lisnaskea Caravan Park (H297373)

BT92 0NZ
☎ 028 6772 1040
dir: Exit Lisnaskea on B514 to Carrybridge, site signed

🚐 🚏 ▲

Open Mar-Sep Last arrival 21.00hrs Last departure 14.00hrs

A pretty riverside site set in peaceful countryside, with well-kept facilities and friendly owners. Fishing is available on the river, and this quiet area is an ideal location for touring the lakes of Fermanagh. A 6 acre site with 43 touring pitches, 43 hardstandings and 8 statics.

AA Pubs & Restaurants nearby: Catalina Restaurant, Lough Erne Resort, Enniskillen 028 6632 3230

Leisure: ⛰
Facilities: 🚿☉✕♿🚻🅿️
Services: 🚐🖨🔒
Within 3 miles: ⛴🏕🎣🖨🅿️♨️
Notes: ⊜

CO TYRONE

DUNGANNON   Map 1 C5

Places to visit

The Argory, Moy, 028 8778 4753, www.nationaltrust.org.uk

Greencastle, Killeel, 028 9181 1491, www.ehsni.gov.uk

Great for kids: Mountjoy Castle, Mountjoy, 028 9023 5000, www.ehsni.gov.uk

▶▶▶ 81% **Dungannon Park** *(H805612)*

Moy Rd BT71 6DY
☎ **028 8772 8690** 📠 **028 8772 9169**
e-mail: dpreception@dungannon.gov.uk
dir: *M1 junct 15, A29, left at 2nd lights*

🚐 £15 🚕 £15 ▲ £10

Open Mar-Oct Last arrival 20.30hrs Last departure 14.00hrs

Modern caravan park in a quiet area of a public park with fishing lake and excellent facilities, especially for disabled visitors. A 2 acre site with 20 touring pitches, 12 hardstandings.

Leisure: 🏊 🎱 🖥

Facilities: 🍴⊙🅿✻👶🕐💵🚿⛱

Services: 🔌🚻🔋

Within 3 miles: ↧✈🎪🎣💰🛍🚶

Notes: Hot & cold drinks, snacks

REPUBLIC OF IRELAND

CO CORK

BALLINSPITTLE   Map 1 B2

Places to visit

Cork City Gaol, Cork, 021 4305022, www.corkcitygaol.com

Great for kids: Muckross House, Gardens and Traditional Farms, Killarney, 064 6670144, www.muckross-house.ie

▶▶▶▶ 74% **Garrettstown House Holiday Park** *(W588445)*

☎ **021 4778156** & **4775286** 📠 **021 4778156**
e-mail: reception@garrettstownhouse.com
dir: *6m from Kinsale, through Ballinspittle, past school & football pitch on main road to beach. Beside stone estate entrance*

🚐 🚕 ▲

Open 4 May-9 Sep (rs Early season-1 Jun shop closed) Last arrival 22.00hrs Last departure noon

Elevated holiday park with tiered camping areas and superb panoramic views. Plenty of on-site amenities, and close to beach and forest park. A 7 acre site with 60 touring pitches, 20 hardstandings and 80 statics.

Leisure: 🏊🎱🎣🖥 **Facilities:** 🍴⊙🅿✻👶🕐💵🐕

Services: 🔌🚻🔋🛢🚽🔋🍺

Within 3 miles: ↧✈💰◎🎣🛍💰🚶

Notes: 🐕 Children's club, crazy golf, video shows, snooker

see advert below

BALLYLICKEY   Map 1 B2

Places to visit

Muckross House, Gardens and Traditional Farms, Killarney, 064 6670144, www.muckross-house.ie

Great for kids: Fota Wildlife Park, Carrigtwohill, 021 4812678, www.fotawildlife.ie

▶▶▶▶ 78% **Eagle Point Caravan and Camping Park** *(V995535)*

☎ **027 50630**
e-mail: eaglepointcamping@eircom.net
dir: *N71 to Bandon, then R586 to Bantry, then N71, 4m to Glengarriff, opposite petrol station*

🚐 🚕 ▲

Open 23 Apr-27 Sep Last arrival 22.00hrs Last departure noon

An immaculate park set in an idyllic position overlooking the rugged bays and mountains of West Cork. Boat launching facilities and small pebble beaches, in an outstandingly beautiful area. A 20 acre site with 125 touring pitches.

AA Pubs & Restaurants nearby: Sea View House Hotel, Ballylickey 027 50073

Leisure: 🏊🎱🖥

Facilities: 🍴⊙✻🕐💵

Services: 🔌🚻🔋♿

Within 3 miles: ↧✈💰🛍🔋

Notes: 🚫 No commercial vehicles, bikes, skates, scooters or jet skis

SERVICES: 🔌 Electric hook up   🧺 Launderette   🍺 Licensed bar   🔥 Calor Gas   ⊘ Camping Gaz   🚽 Toilet fluid   🍽 Café/Restaurant   🍔 Fast Food/Takeaway   🔋 Battery charging   🍼 Baby care   ♿ Motorvan service point   **ABBREVIATIONS:** BH/bank hols-bank holidays   Etr-Easter   Whit-Whitsun   dep-departure   fr-from   hrs-hours   m-mile   mdnt-midnight   rdbt-roundabout   rs-restricted service   wk-week   wknd-weekend   🚫 No credit cards   🚫 no dogs   See page 7 for details of the AA Camping Card Scheme

CO DONEGAL

PORTNOO
Map 1 B5

Places to visit

Glebe House and Gallery, Letterkenny, 074 9137071, www.glebegallery@opw.ie

Tower Museum, Londonderry, 028 7137 2411, www.derrycity.gov.uk/museums

AA CAMPING CARD SITE

▶▶ 62% Boyle's Caravan Park

(G702990)

☎ 074 9545131 & 086 8523131
📄 074 9545130
e-mail: pboylecaravans@gmail.com
dir: *Exit N56 at Ardra onto R261 for 6m. Follow signs for Santa Anna Drive*

🚐 🚐 Å

Open 18 Mar-Oct Last arrival 23.00hrs Last departure 11.00hrs

Set at Narin Beach and close to a huge selection of water activities on a magnificent stretch of the Atlantic. This open park nestles among the sand dunes, and offers well-maintained facilities. A 1.5 acre site with 20 touring pitches and 80 statics.

AA Pubs & Restaurants nearby: Castle Murray House & Restaurant, Dunkineely 074 9737022

Facilities: 🌂⊙✳🕭🕒💲🐾

Services: 🔌🍴🎒🌱🍽🚮

Within 3 miles: 🎣🏊🐎🍸🎱🎮♺

Notes: ⊘ No skateboards. 1.5m Blue Flag beach

CO DUBLIN

CLONDALKIN
Map 1 D4

Places to visit

Castletown, Celbridge, 01 6288252, www.heritageireland.ie

Irish Museum of Modern Art, Dublin, 01 6129900, www.imma.ie

Great for kids: Dublin Zoo, Dublin, 01 4748900, www.dublinzoo.ie

▶▶▶▶ 73% Camac Valley Tourist Caravan & Camping Park *(0056300)*

Naas Rd, Clondalkin
☎ 01 4640644 📄 01 4640643
e-mail: info@camacvalley.com
dir: *M50 junct 9, W on N7, site on right of dual carriageway after 2km. Site signed from N7*

* 🚐 €24-€26 🚐 €22-€25 Å €10-€25

Open all year Last arrival anytime Last departure noon

A pleasant, lightly wooded park with good facilities, security and layout, situated within an hour's drive, or a bus ride, from city centre. A 15 acre site with 163 touring pitches, 113 hardstandings.

AA Pubs & Restaurants nearby: Finnstown Country House Hotel, Lucan 01 6010700

Leisure: ⚠

Facilities: 🌂⊙℗✳🕭🕒💲🍴🐾

Services: 🔌🍴🌱🎽🚮

Within 3 miles: 🎣🏨🐎🎱🎮♺

CO MAYO

CASTLEBAR
Map 1 B4

Places to visit

King House - Georgian Museum and Military Barracks, Boyle, 071 9663242, www.kinghouse.ie

▶▶▶▶ 74% Lough Lannagh Caravan Park *(M140890)*

Old Westport Rd
☎ 094 9027111 📄 094 9027295
e-mail: info@loughlannagh.ie
web: www.loughlannagh.ie
dir: *N5/N60/N84 to Castlebar. At ring road follow signs for Westport. Signs for Lough Lannagh Village on all approach roads to Westport rdbt*

🚐 €21-€31 🚐 €21-€31 Å €21-€31

Open 22 Apr-Sep Last arrival 18.00hrs Last departure 10.00hrs

This park is part of the Lough Lannagh Village which is situated in a wooded area a short walk from Castlebar. Leisure facilities include a purpose-built fitness and relaxation centre, tennis courts, children's play area and café. A 2.5 acre site with 20 touring pitches, 20 hardstandings.

AA Pubs & Restaurants nearby: Knockranny House Hotel, Westport 098 28600

Bluewave Restaurant, Carlton Atlantic Coast Hotel, Westport 098 29000

Leisure: 🎾

Facilities: 🛁🌂⊙℗✳🕭🍴🐾

Services: 🔌🍴🍽🚮

Within 3 miles: 🎣🏊🏨🐎🎱🎮♺

Notes: No pets Jul & Aug. Use of fitness club, table tennis, boules & outdoor tennis. Wi-fi

KNOCK
Map 1 B4

Places to visit
King House - Georgian Museum and Military Barracks, Boyle, 071 9663242, www.kinghouse.ie

AA CAMPING CARD SITE

►►► 77% Knock Caravan and Camping Park (M408828)

Claremorris Rd
☎ 094 9388100 📠 094 9388295
e-mail: caravanpark@knock-shrine.ie
dir: From rdbt in Knock, through town. Site entrance on left 1km, opposite petrol station

🚐 🚌 Å

Open Mar-Nov Last arrival 22.00hrs Last departure noon

A pleasant, very well maintained caravan park within the grounds of Knock Shrine, offering spacious terraced pitches and excellent facilities. A 10 acre site with 88 touring pitches, 88 hardstandings and 12 statics.

Leisure: 🎢 🎣 ⌂
Facilities: 🎢⊙🅿✳♿⊙🚿🎯
Services: 🔌🖸🔥🖊️🅃🚼⛽
Within 3 miles: ↨🖊️🖸🖸∪
Notes: Dogs must be kept on leads. Wi-fi

CO ROSCOMMON

BOYLE
Map 1 B4

Places to visit
King House - Georgian Museum and Military Barracks, Boyle, 071 9663242, www.kinghouse.ie

Florence Court, Enniskillen, 028 6634 8249, www.nationaltrust.org.uk

►►► 65% Lough Key Caravan & Camping Park (G846039)

Lough Key Forest Park
☎ 071 9662212 📠 071 9673140
e-mail: info@loughkey.ie
web: www.loughkey.ie
dir: Site 3km E of Boyle on N4. Follow Lough Key Forest Park signs, site within grounds. Approx 0.5km from entrance

🚐 🚌 Å

Open Apr-20 Sep Last arrival 18.00hrs Last departure noon

Peaceful and very secluded site within the extensive grounds of a beautiful forest park. Lough Key offers boat trips and waterside walks, and there is a viewing tower. A 15 acre site with 72 touring pitches, 52 hardstandings.

Leisure: 🎢
Facilities: 🚿🎢⊙♿⊙🚿🎯
Services: 🔌🖸
Within 3 miles: ↨🚴🖊️🖸🖸
Notes: ⊗ No cars by tents

CO WATERFORD

CLONEA
Map 1 C2

Places to visit
Waterford Crystal Visitor Centre, Waterford, 051 332500, www.waterfordvisitorcentre.com

Brú Ború Heritage Centre, Cashel, 062 61122, www.comhaltas.com

Great for kids: Johnstown Castle Garden, Wexford, 053 9184671, www.irishagrimuseum.ie

►►► 77% Casey's Caravan & Camping Park (X320937)

☎ 058 41919 📠 058 41919
dir: From R675 (Dungarvan road), follow signs to Clonea Bay. Site at end of road

🚐 🚌 Å

Open 21 Apr-11 Sep Last arrival 21.30hrs Last departure noon

A spacious, well-kept park with excellent toilet facilities, situated next to the beach. A 4.5 acre site with 111 touring pitches, 34 hardstandings and 170 statics.

Leisure: 🎢 🎣 ⌂
Facilities: 🎢⊙🅿✳♿🖸
Services: 🔌🔥🖊️⛽
Within 3 miles: ↨🚴🖽🖊️🖸
Notes: ⊗ Dogs must be on leads at all times. Crazy golf, games room & tiny tots' play area

SERVICES: 🔌 Electric hook up 🖸 Launderette 🍸 Licensed bar 🔥 Calor Gas 🖊️ Camping Gaz 🅃 Toilet fluid 🍽️ Café/Restaurant 🍔 Fast Food/Takeaway 🔋 Battery charging 🚼 Baby care ⛽ Motorvan service point ABBREVIATIONS: BH/bank hols-bank holidays Etr-Easter Whit-Whitsun dep-departure fr-from hrs-hours m-mile mdnt-midnight rdbt-roundabout rs-restricted service wk-week wknd-weekend ⊗ No credit cards ⊗ no dogs See page 7 for details of the AA Camping Card Scheme

WALKS & CYCLE RIDES
Contents

WALKING

All the walks are suitable for families, but less experienced family groups, especially those with younger children, should try the shorter or easier walks first. Route finding is usually straightforward, but the maps are for guidance only and we recommend that you always take the suggested Ordnance Survey map with you.

Risks

Although each walk has been researched with a view to minimising any risks, no walk in the countryside can be considered to be completely free from risk. Walking in the outdoors will always require a degree of common sense and judgement to ensure safety, especially for young children.

- Be particularly careful on cliff paths and in upland terrain, where the consequences of a slip can be serious.
- Remember to check tidal conditions before walking on the seashore.
- Some sections of routes are by, or cross, busy roads. Remember traffic is a danger even on minor country lanes.
- Be careful around farmyard machinery and livestock.
- Be aware of the consequences of changes in the weather and check the forecast before you set out. Ensure the whole family is properly equipped, wearing appropriate clothing and a good pair of boots or sturdy walking shoes. Take waterproof clothing with you and carry spare clothing and a torch if you are walking in the winter months. Remember the weather can change quickly at any time of the year, and in moorland and heathland areas, mist and fog can make route finding much harder. In summer, take account of the heat and sun by wearing a hat and carrying enough water.
- On walks away from centres of population you should carry a whistle and survival bag. If you do have an accident requiring emergency services, make a note of your position as accurately as possible and dial 999.

CYCLING

Cycling is a fun activity which children love, and teaching your child to ride a bike, and going on family cycling trips, are rewarding experiences. Not only is cycling a great way to travel, but as a regular form of exercise it can make an invaluable contribution to a child's health and fitness, and increase their confidence and independence.

The growth of motor traffic has made Britain's roads increasingly dangerous and unattractive to cyclists. Cycling with children is an added responsibility and, as with everything, there is a risk when taking them out cycling. However, in recent years measures have been taken to address this, including the on-going development of the National Cycle Network (more than 8,000 miles utilising quiet lanes and traffic-free paths) and local designated off-road routes for families, such as converted railway lines, canal tow paths and forest tracks.

In devising the cycle rides included in this guide, every effort has been made to use these designated cycle paths, or to link them with quiet country lanes and waymarked byways and bridleways. Unavoidably, in a few cases, some relatively busy B-roads link the quieter, more attractive routes.

Taking care on the road

- Ride in single file on narrow and busy roads.
- Be alert, look and listen for traffic, especially on narrow lanes and blind bends and be extra careful when descending steep hills, as loose gravel can lead to an accident.
- In wet weather make sure you keep a good distance between you and other riders.
- Make sure you indicate your intentions clearly.
- Brush up on The Highway Code before venturing out on to the road.

Off-road safety code of conduct

- Only ride where it is legal to do so. It is forbidden to cycle on public footpaths. The only 'rights of way' open to cyclists are bridleways and unsurfaced tracks, known as byways, which are open to all traffic.
- Canal tow paths: you need a permit to cycle on some stretches of tow path (www.waterscape.com). Remember that access paths can be steep and slippery and always get off and push your bike under low bridges and by locks.
- Always yield to walkers and horses, giving adequate warning of your approach.
- Don't expect to cycle at high speeds.
- Keep to the main trail to avoid any unnecessary erosion

to the area beside the trail and to prevent skidding, especially if it is wet.

- Remember the Countryside Code. (www.naturalengland.org.uk)

Cycling with children
Children can use a child seat from the age of eight months, or from the time they can hold themselves upright. A number of child seats fit on the front or rear of a bike, and it's worth investigating towable two-seat trailers. 'Trailer bicycles', suitable for five- to ten-year-olds, can be attached to the rear of an adult's bike, so that the adult has control, allowing the child to pedal if he/she wishes. Family cycling can be made easier by using a tandem, as it can carry a child seat and tow trailers. 'Kiddy-cranks' for shorter legs can be fitted to the rear seat tube, enabling either parent to take their child out cycling. For older children it is better to purchase the right size bike: an oversized bike will be difficult to control, and potentially dangerous.

Preparing your bicycle
Basic routine includes checking the wheels for broken spokes or excess play in the bearings, and checking for punctures, undue tyre wear and the correct tyre pressures. Ensure that the brake blocks are firmly in place and not worn, and that cables are not frayed or too slack. Lubricate hubs, pedals, gear mechanisms and cables. Make sure you have a pump, a bell, a rear rack to carry panniers and, if cycling at night, a set of working lights.

Preparing yourself
Equipping the family with cycling clothing need not be expensive; comfort is the key. Essential items for cycling are padded cycling shorts, warm stretch leggings (avoid tight-fitting and seamed trousers like jeans or baggy tracksuit trousers that may become caught in the chain), stiff-soled training shoes, and a wind/waterproof jacket. Fingerless gloves are comfortable.

A cycling helmet provides essential protection and are essential for young children learning to cycle.

Wrap your child up with several layers in colder weather. Make sure you and those with you are easily visible by all road users, by wearing light-coloured or luminous clothing in daylight and reflective strips or sashes in failing light and when it is dark.

What to take with you
Invest in a pair of medium-sized panniers (rucksacks can affect balance) to carry the necessary gear for the day. Take extra clothes with you, the amount depending on the season, and always pack a light wind/waterproof jacket. Carry a basic tool kit (tyre levers, adjustable spanner, a small screwdriver, puncture repair kit, a set of Allen keys) and practical spares, such as an inner tube, a universal brake/gear cable, and a selection of nuts and bolts. Also, always take a pump and a strong lock.

Cycling, especially in hilly terrain and off-road, saps energy, so take enough food and drink. Always carry plenty of water, especially in hot and humid weather. Consume high-energy snacks like cereal bars, cake or fruits, eating little and often to combat feeling weak and tired. Remember that children get thirsty (and hungry) much more quickly than adults so always have food and diluted juices available for them.

And finally, the most important advice of all – enjoy yourselves!

Useful cycling websites
- National Cycle Network: www.sustrans.org.uk www.nationalcyclenetwork.org.uk
- British Waterways (tow path cycling): www.waterscape.com
- Forestry Commission (for cycling on Forestry Commission woodland): www.forestry.gov.uk/recreation
- Cyclists Touring Club: www.ctc.org.uk

▷

WALKS & CYCLE RIDES

continued

Each walk and cycle ride starts with a panel giving essential information, including the distance, terrain, nature of the paths, and where to park your car.

WALKS AND CYCLE ROUTES

Minimum time: The time stated for each route is the estimated minimum time that a reasonably fit family group would take to complete the circuit. This does not include rest or refreshment stops.

Maps: Each main route is shown on a detailed map. However, some detail is lost because of the scale. For this reason, we always recommend that you use the maps alongside the suggested Ordnance Survey (OS) map.

Start/Finish: Indicates the start and finish point and parking. The six-figure grid reference prefixed by two letters refers to a 100km square of the National Grid. You'll find more information on grid references on most OS maps.

Level of difficulty: The walks and cycle rides have been graded from 1 to 3. Easier routes, such as those with little total ascent, on easy footpaths or level trails, or those covering shorter distances are graded 1. The hardest routes, either because they include a lot of ascent, greater distances, or are in hilly, more demanding terrains, are graded 3.

Parking: Local parking information for the walks.

Tourist information: A contact number for the nearest tourist information office is provided to help find local information.

Cycle hire: For the cycle rides, this lists, within reason, the nearest cycle hire shop/centre.

❶ This highlights at a glance any potential difficulties or hazards along the route. If a particular route is suitable for older, fitter children it says so here.

All the walks and cycle rides featured in this guide appear in the *AA 365 Pub Walks and Cycle Rides*. This is a comprehensive ring-binder format directory offering a vast collection of routes for the whole family.
See the AA website for more details
http://shop.theaa.com/store/anywhere-and-everywhere

CYCLE 1
The Camel Trail – Edmonton to Padstow

Fabulous views and wonderful birdlife make this section of the Camel Trail a delight at any time of year.

Minimum time: 2hrs
Ride length: 10 miles/16.1km
Difficulty level: ✦✦✦
Map: OS Explorer 106 Newquay & Padstow
Start/finish: The Quarryman Inn, Edmonton; grid ref: SW 964727
Trails/tracks: well-surfaced former railway track
Landscape: river estuary, rolling farmland
Public toilets: Padstow
Tourist information: Padstow, tel 01841 533449
Cycle hire: Camel Trail Cycle Hire, Wadebridge, tel 01208 814104

❶ Padstow is very busy at holiday times – leave your bikes at the secure lock-up on the quay and go into town on foot

Getting to the start

Edmonton is west of Wadebridge. Bypass Wadebridge on the A39 signed 'St Columb Major/Padstow'. About 1 mile (1.6km) after crossing the Camel turn right, before Whitecross, on a lane signed 'Edmonton'.

Why do this cycle ride?

If you prefer to avoid Wadebridge, try this route to access the lower part of the Camel Trail. It is busier than the Dunmere to Wadebridge stretch, but the views make it worthwhile, and starting from the Quarryman's Arms is a bonus. If you want to keep away from crowds of people, turn round on the edge of Padstow, or just dive in quickly for an ice cream. If you like birdlife don't forget your binoculars.

DID YOU KNOW?

Although the mysteries of Tintagel Castle have never been satisfactorily explained, recent excavations have revealed Dark Age (AD 500–1000) connections between Spain and Cornwall. Additionally, the discovery of 'Arthnou' stone suggests that this was a royal place for the Dark Age rulers of Cornwall.

DID YOU KNOW?

The ferry across the Camel estuary linking Padstow with Rock is one of the oldest ferry routes in the country. There has been some form of crossing here since 1337.

Padstow and Prideaux Place

Although Padstow is frequently almost overrun with visitors – especially so since chef Rick Stein took up residence – it is still an attractive little town with an interesting maritime history. St Petroc is said to have come here from Wales in the 6th century AD and founded a monastery which was later sacked by the Vikings in the 10th century. The name Padstow comes from 'Petroc stow' (Petroc's church). Being the only decent harbour on the north coast between Bude and St Ives, Padstow was once the fourth most important port in the country, exporting copper and tin, slate and farm produce. Padstow's famous ancient and pagan Obby Oss ceremony takes place every year on May Day. Rumour has it that it even deterred a party of raiding Frenchmen during the Hundred Years' War!

The Prideaux family – whose origins date back to the 11th century – built their home, Prideaux Place, above the town in the 16th century, and their descendants still live there. This beautiful Elizabethan mansion – now open to the public – is surrounded by gardens laid out in Georgian and Victorian times. A tunnel, giving the family private access, leads from the grounds to St Petroc's Church.

Cycle Directions

1 The Quarryman Inn is a fascinating place. Behind the pub are two terraces of stone cottages, originally homes for workers at the quarries (Point **3**); when these fell into disuse in the early 20th century the building became a TB isolation hospital. Today it is a very welcoming pub. From the car park turn right. At the crossroads turn left and enjoy a lovely downhill run, with increasingly good views over the River Camel and rolling farmland beyond. The Camel was known as the Allen river until 1870, thought to derive from the Irish word alain, for beautiful: it's clear to see why. Pass through the hamlet at Tregunna and follow the lane over a bridge to its end. Turn right down a narrow earthy path to reach the trail.

2 Turn right and follow the trail along the edge of the estuary. At low tide it's almost like cycling along the edge of a beach as the river is flanked by broad expanses of sand and the views are superb. The creeks and sandbanks attract wintering wildfowl – widgeon, goldeneye, long tailed duck – as well as many divers and waders, spring and autumn migrants. Look out for curlew, oystercatcher, shelduck and little egret. One of the main reasons for constructing the railway was to transport sea sand, rich in lime, from the estuary, to fertilise farmland away from the coast. Granite, slate, tin, iron and copper from mines on Bodmin Moor were exported.

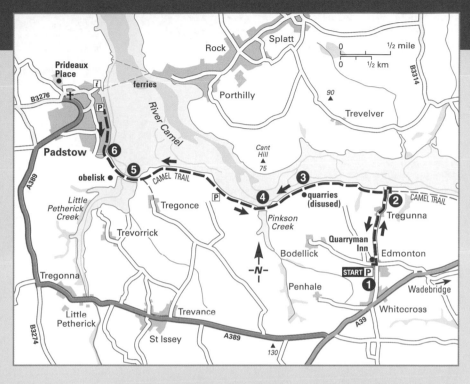

3 A long cutting ends at the spoil heaps of the old slate quarries, with rounded, wooded Cant Hill opposite. The estuary is widening as it approaches the sea; there's a glimpse of Padstow ahead on the left bank. The mouth of the Camel Estuary is marred by the notorious Doom Bar, a shifting sandbank responsible for more than 300 shipwrecks from 1760 to 1920. If you're cycling the Camel Trail on a sunny day it's hard to imagine such disasters.

4 Continue past Pinkson Creek – you may see herons – and continue on to pass the parking area at Oldtown Cove. Once through the next cutting you'll get fantastic views towards Rock, on the other side of the estuary, with Brea Hill and Daymer Bay beyond, and out to the open sea. The trail bears away from the estuary through a cutting.

5 Cross the bridge over Little Petherick Creek. The Saints' Way, a 30-mile (48km) walking route, links Fowey on the south coast with Padstow's St Petroc's Church. It runs along the edge of the creek and past the obelisk (commemorating Queen Victoria's jubilee in 1887) on Dennis Hill, seen ahead. The creek is also an important habitat for little egret and a good range of wading birds.

6 Follow the trail past a lake on the left and then past houses on the edge of Padstow, with moored boats on the water right. Rock, opposite, is a popular sailing and watersports venue, and there's always masses to watch on the water. The trail ends at the quay and car park; you should dismount at this point to explore the town. Retrace your tracks along the Camel Trail to Edmonton.

DID YOU KNOW?

Prideaux Place was used as a location for Trevor Nunn's film version of *Twelfth Night*, and has often featured in film and television productions based on the work of Rosamunde Pilcher.

WALK 1
To Nare Head and Veryan

A fine coastal and field walk through some of South Cornwall's more remote and endearing landscapes.

Minimum time: 3hrs
Walk length: 5 miles/8km
Difficulty level: ✚✚✚
Map: OS Explorer 105 Falmouth & Mevagissey
Start/finish: The Quarryman Inn, Edmonton; grid ref: SW 906384
Paths: Good coastal footpath, field paths and quiet lanes. Field stiles are often overgrown, 30 stiles
Landscape: vegetated coast with some cliffs, mainly flat fields on inland section
Parking: Carne Beach car park. Large National Trust car park behind beach
Public toilets: Carne Beach, Portloe, Veryan
Tourist information: Truro, tel 01872 274555
🛈 The coast path can be slippery after rain. Steep sections of coast/cliff path make the early stages of this walk suitable only for older, fitter children

Getting to the start

From the A39 east of Truro take the A3078 for Tregony and St Mawes. Pass through Tregony then, at a junction by a petrol station, turn left for Veryan. Follow signs into the village, pass the church and the New Inn, following signs for the Nare Hotel. Continue for 2 miles (3.2km), pass the hotel and drop down to Carne Beach and the car park.

There are parts of the Cornish coast that seem especially remote, where main roads have been kept at a distance and where development hasn't gone much beyond farming and sea going. The coast between Gerrans Bay and Veryan Bay, with Nare Head at its centre, is one such place.

Paradoe

The walk begins at the seasonally popular Carne Beach. A steady hike along the coast path soon leads to a steep descent into the narrow Paradoe Cove. On a spur of land above the sea is the ruin of a small cottage. This was the home of Mallet, a 19th-century fisherman, who lived in this lonely spot, fishing from 'Mallet's Cove', and returning at weekends to his wife at Veryan. Eventually Mallet emigrated to Australia – without his wife. The little ruined cottage above the restless sea still speaks of a life of extraordinary detachment.

Portloe

From Paradoe it is a long, punishing climb to the flat top of Nare Head. Beyond the Head a ramble takes you along the coast past the steep Rosen Cliff and by lonely coves. Offshore lies the formidable Gull Rock, a busy seabird colony. The route leads to the fishing village of Portloe. From here, you head inland into a lost world of little fields and meadows that straggle across country to Veryan.

Ancient Landmark

From Veryan the route wanders back towards the sea, past the ancient landmark of Carne Beacon, a Bronze Age burial site that saw later service as a signal station, a triangulation point and as a World War II observation post. A few fields away lies 'Veryan Castle', known also as 'The Ringarounds', the site of a late Iron Age farming settlement. From the high ground the route leads down to the coast again.

> **DID YOU KNOW?**
> St Symphorian is little known in England, but many churches in France are dedicated to him, as is Veryan's church. He came from Autun in Burgundy and was martyred in AD 282 for protesting against the worship of the goddess Cybele.

Walk Directions

1 Turn left out of the car park and walk up the road, with care. Just past the steep bend, turn off right and go up some steps and on to the coast path. Follow the coast path to Paradoe Cove and then continue past scenic Nare Head.

2 Above Kiberick Cove go through a gap in a wall. For the main route keep ahead through a dip to reach a stile. Follow the coast path to Portloe. Go left up the road from the cove, past the Ship Inn.

3 Just after a sharp left-hand bend, and where the road narrows, go over a high step stile on the right. Cross a field to a stile, then follow the next field-edge. Pass a gate, then, in a few paces, go right and over a stile. Cross the next field to reach a stile into a lane.

4 Go right along the road past Camels Farm for 200yds (183mtrs), then go left over a stile and follow the field-edge to another stile. Follow the next field-edge, then just before the field corner, go right over a stile. Turn left through a gap, then go diagonally right across the next two fields to a stile. At a road junction, continue along the road signposted 'Carne and Pendower'.

5 Just past Tregamenna Manor Farm, on a bend, go over a stile by a gate. Cut across the corner of the field, then go right over a stile. Cross the next field to a stile and then continue to a T-junction with a lane. (Turn right to visit Veryan.)

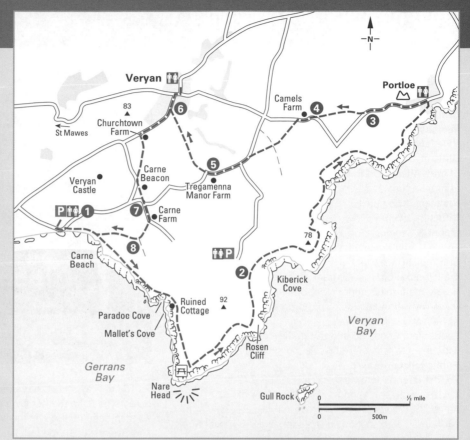

6 If you're not visiting Veryan village, turn left, then, just past Churchtown Farm, go left again over a stile. Follow the edge of the field to a stile into a lane. Go immediately left over two stiles, then follow a path, past Carne Beacon, to a lane.

7 At a corner junction keep ahead down the lane, signposted 'Carne Village Only'. Bear right down a driveway past Beacon Cottage. Go through the gate signposted 'Defined Footpaths Nos 44 & 45'. Follow the track round to the right between a garage and house and then follow a grassy track, keeping ahead at a junction signposted

'Carne Beach'. Go through a gate (put dogs on leads here, please) and follow a path alongside a grassy bank and fence.

8 Abreast of an old wooden gate up on the right, bear away to the left and then walk downhill

through the scrub, (the path isn't evident at first), and soon pick up a path that leads through gorse to join the coast path and return back to Carne Beach and the car park at the start of the walk.

WHILE YOU ARE THERE

King Harry Ferry is one of only seven chain ferries operating in England. It provides a vital and picturesque link between the Roseland peninsula and Feock, saving up to 30 miles (48km) on a round trip to Truro.

The ferry's name is shrouded in mystery, but is possibly linked with Henry VIII. One story is that the king spent his honeymoon with Anne Boleyn at St Mawes Castle, and signed a charter for the ferry during his visit.

CYCLE 2
From Keswick to Threlkeld

A linear ride along an old railway, with an optional return via Lakeland's greatest ancient site.

Minimum time: 1hr 30min
Ride length: 9 miles/14.5km
Difficulty level: ✦✦✦
Shorter Alternative Route
Minimum time: 1hr
Ride length: 8 miles/12.9km
Difficulty level: ✦✦✦
Map: OS Explorer OL4 The English Lakes (NW) and OL5 The English Lakes (NE)
Start/finish: Keswick Leisure Centre; grid ref: NY 269238
Trails/tracks: old railway track, short section of cycle track beside main road, minor road; optional return on minor roads with short section of busy A road (or walk down pavement alongside)
Landscape: woodland and river valley; open farmland with views to fells on return via stone circle
Public toilets: Keswick
Tourist information: Keswick, tel 01768 772645
Cycle hire: Keswick Mountain Bikes, Keswick, tel 01768 775202
❶ Railway path section suitable for all ages. If continuing into Threlkeld, suitability: children 6+; if returning via stone circle, suitability: children 10+

Getting to the start

Follow the A66 to a roundabout north west of Keswick. Take the A5271 towards the town. After 300yds (274mtrs) turn left, signposted 'Leisure Pool' and roadside parking.

Why do this cycle ride?

This route crosses and recrosses the river, running through woodland. Return the same way take the climb to Castlerigg Stone Circle.

The Greta Valley

The railway to Keswick was completed in 1864, having taken just 18 months to build, at a total cost of £267,000 for 31 miles (50km), and with 135 bridges. Goods traffic declined quite early in its life. Passenger numbers peaked in 1913 at 182,000, but never really recovered after World War One, though the line struggled on until it finally closed in 1972.

The railway route passes the bobbin mill site at Low Briery. The Lake District once produced half of all the wooden bobbins used by the world's textile industry, and Low Briery alone exported 40 million of these every year. Whether you cycle there, drive there or take the bus, Castlerigg Stone Circle is a 'must-see' site. It may not be the most impressive such circle in Britain, but it's hard to think of one that has a finer location. Best of all, come early in the morning or late in the evening when there are few others around and your imagination can have free rein. It was probably built around 3000 BC, and no one today knows exactly what it was for, although significant astronomical alignments have been identified.

DID YOU KNOW?

There are four islands on the lake, all owned by the National Trust. The largest and most northerly of the four is Derwent Isle. Once owned by Fountains Abbey it was bought by German miners from the Company of Royal Mines in 1569. The island and part of its grand 18th-century house are open to visitors on a handful of days during the year.

Cycle Directions

1 Ride down towards the Leisure Centre and bear left, signed Keswick Railway Footpath, past the former railway station, now a smart hotel. The old trackbed leads on to a bridge over the river and then over the A5271. Pass a housing estate on the left, then climb – more steeply than you'd expect from a railway track (the route here was disrupted by the construction of the A66 bypass and bridge). There's a National Cycle Network/C2C sign just before the route goes under Greta Bridge. At the end of an unusual elevated boardwalk section, look right and you can just see the top of a stone arch, once the mouth of a tunnel, indicating the original line of the railway. Continue with views of the river then past the caravans of Low Briery. Go under a bridge and pass an information board about the former bobbin mill.

2 Continue across a bridge over the River Greta, seemingly a simple flat span but actually supported by an inverted ironwork arch. There's a second, similar bridge, and then a third with its arch 'right side up'. Just before the fourth bridge an old railway hut is now a shelter and information point. The bridge overlooks the junction of the river with Glenderaterra Beck. Cross another inverted bridge, then go through a short tunnel (no need for lights). There's another bridge, another information shelter and then a cutting. Cross another bridge and make a short climb, where the

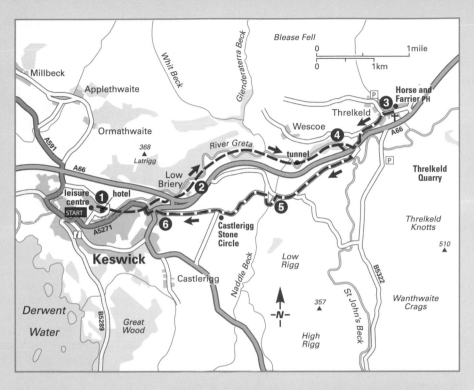

original line of the railway has again been obliterated by the A66. Emerge alongside the busy road on a separate cycle track. After about 200yds (183mtrs) swing left on the minor road to Threlkeld, and follow it into the village, past the church, to the Horse and Farrier.

3 Retrace the route as far as the last bridge you crossed, and go over. (You can, of course, return all the way along the railway track from this point.)

4 About 30yds (27mtrs) past the bridge, turn sharp left through a small gate. A steep drop down and a bumpy path take you under the A66 and soon lead out to a

road. Turn right and climb, with good views of St John's in the Vale and Helvellyn. Make a sweeping descent and turn left just before it levels out.

5 Swing round through a little valley, then turn left again and climb steadily, now looking down the Naddle Valley. The climb is quite long, levelling out just as the stone circle appears in a field on the left. Almost at once the road sweeps down again. Drop down to a T-junction on the outskirts of Keswick.

6 Families may feel safer walking the next short section. Follow the road left to another

T-junction, then turn right down the hill. Round the first bend and just before a bridge with slate parapets go left round a barrier onto a gravel path leading down onto the railway track and so back to the start.

WALK 2
From Patterdale by Ullswater

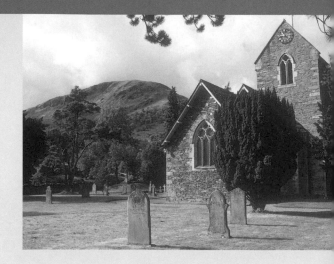

Along the shores of Ullswater to Silver Point, a spectacular viewpoint.

Minimum time: 1hr 30min
Walk length: 4 miles/6.4km
Difficulty level: ✦✦✦
Map: OS Explorer OL5 The English Lakes (NE)
Start/finish: Grid reference: NY 396159
Paths: Stony tracks and paths, no stiles
Landscape: Lake and fell views, mixed woodland
Parking: Pay-and-display car park opposite Patterdale Hotel
Public toilets: opposite White Lion in Patterdale
Tourist information: Ullswater (Glenridding), tel: 017684 82414
🛈 Rough tracks with some steep sections.
Suitability: children 8+

Getting to the start
Patterdale village lies at the southern tip of Ullswater, stretched along the A592.

The elongated hamlet of Patterdale has a rugged, mountain quality. A perfect contrast to the splendour of Ullswater, whose southern shore lies hardly a stone's throw away. This walk strolls through mixed woodland and open aspect above the shores of the lake to visit the famed viewpoint of Silver Point. The adventurous may wish to make the scramble to the top of Silver Crag, as did horsedrawn coach parties of old, for a better view of the lake.

Ullswater
Undoubtedly one of the loveliest of the lakes, it is Lakeland's second largest lake. Its waters are exceptionally clear and in the deepest part of the lake, off Howtown, lives a curious fish called the schelly; a creature akin to a freshwater herring.

Poetic Preservation
The preservation of the lake in its present form is despite the fact that it supplies water to Manchester; the workings for the extraction are hidden underground and designed so that it is impossible to lower the water level beyond an agreed limit.

Among the trees, beside the shore, it was the daffodils that inspired William Wordsworth's most widely known poem, I wandered lonely as a cloud or Daffodils (1807). His sister Dorothy recorded the event vividly in her diary: 'I never saw daffodils so beautiful. They grew among the mossy stones about and around them, some rested their heads upon these stones as on a pillar for weariness and the rest tossed and reeled and danced and seemed as if they verily laughed with the wind'. There is no doubt that this later helped William to pen his famous verse.

WHILE YOU ARE THERE
After reaching the famed viewpoint of Silver Point, the adventurous may also wish to make the scramble to the top of Silver Crag, as did the horsedrawn coach parties of old, for an even better view over the lake.

DID YOU KNOW?
The elongated hamlet of Patterdale has a rugged, mountain quality. Sited below the mighty Helvellyn massif its straggle of houses, inn, hotel, mountain rescue base, church and school have a certain bleakness about them. A perfect contrast to the splendour that is Ullswater, whose southern shore lies hardly a stone's throw away.

Walk Directions

1 From the car park walk to the road and turn right towards the shore of Ullswater. Pass the school to a track leading off right, through the buildings. Follow the unsurfaced track over a bridge and continue through the buildings of Side Farm to join another unsurfaced track.

2 Turn left along the undulating track, with a stone wall to the left, and pass through mixed woodland, predominantly oak and ash, before open fellside appears above. Proceed along the path above the campsite and pass a stand of larch before descending to cross a little stream above the buildings of Blowick, seen through the trees below. The path ascends again to crest a craggy knoll above the woods of Devil's Chimney. Make a steep descent following the path through the rocks before it levels to traverse beneath the craggy heights of Silver Crag. A slight ascent, passing some fine holly trees, gains the shoulder of Silver Point and an outstanding view of Ullswater.

3 Follow the path, which sweeps beneath the end of Silver Crag and continue to pass a small stream before a steep stony path, eroded in places, breaks off to the right. Ascend this, climbing diagonally right, through the juniper bushes. Gain the narrow gap which separates Silver Crag to the right from the main hillside of Birk Fell to the left. This little valley is quite boggy and holds a small tarnlet.

4 If you don't care for steep, exposed ground, follow the high narrow path to make a gradual descent south in the direction of Patterdale. But for those with a head for heights, a short steep scramble leads to the top of Silver Crag and a wonderful view. Care must be exercised for steep ground lies in all directions. Descend back to the ravine and the main path by the same route. The path is easy though it traverses the open fellside and may be boggy in places. Pass open quarry workings, where there is a large unfenced hole next to the path (take care), and continue on, to cross over the slate scree of a larger quarry. Bear right to descend by a stream and cross a little footbridge leading to the gate at the end of a track.

5 Go left through the gate and follow the lane which leads through the meadows. Cross the bridge and join the road. Bear right through Patterdale to the car park.

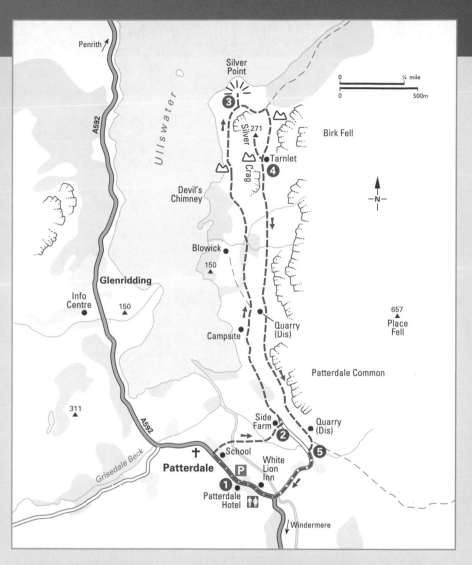

CYCLE 3
Along the Tissington Trail

An easy ride from the Tissington estate village along an old railway line above the secluded valley of the Bletch Brook.

Minimum time: 3hrs 30min
Ride length: 16 miles/25.7km
Difficulty level: ✚✚✚
Shorter Alternative Route
Minimum time: 1hr 30min
Ride length: 6 miles/9.7km
Difficulty level: ✚✚✚
Map: OS Explorer OL24 White Peak
Start/finish: Tissington Old Station, grid ref SK 177520
Trails/tracks: old railway trackbed, lanes in Tissington village
Landscape: limestone plateau of the White Peak, extensive views
Public toilets: Tissington and Hartington old stations
Tourist information: Ashbourne, tel 01335 343666
Cycle hire: Peak Cycle Hire, Mapleton Lane, Ashbourne, Derbyshire, tel 01335 343156, www.peakdistrict.org

Getting to the start

Tissington is signposted off the A515 Ashbourne to Buxton road, a few miles north of Ashbourne. Pass the pond in the village and bear right to find the gated entrance to the Tissington Trail car park.

Why do this cycle ride?

This is one of England's most famous cycling trails and, as it is an old railway line, you can simply choose just when and where to turn round and return to the start. We've suggested heading north, but you could as easily head south to the pleasant market town of Ashbourne, with its antique shops and bookshops. Going north offers a short option along a wooded route followed by a contrasting, airy route through cuttings and along embankments. It's your choice!

Dew Ponds

Once beyond the old station at Alsop, one feature of the landscape you'll notice along the route are the occasional small ponds in the pastures – these are dew ponds. The name comes from the belief that morning dew would

provide sufficient water for cattle and sheep to drink. In days gone by these would be hollows dug out and lined with clay to stop the water from draining away. As this is an area where the rock is predominantly porous limestone, rainwater seeps away and surface water is very rare. The modern-day versions are watertight and they don't rely on dew, either, as they are regularly topped up by the farmers.

Summertime on the Tissington Trail sees a profusion of butterflies. The Common Blue is one of the most noticeable. This very small insect feeds largely on clover flowers and the bright yellow flowers of bird's foot trefoil, a low-growing plant that flourishes in limestone areas. Another butterfly to look out for is the colourful Red Admiral which lays its eggs on nettles, the food plant of the caterpillar.

Cycle Directions

❶ The Tissington car park is at the site of the old railway station. Take time to find the information board which has a fine picture of the place in its heyday. There's also a village information board here; the village centre is only a short cycle away and it's well worth taking the loop before starting out. Turn left from the car park entrance, then right along Chapel Lane. This passes one of the five wells that are dressed in the village during the famous Well Dressing Ceremony held in May on Ascension Day. The lane rises gently to a junction at the top of the village. Turn left to drop down the main street, lined by greens and passing Tissington Hall and more wells. At the bottom keep left,

passing the village pond before swinging right to return to the car park. Here turn left, passing beneath a bridge to join the old trackbed, which starts a long, easy climb.

❷ This initial stretch is through a wooded cutting, soon shallowing to offer the occasional view through the trees across the glorious countryside here at the southern end of the National Park. The panorama sweeps across the peaceful valley of the Bletch Brook to take in the high ridge of rough pastures above Ballidon to the right.

❸ The first natural place to turn around to return to Tissington is the car park and picnic area at the former Alsop Station. This would make a round trip of 6 miles (9.7km) and take perhaps 1.5 hours – and it's downhill virtually all the way back!

4 It's well worth continuing north, however, as once the old railway passes beneath the main road, the character of the Trail changes, and a more open terrain offers different views and experiences. The track continues its gentle climb, soon crossing the first of many embankments. There are grand views left (west) across the rolling pastureland of the White Peak towards the higher, darker hills that characterise the Staffordshire moorlands, forming the western horizon. Closer to hand are round-topped hills capped by crowns of trees.

5 Off to your left, the village of Biggin-by-Hartington soon appears – notice the old army huts down to the left, still put to good use as storerooms. In the distance and looking north, you may pick out the distinctive knolls of limestone near Longnor, Chrome Hill and Parkhouse Hill. The strand of cuttings and embankments continues towards the next logical turning point, Hartington Old Station. Here, the former signal box has been preserved; climb the steps to view the old points and levers.

6 This is the ideal place to turn round and retrace the route back to the car park at Tissington.

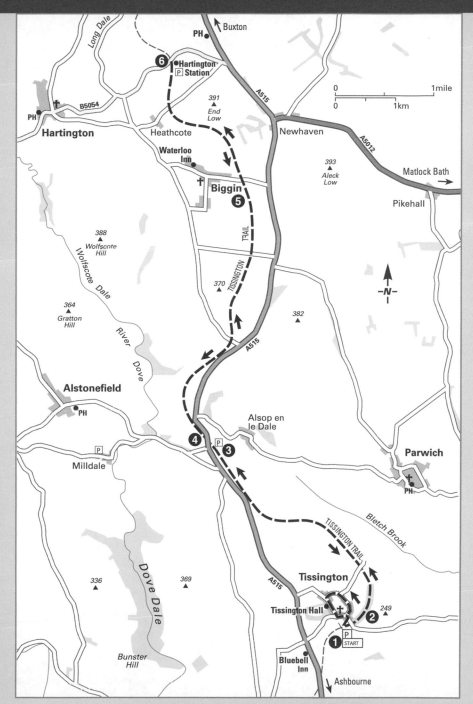

Following the ever-changing River Wye from Ashford-in-the-Water through lovely Monsal Dale.

Minimum time: 3hrs 30min
Walk length: 5.5 miles/8.8km
Difficulty level: ✚✚✚
Map: OS Explorer OL24 White Peak
Start/finish: Grid reference: SK 194696
Paths: Well-defined paths and tracks throughout, lots of stiles
Landscape: Limestone dales and high pasture
Parking: Ashford-in-the-Water car park
Public toilets: At car park
Tourist information: Bakewell, tel 01629 813227
❶ Parents should keep a close eye on children whilst in the vicinity of the Monsal Head Viaduct. There's a short, steady climb in Point ❺. Take care crossing the A6

Getting to the start

Ashford-in-the-Water is signposted off the main A6 road a few miles north west of Bakewell. In the village pass the Bull's Head pub on your right and take Court Lane, the next narrow road on the right to the car park.

The Wye is a chameleon among rivers. Rising as a peaty stream from Axe Edge, it rushes downhill, only to be confined by the concrete and tarmac of Buxton, a spa town, and the quarries to the east. Beyond Chee Dale it gets renewed vigour and cuts a deep gorge through beds of limestone, finally to calm down again among the gentle fields and hill slopes of Bakewell. The finest stretch of the river valley must be around Monsal Head, and the best approach is from Ashford-in-the-Water, one of Derbyshire's prettiest villages.

Monsal Dale

After passing through Ashford's streets the route climbs to high pastures that give no clue as to the whereabouts of Monsal Dale. But suddenly you reach the last wall and the ground falls away into a deep wooded gorge. John Ruskin was so taken with this beauty that he likened it to the Vale of Tempe: 'you might have seen the Gods there morning and evening – Apollo and the sweet Muses of light – walking in fair procession on the lawns of it and to and fro among the pinnacles of its crags'.

The Midland Railway

It's just a short walk along the rim to reach one of Derbyshire's best-known viewpoints, where the Monsal Viaduct spans the gorge. Built in 1867 as part of the Midland Railway's line to Buxton, the five-arched, stone-built viaduct is nearly 80ft (25mtrs) high. But the building of this railway angered Ruskin. He continued, 'you blasted its rocks away, heaped thousands of tons of shale into its lovely stream. The valley is gone and the Gods with it'.

The line closed in 1968 and the rails were ripped out, leaving only the trackbed and the bridges. Ironically, today's conservationists believe that those are worth saving and have slapped a conservation order on the viaduct. The trackbed is used as a recreational route for walkers and cyclists – the Monsal Trail. The walk continues over the viaduct, giving bird's-eye views of the river and the lawn-like surrounding pastures. It then descends to the river bank, following it westwards beneath the prominent peak of Fin Cop. The valley curves like a sickle, while the path weaves in and out of thickets, and by wetlands where tall bulrushes and irises grow. After crossing the A6 the route takes you into the mouth of Deep Dale then the shade of Great Shacklow Wood. Just past some pools filled with trout there's an entrance to the Magpie Mine Sough. The tunnel was built in 1873 to drain the Magpie Lead Mines at nearby Sheldon. Magpie was worked intermittently for over 300 years before finally closing in the 1960s. It's believed to be haunted by the ghosts of miners from the neighbouring Redsoil Mine who tragically died underground in a dispute with the Magpie men.

WHILE YOU ARE THERE

Bakewell, next door to Ashford, is well worth a visit. The spired church of All Saints looks down on this bustling town, which is built round a fine 14th-century bridge over the River Wye. The 13th-century church, refurbished in Victorian times, has many interesting monuments, including one in the Vernon Chapel dedicated to Sir George Vernon who was known as 'King of the Peak' because of his famed lavish hospitality. The Bakewell Show, held in August, is claimed to be the longest continuous running agricultural show in England.

Walk Directions

1 From Ashford-in-the-Water car park, walk out to the road and turn right to walk along Vicarage Lane. After 100yds (91mtrs), a footpath on the left doubles back left, then swings sharp right to continue along a ginnel behind a row of houses. Beyond a stile the path enters a field.

2 Head for a stile in the top left corner, then veer slightly right to locate a stile allowing the route to go on to Pennyunk Lane. This walled stony track winds among high pastures. At its end go left uphill along a field-edge. At the top it joins another track, heading north (right) towards the rim of Monsal Dale. The path runs along the top edge of the deep wooded dale to reach the car park at Monsal Head.

3 Take the path marked 'Viaduct and Monsal Trail' here – this way you get to walk across the viaduct. On the other side of the viaduct go through a gate on the left. Ignore the path climbing west up the hillside, but descend south-west on a grassy path raking through scrub woods down into the valley. This shouldn't be confused with the steep eroded path plummeting to the foot of the viaduct.

4 Now you walk down the pleasant valley. The right of way is well away from the river at first but most walkers trace the river bank to emerge at Lees Bottom and a roadside stile.

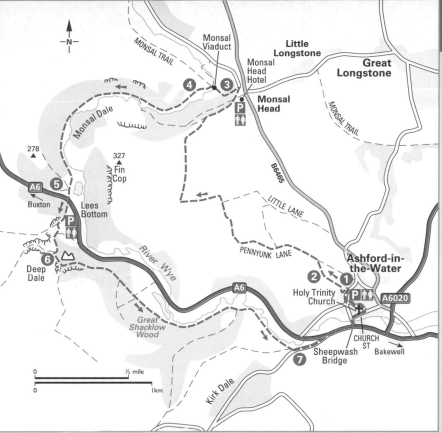

5 Cross the A6 with great care and go through the White Lodge car park on the path the other side, where the route back to Ashford begins. Beyond the gate carry on along the path, ignoring the turning to Toddington. Go over a wall stile, then up to a rocky path, forking left for the path into Great Shacklow Wood, signed 'Ashford'.

6 The path now climbs steeply through the trees and stony ground to another gate. Ignore the turning right for Sheldon and continue straight ahead, following a fine ledge path along the steep wooded slopes. Eventually the path comes down to the river, past an old mill,

before joining a minor road at the bottom of Kirk Dale.

7 Turn left along the road, down to the A6 and turn right towards Ashford. Leave the road to cross Sheepwash Bridge. Turn right along Church Street, then left along Court Lane to the car park.

WALK 4
From Seatown to Golden Cap

Climb a fine top, owned by one of the country's most popular charities.

Minimum time: 2hrs 30min
Walk length: 4 miles/6.4km
Difficulty level: ✚✚✚
Map: OS Explorer 116 Lyme Regis & Bridport
Start/finish: Grid reference: SY 420917
Paths: Field tracks, country lanes, steep zig-zag gravel path, 5 stiles
Landscape: windswept coastline of lumps and bumps
Parking: Car park (charge) above gravel beach in Seatown; beware, can flood in stormy weather
Public toilets: At end of road, Seatown
Tourist information: Bridport, tel: 01308 424901
❗ Long, steep ascent to the top of Golden Cap; steep descent on longer loop; suitable for fit, older children

Getting to the start

To reach Seatown, take the signed lane opposite the church in Chideock, a small village on the A35 between Bridport and Lyme Regis, 3 miles (4.8km) west of Bridport. Arrive early in summertime to ensure a space in the car park.

Golden Cap is the rather obvious name for a high, flat-topped hill of deep orange sandstone on the cliffs between Charmouth and Bridport. It represents the tail end of a vein of warm-coloured sandstone. The Cap is the highest point on the south coast, at 627ft (191mtrs), with views along the shore to the tip of Portland Bill in one direction and to Start Point in the other. Inland, you can see Pilsdon Pen.

Important Habitat

Climbing towards the top, you pass from neat fields, through a line of wind-scoured oak trees, into an area of high heathland, walking up through bracken, heather, bilberry and blackberry, alive with songbirds. The loose undercliff on the seaward side creates a different habitat. In botanical and wildlife terms, Golden Cap is one of the richest natural properties in the National Trust's portfolio.

Earl of Antrim

On the very top of Golden Cap itself is a simple memorial to the Earl of Antrim, chairman of the Trust in the 1960s and 1970s. It was he who spearheaded its 1965 appeal campaign, named 'Enterprise Neptune', to purchase sections of unspoiled coastline before the developers moved in. Golden Cap was part of this and over the years the Trust has continued to buy up pockets of land all around, with the aim of preserving the traditional field pattern that exists in the area between Eype and Lyme Regis.

Its acquisition includes the ruined Chapel of St Gabriel's (little more than a low shell with a porch to one side) and the neighbouring row of thatched cottages that have been smartly refurbished and are let out as visitor accommodation. They are all that remains of the fishing village of Stanton St Gabriel, sheltering in the valley behind the cliffs, which was largely abandoned after the coast road was rerouted inland in 1824; the chapel was derelict long before this.

Walk Directions

1 Walk back up through Seatown. Cross a stile on the left, on to the footpath, signposted 'Coast Path Diversion'. Cross a stile at the end, carry on across the field to cross a stile and footbridge into woodland. Cross a stile at the other side and bear right up the hill, signposted 'Golden Cap'.

2 Where the track forks by a bench keep left. Go through some trees and over a stile. Bear left, straight across the open hillside, with Golden Cap ahead of you. Pass through a line of trees and walk up the fence. Go up some steps, cross a stile and continue ahead. At the fingerpost go left through a gate to follow the path of shallow steps up through bracken, heather, bilberry and bramble to the top of Golden Cap.

3 Pass the trig point and turn right along the top. Pass the stone memorial to the Earl of Antrim. At a marker stone turn right and follow the zig-zag path steeply downhill, enjoying great views along the bay to Charmouth and Lyme Regis. Go through a gate and bear right over the field towards the ruined St Gabriel's Chapel. In the bottom corner turn down through a

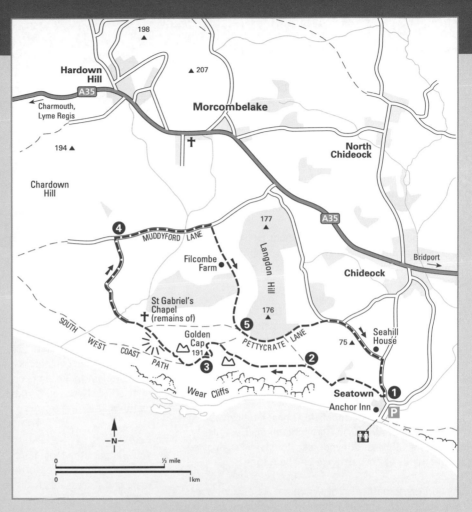

gate, passing the ruins on your right, then go through a second gate. Go down the track, passing cottages on the left, and bear right up the farm road, signed to 'Morcombelake'. Follow this up between high banks and hedges. Continue through a gateway.

4 At the road junction, turn right down Muddyford Lane, signed 'Langdon Hill'. Pass the gate of Shedbush

Farm and continue straight up the hill. Turn right up a concreted lane towards Filcombe Farm. Follow blue markers through the farmyard, bearing left through two gates. Walk up the track, go along the right edge of the first field and across the next field. Head left over the top of the green saddle between Langdon Hill and Golden Cap.

5 Go left through a gate in the corner and down a track (Pettycrate Lane) beside the woods, signed 'Seatown'. Ignore a footpath over a stile to the right. At a junction of tracks keep right, downhill. Pass Seahill House on the left and turn right, on to a road. Continue down the road into Seatown village to return to your car.

WALK 5
New Forest trails around Bank

Ancient oaks, towering conifers and historic inclosures are on the route.

Minimum time: 4hrs
Walk length: 8 miles/12.9km
Difficulty level: +++
Map: OS Explorer OL22 New Forest
Start/finish: Grid reference: SU 266057
Paths: Grass and gravel forest tracks, heathland paths, some roads
Landscape: Ornamental Drive, ancient forest inclosures and heathland
Parking: Brock Hill Forestry Commission car park, just off A35
Public toilets: Blackwater car park
Tourist information: Lyndhurst, tel: 023 8028 2269
❶ Extreme caution needed when crossing the busy A35 (twice). Blind bends on the lane through Bank. Follow directions carefully – unsigned paths, tracks and forest rides

Getting to the start
Look for signs to the Rhinefield Ornamental Drive, off the A35 Lyndhurst-to-Christchurch road, 3 miles (4.8km) south west of Lyndhurst. Parking is signposted on the right, a short distance off the A35.

A short drive south-west of Lyndhurst are ancient woods of oak and beech, notably Bolderwood. Here you are in the true heart of the New Forest and this fascinating loop walk explores this rich landscape.

Finest Relics of Woodland
Unenclosed woodlands such as Whitley Wood are among the finest relics of unspoilt deciduous forest in Western Europe. Hummocky green lawns and paths meander

> **DID YOU KNOW?**
> Charcoal-burning is one of the oldest industries in England, and was one of the commoners' rights. Elizabeth I encouraged the use of coal and passed an act that forbade felling timber for burning, so helping to bring about the industry's decline.

beneath giant beech trees and beside stands of ancient holly and contorted oaks, and through peaceful, sunny glades edged with elegant silver birch. 'Inclosures' are areas of managed woodlands where young trees are protected from deer and ponies. Areas of oak trees were first inclosed in the late 17th century to provide timber required for the construction and shipbuilding industries. Holidays Hill Inclosure is one of the forest's oldest, dating from 1676. Here you'll find 300-year-old oak trees that matured after iron replaced wood in ships.

Famous Forest Sights
You will pass the most famous and probably the oldest tree in the forest, the Knightwood Oak. Believed to be 350 years old, it owes its great age to pollarding (cutting back) its limbs to encourage new branches for fuel and charcoal. Pollarding was made illegal in 1698 as full-grown trees were needed to provide timber for shipbuilding, so any oak or beech tree that show signs of having been pollarded is of a great age. Marvel at the girth of this fine oak, a massive 24ft (7.3mtrs), before walking through Holidays Hill Inclosure.

Close to Millyford Bridge and Highland Water stands the Portugese Fireplace, a memorial to the work of a Portugese Army unit, deployed during World War I to cut timber for pit-props. The flint fireplace was their cookhouse. Returning through Holidays Hill Inclosure you will join a 'reptile trail' and several marker posts, each carved with a different type of British reptile, lead to the New Forest reptillary. Set up to breed rarer species for the wild, including the sand lizard and smooth snake. Here you can to view some of the forest's more elusive inhabitants.

Walk Directions

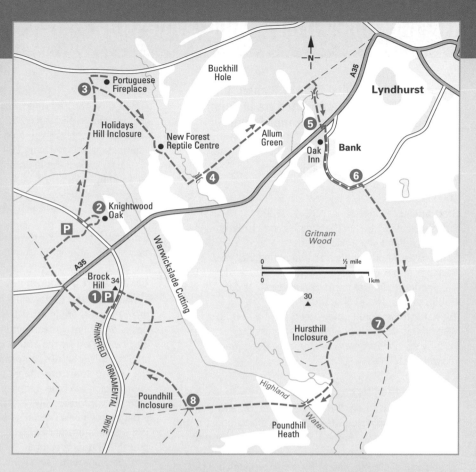

1 Take the gravel path at the southern end of the car park (beyond the information post), parallel with the road. In 100yds (91mtrs) turn right just before a bench seat and descend to a gravel track. Cross straight over; then, where the path curves left, keep ahead to reach a gate and the A35. Cross over the A35 (take care), go through a gate and keep to the path, uphill to a junction. Turn right and follow the path to Knightwood Oak car park, then follow the sign to the Knightwood Oak itself.

2 Return towards the car park and bear right along the road. Turn right again after a few paces, on to a path into mixed woodland. Cross a stream and soon reach a gravel track. Bear right and keep to this trail, passing red marker posts, to a fork. Keep left to a gate and road. Turn right to view the Portuguese Fireplace.

3 Return through Holidays Hill Inclosure to the fork of tracks. Bear left and follow this track to the New Forest Reptile Centre. Try to visit on a hot sunny day, when the cold-blooded reptiles are more active. Walk along the access drive past a cottage, date 1811, then, at a barrier on your left, drop down on to a path and follow it across a bridge.

4 Keep to the main path for 0.75 mile (1.2km), skirting the walls to Allum Green and several clearings,

then gently climb through trees to a defined crossing of paths and turn right. Shortly, bear half right across a clearing and concrete footbridge, then continue through the woodland edge to an electricity pole. Bear right for 20yds (18mtrs), then left through a gate to the A35.

5 Turn left and almost immediately right across the road to a gate. Walk ahead to a garden boundary, then turn right. The narrow path leads to a lane t Bank. Turn right, pass the Oak Inn and through Bank.

6 Just beyond the cattle grid, turn right through a gate on to a gravelled track towards Brockenhurst. Follow this track for nearly a mile (1.4km) to a junction at a small green.

7 Fork right towards Brockenhurst, and enter Hursthill Inclosure at a gate. Drop down past a turning on the right, then climb again and bear left at a fork. Keep to the waymarked track as it drops past another turning on the right and leaves Hursthill Inclosure at a gate. Walk the long straight track to the bridge over Highland Water, and follow the track round

to the right. Soon a gate leads the waymarked trail into Poundhill Inclosure, and another straight section brings you to a five-way junction at waymark post 24.

8 Turn right here. Ignore all turnings, and follow the track as it turns sharp right and winds its way to a junction with the Ornamental Drive. Turn left for the last 100 yards (91mtrs) back to the car park.

WALK 6
The Mortimer Trail around Aymestrey

What have 'Capability' Brown, Richard Payne Knight and Hanson Aggregates got in common? Find out on this brief walk through time.

Minimum time: 2hrs 30min
Walk length: 4.75 miles/7.7km
Difficulty level: ✚✚✚
Map: OS Explorer 203 Ludlow
Start/finish: Grid reference: SO 426658
Paths: Excellent tracks, field paths, minor roads, steep woodland sections, 11 stiles
Landscape: wooded hills and undulating pastures
Parking: At old quarry entrance, on east side of A4110, 0.25 mile (400mtrs) north of Aymestrey Bridge
Public toilets: None on route
Tourist information: Ludlow, tel 01584 875053
🅳 Several steep climbs, busy road crossing, lengthy section of quiet country lane. Not suitable for young children

Getting to the start
Aymestrey is on the A4110 between Ludlow and Hereford. The layby/parking area where the walk starts is just to the north of the village, on the right coming from the south.

Shobdon Airfield was one of the many airfields built in 1940, as part of wartime preparations. The government compulsorily purchased the modest, privately owned quarry at Aymestrey, ensuring a local supply of stone for the airfield. In its latter years, the quarry was run by Hanson Aggregates.

I don't suppose that anyone at Hanson Aggregates expects, in the fullness of time, to be remembered for their landscape architecture in the same way as the ubiquitous

Lancelot 'Capability' Brown, or Richard Payne Knight, but they should at least be commended for trying.

Landscape Continuum
Towards the end of the walk, as you descend to the former quarry area, there is little to indicate that the landscape has been recently manufactured, although your curiosity may be alerted by the absence of any substantial trees. Unlike many quarries, however, the plan here was to return the land to a mixture of agricultural use and woodland.

In geological time, man's quarrying is scarcely a moment. Unfortunately, working out a quarry can take up a fair amount of a person's lifetime – people tend not to like quarries in their backyards, so quarries often get a bad press. The quarry companies will argue that 'restoration' and 'environmental sensitivity' were among their objectives a decade or two before their current fashionability, and that, far more often than not, sand and gravel quarries are returned to a level of agricultural utility that at least equals the one before.

Glacial Gorge
West of Aymestrey the River Lugg runs in a small but spectacular gorge. This is a glacial overflow channel that exploited a fault in the rock, associated with the glacial Wigmore Lake. The paucity of contours on the suggested map a few grid squares to the north shows the position of the former lake. At Mortimer's Cross, Richard of York's son Edward defeated the Lancastrian army in 1461 in one of the battles that changed the course of the Wars of the Roses (Edward was crowned King later that year). The battle site is 0.5 mile (800mtrs) south of the road junction named Mortimer's Cross. The cross itself dates from 1799.

Walk Directions

1 Walk up the access road for 750yds (686mtrs), until just before a junction of tracks. Note a stile on the right – your route returns over this.

2 Turn left then, in 25yds (23mtrs), curve right, passing a house with a stone wall relic in its garden. Shortly curve left to walk through Yatton, to a T-junction. Turn left to the A4110. Cross to a stile, striking across this field to a gap. In the next field veer left to skirt round the right edge of (not over) an oak and ash embankment, to find a corner stile. Walk up the left edge of this field but, at the brow, where it bends for 70yds (64mtrs) to a corner, take a stile in the hedge to walk along its other side. Within 60yds (55mtrs) you will be on a clear path, steeply down through woodland, a ravine on your left. Join a rough driveway to a minor road. (The glacial overflow channel is directly ahead.)

3 Turn left here, joining the Mortimer Trail. Enjoy this wooded, riverside lane for nearly 0.75 mile (1.2km), to reach the A4110 again. Cross, then walk for just 25yds (23mtrs) to the right. (The Riverside Inn is about 175yds/160mtrs further.) Take a raised green track, heading for the hills. Then go diagonally across two fields, to a stile and wooden steps.

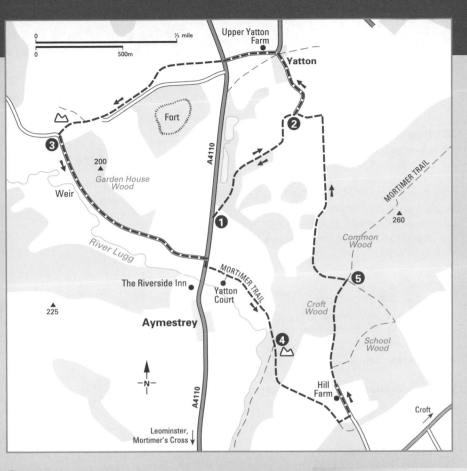

4 Within a few paces fork left to ascend steeply through the trees. Leave by a stile, to cross two meadows diagonally. Over a double stile, walk along the left-hand edge of a field, still heading downhill. At the trees turn left. Soon reach a tarmac road. Turn left along the road, now going back uphill. Beyond Hill Farm, enter the Croft Estate. Walk along this hard gravel track. After 110yds (100mtrs), ignore a right fork but, 550yds (503mtrs) further on, you must leave it. This spot is identified where deciduous trees give way to conifers on the

left and you see a Mortimer Trail marker post on the wide ride between larches and evergreens on the right.

5 Turn left (there is no signpost). Within 110yds (100mtrs) go half right and more steeply down on an aged access track. Within 250yds (229mtrs) look out for a modern wooden gate, waymarked, leading out of the woods. Walk along its right-hand edge. Walk briefly in trees then out and, at the far corner, within the field, turn left to Point **2**. Retrace your steps to the start.

An easy-going walk, yet fascinating with its continuous changes of scenery.

Minimum time: 2hrs
Walk length: 5.5 miles/8.8km
Difficulty level: ✚✚✚
Map: OS Explorer OL7 The English Lakes (SE)
Start/finish: Grid reference: SD 472759
Paths: Little bit of everything, 9 stiles
Landscape: Woodland, pasture and shoreline
Parking: Small National Trust car park for Eaves Wood
Public toilets: In Silverdale village
Tourist information: Lancaster, tel 01524 32878

Getting to the start

Silverdale clings to the northern edge of Lancashire, a few miles north of Carnforth off the A6 and the M6 (junction 35), and looks across the great expanse of Morecambe Bay to the Furness peninsula.

The Arnside–Silverdale Area of Outstanding Natural Beauty (AONB) is barely longer than its name, yet intricate and exquisite.

A Mosaic of Habitats

The AONB covers a mere 29 square miles (75sq km) yet includes rocky coastline, salt marsh, wetland, pasture, woodland, heathland, crags and quarries, and some attractive villages, principally Silverdale in Lancashire and Arnside in Cumbria. With such a mosaic of habitats, it's no surprise that the area is rich in wildlife – more than half of all British flowering plant species are found here.

There's a fine start, through Eaves Wood with its yew trees and impressive beech ring, then the route sidles through the back lanes of Silverdale before reaching the coast. The channels of Morecambe Bay shift over time and so does the shoreline. The band of salt marsh around the Cove has shrunk drastically in the last few years. At high tide the rocky foreshore may be impassable, in which case follow an alternative footpath across open fields of The Lots safely above the shore.

LEIGHTON HALL

Early Gillow furniture is displayed among other treasures in the fine interior of this neo-Gothic mansion where entertaining guides reveal the history of the house and its occupants. Outside, a large collection of birds of prey can be seen, and flying displays are given each afternoon. There is landscaped parkland as well as a pretty 19th-century walled garden, a maze and woodland walks.

By the Sea

The route avoids a tricky section of the coast south of Silverdale, returning to the shore near Jenny Brown's Point. The breakwater running out to sea recalls a failed 19th-century land reclamation scheme. Just around the corner stands the tall chimney of a copper smelting mill that operated around 200 years ago.

Springs and Meadows

After Heald Brow comes Woodwell, the first of three springs on the walk. At Woodwell the water issues from the crag above the square pool. This was used for watering cattle but now you're more likely to see dragonflies. Woodwell and the other 'wells' around Silverdale are found where the water-permeable limestone is interrupted by a band of impermeable material such as clay. Rainfall generally sinks quickly into limestone and there are no surface streams over most of the area, so the springs were of vital importance. This rapid drainage also means that few of the footpaths are persistently muddy, even after heavy rain.

Lambert's Meadow, however, is usually damp. It sits in a hollow where fine wind-blown silt (known as loess) accumulated after the last ice age. The soil is dark and acidic, very different from that formed on the limestone, and the plant community is different too.

Walk Directions

1 From the end of the National Trust car park at Eaves Wood, follow the footpath to reach a T-junction. Go right a few paces and then turn left, climbing gently. Keep left to the beech ring, then straight on. Just beyond a junction veer left to a wall and continue walking on this line to a lane.

2 Cross on to a track signed 'Cove Road'. Keep ahead down a narrow path (Wallings Lane), a drive, another track and then another narrow path to a wider road. After 200yds (183mtrs) go left down Cove Road.

3 From the Cove walk leftward, below the cliffs, to the shore. Walk up the road to Beach Garage then take the footpath alongside. (If high tide makes this route impassable follow the easy footpath across the fields above.)

4 At the next road turn right for 600yds (549mtrs) then bear right down Gibraltar Lane for 350yds (320mtrs). Enter the National Trust property of Jack Scout.

5 Descend left to the lime kiln then follow a narrowing path directly away from it. This swings left above a steep drop and descends. Follow a broad green path to a gate. After 150yds (137mtrs), another gate leads into the lane. At its end continue below Brown's Houses along the edge of the salt marsh to a stile. Go up slightly, then along to a signpost.

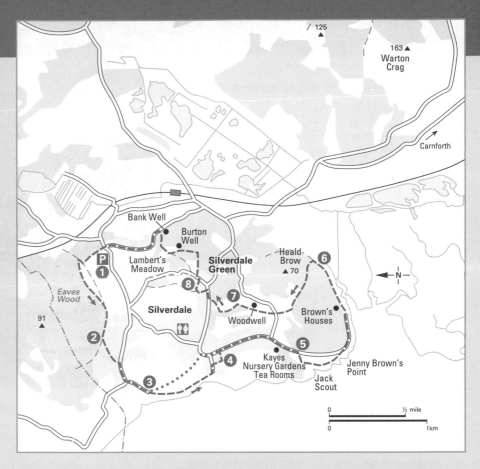

6 Turn left, climbing steeply to a gate. The gradient eases, over rock and through a lightly wooded area into the open. Go left to a stile then follow a wall down and into a small wood. Follow a track down right. Cross the road to a gap in the wall, descend, then walk below the crags to Woodwell.

7 The path signed 'The Green via cliff path' leads to a rocky staircase. At the top go ahead to join a broader path. Follow it left, slant right, then continue into woodland. A stile on the right and a narrow section lead to a road. Go right 150yds (137mtrs), then left into The Green. Keep right at a junction then join a wider road.

8 Go left for 75yds (69mtrs) then right, signposted 'Burton Well Lambert's Meadow'. The track soon descends then swings left, passing Burton Well on the right. Cross a stile into Lambert's Meadow, then go right, over a footbridge to a gate. Climb up, with some steps, and continue more easily to a fork. Go left alongside a pool (Bank Well) into a lane. Go left and at the end the car park is virtually opposite.

DID YOU KNOW?

Just across the border in Cumbria you'll find the Lakeland Wildlife Oasis. The mix of interactive, educational displays and the wildlife is irresistible for children who can get up close to all sorts of creatures, from meerkats to butterflies. The centre participates in breeding programmes for endangered species.

Walk along the sea defences to some of the finest bird reserves in the country

Minimum time: 2hrs
Walk length: 4.5 miles/7.2km
Difficulty level: ✚✚✚
Map: OS Explorer 251 Norfolk Coast Central
Start/finish: Grid reference: TG 028442
Paths: Footpaths with some paved lanes, can flood in winter
Landscape: Salt marshes, scrubby meadows and farmland
Parking: Carnser (pay) car park, on seafront opposite Blakeney Guildhall and Manor Hotel
Public toilets: Across road from Carnser car park
Tourist information: Holt, tel 0870 225 48551
❶ The lane from Wiveton to Blakeney can be busy

Getting to the start
Blakeney is situated off the A149 coast road between Wells-next-the-Sea and Cromer. Turn left down the High Street to locate the car park on the Quay.

Blakeney was a prosperous port in medieval times, but went into decline when its sea channels began to silt up. However, although the merchants decried the slow accumulation of salt marsh and sand bars, birds began to flock here in their thousands. By Victorian times it had become such a favoured spot with feathered migrants that it became known as the place to go shooting and collecting. Some sportsmen just wanted to kill the many waterfowl, while others were more interested in trophy collecting – looking for species that were rare or little-known. The maxim 'what's hit is history; what's missed is mystery' was very characteristic of the Victorians' attitude to biological science. Many of these hapless birds ended up stuffed in museums or private collections.

Nature Reserve
After many years of bloody slaughter the National Trust arrived in 1912 and purchased the area from Cley Beach to the tip of the sand and shingle peninsula of Blakeney Point. It became one of the first nature reserves to be safeguarded in Britain. Today it is a fabulous place for a walk, regardless of whether you are interested in

ornithology. A bright summer day will show you glittering streams, salt-scented grasses waving gently in the breeze and pretty-sailed yachts bobbing in the distance. By contrast, a wet and windy day in winter will reveal the stark beauty of this place, with the distant roar of white-capped waves pounding the beach, rain-drenched vegetation and a menacing low-hung sky filled with scudding clouds. It doesn't matter what the weather is like at Blakeney, because a walk here is always invigorating.

Although these days we regard the Victorians' wholesale slaughter with distaste, they did leave behind them a legacy of valuable information. It was 19th-century trophy hunters who saw the Pallas' warbler and the yellow-breasted bunting in Britain for the first time – and they were seen at Blakeney. A little later, when the Cley Bird Observatory operated here between 1949 and 1963, the first subalpine warbler in Norfolk was captured and ringed.

The Victorians' records tell us that a good many red-spotted bluethroats appeared in September and October, and any collector who happened to visit then was almost certain to bag one. In the 1950s the observatory discovered that these were becoming rare at this time of year. Today, bluethroats are regular spring visitors.

Walk Directions

1 From the car park head for the wildfowl conservation project, a fenced-off area teeming with ducks, geese and widgeon. A species list has been mounted on one side, so you can see how many you can spot. Take the path marked Norfolk Coast Path out towards the marshes. This raised bank is part of the sea defences, and is managed by the Environment Agency. Eventually, you have salt marshes on both sides.

2 At the turning, head east. Carmelite friars once lived around here, although there is little to see of their chapel, the remains of which are located just after you turn by the wooden staithe (landing stage) to head south again. This part of the walk is excellent for spotting kittiwakes and terns in late summer. Also, look for Sabine's gull, manx and sooty shearwaters, godwits, turnstones and curlews. The path leads you past Cley Windmill, built in 1810 and which last operated in 1919. It is open to visitors if you have time to visit, and you can climb to the top to enjoy the superb view across the marshes.

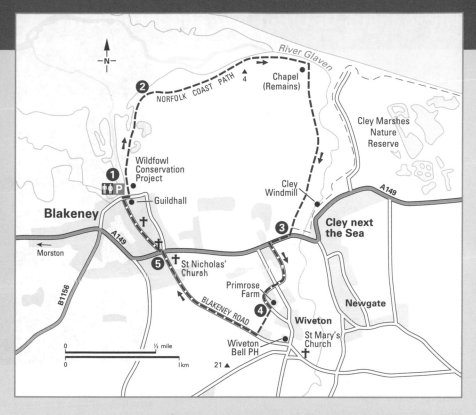

Follow signs for the Norfolk Coast Path until you reach the A149.

3 Cross the A149 to the pavement opposite, then turn right. Take the first left after crossing the little creek. Eventually you reach the cobblestone houses of Wiveton and a crossroads; keep ahead.

4 Take the grassy track opposite Primrose Farm, to a T-junction. This is Blakeney Road; turn right along it. However, if you want refreshments before the homeward stretch, turn left and walk a short way to the Wiveton Bell. The lane is wide and ahead you will see St Nicholas' Church nestling among trees. This dates from the 13th century, but was extended in the 14th. Its two towers served as navigation beacons for sailors, and the east, narrower one is floodlit at night.

5 At the A149 there are two lanes opposite you. Take the High Street fork on the left to walk through the centre of Blakeney village. Many cottages are owned by the Blakeney Neighbourhood Housing Society, which rents homes to those locals unable to buy their own. Don't miss the 14th-century Guildhall undercroft at the bottom of Mariner's Hill. After you have explored the area, continue to the car park.

DID YOU KNOW?

Cley next the Sea is not next to the sea any more, and has not been since the reclaiming of the marshland for pasture in the 17th century left it a mile (1.6km) or so inland. In earlier days Cley was an important port at the mouth of the River Glaven, ranking second only to King's Lynn on this coast.

Take a stroll through one of Oxfordshire's loveliest villages before exploring undulating countryside to the south.

Minimum time: 1hr 45min
Walk length: 4 miles/6.4km
Difficulty level: ✚✚✚
Map: OS Explorer 191 Banbury, Bicester & Chipping Norton
Start/finish: Grid reference: SP 395294
Paths: Field paths and tracks, stretches of quiet road, 5 stiles
Landscape: Rolling parkland and farmland on edge of Cotswolds
Parking: Free car park in Great Tew
Public toilets: None en route
Tourist information: Chipping Norton, tel 01608 644379
🚫 Paths at the edge of some crop fields may become overgrown in summer and may be difficult for young children

Getting to the start
Great Tew stands alongside the B4022, just south of its junction with the A361 and 7 miles (11.3km) southwest of Banbury. There is a small car park on the edge of the village beside the lane as it enters from the north.

Arthur Mee, in his book The King's England – Oxfordshire, says that 'if our England is a garden, Great Tew is one of its rare plots.' Most would agree. The village is a gem.

The Fall and Rise of Great Tew
Designed as an estate village in the 19th century, with the intention of blending architectural beauty with agricultural management, Great Tew went into decline and virtually

became derelict. However, the village has been given a new lease of life, with many of the cottages restored, and it is now a designated Conservation Area.

The village has a long history and in later years the village became closely associated with Lucius Carey, 2nd Viscount Falkland. A later owner, G F Stratton, who inherited Great Tew in 1800, resided in a rather modest late 17th- or early 18th-century house, but during the early years of the 19th century, Stratton engaged in an ill-fated experiment in estate management.

The estate changed hands several times before being acquired by Matthew Robinson Boulton. Farms were rebuilt, cottages were re-thatched and features such as mullioned windows and stone door heads were added. The estate was the Boulton family home for many years. Between 1914 and 1962 Great Tew was administered by trustees, but by now the estate was all but abandoned.

Robb to the Rescue
It was Major Eustace Robb, an old Etonian and descendant of the Boulton family, who moved to the village with the aim of halting its steady decline. His efforts certainly paid off. A stroll through the village today is marked by a conspicuous air of affluence.

Walk Directions

1 From the car park turn left, pass the village turning and take the footpath over a stile on the right, signposted 'Little Tew'. Go diagonally across the field, heading for farm outbuildings on the brow of the hill. Cross a stile in front of silos and continue ahead to a gate and stile. Keep the field boundary on the right, following it to a pair of galvanised gates and a stile leading out to the road at a junction.

2 Cross over and take the path, again signposted to Little Tew. Head diagonally across the field, passing to the right of a transmitter. On reaching the road, turn right and walk down the hill into Little Tew. Pass through the village and turn left at the turning for Enstone. On the corner is the Church of St John the Evangelist.

3 Follow the road out of Little Tew for 0.5 mile (800mtrs) and look for the entrance to The Lodge on the left. Continue downhill to white railings, then turn immediately left at an opening in the hedge into a field. Keep along the left boundary and make for a gate in the field corner. Continue ahead on the grassy path, passing a house over on the left. Keep ahead on the clear track to a kissing gate on to the road.

4 Cross and follow the track signposted to Sandford. Keep alongside trees and where it curves left towards Tracey Barn, keep ahead on the permissive path

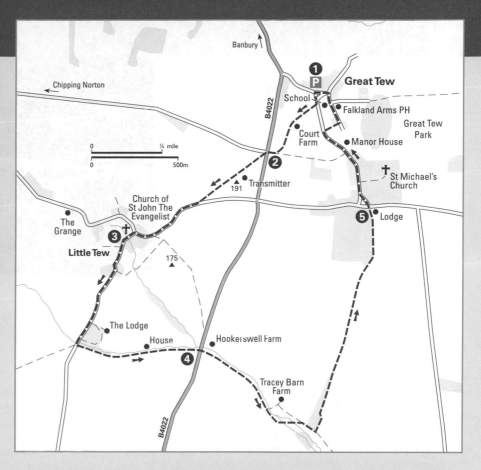

to a stile. Walk across the field, cross a footbridge, then a stile and turn right to reach a gate by some trees. Continue for a few paces to a gate and waymark on the left. Take the path, keeping a belt of woodland and the field-edge on your left. Beyond the trees, continue ahead into the next field, again beside a tongue of woodland. Pass into the next field and continue alongside trees. Approach a lodge and keep to the left of it.

5 Follow the drive to meet the road, cross over to the junction and take the turning signposted for Great Tew. Pass the entrance to St Michael's Church, which lies peacefully amid the trees of the parkland on the right . Before the school take the fenced path

on the right into the village. Turn left at the road and walk past the Falkand Arms, soon to follow the road left back to the car park.

THE THIRD TEW

Tiny Duns Tew lies 5 miles (8km) east of its Great and Little namesakes. It is recorded that in 1841 this village supported no less than four tailors, four shoemakers, three blacksmiths, two grocers, two bakers and a butcher, not to mention various carpenters, wheelwrights and roofers. Although still a thriving community, it can no longer support even a village shop.

Visit one of the 'oldest' bridges in the world, set in a quiet valley clothed in ancient woodland.

Minimum time: 2hrs 30min
Walk length: 5.25 miles/8.4km
Difficulty level: ✦✦✦
Map: OS Explorer OL 9 Exmoor
Start/finish: Grid reference: SS 872323
Paths: Riverside paths and field tracks, some open moor, no stiles
Landscape: Wooded river valley and pasture slopes above
Parking: Just over 0.25 mile (400m) east of Tarr Steps – can be full in summer. (Parking at Tarr Steps for disabled people only.)
Public toilets: At car park

Getting to the start
From B3223 take road signed Liscombe. Through Liscombe to car park on right.

This is the longest and best clapper stone bridge in Britain; as such it featured on a postage stamp in 1968. (The others in the set were the stone military bridge at Aberfeldy; Telford's Menai Bridge; and a concrete viaduct on the M4.) Bronze Age trackways converge on to this river crossing, suggesting that the bridge itself may be about 4,000 years old. Given that it gets swept away and rebuilt after every major flood, this date for its construction is pure guesswork – or, to use the archaeological term, 'conjectural'. It is still arguably Europe's oldest bridge.

'Cleaca' Bridge
The name 'clapper' probably comes from the Saxon 'cleaca', meaning stepping stones. The first clapper bridges arose as stone slabs laid across the top of existing stepping stones. With a serviceable ford alongside, this one is clearly a luxury rather than a necessity. It is only

WHILE YOU ARE THERE
The thatched village of Winsford is delightful in itself but poses a problem in mathematics: is it possible to walk over all of its seven bridges without passing over any of them twice?

because the local sedimentary rocks form such suitable slabs that it was built at all. At 59yds (54mtrs), Tarr Steps is by far the longest of the 40 or so clapper bridges left in Britain.

Right of Way
As the bridge is a public highway you could, in theory, be entitled to ride your bicycle across it. Quite clearly, the damage you might do to yourself by falling off the bridge could be very serious. That said, the feat is not as hard as it looks – the secret seems to lie in avoiding catching the front wheel in the slots where the bridge top consists of two separate, parallel stones. The ford alongside is popular with horse-riders and canoeists, though The Highway Code does not seem to specify who gives way when the one meets the other. It's always very pleasing to see these three non-motorised forms of transport in action together, while motorists are unable to make it down the congested narrow road.

The Woods
Local legend gives the bridge a devilish origin. Apparently Satan himself built it for sunbathing on. The shady groves of ancient woodland, that drove him into the middle of the river, form probably the best birding terrain in the country – you need only to sit or stand quietly in the shadow of a tree trunk and wait for the birds to parade before you. It's also good for the birds, offering them safety from hawks and buzzards, plenty of nest sites, insects to eat and open flight paths between the branches.

Walk Directions

1 Leave the bottom of the car park by the left-hand junction, signposted 'Scenic Path'. This takes you down to the left of the road to the Little River, crossing two footbridges on its way to Tarr Steps, over the River Barle, ahead.

2 Cross the Steps, turning upstream at the far side (signed 'North Barton Wood'). Follow a wide river bank path past what looks like a wire footbridge but is, in fact, a device for intercepting floating trees in times of flood. After 0.75 mile (1.2km) cross a side-stream on a stone bridge (mini Tarr Steps), and immediately afterwards a long footbridge over the River Barle.

3 Cross, and continue upstream, with the river now on the left. After 0.75 mile (1.2km) the path crosses a small wooden footbridge, and then divides at a signpost.

4 Turn right, uphill, signed 'Winsford Hill'. A wide path goes up through the woods with a stream on its right. Where it meets a track turn briefly right to ford the stream, then continue uphill on a narrower signed path. At a low bank with beech trees turn right to a gate and follow the foot of a field to a tarred lane. Go up this to a cattle grid on to open moor. Here, bear right on a faint track that heads up between gorse bushes. After 250yds (229mtrs) it reaches a 4-way signpost.

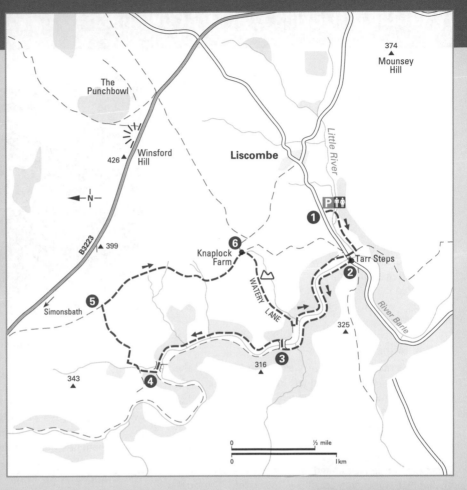

5 Turn right ('Knaplock') and slant down to a hedge corner. The route follows the foot of the open moor, but is about to divert up left to avoid some bog. After 170yds (155mtrs) a sign points back down to the moor-foot banking. A beech bank crosses ahead: aim for a gate at the lower end of this, where a soft track leads forward, with occasional blue paint-spots. After 0.25 mile (400mtrs) the track turns downhill, then back to the left. It becomes firmer and drier as it reaches Knaplock Farm.

6 Among the farm buildings turn downhill signed 'Tarr Steps', to exit on a muddy farm track. This develops into a steep, narrow and stony track, Watery Lane. After its initial descent it becomes a smooth path down to the River Barle. Turn left, downstream. When the path rises a little above the river, look out for a fork on the right, signed 'Footpath'. This rejoins the river to pass through an open field that's just right for a more comfortable sunbathe than the busy Tarr Steps. Cross the road and a small footbridge, then turn left up the path to the car park.

WALK 11
A circuit of Devil's Dyke by Poynings

A fine walk with glimpses over the most famous of all the dry chalk valleys.

Minimum time: 1hr 30min
Walk length: 2.75 miles/4.4km
Difficulty level: ✚✚✚
Map: OS Explorer 122 Brighton & Hove
Start/finish: Grid reference: TQ 269112
Paths: Field and woodland paths, 7 stiles
Landscape: Chalk grassland, steep escarpment and woodland
Parking: Summer Down free car park
Public toilets: By Devil's Dyke pub
Tourist information: Brighton, tel: 0906 711 2255 (charges apply)
❶ Steep steps up the South Downs. Suitable for fitter, older children.

Getting to the start

Poynings is north of Brighton, west of the A23. Take the A281 for Henfield, then turn left for Poynings. Turn left in front of the church, then at the next T-junction, turn right. Follow this road for about 1 mile (1.6km) and turn right, signposted 'Dyke'. The car park is on the right after about 500yds (457mtrs).

Sussex is rich in legend and folklore and the Devil and his fiendish works crop up all over the county. The local landmark of Devil's Dyke is a prime example – blending the beauty of the South Downs with the mystery of ancient mythology.

Disturbed by a Candle

Devil's Dyke is a geological quirk, a spectacular, steep-sided downland combe or cleft 300ft (91mtrs) deep and 0.5 mile (800mtrs) long. According to legend, it was dug

by the Devil as part of a trench extending to the sea. The idea was to try to flood the area with sea water and, in so doing, destroy the churches of the Weald. However, the Devil was disturbed by a woman carrying a candle. Mistaking this for the dawn, he disappeared, leaving his work unfinished. It's a charming tale, but it was most likely to have been cut by glacial meltwaters when the ground was permanently frozen in the Ice Age.

The Grandest View in the World

Is how the artist Constable described the view here. Rising to over 600ft (180mtrs), the views stretch for miles in all directions. The Clayton Windmills are visible on a clear day, as are Chanctonbury Ring, Haywards Heath and Ashdown Forest.

Devil's Dyke has long been a tourist honeypot and assumes the feel of a seaside resort at the height of the season. But don't let the crowds put you off. The views more than make up for the invasion of visitors, and away from the chalk slopes and the car park the walk soon heads for more peaceful surroundings.

Beginning on Summer Down, on the South Downs Way, you drop down gradually to Poynings village where there may be time for a welcome pint at the Royal Oak. Rest here because it's a long, steep climb to the Devil's Dyke pub. The last leg of the walk is gentle and relaxing by comparison.

Walk Directions

1 From the car park go through the kissing gate, then veer right. Join the South Downs Way and follow it alongside lines of trees. Soon the path curves left and drops down to a road. Part company with the South Downs Way here, as it crosses to join the private road to Saddlescombe Farm, and follow the verge for about 75yds (68mtrs). Bear left at the footpath sign and drop down the bank to a stile.

2 Follow the line of the tarmac lane as it curves right to a waymark. Leave the lane and walk alongside power lines, keeping the line of trees and bushes on the right. Look for a narrow path disappearing into the vegetation and make for a stile. Go down some steps into the woods and turn right at a junction with a bridleway. Take the path running off half left and follow it between fields and a wooded dell. Pass over a stile and continue to a stile in the left boundary. Cross a footbridge to a further stile and now turn right towards Poynings.

3 Head for a gate and footpath sign and turn left at the road. Follow the parallel path along to the Royal Oak and then continue to Dyke Lane on the left. Follow the tarmac bridleway and soon it narrows to a path. At a fork, by a National Trust sign, veer right and climb the steps.

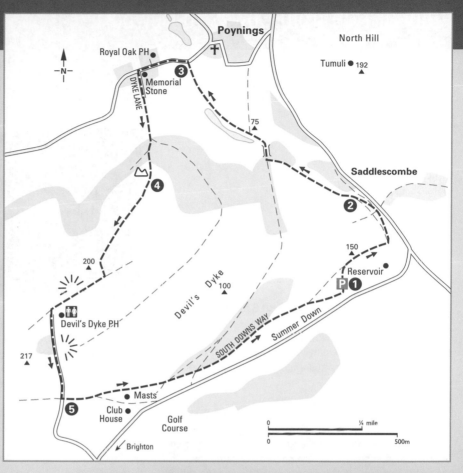

4 Follow the path up to a gate and continue up the stairs. From the higher ground there are breathtaking views. Make for a kissing gate and head up the slope towards the inn. Keep the Devil's Dyke pub on your left and take the road round to the left, passing a bridleway on the left. Follow the path parallel to the road.

5 Head for the South Downs Way and turn left by a National Trust sign for Summer Down to a stile and gate. Follow the trail, keeping Devil's Dyke down left, to eventually reach a stile into the car park.

Take a return trip down this scenic old railway trail beside the River Medina, on the Isle of Wight.

Minimum time: 1hr 45min
Ride length: 8 miles/12.9km
Difficulty level: ✚✚✚
Map: OS Explorer OL 29 Isle of Wight
Start/finish: Medina Road pay-and-display car park, West Cowes; grid ref: SZ 499956
Trails/tracks: back streets of Cowes, tarred and level cycle track
Landscape: wooded, riverside trail
Public toilets: Medina Road, Cowes, also The Quay, Newport
Tourist information: Cowes tel: 01983 813818
Cycle hire: Funation Cycle Hire, Cowes, tel: 01983 200300; www.funation.co.uk
❶ One short hill at the start and two sections of public road. Ideal for beginners and children aged eight and over

Getting to the start

On the island, take the A3020 from Newport to West Cowes and follow signs to the floating bridge. Passengers arriving with their bikes on the Red Funnel car ferry from Southampton should follow the one-way system around to the right, and cross the floating bridge to begin the ride in Medina Road, West Cowes.

Why do this cycle ride?

This ride makes a relaxed day out, with easy access from the mainland, too. There's a lot to see from the safe, level trail, which follows the National Cycle Network route along the former Cowes-to-Newport railway line. Route finding is straightforward, and you'll enjoy some lovely views across the River Medina, with plenty of opportunities for birdwatching.

The Ryde

Half way up the river you'll see a sad relic of former glory stuck in the mud. It's the Ryde, a paddle steamer built on Clydeside for the Southern Railway Company's Portsmouth-to-Ryde ferry services, and launched in 1937. Soon after the outbreak of the Second World War in 1939, the ship was requisitioned and converted for use as a Royal Navy minesweeper. Later Ryde was refitted with anti-aircraft weapons, and saw service defending the Normandy beaches during the D-Day invasion of Europe.

After the war Ryde returned to her work as an Isle of Wight ferry, but within a few years she was eclipsed by the more modern motor vessels built to replace wartime casualties. The old paddle ship found herself downgraded to summer relief duties, excursions and charters around the Solent, before she was finally withdrawn from active duty in 1968. After a couple of years moored on the River Thames as a tourist attraction, Ryde returned to the Isle of Wight and was converted for use as a nightclub at the Island Harbour Marina, on the east bank of the River Medina. In 1977 she was seriously damaged by fire and, by the mid-1990s, Ryde lay derelict and neglected in her mud berth. Following a recent survey, there are hopes that funds might be raised to restore the old paddle steamer as a passenger-carrying vessel.

DID YOU KNOW?
As well as cycle routes, the Isle of Wight has over 500 miles (805km) of well-maintained and signposted footpaths and around 30 miles (48km) of Heritage Coastline. More than half the island is a designated Area of Outstanding Natural Beauty.

Cycle Directions

1 From Medina Road turn into Bridge Road, signposted 'Newport via cycleway'. Follow the road all the way to the mini-roundabout at the top of the hill and turn left into Arctic Road, still following the signposted cycle route. Pass the UK Sailing Academy on your left and continue to the very end of the road.

2 Zig-zag right and left as the cycle route joins the old railway line, which edges its way clear of industrial Cowes through a tunnel of oak, birch and ash trees. Pass the signposted footpath to Northwood on your right and, a little further on, look out for the broken remains of an old iron and timber bridge.

3 Beyond the bridge, look out for a distinctive spire and pinnacles poking above the trees across the river. Standing little more than 0.5 mile (800mtrs) from the gates of Osborne House, St Mildred's church at Whippingham was remodelled in the mid-18th century for use by the royal family. Queen Victoria gave many of the furnishings, and a permanent exhibition in the churchyard recounts the story of this extraordinary building. Continue ahead along the track.

4 Now the views begin to open up, and between Pinkmead and Stag Lane you'll spot the old Ryde paddle steamer slowly rusting in her mud berth at Island Harbour Marina on the opposite bank. This

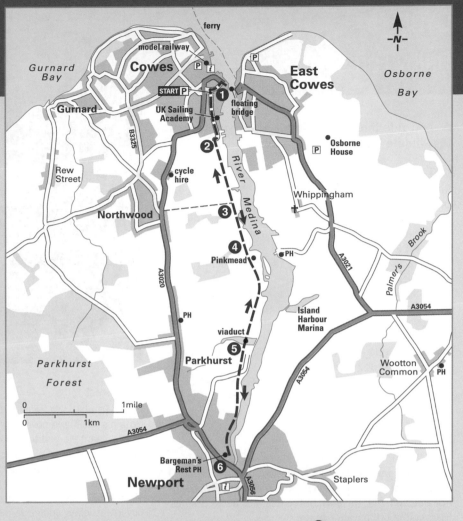

is a good area for wildlife – the hedges are thick with blackthorn, dog rose and crab apple, and in summer you'll see dragonflies and red admiral butterflies fluttering above the path. Listen, too, for the plaintive call of curlews, which use their long curved beaks to probe the mudflats for worms.

5 Now the trail crosses the old trestle viaduct that once carried the railway over Dodnor Creek. This area of open water, marsh and woodland was created in the 1790s when the creek was dammed to provide power for a proposed tide mill. The creek

is protected as a local nature reserve and you may see reed warblers, coots, moorhens and grey herons. Beyond the creek the cycleway climbs briefly across Dodnor Lane and approaches the modern industrial buildings on the outskirts of Newport. Soon, reach the white gate at the end of the traffic-free route. Stop here, then continue straight ahead as far as the post-box on the corner of Hurstake Road. Turn left, signed to The Bargeman's Rest, and bear right at the bottom of the hill for the final 300yds (274mtrs) to the pub.

6 Here you can take a well-earned break before retracing your outward route back to Cowes.

WHILE YOU ARE THERE

The cycle route passes close to HM Prison Parkhurst, which accommodates more than 500 prisoners. It was first built as a military hospital in 1805, then later transformed to a prison for boys awaiting deportation, mainly to Australia, as part of the Parkhurst Act of 1835.

CYCLE 5
Dalby Forest

A short ride through the forest where you seek the wildlife that's watching you.

Minimum time: 2hrs
Ride length: 6 miles/9.7km
Difficulty level: ✚✚✚
Map: OS Explorer OL27 North York Moors Eastern Area
Start/finish: car park at Adderstone Field, Dalby Forest; grid ref: SE 883897
Trails/tracks: forestry roads and a few narrow paths, mostly well graded
Landscape: river estuary, rolling farmland
Public toilets: Visitor Centre, Lower Dalby (none en route)
Tourist information: Dalby Forest Visitor Centre, tel 01751 460295
Cycle hire: Cycle Hire Kiosk next to Visitor Centre, Low Dalby, tel 01751 460400

❗ There's a short, rough and slightly downhill section of track at the start. The forest drive road needs to be crossed with care twice

Getting to the start

From the A170 at Thornton le Dale head north on a minor road signed the Dalby Forest, then turn off right on the Dalby Forest Drive, where you'll come to the tollbooths. Adderstone Field, the start of the ride, lies about 5 miles (8km) beyond the visitor centre.

Why do this cycle ride?

It's a good introduction to forest tracks, with just a few hilly bits to get your pulse racing, but nothing frightening to put off the inexperienced. There's lots of wildlife for the observant cyclist.

DID YOU KNOW?

If you cycle this route in summer you're likely to hear the distinctive song of the chiffchaff. Seen in open woodland, copses and hedgerows, the adults are a dull brownish-olive above with pale yellow below merging into buff on the flanks, and with dark legs. The sexes are similar and juveniles resemble adults but are a little browner above with warmer yellow underparts. They have a persistent hweet hweet call and chiffchaff song.

The Forest

In 1919, when the Forestry Commission was founded, Britain's woodland cover had shrunk to around 5 per cent, which meant we had to import large quantities of timber to meet the increasing needs of industry. In Yorkshire they turned to Dalby on the south east corner of the North York Moors. The area, once part of the Royal Hunting Forest of Pickering, had degenerated into boggy heathland, poverty-stricken upland farms and a huge rabbit warren that provided fur for a felt hat industry. Several streams drained the moorland plateau and flowed south west into Dalby Beck, forming a rigg and dale landscape. Scrub oak and birch clustered around these streams, but in general the ground was only suitable for conifers. By 1921 the planting began and within years over 8,500 acres (3,442ha) of Sitka Spruce and Scots Pine had covered the ground.

Conservationists hated these new forests, complaining that wildlife had been decimated, but today, if you stay quiet and look hard enough, you'll see that it's really quite abundant. In quieter corners you may stumble upon the Bambi-like roe deer. Many of the mammals, such as the pygmy shrew and the otter, stay clear of humans and it's bird-life you're more likely to spot. Besides the common blue tits, you're quite likely to see a wading heron, or a tiny warbler such as that summer visitor, the chiffchaf, so called because of its birdsong.

The Dalby Forest Visitor Centre is situated adjacent to the forest village of Low Dalby. This is where you'll get information about Dalby and other forests in the area, plus maps and booklets about the various walking and cycle trails. Refreshments are available and there are picnic tables and toilets. The visitor centre is open daily from Easter to the end of October.

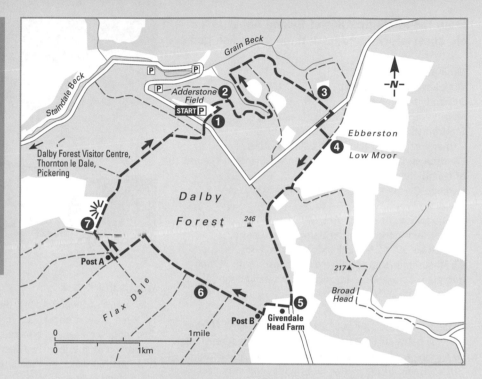

Cycle Directions

❶ The green cycle route begins beyond the trees at the south east end of the large Adderstone Field (the furthest from the visitor centre). Here you turn left along a narrow slightly downhill track. Though still easy, it's the most difficult section of the route – use gentle braking if you're a little unsure. Ignore two lesser, unsigned left fork tracks.

❷ Turn right along a much wider forestry track which takes a winding course round the afforested valley of Worry Gill. Where the more demanding red route goes off on a rough track to the right, your green route goes straight on, still using a well-graded track.

❸ Where a track doubles back, go straight on up a steady hill before meeting the forest drive again. Cross this with care – it can be quite busy on summer weekends – before turning right along it for 200yds (183mtrs). Turn left along a narrow path signed with red and green waymarkers and just before a 30 mile per hour speed limit sign (hope you were not speeding!). If you're early and it's summer, you may be able to dally and eat some of the bilberries that grow beside the path.

❹ The path reaches a flinted road at the south east edge of the forest. Turn right along this then left at the next junction. Looking left, you'll see the rougher high pastures of Ebberston Low Moor decline to the greener, more fertile fields of the Vale of Pickering.

❺ Turn right just before reaching Givendale Head Farm along a rutted farm track with a grassy island in the middle. Turn right at the next junction (Post B) on a downhill section, followed by an uphill one where you're joined by a farm track from the left.

❻ A long hill follows to a wide junction where you go straight on along a tarred lane. A sign tells you that you're now at the head of Flaxdale. Stay with the tarred lane at the next bend and junction. Turn right at the crossroads along a long sandy track (Post A), then right again at the next junction. Note the linear earthwork to both left and right – nobody seems to know the exact origins of these.

❼ After going straight on at the next junction past a fine stand of Scots pines, you get fine views over the farm pastures of High Rigg to Levisham Moor. There's another downhill section followed by an uphill one. Take a right fork at Newclose Rigg. Where the red route goes straight on, your green route veers right along the main track. There's a downhill left curve beyond which you take the upper right fork, which brings the route back to the forest drive opposite Adderstone field.

From the romantic ruins of Byland Abbey to an old observatory – and back through the fish pond.

Minimum time: 2hrs 30min
Walk length: 5 miles/8km
Difficulty level: ✚✚✚
Map: OS Explorer OL26 North York Moors – Western
Start/finish: Grid reference: SE 548789
Paths: Woodland tracks, field paths, 8 stiles
Landscape: Undulating pasture and woodland on slopes of Hambleton Hills
Parking: Car park beside Abbey Inn in Byland for abbey visitors
Public toilets: At Byland Abbey
Tourist information: Sutton Bank Visitor Centre, tel 01845 597426 (weekends only Jan–Feb)
🅳 In summer some paths may be choked with nettles and giant hogweed, so unsuitable for small children

Getting to the start

Byland Abbey is 2 miles (3.2km) south of the A170 road halfway between Thirsk and Helmsley. It is best reached by turning south off the A170 3 miles (4.8km) east of Sutton Bank. In the village turn right by the inn to access the signed car park.

In 1134 a party of Savigniac monks set out from their English mother house in Furness on the west coast of Cumbria to found a new monastery. Forty-three years and six moves later, Byland was founded as their permanent home, and by then they had become part of the Cistercian Order.

The Abbey Buildings

The most impressive parts of the ruins remaining today are in the church – and especially the remnants of the fine rose window in the west front. Beneath it, the main door leads into the nave, the lay brothers' portion of the church. The monks used the east end. Although the walls of the south transept collapsed in 1822, that area of the church still retains one of Byland's greatest treasures – the geometrically tiled floors, with their delicate patterns in red, cream and black.

Work and Pray

The monks at Byland Abbey, like all of their Cistercian brethren, rose at about 2am for the first service, Vigil. Two more services and a meeting followed before they had lunch at midday. They spent the afternoon working at their allotted tasks, and there were three more services, after which they went to bed, at around 8:30pm. The choir monks did some of the manual work in the abbey and on its estate, but the Cistercians also had lay brothers to work for them.

The lay brothers were vital to the success of the monasteries. They also took vows (though much simpler ones than the monks) and had their own church services. The Black Death in the 14th century, which radically changed the supply of agricultural labour, effectively ended the tradition of lay brothers in English monasteries.

Oldstead Observatory

At the highest point of the walk is Oldstead Observatory, built on the splendidly-named Mount Snever by John Wormald, who lived at Oldstead Hall in the valley below. It was a celebration, as the rather worn inscription tells us, of Queen Victoria's accession to the throne. At just over 40ft (12mtrs) high, 1,146ft (349mtrs) above sea level, it is high enough to scan the heavens, though history does not record if Mr Wormald made any startling astronomical discoveries.

Walk Directions

1 Visit the abbey, then leave beside the ticket office and turn right along the abbey's north side. Opposite a public footpath sign, go left through a gateway and after 10yds (9mtrs) right, over a stile. Cross the field to a second stile, then bear half left uphill to a waymarked gate behind a bench. Go through two more gates and on to a metalled lane.

2 Turn left. At the top of the lane go through a gate signed 'Cam Farm, Observatory'. The path climbs then leaves the wood edge to rise to a terrace. After a stile, take the left-hand path, following Cam Farm. Go straight on at two junctions, uphill, to reach a large open space.

3 Turn right and, just before a waymarked metal gate, turn left along the wood edge. Follow the path to Oldstead Observatory, bearing left through the wood. Pass to the left of the Observatory, go down a slope and follow the path running steeply downhill to reach a signpost.

4 Turn right on the track, signed 'Oldstead'. Follow the track as it curves left to become a metalled lane. Turn left at the T-junction, and left again on to the road by a seat. Just before the road narrows sign, turn left.

5 Go through some gateposts and over a cattle grid. Then, as the avenue of trees ends, take a signposted footpath to the right,

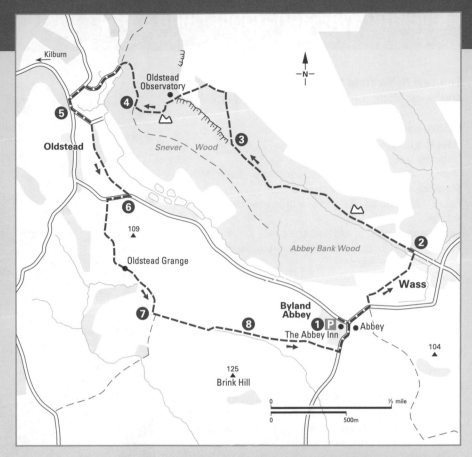

uphill. Climb up to a stile, bending around to the left beside the woodland to a gate. After the next gate, go ahead, through two more gates and on to a metalled road.

6 Turn right then, just beyond the road sign which indicates a bend, take a track to the left by the Oldstead Grange sign. Pass the house and go between barns and through a gateway. Bear right downhill on the track, bending right on a track to a gateway with a waymarked tree.

7 Immediately after the gateway, turn left and go through the wood to a Byland Abbey signpost. Follow

the path ahead as it bends left by another sign, go over a stile and down the field with the hedge on your left, bending left then right at the end to another signpost. Go through an opening beside a metal gate and along the field with a hedge on your right.

8 Go over two stiles then bear slightly left to another stile. Cross the field to a signpost in the hedge by a metal gate. Follow the fence, then on to the road by a wooden stile. Turn left back to the car park.

WHILE YOU ARE THERE

Take a trip to nearby Kilburn to the Mouseman Visitor Centre. This is where Robert Thompson, born in 1867, created his renowned furniture, each piece carved with his characteristic mouse. Oak furniture is still made by his successors, and the centre demonstrates the history of the firm and its work.

WALK 13
Cleveland Way and Robin Hood's Bay

Through fields from this obscurely named village and back along part of the Cleveland Way.

Minimum time: 2hrs 30min
Walk length: 5.5 miles/8.8km
Difficulty level: ✚✚✚
Map: OS Explorer OL27 North York Moors – Eastern
Start/finish: Grid reference: NZ 950055
Paths: Field and coastal paths, a little road walking, 4 stiles
Landscape: Farmland and fine coastline
Parking: Car park at top of hill into Robin Hood's Bay, by the old railway station
Public toilets: at car park
Tourist information: Whitby, tel 01947 602674
❗Take care on the road at the beginning of the walk. Keep well away from the friable cliff edges

Getting to the start

The old smugglers' village at Robin Hood's Bay huddles in a coastal hollow at the end of the B1447. It can be accessed from High Hawsker on the A171 Whitby to Scarborough road. There are two main car parks, both off to the right of the B road in the upper part of the village. The lower streets are access only.

Walking the coastal path north of Robin Hood's Bay, you soon notice how the sea is encroaching on the land. The Cleveland Way, which runs in a huge clockwise arc from near Helmsley to Filey, has frequently to be redefined as sections of once-solid path slip down the cliffs into the sea.

DID YOU KNOW?

In 1800 everyone who lived in the Bay was, supposedly, involved with smuggling. The geography of the village gave it several advantages. The approach by sea was, usually, the easiest way to the village; landward, it was defended by bleak moorland and a steep approach. The villagers linked their cellars, so that (it is said) contraband could be landed on shore and passed from house to house before being spirited away.

Robin Hood's Bay

Robin Hood's Bay is perhaps the most picturesque of the Yorkshire Coast's fishing villages – a tumble of pantiled cottages that stagger down the narrow gully cut by the King's Beck. Narrow courtyards give access to tiny cottages, whose front doors look over their neighbours' roofs. Vertiginous stone steps link the different levels. One of the narrow ways, called The Bolts, was built in 1709, to enable local men to evade either the customs officers or the naval pressgangs – or perhaps both. Down at the shore, boats are still drawn up on the Landing, though they are more likely to be pleasure craft than working vessels.

Walk Directions

1 From the car park, return via the entry road to the main road. Turn left up the hill out of the village. Just after the road bends round to the left, take a signed footpath to the right over a stile. Walk up the fields over three stiles to a lane.

2 Turn right. Go left through a signed metal gate. At the end of the field the path bends right to a waymarked gate in the hedge on your left. Continue down the next field with a stone wall on your left. Again, go right at the end of the field and over a stile into a green lane.

3 Cross to another waymarked stile and continue along the field edge with a wall on your right. At the field end, go over a stile on your right, then make for a waymarked gate diagonally left.

4 Walk towards the farm, through a gate and take the waymarked track through the farmyard. Continue with a wall on your right, through a gate and on to a track that eventually bends left to a waymarked stile.

5 Continue to another stile before a footbridge over a beck. Cross the bridge, then bear right across the hedge line, following the waymarker, then diagonally right towards the next waymarker and a signpost for Hawsker. Cross the stream and bear right. As the hedge to your right curves left,

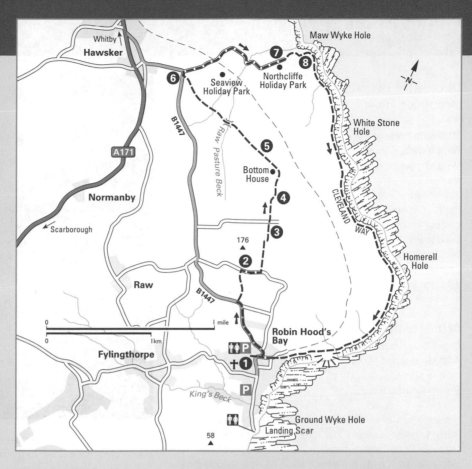

go through a gap on the right and over a signed stile, walking straight ahead through the field to another stile on to the main road.

6 Go right and right again, following the footpath sign, up the metalled lane towards the holiday parks. Pass Seaview Holiday Park, cross the former railway track and continue along the lane, which bends right, goes downhill, crosses a stream and ascends to Northcliffe Holiday Park.

7 Follow the Robin Hood's Bay sign right, and follow the metalled road, bending left beside a gate

and down through the caravans. Just beyond them, leave the track to bear left to a waymarked path. Follow the path towards the coastline, to a signpost.

8 Turn right along the Cleveland Way for 2.5 miles (4km). The footpath goes through a kissing

gate and over three stiles, then through two more kissing gates. It passes through the Rocket Post Field by two more gates. Continue to follow the path as it goes past houses and ahead along a road to the main road. The car park is opposite.

WHILE YOU ARE THERE

Explore further along the coast to Ravenscar, a headland where the Romans built a signal station. In the middle of the 19th century a new resort, a rival to Scarborough, was begun here, then abandoned. The streets are still there, but only one row of houses was constructed.

Discovering the valley where rocks and the mountains are still all important.

Minimum time: 2hrs
Walk length: 4 miles/6.4km
Difficulty level: +++
Map: OS Explorer OL17 Snowdon
Start/finish: Grid reference: SJ 720582
Paths: Generally clear and surfaced but can be wet in places, 9 stiles
Landscape: Woodland, wetland and high pasture
Public toilets: Behind Joe Brown's shop at Capel Curig
Tourist information: Betws-y-Coed, tel: 01690 710426
❶ Care to taken if climbing the craggy outcrop (Y Pincin) and beside the River Llugwy

Getting to the start
Capel Curig is located at the junction of the A5 and A4086, 6 miles (10.1km) west of Betws-y-Coed. The car park is signed just north of the road junction, behind Joe Brown's outdoor shop.

Nowhere has one village been so strung out – Capel Curig's sparse cottages and inns stretch 6 miles (9.7km) between Pont-Cyfyng, beneath Moel Siabod, to the Pen y Gwryd, beneath Glyder Fawr. The well-spaced inns there first served quarrymen from the barracks of Siabod and the miners from the copper mines of Snowdon, and later walkers and climbers. These inns were a convenient meeting place for those pioneering new routes on the crags. Quickly Capel Curig became the Zermatt of Wales, and Snowdon, the Matterhorn. In the 1950s the Pen y Gwryd Inn, run by enthusiast Chris Biggs, became a centre for planning Alpine and Himalayan expeditions. Here Lord Hunt and his team, who in 1953 were the first to climb to the summit of Everest, met to make the final preparations before departing for their daring climb in Nepal.

In the Steps of the Brave
This walk rounds the valley, taking in views of the wide sweep of mountains that surround Capel Curig and the Llugwy Valley. There's an optional scramble to Capel's pinnacle, Y Pincin, where you can see the five distinctive peaks of Snowdon reflected below in the twin lakes of Mymbyr.

You continue through mature oak woods, before descending back down to the boisterous river. In front of the Ty'n y Coed Inn they have one of the old London to Holyhead stagecoaches on display. After crossing the river at Pont-Cyfyng you follow its banks for a short while, then go over crag, across pasture and through the woods. You come out by a footbridge on the shores of Llynnau Mymbyr, and again you see Snowdon reflected in glass-like waters. On the other side of the bridge at the Plas y Brenin National Mountain Centre, the next generation of mountaineers are in training.

THE UGLY HOUSE
Midway between Capel Curig and Betws-y-Coed, beside the A5, stands Ty Hyll – better known as the Ugly House. Built of lumpy, irregular stones, the cottage is said to be an example of a 15th-century dwelling built hastily in order to cash in on freehold rights to common land. It's now home to the Snowdonia Society (open Easter–October, tel 01690 720287).

Walk Directions

1 The path begins at a ladder stile by the war memorial on the A5 and climbs towards Y Pincin, a large craggy outcrop cloaked in wood and bracken. Go over another stile and keep to the left of the outcrop. Those who want to go to the top should do so from the north-east, where the gradients are easier. It's fun, but take care! You'll need to retrace your steps to the main route.

2 Continue east through woods and across marshy ground, keeping well to the right of the great crags of Clogwyn-mawr. On reaching a couple of ladder stiles, ignore the footpath, right, back down to the road, but maintain your direction across the hillside.

3 Just beyond a footbridge over Nant y Geuallt, leave the main footpath and follow a less well-defined one, with marker posts, across marshy ground. This path veers south-east to cross another stream before coming to a prominent track.

4 Turn right along the track, go over a ladder stile, then at a four-way meeting of paths head left. Follow the path descending into some woods. Take the right-hand fork descending to the road near Ty'n y Coed Inn.

5 Turn left down the road, then right, along the lane over Pont-Cyfyng. Go right again beyond the bridge to follow a footpath

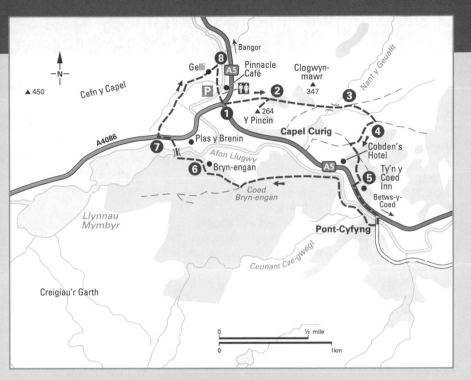

that traces the Llugwy to another bridge opposite Cobdens Hotel. Don't cross this time, but scramble left over some rocks before continuing through the woods of Coed Bryn-engan, where the path soon becomes a wide track.

6 After passing the cottage of Bryn-engan, the track comes to the bridge at the head of the Mymbyr lakes. Turn right across it, then go left along the road for a short way.

7 Cross over the road to reach the next ladder stile and then take a track straight ahead, soon swinging right to hug the foot of the southern Glyder slopes.

8 When you get beyond Gelli farm turn right to follow the cart track back to reach the car park.

WHILE YOU ARE THERE
A 7-mile (11.3km) loop south of Capel Curig takes in the rocky peak of Moel Siabod. It's an exhilarating climb, and the views to the Horseshoe and the major peaks of Snowdon are fabulous.

An undemanding tour of the cliff tops, beaches and lakes at the southernmost point of the Pembrokeshire Coast National Park.

Minimum time: 2hrs 30min
Walk length: 6 miles/9.7km
Difficulty level: ✚✚✚
Map: OS Explorer OL36 South Pembrokeshire
Start/finish: Grid reference: SR 976938
Paths: Easy coast path, quiet lanes and well trodden waterside walkways, no stiles
Landscape: Magnificent limestone headlands, secluded beaches and tranquil waterways
Parking: National Trust car park above Broad Haven Beach
Public toilets: At start and at Stackpole Quay
Tourist information: Pembroke, tel 01646 622388
🛈 Take care with children on the cliff edge and beside the lake

Getting to the start

From the Pembroke one-way system take the B4319 south for Bosherton and Angle. Pass through St Petrox, ignore the lane left for Stackpole and take the next left for Bosherton. In the village follow the sign left for Broad Haven Beach. The car park (pay in summer) is at the end of the lane.

The limestone headlands of St Govan's and Stackpole, some of the most impressive coastline in South Pembrokeshire, have grass-covered, plateau-like tops. The cliffs, however, make up only a short section of a varied walk that crosses two of the region's finest beaches and also explores some beautiful inland waters.

DID YOU KNOW?

The saint after whom St Govan's Head is named is thought to have been an Irish contemporary of St David. The story goes that he was hiding from pirates in the cleft of rock where his chapel is now wedged, when a crack miraculously opened in the floor. He entered the crack and it closed behind him, opening once more when the danger had passed.

WHILE YOU ARE THERE

East along the coast lies the magnificent 13th-century Manorbier Castle (open April– September). The medieval scholar Giraldus Cambrensis, famous for his accounts of everyday life and people in Wales, was born here in around 1146.

Quiet Bay

The beach is a broad gem of white sand, backed by rolling dunes and flanked by impressive headlands. Barafundle Bay is equally as picturesque, but also benefits from a lack of road access that keeps it relatively quiet for most of the year. The final attraction of this simple circuit is the three-fingered waterway that probes deeply inland from Broad Haven. The wooded shores and calm waters make a refreshing change from the wildness of the coast.

The Headlands

The cliffs between Linney Head, closed to the public as part of the MOD firing range, and Stackpole Head comprise some of the best limestone coastal scenery in Britain. Exposed to the full force of the Atlantic at their feet, they are often overhanging and contain caves and blowholes. A few sea stacks have survived – Church Rock, just off Broad Haven Beach, is one of the finest. The area is also popular for rock climbing.

Bosherston Lily Ponds

A series of interconnecting lakes was created at the turn of the 19th century by the then owner of the Stackpole Estate. A small tidal creek was damned, which flooded three tributary valleys. Subsequent sand drift has created a large marram grass-covered dune system behind the beach. The lakes are abundant in wildlife, with herons, swans, ducks, moorhens, coots and kingfishers. The Lily Ponds, the two westerly fingers, are a National Nature Reserve. The lilies are at their best in June, while the woodland is a magnificent spectacle in spring and autumn.

Walk Directions

1 From the car park above Broad Haven Beach, head back to the National Trust building at the head of the lane and bear right, down a set of steps, to reach the beach. Cross the beach and keep left to walk up the creek to a footbridge.

2 Go over this and bear right to walk above rocky outcrops, above the beach, to a gate. Follow the grassy path around the headland and then back inland to another gate above Saddle Bay. Continue around a large blowhole and up to a gate above a deeply cloven zawn (cleft), known as the Raming Hole.

3 Go through the gate and hug the coastline on your right to walk around Stackpole Head. As you turn back inland, pass a blowhole and then go through a gate to drop down to Barafundle Bay. Cross the back of the beach and climb up the steps on the other side to an archway in the wall. Continue around to Stackpole Quay.

4 Turn left, above the tiny harbour, and drop to pass the Old Boathouse Tearoom on your left before turning sharp right on to a road. Follow this past some buildings on the right and up to a T-junction, where you turn left.

5 Drop down into Stackpole village, pass the Stackpole Inn on the right, and continue around a series of bends until you come to a road on the left, over a bridge.

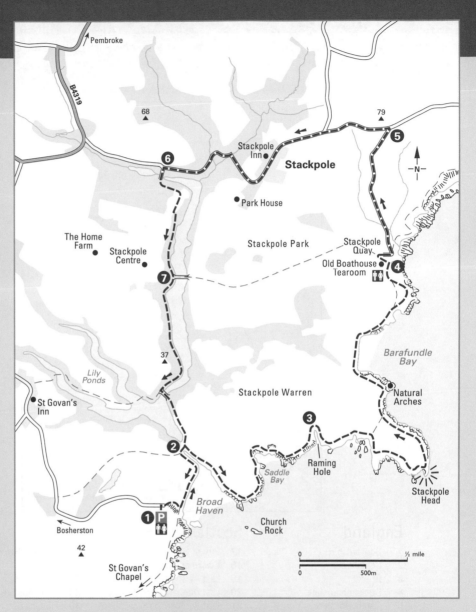

6 Cross the bridge and then bear left to follow a good path along the side of the lake. This leads through one kissing gate to a second, where you bear right, up a short steep section. Continue easily again to a bridge.

7 Don't cross the bridge, but drop down on to a narrow path that keeps straight ahead and follow it with the lake on your left-hand side. Continue ahead to reach another bridge, cross it, then carry on with the lake now on your right. This path leads to the footbridge that you crossed at Point **2**. Retrace your steps across the beach and up the steps back to the car park

County Maps

The county map shown here will help you identify the counties within each country. You can look up each county in the guide using the county names at the top of each page. To find towns featured in the guide use the atlas and the index.

England

1 Bedfordshire
2 Berkshire
3 Bristol
4 Buckinghamshire
5 Cambridgeshire
6 Greater Manchester
7 Herefordshire
8 Hertfordshire
9 Leicestershire
10 Northamptonshire
11 Nottinghamshire
12 Rutland
13 Staffordshire
14 Warwickshire
15 West Midlands
16 Worcestershire

Scotland

17 City of Glasgow
18 Clackmannanshire
19 East Ayrshire
20 East Dunbartonshire
21 East Renfrewshire
22 Perth & Kinross
23 Renfrewshire
24 South Lanarkshire
25 West Dunbartonshire

Wales

26 Blaenau Gwent
27 Bridgend
28 Caerphilly
29 Denbighshire
30 Flintshire
31 Merthyr Tydfil
32 Monmouthshire
33 Neath Port Talbot
34 Newport
35 Rhondda Cynon Taff
36 Torfaen
37 Vale of Glamorgan
38 Wrexham

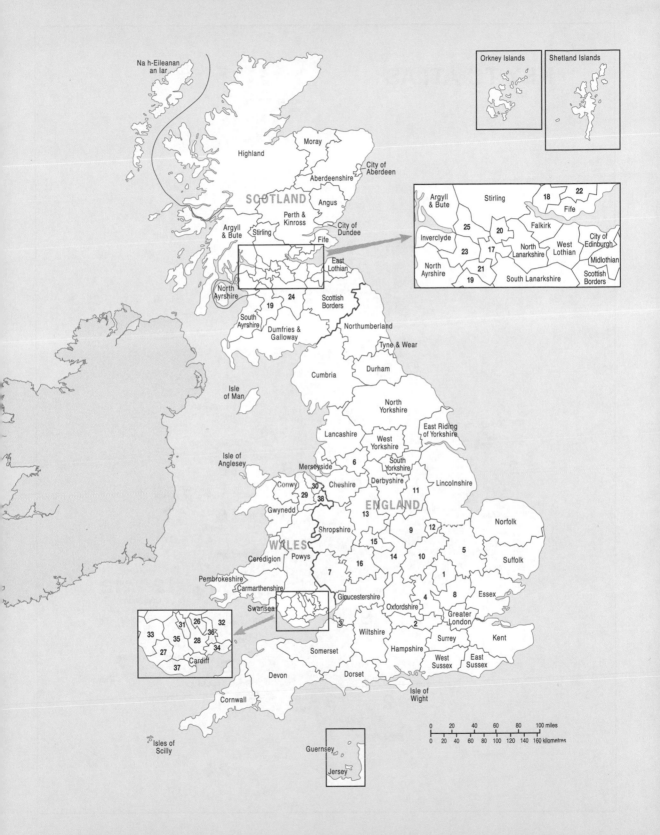

Orkney Islands

Shetland Islands

Na h-Eileanan
an Iar

Highland

Moray

SCOTLAND

Aberdeenshire

City of
Aberdeen

Angus

Perth &
Kinross

City of
Dundee

Argyll
& Bute

Stirling

Fife

East
Lothian

Argyll
& Bute

Stirling

18

22

Fife

25

20

Falkirk

Inverclyde

23

17

North
Lanarkshire

West
Lothian

City of
Edinburgh

North
Ayrshire

North
Ayrshire

24

Scottish
Borders

21

19

South Lanarkshire

Midlothian

Scottish
Borders

19

South
Ayrshire

Dumfries &
Galloway

Northumberland

Tyne & Wear

Cumbria

Durham

Isle
of Man

North
Yorkshire

East Riding
of Yorkshire

Lancashire

West
Yorkshire

Isle of
Anglesey

Merseyside

6

South
Yorkshire

Lincolnshire

Conwy

30

Cheshire

Derbyshire

11

29

38

Gwynedd

13

ENGLAND

Norfolk

Shropshire

9

12

Ceredigion

WALES

Powys

15

14

10

5

Suffolk

Pembrokeshire

16

7

1

Carmarthenshire

Gloucestershire

4

8

Essex

Swansea

3

Oxfordshire

2

Greater
London

31

26

32

Wiltshire

Kent

33

35

28

36

Somerset

Hampshire

Surrey

27

34

Cardiff

West
Sussex

East
Sussex

37

Devon

Dorset

Isle of
Wight

Cornwall

Isles of
Scilly

Guernsey

Jersey

0   20   40   60   80   100 miles

0   20 40 60 80 100 120 140 160 kilometres

KEY TO ATLAS

Shetland Islands

24

Orkney Islands

22 Inverness

23 Aberdeen

Fort William

Perth

Edinburgh

20 Glasgow **21**

Stranraer

Newcastle upon Tyne

Londonderry Larne

Belfast

Isle of Man

Carlisle

Middlesbrough

24 **18** Kendal **19**

1

Galway Dublin

Leeds York Kingston upon Hull

Manchester **16** **17**

Holyhead Liverpool

Limerick

Sheffield

Rosslare

Lincoln

Cork

Nottingham

Aberystwyth

Norwich

12 **13**

8 **9** **10** Birmingham **11**

Cambridge

Carmarthen

Gloucester Colchester

Cardiff Oxford LONDON

Bristol Guildford **6** **7**

4 **5** Maidstone

Barnstaple Taunton Southampton Dover

2 **3** Bournemouth Brighton

Plymouth Exeter

Penzance

Isles of Scilly

Channel Islands **24**

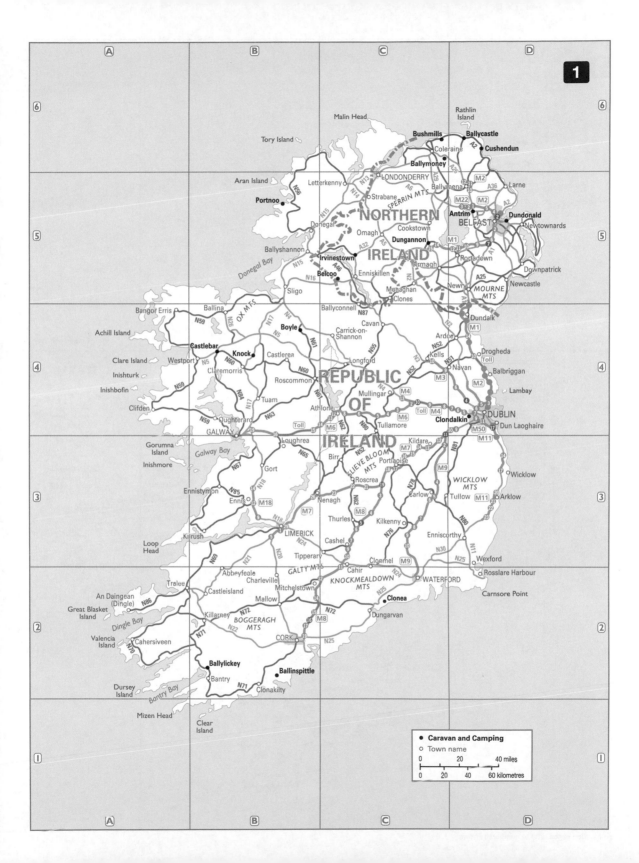

2

Legend

M6	Motorway/toll motorway	
	Motorway junction full/restricted. Service area	
A33	Primary route single/dual carriageway	
A34	Other A road single/dual carriageway	
B3400	B road	
	Unclassified road	
V	Vehicle ferry	
C	Fast vehicle ferry or catamaran	

● Edale	Caravan and Camping
● Corpach	AA Campsite Award Winner
○ Oundle	Town/Village name
	National boundary
ESSEX	English county name & boundary
CONWY	Welsh county name & boundary
MORAY	Scottish county name & boundary
	National Park

Lundy

Hartland Point

Hartland

Morwenstow

Kilkhampton

Bude

Bude Bay

Widemouth Bay · Bridgerule

Stratton

Week St Mary

Crackington Haven · Jacobstow

Boscastle

Tintagel · Otterham

Delabole

Camelford

Bolventor

BODMIN MOOR

Blisland

ISLES OF SCILLY

Bryher

New Grimsby

Tresco · St Martin's

Higher Town

Hugh Town · **St Mary's**

Old Town

Middle Town

St Agnes

ISLES OF SCILLY

SV

Port Isaac

Pendoggett

Polzeath

St Minver

Harlyn · Rock · St Tudy

St Merryn · **Padstow**

Porthcothan · **Wadebridge**

Rumford · Ruthernbridge

Mawgan Porth · St Mawgan

Watergate Bay · St Columb Major

Newquay

West Pentire

Holywell Bay · Cubert

Rejerrah · Goonhavern

Perranporth

St Agnes

Porthtowan

Portreath

St Ives Bay

St Ives · Gwithian

Zennor

Lelant · Hayle

Leedstown

Redruth

Camborne

Truro

Roche · Bugle

Indian Queens

Summercourt

Ladock

Marazanvose

St Stephen

Grampound

Tregony

Portloe

Luxulyan · Lostwithiel

St Austell

St Blazey Gate · St Blazey

Carlyon Bay · **Fowey** · Polruan

Pentewan

Mevagissey

Gorran · Gorran Haven

C O R N W A L L

Bodmin

St Cleer

Dobwalls

Liskeard

St Keyne

Pelynt

Widegates

Looe

Polperro

Blackwater

St Day

Carnon Downs

Falmouth

St Just-in-Roseland

Portscatho

St Mawes

Penryn

Edgcumbe

St Just · **Penzance**

Marazion

Rosudgeon · Ashton

Praa Sands

Helston

Constantine

Mawnan Smith

Gweek

LAND'S END

Land's End

St Buryan

Newlyn

Mousehole

Porthleven

Manaccan

St Keverne

Sennen

Porthcurno · Treen

Mullion

Coverack

Kennack Sands

Cadgwith

Lizard

Lizard Point

SW

Lau...

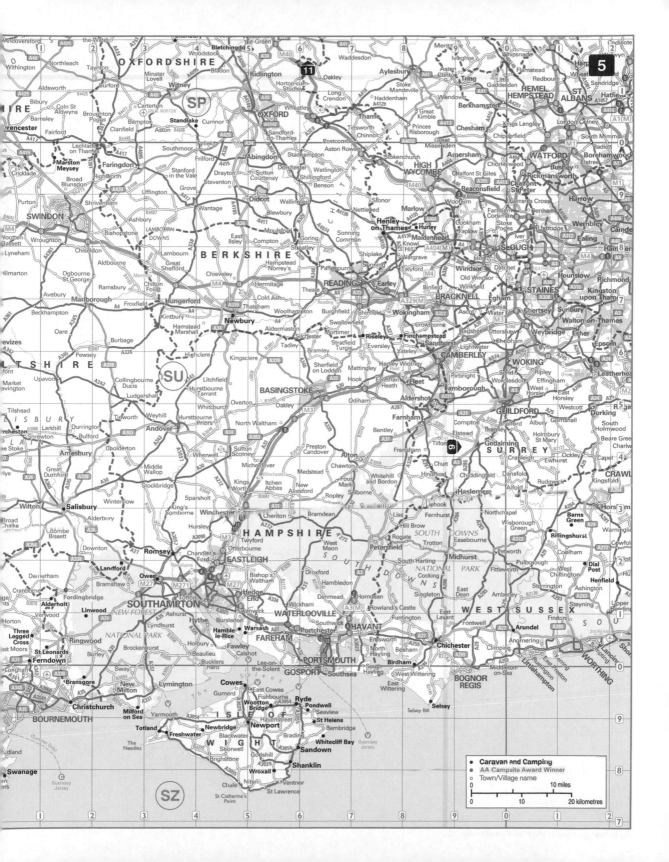

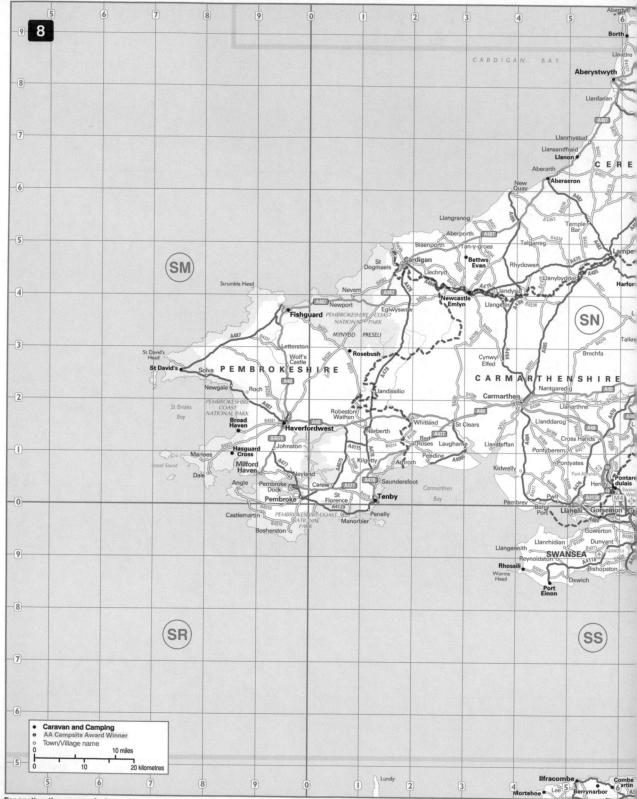

CARDIGAN BAY

Aberdyfi
Borth
Llandre
Aberystwyth
Llanfarian
Llanrhystud
Llansantffraid
Llanon
Aberarth
New Quay
Aberaeron
CERE

Llangranog
Aberporth
Blaenporth
Tan-y-groes
Talgarreg
Temple Bar
Lampe

SM

Strumble Head

St Dogmaels
Cardigan
Bettws Evan
Rhydowen
Llanybydder
Harfor

Nevern
Newport
Llechryd
Newcastle Emlyn
Llangeler
Llandysul

SN

Fishguard
PEMBROKESHIRE COAST NATIONAL PARK
Eglwyswrw
Talley
Cynwyl Elfed
Brechfa

MYNYDD PRESELI

Letterston
Wolf's Castle
Rosebush

St David's Head
St David's
Solva
PEMBROKESHIRE
CARMARTHENSHIRE
Nantgaredig
Carmarthen

Newgale
Roch
Llandissilio
Llanarthne

PEMBROKESHIRE COAST NATIONAL PARK
Robeston Wathen
Llanddarog
Cross Hands
Pontyberem
Pontyates

St Brides Bay
Broad Haven
Haverfordwest
Narberth
Whitland
St Clears
Llansteffan

Marloes
Hasguard Cross
Johnston
Red Roses
Laugharne
Kidwelly
Pontar dulais
Swans

Broad Sound
Milford Haven
Neyland
Kilgetty
Amroth
Pendine
Pembrey
Pwll
Llanelli
Gorseinon

Dale
Angle
Pembroke Dock
Carew
St Florence
Saundersfoot
Carmarthen Bay
Burry Port
Gowerton
Dunvant

Pembroke
Tenby
Pembrey
M4

Castlemartin
PEMBROKESHIRE COAST NATIONAL PARK
Penally
Manorbier
Llangennith
Llanrhidian
SWANSEA
Bishopston

Bosherston
Reynoldston
Rhossili
Worms Head
Oxwich

SR

Port Einon

SS

Caravan and Camping
AA Campsite Award Winner
Town/Village name

0   10 miles
0   10   20 kilometres

Lundy
Ilfracombe
Combe artin
Mortehoe
Lee
Berrynarbor

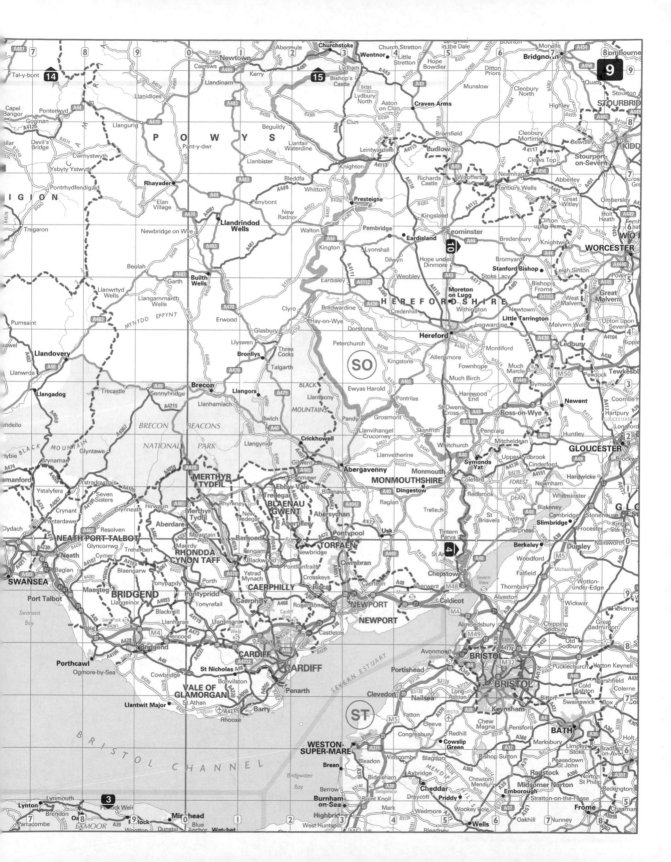

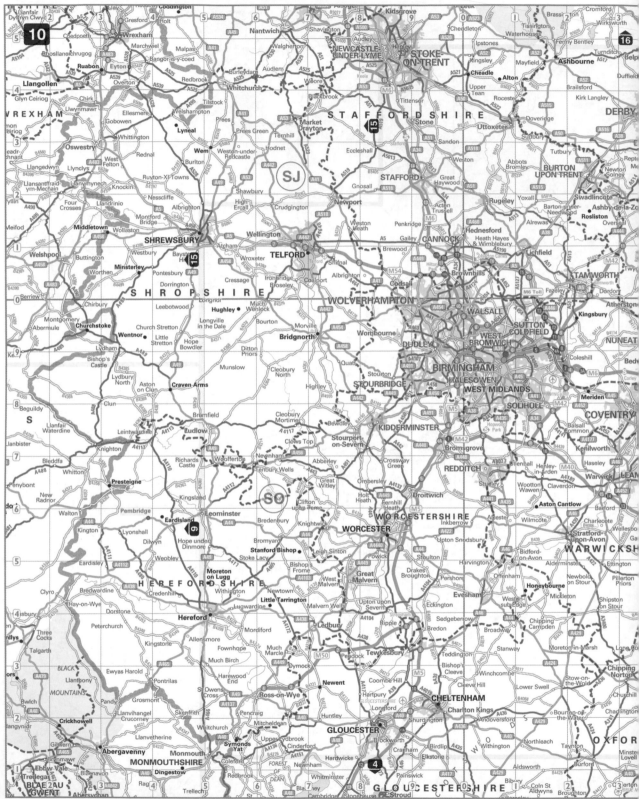

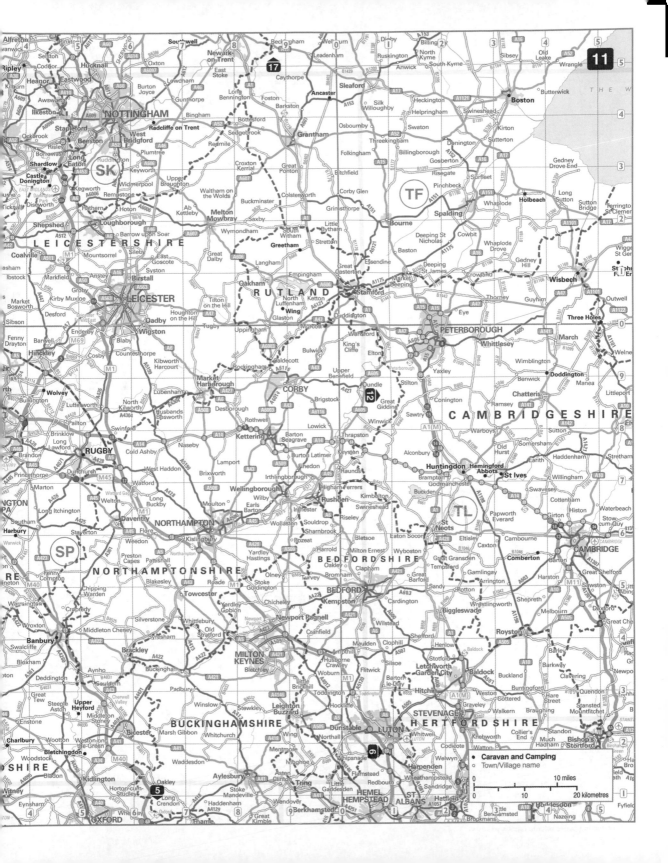

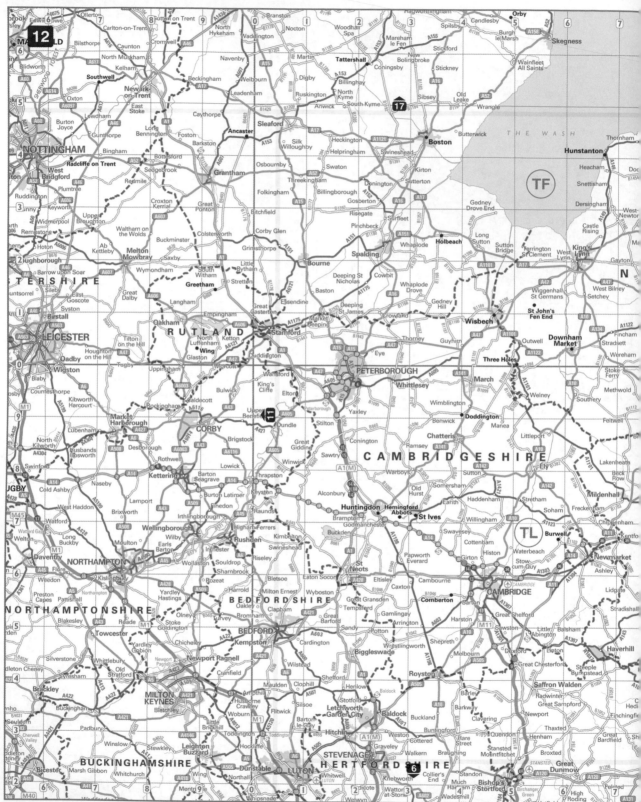

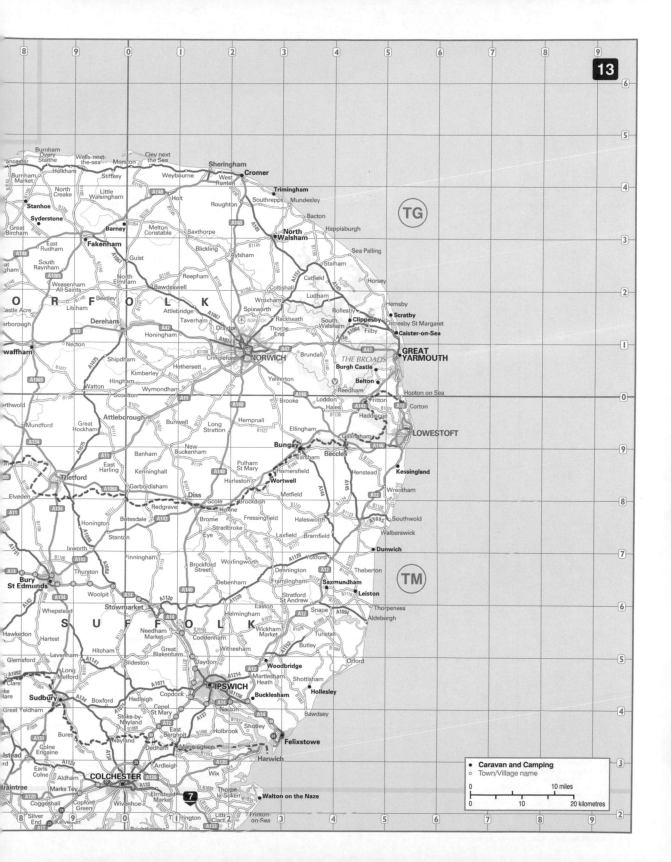

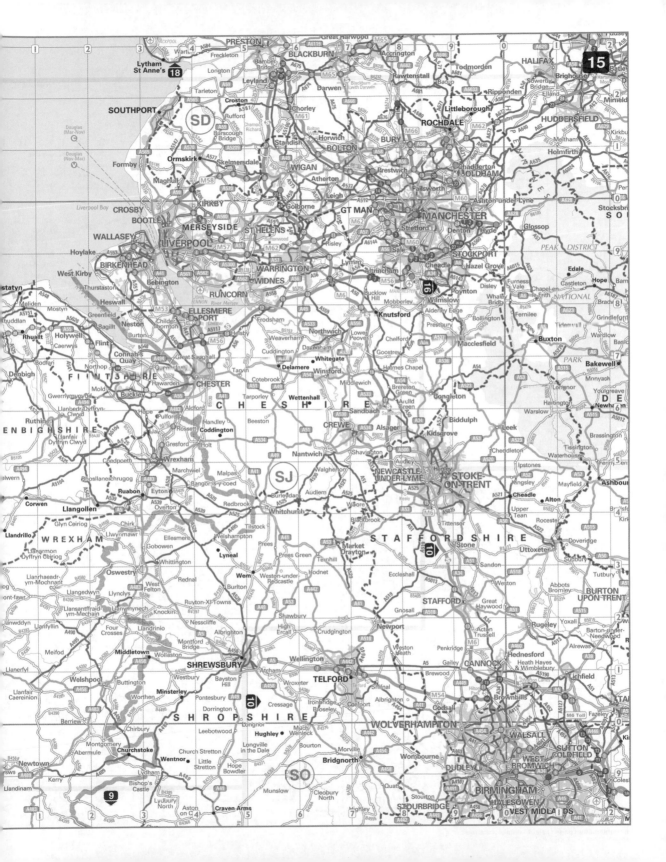

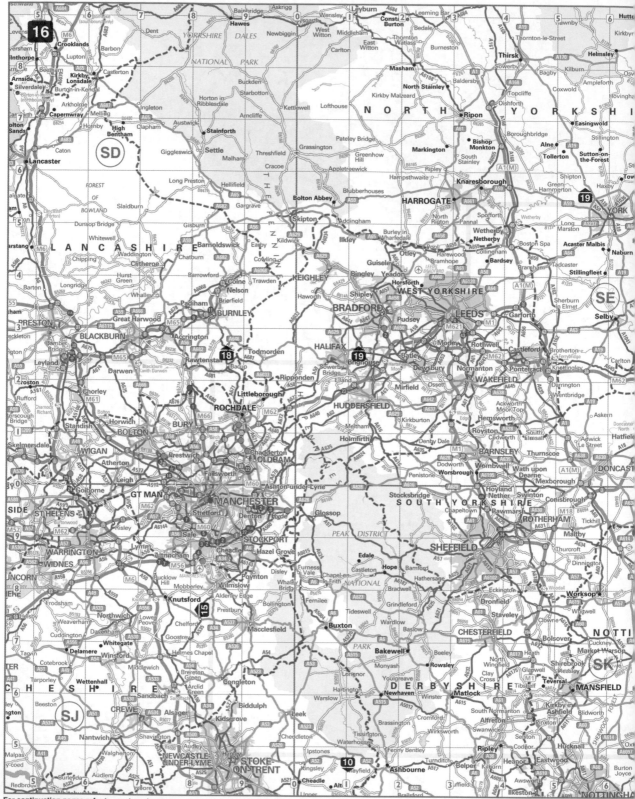

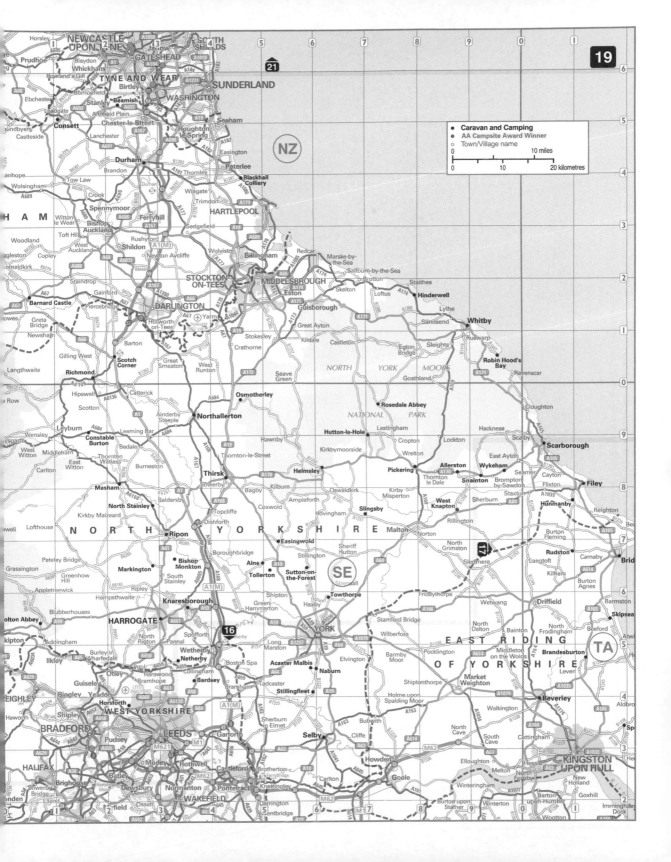

22

Point of Ardnamurchan
Acharacle
Fort Wil**2**m

Kinlochleven
Kinloch Rannoch
PERTH KIN

Coll
Arinagour
Tobermory
Ballachulish
Glencoe
Duror

Tiree
Scarinish
ISLE
Lochaline
A828

Ulva
OF
Craignure
Lismore
A828

NM
MULL
Kerrera
Oban
Tyndrum
NN
Killin
Lulb

Iona
Fionnphort
A849
Firth of Lorne
Dalmally
Crianlarich
Lochearnhead

ARGYLL AND
BUTE
Inveraray
LOCH LOMOND
Strathyre
STIRLING

Luing
AND THE TROSSACHS
Callande

Scarba
Aberfoyle
STI

Colonsay
Scalasaig
NATIONAL PARK

Oronsay
Lochgilphead
Glendaruel
Helensburgh
Balloch
W DUNS
Aucher

Kilsy

JURA
Dunoon
Colintraive
GREENOCK
Dumbarton
E DUNS

Port Askaig
Sound of Jura
Tarbert
Bute
INVER
M8
C GLAS

Kennacraig
Rothesay
RENS PAISLEY
GLASGOW

ISLAY
Claonaig
Great Cumbrae Island
Largs
E RENS
EAST KILBRIDE

Portnahaven
Gigha
Sound of Bute
Kilbirnie
Beith
M77

Port Ellen
NR
Lochranza
NORTH AYRSHIRE
Stewarton
Strathaven
S LAN

Carradale
Ardrossan
Kilwinning
NS

ARRAN
Saltcoats
Irvine
KILMARNOCK

Brodick
Troon
Galston

Machrihanish
Lamlash
Prestwick
EAST AYRSHIRE

Campbeltown
Ayr
Coylton
Cumnock

Maybole

Mull of Kintyre
SOUTH AYRSHIRE

Ailsa Craig
Girvan

Ballantrae
DUMF GA

Barrhill
Bargrennan
New Galloway
Parto

NX
Newton Stewart
Creetown

NW
Gatehouse of Fleet

Stranraer
Wigtown
Kirkcudbright

Portpatrick
Sandhead
Wigtown Bay
Brighouse Bay

Luce Bay
Port William

Drummore
Whithorn

Mull of Galloway
Burrow Head

C EDIN	City of Edinburgh
C GLAS	City of Glasgow
CLACKS	Clackmannanshire
C DUND	City of Dundee
E DUNS	East Dunbartonshire
E RENS	East Renfrewshire
INVER	Inverclyde
MDLOTH	Midlothian
N LANS	North Lanarkshire
RENS	Renfrewshire
W DUNS	West Dunbartonshire
W LOTH	West Lothian

North Channel

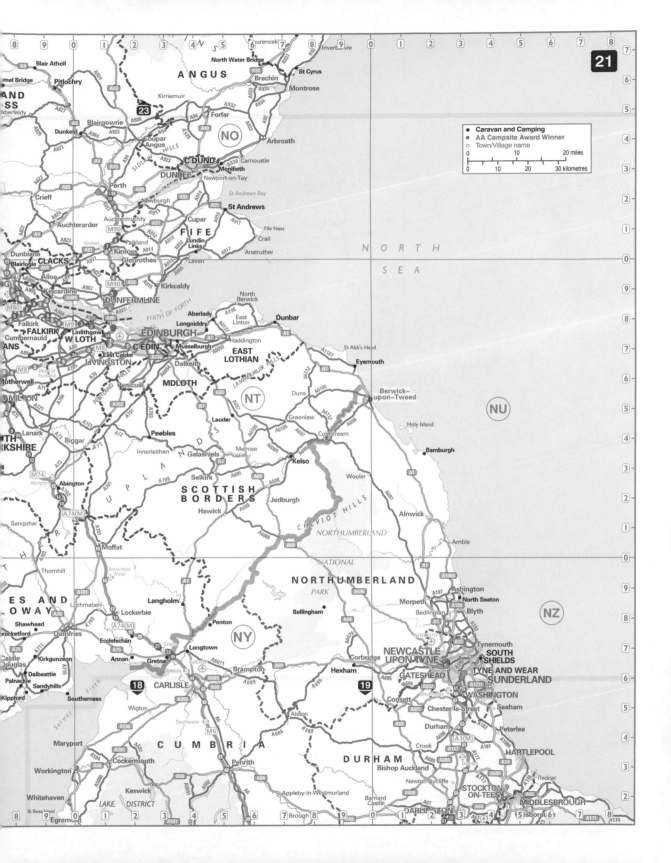

Cape Wrath

Rudha Rhobhanais
(Butt of Lewis)
Port Nìs
(Port of Ness)
Cellar Head

Handa Island
Scourie

NA

NB

Great
Bernera

Carlabhagh
(Carloway)

Steòrnabhagh
(Stornoway)

LEWIS

OF

STORNOWAY

Tiumpan
Head

Lochinver

Technadamph

ISLE

**NA H–EILEANAN
AN IAR**

Scarp

Taransay

Tairbeart
(Tarbert)

Scalpay

Gruinard
Bay

Ullapool

HARRIS

OUTER

Pabbay

Boreray

Berneray

Gairloch

Loch nam Madadh
(Lochmaddy)

Uig

Kinlochewe

Achnasheen

NORTH UIST

HEBRIDES

NG

NF

Benbecula

Ronay

Wiay

Dunvegan

Edinbane

Portree

Raasay

Inner Sound

Balmacara

**SOUTH
UIST**

ISLE

OF

Scalpay

Kyle of
Lochalsh

Cannich

Drynoch

SKYE

WEST

Loch Baghasdail
(Lochboisdale)

Soay

Cuillin Sound

Ardvasar

Sound of Sleat

Eriskay

BARRA

Canna

Rùm

Mallaig

Invergarry

Bàgh a Chaisteil
(Castlebay)

Sandray

Eigg

Arisaig

Corpach

Spean
Bridge

Mingulay

Muck

Fort William

NL

INNER

Point of
Ardnamurchan

NM

Acharacle

Kinlochleven

Coll

HEBRIDES

Arinagour

Tobermory

Ballachulish

Glencoe

Duror

Tiree

Scarinish

20

ISLE

Lochaline

Lismore

Ulva

OF

Craignure

Iona

MULL

Kerrera

Oban

Dalmally

Crianlarich

Fionnphort

Lorne

THE MINCH

THE LITTLE MINCH

NORTH

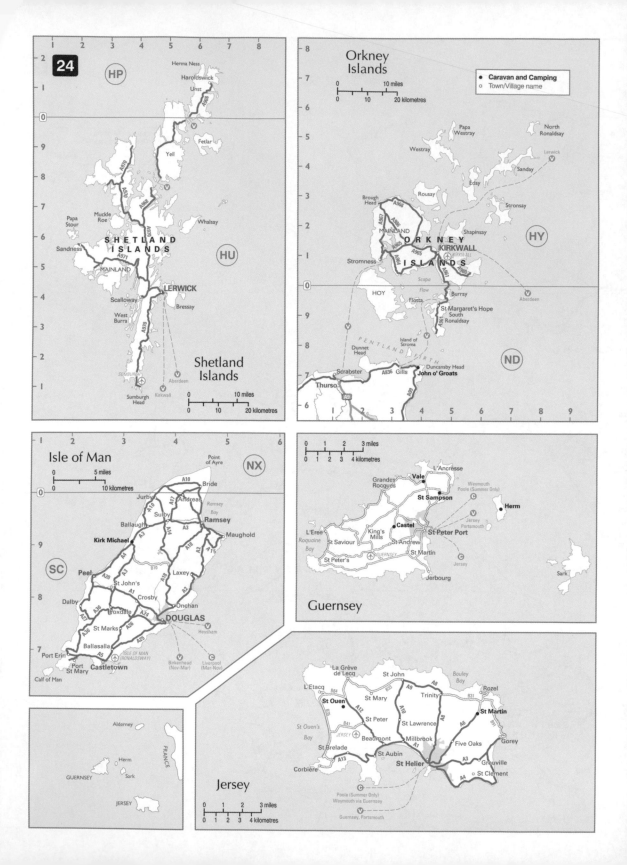

AA Camping Card Sites

The following list shows AA rated campsites that accept the new AA Camping Card which is valid until 31st January 2012.
See page 7 for further details of the card.

ENGLAND

BERKSHIRE
FINCHAMPSTEAD
California Chalet & Touring Park
0118 973 3928

CAMBRIDGESHIRE
ST IVES
Stroud Hill Park
01487 741333

CHESHIRE
CODDINGTON
Manor Wood Country CP
01829 782990
DELAMERE
Fishpool Farm CP
01606 883970
WETTENHALL
New Farm CP
01270 528213

CORNWALL & ISLES OF SCILLY
BRYHER
Bryher Camp Site
01720 422559
BUDE
Widemouth Fields C&C Park
01288 361351
Wooda Farm Holiday Park
01288 352069
GOONHAVERN
Roseville Holiday Park
01872 572448
Penrose Holiday Park
01872 573185
HAYLE
Higher Trevaskis C&C Park
01209 831736
HELSTON
Poldown CP
01326 574560

KILKHAMPTON
Upper Tamar Lake
01288 321712
LANDRAKE
Dolbeare Park C&C
01752 851332
LANIVET
Mena C&C Park
01208 831845
LOOE
Tencreek Holiday Park
01503 262447
MARAZION
Wheal Rodney Holiday Park
01736 710605
MEVAGISSEY
Seaview International Holiday Park
01726 843425
PERRANPORTH
Higher Golla Touring & CP
01872 573963
POLRUAN
Polruan Holidays - C&C
01726 870263
PORTHTOWAN
Wheal Rose C&C Park
01209 891496
PORTREATH
Tehidy Holiday Park
01209 216489
REDRUTH
Cambrose Touring Park
01209 890747
REJERRAH
Newperran Holiday Park
01872 572407
ST AGNES
Beacon Cottage Farm Touring Park
01872 552347
ST JUST [NR LAND'S END]
Trevaylor C&C Park
01736 787016
Secret Garden C&C Park
01736 788301
SUMMERCOURT
Carvynick Country Club
01872 510716

TORPOINT
Whitsand Bay Lodge & Touring Park
01752 822597
TRURO
Cosawes Park
01872 863724
WADEBRIDGE
St Mabyn Holiday Park
01208 841677
WATERGATE BAY
Watergate Bay Touring Park
01637 860387
WIDEMOUTH BAY
Cornish Coasts C&C Park
01288 361380

CUMBRIA
APPLEBY-IN-WESTMORLAND
Wild Rose Park
017683 51077
HOLMROOK
Seven Acres CP
01946 822777
KESWICK
Burns Farm CP
017687 79225
PATTERDALE
Sykeside CP
017684 82239
PENRITH
Flusco Wood
017684 80020
POOLEY BRIDGE
Park Foot C&C Park
017684 86309
WATERMILLOCK
Cove C&C Park
017684 86549

DERBYSHIRE
BAKEWELL
Greenhills Holiday Park
01629 813052
BUXTON
Lime Tree Park
01298 22988
Beech Croft Farm
01298 85330

AA Camping Card Sites *continued*

DEVON

ASHBURTON
River Dart Country Park
01364 652511

AXMINSTER
Hawkchurch Country Park
01297 678402

BERRYNARBOR
Mill Park
01271 882647

BROADWOODWIDGER
Roadford Lake
01409 211507

CHAPMANS WELL
Chapmanswell CP
01409 211382

COMBE MARTIN
Newberry Valley Park
01271 882334

DARTMOUTH
Woodlands Grove C&C Park
01803 712598

DAWLISH
Lady's Mile Holiday Park
0845 026 7252
Leadstone Camping
01626 864411

EAST ALLINGTON
Mounts Farm Touring Park
01548 521591

EAST ANSTEY
Zeacombe House CP
01398 341279

HOLSWORTHY
Headon Farm Caravan Site
01409 254477
Tamarstone Farm
01288 381734

ILFRACOMBE
Hele Valley Holiday Park
01271 862460

KENTISBEARE
Forest Glade Holiday Park
01404 841381

LYNTON
Channel View C&C Park
01598 753349

MORTEHOE
Easewell Farm HP & Golf Club
01271 870343
Twitchen House Holiday Park
01271 870343

NEWTON ABBOT
Dornafield
01803 812732
Ross Park
01803 812983

PAIGNTON
Beverley Parks C&C Park
01803 661979
Whitehill Country Park
01803 782338

SHALDON
Coast View Holiday Park
01626 872392

SIDMOUTH
Oakdown Holiday Park
01297 680387

SOUTH MOLTON
Riverside C&C Park
01769 579269

TAVISTOCK
Harford Bridge Holiday Park
01822 810349
Langstone Manor Camping & CP
01822 613371

TEDBURN ST MARY
Springfield Holiday Park
01647 24242

WOOLACOMBE
Golden Coast Holiday Park
01271 870343
Woolacombe Bay Holiday Village
01271 870343

DORSET

BRIDPORT
Highlands End Holiday Park
01308 422139
Bingham Grange Touring & CP
01308 488234

CHARMOUTH
Newlands C&C Park
01297 560259

CHIDEOCK
Golden Cap Holiday Park
01308 422139

FERNDOWN
St Leonards Farm C&C Park
01202 872637

LYME REGIS
Hook Farm C&C Park
01297 442801

ORGANFORD
Pear Tree Holiday Park
01202 622434

OWERMOIGNE
Sandyholme Holiday Park
01308 422139

PUNCKNOWLE
Home Farm C&C
01308 897258

ST LEONARDS
Shamba Holidays
01202 873302

SHAFTESBURY
Blackmore Vale C&C Park
01747 851523

WIMBORNE MINSTER
Charris Camping & CP
01202 885970

ESSEX

CANEWDON
Riverside Village Holiday Park
01702 258297

GLOUCESTERSHIRE

CIRENCESTER
Mayfield Touring Park
01285 831301

HAMPSHIRE

HAMBLE-LE-RICE
Riverside Holidays
023 8045 3220

ROMSEY
Hill Farm CP
01794 340402

KENT

FOLKESTONE
Little Switzerland C&C Site
01303 252168

WHITSTABLE
Homing Park
01227 771777

LANCASHIRE
BOLTON LE SANDS
Bay View Holiday Park
01524 732854
MORECAMBE
Venture CP
01524 412986
SILVERDALE
Silverdale CP
01524 701508

LINCOLNSHIRE
GREAT CARLTON
West End Farm
01507 450949
LANGWORTH
Lakeside CP
01522 753200
MABLETHORPE
Kirkstead Holiday Park
01507 441483
SALTFLEETBY ST PETER
Saltfleetby Fisheries
01507 338272

MERSEYSIDE
SOUTHPORT
Riverside Holiday Park
01704 228886

NORFOLK
CLIPPESBY
Clippesby Hall
01493 367800
SWAFFHAM
Breckland Meadows Touring Park
01760 721246
WORTWELL
Little Lakeland CP
01986 788646

NOTTINGHAMSHIRE
MANSFIELD
Tall Trees Park Homes
01623 626503
TUXFORD
Orchard Park Touring C&C Park
01777 870228
WORKSOP
Riverside CP
01909 474118

OXFORDSHIRE
HENLEY-ON-THAMES
Swiss Farm Touring & Camping
01491 573419
STANDLAKE
Lincoln Farm Park Oxfordshire
01865 300239
UPPER HEYFORD
Heyford Leys Camping Park
01869 232048

SHROPSHIRE
HUGHLEY
Mill Farm Holiday Park
01746 785208
SHREWSBURY
Beaconsfield Farm CP
01939 210370
WEM
Lower Lacon CP
01939 232376

SOMERSET
BATH
Newton Mill Holiday Park
01225 333909
CHARD
Alpine Grove Touring Park
01460 63479
CHEDDAR
Broadway House Holiday Park
01934 742610
CROWCOMBE
Quantock Orchard CP
01984 618618
DULVERTON
Wimbleball Lake
01398 371257
EMBOROUGH
Old Down Touring Park
01761 232355
MARTOCK
Southfork CP
01935 825661
PORLOCK
Porlock CP
01643 862269
SHEPTON MALLET
Greenacres Camping
01749 890497

SUFFOLK
KESSINGLAND
Heathland Beach CP
01502 740337
LEISTON
Cakes & Ale
01728 831655
WOODBRIDGE
Moon & Sixpence
01473 736650

SUSSEX, EAST
PEVENSEY BAY
Bay View Park
01323 768688

SUSSEX, WEST
ARUNDEL
Ship & Anchor Marina
01243 551262
BARNS GREEN
Sumners Ponds Fishery & Campsite
01403 732539
DIAL POST
Honeybridge Park
01403 710923

WIGHT, ISLE OF
SHANKLIN
Ninham Country Holidays
01983 864243

WILTSHIRE
MARSTON MEYSEY
Second Chance Touring Park
01285 810675
WESTBURY
Brokerswood Country Park
01373 822238

YORKSHIRE, NORTH
NORTHALLERTON
Otterington Park
01609 780656
SCARBOROUGH
Scalby Close Park
01723 365908
Killerby Old Hall
01723 583799
THIRSK
Hillside CP
01845 537349

AA Camping Card Sites *continued*

TOWTHORPE
York Touring Caravan Site
01904 499275
WYKEHAM
St Helens CP
01723 862771

CHANNEL ISLANDS

JERSEY
ST MARTIN
Beuvelande Camp Site
01534 853575

SCOTLAND

ABERDEENSHIRE
HUNTLY
Huntly Castle CP
01466 794999

DUMFRIES & GALLOWAY
CROCKETFORD
The Park of Brandedleys
01387 266700
GATEHOUSE OF FLEET
Anwoth Caravan Site
01557 814333
KIPPFORD
Kippford Holiday Park
01556 620636
KIRKGUNZEON
Mossband CP
01387 760505
STRANRAER
Aird Donald CP
01776 702025

HIGHLAND
GAIRLOCH
Gairloch CP
01445 712373

MORAY
ABERLOUR
Aberlour Gardens CP
01340 871586

PERTH & KINROSS
TUMMEL BRIDGE
Tummel Valley Holiday Park
0844 335 3756

WEST DUNBARTONSHIRE
BALLOCH
Lomond Woods Holiday Park
01389 755000

WALES

CEREDIGION
ABERAERON
Aeron Coast CP
01545 570349
ABERYSTWYTH
Ocean View CP
01970 828425

CONWY
BETWS-YN-RHOS
Plas Farm CP
01492 680254

DENBIGHSHIRE
RHUALLT
Penisar Mynydd CP
01745 582227

GWYNEDD
BALA
Pen-Y-Bont Touring Park
01678 520549
BARMOUTH
Hendre Mynach Touring C&C Park
01341 280262
CRICCIETH
Tyddyn Morthwyl C&C Site
01766 522115
DINAS DINLLE
Dinlle CP
01286 830324
LLANDWROG
White Tower CP
01286 830649
LLANGIAN
Tanrallt Farm
01758 713527
TALSARNAU
Barcdy Touring C&C Park
01766 770736
TAL-Y-BONT
Islawrffordd CP
01341 247269

PEMBROKESHIRE
HASGUARD CROSS
Redlands Touring C&C Park
01437 781300
ST DAVID'S
Tretio C&C Park
01437 781600
TENBY
Wood Park Caravans
0845 129 8314

POWYS
BRONLLYS
Anchorage CP
01874 711246
LLANDRINDOD WELLS
Disserth C&C Park
01597 860277
MIDDLETOWN
Bank Farm CP
01938 570526

WREXHAM
EYTON
The Plassey Leisure Park
01978 780277

NORTHERN IRELAND

CO ANTRIM
BUSHMILLS
Ballyness CP
028 2073 2393

REPUBLIC OF IRELAND

CO DONEGAL
PORTNOO
Boyle's CP
074 9545131

CO MAYO
KNOCK
Knock C&C Park
094 9388100

Index

Entries are listed alphabetically by town name, then campsite name. The following abbreviations have been used
C&C - Caravan & Campsite; HP - Holiday Park; CP - Caravan Park; C&C Club - Camping & Caravanning Club Site

The AA Media Ltd would like to thank the following photographers, companies and picture libraries for their assistance in the preparation of this book.

Abbreviations for the picture credits are as follows: (t) top; (b) bottom; (l) left; (r) right; (c) centre; (AA) AA World Travel Library.

1 Outwell; 2 AA/J Tims; 3 AA/J Tims; 9 AA/A Burton; 10l Colman; 10r Outwell; 15 AA/A J Hopkins; 16 Silverdale Caravan Park; 17t Linnhe Lochside Holidays; 17b Plassey Leisure Park; 19t Oakdown Holiday Park; 19c Sandy Balls Holiday Centre; 19b Townsend Touring Park; 21t Skelwith Fold Caravan Park; 21c Ord House Country Park; 21b Church Farm Caravan and Camping Park; 22/23 South Penquite Farm; 24 Woodclose Caravan Park; 25 South Penquite Farm; 26l Rebecca Boys; 26r South Penquite Farm; 27 AA/J Wood; 28 AA/J Tims; 29 AA/J Tims; 30t Colman; 30b AA/J Tims; 31c Colman; 31b AA/J Tims; 32 Gelert Ltd; 33 AA/J Tims; 34/35 AA/J Tims; 35 Elddis; 36t Colin Church; 36c Baileys Caravans; 36b Baileys Caravans; 37t AA/J Tims; 37c AA; 37b Elddis; 38 Outwell; 39 AA/J Freeman; 40 AA/A Burton; 41 Eskdale Caravan and Camping Club Site; 43 AA/J Tims; 45 Outwell; 47 AA/N Hicks; 50b AA/S Anderson; 52/53 AA/A Burton; 54/55 AA/J Smith; 56/57 AA/M Bauer; 58/59 AA/C Coe; 60/61 AA/T Marsh; 62/63 AA/J Wood; 64 AA/C Jones; 65 AA/J Wood; 115 AA/J Wood; 116 AA/A Mockford & N Bonetti; 118 AA/T Mackie; 119 AA/A Mockford & N Bonetti; 134/135 AA/T Mackie; 136 AA/T Mackie; 137 AA/A Midgley; 141 AA/T Mackie; 142 AA/N Hicks; 143 AA/G Edwardes; 144 AA/N Hicks; 145 AA/G Edwardes; 173 AA/N Hicks; 175 AA/N Hicks; 176 AA/M Jourdan; 177 AA/M Jourdan; 178 AA/M Jourdan; 187 AA/C Jones; 227 AA/N Setchfield; 228 AA/T Mackie; 230 AA/T Mackie; 231t AA/T Mackie; 231c AA/T Mackie; 250 AA/R Ireland; 252 AA/C Jones; 253 AA/R Moss; 268 AA/T Mackie; 270 AA/T Mackie; 271 AA/T Mackie; 277 AA/T Mackie; 278/279 AA/J Miller; 280 AA/J Miller; 281 AA/P Baker; 289 AA/C Jones; 290/291 AA/S McBride; 292 AA/A Burton; 293l AA/A Burton; 293r AA/A Burton; 301 AA/S Day; 303 AA/M Moody; 304/305 AA/T Mackie; 306t AA/M Kipling; 306b AA/M Kipling; 307 AA/M Kipling; 336/337 AA/M Hamblin; 338 AA/S Whitehorne; 339 AA/D W Robertson; 367 AA/A J Hopkins; 370/371 AA/S Lewis; 372 AA/M Moody; 373 AA/N Jenkins; 404 AA/I Burgum; 405 AA/R Eames; 414 AA/A Burton; 414 AA/T Souter; 417 AA/T Mackie; 420 AA/R Moss; 422 AA/J Wood; 424 AA/S Day; 426 AA/S King; 431 AA/T Mackie; 432 AA/R Czaja; 434 AA/A Burton; 437 AA/N Channer; 440 AA/T Mackie; 441 AA/T Mackie; 442 AA/V Greaves; 444 AA/W Voysey; 445 AA/R Moss; 446 AA/J Miller; 447 AA/J Miller; 448 AA/A Burton; 450 AA/J Morrison; 452 AA/J Morrison; 454 AA/M Kipling; 456 AA/C Jones; 457 AA/S Watkins;

Every effort has been made to trace the copyright holders, and we apologise in advance for any accidental errors. We would be happy to apply any corrections in the following edition of this publication.

Can you recommend a good pub to us?

In this edition of the guide we have included a selection of pubs that appear in the current AA Pub Guide which we think might be useful to know about when you are camping. Many of these pubs have been recommended to us by readers for the excellent quality of the food and for the range of beers on offer.

Such pubs close to AA inspected campsites prove harder to source in some areas than others, and that's where we are hoping you can help us.

If you have found a good (and easily accessible) pub that is within a ten mile radius of the site you stayed at, please take a few minutes to fill in this form and tell us about it. The pub might then appear in future editions of both the AA Caravan & Camping Guide and the AA Pub Guide.

PLEASE COMPLETE IN BLOCK CAPITALS

Date:

Your name:

Your address:

Post code

Your e-mail address:

Name and location of site you stayed at:

Name of recommended pub:

Location or address of pub:

Why are you recommending this pub? (Please use the space overleaf or a separate sheet if necessary)

Please return this form to:
The Editor, AA Caravan & Camping Britain & Ireland
Lifestyle Guides, The Automobile Association
13th Floor, Fanum House, Basingstoke RG21 4EA

Or fax: 01256 492433
Or e-mail: lifestyleguides@theAA.com

We may use information we hold about you to write, e-mail or telephone you about other products and services offered by us and our carefully selected partners, but we can assure you that we will not disclose it to third parties.
Please tick here ☐ if you DO NOT wish to receive details of other products or services from the AA.

Can you recommend a good pub to us? *continued*

Please send this form to:
Editor, AA Caravan & Camping Britain & Ireland,
Lifestyle Guides,
The Automobile Association,
13th Floor,
Fanum House,
Basingstoke RG21 4EA

Readers' Report Form

e-mail: lifestyleguides@theAA.com

Please use this form to tell us about any site you have visited, whether it is in the guide or not currently listed. Feedback from readers helps us to keep our guide accurate and up to date. However, if you have a complaint to make during your visit, we recommend that you discuss the matter with the management there and then, so that they have a chance to put things right before your visit is spoilt. The AA does not undertake to arbitrate between you and the site's management, or to obtain compensation or engage in protracted correspondence.

PLEASE COMPLETE IN BLOCK CAPITALS

Date:

Your name:

Your address:

Post code

Your e-mail address:

Name and address of site/park:

Comments

(please attach a separate sheet if necessary)

We may use information we hold about you to write, e-mail or telephone you about other products and services offered by us and our carefully selected partners, but we can assure you that we will not disclose it to third parties.
Please tick here ☐ if you DO NOT wish to receive details of other products or services from the AA.   PTO

Readers' Report Form *continued*

Have you bought this Guide before?   Yes   No

How often do you visit a caravan park or camp site? (circle one choice)

once a year   twice a year   3 times a year   more than 3 times a year

How long do you generally stay at a park or site? (circle one choice)

one night   up to a week   1 week

2 weeks   over 2 weeks

Do you have a:

tent   caravan   motorhome

Which of the following is most important when choosing a site? (circle one choice)

location   toilet/washing facilities   personal recommendation

leisure facilities   other

Do you buy any other camping guides? If so, which ones? _____

_____

_____

_____

Please answer these questions to help us make improvements to the guide:

Have you read the introductory pages and features in this guide?   Yes   No

Do you use the location atlas in this guide?   Yes   No

Which of the following most influences your choice of site/park from this guide? (circle one choice)

gazetteer entry information and description   photograph   advertisement

Do you have any suggestions to improve the guide? _____

_____

_____

_____

Thank you for returning this form

Please send this form to:
Editor, AA Caravan & Camping Britain & Ireland,
Lifestyle Guides,
The Automobile Association,
13th Floor,
Fanum House,
Basingstoke RG21 4EA

Readers' Report Form

e-mail: lifestyleguides@theAA.com

Please use this form to tell us about any site you have visited, whether it is in the guide or not currently listed. Feedback from readers helps us to keep our guide accurate and up to date. However, if you have a complaint to make during your visit, we recommend that you discuss the matter with the management there and then, so that they have a chance to put things right before your visit is spoilt. The AA does not undertake to arbitrate between you and the site's management, or to obtain compensation or engage in protracted correspondence.

PLEASE COMPLETE IN BLOCK CAPITALS

Date:

Your name:

Your address:

Post code

Your e-mail address:

Name and address of site/park:

Comments

(please attach a separate sheet if necessary)

We may use information we hold about you to write, e-mail or telephone you about other products and services offered by us and our carefully selected partners, but we can assure you that we will not disclose it to third parties.
Please tick here ☐ if you DO NOT wish to receive details of other products or services from the AA.   PTO

Readers' Report Form *continued*

Have you bought this Guide before?   Yes   No

How often do you visit a caravan park or camp site? (circle one choice)

once a year   twice a year   3 times a year   more than 3 times a year

How long do you generally stay at a park or site? (circle one choice)

one night   up to a week   1 week

2 weeks   over 2 weeks

Do you have a:

tent   caravan   motorhome

Which of the following is most important when choosing a site? (circle one choice)

location   toilet/washing facilities   personal recommendation

leisure facilities   other

Do you buy any other camping guides? If so, which ones? _____
_____
_____
_____

Please answer these questions to help us make improvements to the guide:

Have you read the introductory pages and features in this guide?   Yes   No

Do you use the location atlas in this guide?   Yes   No

Which of the following most influences your choice of site/park from this guide? (circle one choice)

gazetteer entry information and description   photograph   advertisement

Do you have any suggestions to improve the guide? _____
_____
_____
_____
_____

Thank you for returning this form